ISBN: 9781313454537

Published by:
HardPress Publishing
8345 NW 66TH ST #2561
MIAMI FL 33166-2626

Email: info@hardpress.net
Web: http://www.hardpress.net

A HISTORY OF ENGLISH PROSODY

MACMILLAN AND CO., Limited
LONDON · BOMBAY · CALCUTTA
MELBOURNE

THE MACMILLAN COMPANY
NEW YORK · BOSTON · CHICAGO
ATLANTA · SAN FRANCISCO

THE MACMILLAN CO. OF CANADA, Ltd.
TORONTO

A HISTORY

OF

ENGLISH PROSODY

FROM THE TWELFTH CENTURY TO THE PRESENT DAY

BY

GEORGE SAINTSBURY

M.A. OXON; HON. LL.D. ABERD.; HON. D.LITT. DURH.; PROFESSOR OF RHETORIC AND
ENGLISH LITERATURE IN THE UNIVERSITY OF EDINBURGH

VOL. II

FROM SHAKESPEARE TO CRABBE

'Maxima and minima.'—*Mathematical Treatise*

MACMILLAN AND CO., LIMITED
ST. MARTIN'S STREET, LONDON
1908

PREFACE

NOT many prefatory words are, I think, necessary to this volume. I have indeed to acknowledge, with the most sincere thanks, the gratifying and almost unhoped-for approval given by some competent and impartial critics to the first. Unfavourable comment seems to have very mainly reduced itself either to a reiteration of the views which prefer German theory to English fact, or to an amplification of the argument, " I know and care very little about this subject ; therefore nobody has any business to write a book, and especially a big book, on it." This latter syllogism is perhaps a little inconclusive ; at any rate, I do not propose to rebut it. Nor would it be of much use to cope directly with those whose prejudices against classical nomenclature and quantitative valuation lead them to deny the possibility of "scanning" Shakespeare and Milton. It is better to disprove the impossibility by the simple expedient of going and doing it. As for the objection, which has actually been made, that this book will not make poets : I can only say, " God forbid that it should attempt to do so !"

One point, however, is of too much importance to be wholly omitted. A reviewer in *The Guardian* (of whom I have no complaint to make on the whole, and who seemed, indeed, to be not so much dissatisfied with my prosodic conclusions as shocked at my Chaucerian heresies) commented on the note at vol. i. p. 299—respecting the more than probable *unconsciousness* of early poets as to their prosodic system—as if it were a "hedge," a kind of afterthought on discovering inconveniences. I can assure him that it was nothing of the kind : but, like other similar separated notes, intended to draw special attention to an important point. In fact, this thing happens to be the hinge and staple of my own critical and prosodic apparatus. Those who cannot see the existence and the value of this silent testimony are in much the same plight with the assailants of formal logic, a hundred years ago and later, who asked if the great arguers from Demosthenes and Plato to Burke and Bentham reasoned in syllogism ? The retort, of course, was, that though every good argument is not syllogistically expressed, or by consciousness syllogistically thought out, every good argument is reducible to syllogism ; and the same, *mutatis mutandis*, is the reply here.

There is nothing over which I have taken more pains than the method of this volume ; and I may respectfully beg readers not to judge it hastily as unmethodical. In some experience of writing, and a very great experience of reading, literary histories, I have found that while there are the usual three courses of apparent and self-justifying system in planning these, they are all, if too rigidly adhered to, productive of great inconveniences. The system of proceeding wholly by Kinds, which has become fashionable recently, looks very "good and godly"—very philosophical and scientific ; but it leads, in some instances at any rate, to the entire destruction of all historical perspective and mapping out, so that contemporary work is separated by hundreds of pages. The opposite plan of adopting strict chronological slices, of leaving an author in the middle of his career without ruth, and picking him up again without ceremony, obviates this difficulty, but substitutes another. You get no complete view of any writer ; you have to patch and piece him together from two or three or more different chapters or even volumes ; and you must be provided with a very clear head, a very good memory, and a copious supply of temper, if you do not get either irretrievably muddled, or driven out of all patience, or both. If, on the other or third hand, you proceed by authors *merely*, the thing becomes rather a dictionary than a history ; and there is the danger—— perhaps the most insidious of all because it is somewhat latent——of obscuring the coincidence of persons, times, kinds, and works. I have endeavoured to meet all these difficulties by adopting no one of the three ways ex- clusively, and proceeding by each as seems to me most likely to give the general sequence of things. No doubt this too is difficult——I daresay I have failed to do it perfectly ; but I am sure it was worth attempting.

Perhaps I should give instances. I have dealt together with the whole prosody of Donne and of Waller, though in each case part of it falls out of the main subject of the chapter in which the treatment appears, because there is an important connection, and one which concerns that main subject, between the parts. . I have separated the treatment of Cowley, because his Pindarics require, as it seems to me, distinct handling. I have given combined and exclusive treatment to the whole work, multifarious as it is, of Shakespeare, Milton, and Dryden, because each of these has prosodic importance and prosodic idiosyncrasy which seem to me to demand this treatment.

But enough of this shadow-fighting : let us speak once more of the real Eugénie Grandet——of Prosody herself.[1]

GEORGE SAINTSBURY.

BATH, *Maundy Thursday*, 1908.

[1] The great bulk of matter which has to be dealt with in this volume has made it necessary to suspend the Appendix system as far as it is concerned. I regret this, because it prevents my giving certain excursus which I have

already prepared to meet direct requests, such as one on the question " What is a foot ? " and another on the point whether the iamb or the trochee is really the staple foot of English poetry. But these and some others will come with greater appropriateness at the end of the whole inquiry on which they are based ; and there is no absolute necessity for an interim survey of rhyme, etc., at the point here reached. As before, I have to give the heartiest thanks to Professors Ker, Elton, and Gregory Smith, for reading my proofs, and for making many valuable suggestions.

CONTENTS

BOOK V

THE TIME OF SHAKESPEARE

CHAPTER I

SHAKESPEARE AND BLANK VERSE

ix

CHAPTER III

THE CONTEMPORARIES AND FOLLOWERS OF SPENSER IN STANZA AND COUPLET

CHAPTER IV

ELIZABETHAN LYRIC AND SONNET—DONNE

CHAPTER V

PROSODISTS

BOOK VI

LATER JACOBEAN AND CAROLINE POETRY

CHAPTER I

MILTON

CHAPTER II

THE BATTLE OF THE COUPLETS

CHAPTER III

THE DECAY OF DRAMATIC BLANK VERSE

CHAPTER IV

CAROLINE LYRIC, PINDARIC, AND STANZA

CHAPTER V

PROSODISTS

BOOK VII

THE AGE OF DRYDEN

CHAPTER I

DRYDEN

CHAPTER II

CONTEMPORARIES OF DRYDEN IN LYRIC, PINDARIC, AND COUPLET

CHAPTER III

THE OCTOSYLLABLE AND THE ANAPÆST—BUTLER, SWIFT, AND PRIOR

CHAPTER IV

PROSODISTS

BOOK VIII

THE EIGHTEENTH CENTURY

CHAPTER I

POPE AND THE LATER COUPLET

ADDENDA AND CORRIGENDA FOR VOL I.

Page xvii.—In strictness I should have included in the list of feet the *Proceleusmatic,* or double pyrrhic, ◡◡◡◡. I do not, however, believe that this is possible in English verse, even as a combination ; and in prose I should feel inclined, if it occurred anywhere, to merge it in a dochmiac.

Page 179, *note.*—I was very sorry to learn that this note was misunderstood by some readers as meaning that Professor Skeat had *not* printed the three texts of Langland apart from each other, and that Whitaker's was the only one in which C could be read alone. Even now I hardly know how to remedy the matter, for the note seems to me quite clear. It means—

That in Dr. Skeat's Clarendon Press edition the three texts appear on the same page or page-opening ;

That in his E.E.T.S. edition they all appear, but are separately printed ;

That Whitaker's contains C *without* A *or* B *in any form or place* ;

Wright's is of course, B, with a certain proportion of A and C variants.

Page 245.—I might, and perhaps should, have added here or at p. 264, the alchemical poets Norton and Ripley, Bradshaw's *Life of St. Werburgh,* Ashby's *Poems,* and one or two others. They have, however, nothing really new for us except to illustrate additionally the break-up of the line and the degradation, more especially, of rhyme-royal.

But perhaps the *St. Werburgh* piece (E.E.T.S.) at least ought to have been mentioned. It is not very specially noteworthy for irregular length of line, though the writer evidently does not trouble himself in the least about this. But it is almost the *ne plus ultra* of sheer prose cut into not very regular lengths, perfunctorily tipped with rhyme, and turned loose. Such books help us, more than anything else, to understand the at first sight unreasonable aversion of some in the next generation or two to rhyme itself.

Page 266.—It might not have been ill to mention the comparative prosodic correctness of the English poems ascribed to Charles d'Orléans, in support of the contention advanced in this context.

Page 335.—If I had written this chapter a little later I should have given a special notice to the rhymed doggerel of *Respublica* (*E.E.T.S.*), which has some peculiarities.

Page 371.—" Inarticulatenesses like the final *e*."   I intend no disrespect to this syllable or vocable in any other language ; especially none to it in German, where it often gives occasion for the most exquisite melody.   But we seem to have lost, if indeed we ever had, the proper pronunciation of it ; and we want broader vowel-sound than we usually have to bring out by contrast that pronunciation, little more than a breath as it should be.   (Compare the final line of Baroness Marie von Ebner - Eschenbach's delightful poemlet *Ein kleines Lied*—

Und eine ganze Seele.)

We can still get something of the kind with the participle -e*d* and a strong vowel sound behind it; but the '*y* sound in "pretty," "pony," etc., is very unmanageable, and we have hardly any other for valued final *e* alone in English.

BOOK V

THE TIME OF SHAKESPEARE

CHAPTER I

SHAKESPEARE AND BLANK VERSE

Retrospect of Chaucer, Surrey, etc.—The line of the University Wits —Shakespeare—The order to be taken with his work—*Titus Andronicus*—*The Comedy of Errors*—*Love's Labour's Lost*— *The Two Gentlemen of Verona*—*Romeo and Juliet*—*A Midsummer Night's Dream*—*All's Well that Ends Well*—The Early Histories and their Doubles—*King John*—The "Doubles" generally—*Henry VI.*—*Richard III.*—*Henry IV.*—*Richard II.* —*The Merchant of Venice* — The later plays—*The Tempest* —The later (?) Comedies—*The Merry Wives*—*Measure for Measure*—*As You Like It*—*Taming of the Shrew*—*Twelfth Night*—*Much Ado*—*The Winter's Tale*—The other English Histories—*Henry V.*—*Henry VIII.*—*Troilus and Cressida*— *Timon of Athens*—*Coriolanus*—*Julius Cæsar*—*Antony and Cleopatra*—The Four Great Tragedies — *Macbeth* — *Hamlet*— *King Lear* — *Othello* — *Cymbeline* — *Pericles* — General considerations—The pause — The trisyllabic foot and its revival —The redundant syllable — Enjambment—The morphology and biology of blank verse—*The Poems*—*Venus and Adonis*— *Lucrece*—*The Sonnets*—Miscellaneous metres, the octosyllable —Decasyllabic couplets—The Songs—Note on *The Passionate Pilgrim*, etc.

IT is perhaps desirable, though some pains were taken to make the point clear long before the close of the last volume,[1] to repeat that the attention paid to Spenser, and the praise bestowed on him, involve no disregard, and still less any disparise, of his fellow-workers in prosody and poetry during the last quarter of the sixteenth century. That he was a great master in both senses—that he gave actual, direct, almost pedagogic instruction to many of these

[1] *E.g.* pp. 330, 333.

3

contemporaries—there can be no doubt whatever. But that they would have achieved, perhaps more slowly and uncertainly, something of the same result without him, there can be as little. Some of them, we know, worked in common with him ; others may very well have worked independently. All shared, in their several degrees, the new afflatus of which he had the greatest share next to Shakespeare's. That great exception, moreover, and others, worked in a direction which he did not even try —putting the "sports" of the first *Visions*[1] aside. With these, and with their master and king, we shall therefore now deal. And we shall first deal—reverting in Spenser's own fashion to some personages of the last volume so as to knit and to exhibit the continuity and vitality of the story—with that almost greatest and certainly most idiosyncratic development of English poetry, the un- rhymed decasyllable or blank verse. Under this we shall consider Shakespeare, and those about Shakespeare, who practised it. But as with Chaucer and Spenser in the past, as with all the greatest in the future, we shall not allow a mere hidebound distinction of kind to prevent us from surveying all the prosodic work of Shakespeare himself in this chapter. For this also will throw out tentacles of connection with what is to come, as well as with what is past, and thus again serve to maintain in evidence the vitality and the continuity of the subject.

Retrospect of Chaucer, Surrey, etc.

Blank verse, to throw back a little, had, as has been noticed, made its appearance in a rather puzzling fashion in Chaucer's prose *Tale of Melibee*. It might, no doubt, be possible to find scattered decasyllables in other early prose, for the iambic is a natural, if not *the* natural rhythm of modern English ; but I do not remember so many together.[2] It is at least no unreasonable supposition that Chaucer, with his head full of the decasyllabic mould, even though he had made up his mind not to *rhyme—i.e.* not

---

[1] Vol. i. pp. 351, 359, 360.

[2] There is, of course, the famous—

And many a song, and many a lecherous lay

in the Palinode to the *Canterbury Tales*, and others.

to give the characteristic of verse as he thought it—
should slip into verse-*rhythm* unintentionally, and perhaps
without even observing it. But the conditions, precedent and
surrounding, of this phenomenon are too absolutely obscure
to make it much worth while to discuss it further.   We
have likewise spoken of Surrey's first regular attempts at
the form, and have noted that, naturally and almost un-
avoidably, there is a tendency in them to make line and
clause coincide, and (as naturally if not quite so inevitably)
no great advance towards the discovery of the secret of
pause-variation.[1]   The same remark applied to the earliest
blank-verse plays, *Gorboduc*, the *Misfortunes*, etc.   And
we saw that even the Marlowe-and-Peele or Peele-and-
Marlowe group, great as was the advance which they
made, never quite achieved that combination of internal
dissimilarity and external communication which is necessary
for the triumph of the vehicle.   But we promised some
more remarks upon this subject, and the time has now
come to give them.

It is probably not superfluous, at the beginning of a
new volume, thus to pick up again the points which were
lightly touched upon in this respect in the last : especially

---

[1] A reviewer reproached me, not without some reason, for neglecting
specially to notice Gascoigne's blank verse in *The Steel Glass*. It was the
usual case of hesitation exactly where to place the notice, ending in its being
placed nowhere.   The sample is chiefly interesting as one of its author's
numerous tentatives in nearly or wholly new style.   It has no very special
characteristics, but shares with all its early kin those of strongly single-moulded
lines, abundant *epanaphora*, etc.   But a specimen should be given :—

> And on their backs they bear both land and fee,
> Castles and towers, revenues and receipts,
> Lordships and manors, fines,—yea farms—and all.
> "What should these be?" (speak you, my lovely lord?)
> They be not men : for why, they have no beards.
> They be no boys, which wear such sidelong gowns.
> They be no gods, for all their gallant gloss.
> They be no devils, I trow, which seem so saintish.
> What be they? women? masking in men's weeds
> With dutchkin doublets and with jerkins jagged?
> With Spanish spangs, and ruffs set out of France,
> With high copt hats and feathers flaunt-a-flaunt?
> They be, so sure, even *woe* to *men* indeed.

There are one or two other instances of non-dramatic blanks within the
sixteenth century, but they are quite unimportant.

that of the main one—the excessively *integral* character of the line in these poets.   The consecrated term of "end-stopped" is open to the objection that it may easily convey a wrong idea—that of end-*punctuated*; and that even if this is escaped, the mere stoppage of the line at the end is not the whole of the matter.   It is true that a very large—an enormous—proportion of their lines have (or ought to have) stops at the end ; but it is also true that many which have not, even in modern editions, and perhaps ought not to have, on any reasonable theory of punctuation, are still end-*lopped* if not -*stopped.*   Here are three examples, selected, according to our favourite principle, almost at haphazard, certainly not on any principle of " packing the jury "—

The line of the University Wits.

> And tempted more than ever creature was
> With wealth, with beauty, and with chivalry.
> > PEELE, *Arraignment of Paris.*

> The framing of this circle on the ground
> Brings whirlwinds, tempests, thunder and light[e]ning.
> > MARLOWE, *Doctor Faustus.*

> That God sends down his hateful wrath for sin
> On such as never heard his prophets speak.
> > LODGE and GREENE (?)
> > *Looking-Glass for London and England.*

Now in none of these distichs, save, perhaps, the first, could a comma properly be placed at the end of the first line ; yet in each there is a certain completeness of clause which shuts the sense in.   Moreover, these plays exhibit something else, not quite so glaringly evident, which will emerge to the attentive reader if he brings his mind's ear to the reading, and still more if he reads aloud.   The lines are not merely stopped at the end, but they are constructed to stop at the end.   They are moulded individually, not collectively.   Even in those very greatest passages cited formerly [1]—the *locus classicus* on poetry in *Tamburlaine*, the death - agony of Faustus, the great

---

[1] Vol. i. pp. 347, 348.

speech of Bathsheba, and the rest—they are literally " some dozen or sixteen *lines* " (is it one of the " points in Hamlet's soul " that he meant this ?), making, it is true, a whole of beauty, but separable into line-parts as Shakespeare's own greatest things are not.   The effect is cumulative ; the poet adds line after line to produce it, as you hitch the grooved weight-disks on a steel-yard.   It is a dropping fire not a volley, a shower not a cascade.   So inherent and ingrained is this characteristic that it survives and neutralises the most audacious enjambment [1] in grammar, which does sometimes occur in these poets.   As for instance in the *Jew of Malta*—

> Three thousand camels, and two hundred yoke
> Of labouring oxen, and five hund[e]red
> She-asses—

where, do what you will, you cannot run the " five hundred she-asses " rhythmically together.

There can be very little question that this peculiarity, surviving and resisting even the immense *poetical* advance which these poets made, is a great disadvantage.   It is least felt in the Faustus speech, because that supreme agony consists with—almost invites—separated and ejaculatory expression.   The Bathsheba passage is mainly description ; and description is of its essence cumulative : while the miraculous utterance of Tamburlaine is, as it were, a succession of half-gasping attempts to express that inexpressible of which it speaks.   But turn to the only less fine

> Leicester, if gentle words would comfort me

of *Edward the Second*.   It also is wonderful ; but how one longs for one minute of Shakespeare to turn it from a string of dazzling beads to a ringed and winged serpent of colour and fire !   Almost every line has an actual stop at the end, and those which have not—for instance

> And so it fares with me, whose dauntless mind
> The ambitious Mortimer would seek to curb—

---

[1] This word has to be used so often that I shall henceforward take the liberty of Anglicising it invariably.

are too stiffly and rigidly constructed towards the close to run on as they should. And if this is the case in the greatest passages of all, what must it be, what is it, in the less great? A perpetual hobble, as it were, in the pace; an ever-officious obstacle and blocking in the wind-stroke or the oarage of poetry. In the worst examples of all, even more unpleasant metaphors suggest themselves; the verses positively *hiccup* in their abrupt severance of rhythm and of meaning. Not that there are not glimpses of better things. After the above-quoted great speech of Edward, and two or three other long ones, less good in the same style, there is one in which Marlowe nearly shakes himself free—

> Oh! would I might! but heaven and earth conspire
> To make me miserable.
>
> He of you all that most desires my blood,
> And will be called the murderer of a king,
> Take it.
>
> And Isabel, whose eyes, being turned to steel,
> Will sooner sparkle fire than shed a tear.

Yet he has not got entirely free of the single-moulded line even here. In another speech (of Isabel's own) he comes even nearer; and it is at least noteworthy that it draws upon her the rebuke of her lover Mortimer—

> Nay, Madam, if you be a warrior,
> You must not grow so passionate in speeches.

Yet the passion had been able to fuse the ordinary *stichomythia*[1] into this—

> Our kindest friends in Belgia have we left
> To cope with friends at home; a heavy case
> When force to force is knit, and sword and glaive
> In civil broils make kin and countrymen
> Slaughter themselves in others, and their sides
> With their own weapons gored! But what's the help?
> Misgoverned kings are cause of all this wreck;

---

[1] The word is, of course, ordinarily and properly used of conversation in alternate single lines. But I employ it here because this conversation necessarily generates a line of the type I am discussing.

> And, Edward, thou art one among them all,
> Whose looseness hath betrayed thy land to spoil,
> Who made the channel overflow with blood
> Of thine own people.

It is to be feared that Mortimer had no ears for " a good metre and a plentiful vein," even from fair and, to him, loving lips. Earlier, in the Herald's speech to Edward, oratory does the task of passion to some extent, as in

> That from your princely person you remove
> This Spenser, as a putrefying branch
> That deads the royal vine.

And of course there would be no difficulty in producing other instances, both from Marlowe himself and from the rest of the group, as in the speech of Jonas in *A Looking-Glass for London and England*—

> Lo ! Israel once that flourished like the vine
> Is barren laid ; the beautiful increase
> Is wholly blent, and irreligious zeal
> Encampeth there where virtue was enthroned ;

or in that of Paris in *The Arraignment*—

> Sacred and just, thou great and dreadful Jove,
> And you, thrice-reverend powers, whom love nor hate
> May wrest awry ; if this to me a man,
> This fortune, fatal be, that I must plead, etc.

But, as a rule, this sort of welding of the lines together, and the tempering and annealing of the line itself that makes it possible, are neglected. They do not seem to have come within the scope and purview of the writer. Even when, as not so very frequently happens, there is a full or at any rate heavy stop in the middle or towards the two ends, it is not utilised for the purpose ; the old *anhelitus* or gasp at the end of the line, occasioned by the omission to take minor inhalation during its course, seems to beset the poet. And, misty as all the chronology of the theatre of the period is, we do know that when Shakespeare came to town, and heard or read the work of these men, this kind of blank-verse rhythm must have been what he read or heard.

Shakespeare.

He did not alter it at once ; even he could not have altered it at once without a miracle, and an unwholesome sort of miracle too. There was no reason why the ordinary laws of growth, which our prosody so admirably exemplifies, should be altered in his case ; and had they been so, even his versification could hardly have displayed that perfect naturalness and infinite variety which it actually possesses, but would have shown only a hard and machine-like consummateness — within limits — after the Racinian or Popian manner. Like Chaucer, like Spenser, Shakespeare, beyond all reasonable doubt, experimented ; and though we shall not here attempt to fix the order of the experiments with the rashness which some have shown, every canon of criticism, external and internal alike, when reasonably applied, gives us sufficient data. Taking the Meres list as the positive and not reasonably disputable *terminus ad quem* externally given, and applying to it

The order to be taken with his work.

(with "exception for errors ") the internal signs of less or more maturity in handling diction and metre alike, we may rank *Titus Andronicus*, the *Comedy of Errors*, and *Love's Labour's Lost* as the earliest ; the *Two Gentlemen of Verona, Romeo and Juliet, A Midsummer Night's Dream*, and *All's Well that Ends Well* (if it is *Love's Labour's Found*) next ; the historical plays mentioned by Meres with the addition (in any degree of "doubtfulness" that the reader may please) of *Henry VI.* overlapping this second batch in no very certain order ; and *The Merchant of Venice*, in part at least, last. But I ought to say that it seems to me pretty certain that some (and perhaps many) of the plays represent very different stages, and were in all probability begun, suspended, and finished with more or less rewriting, sometimes at long intervals.[1]

---

[1] In making the above order (which Heaven forefend that I should propose as "matter of breviary"!) I have been guided, as is surely here not improper, mainly by the plain evidences of prosodic improvement. As for *Titus Andronicus*, the statement of Meres is sufficient evidence to me that Shakespeare did write on the subject : and I have myself read Shakespeare (ever since I could read anything) to no purpose if there is anything in the play we have that Shakespeare might not have written, though I do not say that it is all his. As for *Henry VI.*, the fantastic attempts that used to be made, twenty or thirty years ago, to parcel it out among the "Wits," have

If Shakespeare did not write the *Titus Andronicus* *Titus Andronicus.* that we have, there was another person living at that time who had a Shakespearian genius, who was passing through exactly the stage that Shakespeare must have passed through, and who is afterwards lost sight of. For the many beauties which chequer its prodigality of horrors are of a distinctly different type from the Marlowesque, are above anything in Kyd and the others at this time, and are still more markedly different from anything in Middleton, Webster, and the rest of the younger generation. But whether Shakespeare wrote it or not, it is of equal value to us as prosodic stuff and stage. For it is almost certainly the work of a man who, either going through the same process as the Marlowe group or studying their work directly, is in the main and consciously working with the same single-verse mould that they worked with. The First Act contains all but five hundred lines ; and though they are not invariably stopped—that is, punctuated—at the end, I have, in reading them over again carefully, detected hardly one that is not of this mould—that does not invite the suspension of voice or of eye at the close of the line. And this prevails throughout the play, even in those numerous fine passages (to my thinking, quite clearly Shakespearian in themselves) which lighten its darkness. The soliloquy of Aaron opening Act II. ; the charming one of Titus at the beginning of the next scene, and that of Tamora in the third ; even the famous and splendid lines of Martius—

> Upon his bloody finger he doth wear ;

the pathetic, if conceited, lamentations of Titus and Marcus over Lavinia ; and the brave rhetorical addresses of Marcus and Lucius at the end,—all bear this impression, indelibly and unmistakably stamped on them.

But the man who wrote them, be he, let it be once

---

had their day. Most of the three parts represent, of course, rehandling of older work ; but again I see no reason to question the fact of Shakespeare having been the rehandler. That many things, especially the part of Margaret as we have it, are his, I dare swear.

more repeated, Shakespeare or another, is a man of genius, if yet only in his nonage, and he represents and has the advantages of a stage farther than Marlowe himself could traverse. Even more distinctly, therefore, than in Marlowe himself does passion (according to the lover of Isabel) or something else run the moulds of his verse together. It may be fanciful to think that he made some resistance to this agency ; but this is just what a conscientious student of style does do. At any rate, there are passages where the fusion has taken place, and we may take two of them—one from the *threnos* above mentioned (there are others there), and the other the well-known proclamation of unbelief by Aaron. The first shows most interestingly how actual punctuation at the end of lines by no means prevents the continuity, if the rises and falls, the weightings and lightenings, within the line are observed :—

> Come, let's fall to ; and, gentle girl, eat this :
> Here is no drink ! Hark, Marcus, what she says ;
> I can interpret all her martyred signs ;
> She says she drinks no other drink but tears,
> Brewed with her sorrow, meshed upon her cheeks.
> Speechless complainer, I will learn thy thought ;
> In thy dumb action will I be as perfect
> As begging hermits in their holy prayers :
> Thou shalt not sigh, nor hold thy stumps to heaven,
> Nor wink, nor nod, nor kneel, nor make a sign,
> But I of these will wrest an alphabet,
> And, by still practice, learn to know thy meaning.

Here is the beginning of the verse-paragraph ; and here, again, is a still better example helped by the use—so rare in Marlowe and the others—of the hendecasyllable :—

> What if I do not ? as, indeed, I do not ;
> Yet, for I know thou art religious,
> And hast a thing within thee, called conscience,
> With twenty popish tricks and ceremonies,
> Which I have seen thee careful to observe,
> Therefore I urge thy oath ; for that I know
> An idiot holds his bauble for a god,
> And keeps the oath which by that god he swears.

If anybody says that this last is so prosodically accomplished that it must be a later insertion, I shall not quarrel with him much ; for he will certainly not damage my argument, but confirm it. It is certain that the verse of the play, as a whole, is "single-moulded" in the sense in which we are using that word. The writer does not yet think of his quantities and pauses as keys, by dwelling on which, or not dwelling on them, he can make connection or break it with the next line, and the next, and the whole symphonic unit. But it is equally certain that there are instances where something of the sort seems to be glimmering upon him.

The *Comedy of Errors* and *Love's Labour's Lost*, especially the latter, supply matter of prosodic interest strikingly different at first sight from that of *Titus Andronicus*; and much more varied, but by no means inconsistent. In *Titus* we have a man who is setting himself—setting his teeth, one may almost say—to the task of carrying out a definite model and pattern in his verse, and who succeeds—almost, if not quite, too well. In the others we have quite conceivably the same man (if that man was Shakespeare) indulging in almost unlimited experiment, constantly breaking out of blank verse altogether, or, if anybody prefers it, only occasionally settling down thereinto. It is, however, extremely noteworthy—indeed, of the first importance—that the staple in blank verse is still the single-moulded line, the line intended to be used cumulatively, and not periodically. That the variety and licence of both, as compared with *Titus*, are at least partly to be accounted for by the fact that both are comedies—that they take the licence which not merely immemorial tradition, but the nature of things, confers on that form in comparison with tragedy—is proper to be mentioned, but can require no insistence.

Of the two, that which actually tickets itself as Comedy *The Comedy* is the less interesting prosodically, as in other ways ; but *of Errors.* its want of interest is only comparative, not positive at all. That much of it is in prose ; that much again,[1]

---

[1] I have always felt pretty sure that we have here some of Shakespeare's very earliest work.

whether in prose or in some sort of verse, is devoted to that *stichomythic* bandying of speech, generally with inordinate word-play, which is the most difficult—perhaps to good digestions the only difficult—thing in Shakespeare to stomach ; these things are obvious to the mere turner of the pages. But the piece opens with a long spell of blank verse, and it is diversified throughout, not only with these long blank-verse set-speeches, which the Senecan tradition fostered, but with blank verse dialogue of all sizes. The staple is still single-moulded, of the kind just analysed, which often coincides with but does not necessitate end-punctuation, while end-punctuation by no means necessitates *it.* The opening speeches of the Duke and Aegeon are almost wholly of this pattern,[1] as are many of those of Adriana and Luciana. Yet the fine *tirade* of the wronged wife (as she thinks herself) to him she thinks her husband—

> Ay ! ay ! Antipholus, look strange and frown—

shows once more the *fusing* power of passion, especially in the extremely beautiful lines :—

> For know, my love, as easy may'st thou fall
> A drop of water in the breaking gulf,
> And take unmingled thence that drop again,
> Without addition or diminishing,
> As take from me thyself, and not me too,

where the secrets of prosodic effect are the inset " my love " ; the pauseless rapidity of the next line, or even two lines ; the stop, given by emotion, not grammar, at " thyself," and the spondee (making with the " not " of the preceding foot almost a *molossus*) of the close.

But besides the prose and the blank verse we find, in the *Comedy of Errors,* what we did not find in *Titus*— an admixture of other metres ; while in the blank verse itself we find frequent *epanaphora*—that favourite Elizabethan device (prosodic quite as much as rhetorical) which has been referred to in the last volume, and which is particularly notable in the great speech of Adriana

---

[1] We shall see that it persists in overture perhaps longer than anywhere else.

quoted above. The additional metres, besides the couplet (constantly, according to custom, at the end of speech and scene, and not seldom elsewhere), include rhymed doggerel of various lengths like that in the early plays—

> O villain ! thou hast stolen both my office and my name,
> The one ne'er got me credit, the other mickle blame :
> If thou hadst been Dromio to-day in my place,
> Thou wouldst have changed thy face for a name or thy name
>   for an ass,

and alternate-rhymed quatrains [1]—

> And may it be that you have quite forgot
> A husband's office ? Shall, Antipholus,
> Even in the spring of love, thy love-springs rot ?
> Shall love, in building, grow so ruinous ?

---

[1] The *locus classicus* for the change of taste in this dramatic metre is, of course, the *Tancred and Gismund* of Robert Wilmot, which, written in quatrains about 1568, was published twenty-four years later (1591) in blank verse (with many couplets, and even some quatrains, still floating about in it), "fresh painted," as the author says in his Dedication to the Inner Temple. The play, in its later form, with some extracts from the MSS. of the earlier, will be found in the seventh volume of Hazlitt's *Dodsley*. Two short parallel passages may be given :—

> *Tancred.*   O dolorous hap, ruthful and all of woe,
>   Alas ! I careful wretch, what resteth me ?
>   Shall I now live, that with these eyes did so
>   Behold my daughter die ? what ? shall I see
>   Her death before my face that was my life,
>   And I to live that was her life's decay ?
>   Shall not this hand reach to this heart the knife
>   That may bereave both sight and life away,
>   And in the shadows dark to seek her ghost
>   And wander there with her ?

This becomes later—

> Now, ruthful, wretched king, what resteth thee ?
> Wilt thou now live wasted with misery ?
> Wilt thou now live that with these eyes did see
> Thy daughter dead ? wilt thou now live to see
> Her funerals that of thy life was stay ?
> Wilt thou now live that wast her life's decay ?
> Shall not this hand reach to this heart the stroke ?

The survival of rhyme in the second passage is curious though not unnatural ; but it is still more curious, though one sees the reason on a moment's thought, that *the quatrains are rather better blank verse than the blank verse itself,* only tagged. The rhyme is in itself superfluous, but it has encouraged the writer to step out of the narrowest line-model. It may be just worth adding that *Romeo and Juliet* is dated by some as early as this very year 1591.

continued for over fifty lines.   But there are no pure
fourteeners, though the doggerel may sometimes simulate
them.

These last the other play supplies, with much else ;
in fact, *Love's Labour's Lost,* so prolific in many ways of
disorderly but dear delights, is unquestionably *the* " place "
for the prosody of the youthful Shakespeare.   There is a
great deal of prose ; some of it approaching Shakespeare's
best in phrase and quality, if full of *péchés de jeunesse* in
diction and otherwise.   There is the doggerel, occurring
chiefly in the speeches of Costard and Nathaniel.   There
are here undoubted fourteeners (or fifteeners with the
double rhyme), which the great Holofernes naturally
prefers [1] to doggerel pure and simple.   There are stately
Alexandrines,[2] most *reviewerishly* criticised by the said
Holofernes, but doing credit to the abilities of Biron.
There are the couplets and the quatrains, solid and split
into conversation, but sometimes of extreme beauty.[3]
There are (what we have not had in either of the other
plays) early and delicious examples of the lyrics with
which we shall deal as a whole presently.   And there
is the blank verse.

This last is so much scattered among the other
experiments that it is far less easy to judge it than in
Titus, and even than in the *Comedy.*   But I think it may
be said without rashness that the single - mould line, the
cumulative and non-periodic line, still holds the field on
the whole.   When he is doing things deliberately, the
poet seems still to cling to it,—in the king's opening

[1] He also " will something affect the letter [alliterate] for it argues
facility," as in

┌play?┐
└praise┘
The preyful princess pierced and pricked a pretty pleasing pricket ;
Some say a sore ; but not a sore, till now made sore with shooting.

[2] If love make me forsworn, how shall I swear to love ?

[3] As those in "Who sees the heavenly Rosaline" which Milton did
not miss—

That like a rude and savage man of Inde
At the first opening of the *gorgeous East,*
Bows not his vassal head and stricken mind,
Kisses the base ground with obedient breast.

harangue especially ; in his formal address to the Princess about business ; in most of the set speeches. But once more the fire kindles ; and passion or satire, love or wit, gets the better of his intention, or makes him intend more nobly. It is in the speeches of Biron, the real hero, and of Rosaline, the real heroine, that this happens most frequently and with most felicity. Biron shakes himself half-free in the self-satire on his love at the end of Act III., and is only prevented from doing so fully in the splendid and famous " Who sees the heavenly Rosaline " (quoted already above) by the fact of his own conceit in choosing the quatrain. But in the long speech which gives the " salve for perjury," the "*placebo* and *dirige*" to his and his companions' self-denying ordinance (IV. iii. 290-365), the battle of the blank-verse lines, the " breaking deep " (to quote Adriana as we quoted Mortimer) melting the icy single verses, is a wonderful spectacle. And the " studies " of his lady at the close, with his own interjected remonstrance, show us the wave of the true blank verse all but free,—rejoicing in its freedom and strengthened in its strength.[1]

[1] For when would you, my liege, or you, or you,
In leaden contemplation have found out
Such fiery numbers as the prompting eyes
Of beauty's tutors have enrich'd you with ?
Other slow arts entirely keep the brain ;
And therefore, finding barren practisers,
Scarce show a harvest of their heavy toil :
But love, first learned in a lady's eyes,
Lives not alone immured in the brain ;
But, with the motion of all elements,
Courses as swift as thought in every power,
And gives to every power a double power,
Above their functions and their offices.
It adds a precious seeing to the eye ;
A lover's eyes will gaze an eagle blind ;
A lover's ear will hear the lowest sound,
When the suspicious head of theft is stopp'd :
Love's feeling is more soft and sensible
Than are the tender horns of cockled snails ;
Love's tongue proves dainty Bacchus gross in taste :
For valour, is not Love a Hercules,
Still climbing trees in the Hesperides ?
Subtle as Sphinx ; as sweet and musical
As bright Apollo's lute, strung with his hair ;

*The Two
Gentlemen of
Verona.*

The other comedy, which comes next to these two in hardly disputable prosodic signs of belonging to an early if not the very earliest stage — *The Two Gentlemen of Verona,*—is perhaps not to be widely separated from them, except by too curious consideration. Yet there are real *differentiae.* We find excursions into doggerel—

> From a pound to a pin, fold it over and over,
> 'Tis threefold too little for carrying a letter to your lover ;

and into pure fourteeners—

> For often have you writ to her and she in modesty,
> Or else for want of idle time, could not again reply,

> And when Love speaks, the voice of all the gods
> Make heaven drowsy with the harmony.
>
> .   .   .   .   .
>
> *Biron.* Studies my lady ? mistress, look on me ;
> Behold the window of my heart, mine eye,
> What humble suit attends thy answer there :
> Impose some service on me for thy love.
> *Ros.* Oft have I heard of you, my Lord Biron,
> Before I saw you ; and the world's large tongue
> Proclaims you for a man replete with mocks,
> Full of comparisons and wounding flouts,
> Which you on all estates will execute
> That lie within the mercy of your wit.
> To weed this wormwood from your fruitful brain,
> And therewithal to win me, if you please,
> Without the which I am not to be won,
> You shall this twelvemonth term from day to day
> Visit the speechless sick and still converse
> With groaning wretches ; and your task shall be,
> With all the fierce endeavour of your wit
> To enforce the pained impotent to smile.
> *Biron.* To move wild laughter in the throat of death ?
> It cannot be ; it is impossible :
> Mirth cannot move a soul in agony.
> *Ros.* Why, that's the way to choke a gibing spirit,
> Whose influence is begot of that loose grace
> Which shallow laughing hearers give to fools :
> A jest's prosperity lies in the ear
> Of him that hears it, never in the tongue
> Of him that makes it : then, if sickly ears,
> Deaf'd with the clamours of their own dear groans,
> Will hear your idle scorns, continue then,
> And I will have you and that fault withal ;
> But if they will not, throw away that spirit,
> And I shall find you empty of that fault,
> Right joyful of your reformation.

as well as stanzas, etc. But they are nothing like so
frequent as in the *Errors* and in *Love's Labour's Lost*.
The blank verse itself, too, is even less run-on than in
either of the others—stop or no stop at the end of the
line, each is formed with a single respiration. Even
Julia's exquisite lines—

> She hath been fairer, Madam, than she is—

which supply the unmistakable Shakespearian sign-manual,
and (with one or two other things) have given the play a
reputation with some good judges that, as a whole, it
hardly deserves—are distinctly of this type. But there is
in these blank-verse passages a curious feature which we
sometimes do not notice, where the verse, as such, is
much more accomplished : and that is the presence of the
redundant syllable. This appears in the first line of
Julia's first soliloquy—

> And yet I would I had o'erlooked the letter,

and there are numerous other examples. Yet it may be
doubted,—when we come upon such a curious piece of
unfinishedness as the quatrain—

> Oh, how this spring of love resembleth
> The uncertain glory of an April day,
> Which now shows all the beauty of the sun,
> And by and by a cloud takes all away!

with its omission to rhyme the first and third lines, and its
*un*skilful repetition of " all,"—whether in the other case
also there is more than the mere carelessness of the novice.

Love's Labour's Lost, to return to it for a moment, is in
a manner Shakespeare's *Shepherd's Kalendar* for prosodic
experiment. But there were more reasons than one why
it should not serve him once for all, why he should still
" box the compass" of verse. In the first place, the
play is a less serious and a more artificial field of art-
experiment than the poem ; and in the second, though, as
we know on good authority, Shakespeare " could be very
serious," still seriousness was not quite uppermost with him
as it was with Spenser. It would scarcely be erroneous

to say that he never outgrew the period of experiment—
at least with blank verse itself.   At any rate, with regard
Romeo and to these early plays, each is, and all are, full of it.   *Romeo*
Juliet. *and Juliet*, for instance, renews for us the interest of
subject, almost of kind, in its relation to prosody.   It is a
tragedy more really tragic than *Titus* itself ; but while
there the tragic gloom is unmixed, here there are large
stretches of pure comedy and others of pure passion, not
necessarily connected with, or tending to, any tragic event
at all.   In short—in the way in which we are, not, I hope,
improperly handling the list—it is our first example of the
great English kind of the tragi - comedy.   Accordingly,
the metre is more varied than in *Titus*, less so than in the
three lighter pieces.   Doggerel does not appear at all :
nor, speaking under correction, do pure fourteeners ; while
—a more surprising thing considering the subject—there
are no lyrics, unless anybody feels inclined to give that
name to Mercutio's snatches.   But there is some stanza-
writing, both in quatrain and sixain (of which latter form
Shakespeare was for a time rather fond), and there is very
much more admixture of rhyme than in any of the plays
we have considered, except in the doggerel passages of
them.   *Romeo and Juliet*, indeed, might be taken as, in
Shakespeare's case, the representative of the battle of the
couplet and of blank verse—they are sometimes almost
at odds with each other.   And those who believe in its
being as early as 1591 might take this for an argument
on their side, though I should not agree with them.

But from and in this battle there arises a curious and
interesting advantage for blank verse itself.   The couplet
as such, though capable of indefinite linking, always tends
rather to stoppage.   But even in the stopped form, the
structure and rhythm of its decasyllable are markedly
different from that of the stopped blank verse ; while in
the linked or enjambed variety that difference is, of course,
largely increased.   The result is that portions of couplet-
verse, small enough not to allow the rhyme to be prominent,
often give a most admirable model for blank verse itself.
For instance, the two and a half lines which follow—

> It seems she hangs upon the cheek of night,
> Like a rich jewel in an Ethiope's ear ;
> Beauty too rich for use—

are actually, and in their original place, part of a pair of couplets, which are continued by three others. But as they have just been printed they make what we call a "blank - verse clause," itself of almost perfect beauty. When a man is Shakespeare, and produces such an effect as that, even when deliberately doing something else, it is unlikely not to strike him : particularly since he is sure to go on doing it. And by and by he will discard the couplet altogether and use this far superior medium.

Accordingly, we find in the play (not to mention again the things already mentioned, the sonnet prologues and the prose) the most curious alternation, or rather intermixture, of the cumulative and the periodic styles of blank-verse decasyllable. Some speeches, like that of the Prince[1] after the opening brawl, seem to have preserved the older model. Friar Laurence also, in his longer utterances, is rather given to it ; and there are many other examples. But Juliet's heart beats throughout to another tune than this sententious clank ; her lover, though less uniformly, is master of the better rhythm also; and Mercutio shows that fancy can act as the solvent no less than passion. From his immortal celebration of Queen Mab, through Juliet's

> Gallop apace, you fiery-footed steeds,

(where the Marlowesque opening changes so wonderfully into the fused music that Marlowe, with all his genius, could hardly reach and never command), to the death-song of Romeo, the new model triumphs. And such a triumph as it obtains in the last (so far as we can guess at the chronology of these pieces) English poetry—nay, the poetry of the world—had not seen. When Dr. Johnson reprehended, in a famous phrase,[2] the mixing of the methods of the poet and the declaimer, he was

---

[1] See what has been said elsewhere as to speeches of this class.
[2] In discussing Milton's verse-paragraph. (*V. inf.* on Johnson himself.)

unconsciously describing the real virtue of the thing—the application, as no other poetic form has ever mastered it, of the double appeal of poetry and rhetoric, the magical order of poetry and the magical *apparent* freedom of rhetoric.   In that exquisite and consummate period—

> Why art thou yet so fair ? shall I believe
> That unsubstantial death is amorous,
> And that the lean abhorrèd monster keeps
> Thee here in dark to be his paramour ?
> *For fear of that, I still will stay with thee :*
> *And never from this palace of dim night*
> *Depart again : here, here will I remain*
> *With worms that are thy chamber-maids ; O, here*
> *Will I set up my everlasting rest,*
> *And shake the yoke of inauspicious stars,*
> *From this world-wearied flesh—*

the poet shows that he has nothing left to learn,—that he has everything to teach, with the exception that the redundant syllable and the trisyllabic foot, not being wanted, do not occur.   The shift, of the pause in the italicised part—fourth syllable in the first line ; practically none in the second ; fourth in the third, but with strong subsidiaries at fifth and sixth ; eighth in the fourth ; hardly any in the next two, and the broken line to finish with—is therefore almost the sole device used of a tangible character ; but the κῶλα, the members of the line, or lines, which these pauses outline, are internally arranged with incomparable subtlety.[1]

A Midsummer Night's Dream.   Next to *Romeo and Juliet* there are strong prosodic reasons for taking *A Midsummer Night's Dream*.   As a non-tragic pendant to the tragic counterpart, it offers a temptation to do so ; and that this is not merely a temptation, is shown by the presence in it of the same admixture of a certain juvenility with power already of the very highest.   Perhaps there is a little touch of

---

[1] I hope many of my readers will excuse what only a few may need— the reminder that I have not the slightest intention of suggesting that Shakespeare said to himself, "Go to : let us put a pause at the *x*th place, that we may produce this or that effect."   Nor do I think that, in the same century, Titian said, "Let us bend such and such of our muscles in such and such a manner that we may draw Ariadne."   But they both did it.

further age in it—more critical and satiric grasp, nicer
composition,—but all this is for another story. Prosodically, it comes in as hardly anything else could. We
must once more remember that we have here the comic
licence of variety ; and the fact that that variety does not
run, as it does in the *Errors* and in *Love's Labour's Lost*,
to doggerel, shows a further advance. The fact that it
does run to great lengths shows that we are still at an
early stage of the poet's development. The beautiful
octosyllables and the serious lyrics we shall take later
with their kin ; but the burlesques of the "tedious, brief
scene" are too important prosodically, and too unique
not to require a short separate treatment at once.

We have seen above (Vol. i. Bk. iii. Ch. I.) that the
original dramatic performances of the guilds indulged in
an extreme prosodic variety, and we have also seen (*ibid.*)
that, in the Interludes and other sixteenth-century successors of these, doggerel of various kinds rode almost
sovereign. Shakespeare seems to have seen his opportunity for a dramatic *Sir Thopas* here, and he certainly
made the most of it. That he is not always original—
that, for instance, the "misperusing" of poor Quince's
Prologue is borrowed from *Ralph Roister Doister*, whose
author (as Thackeray says of another subject) no doubt
borrowed it from somebody else — does not matter.
The absurdity combined with the prosodic correctness
and almost ease of the stanzas, the couplets, and the
short-lined lyrics is *impayable*, except with recognition of
its merits, and of the indication which it gives of its
author's prosodic progress.

In the body of the play there is a good deal of rhymed
couplet, just as there is in *Romeo and Juliet* ; but in the
blank-verse staple there is a most remarkable change.
In the tragedy, as we saw, the crude and the perfect
blank verse—the medium which is still made up, like a
surveyor's measuring-chain, of units linked together, and
that which is as integral and undulating as a serpent—
alternate with each other. Such alternation is not absent
in *A Midsummer Night's Dream*, but the live variety has

altogether the upper hand. Even the short opening speeches [1] of Theseus and Hippolyta are couched in it : and though the Duke's second speech falls back rather into the older strain of these set harangues, that of Egeus (which follows so quickly, and which in any earlier play would probably, as we have seen, have been quite of the chain-pattern) is not. But in the great Oberon-and-Titania passage of the Second Act comes one of the most important *loci* for our purpose. Most of this would earlier have been in the stiffer form, for the speeches are long and set. Nor is this form quite absent ; but it is constantly fused, not, as in some other pieces that we have seen, by passion or by fancy, so much as by the poet's growing facility in the other and higher kind, and his conscious, or unconscious, conviction that it *is* the higher. Redundant syllables and trisyllabic feet are still absent, as a rule ; but in other ways the newer kind is victorious, and the older (see Puck's speech in Act III. Sc. ii.) seems actually to be taking refuge in the couplet passages when it has been driven out of its ancient stronghold of " blanks "—a most curious instance of the " exchange of rapiers." The rhymed part of the central scene of confusion goes out of its way to be single-moulded. Helena's pathetic blank-verse appeals are almost completely interknitted. So, too, *indignatio facit* " blancos " *versus* for Hermia later ; and her passion gets in even the trisyllabic foot in—

And with | her per|*sonage* [2] *her* | tall per|sonage.

All's Well that Ends Well. The most puzzling and (but for Parolles and, perhaps, Lafeu) the most un-Shakespearian of all the plays, *All's Well that Ends Well*, although it is not exactly a puzzle prosodically, is not very easy to place in the combined respect of prosody and chronology. There is none of the early medley—prose, blank verse, and the usual drop

---

[1] This is probably because they *are* short, and not of the tirade or harangue kind.

[2] On what some people call an extra-metrical syllable here, to escape the abhorred trisyllabic foot, see later. As for others, who would read " pursnidge " in one place and the proper word in the other, *non ragioniam*.

into couplet pretty well exhaust its variety. But the man who wrote it, whosoever he was, and at whatsoever time he wrote, seems to be experimenting with blank verse itself in a rather different fashion from that which we find in any other play, earlier or later. Thus the King's speech in II. iii.—

> 'Tis only title thou disdain'st in her, the which—

(an Alexandrine, in itself noteworthy) is evidently written with a definite attempt to break up the lines—

> In differences so mighty.   If she be
> .   .   .   .   .
> It is a dropsied honour.   Good alone
> Is good without a name.   Vileness is so :
> The property by what it is should go,
> Not by the title.

But, it will be observed, the speaker has already dropped into rhyme, in which he continues to the end of the speech ; and his junctures want the nail—they are harsh and grating. Yet there are attempts here, much more often than earlier, at the other great devices for variation— trisyllabic feet and redundant syllables—besides occasional Alexandrines, as noted.[1]

---

[1] Two curiously ugly but representative speeches follow each other in II. i. :—

> *King.*   I knew him.
> *Hel.* The rather will I spare my praises towards him ;
> Knowing him is enough.   On's bed of death
> Many receipts he gave me ; chiefly one,
> Which, as the dearest issue of his practice,
> And of his old experience the only darling,
> He bade me store up, as a triple eye,
> Safer than mine own two, more dear ; I have so ;
> And, hearing your high majesty is touch'd
> With that malignant cause wherein the honour
> Of my dear father's gift stands chief in power,
> I come to tender it and my appliance
> With all bound humbleness.
> *King.*   We thank you, maiden ;
> But may not be so credulous of cure,
> When our most learned doctors leave us and
> The congregated college have concluded
> That labouring art can never ransom nature
> From her inaidible estate ; I say we must not
> So stain our judgement, or corrupt our hope,

The early historical plays mentioned by Meres, and the enigmatical *Henry VI.* batch, will be best taken together from the prosodic point of view. As is well known, Shakespeare's part in most of them is mixed up with other and probably earlier work, to a rather bewildering extent. But it is the great advantage of our subject and our method that the question of authorship hardly concerns us at all, or only indirectly and secondarily. It is the "Progress of Prosody" which the present writer, not being able to "sing," is ambitious to "say." And of this progress there is plentiful and interesting evidence in comparing the two sets. The blank verse, for instance, of *The Troublesome Raigne of King John* is, as is that of all the doubles,[1] strongly of the "University," the single-moulded, the cumulative type. Nor has Shakespeare himself quite, though he has partly, broken with the type —he is in the *Romeo and Juliet* not the *Titus Andronicus* stage of his apprenticeship. When he sees a possible good line, if it is only a string of names like

> That England, Ireland, Poitiers, Anjou, Touraine, Maine,

he takes and turns it into an actually good one of the same type—

> To Ireland, Poitiers, Anjou, Touraine, Maine.

> To prostitute our past-cure malady
> To empirics, or to dissever so
> Our great self and our credit, to esteem
> A senseless help when help past sense we deem.

For trisyllabics see Helena's speech to the widow at the end of Act III.—

> When I have found it.   The count he woos your daughter,

> Resolved to carry her : let her in fine consent,

> Since the first father wore it : this ring he holds.

All at the cæsura; all explicable, if anybody likes such things, as "extrametrical"; all exceedingly ugly; but all, according to my notation, distinctly trisyllabic.   The author of all these things is clearly experimenting; but his *Love's Labour* is not yet *Won*, though we take his play here on the chance that Meres may have so named it.

[1] I use for this work Hazlitt's reprint, with additions, of Collier's *Shakespeare's Library*, 6 vols., London, 1875.

But generally he re-founds the metre as completely as *King John.* the diction; and the dull stump of the original changes into the passionate or fanciful airs of the rehandling as if by miracle. The form of the blank verse is still of the austerer kind, but in that kind it gives some of his greatest and best known triumphs, proceeding from still cumulative specimens (though the cumulation is here disguised by the Bastard's abundant fancy), like Falcon-bridge's soliloquy on his Lackland Knighthood, through the stately tirades of the kings and the First Citizen, through Constance's never-to-be-hackneyed despair, and the other famous pieces, all slightly single-line in their constitution, till, as usual, the greatest passion of all brings the point of projection with it, and an impeccable specimen in the later kind is given by the wonderful lines which wrest pity for almost the vilest of all heroes—

> Poison'd,—ill fare—dead, forsook, cast off: [1]
> And none of you will bid the winter come
> To thrust his icy fingers in my maw,
> Nor let my kingdom's rivers take their course
> Through my burn'd bosom, nor entreat the north
> To make his bleak winds kiss my parched lips
> And comfort me with cold.[2]

As for the "rough copy" plays themselves, com-paratively few remarks must serve them, though it would be interesting (to the writer, that is to say) to be much more diffuse. They stand in three classes prosodically. *The True Tragedy of Richard III.* and *The Famous Victories of Henry V.* are in almost the lowest stage of blank-verse doggerel, as we may call it, though they acquire considerable interest, when we compare them with that other stage to which we shall come in the decadence of blank verse itself, some half century later. It will not, of course, do to judge them merely as printed; for some of the prose passages are clearly verse in intention, and many of the verse passages were probably meant to be simple prose. It is, however, rare that even a tolerable single

The Doubles generally.

---

[1] Note the "pause-foot" or half-foot here in the first line.
[2] The actually last speech ("O cousin, thou art come") is single-moulded again.

line emerges, while a tolerable batch of lines is almost unknown. *The Troublesome Raigne*, on the other hand, is a very fair, though by no means a first-rate specimen of the chain-stitch blank verse of the Wits. And in the two parts of the *Contention*, compared with the three of *Henry VI.*, we have one of the most attractive special prosodic studies imaginable, though one of which only the general results can be indicated here.

Henry VI.   Generally speaking, the process of editing is performed by persons who have not genius, upon persons who have.[1] Here the positions are capitally and signally reversed. One parallel (from the great passage of the Cardinal's death) will prove this as well as fifty. The *Contention* has—

> Lord Cardinal, if thou diest assured of Heavenly bliss
> Hold up thy hand and make some sign to us.
> Oh, see ! he dies, and makes no sign at all !
> Oh God ! forgive his soul !

In *Henry VI.* it is—

> Lord Cardinal ! if thou think'st on Heaven's bliss,
> Hold up thy hand ; make signal of thy hope !
> He dies and makes no sign.   O God ! forgive him !

Shakespeare for a thousand ducats : even *Aut Diabolus* being out of the question in the circumstances.[2]

Richard III.   Of the other historical plays mentioned by Meres, *Richard the Third*, despite the glorious things that it contains, bears the earliest appearance prosodically. The splendid opening soliloquy of Gloucester still has the pant, the gasp, of the older model, and its intrinsic uniformity ; and so have Anne's Prologue and Gloucester's own central speech in the incomparable wooing-scene,

---

[1] I believe I have edited enough myself to say this without impertinence to others.

[2] If space permitted, many other things in this most interesting trilogy would be discussed. The great Towton speech of the King, III. ɪɪ. v. (" This battle fares like to the morning's war "), is a text for a complete sermon on Shakespeare's blank verse in the apprenticeship period ; and it would not be difficult to make up the " fifty " referred to in the text. I own to very great affection for *Henry VI.* It is a historical novel of the best kind, with the joy of verse added.

which is the triumph of impossibility made probable as far as dramatic character is concerned ; and the Prince's Mephistophelian conclusion thereto.   Even Margaret's magnificent

> I called thee, then, vain flourish of my fortune

is the very paragon of the style. Marlowe himself, though he shoots higher for a little space here and there, never holds the heavens of declamation in which passion does *not* sleep, so royally and long.[1] Only in the two *apices* of the whole, the Clarence passage and Richard's desperate awakening (with perhaps the repentant death-words of Edward) is the other and greater method tried with complete success ; and even in these the mould of the verse tends towards rigidity. It is as if Shakespeare, in this chronologically final division of the long pageant of historic tragedy which his predecessors had attempted with such varying success, determined to give the method of those predecessors its full chance—to get out of it everything that could be got—and so an end.

It would be in accordance with such a plan that the *Henry IV.* play is almost wholly in verse. In *Henry IV.*, on the other hand, the best and most characteristic passages, as was necessitated by the grasp of comedy which the author had now made sure, are wholly in prose, or versed only in snatches which are mainly burlesque. The blank verse would seem to have received no very special attention ; and though a good deal of it is in the older model, the newer seems to come from him less of deliberate purpose than because his hand was getting accustomed to it. The King opens (as usual) in the one, and Hotspur denies

---

[1] If the play were not among the most universally known even of Shake-speare's, I think I must have quoted this gorgeous tirade. It has redundant syllables (six out of some thirty) ; but, as we have seen, though the frequency of these is a mark of lateness, their occasional occurrence does not prevent a piece being early. And they are mostly " very little ones " :—fort*u*ne, bub*b*le, broth*e*rs, wid*ow*, sor*row*. There is one trisyllabic foot (the flat|tering in|dex), but it is easily slurred. On the other hand, the "single-mould" is all but universal ; *epanaphora* (which disjoins the lines specially) is prominent, and it bears the full hall-mark of the workshop of which it is one of the greatest triumphs.

that he denied his prisoners in the other. But he himself relapses in the "Cankered Bolingbroke" harangue to his father and uncle, and comes back again in his satire on Glendower. Lady Percy is very nearly perfect in the newer numbers, when she tries to keep her father-in-law from rushing on his fate ; and the King is between the two in his celebrated apostrophe to Sleep : while the Prince, as is fitting, "likes the youngest best," in his to the Crown. In fact the poet is by this time nearly at mastery of the newer measure in its older form—that which has got over the stand-off disposition of the lines towards each other, but has not yet completely achieved variety of music and structure in the lines themselves.

Richard II.   The prosodic, like the other interest of *Richard II.*, arising from the comparison with Marlowe on the other hapless "Second," is exceptional, and it can hardly escape any reader who has got beyond the state of thinking prosody pedantry.   There can, of course, be not the slightest doubt that it was written under the influence of the hardly older but rather more precocious poet and his fellows ; nor is there any play which is more likely to have been the direct occasion of Greene's splenetic outburst.   The single-line model is conspicuous throughout ; and there are few finer instances of it anywhere than in the famous "rally" of Gaunt and his exiled son—

> All places that the eye of Heaven visits
>
> O who can hold a fire in his hand,[1]

to the King's final soliloquy just before his murder. But whereas in *Titus Andronicus* this model showed but a few marks of approaching change by fusion, here these marks are ubiquitous. Even in some of the passages just referred to they appear. It is specially curious to notice how, in the great patriotic speech of Gaunt, the central

---

[1] Both these are good instances of the distinction I have tried to draw between the "single-moulded" and the merely "end-stopped" line.

passage,[1] although almost every line is self-enclosed *as* a line, the paragraph-effect is given in a way that Marlowe hardly ever attains, by the variation of the pause, the weighting of different parts of the line by the quicksilver power of specially sonorous or important words, and sometimes by a cunning parenthetic device which makes the voice hurry over parts of a line, or whole lines, so as to connect, rhythmically as in sense, what comes after with what comes before. Indeed the rhetorical - poetical " colour " which Shakespeare has conveyed to his blank verse in this play, may vie with almost anything later ; though the actual drawing and composition of the lines are less varied and delicate. This is the case with Richard's speech to Aumerle, his despairing reception of the news of the death of his friends, and his other " epideictics." And it is worth observing that the charge, so often brought against this play, that the rhetorical character rather outvies the strictly poetical, whether just or not (which does not concern us), connects itself very interestingly with the undoubted prosodic symptoms and stage of it. It is the work of a man at once striving

[1] This royal throne of kings, this scepter'd isle,
This earth of majesty, this seat of Mars,
This other Eden, demi-paradise,
This fortress built by Nature for herself
Against infection and the hand of war,
This happy breed of men, this little world,
This precious stone set in the silver sea,
Which serves it in the office of a wall
Or as a moat defensive to a house,
Against the envy of less happier lands,
This blessed plot, this earth, this realm, this England,
This nurse, this teeming womb of royal kings,
Fear'd by their breed and famous by their birth,
Renowned for their deeds as far from home,
For Christian service and true chivalry,
As is the sepulchre in stubborn Jewry
Of the world's ransom, blessed Mary's Son,
This land of such dear souls, this dear dear land,
Dear for her reputation through the world,
Is now leased out, I die pronouncing it,
Like to a tenement or pelting farm :
England, bound in with the triumphant sea,
Whose rocky shore beats back the envious siege
Of watery Neptune, is now bound in with shame,
With inky blots and rotten parchment bonds.

(whether consciously or not does not in the least matter) to write up to a certain model, *and beyond it.* Nobody, not even Shakespeare, could do this without producing a certain effect of artifice and labour.

The Merchant of Venice.   The last of the Meres-mentioned plays, *The Merchant of Venice*, from its being one of the most popular of all, both in stage and study, has also been one of those which have attracted the most prosodic attention. It has, however, from this point of view unnecessarily puzzled those who are unhappy unless they can assign a date, and a fixed one, to each play as a whole. As for me, I judge, *securus*, that it is one of those which represent not necessarily very long intervals, but certainly intervals, of work, with correspondingly different stages of study, practice, and accomplishment. Not even *A Midsummer Night's Dream*, though the actual variety of metre in it may be greater, has passages representing such different grades of apprenticeship and craftsmanship. The Casket scenes, especially those with Morocco and Arragon, are notoriously of the earlier type — not directly Marlowesque, for there is much more enjambment than in Marlowe, but sententious and staccato for all that enjambment. Not a few of the earlier set speeches, especially that of Salarino about the dangers of the sea, are of the half-and-half kind : while not merely Portia's diploma-piece for her doctor's gown but many other speeches of hers, nearly all of Shylock's, and much else, are on the perfectly or almost perfectly fused model — not far from *Antony and Cleopatra* itself.

The later plays.   After Meres's list we have, in fact, no thoroughly satisfactory dates for Shakespearian production ; though we know too well when that production must have stopped. The apparently more certain evidences of entries of licensing or printing, the order of performance, and the infinitely uncertain ones of allusion to events which commentators have worked so hard, would be treacherous testimony for us anyhow ; and, as it happens, we do not want them. The actual prosodic progress —from a *pot-pourri* of metres with stiff blank verse, or from the latter alone, to a complete command of blank verse itself; and then, perhaps, a slight tendency, not exactly to abuse but to use very lavishly the redundant syllable—is logically too convincing and too well supported by the general comparison of the plays before 1598 with the plays after it, to need much argument. Having once laid down the law of it, a slight survey of these plays themselves, for the most part in their canonical (though most certainly *not* chronological order), will suffice.[1]

Whatever the heretical eccentrics who deny the late- *The Tempest.* ness of *The Tempest* may have to say for themselves (I have never been able to discover in it anything of value) on other grounds, it is certain that they can derive no countenance from prosody. It is simply impossible, to any one who has made a careful prosodic study of the plays in the Meres list, that *The Tempest* should be early. There is hardly so much as a trace of the old staccato line, even in passages such as Ariel's to the "three men of sin," and some of Prospero's which would, in the early period, have irresistibly invited it. The couplets of the Masque, indeed, show something of the type; but there is no reason whatever why *these* should not have been written earlier, and perhaps without any view to their actual place of appearance. On the other hand, the actual type is of the most advanced kind—the "fingering" of the overlapped lines exhibiting absolutely perfect mastery, and the abundant redundances indicating that tendency, almost to take liberties with licence, which was to prove so dangerous when the wand slipped out of Prospero's hand.[2]

[1] I fear my arrangement may prove teasing to some readers; but I do not see my way to alteration. For I wish at any cost to avoid a hard-and-fast ordering, even on purely prosodic grounds, inasmuch as I do not believe in the possibility of such a thing on any; and I wish to respect, as far as possible, the solid facts of the Meres list, the Folio contents, and the parallelism of the inside and outside *Histories*.

[2] This is not a *Beauties of Shakespeare*; but it can hardly be inexcusable to note that the very Mount Everest of the blank verse region—the passage that is "rounded with a sleep," the deepest peace over the highest peak—occurs in *The Tempest*.

The later (?)
Comedies.
The Merry Wives.
The Merry Wives (we shall silently pass over the plays already mentioned) is very largely prose, or blank verse of the masterly prose-verse style elsewhere to be noted. The exceptions are not prosodically very remarkable, but rather of the accomplished early time than of a later.

Measure for Measure.
Measure for Measure, however, is, in prosodic as in other respects, something of a puzzle. It is generally taken as a rather late play. I have always myself been pretty sure, for reasons by no means wholly prosodic, that it is in part an early one. For instance, Shakespeare surely never drew Pompey *after* he had conceived his greater clowns, nor Lucio *after* he had drawn Benedick or even Sir Toby. But the blank verse is certainly mixed. None of it, perhaps, is of the earliest type, and some of it is, if not of the latest, of a late kind, as in the terror-struck eloquence of Claudio, and the Duke's great but ineffectual exhortation which precedes it. But in some places—especially in the opening passages, where the same Duke unfolds his exceedingly unstatesmanlike design, and that a little later when he reveals the rather ungenerous reason of it to Friar Thomas—there are all the marks of imperfect accomplishment. Abrupt ends occur side by side with divided middles ; large redundancy with a stiff and sententious form of the individual line. Judging by prosody only, one would say that the play had been more than once begun, and more than once left off.

As You Like It.
There is nothing of this kind about *As You Like It*, which is "of the Cabinet" ; a capital example of the plays where the poet, whatever he wants to do prosodically, does it without the slightest difficulty, and with perfect success. It has, as befits a comedy, much prose ; but as soon as it suits the author to drop into poetry, his blank verse is of the absolutely perfect type—so easy that it alternates with prose itself without any sense of jar, and yet perfectly modulated and rhythmed. There is not a very great deal of redundancy ; it is not late enough for that. But the poet never hesitates at the

extra-syllable when he wants it, and never fails to want it to good purpose. If there is anywhere a falling back on the stopped type it is, perhaps, in Phoebe's

> I would not be thy executioner;

and there, as elsewhere, it is probably done on purpose.

In *The Taming of the Shrew*, on the other hand, *Taming of the Shrew.* which is certainly earlier, this type is paramount : not indeed of the stiffest, but much suppled and eased by the genius of the adapter-author, and found side by side with much jointed conversation-verse of a fairly accomplished kind.

Twelfth Night puts itself behind (that is to say, before) *Twelfth Night.* *As You Like It* by a somewhat greater predominance of the self-centred line, with the tendency (which seems to accompany that predominance, but which is, of course, a cause precedent rather than a result of it) towards constant dropping into rhyme. The very beautiful opening speech of the Duke is of this kind ; yet it is imperatively necessary to observe that though there is somewhat too much of a tendency to turn the bullets out and nip off their junction singly, yet there is the fullest sense of the importance of varying them individually. The opening speeches of all Shakespeare's plays, except the very earliest, are almost invariably documents for this process of pause-variation. The "end-stopping," however, continues. It is notorious (the warning must again be repeated that it is not identical with end-punctuation) in Viola's prettiest sighings ; in Olivia's stateliness and surrender alike ; almost (though of course not quite) everywhere. At the same time, the very large amount of prose in the play curtails the opportunity of variation. And the same is the case with *Much Ado about Nothing*, *Much Ado.* which was, therefore, omitted from its proper place in the folio list. Except that *Twelfth Night* is the purest comedy and *Much Ado* very nearly tragic, these plays ,run indeed very much in a curricle prosodically, though the last named is a little the more mature. The principal blank-verse scene—that of the false accusation brought against Hero in the church, and the council held after it—is very well illustrative of the later form of stopped verse, which has actually chipped itself free to a great extent from the mere shell of the earlier mould, but has not yet fully spread and freely used the wings of rhythmical undulation.[1]

The Winter's Tale.   In *The Winter's Tale* we have blank verse of the very latest kind, which shows what it can do poetically in the famous and incomparable flower-speech of Perdita, but is on the whole (for Shakespeare was an experimenter to all but the last) rather more loose-girt than the medium of *The Tempest.* The writer not only indulges in the redundant syllable freely, but is particularly fond of making his coupling foot with the next line redundant [2]— a distinctly hazardous *tour de force* which, when attempted in the next generation, had much to do with the un- buttoning and unbuckling of blank verse altogether. So, too, he is also fond of fashioning this union [3] out of the conjunction " and "—a perfectly justifiable thing, except in the eyes or ears of those who, to this day, do not know what Stanyhurst knew three hundred years ago and more, the double quantity of that useful monosyllable and others ; but, again, a dangerous one in unskilful hands. There is almost a redundance of redundances themselves : though one may trust the master one cannot trust his scholars not to forget that, when licences and exceptions go beyond a certain proportion, they lose their own justification as variety, and do not often acquire a fresh one as norm. There might be some reason for thinking *The Winter's Tale* Shakespeare's first experiment in very

---

[1] To attempt to " place " this batch (with *The Merchant of Venice*) too exactly would be to commit the very fault which seems to me gravest in the usual commentator. *The Taming of the Shrew* ought to be the earliest ; *As You Like It* must be the latest. *Twelfth Night* and *Much Ado* should come between them, and are much of a piece in themselves and with each other. *The Merry Wives* stands alone. In *The Merchant of Venice* and *Measure for Measure* early and late work are pretty clearly mingled.

[2] Leontes opening his free arms and weeping
His welcome forth.

[3]   .   .   .   bold oxlips and
The crown-imperial.

free redundance and overlapping combined : perhaps one
made very much earlier than is usually thought, and kept
back.   Nor would this lack support in some non-prosodic
aspects of the play.[1]

Most of the English " Histories " come into Meres's
list, and have thus been discussed, as well as *Henry VI.*,
which is not there.   *Henry V.*—resting, as it does, in
part on old work, but in its most remarkable passages
pure Shakespeare—is prosodically of a late, but not
the very latest portion of the first stage.   The single-
verse mould is still, so to speak, the handiest that the
author finds to pour his verse into ; and he uses hardly
any other in the set scenes of the First and Second Acts
respecting the claim to the French crown and the Scroop
conspiracy, the chorus-prologues, etc.   But he passes
into the fused form as before, when passion rather than
pomp requires expression : as in the great soliloquy
" Upon the King."   Indeed, and for obvious reasons,
Shakespeare's soliloquies, as they are among his most
characteristic passages in other respects, are also of the
first importance as prosodic " places."   The bold picture

The other English Histories.

Henry V.

[1] A longer specimen should, perhaps, be given, as the prosodic character
of the play is peculiar :—

> *Flo.* So call it : but it does fulfil my vow ;
> I needs must think it honesty.   Camillo,
> Not for Bohemia, nor the pomp that may
> Be thereat glean'd, for all the sun sees or
> The close earth wombs or the profound seas hide
> In unknown fathoms, will I break my oath ;
> To this my fair beloved : therefore, I pray you,
> As you have ever been my father's honour'd friend,
> When he shall miss me,—as, in faith, I mean not
> To see him any more,—cast your good counsels
> Upon his passion : let myself and fortune
> Tug for the time to come.   This you may know
> And so deliver, I am put to sea
> With her whom here I cannot hold on shore ;
> And most opportune to our need I have
> A vessel rides fast by, but not prepared
> For this design.   What course I mean to hold
> Shall nothing benefit your knowledge, nor
> Concern me the reporting.

This connects itself, rather remarkably, with the *All's Well that Ends Well*
passages cited above.

of the wretchedness of the English army by Grandpré— a thing resembling Victor Hugo's sketches with pen-ends —is half-and-half, as is also the hackneyed (if it could be hackneyed) address to "my cousin Westmoreland"; while in Burgundy's oration towards the close, the older model has the speech pretty much to itself. The Sonnet-Epilogue by the Chorus is noteworthy, and reminds us of the Sonnet-Prologues to the first two acts of *Romeo and Juliet.*

Henry VIII.   As for *Henry VIII.*, the suspicions of at least collaboration therein are well known. A good deal of it *must* be Shakespeare's; the fall [1] of Wolsey and the death of Katharine are his in thought, in diction, and in prosody, as surely as if we had his autograph assertion of the fact, signed and witnessed by Fletcher and Ben Jonson, and the witnesses' signatures attested by a succession of endorsements for each generation to the present day. The Prologue has, indeed, no such ring, and this might have been added; but I do not see much else that fails to come up to the test. The whole play, however, is well known to be as full of hendecasyllables as one of Beaumont and Fletcher's own, and the overlapping even exceeds the redundancy. It is therefore impossible that it should not be late.

Troilus and Cressida.   It is equally impossible, to pass to the classical plays, that *Troilus and Cressida*, in part at least, should not be early; and it must be remembered that the fact of Meres *not* mentioning a play is not final. But it belongs to the class in which, though the bullet-mould verse (as it has been called) is still predominant, there are already redundant endings, full pauses in the middle of lines, and even some direct enjambment between line and line. The piece also, as is well known, is full of the long set tirades— almost soliloquies—couched in very rhetorical, and even bombastic language, which are characteristic of the

---

[1] Even the "farewell," which seems to some so eminently Fletcherian, is to me, after recent and copious re-readings of "B. and F.," Fletcher *plus* some more potent spirit prosodically as otherwise, if it is Fletcher at all. The further discussion of this seems to me rather for editors of the two dramatists.

University Wits.   And something of this comes in the modernest touch of the whole, the fine

> Time hath, my lord, a wallet at his back,

of Ulysses, which may stand as a capital specimen of Shakespeare's blank verse just before it had attained its highest point of ease, without ceasing in the least to be well girt ; while nearly as much may be said of Troilus's passionate repudiation of the identity of " Diomed's Cressida " with his own.

But the other Greek tragedy — to violate the folio order a little, here as elsewhere, for convenience' sake — though somewhat of a puzzle in many ways, is certainly of a later date than *Troilus* prosodically.   The great prosodic note of *Timon* is that pause which shocked Guest[1] *Timon of* so irreconcilably, and which shows the final mastery of *Athens.* the whole secret—

> .   .   .   . Dead
> Is noble Timon.

But this, though a special grace, a single flower or feather in the cap, is not in any discordance with the general prosodic character of the garment.   From the first conversation of Painter and Poet to the funeral speech of Alcibiades, in which the tolling-bell pause above quoted occurs, the blank verse is of the thoroughly fused, matured, accomplished type, whether in jointed or in single speech. There is some but not much redundance and enjambment, rather, it would seem, for convenience than deliberately used.

The three Roman plays, on the other hand, exhibit, probably because they were actually written in their proper chronological sequence,[2] a steady rise in prosodic mastery.

---

[1] *English Rhythms*, ed. Skeat, p. 153.   "Opposed to every principle of accentual rhythm," he says, and perhaps he is right.   But in that case the principles of accentual rhythm are obviously themselves opposed to the best English poetry.

[2] It is usual to regard *Julius Cæsar* as the earliest by some seven years, but the evidence for its date is weak, and that for the late dates of the others weaker.   On the other hand, the " cragginess " of *Coriolanus* in parts seems to me much more like a partial and probable break-up of the rock-wall of *Titus* than an experiment later than the smoothness of *Julius Cæsar*.

Coriolanus.   In *Coriolanus* we are already far from the at least pseudo-Roman *Titus Andronicus*; but *Antony and Cleopatra* shows the blank verse of Shakespeare at its absolute zenith. "My name is Caius Marcius," "All places yield to him," and the great supplication-rebukes of Volumnia are so good that, considering them singly, a critic might say they could not be better. If a suspicion of want of ease, of absence of variety, of the declamatory occurs to us, it is only on the "rascally, comparative" principle, because the *Julius Cæsar.* same writer has given us things more perfect. In *Julius Cæsar* variety itself, colour, flexibility, a dozen other qualities of attraction reinforce and complicate the Coriolanian dignity. The appeal of Marullus, partisan as it is, sets the note, or one of the numerous notes, of brilliant phrase married to concerted verse; and all the great passages, that literally every schoolboy knows, carry it on to the end. It might seem impossible to improve on *Antony and* this; but I sincerely think that *Antony and Cleopatra* *Cleopatra.* does show an improvement, and the last possible. The very opening speech, poetical enough, but, as was fitting, somewhat rhetorically poetical in substance, displays such cunning and science of pause and line-weighting that it is perhaps worth taking as the specimen thereof.[1] The poet plays on the ten lines as if they were the strings, separate but in harmony, of a ten-stringed lyre. There is hardly any prose—none, in fact, save in the one purely

---

[1] Nay, || but this dotage of our general's
O'erflows the measure : || those his goodly eyes,
That o'er the files | and musters of the war
Have glowed like plated Mars, || now bend, | now turn,
The office and devotion of their view
Upon a tawny front : || his captain's heart,
Which | in the scuffles of great fights | hath burst
The buckles on his breast, || rene[a]g[u]es all temper,
And is become | the bellows and the fan
To cool a gipsy's lust.

(Here the double division marks indicate stronger, and the single lighter, *pauses*—*not*, as usually in the latter case, *feet*.) Attention may also be called to the set speeches of Octavius on different occasions. They are usually in very artful verse, strongly but variously broken by middle pauses; extremely effective, but with the *art* obviously emphasised to suit the character. *Cf.* especially the opening of III. vi. and the speeches to Octavia later.

comic passage,—but Shakespeare moulds his blank verse so impeccably that it never sounds unnatural in doing prose office.   And when it does its own, it is indeed far above singing.   Rhyme is great and good ; no one who has done me the honour to read my first volume will doubt my allegiance to it.   Stanza is good ; I may say the same of that.   But no rhyme, no stanza, could have given us such a piece of pure and absolute poetry—that is to say, of language in metrical form—as

> Peace ! Peace !
> Dost thou not see my baby at my breast,
> That sucks the nurse asleep ?

The serpent of old Nile dies true to herself in the marvellous winding of this dying fall, which, while it is one of the greatest things in poetry, is an absolute pattern, a school-model and sampler of all but the whole secret of blank-verse fashion in pause, and cadence, and composition.

The first of the four great romantic tragedies, as it is one of the best known both to audiences and readers, so it is one of the fullest of puzzles, not least prosodically, to critics.   Nowhere has Shakespeare shown either the infinite resources of blank verse, or his own infinite command[1] of them, more completely and victoriously than in *Macbeth*.   Not only do all the great single speeches— from Lady Macbeth's " The raven himself is hoarse " to that ineffable lament of her husband's for her, which some equally but differently ineffable persons regard as a callous put-by, and Siward's epitaph on his son—exhibit these two things as he only could exhibit or has exhibited them ; but the jointed work of, say, the banquet scene, is not inferior.   Still, mainly but not merely in the singular overture, there are passages of a far older and less accomplished type.   In the curious bombast of the Sergeant, in Ross's first entrance, and (which, I think, has been less noticed) almost everywhere where the Thanes appear, we have, if not full, yet distinct, examples of the gasp-line, unmodulated and unsymphonised, the line weighted with

The Four Great Tragedies.

Macbeth.

---

[1] For more on this command and these resources, see the general remarks which will follow this detailed comment.

fixed plummets or pledgets of lead, and not with coursing quicksilver.   Half-a-dozen different conclusions might be drawn from these facts as to the origin, the date, and other things which concern a different method of inquiry from ours.   It is enough for us to point out that they exist.

Hamlet.   The "points in Hamlet's soul" are a byword ; and the points which make *Hamlet* its author's capital play are scarcely less numerous, or less disputable.   On one point concerning it, however, one may pronounce with some positiveness.   The play, in its recognised form, is the work of a man for whom blank verse has no further secrets, who has every trick of it literally at his finger's ends ; and who, moreover, is not yet under the influence of any mannerism which impairs the universality of his handling of the medium.   Except that he is not so prodigal of the trisyllabic foot as he might be, and, as sometimes elsewhere, restricts it mainly to that interesting but tell-tale use at the cæsura on which we speak presently, there is hardly a single device that he does not employ copiously ; and he employs them all with a very minimum of effort.   In particular, he has now so completely got under his command the jointed blank verse of conversation, that he really has no need of prose.   He uses it, of course ; *Hamlet* is hardly a greater place for anything Shakespearian than for the Shakespearian prose ; but he need not have used it.   The First Act has many passages where prose would do just as well as verse, but where the actual easy jointed verse does just as well as prose.   He can still, when he chooses and thinks it appropriate, use the old staccato form.[1]   The King's opening harangue in Act I. Sc. ii. is mainly in this, and it recurs at intervals up to Horatio's closing observations. But it is quite evidently not an obsession from which the writer with difficulty escapes, or an object at which he dutifully aims ; it is something that he does because he likes and chooses to do it.   Elsewhere, in Hamlet's great soliloquies, and indeed constantly, he chooses to do something quite different——he has the paragraph style as

---

[1] As, for instance, in the inset play with obvious reason.

completely at command as the staccato or the mosaic, and uses it at his pleasure, and for ours.

Even these things, however, do not show the terms of absolute and intimate familiarity on which the medium and the craftsman now are, so well as another. The variation of the pause, the breaking of the line, the use of the redundant syllable both at end and cæsura, and the trisyllabic foot improved from this latter, are all great things in the perfecting of the decasyllable. But, to paradox it a little, the greatest evidence of the triumph of this decasyllable is to be found in the lines which are not decasyllabic ; in those which exceed and become Alexandrines, more or less regular, of which there are not a few ; and in the fragments, falling short of decasyllabic length, of which there are many.[1] For these are evidently *not* like the excessive or defective lines in fifteenth and even mid-sixteenth-century verse—blundering attempts to be regular ; but quite deliberate indulgences in excess or defect over or under a regular norm which is so pervading, so thoroughly marked, that it carries them off on its wings. In the whole First Act of *Hamlet* (I have just read it through for the purpose, scanning every line) there is not a single unmetrical verse or fragment of verse, nor any licence unsanctioned by the general principles of which we are watching the evolution in this treatise, except that (certainly sanctionable by them) of using lines longer or shorter than the norm when the poet chooses to do so. To read *Hamlet*, and think of *Titus Andronicus* or *Love's Labour's Lost*, is a most quaint and pleasing experience; to read *Hamlet* and then one of Marlowe's plays, remembering that the poets were of the same age, that they were not so very unequally matched in quality, whatever may be the case with quantity, of genius, and that scarcely more than fifteen years can by any possibility have elapsed between the pieces, may make one simply marvel.

---

[1] This is a point of importance, and may be misunderstood by those who have not accustomed themselves to note the difference between poetical and prosodic rhythm. What I mean is that the incomplete lines, of which there are many, even in I. i., *all scan regularly as far as they go*, like those found here and there in Virgil.

44   *THE TIME OF SHAKESPEARE*   BOOK V

King Lear.   There are some peculiarities in the blank verse of
King Lear. Instead of the set speeches in the earlier
part of the play showing—as we have seen is sometimes
the case, even in pieces pretty late in date and pretty far
advanced in accomplishment — a tendency towards the
stiffened model, the decasyllables of Lear's ill-judged and
ill-fated bid for his daughters' hypocrisy are of the very
finest type.   They run into each other less than the
probably still later model of *The Winter's Tale*, and
Cymbeline, and *The Tempest*; but they are even fuller of
trisyllabic feet, and the lines extend not merely to the
Alexandrine but to the fourteener.[1] The speeches, evidently
conned beforehand, of Goneril and Regan, lack this luxuriance, and Lear's rage at Cordelia's fractiousness (one fears it
must be called so, and it supplies in her case the ἁμαρτία
of the play) acts as a kind of styptic to it.   But it recurs
in him and in others, though not in all, and not always
in those who use it.   It is the properest of all possible
media for the splendid central scenes, and especially for
that more than Æschylean opening which the late
Professor Bain,[2] though acknowledging it to be one of
the loftiest flights of Shakespeare's sublimity, thought
"wanting in dignity," " improperly arranged" ("hurricane,"
it seems, ought to have preceded "cataract "), "powerful
but extravagant," "containing epithets not specially applicable," and " barely redeemed from feebleness."   Well as
it is known, we must give this so loftily feeble piece—

> Blow, winds, and crack your cheeks ! rage ! blow !
> You cataracts and hurricanoes, spout
> Till you have drench'd our steeples, drown'd the cocks !
> You sulphurous and thought-executing fires,
> Vaunt-couriers to oak-cleaving thunderbolts,
> Singe my white head !   And thou, all-shaking thunder,
> Smite flat the thick rotundity o' the world !
> Crack nature's moulds, all germens spill at once,
> That make ingrateful man !

Here the monosyllabic feet in " rage " and " blow," the
trisyllabic (nearly if not quite tribrachs) at " sul|phurous

---

[1] May be prevented now.   The princes, France and Burgundy.
[2] *Rhetoric and Composition*, i. 105.   ,

and," and " vaunt cou|riers to " | and " rotun|dity o' | the
world "—are the *clous* or the hinges of the metrical composition.   It is not for nothing that the equally famous
description of the cliff is in regular, cunningly jointed, but
swiftly moving verse, a sort of under-the-breath of appre-
hension, as if boisterous speaking might bring danger ;
nor that the broken verse (really " broken ") of Lear's
invective on women resolves itself at last into sheer prose ;
nor that Edmund supplies a hardly less perfect example
in little than Cleopatra's, with—

> Thou hast spoken right : 'tis true   .
> The wheel has come full circle : I am here ;

nor that Lear's last moan, before his agony chokes him,
is represented by the incomparable audacity and the more
incomparable success of the five-times-repeated trochee
" Never ! "   Once more there is no spirit from the infinite
deep of prosodic possibility that the poet cannot call, and
none that dare disobey the calling.

The agony in *Othello* is not finally abated, because *Othello.*
Desdemona is a more entirely innocent victim than Cordelia,
and the ἁμαρτία of the Moor is far more pardonable than
that of Lear.   But the matter of the play is much more
varied ; and whereas, in *Lear*, the actual tragedy begins
almost at once, and is hardly medicable, the author of
Much Ado about Nothing would not have found it a very
difficult matter to turn *Othello* into a tragi-comedy, though
the present phase of dramatic taste would of course have
been shocked at this.   Therefore the play requires greater
variety of medium also, and has it.   At this time, moreover, Shakespeare was evidently expert in, and fond of,
the very freest and at the same time the very purest form
of his verse.   Iago is, in fact, the great master of it.
Few people have ever denied " mine ancient " brains, and
some have thought that, if he had not been such a villain,
he might have been a very good fellow.   He is certainly
both good and great at verse.   His two chief opening
speeches are actually the text and *locus* for this kind of it,
as well as for demonstrating the extraordinary and hardly

comprehensible error of those who will not have "feet"
in Shakespearian, or in any, scansion.   The excursions
outwards and the withdrawals inward from the norm
are almost infinite ; but they are animated and regulated
by the presence of that norm in foot and verse alike.
The extreme freedom of the type is appropriately modified
in the interview with Brabantio, and in what we may call
the "Court-of-Honour" scene, but it subsists to some
extent throughout.   Some of the characters—Montano
and the Two Gentlemen, for instance—make a little
return to the "bumbasted out" blank verse ; while Iago
in his soliloquies is rather more regular than *Hamlet*,
precisely because he is less natural.   But Desdemona's
perfect naturalness makes her almost as excursive as her
great enemy in his virtuoso moods.   And all—Iago himself in the fiend's aside "not poppy nor mandragora,"
Othello in his farewell to peace of mind, Desdemona in
her sorrow at his change, and still more and most of all
the Moor in his agony of remorse—can employ the sedater,
but perfectly motioned and well-breathed model to perfection.   Yet in that other of the *apices* of the impregnable
and only from afar beholdable places of poetry with
which the play closes, there is a sort of return to the
elastic verse.   Othello hurries over or lengthens out—

> Nor set down aught | in malice : | then must you speak,

and

> Richer | than all | his tribe ; | of one | whose sub|dued eyes.

But there is no irregular throb in the steady pulse and
purpose of the period from " Set you down this," to
" And smote him " ; though the sob of the trisyllable may
return in the final

> I kissed | thee ere | I killed | thee : no way | but this.

Cymbeline.   *Cymbeline*—a play of which more foolish people have
said more foolish things [1] perhaps than even of any other

---

[1] I think the palm is perhaps due to a mysterious person at Calcutta who,
as I learn from Mr. Bertram Dobell's *Catalogue of Privately Printed Books*,
requested to be informed, in the year 1841, " What can be more drivelling than
the ' Dirge on Fidele '—a subject of which Collins has shown the poetical

play of Shakespeare (if that be possible)—does not tax the instrument to the superhuman extent of *Othello*. And the late type of verse—rather loose than merely free—which it shares with some others, suits well enough, and breaks into prose quite naturally and easily when the poet feels inclined for even more of " dressing-gown-and-slippers " liberty. But he never forgets civility ; and is always duly garbed for a ceremonious occasion. Iachimo resembles his spiritual and perhaps natural clansman—certainly compatriot—Iago, in being able to run the gamut of blank verse perfectly ; Imogen's is as gracious as her nature ; the Queen's has a treacherous stateliness ; the most orderly pattern is perhaps found in the scene with the banished family ; the most powerful in that which follows between Imogen and Pisanio ; while the sweetest is Guiderius' companion flower-piece to Perdita's in the play which is itself the pendant to *Cymbeline* prosodically. But the most accomplished is Iachimo's at the accomplishment of his treason ; and this is not of the very loosest model.

Nor shall we omit *Pericles*, of the authorship of which *Pericles.* (at least as far as concerns the greater part of it) I have never had the slightest doubt. But it was ·evidently a derelict in some way. Not merely the extremely *décousu* character of the plot, and the absence of any distinct character-drawing, but the importance and peculiarity of the chorus, show earliness ; and so does the blank verse, though this is not exactly of the earliest. The first

---

capabilities ? " Now certainly Collins, at his best, is a poet whom it is not absurd to mention in the same sentence with Shakespeare, different though the magnitude of their stars may be. But the "drivel" of

> Fear no more the heat o' the sun
> Nor the furious winter's rages,

and the " poetry " of

> To fair Fidele's grassy tomb
> Soft maids and village hinds shall come

(which is hardly at the best eighteenth century level in its gradus epithets and mawkish sweetness), is a very comfortable comparison. It would be interesting to know the gentleman's name, and whether he left a family. His spiritual descendants are certainly still with us.

speeches, especially the soliloquies, of Pericles himself are distinctly but not exclusively stopped ; and there is plenty of redundance in them. So also is it with Cleon's in the famine. But when the storm comes, the Prince, both in his opening and in the beautiful

> A terrible childbed hast thou had, my dear,

adopts a very much freer model—indeed, one almost as free as that of the great Quadrilateral. There is, how- ever, little new for us here, though we must return to the important octosyllables.

General considerations. In the foregoing survey of Shakespeare's plays I have given some general idea of the way in which the operation of the various agencies shows itself, with (as far as possible) the order of their succession. Really, though chrono- logical illustration is interesting and corroborative, it is in a way superfluous, because we can see without it how the employment of them would grow on the hands of such an artist. Of *deliberate* experimenting with any or all of them there would probably not be very much ; the man who wrote " Rebellion lay in his way, and he found it," has dispensed us from any such vain imagination. These things lay in *his* way ; and he found them, and made the most of them. That " most " also has been illustrated freely. But it is perhaps desirable to give it an account of something the same kind as that which has been given to the style which was its matrix and crude form.

The completed Shakespearian blank verse, as we see it maturing in the later early, and middle plays, and matured in the four great tragedies and in *Antony and Cleopatra*, preserves the iambic decasyllable as norm inviolably ; never instals any other, and makes everything that it admits hold of that. But the strict minimum is infinitely varied, and, even when kept, is entirely stripped of its monotonous and stable character, and made to understand that it must be Protean in itself, and ready to enter into infinite combinations with its neighbours. The great agency in this, beyond all doubt, is the

manipulation of the pause.   Not that Shakespeare is, as
some have vainly thought, to be scanned by " staves "—
staves " knapped," as the good old Biblical word has it,
almost as bluntly as the old alliterative verses themselves.
The futility of this notion is shown, in a way which makes
it wonderful that it should ever have been entertained by
anybody, in the fact that a very large proportion of
Shakespeare's lines have no real pause at all, are " staves "
of themselves, and hardly even that, so unbroken is the
rhythmical current of the adjacent lines from and into
them.   This doing away with middle- and end-pause
alike is at least as important as the variation of the
middle, and, in fact, is but an extension of it.

The normal blank-verse line of the origins, as Shakespeare took it over from Surrey, Sackville, and even the
Wits, was a strict " decasyllabon " of five iambics, with a
cæsura somewhat carefully observed about the middle,
and self-inclosed in a manner not easy to make plain by
individual examples, or by any process of overt analysis,
but sensible to any ear of the slightest delicacy when a
few specimens have been read.   It sometimes admitted a
sort of redundance or " weak ending," not merely in
words which were then really monosyllables, like " heaven,"
but in those which were trochaic-tipped with a very short
final syllable, like " glory."   This licence, however, did
not in the least affect its general structure.   It by no
means always concluded with even a comma (though it
mostly did do so) ; but the grammatical running on did
not in the least interfere with the metrical snapping off.
It tolerated pretty strong stops in the middle of the line,
but these also (so much stronger was the obsession of
line-integrity) did not interfere with the sunk ditch of the
line-end.   Thus, even when, as in the great passages
of Peele and Marlowe, the unity of thought and imagination made the paragraph quite *poetically* distinct, this
paragraph was never a real verse-period of the larger
kind ; there was no composition in the purely rhythmical
and metrical conception of the verse.   To put the thing
extremely—extravagantly, some would say—the delivery

of this paragraph to a person who did not understand the language would have conveyed to him the idea of some dozen or sixteen verses, individually perhaps melodious, but not *regimented*, not worked into any kind of *symphony*. This sort of blank verse we find in all the writers named above exclusively, with the exceptions (and others, of course), also noted above, in Marlowe and his mates, when the rough strife of poetry bursts its way through the iron gates of metre. We find it also in *Titus Andronicus*, in the *Comedy of Errors*, in *Love's Labour's Lost*, in the early rehandled " Histories," and elsewhere in Shakespeare himself.

But, as partly noted, there are certain features even in this rigid and early model which are at war with the self-contained single line and the merely cumulative batch of lines. They may be kept under as long as the poet's chief aim is to *secure* his decasyllabon, to keep it from doggerel on the one hand, and, on the other, to make it independent of the warning bell of rhyme at the end. But when practice, in himself to speak and in his readers to hear, has made the blank decasyllabic effect familiar— when it need not be strictly uniform in order to obtain recognition—these features assert themselves. The first of these probably, and the most insidious, but also the most revolutionary, is the redundant syllable. It is of an ancient house ; we had ourselves fifteeners before we had fourteeners, and in all prosodies from Greek downwards there has been a tendency to regard the last place in a line as a place of licence and liberty. It is curiously unassuming ; in words (to keep the same examples) not merely like " heaven," but like " glory," it is a sort of " breath " only, something that you do not count, but just smuggle in with its companion. Yet, as we shall see presently, it is a very Trojan Horse in reality. Then there is the stop, full or other, in the middle of the line. This also is innocent-seeming. What is it but a mere grammatical emphasising of the cæsura itself, recognised of Gascoigne and all good people long before the first of the Wits had trodden or supplied the stage ? Next probably—but it need hardly be said that I stand not upon the order—comes the intermixture of rhyme, a thing which the greatest blank verse will frown upon, but which is so likely as a relapse, so convenient as a " cue-tip," so pleasant to the as yet unaccustomed ear of the ground-lings ; and which, be it remembered, almost necessitates a sort of junction between two lines, though it may favour the closing of the couplets.   All these are things apparently compatible—certainly found—with the stiffest of the drumming decasyllabons, yet secret solvents of their stiffness.

Other things, still not ostensibly revolutionary, next suggest themselves.   We have seen in the last volume, that mediæval poets, whether through inexpertness or by experiment, and fifteenth - century poets through clumsiness, largely curtailed or extended the normal length of the line ; that there are Alexandrines even in Chaucer, while—a point to which the Renaissance was likely to pay more attention—there are undoubtedly incomplete lines in Virgil.   Why not avail oneself of these licences?   Even Marlowe had done so now and then.   Why not?   But if you do, your sacred integer of ten syllables is rudely touched.   Once more, again, you have recognised, and had formally recognised for you,[1] the duty of making a sort of fold or crease in each verse at the fourth, fifth, or neighbouring syllable.   It is inconvenient, as well as monotonous always to do it at the same place ; yet when you begin to vary that place, is not the structure of the line troubled, though beneficently so?   And is there not somehow a kind of rhythmic conspiracy in the successive lines where you vary it?   Then, too, there comes the power of words.   Important or beautiful words, adjusted, spaced, accumulated, give brilliancy, splendour, weight to the line.   But the line is so short.   Why cut the necklace into lengths?   Why not make the stars constellations?

And, lastly, there is the trisyllabic foot.

---

[1] On this and other references of the kind see the chapter on " Prosodists " in this Book.

I trust I may repeat (after the not of course unanimous but fairly general acknowledgment of critics, that the preceding volume has made something of a case for it) that the trisyllabic foot is ubiquitous in English verse from 1200 to 1500, and that nothing but the reaction from the anarchy of doggerel brought about later, the partial and only partial reprobation thereof. But there is no need to have recourse to this, though from the historical point of view it cannot be omitted. In blank verse, and especially in dramatic blank verse—when once the practitioner has got rid of his fear of losing the guide-rope, if he step out of the strict iamb—it *must*, in English, appear. It does appear ; and with it disappears the mere rub-a-dub of the decasyllabon.

The pause.
In arranging the pause—at any syllable from first to ninth, and at no syllable at all, not even tenth—he is helped infinitely by that distribution of the weight of words, rather after the fashion of quicksilver in a reed than of leaden bracelets fastened at intervals round a stick, which has been more than once referred to. Nobody has approached Shakespeare—Tennyson has perhaps come nearest, for Milton's verse is too uniformly stately for comparison—in this mastery of poetical conjuring with word and line, a mastery of which he had more than a glimpse as early as *Romeo and Juliet*, and of which he gave the final and perfect display in *The Tempest*. The lines rise, fall, sweep, wave, dart straight forward, are arrested in mid-air, insinuate themselves in serpentine fashion as if in sword-play against an invisible adversary.

But these effects of weight, lightness, pungency, arresting power, and so forth, are at least partly caused— are certainly assisted immensely—by two other things, the redundant ending and the trisyllabic foot. The first chiefly gives variety ; the second variety *and* flexibility as nothing else could do ; while variety again is lent by the shortened fragment-verses and the elongated Alexandrines and fourteeners, or by verses with several trisyllabic feet in them. How these various devices may be made to subserve particular effects of meaning, shades of passion,

and the like, need not be much dwelt on.   This is a form
of prosodic study which has always commended itself to
the multitude as much as, perhaps almost more than, it
should.   But as to the way in which the use of the
trisyllabic foot grew, I have a theory which is doubtless
not new but about which I have not seen much written.

It has been observed before, that, according to the The trisyllabic
principles of this book, "extra-metrical" syllables, anywhere foot and its
revival.
but at the end or middle of the verse, are a confession, as
the case may be, of impotence on the part of the poet
if they exist, of the critic, if they are supposed to exist.
And no great admiration has been hinted of the extra-
metrical syllable at the middle in any case.   I believe,
however, that at this critical moment in the history of
blank verse and, through the influence of this on rhyme,
in the history of English poetry generally, the mistake or
laches of indulging in this internal excrescence brought
about a great good.   A large, a very large, number of
lines could be pointed out where such a syllable is almost
undoubtedly intended by the poet (supposing he thought
about it at all) as a licence of the kind, and not to be
carried on to the other half of the line.   As such, the effect
is almost always ugly ; it can only be admired by those
persons (with whom the present writer most heartily
differs, though he has been confused with them) who
think that an irregularity *must* be an improvement, that
a mole *must* be a beauty, that discord *must* be
harmonious.   But such an ear as Shakespeare's could
not fail to perceive that this ugliness could be turned into
a beauty by simply effecting the connection, and fusing
the derelict syllable with the following iamb to make an
harmonious anapæst.[1]   And this, I have myself not the
slightest doubt, was, in his and other cases, the actual
genesis (whether consciously and deliberately carried out
does not, once more, in the least matter) of the revived
trisyllabic foot which Gascoigne had bewailed as dead.
And so the discord *was* made harmonious ; the mole *did*

---

[1] Those who like amphibrachs may, of course, join it to the preceding,
not the following, iamb.   To my ear this arrangement is generally inferior.

become a beauty ; and the irregularity *was* the foundation of the larger and nobler Rule. The process, in fact, is one of the best examples of that operation of growth and life to which the people who say that the ballad writers never thought about contending for the liberty of this very trisyllabic foot itself, seem insensible. I do not know whether the wind thinks about blowing or the flower about growing, but I know that they blow and grow.

The redundant syllable. The use at the end of the syllable, redundant or extra-metrical—if we must have the word, though to me extra-metre is no metre—has a different history. At the middle it is very rarely a beauty ; perhaps never, unless it can be " carried over " as just described. At the end it is often beautiful ; and, whether beauty or not, is almost inevitable now and then, and most useful constantly. Further, it is a most powerful and important instrument of variation— a natural link or remedy against line - isolation, far-descended as has been said, and of other excellent differences. But it is something of a Delilah—who was herself apparently of a good Philistine family, and is known to have had exceptional attractions as a person. Indeed, the parable or parallel works out with remarkable exactness ; for it is a very considerable time before Delilah takes away Samson's strength, and the means whereby she does so are mysterious. It can hardly be said (though one may feel a vague sense of danger) that in Shakespeare's own probably latest plays, where he indulges himself with the redundant line, Samson is anything but Samson still. There are passages on passages in Beau-mont and Fletcher themselves—notably that magnificent piece in *The False One*, which is one of the purplest patches in the coat of Elizabethan drama—where the hendecasyllable has it nearly all its own way, with no harm and much good. But Delilah is still Delilah ; and she is too much for Samson—the verse if not the verse-smith—at last.

Enjambment. She takes indeed two forms : for much the same as has been said of the redundant syllable may be said of enjambment or overlapping. This, indeed, is rather the special Delilah of the couplet than of blank verse, but each kind has to be very wary when it visits the vale of Sorek in this manner also. Opportunity of delight and occasion for display of power as it is to the verse that keeps itself strong and wide awake, overlapping is a place of slipping, and may be a pit of destruction, to the loose-girt and careless versifier. And it has, in common with redundancy and with the use of trisyllabic feet, the special danger that it is perfectly easy to do it badly. Anybody, as soon as these devices are once recognised, can practise them after a fashion, and everybody proceeds to do so : whence come things for tears.

But the offence is his by whom the offence cometh ; and Shakespeare in his complete work showed that there was no necessity of offence at all, while there was the possibility (and in his case the accomplishment) of infinite beauty. Foolish things have, no doubt, been said—in fact they are not unfrequently said at the present moment —as to the superiority of blank verse to rhyme ; and we shall have to deal with them, and with those from Milton downwards who have been and are guilty of them, as they occur. At present it is sufficient to point out, first, that the misvaluation is merely a case of the common inability to like two good things without putting them into unjust balances and weighing them against each other with unstamped weights. Secondly, that, for this purpose and that, blank verse is *not* superior to rhyme but demonstrably inferior. It will not do—at least it has not done—for strict lyric, as the moderate success even of Campion or Collins, and the failure of almost everybody else, have well shown. It is a great question whether it is not a very dangerous medium even for long narrative poems. But for *short* narratives : for short reflective, descriptive, didactic, and other pieces of various kinds : and for every kind of drama, or even partially dramatic matter, it is, in English, the predestined medium, hammered out at first by a full generation and more of partly unsuccessful, never more than partly successful, pioneers and journeymen, chipped into perfect

The morphology and bio-logy of blank verse.

form by the master Shakespeare, in probably not half a
generation longer.   Its extraordinary and unique success
in English—for German blank verse, good as it can be,
is far inferior, especially in variety and music ; and I know
no thirdsman that deserves to rank—is probably due to
the fact that our language, though perhaps singly accented,
is not singly emphasised ; that it provides a large number
of sufficient resting-places for the voice, but does not require
(or, except as an exception, allow) long dwelling on any.
The way in which not merely the French but almost all
continental nations hurry over half-a-dozen or a dozen
syllables, and then plunge on the succeeding one with
a volley of exploding and shrapnel-like emphasis, utterly
ruins blank verse, whether as articulately delivered, or
as read with that inarticulate but exactly proportioned
following of actual delivery which is necessary for
prosodic appreciation.   It is one of the worst faults of
the stress- or accent- or beat-system, as opposed to the
foot, that it vulgarises and impoverishes this great metre,
where the unstressed syllables are no less important than
the stressed.   It is essential to blank verse that no part
of it should be killed, and none brought into convulsive
and galvanic activity : otherwise the delicate and complicated or simple and yet substantial melody is jarred
and jangled out of all tune and time.   Yet what infinite
variety of time and tune can be got out of it—not by
" getting up stairs " on the instrument, and flinging oneself
down again, but by evoking the infinite variety of its
tones Shakespeare, Milton, Thomson, Shelley, Tennyson,
Browning, have shown us.   But the greatest of these,
and the first, and the master of all the rest in even the
details and peculiarities in which each is himself a master,
is Shakespeare.

The Poems.   It would be a pity not to pursue this mastery, without
a break, into the other and minor departments in which
it is shown, even though we may have to recur to the
subject hereafter.   It is, in fact, all the more important
and almost necessary to do so, in that the earliest
documents, certainly dated, of Shakespeare's prosodic

practice that we have, are non-dramatic. We may date by guesswork any existing dramatic passages of the earlier blank-verse type, such as those which excited Greene's spleen certainly, and his envy not improbably, as much before 1593 as we like ; but we *know* nothing dramatic of Shakespeare's before that time, and hardly anything for five years after it. *Venus and Adonis*, on the other hand, and *Lucrece* are assured facts of that year, 1593, and its successor. Now at the date of the earlier *The Faerie Queene* was but three years old, and *The Shepherd's Kalendar* itself but thirteen ; while the great sonnet-outburst was only beginning, and Drayton, the chief non-dramatic poet of Shakespeare's exact generation, had published nothing previously but the *Harmony of the Church.*

To say that the sixains of *Venus and Adonis* and the rhyme-royal of *Lucrece* are perfect, would be mere " blind affection," as Ben Jonson says. They are not ; and they would be much less interesting if they were. For in that case the experienced and unsatisfactory critic would expect with a rueful certainty, what has happened in so many other cases of mocking-birds, who can learn anything but do nothing. The individual verses of the *Venus* have the mark which we have seen so often before, and which is an infallible symptom of the desire at any cost, however unconsciously, to get rid of the abominable looseness of preceding generations—the mark of excessive self-completion, of what we have called the bullet-mould. Just as in the blanks, this effect is independent of mere punctuation at the verse end ; you will find it in such a line as—

> The studded bridle on a ragged bough

where there is no stop at all, not so much as a comma. And in the same way the final couplet is apt to be too much isolated from the quatrain—a thing which, as has been also pointed out, was a valuable school for the continuous stopped couplet itself, but which is not always a beauty in the stanza. But here, also, the dæmonic

Venus and Adonis.

element in Shakespeare shows itself, and here, fortunately, we can say that it shows itself at once. While he is musing over the supposed requirements of the metre the fire kindles, and the metre itself is transposed, transformed, transfused, under his hand. Spenser had begun the *Kalendar* with this very stave thirteen years before, and had done nobly with it. But though perhaps the stanza "Thou barren, etc.," formerly quoted, has a certain marmoreal dignity which the more passionate and human strains of the *Venus* do not invite, the advance in this direction of passionate humanity represented by prosodic movement is very great. It is no wonder that musicians should have seen the extraordinarily lyrical movement of " Bid me discourse," or that painters and naturalists should have acknowledged the astonishing feats of the episode of the horse. But the evidences of prosodic adequacy are omniform and omnipresent. In the single and early line—

> Ten kisses short as one, one long as twenty,

there is, when we consider the stage both of the poetry and of the poet, an almost uncanny mastery in the location of the pause, the distribution of the words of the hemistich, and the adoption of the redundant syllable. So with the trisyllabic centre of

> Leading him *prisoner* in a red rose chain,

and the fingering of the vowels and of the suggested trochees in

> Her two blue | windows | faintly | she upheaveth.

Rhyme-royal is a far finer measure than the sixain ; but, as we have noted already, it seems to be rather a capricious mistress, and not to reward all its lovers equally. Certainly Shakespeare does not get out of it, in proportion to its possibilities, quite the effect which, at a yet earlier stage, he produces with the other. Indeed, *Lucrece.* one might not be unjustified in the suspicion that *Lucrece*, though the later published, was the earlier written of the two. There are more of the mere tricks, rhetorical rather

than poetical, of *epanaphora* and the like : the separate
model of the lines is more constantly maintained ; and
the tetremimeral cæsura, which, as we can guess from
Gascoigne's warning, was a sort of fetich with rhyme-royal
writers, imposes its monotonous clutch too often.   It is
more like a school-exercise than anything else of Shakespeare's, though it is the exercise of a very remarkable
schoolboy indeed.   Besides, the perfection to which
rhyme-royal had been brought already, and by others, at
once made the exercise easy, and deprives it of interest.
It was probably the sense that, after Chaucer and
Sackville, little more was to be done with it that made
Spenser reject it for his great work, and even Shakespeare
could not, or at least did not, prove him wrong.

Very different is it with the *Sonnets*.   We are, of *The Sonnets.*
course, free here from the self-sought obsessions in respect
of subject or object which beset so many students of
these marvellous compositions.   It is enough for us that
they exist, and that Meres's reference shows that at any
rate some of them existed at a pretty early period of
Shakespeare's career ; while the general—not of course
quite universal—equality of the model makes it very
unnecessary to disturb ourselves with the futile inquiry
whether any, and if so which, of them were not or might
not have been handed about among his private friends
before 1598.   Here the poet has a medium which is
absolutely congenial to him, and with which, as with
blank verse, he can do anything he likes.   With his usual
sagacity he chooses the English form, and prefers its
extremest variety—that of the three quatrains and couplet,
without any interlacing rhyme.   Nevertheless he gives
the full sonnet-*effect* — not merely by the distribution
(which he does not always observe, though he often does)
of octave and sestet *subject*, but very mainly by that same
extraordinary symphonising of the prosodic effects of
individual and batched verses, which was his secret in
blank verse itself.   If it seem surprising that so difficult
and subtle a medium should be mastered so early, let it
be remembered that the single-line mould, properly used,

is by no means unsuitable to the sonnet, the effect of which is definitely cumulative.   We have no certain or even probable sonnets of Marlowe's, for the three coarse but fairly vigorous ones by "Ignoto," usually printed with his works, are very unlikely to be his.   But if he had written any he would not have had to alter his mode of line much in itself.   He would, however, have had to adjust it relatively, as he seldom did, and as Shakespeare began to do from the first, by weighting it variously, by applying what we have called the "quicksilver" touch.

It is by this combined cumulative and diversifying effect, this beating up against the wind as it were,[1] that the ordinary and extraordinary "tower" of these sonnets is produced ; and this tower is to some readers their great and inexhaustible charm.   No matter what the subject is, the " man right fair " or " the woman coloured ill," the incidents of daily joy and chagrin, or those illimitable meditations on life and love and thought at large which eternise the more ephemeral things,—the process, prosodic and poetic, is more or less the same, though carefully kept from monotony.   In the very first lines there is the spread and beating of the wing ; the flight rises till the end of the douzain, when it stoops or sinks quietly to the close in the couplet.   The intermediate devices by which this effect is produced are, as always with Shakespeare, hard to particularise.   Here, as in the kindred region of pure style, he has so little mannerism, that it is easier to apprehend than to analyse his manner.   It may be a coincidence, or it may not, that in a very large proportion of the openings what we may call a bastard cæsura, or ending of a word without much metrical scission at the third syllable, precedes a strictly metrical one at the fourth.[2]   Another point is that, throughout, full stops or

---

[1] Shakespeare, like a sensible man as he was, did not care a rush about the consecutiveness of his own metaphors ; indeed it is doubtful whether any sensible man, except Théophile Gautier, ever did.

[2] In other words the fourth half-foot is constantly monosyllabic.   "Look in thy glass" (iii.) is the first, and there are a dozen others in the first two dozen sonnets.

their equivalents in mid-line are extremely rare, and even at the end not common, till the twelfth, so that the run of the whole is uninterrupted, though its rhythm is constantly diversified. Redundant syllables are very rare, except where, as in lxxxvii., they are accumulated with evident purpose. The trisyllabic foot, though used with wonderful effect sometimes, is used very sparingly. On the whole Shakespeare seems here to have had for his object, or at any rate to have achieved as his effect, the varying of the line with as little as possible breach or ruffling of it. He allows himself a flash or blaze of summer lightning now and then, but no fussing with continual crackers. All the prosodic handling is subdued to give that steady passionate musing—that " emotion recollected in tranquillity "—which is characteristic of the best sonnets, and of his more than almost of any others. Of mere " sports," such as the octosyllabic cxlv., it is hardly necessary to speak.

There remain to be discussed the miscellaneous metres *Miscellaneous* in the Plays themselves, and the Songs. Of the former *metres.* not very much need be said. The fourteeners, the doggerel, the stanzas, the octosyllables, and the rhymed couplets are quite clearly makeshifts and stopgaps, dictated not (with a possible exception in the last case) by the poet's sense that they make good dramatic media, but at the most by an experimentalising tendency, at the least by mere noviceship and the following of others. It is, however, really curious how the faculty of turning everything touched more or less to gold, appears here also. Into the doggerel and the fourteeners, especially in *Love's Labour's Lost,* as well as into the short stanza-verse of *A Midsummer Night's Dream,* Shakespeare infuses an inimitable touch of parody which had not been seen in English prosodic handling since *Sir Thopas* ; and like Chaucer he takes care to make his parody particularly smooth and correct in its very absurdity. The octosyllables *The octo-* (mostly shortened to trochaic heptasyllables, and so *syllable.* patterning that delightful variation for the future) of the close of the *Dream,* of the Epilogue of *The Tempest,* of the scrolls in *The Merchant of Venice* and *As You Like It*, of the Gower Prologues (some of them among the most Shakespearian things in the play), in *Pericles*, show an absolute command of this old and charming measure, so easy in appearance, so difficult to preserve from sing-song and prose in reality. The stanza-speeches of the early and middle-early plays are too few and too unim-

Decasyllabic portant to require much attention. But the decasyllabic
couplets. couplets are in a somewhat different position, considering the abiding importance of that vehicle in English. This importance is, of course, somewhat diminished by the fact that they are almost entirely, either as has been said, makeshifts, or else dictated by the well-known cue-purpose—the desire to wind up a scene, or part of a scene, with a ring-beat agreeable to the audience and convenient to the actors. It will, however, be at once evident that this latter object of itself prescribes a certain decision and precision in the sound, as well as in the sense of the distichs, and so makes them inevitable patterns and stimulants in the cultivation of the stopped and epigrammatic form. Many of the most emphatic and clearest-ringing passages in Shakespeare—for instance, Iago's mocking praise of women and his half-triumphant, half-apprehensive anticipation of the night of murder—take this form. In the early and middle-early plays, as we have seen, and sometimes later for an object (as in the cases just mentioned), not merely end-couplets but whole passages fall into rhyme ; but the couplet is most commonly [1] of the stopped form—which indeed the poet had practised in his two earliest positively known works, both of them non-dramatic, as *code* to the sixain and the rhyme-royal. When, on the other hand, he wanted to overlap, his growing sense of the possibilities of blank verse made him independent of the couplet, or positively disinclined to it. Thus, in the battle which we are shortly to witness, his powerful influence and example is, by a rather quaint accident, on the side of the less Romantic form as against the more Romantic.

---

[1] Not, of course, always.

If good wine needs no bush, pure nectar needs it still less ; and who shall praise Shakespeare's songs ? Yet they touch us too nearly to be entirely passed over. It is at least remarkable that, except Peele in a few places, and Lyly (with whom he has a connection—never, of course, missed, but perhaps, on the whole, rather under-than over-valued), Shakespeare's predecessors do not seem to have thoroughly appreciated the charm of the lyric element, which he and his successors were to make a feature of the Elizabethan drama, and one of the loveliest. This is all the more remarkable in that two of them, Lodge and Greene, are prodigal of beautiful songs in their prose work. Marlowe has no songs, nor, I think, has Kyd any worth speaking of. Even Peele, himself a perfect master of them, does not use them in every play.

But Shakespeare employs the lyre, and shows his skill in it, from the very first—" Who is Sylvia ? " in *The Two Gentlemen*, and "When daisies pied" in *Love's Labour's Lost*—to Ariel's ineffable music at the very last. We shall deal with the whole subject of this song-cycle presently, but it is proper and important to observe here that Shakespeare's absolute prosodic mastery is hardly in any division more conspicuous. We saw, in dealing with the pre-Shakespearian Miscellanies, that the endeavour to match words to music had already communicated a great apparent variety to measure ; but that prosodic development had not quite kept pace with musical adaptation. If, on the other hand, we turn to the now well-known music-books, we shall find that the more exquisite word-masters—Campion, "those about Jones," and others—do not so very often (though, of course, they do sometimes) affect very zig-zaggy formulas. But Shakespeare, from first to last, seems to have had entirely at his command the " wood notes wild " that Milton (a skilled musician, remember, as well as, which is a very different thing, a prosodist, inferior to hardly anybody but Shakespeare himself) recognised in him. I suppose it is probable, though I do not think it at all certain, that he may have always written to existing airs,[1] but, unless I mistake, these airs do not exist in at least the great majority of cases.   Nor are the well-known modern settings (with a few exceptions, such as the well-known " Under the greenwood tree ") by any means self-imposing or authoritative to a carefully trained prosodic ear.   On the other hand, to such an ear, there is hardly one of these songs that does not carry its own prosodic. music with it, infallibly and exquisitely married.   Here Shakespeare indeed " fulfils all numbers."   There is no better text for that iambic-trochaic substitution, with which the accent people make such wild work, than Ariel's first and greatest song.   Nobody had yet used a trisyllabic foot, which, in its connection with hitherto unbroken trochees, may be allowed to be dactylic, as in the " Merrily, merrily " of his last.   But these, it may be said, are absolute masterpieces—the last achievement of many a tentative.   Next door, so to speak, in place, perhaps twenty years or more earlier in time, comes " Who is Sylvia ? " where the proper name itself and the use of it are simply " signatures," guarantees of prosodic omnipotence, endorsed by the double rhymes of the even lines.   From this point of view the arrangement of the folio is a positive advantage, because it shows us how personal and immediate this gift was.   Even if some of the songs, not merely the one or two which are well known to occur elsewhere, were not his own, the general character of all is too uniform and unmistakable to present any difficulty.   " Take, oh ! take," the triumph of the pathetic use of the trochee ; the lighter use of the same foot in " Sigh no more " ; and the passing-bell variation in the dirge on Hero (where we must scan, not as in " Merrily, | merrily," | but " Heavi|-ly, | heavi|-ly ") ; the new trick of common measure in Moth's " If she be made of white and red " ; and the perfect employment of the " bob " refrain in " When daisies pied " and (with a difference) in " Tell me where is fancy bred ? " —all these things are pure prosody.   They do not want

---

[1] Sir Frederick Bridge, I think, recently handled this interesting subject, but I have merely seen a newspaper report of what he said.

music at all, though they will greet her very civilly when she comes, and make her welcome—if she deserves it. And this is still more the case with the twin triumphs of *As You Like It*, of which, as a matter of fact, though " Under the greenwood tree " has been mated without too much derogation, " Blow, blow, thou winter wind " still awaits an Audrey in notes that shall be its own, and *not* a poor thing.

But, luckily, all these things are well known, and our not too abundant space should be saved for others that are not quite so. Let it suffice to say, in conclusion, that, blank verse or song, sonnet or stanza, Shakespeare achieves everything that he touches ; that he foots it everywhere with perfect featness ; and that he always does *foot* it. His harmonies and melodies are reducible to the nicely constructed and regularly equivalenced group, not to the haphazard and blundering accent scheme. They are independent of music, though quite willing to unite with it. They require no fantastic laws of sound to explain them. The poet simply puts his hand into the exhaustless lucky-bag of English words, and arranges them — trochee and iamb and anapæst regularly, spondee and dactyl and even tribrach when he chooses—at his pleasure and for ours.

NOTE ON *THE PASSIONATE PILGRIM*, ETC.

IT seems unnecessary to say much on the partly contentious
"minors" of *The Passionate Pilgrim*, etc.   There are things in
both sonnet- and song-form amply worthy of Shakespeare, and
there are few more curious instances of the way in which the
mathematically same metre can receive an infinite prosodic
difference than the fall of

> King Pan|dion, | he is | dead,

and the rise of

> Let | the bird | of loud|est lay

(which fall and rise, be it observed, are inappreciable on the
stress-system).   But they hardly give, in themselves, anything
prosodic that we cannot find elsewhere, and they are doubtfully
Shakespeare's as far as proof goes.

CHAPTER II

THE OTHER " ELIZABETHAN " DRAMATISTS

The shortness of the blank-verse season—And its causes—The
practitioners — Jonson — Chapman — Marston — Dekker —
Webster—Rowley—Middleton—Heywood—Tourneur—Day
—The minors—General remarks—Note on Shakespearian
" Doubtful " Plays.

IT would obviously be impossible, and if possible it would The shortness
of the blank-
verse season. be supererogatory, to go through the entire works of the
contemporaries of Shakespeare with the same minuteness
which has been observed in dealing with Shakespeare
himself, or even with as much as has been allotted to his
predecessors. The very object, or one of the objects, of
that minuteness in his case, was to render such an
expatiation unnecessary. For he touched, at one time or
another, almost all possible forms of blank verse: and it
would skill but little to trace them out here as they recur
in individual cases, though editors of the individual works
may very properly do so. That something like such a
tracing has gone to the preparation of this book the
reader may be assured—that only the results should be
supplied in the composition of it he may justly claim. I
believe there is not a playwright, from Chapman and
Jonson to Goff and Glapthorne, whom I have not considered in order to draw up these summaries ; but I cannot
think it necessary to march them all across my limited
stage that each may answer " Here ! " Indeed, too
meticulous a review might positively obscure one of the
most important facts to be brought out by it—the
extremely rapid passing of the flower of blank verse. It

did not come very rapidly into full beauty—there are some forty years between *Gorboduc* and *Hamlet.* But before another forty had passed it was all overblown : it may be questioned whether its best bloom was not over in half the time.

And its causes.

That this must almost necessarily be the case with a form depending so much on individual genius, admitting so many and such perilous licences and varieties, is obvious enough. To get *immortelles,* here as elsewhere, you must sacrifice a good deal in colour, odour, and shape. But there were certain particular causes which at this time hastened its decay ; and these it must be our business to bring out by or from the usual survey of the contents of the subject, if but a summary one. And first of Ben.[1]

The practitioners— Jonson.

That Ben Jonson was a great master, and probably one of our first conscious and deliberate masters, of prosody, must be clear to any one who has even the slightest knowledge of his work ; and especially of the exquisite lyrics which will be handled later. But if we had only his regular plays (the masques are really part of the lyrics) it might not be easy to speak so highly of him in this particular respect. He uses a very great deal of prose—admirable prose too—but with that we have nothing to do. And when he comes to blank verse the atmosphere of prose seems to remain with him. It is correct enough : in fact it is too correct, in the earlier plays at least, while though in the later there is much more liberty taken with the number of syllables, and though both in earlier and later there is no lack of redundance, real flexibility and ease are seldom gained. It is curious that the single mould still prevails—in fact, as we shall see, it is very rarely got rid of ; and even strong middle pauses, not always rigidly " middle," do not succeed in giving the poetic-prosodic *phrase,* the many-centredness of which is Shakespeare's secret. Where Jonson's blank verse is really fine, it is usually in rather

---

[1] A great deal of work has been recently done on Jonson both in England, in America, and in France. I have a fair acquaintance with this. For our purpose, however, it is not necessary to go beyond the three-volume Gifford-Cunningham edition, published originally by Hotten (London, *n.d.*).

long and rather rhetorical *tirades* — pieces of verse-declamation which, no doubt, had a great effect on Dryden afterwards, and which would have gone as well or better in the couplet. Indeed, if we did not know that he thought couplets "the bravest sort of verses," we could have guessed it. His own couplet pieces, such as the famous eulogy of Shakespeare himself, quite carry out this idea. But for all this no disrespect is intended to the actual "blanks." *Sejanus* is perhaps the chief place for a blank-verse line which marks the transition from Marlowe to Dryden himself in might and weight ; while it is not a little noticeable that in the fine speech[1] of Arruntius here, and in others, the *polycentric* state is by no means ill-attained.

The fact is (and though a certain kind of commentator would take it as a natural result of the traditional hardness and ruggedness of Ben's disposition, it is a most surprising contrast with the sweetness of his lyrics) that all his blank verse is *hard*, though all is not rugged. From *Every Man in his Humour* or *The Case is Altered*, whichever he may have really written first, to the fragment of *The Fall of Mortimer*, we have nearly forty years' practice in the medium. Some of the best passages are really fine ; not merely the speech of Arruntius just glanced at, which is really in the noblest Roman tone ; not merely the brilliant extravagance of Sir Epicure's sensual visions in *The Alchemist* ;[2] not merely Catiline's great speech to

---

[1] Or speeches, as they actually meet the eye in Act IV. Sc. v. But that which begins as a soliloquy—

> Still dost thou suffer, Heaven ? will no flame,
> No heat of sin, make thy just wrath to boil
> In thy distempered bosom, and o'erflow
> The pitchy blazes of impiety ?

is really continued, after not a little dialogue and incident, by

> I would begin to study 'em, if I thought
> They would secure me, etc.,

and

> He is our monster : forfeited to vice
> So far, as no racked virtue can redeem him,

and the rest.

[2] And roll us dry in gossamer and roses

is a good example here.

the soldiers when he is driven to bay,[1] and some of the long and undramatic but powerful *tirades* of *Cynthia's Revels*, and the *Poetaster*, and *Volpone*, and *The Devil's an Ass*, and even the "dotages"; but very many smaller and shorter passages scattered everywhere. Still, the hardness is everywhere too; the verse is rock or metal, not flesh.

And what is most curious and interesting of all is that at the touch of rhyme the rock, the metal, *becomes* flesh. I do not refer to the inserted lyrics, though the choruses interspersed in the austere verse of *Catiline*, grave as they are, would almost prove my point. This is illustrated over and over again in the exquisite *Sad Shepherd*, where the drops into rhyming are very well worth comparison with those in the not wholly dissimilar *Midsummer Nights' Dream*. The youthful Shakespeare is constantly making the change, because he has not made up his mind which is the best vehicle; but his verse is equally poetical in both, and such lines as

> Fall in the fresh lap of the crimson rose,

or

> The summer still doth tend upon my state,

want no rhyme and, in the first case, have no rhyme, to bring out their sweetness. The veteran Jonson wishes to soften his verse and does it, but only by the help of the dulcifier, of which he knew the use so well in other metres. Even when he does soften the blanks themselves a little as in the beautiful Earine passage suggested by Martial, he has (after the first line) to start himself with rhyme.[2]

---

[1] *V.v.* I never yet knew, soldiers, that in fight
      Words added virtue unto valiant men, etc.,

with the splendid touch (where the use of redundance is noticeable) towards the end—

      Methinks I see Death and the Furies waiting :
      What we will do, and all the Heaven at leisure
      For this great spectacle.

The fine description of the battle itself by Petreius should be added.

[2] In the speech, "A spring, now she is dead," *ten* lines out of the *thirty* rhyme. Large passages, of course, rhyme continuously.

Some, it is known, would make *The Sad Shepherd* his latest thing; it is certainly very late, and this taking refuge in rhyme is very noteworthy. But an even greater instance of Ben Jonson's anticipation of the second half of the century, at the very moment when he was so largely influencing the first, is to be found in the other fragment—the *Mortimer* one—which was to have been in blank verse with choric interludes, less purely lyrical than those of *Catiline,* and not, it would seem, entirely unlike *Samson Agonistes.* A slice of the opening tirade, and of the short conversation with Isabel, which together make up all we have of the play, is given below with a special purpose.[1] Unless I am singularly deceived — and the impression was certainly a spontaneous and genuine one, proceeding from no precedent theory — there is noticeable in this, as in the work of hardly any other really Elizabethan writer, even Shirley, that curious false note which pervades all our modern dramatic blank verse, no matter whether it be Lamb's or Landor's, Taylor's or Tennyson's, not to speak of that of living persons. It is

---

[1] *Mort.* There is a fate that flies with towering spirits
Home to the mark, and never checks at conscience.
Poor plodding priests, and preaching friars may make
Their hollow pulpits, and the empty aisles
Of churches ring with that round word : but we
That draw the subtile and more piercing air
In that sublimèd region of a court,
Know all is good we make so ; and go on
Secured by the prosperity of our virtues.

    .   .   .   .

  Isab. My Lord ! Sweet Mortimer !
  Mort.   My queen ! my mistress !
My sovereign, nay, my goddess and my Juno !
What name or title, as a mark of power
Upon me, should I give you?
  Isab.   Isabel !
Your Isabel, and you my Mortimer,
Which are the marks of parity not power.
And these are titles best become our love.
  Mort. Can you fall under those?
  Isab.   Yes, and be happy !

The triumphant arrogance of the favourite and the passion of the queen are both fine. I agree with Whalley (though not quite for his reasons) in regretting the loss of the rest bitterly. But I think the extract justifies the text with the exception of the disjoined "Isabel—*your* Isabel," and that is a touch of nature borrowed from nature itself, not art.

good poetically but not good dramatically ; it is evidently
written in nature, if not in intention, to be read rather
than heard.   And this, which declares itself so strangely
in the decayed fragment of this last work, is probably
what has really been the matter all through.   If we were
playing the old children's game of " Animal, vegetable, or
mineral ? " in respect to Jonson's prosody, I should say,
when questioned about his lyrics, " Animal, and of all but
the very highest animation " ; of his couplets, " Vegetable,
and first-rate vegetable"; but of his blank verse, " Mineral :
weighty, useful, sometimes brilliant, but not alive." [1]

It has been said that the general mark of Ben's blanks
is not exactly ruggedness, but *is* hardness.   On the other
Chapman. hand, " Georgius Chapmannus Homeri Metaphrastes " is
nothing if not rugged.   The splendour of his best verse,
both in meaning and in a certain sense of poetic expression, is undoubted—it surpasses, in this blank verse division,
Jonson's own.   Dryden's earlier judgment was better, in
some ways, when he approved Chapman's " Delilahs of
the imagination," than his later, when he thought them
bombast.   Yet they *are* bombast ; and bombast not
smoothly puffed out but packed and stuffed with knotty,
knarry phrase, jagged in outline like a bag of nails.   His
early adherence to the University Wits, and his discipleship to Marlowe in particular, could hardly fail to give
him an affection for the single-moulded line, whether
redundant or not, and for mighty words rather disdainfully
cast before the reader than complaisantly prepared for his
delight.   And though the dates of his work are not quite
certain, we can see this general mould prevailing from
The Blind Beggar of Alexandria, which is at least as old
as our first certain date for Shakespeare (Meres's mention
in 1598), to the very late and collaborative tragedy of
Philip Chabot, and the (if we take them in) very doubtful
Alphonsus and *Revenge for Honour*.   In fact, the similarity

---

[1] It ought to be unnecessary, but I fear it is not, to observe that this
judgment is altogether *ad hoc.*   It must be supplemented with what is said
on the other poems, and even when thus supplemented it must not be taken
as a judgment on the whole Ben.   There are few, I think, who rate him
higher than I do.

of the versification, especially in such late plays, is one of
the main arguments for the usually accepted canon of
Chapman's works. It may be studied almost anywhere
with fair confidence of its being representative ; and that
being the case, the undoubted centre and citadel of the
position—the *Bussy* and *Byron* pieces—form a sufficient
field of observation for those who do not care to undertake the very paying trouble, but the certainly rather
troublesome process, of reading Chapman through.

But no one who wishes to be a real student should
omit to read at least these four plays through.[1] The great
places in them are, in the first D'Ambois play, the account
of Bussy's duel with Barrisor ; the powerful and libellous
passage about women and the moon ; the wild rants of
Montsurry when he discovers his disgrace ; the famous
incantation passage. In the *Revenge*, Tamyra's soliloquy,
several of Clermont's meditative speeches (though some of
these are rhymed), and the notably Senecan overture of
the Fifth Act by the ghost of Bussy, should be studied.
In the Byron pair, attention may be paid to at least a
dozen set harangues (for this is the most sententious of the
plays) from the early one,

> Now by my dearest marquisate of Saluces,

onward.

In all these passages, whether the subject be declamatory
or meditative, the structure of the verse is remarkably
similar; as may be seen from the extracts below.[2] It most

---

[1] The Bussy pair are now accessible, carefully edited, in Mr. Boas's edition
(Boston, U.S.A., and London, 1905). For the others and the rest of Chapman,
the three-volume edition (London, 1874), which contains Mr. Swinburne's
famous Introduction, is still the best place of resort. Some have specially
compared *The Gentleman Usher* with *Love's Labour's Lost*, and the comparison
is not unjustified prosodically.

[2] (*a*) (The close of the D'Ambois-Barrisor duel.)

> Then, as in Arden I have seen an oak,
> Long shook with tempests, and his lofty top
> Bent to his root, which being at length made loose
> (Even groaning with his weight), he 'gan to nod
> This way and that : as loth his curlèd brows
> (Which he had oft wrapt in the sky with storms)
> Should stoop : and yet his radical fibres burst,
> Storm-like he fell and hid the fear-cold earth.
>
> *B. d'Amb.* II. i.

resembles, in the long and varied phases of Shakespeare's blank verse, that of *Romeo and Juliet*, where the "Wits" model is beginning to be made more supple and springy. But the suppleness and spring, which even there Shakespeare attains, are not, and never were to be, within Chapman's reach ; and though he never quite fell back to the stages of *Andronicus*, or, to take an outside example, of *Jeronimo*, he is always suggesting that such a relapse is possible. At the same time he has preserved or recovered, as no other dramatist did preserve or recover, the cloudy magnificence, the " sulphurous and thought-executing fire " of these earlier writers ; while the thought itself that this volcanic expression executes, is Jacobean instead of Elizabethan—deeper and wider, if rather more artificial, than Marlowe's.

Marston.   Both Jonson and Chapman are verse-smiths in such long practice, and of such varied exercise, that it seemed worth while to deal with them in some circumstance ; especially as both are known to have been scholars and critics as well as poets.[1] But most of the Elizabethan dramatists, even some who may claim to be *majorum gentium*, though they may in this respect provide cobweb-spinning for the thesis-writer, hardly supply the historian with material for solid work. The lessons of the body of their production are invaluable ; the details in special

---

(*b*) (Women and the Moon.)

    For as the moon, of all things God created,
    Not only is the most appropriate image,
    Or glass to show them how they wax and wane ;
    But in her height and motion likewise bears
    Imperial influences that command
    In all their powers and make them wax and wane,
    So women that, of all things made of nothing,
    Are the most perfect idols of the moon,
    (Or still unweaned sweet moon-calves with white faces),
    Not only are patterns of change to men,
    But as the tender moonshine of their beauties
    Clears or is cloudy, make men glad or sad—
    So thus they rule in men, not men in them.
                        Ibid. IV. i.

I wish there were room to quote all the passages referred to in the text.

[1] Once more *vide* chapter on " Prosodists," and, for Chapman, *inf.* p. 111.

cases may be lightly passed over.[1] We know, for instance, of Marston, that his not inconsiderable work was the fruit of but a few years of his youth and earlier manhood. The couplets of his boyish satires, though extremely rough in language, and sometimes almost unintelligible, by no means push the licence of *prosodic* roughness to any great extreme ; and the sixains of *Pygmalion* are almost smooth. But in all, the line has a tendency to be singly-moulded ; and this is also the characteristic of the blank verse, in the plays where there is a good deal of prose.   It is not (the caution has constantly to be repeated) that the sense does not often overrun ; but that the line-tension is not adjusted to the overrunning.   He does not by any means indulge largely in extended or shortened lines, generally dropping into prose when he leaves off set verse. And he seems also to have a positive distaste for the redundant syllable.   You may read pages on pages without finding a single one ; and when one comes it is odds but it is a word like " bosom," or some other of the kind, which almost offers to shut itself up into a monosyllable. It is, in fact, something of an argument (though, of course, no strong one) against *The Insatiate Countess* being his, that redundant syllables are rather common in it.

The extensive, and in great part delightful, work of Dekker. Dekker is so much dashed and brewed with collaboration, and we have (excepting the lyrics which are almost certainly his, and which will be dealt with elsewhere) so little non-dramatic verse to help us in distinguishing, that it is very difficult to speak positively of his blanks—especially as the editions of them are of the most uncertain character for all but adventurous theorists.   That he was a prolific prose writer we do know ; and it cannot be quite for nothing that he slips into prose in his plays, even more easily and frequently than his fellow in Ben's black-books, Marston.   But no one who has learnt what literary evidence is, can be otherwise than shy of basing conclusions on (for instance) such contrasted facts, as that in

---

[1] In *giving* the account, that is to say ; not, of course, in preparing to give it.

Old Fortunatus you get splendid single lines, and even
passages which as a whole are splendid, hitched with
breakdowns which are quite unaccountable ; and so
with all the rest.   Repeated reading of Dekker, now
designedly combined with reading of the plays in which
he collaborated with Middleton, Rowley, Massinger, or
Ford, now taking his writings as a whole, and now passing
to theirs as wholes likewise, is a process which is indispensable to any judgment that is to be sound, but most
likely to suspend positive judgment altogether.   I should
say that Dekker was more inclined to the redundant
syllable than Marston ; rather given to drop into couplet
and even alternate rhyme without any intention of keeping
either up ; but capable of rising now and then to an
almost Shakespearian *weaving* of a blank-verse passage,
though he too rarely gave himself the trouble to do so.

Webster.   Webster is to some extent, and only to some, less of
a puzzle ; for though he probably wrote a great deal in
collaboration, we have little of it, and his practically
undoubted work in verse is substantial.   Nor have
we any certain *prose* work of any size from his hand.
Discarding the batch written with " Thomas Dickers,"
and taking the four plays which are probably his own
—*The White Devil, The Duchess of Malfy, The Devil's
Law Case*, and *Appius and Virginia*—we find a difference between the pairs that make up the quartette.
The two great Romantic tragedies, infinitely above the
others as poetry, are among the most irregular productions,
prosodically speaking, of all the great age ; the others
are much less so, and *Appius and Virginia*, whether in
compliment to its classical subject or not, is almost
regular.   It is not certain that this is not accidental, but
it is at least remarkable.   Refining further, one might
say that *The Devil's Law Case* stands nearer to the great
plays than to *Appius and Virginia*.   This last, when it
is not prose, is fairly regular blank verse of the middle
kind, neither as wooden as the earlier, nor as limber, and
sometimes limp, as the later.   But in the *Devil* and the
Duchess we find what was found in Dekker more notice-

ably still. Save rarely, and that in unimportant as well as in important speeches, the author seems hardly able to rouse himself to the composition of even a miniature tirade of regular verse. Prose, pure and simple ; verse which is half-prose, or itself prose a little versified ; and casual snatches of pure verse, seem to serve his turn indifferently. In fact, if there were not in these two writers such strange soars of poetry, one might sometimes think that they were not poets after all—that it was pain and grief to them to write verse, and that they shirked it as much as possible.

In Rowley,[1] on the other hand, it is not quite unsafe to suspect little or no liking or faculty for verse at all. The chief plays attributed to him [2] without a collaborator, *A New Wonder* and *A Match at Midnight*, have little verse, and what they have is of a most pedestrian character ; while he generally associated with persons who had demonstrably, or almost so, a greater faculty for verse than himself. Whether, indeed, it was quite safe (as was done some years ago ingeniously in a pretty book,[3] and to an effect not unpleasing) to carve all or most of the verse in *A Cure for a Cuckold*, and set it down to Webster, I have doubted considerably since I began the comparisons necessary for this inquiry. But there certainly is not much reason for setting it down to Rowley, while, as will be seen, there is very strong reason

Rowley.

---

[1] *William* Rowley. His namesake Samuel is of too little importance to need comment here, and has left too little work to justify any. I may perhaps put in a *caveat lector* against the practice, common with the wilder commentator, and not quite unknown among the soberer sort, of dogmatising on the authorship of parts of plays, in the case of some writers from whom we have little and undistinguished original and certain work. The almost frantic folly with which little bits of this and that play used to be dealt out among half-a-dozen different authors, as rapidly and surely as a good dealer distributes cards, has indeed rather gone out of fashion. But I cannot agree with authorities whom I respect in assigning, for instance, parts of *Timon* and *Titus Andronicus* to such a person as George Wilkins on prosodic grounds. We really have not enough to go upon.

[2] We have been waiting, not *quite* twenty years, for Mr. Bullen to complete his second series of *Old Plays* with Rowley. Seven volumes are good, but eight are better.

[3] *Love's Graduate* (Oxford : Daniel Press, 1885), executed by Mr. S. E. Spring Rice on the suggestion and with the collaboration of Mr. Edmund Gosse.

for setting most of the verse in the rather numerous plays which he wrote with Middleton to the credit of this latter. So, too, the Dekker and Webster collaborations manifestly tempt to "hariolation." *Westward Ho!* in particular, with its immense over-proportion of prose, suddenly breaking into a verse, and rather fine verse, is something of a curiosity ; while *Northward Ho!* after an early passage (not a whole scene) of passionate verse, is, except for a few cue-tags and the like, consistently prose to the end.

Middleton.   The same difficulties recur in the far larger work of Middleton himself, except that we know that Middleton was very much less of a prose writer [1] (out of plays) than Dekker ; and that we also know that he had been in his youth a copious practitioner in verse.   I have no wish to recant the censure which, twenty years ago,[2] I passed on *Microcynicon* and the version of the *Book of Wisdom*, though I cannot quite agree with Mr. Bullen and say that it is "the most damnable piece of flatness that has ever fallen in my way." The flats extend behind me far too widely and too variously for that.   The satires are not good satires, and the paraphrase turns an admirable book into a very dull one.   But what is important to us is that neither is positively bad as verse.   The couplets of the *Microcynicon*[3] show that Middleton adopted the half-way house of the couplet, neither distinctly stopped nor distinctly enjambed, and lived in it with ease.   Nor was he ever at a loss for such verse in his nearly thirty years' usage of the stage.   Some couplets, indeed, in his later *Triumphs*, etc. (*v. inf.*), are by no means bad.   So, too, the sixains of the *Paraphrase*, however " wersh " they may be in phrasing and expression, are by no means of

---

[1] He *did* write prose, of course.
[2] *Elizabethan Literature*, p. 267.
[3] The opening will do well enough.   I use, of course, Mr. Bullen's excellent edition (London, 1886) :—

> Time was when down-declining, toothless age
> Was of a holy and divine presage,
> Divining, prudent, and foretelling truth,
> In sacred points instructing wandering youth.

the lowest, or even of a very low, class as metre.[1]   They
could not have been written, as they were, during Spenser's
lifetime, and not so very long after the second instalment
of the *Faerie Queene* appeared, except by a man who had
either given very considerable heed to the new master, or
masters, of verse, or else had been born with something
more than an average faculty for it.   When we take
account of this, and when we consider the facts noted
above as to Middleton's most frequent collaborators,
Dekker and Rowley, we shall be in a position to judge
the probable qualities of his play-verse—not, indeed, with
the rash dogmatism which has been so often indulged in
on this subject, but with a reasonable hope of not going
too far wrong.

And we do accordingly find that in the large number
of plays attributed to Middleton, whether alone or in
collaboration, some hand which was perfectly facile at
blank verse is at work.   The importance of couplet
preparation for blank-verse writing is beyond all question ;
and in plays of the *Blurt Master Constable* type, in which
he is so prolific, and which in others' hands tend more
and more to prose, it seems all one to Middleton whether
he writes prose or verse ;   though even when the theme
seems to invite prose he often versifies.   In fact, his case
is exactly the opposite of those just mentioned.   Webster
and Dekker can write finer verse than all, save a very
little, of his ;   but they never seem to write it with ease,
and sometimes make most botcherly work of it.   *He* has
the pen of a ready verse-writer, and by no means of one
over ready.   In that other curious class of " strapped-
together " plays—where a comic underplot, generally in
prose, is simply tied neck and heels, without the faintest
attempt to secure a more intimate union, to a tragic plot
in verse—his are eminent for the excellence of the verse-

[1]   Like as the traces of appearing clouds
      Gives way when Titan re-salutes the sea,
    With new-changed flames gilding the ocean's floods,
      Kissing the cabinet where Thetis lay :
    So fares our life, when death doth give the wound
    Our life is led by death, a captive bound.

passages. Besides the great one in *The Changeling*, which nobody need have refused to sign :[1] besides others in *The Mayor of Queenborough* : the famous *loci* of *Women beware Women* and *A Fair Quarrel* give admirable illustration of Middleton's blank verse ; as do things yet different in *The Witch* and the *Game of Chess* and *The Spanish Gipsy*. On the whole, however, this blank verse, as indeed might be expected from what has been said of it, is rather excellently competent than excellently distinguished. It has no very salient characteristic of its own ; but something of that minor universality which brings its author some way towards Shakespeare on one side, as poignancy and humanity bring Webster and Dekker on others.

Heywood.   This is even more the case with the "prose Shakespeare" ; and it certainly should prevent one of the interpretations of that rather idly discussed phrase from even suggesting itself to any one who knows Heywood. He is, perhaps, of all the great class to which he belongs, the one to whom it seems least difficult to drop into fluent, easy, not very distinguished,[2] but by no means unaccomplished blank verse. The impression left upon me by repeated readings is, in Middleton's case, as I have said, that it was as easy for him to write in verse as not ; in Webster's and Dekker's, that it was not so easy ; in Heywood's, that it was easier. There is of course plenty

[1] The scene between Beatrice and De Flores. It is too long to quote here, but I may observe that it will be found in my *Elizabethan Literature* (p. 270 and ff.) at only a page or so's distance from the long passage in *Vittoria Corombona*, made earlier famous by Lamb (who somehow left De Flores for the less exquisite but more catholic criticism of Leigh Hunt to find). These extracts, which would together fill at least four of the present pages, will show better than any snippets can do the remarkable prosodic difference between these two great acolytes of Shakespeare—Webster fluttering up and down from lyric soar to almost prosaic "patter" ; Middleton keeping a steady, though by no means monotonous, flight of well-grasped blank verse with the occasional couplet-tags.

[2] A word of caution on the use, here and elsewhere, of this phrase "undistinguished." It does not mean that there are not in almost all these dramatists lines and sometimes passages of extreme distinction as poetry— distinction which is not wholly unconnected (as indeed it never can be) with prosodic qualities. But in these cases "facit *inspiratio* versus." It is not art that does it.

of actual prose in him ; but there is a great deal more verse where prose would do just as well.   Everywhere— in his rather pedestrian chronicle-plays ; in the wild jumble of farcical songs and serious dialogue called *The Rape of Lucrece* ; in his endless *Ages* and dramatic dialoguings of classical mythology,—things that show us better than anything else what an all-absorbing and all-returning vortex this drama was ; in the travel-plays (again symptoms) of which he is the best master ; and in the domestic dramas of which Lamb was thinking, and of which the *Woman Killed with Kindness* is the chief,— in all these the characteristic appears.   Heywood has a sort of *tap* of blank verse, not at all bad, which he can turn on at any time and the cistern whereof never runs dry or foul.   But there *is* something of a tap-and-cistern quality about it, and it is never the earth-born and heaven-seeking fountain of Shakespeare.

The connection between practice in couplet or stanza   Tourneur. verse and " blanks " reappears in Cyril Tourneur.   I do not, indeed, recognise in him that quasi-Shakespearian variety of verse which some have seen : at any rate, his variety seems to me a variety of carelessness, rather than a variety of art.   But he has, to a specially large extent, that " versification of inspiration " which has just been referred to ; and it is doubtless assisted in him by the practice above mentioned.   *The Transformed Metamorphosis*, though it reads almost like a designed parody of the most extravagant style of the period, and though its diction is an undigested mishmash of terms which would have made the Limousin scholar embrace Cyril as a brother, is very far from being bad verse—is, indeed, here and there very fine verse.   And the enjambed couplets of the *Funeral Poem on Vere* and the *Death of Prince Henry* display similar capacity.   The consequence is that when he will give himself time, he has not the least difficulty (even in that wild nightmare, the *Atheist's Tragedy*, much more in the *Revenger's*) in producing admirable specimens of the more rhetorical and *pavanesque* blank verse.   It is, however, noticeable in him as in the others of this division, that when the blank verse is highest the couplets are nighest—as for instance in the fine speech of that " ancient damnation " Castiza's mother.[1] We know the dividing line in Shakespeare between the plays where he, too, suffers from this inability to keep the clue, and those where he does not. Of most of those with whom we are now dealing it may be said that they have not passed that line.

Day. One who has certainly not passed it, but on the contrary is far on the other side—one, for all this, of the " best versers " among Shakespeare's middle contemporaries—is the last of those contemporaries to whom we shall here give specific mention. John Day,[2] the author of *The Isle of Gulls* and the *Parliament of Bees*, can write blank verse ; indeed, the people who like such things might select a line in the *Beggar of Bethnal Green*—

> Eyeless, handless, footless, comfortless,

as an attempt to naturalise in blank verse the " Chaucerian acephalic," or something else of the same comforting, if footless as well as headless, terminological kind. But he is consistently ill at ease in this variety of numbers ; and though he writes prose fairly and frequently, it is not for prose that he quits them. It is for the beloved octosyllabic and decasyllabic couplets which nearly compose the *Parliament*, and which he wields always with facility and sometimes with distinguished grace. But it is not

---

[1] That beginning " Dishonourable Act," Act II. Scene i., of *The Revenger's Tragedy* (Tourneur's *Works*, ed. Churton Collins, vol. ii. p. 47 : London, 1878). Most of Vindice's own harangues and soliloquies have the same composite character.

[2] Nobody has yet superseded, or is soon likely to supersede, that edition of Mr. Bullen's (London, 1881), which gave such pleasure to its subscribers, and gives it still. But the *Parliament* will be found in a volume (entitled from *Nero*) of miscellaneous plays in the extremely useful *Mermaid Series*, which will also, for the more important single authors, to no small extent serve as a companion to the present survey. Even Lamb's *Specimens*, however, short as they are, will illustrate what has been said in the cases where there has been no room for illustration here ; the examples in that excellent collection, Knight's *Half-Hours with the Best Authors*, which has, I believe, been reprinted, or in Chambers's *Cyclopædia of English Literature*, still better ; and those in Mr. Williams's *Specimens of the Elizabethan Drama* (Oxford, 1905), best of all.

when he is giving himself up to them that his love for them is most remarkable. He cannot keep them out of blank verse itself. I think it would be very difficult to find a single long speech of Day's, which he seems to have written with any gusto at all, and which is wholly blank ; while it would, on the other hand, hardly be necessary to turn over more than a page or two to find the couplet cropping up.

I do not think it necessary to attempt to characterise The minors. the prosody of still lesser writers or of anonymous plays ; and I have already put in a *caveat* as to generalisations about authorship. But there are generalisations of another and much safer kind which this process fairly validates, and to some of these we may pass. Of the writers mentioned in this chapter, and of the much larger number glanced at in the last paragraph, Jonson and Chapman stand somewhat apart, for reasons given already. And both they and some others lived long enough to be affected by changes which we shall see, in their more direct and exclusive subjects, hereafter. But even they, to some extent, and the others in varying but much greater degrees, exhibit some general characteristics in relation to prosody generally, and blank verse in particular, which we may now briefly notice, using Shakespeare and the remarks already made in the last chapter on his blank verse as an admitted standard and system of comparison, not as a mere excuse for belauding or belittling.

In the first place, all, or almost all, represent the General literary generation which saw the process of the *establish-* remarks. *ment* of blank verse as the dramatic staple. Only Chapman could claim to be of the actual *conquistadores* in point of date, and it does not seem that he began drama very early. The University Wits had dropped off very soon— except Lodge, who was the least dramatic of all, it is doubtful whether one lived into more than the first year or two of the seventeenth century. Moreover, when most of the present subjects came into dramatic work, " our fellow Shakespeare " had already put all these Wits, dead and alive, down, by developing blank verse itself all

but to its full, if not to its absolutely full, capacity.   But
though he was the elder of most of them in years, he
was too much their fellow to impose upon them as a
master.   Tourneur has been thought to be a direct
disciple ; but I should rather doubt it.   So has Webster ;
but in that case Webster's well-known reference has
about it a disingenuousness which one does not somehow
" see " in the author of Webster's works.   Heywood and
Middleton are in the precincts of Shakespeare, but not
close to him metrically ; the rest further still from the
prosodic point of view.   And I shall proceed to expound
that point of view, only repeating the caution about Ben
and Chapman.   Undoubtedly Ben wrote his blank verse
with deliberate art, but his alleged hankering after the
couplet is a precious tell-tale.   And the ruggedness of
Chapman, his ineradicable preference for cragginess of
speech and thought, must have affected every metre with
him, as it did, till it was half-liquefied by the volcanic
rush and volume of the fourteener and of Homer.

The others, speaking largely, nowhere show a greater
contrast with Shakespeare than in the point of regarding
blank verse as an art, and getting the utmost out of it in
variety, as well as in power of accomplishment.   It is,
except perhaps in the case of Day, their staple, or at
least their staple verse—the main, if not the only, wear
prosodically.   They show, save for special purposes, very
little trace of a desire to relapse into doggerel or fourteeners.   They (with the same exception) use couplet only for a change, though with varying frequency.
Moreover, they are not rigidly limited to one form of
blank verse.   They know and occasionally use most of
its varieties.   The earlier of them—and perhaps all of
them in their earlier work—incline to the single-moulded
form, are not very lavish of redundant syllables or trisyllabic feet, nor very skilful in the verse paragraph.
But in more or less degree, with more or less intention,
they drop into all these things at times.   Yet, in regard
to the capacities of their instrument, they have neither
the devotion of the virtuoso nor the keen sense of results

belonging to the craftsman. Some of them, as has been noted, use it with a sort of appearance of reluctance or effort : let it drop willingly, and take refuge in prose or in the couplet as idiosyncrasy may suggest. Some of them, as has been noted likewise, have command of it up to a certain point, show no inclination to disuse it, but seldom get its very finest tones, and hardly ever use these tones as a means of furthering their poetical and dramatic conceptions. It is the fashion to write blank verse ; they write blank verse ; and they do it in different measure and degree pretty well, or even very well. But that is all. It is with them nowhere near decadence, though it is sometimes short of accomplishment ; but it is never constantly, or for any length of time, at its height.

It is here that the comparison with Shakespeare, if used in the right way—for instruction of prosodic life and example of prosodic manners, not for giving prizes to that boy and stripes to this—comes in with such effect. In most, if not all, of these writers we find passages of fine blank verse—passages where the verse, and even the particular kind of verse, contributes un-doubtedly to the sum of poetic achievement reached and of poetic pleasure given. But this part of the work is vague and indeterminate, and it is not extraordinarily large. We scarcely ever (as in Shakespeare's great places, by the score and hundred, we can, if we choose) regard the thing as what, in Fanny Burney's day, musical people called a " lesson "—a definite accomplishment of art, inseparably, but not quite inextricably, combined with a simple appeal to the gratification of the senses and the intellect. Extension and curtailment of line ; insertion or omission of trisyllabic feet and redundant endings ; variation of pause ; enlarging or compressing of the bulk of the poetic clause : these things, of course, appear after a fashion, because they cannot but appear ; because they are, after all, the natural and irresistible prosodic outlets or mouthpieces of a certain sense and sentiment. But they appear as unpremeditated, almost as if accidental.

So, and much more, we find comparatively little of

that concordat, or give-and-take, between prose and blank verse which is perhaps the most wonderful thing in Shakespeare. As we noted above, there are passages in *Hamlet* (and, for the matter of that, in most plays of the period of perfection) where complete blank verse, segments of blank verse, and positive prose are dovetailed together in the most inconceivable fashion, so that you never stumble, but always glide easily from one to the other.

Now, that is exactly what, in these contemporaries, or most of them, you do *not* find. In the mixed scenes of some of them, if, again, not of all, the verse suggests a sort of shame-faced reflection on the writer's part—" We really *must* pull ourselves together ! "—the prose a fit of recklessness—" Oh, this blank verse is really too much trouble ; let us prose it for a while ! "

Still, in all of them there is, be it repeated, no " decadence " ; and at the best they all, or nearly all, have that indefinable command of really dramatic " blanks " which has never been recovered since Dryden, or perhaps (for his is, in the main, a marvellous galvanisation of the dying thing) since Shirley. The characteristics of it, or of this form of it, will be best summed up in juxtaposition with others in the Interchapters ; but we have here given what attention seemed proper to the evidence.

NOTE ON SHAKESPEARIAN "DOUBTFUL" PLAYS

I HAVE not thought it necessary to discuss the prosody of the vague and floating body of Shakespearian "Doubtfuls." To do so, with any profit, would require examination at least as full as that given above to the genuine dramas; and this is practically out of the question. Nor do any of them raise new or independent prosodic questions, interesting as the prosody, say of *Edward III.*, may be in itself, and as bearing on the authorship. To distinguish between that which is incumbent on a historian of English Prosody, and that which properly concerns an editor of individual works or writers, has been one of my chief cares in this book.

CHAPTER III

THE CONTEMPORARIES AND FOLLOWERS OF SPENSER
IN STANZA AND COUPLET

Retrospect on Spenser's comparative position—Dyer—Raleigh—
Greville—Sidney—The *Arcadia* verse—*Astrophel and Stella*,
etc. — Marlowe — Drayton — The *Polyolbion* — His narrative
stanzas—His couplet—His lyrics—Daniel—Davies—Chapman
—His minor metres—His fourteener—Its predecessors—Phaer,
Golding, etc.—Southwell and Warner—Chapman's comments
on his own verse—Jonson—The Fletchers—Giles—Phineas—
Browne — His dealings with Occleve—His " sevens "—His
enjambed couplet—Wither—His longer couplet in " Alresford
Pool " — His shorter — Sylvester and Basse — The Scottish
Jacobeans—Ayton, Ker, and Hannay—Drummond—Stirling—
Note on the Satirists.

Retrospect on Spenser's comparative position.

ALTHOUGH the point was carefully guarded in the last
volume, it may be well to repeat in this that the separation
and previous treatment of Spenser by no means implies
that he is the absolute forerunner and conscious pattern
of all those who write contemporaneously with him in
the two great decades from 1580 to 1600. It is indeed
certain that some, and probable that nearly all, *did* receive
at his " noble and most artful hands " (to use Davenant's
superlatively felicitous description of them) the gifts of
the new spirit and the new form of poetry. But, to
a very large extent also, the spirit and the form
came upon him and upon them as fellow-recipients ;
though he had so much the largest share that he could
dispense to others as well as keep for himself. And we
are so much accustomed to treat him as something remote
and afar, even from the great company of these contemporaries—he died so prematurely, and some who were but

a few years his juniors lived to experience and take part in such different phases of poetic development — that perhaps there is a tendency to overlook the fact of the contemporaneousness. Yet there is no doubt that Sidney and Greville, Raleigh and Dyer, were his fellow-students rather than his pupils ; although Marlowe's heart of flame must have been kindled by the *Shepherd's Kalendar*, it was ashes before the *Amoretti*, and *Colin Clout*, and the two great Odes, and the *Four Hymns*, and the last half of the *Faerie Queene* itself appeared. While, not to multiply instances and double propositions, Daniel and Drayton (probably both personal friends) had done much of their most notable work, and Davies (not improbably a friend also) had completed almost all his too brief performance, before Spenser died on New Year's Day of the penultimate year of the century.

Of the four whom, as we have said, dates and facts generally exclude from mere discipleship, all but one give us rather less to say in a History of Prosody than they would give in a History of Poetry. Dyer's few and Dyer. decently famous things are pure lyric, and exhibit prosodically, as perhaps otherwise, the old respectable reformation of Turberville and Gascoigne, lightened and freshened a little by the new breath of fancy. Raleigh—— Raleigh. who actually published verse before Spenser had published any, save the enigmatical deliverances to " Voluptuous Worldlings "—exhibits at first, and retains to the last of his too scanty but intensely interesting and rather puzzling work, a certain *ærugo* of antiquity. If he wrote—one has unluckily in so many cases to say " if "—" As you came from the Holy Land," he had the dateless ballad note, as it is alike in the anonyms of the fifteenth century, and in Blake, and in " Proud Maisie." The last verses in the Gatehouse blend Donne with Sackville in certain tones, but add a burden, an " underhum " which is that of the despised vaunt-couriers of the first twenty-five years of Elizabeth ; and there is the same in " The Lie." Once more, Gascoigne and Turberville would have written it, if they could. He experiments a good deal, as in the

curious " Fain would I, but I dare not," where exact
prosodic arrangement is rather optional, though its general
lines are clear ; and in the strange variety (which suggests
well enough the imagined presence of the Shadow of
Death, though that presence seems actually to have been
set back) of " Give me my scallop-shell of Quiet." *Cynthia*
seems to have been in various metres, quatrains, and
tercets, and what not, including, unless the copyist has
mistaken, a very curious section of Alexandrines ; while
the Sidney epitaph (once more doubtful) gives us the *In
Memoriam* quatrain, but with decasyllabic, not octosyllabic,
lines, and may perhaps have suggested to Jonson the
happy, though by himself apparently unvalued, thought, of
razing the clumsy galleon to a gallant frigate.[1]

Greville.   Fulke Greville [2] would not be Fulke Greville if he
were not difficult, at any rate in appearance ; and his
difficulty extends to his prosody.   There are flippant
persons who have asked why he should have written
Alaham and *Mustapha* at all ? It is certainly not flippant
to ask the question why he wrote these singular things in
such a still more singular confusion of metre.   Not only
does he never seem to know whether he means to write
blank verse, couplet, terza rima, quatrain, or extended
stanza, but it may almost be said that he apparently
seems to mean to write them all at the same time, or to
have written the things separately in each form and then
made a sort of *pot-pourri* of the variants.   Again and again
one form seems to emerge from the chaos, only to vanish
again.   The intelligent and candid Langbaine shows that
he may (without irony this time) be also called "ingenuous,"
by observing of *Alaham* that " 'Tis mostly written in

---

[1] Both Dyer and Raleigh, with many others, will be found in Dr. Hannah's
admirable *Courtly Poets*, more than once printed in the " Aldine " series.   How
easily the Sidney piece "shuts up" into pure *In Memoriam*, the following
verse shows :—

> Drawn was thy race [aright] from princely line :
> Nor less [than men] by gifts that nature gave,
> The [common] mother that all creatures have,
> Doth virtue show, and [princely] lineage shine.

[2] Ed. Grosart, 4 vols.   Privately printed, 1870.

rhyme." 'Tis ; but in rhyme of what sort it would have puzzled the amiable Gerard to tell. The choruses, on the other hand, are mostly downright "poulter's measure" here ; while in *Mustapha*, the dialogue of which is the same jumble as that in *Alaham*, they take various stanza-forms. These stanza-forms are also used correctly enough in the almost equally strange "treatise" poems of *Monarchy* and *Religion* ; but it is, of course, on *Cœlica* that Brooke's prosodic, not less than his poetic, interest rests. Its "sonnets," though there are a few actual quatorzains among them, adopt that form so rarely, and with such an obvious absence of any recognition of an even prerogative right in it, that they are better not classed with sonnets generally. It is quite clear from them that any prosodic oddities of which Greville may be guilty elsewhere are merely his fun. He is bound as an Areopagite to try "versing" sometimes. But (and this is really funny as well as instructive) the central poetic heat which he had in such great measure, and the superficial case-hardening of obstinate idiosyncrasy which he had in no less, combine to transform the thing. He tries to write sapphics, and in lieu of the abortions or burlesques which generally result[1] from that attempt in English, lo and behold ! we have a really lively thing in true English metre,[2] where the natural scansion is three five-foot iambics with redundant ending, and one two-foot ditto. Since the alliterative rebels capitulated to rhymed stanza, more than two centuries earlier, there is no more agreeable instance of the triumph of the right. But Brooke has plenty of other interesting prosodic things in this charming collection—the combination in which of strangeness, sweet-

---

[1] Mr. Swinburne's

> All the night sleep came not upon my eyelids

is, of course, the great exception. But the least unnatural sapphics in any modern language seem to me Carducci's in Italian.

[2] Eyes, why | did you | bring un|to me | these gra|ces ?
Graced to | yield won|der out | of her | true mea|sure ;
Measure | of all | joys ! stay | to fan|cy tra|ces
Model | of plea|sure.

ness, and strength makes it more fascinating every time it
is read, though one must acknowledge that Brooke leaves
his readers to do a good deal that a poet is usually supposed
to do ready to their hand.   When he shifts from the
sinewy decasyllables of his opening pieces to the exquisite
lightness of such things as—

> You little stars that be in skies,
>   All glory in Apollo's glory,
> In whose aspects conjoinèd lies
>   The Heaven's will, and Nature's story :

when he breaks out into that astonishing expostulation—

> 1, with whose colours Myra dressed her head !

and puts fire into the too commonly slow and languid
sixain ; or when he once more takes the lighter and more
fantastic touch in

> Faction that ever dwells
> In courts where Wit excels,
>   Hath set defiance :
> Fortune and Love have sworn
> That they were never born,
>   Of one alliance :

when he helps to start the mixed eights and sevens which
were to give delightful things for forty years to come, with

> In the time when herbs and flowers
> Springing out of melting powers,—

in all these cases and many others we see that there is
more than experiment, much as there is of that—there is
achievement also.

The great achiever, however, as well as the great
experimenter of the group is, of course, " Astrophel " himself.   He appears, with all his graciousness, to have been
a person who had distinct opinions of his own, and was
by no means likely to be led by anybody ; nor, be it
remembered, did he apparently know Spenser very early ;
nor did his fancy lead him, by any means, in exactly or

nearly the same paths. By the date of Sidney's death
the greater poet had at least published no original sonnets,
he had quite clearly got over his passing fancy for
classical "versing," and he never at any time seems to
have been given at all to the shorter and slighter lyric
measures. Now Sidney's work may be divided almost
completely under these three heads ; and not merely from
this fact, but from the much less precisely definable but
really more trustworthy *aura* and atmosphere of the two
men's work, I should judge that, with whatever understanding and appreciation of each other, they worked almost
independently, though almost all others worked more or
less dependently on them. For this latter reason, as it
affects Sidney, his sonnets and songs as well as those of
Greville may be separated from the main and later flower-
heap of Elizabethan sonnet and lyric, while the interesting
but impossible division of "versing" almost necessarily
finds a place here.

" Interesting but impossible " ; and as nobody better
than Sidney could give the interest, so nobody could
better expose the impossibility. Spenser, as we have
seen, " cohorresced and evaded " early. Sidney had
hardly time for this pusillanimity ; and it is not certain
that he would ever have shared it, for the *Defence-
Apology* shows that he was much eaten up of neo-classic
delusions. And it is noticeable that the rhythms do not
in his hands, as in those of his friend Fulke Greville,
suffer a happy change into true English prosody. They
play the strict and lamentable game.

Indeed, the mixture of them in *The Countess of*
Pembroke's Arcadia,[1] with other things equally characteristic of the time, makes this pretty extensive collection
of verse one of the main *points de repère* in the history of
English prosody. The thing could not have been done
—at least by any one with a quarter of Sidney's critical
and poetical genius—after Spenser. If we compare it

---

[1] The *Arcadia* verse is most conveniently extracted and set together in
Dr. Grosart's "Fuller Worthies" edition of the *Poems* (2 vols., 1873),
and there fills some 180 pages.

with *The Shepherd's Kalendar* it shows us clearly how far
Spenser was ahead of and above his friend in the combination of these two gifts.   A quatorzain in poulter's
measure is followed by an ordinary decasyllabic one ;
that by a decasyllabic dizain on sonnet (*English* sonnet)
principles ; and this again by a sixain similarly arranged,
but in octosyllabics.   Then comes a song ; then continuous
Alexandrines which were no doubt intended for classical
iambic trimeters, and which dwindle to tens admitting
lyrical admixtures.   At last Sidney takes up " the burden
of the South "—the regular classical metres themselves.
And which are the worse, Dorus his Elegiacs, or Zelmane
her Sapphics, is a question which might be referred to a
mixed committee of Ancients and Moderns—say Bavius,
Codrus, Sternhold and Hopkins, with Alaric Attila Watts
for chairman.   The comparison of these Sapphics [1] with
Greville's is really most luminous.   The pair, however
(Dorus and Zelmane, I mean), are quite satisfied with
themselves ; and proceed to an enormous dialogue in
pure hexameters, clattering like the pans and the pots to
which Lockhart (though not quite in that sense) compared
Alaric Attila's own verses.   Of course, Sidney being
Sidney, there cannot but be some poetry even here ; and
much more in the native or naturalised metres which he
still combines with this unnatural and unnaturalisable
" rhythm of the foreigner."   And there is, of course,
always the delight, the " rock in the weary land," of

> What tongue can her perfections tell,

or

> Why dost thou haste away,
> O Titan fair, the giver of the day ?

and the like after the grotesques.   But both divisions are
equal documents for the fact that, in prosody, Sir Philip

---

[1] Thus, not ending, ends the due praise of her praise.
Fleshly veil consumes ; but a soul hath his life
Which is held in love ; love it is that hath joined
     Life to this our soul.

This is either very bad " Needy Knife-grinder," or else mere prose.

was still Sir Philip the Seeker; and that he was not sure when he had found.

Yet he had found, and greatly, even in these very *Astrophel and Stella*, etc. *Arcadia* poems; and much more in *Astrophel and Stella* and in some of his miscellanies. There cannot be much doubt that though Wyatt and Surrey introduced the sonnet into English, it was Sidney who made it popular, determined its form, sowed its seed broadcast among the fertile poetic soil of the time. It is not necessary to lay much stress on the highly respectable argument that Sidney could not possibly have written sonnets to a married woman, in order to carry the date of the Stella series back to 1580 or earlier. The Fury with the abhorred shears herself cuts off all possibility of their being later than 1586; and by that time nothing of any merit in the kind but Watson's *Hecatompathia* had made its appearance. No doubt Watson's frigidity helped the vogue of this incomparable form as well as Sidney's fire; but it must be remembered that the *Hecatompathia* pieces are not quatorzains at all, though the *Tears of Fancy* are. Here also Sidney experiments; he cannot help it. He uses Alexandrines; and at least tries the Petrarchian form. But in the main he is a true English sonneteer; and we shall return to him as such.

The songs, on the other hand, are free, and almost make amends for Spenser's reluctance to enjoy such liberty. There was nobody in English, not even Chaucer, from whom Sidney could have learnt the art of playing on a word for its sound and echo as he does in the first song on the word *You*; and, old as double rhymes are, they had never been made to yield quite such sweetness. The enclosed rhymes of the Second; the trochaic intermixture of the Fourth; the dainty "sixes of six" in the Sixth; the quaint quintets of the Ninth,—all these things show that English prosody has entered into her kingdom, and is exploring the riches thereof. And outside of *Astrophel* the same thing is shown by the indignant concert of "Love is dead," the charming *Guitare* (it is actually "to a Spanish tune") "O fair! O sweet! when

I do look on thee,"[1] and the sober rapture of that other to *Wilhelmus Van Nassau.*[2] He had found ; and he taught all fit seekers how to find likewise.

Marlowe.   There is perhaps no more extraordinary instance, both of the intrinsic power of metre and of its strange faculty of adapting itself to the genius of the individual, than the non-dramatic verse of Marlowe.   Except the famous "Come live with me" (which has more charm than character, and might have been written by anybody who could have written it at the time when it was written) and a few doubtful, or not doubtful, epigrams and sonnets, all this verse is couched in the rhymed couplet—original and gorgeous in *Hero and Leander*, adapted and familiar in the Ovidian *Elegies*.   In both, with an extraordinary unity in diversity, the character of the verse is as opposite as possible to that of Marlowe's "blanks."   That the quality of the poetry is the same only makes the thing more interesting.   In his plays Marlowe, as we have seen, though he discards and obliterates the mere stump of *Gorboduc* (once more let us not forget the contrast of this and Sackville's rhyme-royal), retains single-mouldedness ; and while he clothes with thunder the neck of his charger, restrains him always to stately paces.   In the poems, at least in *Hero and Leander*, the verse melts and ripples, or

[1] O fair ! O sweet ! when I do look on thee,
In whom all joys so well agree,
Heart and soul do sing in me.
This you hear is not my tongue,
Which once said what I conceivèd,
For it was of use bereavèd,
With a cruel answer stung.
No : though tongue to roof be cleavèd,
Fearing lest he chastised be,
Heart and soul do sing in me.

In these lines iamb and trochee play cat's-cradle together quite ravishingly.

[2] Who hath his fancy pleasèd
With fruits of happy sight,
Let here his eyes be raisèd
On Nature's sweetest light ;
A light which doth dissever
And yet unite the eyes—
A light which, dying never,
Is cause the looker dies.

canters and dances (whatever metaphor be preferred) with unceasing mobility.   There can be very little doubt that this most fascinating and popular poem was the instigator of Browne and others in the relaxed and enjambed couplet at the earlier part of the next century ; it may even have had something to do with *Thealma and Clearchus* (if *Thealma and Clearchus* is as early as it ought to be to carry out Walton's attribution) ; and good wits have thought that it influenced Keats quite as much as any later example.   The couplet is more distinctly enjambed in *Hero and Leander*, more often (as its connection with the elegiac almost necessitated), stopped in the Ovidian translations, but there is the same mobility in each.   For splendour of vowel-colour and music the fragment of a heroic poem, of course, stands alone.[1]

It is not easy to exaggerate the prosodic importance Drayton. of Drayton, though it is an importance very difficult to illustrate, and not very easy even to estimate, so long as we have no complete edition of his immense work in its proper chronological order, and with its unusually numerous variants of correction, substitution, addition, and omission.[2]   That he wrote verse steadily for some forty

---

[1] Even a mere scrap may show this—

> On this feast-day—O cursèd day and hour !—
> Went Hero thorough Sestos from her tower
> To Venus' temple, where, unhappily,
> As after chanced, they did each other spy.
> So fair a church as this Venus had none :
> The walls were of discoloured jasper-stone,
> Wherein was Proteus carved ; and overhead
> A lively vine of green sea-agate spread,
> Where by one hand light-headed Bacchus hung,
> And with the other wine from grapes out-wrung.

Or better still, but shorter, the passage in the second Sestiad—

> Where the ground,
> Was strewed with pearl, and in low coral groves
> Sweet-singing mermaids sported with their loves
> On heaps of heavy gold.

[2] The only thing to do at present is to take the collection (*not* complete) in Chalmers, or the Spenser Society's issues, with Hooper's *Harmony of the Church* and Professor Elton's *Michael Drayton* (London, 1905), and "combine the information" as best may be done.   But we are promised a complete issue in the "Cambridge Poets," which have already completed Prior and Crabbe ; and a good collection of the *Minor Poems* has appeared (ed. Cyril Brett, Oxford, 1907) while this book was in the press.

years ; that he had, despite his sturdy and rather re-
calcitrant temperament, a singular faculty of catching,
and even of anticipating, the *aura* of the time, so that he
is by turns representative of strictly Elizabethan, of
Jacobean, and even of Caroline poetry ; that, unlike
many voluminous poets, he seems to have been not in
the least " thirled," as the Scotch say, to one particular
metre,—all these things are in his favour from our point
of view.   But what is even more so is that, as in the poet
who was born just to succeed him, and who resembles
him in so many ways—Dryden,—and as in one or two
others of the difficult class between the absolute " Firsts "
and the unpromotable " Seconds," his redoubtable craftsmanship wrestles with, and often conquers, in this respect
as in others, the difficulties over which his mere genius
would not enable him to prevail.   Like nearly all such,
he seems to have been an untiring experimenter; perhaps
a little exposed to the danger of those who have the
Ulyssean indefatigableness without the Ulyssean astute-
ness, and who therefore persevere in experiments promis-
ing no great success, but in this very point infinitely
superior to those who are too clever to dare at all.   It
may be added that, at one time at any rate, Drayton
was a very popular poet—though, like nearly all very
popular poets, he had to pay later for his popularity,—
and that he holds a great position in what was *the*
prosodic business of the early seventeenth century, the
question of the couplet.

One of his experiments—about the most daring and
the most sustained forlorn hope in all prosodic history—
we may as well despatch first.   One seems to detect,
even in some of Drayton's few but faithful champions, a
kind of wish that he had not written it ; while those who
are not the elect dismiss it (probably on very slight
acquaintance) as a respectable, or not even respectable,
monstrosity.   I cannot agree with either of these views.
In some moods I am a very little prouder of being an
The   Englishman than I should have been if the *Polyolbion*
Polyolbion. did not exist—if the " strange Herculean task," so worthy

in itself of any Hercules, had been grappled with in a less Herculean manner.   But, speaking as a mere pros-odist, I must of course confess that the continuous Alexandrine, seriously treated at very great length, is an impossible metre in English.[1]   I do not believe that any line longer than a fairly elastic decasyllable will do as such a vehicle in our language : unless, indeed, it be the old fourteener.   For there is nothing of which English is so impatient as monotony, or of which it is so avid as variety.   If you pause the Alexandrine exactly at the middle, you cannot escape monotony ; and if you attempt a variable pause, "sixes and sevens," literally as well as metaphorically, will be the result.   Whether any poet has ever tried equivalenced Alexandrines copiously and with success, I do not at present remember ; but I should not augur well of the experiment.

At the same time, I am bound to say that it is not impossible to establish a "*Polyolbion* habit," in which, as the medical persons say, this Alexandrine is well borne. You must observe cæsura in reading ; but it becomes by degrees as tolerable as that of the Popian couplet, if not a little more so, and is certainly not much more mono-tonous.   In consequence, probably, of the hugeness of his task, which precluded nicety of revision, Drayton has not always distributed prosodic phrase as happily as he might ; for instance, the two halves—

> Her brave Pegasian steed
> The wonder of the West,

(for the Berkshire White Horse) would have made an admirable line if put together.   But he has often done this ; and if his selection was originally wrong, it was *non ingratus error*.[2]

---

[1] Sidney's Alexandrines (the chief examples that may be quoted against me at this time) do *not* run to any great length.   For the reasons of its better success in *Fifine at the Fair* we may wait till we come to that poem.

[2] Here is a fairly average specimen :—

> Whenas the pliant Muse, with fair and even flight,
> Betwixt her silver wings is wafted to the Wight,—
> That Isle, which jutting out into the sea so far,
> Her offspring traineth up in exercise of war ;

Not a great deal need be said of the octaves, in which he, like Daniel, couched his principal " history," *The Barons' Wars*, and in which he also wrote some of the minor ones—*The Miseries of Queen Margaret, The Battle* (to be most sedulously distinguished from the *Ballad*) *of Agincourt*, etc. ; or of the rhyme-royal of others—*Robert Duke of Normandy, Matilda the Fair*, etc. ; or of the sixains of yet others. Spenser had once for all taught poets who were teachable the outward form and fashion of these things—had supplied them with the perfect art of poetical bottle-making in stanzas. They had to fill the bottles with their own wine, of course, and the vintages and growths differed. But, as a rule, they ran the bottles themselves into very much the same moulds. Drayton (whose special interest as a *conscious* prosodist will occupy us later) seems to me to have been least happy in these numbers ; they encouraged his tendency to be prosaic in a different fashion from that in which they encouraged Daniel's, but to much the same degree. It is, no doubt, wrong ; but I can never open *The Miseries of Queen Margaret* without having in mine ear certain blank-verse lines written perhaps not so long before by (as I feel sure) another Warwickshire man—

> I called thee then, vain shadow of my fortune.

And I find it difficult to read flat octaves that day any more. But flatness and Drayton are, fortunately, only occasional companions. She comes on him when he is

> Weary, forswat, and vill of vayn

Those pirates to put back, that oft purloin her trade,
Or Spaniards or the French attempting to invade.
Of all the southern isles she holds the highest place,
And evermore hath been the great'st in Britain's grace.
Not one of all her nymphs her sovereign fav'reth thus,
Embraced in the arms of old Oceanus.
For none of her account so near her bosom stand,
'Twixt Penwith's furthest point and Goodwin's queachy sand.

Drayton, as in this last line, often manages his frequent proper names with great skill. I think Macaulay learnt the trick for *The Armada* from him, as. well as from Æschylus.

at dogged task-work ; but he shakes her off when he is
himself.   It is in his couplet and his numerous lyrical
experiments that his great prosodic value and interest
lie, and to these we may now turn.

His importance in the couplet has been, and must His couplet.
always be, more and more recognised the more he is
studied ; but there are few points on which the promised
complete edition, with various readings and forms, is
more required.   In *Idea, The Shepherd's Garland* (as later
entitled, *Pastorals containing Eclogues*), there are no
pieces wholly in couplet, but there are several in stanzas
with final couplet.   Now this, as has been and will be
said and seen, always acts as an encouragement, sometimes a very strong encouragement, to closing the form.
And the *Legend of Gaveston*, which is possibly of 1593,
the year of the death of Marlowe, and two years after
Spenser's *Complaints* with *Mother Hubberd*, is again in
such a stanza—sixains this time.   The final couplets
here are usually sententious and self-enclosed ; but they
often have double rhymes, which tends towards enjambment.   *Matilda*, which follows, extends itself to rhyme-
royal, and here the couplet again dogs the step.   So it
does even in the sonnets of *Idea*.   And so again the
rhyme-royal of *Mortimeriados*, the first version of *The
Barons' Wars*, was expanded into octave in the second,
and the couplet of the octave is of all the most insinuat-
ing, if not positively self-imposing.   (Is there anything
in the fact that Fairfax came between ?)   And though
the new legend, *Robert of Normandy*, which accompanied
Matilda and *Gaveston* in 1596, is in rhyme-royal, *ecce
iterum* the couplet.   Meanwhile he had actually tried it
by itself in a poem (which he never re-issued, though he
used parts of it in *The Man in the Moon*, and which is
not to be found in the most accessible editions of his
works), *Endimion and Phœbe*.   There is no doubt that Mr.
Elton is right in associating this with *Hero and Leander*.
Even without Drayton's known and attested admiration
for Marlowe, it would be certain.   But there is here much
less tendency to enjambment, and when Drayton returned

to the metre in *England's Heroical Epistles* there was less
still.   He is constantly emphatic, and not seldom positively antithetic.   Now, emphasis and antithesis are the
certain begetters of closure.   And always he held nearer
to this closed model than to the other, though you may
find things in him that might almost be Waller, and
things that might almost be Browne, for date and
character combined.

His lyrics.   He, however, like Jonson and not a few others, is an
instance of how easily sturdy and even rugged natures
can adjust themselves to the lightest and most delicate
versification.   Apparently, when he resolved to write the
Polyolbion, he wisely determined, being already provided
with the famous "something craggy to break his mind
upon," to provide himself likewise with something flowery
on which to rest it.   As Mr. Elton says, his lyric gift
came late, but the light of the eventide was coloured fair.
The Odes, the *Muses' Elizium*, *Nymphidia*, and the other
poems which he wrote in lighter measures during the last
five-and-twenty years of his life, are very charming things,
and hardly more than one of them can be said to be
known as it deserves.   How much the measure has to
do with the admirable excellence of the *Ballad of Agincourt* need only be urged upon persons who are incapable
of understanding what is urged on them.   Out of the
drama, poets were at this time so very shy of trisyllabic
feet, especially as regular things, that one at once sees
Drayton's mastery and independence, while no fit reader
has ever missed the triumph of

Ferrers and Fanhope.[1]

But Drayton has plenty more things besides this for
bow and lyre.   He is still in the period of experiment,

---

[1] I do not think I need apologise very much for occasionally suggesting
"off" prosodic considerations to my readers.   Some of them may like to
contrast the Ballad with Carducci's *Satana*.   I need not "sign-post" the
agreements and differences.   Of course Carducci did not introduce this metre,
which is an old one in Italy.   In fact, Mitford long ago actually compared
Drayton (in the "Sirena" piece) and Metastasio, though, I regret to say, with
not a little misunderstanding of the English beauty.

and sometimes he strikes them into jangle, but very seldom. His lyrical "Why not?"[1] is not the happiest piece of verse, and he should not have praised that dreadful person Soothern. But 'tis astonishing how much pleasanter it is to hear a good writer praise a bad one than to hear a bad writer blame a good! The splendid "New Year,"[2] where Mr. Elton has not failed to notice a Swinburnian touch; the pretty "Valentine" (many good things went out with St. Valentine); "The Heart"[3] (could he possibly have known Alexander Scott?); "The Virginia Voyage,"[4] even the Skeltonics,[5]

[1] And why not I, as he
That's greatest, if as free
(In sundry strains that strive
Since there so many be),
The old lyric kind revive?

I will: yea, and I may.
Who shall oppose my way?
For what is he alone,
That of himself can say,
He's heir of Helicon?

[2] Rich statue, double-faced,
With marble temples graced,
To raise thy godhead higher,
In flames where altars shining
Before thy priests divining
Do od'rous flames expire.

.   .   .   .

Give her th' Eoan brightness
Winged with that subtle lightness
That doth transpierce the air;
The roses of the morning
The rising heaven adorning
To mesh with flames of hair.

[3] If thus we needs must go,
What shall our one heart do,
This one made of our two?

[4] Britons! you stay too long,
Quickly aboard bestow you,
And with a merry gale
Swell your stretched sail,
With vows as strong
As winds that blow you.

[5] The Muse should be sprightly,
Yet not handling lightly
Things grave, etc.

are all documents for us of the paradise of lyric song that
was to atone for other not at all paradisaical things in
England for the next fifty years.   And there are delightful
things in the " Nymphals " of the *Muses' Elizium*—a use
of the common measure not quite reaching the ineffableness
which was (perhaps had been already) introduced by Ben
or Donne, but a form of its own, quietly musical—and the
curious variation on the Agincourt measure in the duet
between Nais and Cloe.[1]   Above all things,

> Near to the silver Trent
> Sirena dwelleth,

exhibits the old trick of knapping verses sweetly as few
other things do.   And as for *Nymphidia*, who shall overpraise the inimitable lightness and childishness of its
rippling melody ?   It is burlesque, of course ; there is no
witchery about it, and its figures are rather puppets
than fairies, and so want puppet music.   But prettier
marionettes you shall hardly find, nor a prettier "marionette
symphony " for them to dance to.

Daniel.   Daniel and Davies, the two poets who are in many
ways closest to Drayton, require rather less notice in this
place : first, because their practice is a good deal less varied
than his ; and secondly, because their even excellence in
this respect rather deserves encomium than necessitates
examination.   The name of Daniel is indeed clear and
venerable in the history of English prosody ; but mainly
on account of the prose-tractate which will be noticed
later in its proper place, as will be his sonnets with their
kind.   Otherwise he is chiefly noticeable as having (he
was of the Sidneian family, as they said then) almost at
once caught the great lesson of prosody which Spenser
had taught.   But the extreme sobriety of Daniel's genius
made it easier for him to be orderly than to be anything
more.   The octave, which is his vehicle in the *History of*

[1] Nais says—

> Cloe, I scorn my rhyme
> Should observe feet or time :
> Now I fall, now I climb—
> What is't I dare not ?

the Civil War, and to which he recurs with evident predilection in other places, is accomplished enough ; but it is rarely inspired or inspiring. The triumph of it— the one really magnificent thing that Daniel did, in the lines to the Countess of Cumberland—

> He that of such a height has built his mind,

comes from the singular coincidence of stately quietism in verse and thought. He has to modulate a theme which would be almost as effective unmodulated, and he does it splendidly ; but the process is rather rhetorical than poetical.[1] He can and does derive from his sonnet practice tender and more strictly poetic notes, as in the opening line of the Lady Anne Clifford poem—

> Unto the tender youth of those fair eyes,

where the adjustment of "tender" and "fair" has the secret ; he can be suddenly fulminant, as in the line which Wordsworth "lifted" like a Borderer as he was—

> Sacred religion ! mother of form and fear.[2]

He can write good rhyme-royal and good sixes, and we may be able to recur to his few lyrics. But on the whole, prosodically speaking, he is more generally *adequate* than anything else. Now adequacy is good, but it is not delicious.

With regard to Sir John Davies it ought never to be forgotten that his poetical work is the product of only a few years of his youth.[3] When this is remembered it may perhaps be allowed that, for prosodic practice, he ranks higher than Daniel. Indeed, of the three works by which he is chiefly known, two have a prosodic originality which cannot but make one think that if Davies had been in the conditions of Drayton he would have been

Davies.

---

[1] Perhaps in connection with this he altered the rhyme scheme to *abcabcdd*, so that each stanza starts with a blank-verse effect.

[2] There are others hardly less good than this in the original *Musophilus.*

[3] *Orchestra* (1594) was written before he was five-and-twenty ; all the rest before the Queen's death, when he was not thirty-five.

at least as important for us, and perhaps more so.
Orchestra—that whimsical, but by no means frivolous
fragment, which combines the information of two very
different kinds of " Academy "—is in rhyme-royal of a
most excellent pattern, less solemn and plangent (indeed
solemnity and plangency were here required, the first but
little, and the last not at all) than Sackville's, but as
resonant, flexible, and full.   Two of its own lines—

> So subtle and so curious was the measure
> With so unlooked-for change in every strain,

may almost be applied to it.   That the more Spenserian
Nosce Teipsum should be in quatrains is again a very
interesting prosodic fact at this early period.   And it is
by no means clear that the metre does not here, to some
extent, justify itself against the objections which will be
brought elsewhere against it as practised by Davenant,
and even by Dryden.   It never can be a good vehicle of
narration, but if—*if*—theological-philosophical argument
is ever to be put into verse at all, this sententious, not
inharmonious, not too involved or too scrappy vehicle
seems good for it.   Still, to see what a verse-smith Davies
was we have chiefly to look to *Astræa*, where the pervading acrostic " Elizabetha Regina " is wrought into two
fives and a six of almost Caroline quaintness and elegance
combined.   It is no wonder that Sir John should have
been fond of dancing, which is indeed very close to
prosody, and like it may be much assisted by, but is by
no means to be dictated to, by music.   On this point he
went a little wrong in *Orchestra* itself, but excusably, for
he never finished or reviewed that poem.[1]

---

[1] Who doth not see the measures of the moon,
   Which thirteen times she danceth every year?
   And ends her pavin thirteen times as soon
   As doth her brother, of whose golden hair
   She borroweth part, and proudly doth it wear :
   Then doth she coyly turn her face aside
   That half her cheek is scarce sometimes descried.

   The quatrains of *Immortality* would require rather too long an extract,
but one of the *Astræa* " Hymns " must be given :—

Large as is the amount of Chapman's non-dramatic Chapman. poetry, a prosodic study of it need deal with but two things—his couplet and his fourteeners; while the handling of the former need not be very protracted.   For the lyre, and even for those stanza measures which always have something of the lyrical in them, he seems to have been less disqualified than disinclined.   The nine-lined couplet-ended staves of *Ovid's Banquet of Sense* are by no means destitute of a grave beauty ; and the *Song of Corinna* therein is not unmusical.   No one need speak prosodic evil of the sixains of *The Amorous Zodiac*, or of the mono-rhymed octosyllabic quatrains of that *Contention of Phillis and Flora* for which Chapman (most original of translators and most given to translations of all original writers, with the exception in both cases of Edward FitzGerald) went to the Middle Ages to fetch.   His sonnets have a rare stateliness ; he can manage divers lyrical measures in his version of Petrarch's *Penitential Psalms*.   In the *Guiana* poem, though he slips into couplets now and then, he means blank verse—a notable thing at that time off the stage.   But these are all mere *hors-d'œuvre* to him.

The reason why it is not necessary to say much of

IX

TO FLORA

E mpress of flowers, tell where away
L ies your sweet court, this merry May,
I n green wide garden alleys :
S ince there the heav'nly powers do play
A nd haunt no other valleys.

B eauty, Virtue, Majesty,
E loquent muses, three times three,
T he new fresh Hours and Graces,
H ave pleasure in this place to be
A bove all other places.

R oses and lilies did them draw,
E re they divine Astræa saw,
G ay flowers they sought for pleasure :
I nstead of gath'ring crowns of flowers,
N ow gather they Astræa's dowers,
A nd bear to Heaven that treasure.

his couplet is that almost everything which has been already said, in the last chapter, of his blank verse, applies to it. It is grave and noble ; nor does it ever allow itself the eccentricities of Donne—the "holes that you may put your hand in" that so did annoy Sir John Beaumont. It is, in this resembling the similar verse of his contemporaries Drayton and Daniel, neither conspicuously stopped nor conspicuously overlapped, though it tries both ways at times. Perhaps—the couplet short of unbridled overlapping effecting this almost *per se*—it is a little less embroiled and obscure than the blank verse of the plays, and it is noteworthy that at its obscurest, as in the famous *Shadow of Night*, it succumbs to the temptation of enjambment most. But the prevailing characteristics are those of thought and action, not of metre. Chapman, in Mr. Swinburne's excellent application, "cannot clear his mouth of pebbles"; but it is the flow of his speech and thought rather than of his verse that the pebbles obstruct, though they prevent this also from being very fluent. Still, there are worse things both in sound and to sight than the ripple round pebbles.

But the metre which Chapman was, if not "born to introduce," born to perfect and consummate as a vehicle of extended narrative was the fourteener. His strong attraction for it is shown by the fact that he absolutely tried both it and the couplet for part of the *Iliad*, and abandoned the latter. That he did not make a similar double attempt or experiment in the case of the *Odyssey* is, I think, sufficiently accounted for by his saturation with the almost pedantic scholarship of the age. The ancients had drawn a distinction between the simple and passionate *Iliad*, the complex and manners-painting *Odyssey*. The old fourteener, with its age-long history, its ballad associations, corresponded to the former description ; the modern and rather sophisticated decasyllabic couplet to the latter. It is true that the *Odyssey* itself contains some of Chapman's best couplet work, but both in itself and as an equivalent for the original it cannot vie with his *Iliad.* I cannot understand how any one

who can read the Greek can tolerate Chapman's *Odyssey*
except as a student : one can read his *Iliad* with the
original sounding in one's ears and say, " Well done our
side ! " The contribution of the prosody to this success
is our business here ; and it is the importance of it which
makes appropriate what was formerly promised—a short
study of the fourteener itself, in connection, but not
merely in connection, with Chapman's employment of it,
and in especial bearing on those earlier attempts to use
it for purposes of translation which were passed over.
For that Chapman was indebted to Phaer and Golding
(to name no others), at least for suggesting the metre to
him, there can be no manner of doubt. Of late years Its
there has been a certain tendency to put up the estimate predecessors
—Phaer,
of these two, especially of Golding, who was also set much Golding, etc.
above Phaer by Warton ; and there has been a stately
reproduction of the *Ovid*.[1] Here are some extracts from
both on which to base criticism.[2]

[1] Ed. Moring and Gollancz (London, 1904).
[2] It may not be an uninteresting connection with "the ancestors" to take
the selections from those passages which Webbe (a great admirer of Phaer) and
Warton respectively admired in the two.

Phaer :—
Three times her hand she *bet*, and three times strake her comely breast ;
Her golden hair she tare and frantic-like with mood opprest ;
She cried " O Jupiter, O God," quoth she, " and shall 'a go ?
Indeed ! and shall 'a flout me thus within my kingdom so ?
Shall not mine armies out, and. all my people them pursue ?
Shall they not spoil their ships and burn them up with vengeance due ?
Out people, out upon them, follow fast with fires and flames—
Set sail aloft, make out with oars, in ships, in boats, in *frames* [rafts ?].
—What speak I ? or where am I ? what furies do me enchant ?
O Dido, woful wretch, now dest'nies fell thy head doth haunt."

Golding :—
The princely palace of the Sun stood gorgeous to behold,
On stately pillars builded high of yellow burnished gold,
Beset with sparkling carbuncles, that like to fire did shine,
The roof was framèd curiously of ivory pure and fine.
The two door-leaves, of silver clear, a radiant light did cast,
But yet the cunning workmanship of things therein far past
The stuff whereof the doors were made. For there a perfect *plat*
Had Vulcan drawn of all the world ; both of the surges that
Embrace the earth with winding waves, and of the steadfast ground,
And of the heaven itself also, that both encloseth round.

" It is not so bad," as Mr. Foker observed of his and Pendennis's libations :
and Phaer at least attains sometimes to trisyllabics, virtual if not intended.

But as a rule, though less than usual in these passages, the defect of all these writers — Golding perhaps escapes it oftener than the others—is what has been elsewhere termed the " lolloping " character of their verse. They seem unable to " lift " it, in the jockey's sense, over the ground.   To shift the metaphor from riding to walking, they all appear to be " down-gyved " like Hamlet in his ill-fated visit to Ophelia, and they shuffle along in the hamper of their nether garments in a truly deplorable manner.   Every now and then, in a short poem, some fire of passion, earthly or heavenly, gets them out of the difficulty, as in Southwell's magnificent *Burning Babe* ; but one feels that it is not far off.   The great place, however, before Chapman for observing the phenomena of the fourteener is, of course, Warner's *Albion's England.* And in this examination it is well not to neglect the mechanical but useful aid of typographical arrangement. The original volume is printed in actual fourteeners, and the present writer, nearly thirty years ago, took care to reproduce this in the extract given in Mr. Ward's *Poets.* But Chalmers, in the not very " gnostical " admiration (as his own time would have said) of that time for ballad, thought fit to balladise the whole,[1] to the great waste of space, and to the great damage, except in a few fragments, of the verse.   The splitting up, however, does make evident—what indeed could have been easily found out by any careful observer without it—certain weaknesses of the metre, unless it is managed with a great deal of art.   If you make a strong break of rhythm at the eighth syllable, as in the unapproached common-measure poems of the earlier seventeenth century, you dislocate your line too much, and prevent the continuity which narrative requires.   If, on the other hand, you make no break at all, the line becomes flaccid and expressionless, and hobbles or ambles along, from unmarked beginning

---

[1] Warton before him had identified Phaer's and Golding's metre with that of Sternhold and Hopkins ; for which, of course, fight might be made. But, as a fact, the continuous fourteener and the common measure distich have differences which are not merely typographical.   Each develops a different side of the common possibilities—and *should* develop it.

to unremarkable end, with the slipshod effect noted above.

To come to Chapman himself: in the first line of the Fourteenth Book—

Not wine nor feasts could lay their soft chains on old Nestor's ear,

we find the annotation, " This first verse, after the first four syllables, is to be read as one of our tens." Now what exactly did he mean by this? and why, whatever he meant, did he take the trouble to say it in this unusual manner? There cannot be much doubt about the answer to either question. He wished to indicate that the cæsura is in an unusual place ; and so, for him, it is. Chapman is ordinarily most punctilious about having a cæsura—not, of course, necessarily a stop in punctuation, but certainly a completion of possible sense and rhythm—at his eighth syllable. Here you can only get such a stop by separating adjective and substantive, which evidently troubled his careful soul ; and accordingly he points out that the division of the line must be *extraordinary* ; that you are not to look for the ordinary rhythm of the fourteener, but to take the first four syllables by themselves and accommodate the rest with the ordinary decasyllabic scansion. Now this very clearly shows that the fact that fourteen syllables do not make an eight-and-six, or a fourteener at pleasure, but that you ought to make up your mind with which charmer you will be happy, had not dawned on his mind. And it also shows that the Gascoignian superstitions (indeed, Chapman was nearer Gascoigne in age than any of his great contemporaries in the Jacobean time) were still rife—that the liberty of prosodising had yet to be preached. His position, in fact, is untenable on his own showing. You cannot, on any theory of prosody that is not a mere go-as-you-please anarchy, intrude a four-and-ten into a company of eights-and-sixes. But both will go together in a team of frank fourteeners as merrily and rhythmically as may be.

But he had not these crotchets always in his head.
The voyage to Chrysa and the beautiful single line—

> But when the lady of the light, the rosy-fingered morn,

which, wisely perceiving his windfall, he repeats ; the
description of Helen in the Third Book with that other
jewel, a couplet this time—

> To set her thoughts at gaze and see, in her clear beauty's flood,
> What choice of glory swum to her yet tender womanhood

(where, as in a thousand other places, it does not in the
least matter whether Chapman writes Homer, the point is
that he writes poetry) ; the fine line-conclusion—

> her bright and *ominous* blaze,

in the passage of the descent of Pallas ; the interesting
double version earlier and later, part of which shall be
given below,[1] of Achilles' speech in the Ninth Book ;
passage after passage of the Battle at the Ships, which
seems to have specially caught Chapman's English
imagination ; the Beguilement of Zeus, an admirable
rendering of that admirable passage which so much
disturbed the prudery of ancient criticasters ; the special
patches of the Prayer of Ajax and the Shield of Achilles,
—Chapman is equal to them all, in gross and in detail,
in general effect and in the jewelry of single verses.

Of course, there are plenty of weak lines to balance

---

[1] 1598 :—

> Nor all the wealth Troy held before the arms she now enfolds,
> Nor what Apollo's stony fane in rocky Pythos holds,
> I value equal to my life, spent with a pleasant mind :
> Oxen, sheep, trivets, crest-deck'd horse, fortune or strength may find,
> But of an human soul no prize nor conquest can be made
> When the white formers of his speech are forced to let it fade.

1611 :—

> Not all the wealth of well-built Troy possess'd when peace was there,
> All that Apollo's marble fane in stony Pythos holds,
> I value equal with the life that my free breast enfolds.
> Sheep, oxen, tripods, crest-deck'd horse, though lost, may come again,
> But when the white guard of our teeth no longer can contain
> Our human soul, away it flies, and once gone, never more
> To her frail mansion any man can his lost powers restore.

these, and the number of them in such a poet as Chapman is a sufficient proof of the insufficiency of the metre for continual use when unequivalenced. The verse, indeed, personifying it as its own time would have loved to do, might rise in righteous wrath and say, "I am not to be blamed for such things as—

<blockquote>
Achilles called a court
Of all the Greeks ; Heaven's white-armed Queen, who, everywhere
  cut short,
Beholding her loved Greeks by death, suggested it ; and he
(All met in one) arose and said, 'Atrides ! now I see ' "—
</blockquote>

where the unconscionable inversion and syntactical muddlement might take place in any metre, equivalenced or rigid, if the poet were careless enough. But when you come, on the opposite page in the current modern edition, to such another line as—

<blockquote>
Bright-cheeked Chryseis. For conduct of all which we must choose,
</blockquote>

the conditions are different. The grammar is quite impeccable, and the composition likewise, but unfortunately the thing, even granting "condùct," is hardly a verse at all. And there are too many like it. The fact, of course, is that pure iambic fourteeners, like blank verse and heroic couplets, can, with a little practice, be written, after a fashion, almost, if not quite, as rapidly as prose. One could not say that Chapman never reminds us of this fact.

Now he himself saw this ; whether he saw that he saw it, is (must it be repeated ?) not of the smallest consequence. He did not see beyond his own age, and therefore did not (as he might have done if only *per impossibile* he had looked before and after to *Gamelyn* and to *Sigurd*) adopt the one device which makes the fourteener a perfect vehicle—free, yet not too free, substitution of anapæsts. But he saw a good deal ; and the result is that though his fourteener cannot be accepted as a perfect medium for so long a poem, it has lifts and bursts which make it a "grand compounder"—something which attains the high degrees without exactly complying with minute or

constant counsels of perfection.   Nay, in his very third
line—

From breasts heroic ; sent them far to that *invisible* cave,

he shows (as also in "ominous" quoted above) that
he felt, if he did not consciously know it, the secret of
the anapæst itself.   From the first, too, and throughout,
he knows as well (there can be no doubt here) the other
secret of the variation of the pause.   It would be a
piquant experiment, but one of those on which millionaires
might spend their money with better reason than any
which can be alleged for their usual spendings, to print,
not the whole (which would be as unfair as printing all
Chatterton with modern spelling), but considerable parts
of the *Iliad* on the principle of dividing the lines ballad-
fashion where the cæsura, in sense or punctuation, corresponds ; straight on as fourteeners where the line is
practically unbroken ; and in stepped fashion where the
pause comes hither or thither of the middle division of
eight and six.   But, short of this open object-lesson of
things *oculis subjecta fidelibus*, it cannot be so very difficult,
for any one who is curious, to read the lines of a fair body
of verse on this principle, and so discover the effect.   The
process should not be disagreeable to any one who has
broken himself to reading in accordance with scansion ;
and nobody who will not do this will ever really appreciate
prosody.

Jonson.   The curious contrast between the hardness of Ben
Jonson's blank verse and the softened quality, sometimes
reaching *ipsa mollities*, of his lyric, has been noted above ;
with the fact that the melting process is shown cumulatively in his handling of that couplet which in language a
little ambiguous (see chapter on *Prosodists*) he extolled so
to Drummond.   That is to say, if you took all the couplet
passages from the plays, and put them together with all
those in the poems, there is a good deal of it.   But the
couplet, from its very nature, requires a very considerable
field of exercise in order to allow it to display any special
qualities ; and for this or that cause Ben did not give it

such a field.   The epigrams are naturally couched in it for the most part ; but it is rather curious that this kind, even with the wide ancient extension which he prided himself on giving to it, by no means invariably, or very often, tempted him to adopt the incisive form which it seems so naturally to invite.   That to Donne comes as near as most ; but, as will be seen below,[1] it is not exemplary.   It cannot be said that the sixth line, whether scanned with elision or with trisyllabic substitution, is euphonious ; in fact, it is nearly as ugly as some of Donne's own in the same kind, and suggests the same contrast of wonder with the impeccable lyrics.   If this was the " hexameter-like breaking " which Ben admired, one can only be glad that he did not practise it oftener. But there cannot be much doubt that the craze for roughness in satire extended to epigram likewise, though neither Catullus nor Martial can be said here to suggest what may seem to be suggested by Horace and Persius. In *The Forest* his prepossession vanishes ; but the beautiful couplets of the "Penshurst" poem are very much enjambed, as are most of the rest, especially the famous Shakespeare-piece.   Indeed, they actually give ground for thinking that " broken " *meant* " enjambed."   But of this elsewhere.

The interest of the Fletcher brothers [2] for us consists The Fletchers. mainly, and that of Giles (perhaps the better poet of the two) wholly, in their interesting if not exactly felicitous

---

[1] Donne, the delight of Phœbus and each muse,
   Who, to thy one, all other brains refuse ;
   Whose every work, of thy most early wit,
   Came forth example, and remains so yet ;
   Longer a-knowing than most wits do live,
   And which no affection praise enough can give !
   To it, thy language, letters, arts, best life,
   Which might with half mankind maintain a strife,
   All which I meant to praise—and yet I would—
   But leave because I cannot as I should.

[2] If the recent attempts to credit Phineas with *Britain's Ida* were well founded, it would be a considerable additional asset for him.   But I do not see any real evidence for the assignment, and it seems to have escaped the assigners that it is an odd sort of argument to say that it must be Phineas's because it is in Giles's stanza.

variations on the Spenserian stanza. These variations
may have been dictated either by mere reverence for the
master, whose influence was so obvious in both, or through
a desire " to create for oneself," or perhaps by a mixture
of the two feelings and a hope to escape disastrous
comparison by slightly innovating. It cannot be said,
despite the extraordinary beauty, in a sort of præ-
Raphaelite kind, of parts of *Christ's Victory* and fewer
parts of the longer *Purple Island*, that either form is a
success. Giles dropped line seven of the Spenserian, but
retained the order of the rhymes and the final Alexandrine.[1] This gives a triplet at the close, which is sometimes not ineffective in itself, but seriously damages both
the individual and the social merits of the stanza. From
the first point of view the extraordinary unity—the
" seamless coat "—of the Spenserian, is broken into
quintet and triplet, inevitably in sound, and by strong
temptation in sense and suggestion, like the octave and
sestet arrangement of a sonnet. From the second, the
accumulation of rhymes in the triplet and the culmination
by the Alexandrine in the same way suggests a much
stronger stop than the couplet-ending, and so arrests and
injures that curious concatenation which, side by side
with its individual integrity, is the glory of the great
novena.

Not satisfied with this, or fearing to touch it (for he
had, and constantly expresses, almost as great a reverence
for the brother who died so long before him as both had
for Spenser), Phineas used the shears still further, and

Giles. (margin)
Phineas. (margin)

[1] This form is also adopted in the curious poem on *St. Mary Magdalene*
(E.E.T.S., London, 1899), but almost certainly as a *following* of Fletcher.
Some would regard it as, in origin, rather a building up of rhyme-royal with
an Alexandrine than as a cutting down of the Spenserian, but I think this
very much less likely. Here is a stanza of Giles's own :—

> The garden like a lady fair was cut,
> That lay as if she slumbered in delight,
> And to the open skies her eyes did shut ;
> The azure fields of Heaven were 'sembled right
> In a large round, set with the flowers of light—
> The flowers-de-luce, and the round sparks of dew,
> That hung upon their azure leaves, did shew
> Like twinkling stars that sparkle in the evening blue.

cut off the last line of the quintet, leaving quatrain and triplet to make up a new seven-line stanza.[1] Whether this is better or worse in itself than the octave of Giles, I am not quite sure. I used to think it more of an improvement than I do now. But I have never varied in considering both as possessing the same faults, when compared with their original. It says something for the power which both these poets have of merging defects of form, and even of subject, in floods of poetic fancy and phrase, that they get over the defects of their form itself. But things so beautiful as those cited would look well in any garment.

The remaining metres of Phineas need slighter notice. He tried in his *Piscatory Eclogues* yet another septet, rhyme-royal with the last line extended to an Alexandrine, his brother's stanza, an ordinary rhyme-royal, sixains, Spenserians with triplet ending, quintets with Alexandrine close, heptasyllabic couplets ; and in his *Miscellanies* various short lyrical mixtures. He is never prosodically incompetent ; but he seems to suffer from a kind of prosodic *fidgetiness*.

William Browne, not one of the strongest of poets, Browne. but also not one of the least engaging, has more appeals than one ; and it so happens that most, if not all, of these concern prosody. That he, when all Middle English poetry save Chaucer was passing into utter neglect, save by a few students, for all but two centuries, read and revived Occleve is something ; that, after these two centuries, he himself was read, and, what is more, followed by Keats, is something more. It would have been lucky if the following had been only prosodic ; for few people can be sorry for Keats's return to enjambment, extravagant as it may be. But there might, with

---

[1] The early morn lets out the peeping day, a
And strewed his path with golden marigolds : b
The moon grows wan, and stars fly all away ; a
Whom Lucifer locks up in wonted folds b
Till light is quenched, and Heaven in seas hath flung c
The headlong day : to the hill the shepherds throng, c
And Thirsil now began to end his task and song.

considerable advantage, have been less in *Endymion* of the overrunning of fable as well as of verse, which is characteristic of *Britannia's Pastorals.*

His dealings with Occleve.

As for the first of these connections in our matter, Browne was the first to print, as part of his own *Shepherd's Pipe,* but with full attribution, Occleve's tale of *Jonathas.* Perhaps the story, though it is one of Occleve's best pieces of work, did not please ; for Browne never carried out his intention of giving the rest, which he says were " all perfect in his hands." One cannot but be sorry that he did not say something about the versification, which looks all the odder beside his own sweet and fluent style. Probably he thought, as almost everybody did for some three centuries, that you were not to expect any system in these old poets. But he showed that he had more grace than many editors of greater name, and more vaunted scholarship, by attempting no mendings. The result, of course, is that poor Occleve, who never had much smoothness to lose, is occasionally robbed even of what he has, as where

> Reigned in Rome, and had*de* son*nes* three,

becomes

> Reigned in Rome, and had sons three ;

or where

> Un*meeble* good right noon, withouten ooth,

is turned, correctly in sense, but to the impairing of the metre, into " un*moveable.*" At the other end, though he reads in one place, " Thus it is said," instead of " Thus saith the book," he keeps to his text so closely as to retain the odd phrase " gyle man," [1] where even modern preciseness expects that " wo " should be supplied. He himself is among the easiest and smoothest of writers, whether in octosyllable or decasyllable. In the honeyed

---

[1] Thus wrecchedly this gyle [wo]man dyed.

eights and sevens [1] of the first as he writes it there is His "sevens."
indeed nothing very new or special ; they were among
the most frequent numbers of all poets from Shakespeare
to Milton.   And the perfection with which not only these
mighty singers, but quite small poets, like Barnfield, and
not very great ones, like Browne himself and Wither, or
giants of hardly lesser than godlike race, like Jonson
and Fletcher, used them, is very remarkable.   On the
other hand, in the enjambed decasyllabic couplet, the
staple metre of *Britannia's Pastorals*, it is not clear that
Browne had any direct master (save perhaps Marlowe),
while he and Wither were the earliest copious practitioners
in it.   It is indeed necessary to repeat the caution that
the thing is no actual novelty.   It appears, and was
bound to appear, as soon as we have any considerable
practice with the couplet, in Chaucer, and it was being
developed by Drayton in the generation before Browne.
But before the second decade of the seventeenth century
it was a variant, a sort of escape.   It was only then that
it became, if not dominant, a serious candidate for domi-
nance, and so, in fact, forced its rival, the stopped form,
into as definite pretensions, which at last triumphed.

It has beyond all question singular charms, especially His enjambed
that one for which the Latins called a woman *morigera*, couplet.
and the French still call her *avenante*, while we used to
call her "coming."   There is nothing stiff or "stand-
off" or abrupt about it ; it meets the poet more than
half-way, and lends itself to any sport of fancy or conceit
in him with untiring complaisance.   Its compass of

---

[1] Here are some nearly pure sevens :—

> See how every stream is dressed
> By her margin with the best
> *Of Flora's gifts : she seems glad*
> For such brooks such flowers she had.
> And the trees are quaintly tired
> With green buds, of all desired ;
> And the hawthorn, every day,
> Spreads some little show of May.
> See the primrose sweetly sit
> By the much-loved violet, etc.

where only l. 3 has not made up its mind, as it easily might, to be eight or
seven.

melody is, of course, far greater than that of its rival: only a very bad poet indeed can be monotonous in it. Adroitly managed, it combines the advantages and powers of the stanza with those of the couplet, and even both with those of the blank verse paragraph to no small extent. For description it has no peer, inasmuch as it escapes the over-*vignetted* effect of the stanza, and the sharp creases, as of a picture folded and not rolled, that are inseparable from the stopped distich. And for the poetry of 1600-1650, with its prodigality of richly figured and coloured conceit—the description, as it were, of the intellect,—it is equally efficacious.[1]

But in the very enumeration of these advantages and charms the suggestion of the other side must be clear to all but dullest wits. Enchantresses are extremely nice persons at times; but they are always dangerous. And this enchantress is notoriously the very Circe of her kind. Ulysses can master her, and perhaps Ulysses is rather unwise if he ever goes away from her to her precise and orderly rival with the everlasting machine-work. But then everybody is not Ulysses. Most of her lovers get pretty soon flustered with the cup of her enchantments, and some of them even undergo the further transformation.

Browne is not Ulysses; but neither is he Gryll. The most remarkable effect of the Circean spells upon him is that glanced at above, and noticeable in almost all practitioners of this form, except (I should say, though some would not) the late Mr. William Morris. There is

---

[1] Here is a passage taken, as I always prefer to do, almost at random :—

> It chanced one morn, clad in a robe of grey,
> And blushing oft, as rising to betray,
> Enticed this lovely maiden from her bed
> (So when the roses have discovered
> Their taintless beauties, flies the early bee
> About the winding alleys merrily)
> Into the wood, and 'twas her usual sport,
> Sitting where most harmonious birds resort,
> To imitate their warbling in Aprill,
> Wrought by the hand of Pan, which she did fill
> Half full of water :

The actual verse-sentence does not end for another half-dozen lines.

no very cogent reason why the liberty of enjambment in verse should lead to confusion in narrative and exposition. After all, whether you give to a particular subdivision of your subject twenty lines in a bundle of ten pairs, or in batches of seven and thirteen, it need not much matter to the conduct of the subject itself. But in practice it does. *Endymion* is bad enough in this respect : the best way is to keep fast hold of Cynthia's hand or waist, and never mind where she is taking you. But its originals leave it far behind. I have found it my duty to make a regular argument of Chamberlayne's *Pharonnida*; and this duty has not been imposed upon me in regard to *Britannia's Pastorals*, so that I am not quite in the same position with regard to the two. But from reading the *Pastorals* more than once or twice, I should say that they, although the shorter, would be in some ways the harder to reduce to *précis*. And much the same is the case with the minor poems of the same class and measure, especially *Thealma and Clearchus*. The contagion of breathlessness and " promiscuousness " seems to spread from the structure of the verse to that of the story. Yet, when one reads such a passage as Wither's " Alresford Pool," which will be given presently, or any one of scores in Browne, such as that which was given above, it is very hard to quarrel with the measure or the method. One floats on away, afar, with such pleasant aimlessness, and in such an agreeable country ! It is a little relaxing perhaps. The charms of the South and of the West are in it. But there are times when one does not exactly consider the northeaster the only " wind of God "—who indeed, according to the more orthodox view, created them all.

Browne, however, by no means confined himself to this one metrical mistress. The *Pastorals* themselves are interspersed with lyrical admixtures of very varied kinds— octosyllables and heptasyllables (though fewer of these) and stanzas of all sorts,[1] and the minor poems swell the

---

[1] The reader will find in Mr. Gordon Goodwin's edition of Browne (London, two vols., 1894) abundant examples, from the wasp-waisted kind, ii. 43 (which is mainly decasyllabic, but contracts itself in the middle), to very

tale of variety. But perhaps the best place of all for Browne's power in irregular metres is the *Inner Temple Masque*, with its often-quoted and extremely beautiful lyrical overture—

Steer hither, steer your wingèd pines,

the completion of which does not come for some time in the original ; and with a large choice of other lyrical metres, including one of those fantasticalities rather favoured by the Elizabethans older and younger—an " Echo Song." In fact, this later but really " pleasant Willy " is a very good example of the way in which his master had in his own words " taught all the woods to answer, and their echoes ring " to tunes and times never imagined before.

Wither.   His almost inseparable companion in literary history, Wither, who was actually his friend, has very much less variety of accomplishment and much volume of actually accomplished verse ; but for this very reason his native woodnote strikes, and, when it was attended to, always has struck, hearers and readers almost more forcibly. Wither illustrated both his pluck and his silliness by collecting [1] all his good poems under the name of *Juvenilia* when he was nearly thirty-five, and publishing hardly anything that was not rubbish later. In fact, out of *The Hymns and Songs of the Church* and *Hallelujah*, it is quite in vain to search the vast desert of his later work for anything good ; and the samples of good hymn-metre and phrase in these two [2] are not abundant. Even the *Juvenilia* themselves contain plenty of warning both of what was to come and of what was not. The whole mass of the satires is worthless prosodic-

beautiful things like " Glide soft, ye silver floods," ii. 96. Note i. 225, for closed couplet, and " Shall I tell you whom I love ? " i. 235, where the honey of the period is admirably combed. Note also i. 285, " As new-born babes," which is especially redolent of Spenser. In fact, all these pieces vividly recall *The Shepherd's Kalendar* with another generation of practice added. *The Shepherd's Pipe* invites this remembrance still more candidly.

[1] The Spenser Society's reprints in the originals must be consulted by those who want all the chaff as well as all the corn. The latter is to be found almost completely in Mr. Arber's *English Garner*.

[2] To be found in the *Library of Old Authors*, ed. Farr (two vols., London. 1856-57).

ally, Wither's rather languid, if not exactly limp couplet, being quite unfitted for use as whip-lash, and not knowing, as Browne's did, how to exchange itself for something else. Nor is it much good in his other pieces for any purpose save description, where, however, it achieves mild triumphs. The already-mentioned picture of Alresford Pool [1] I must always regard as one of the most perfect things of its kind in English, if not in any language.   The actual place, it is true, is very pretty ;   and nobody would ever think that it is anything but a natural lake, though as a · matter of fact it is the work of one of the benighted priests of the slothful and ignorant Middle Ages, intended (and for ages serving) as an instrument of public utility and health.   But Wither has heightened its beauty a little, though quite in a legitimate and Turneresque manner, and has ·rendered the whole thing magisterially.   It would be impossible to suit the texture and colour of the metrical garment more perfectly to the body of the picture.

His longer couplet in "Alresford Pool."

Still there is no doubt that it is not the decasyllabic couplet, enjambed or other, which gives Wither his shrine in the west front of the Church of St. Prosodia, and almost entitles him to a special chapel or chantry inside.   His claims rest on the shorter distich, which is so faithful to the trochaic cadence and the seven-syllable norm that,

His shorter.

[1] For pleasant was that Pool ; and near it then
Was neither rotten marsh nor boggy fen ;
It was not overgrown with boisterous sedge,
Nor grew there rudely, then, along the edge
A bending willow, nor a prickly bush,
Nor broad-leaved flag, nor reed, nor knotty rush.
But here, well ordered, was a grove with bowers ;
There, grassy plots set round about with flowers.
Here you might, through the water, see the land
Appear strewed o'er with white or yellow sand.
Yon, deeper was it ; and the wind, by whiffs,
Would make it rise and wash the little cliffs ;
On which, oft pluming, sate unfrightened then
The gaggling wild goose and the snow-white swan,
With all those flocks of fowl which, to this day,
Upon these quiet waters breed and play.

The prosodic note of this (which no one perhaps has later caught so well as Mr. William Morris) is not enjambment, so much as a varied valuing of pause and clause, which *distributes* the harmony otherwise than merely by couplets.

although it has the very same line which more generally serves as a change for the iambic octosyllable, and is probably a mere derivative therefrom, seems in such examples as these, with the patronage of Shakespeare before and over it, almost to deserve a separate establishment and title.[1]   The name just mentioned, and others mentioned before, would of themselves negative any idea of regarding Wither as the chief practitioner of this.   But he may be the most representative without being the chief, and I think he is.   When he tries others, as in some of the " Sonnets " of *Philarete*, he is at best unimportant ; but when he returns to this, either arranged simply (and best so), or alternately rhymed, or set in stanza form, he rises at once.   It is his mother-metre : he cannot touch it without deriving strength and inspiration from the touch. Even here, of course, he cannot conquer his nature, and put in the light ringing measure the fire as well as light of Shakespeare in *A Midsummer Night's Dream* or the *Pericles* choruses, the quintessenced elixir of Fletcher or of Herrick.   His, even more than Browne's, is really a " shepherd's pipe," the ideal utterance of the impossible but agreeable person with crooks and garlands, in the equally impossible but agreeable country in which ribbons never grow faded and sheep are always fresh from the washing.   Yet he does it with the least possible touch of artificiality.   Wither is no Watteau : he may not have so much art, but he has much less flagrant artifice.   And his prosody at this time is just what it ought to be to suit Arcadia.   In the dreary dotages of his later years he returned almost exclusively to the decasyllabic couplet.

A few remarks on the prosody of two other poets in

---

[1] One example is hardly better than another, though one may contain an individually happier phrase than another. This (though it has none such) will do :—

Then shall cowardly Despair	As to live in such a time,
Let the most unblemished fair,	In so rude, so dull a clime,
For default of some poor art	Where no spirit can ascend
Which her favour may impart,	High enough to apprehend
And the sweetest Beauty fade	Her unprizèd excellence,
That was ever born or made?	Which lies hid from common sense ?
Shall, of all the fair ones, she	Never shall a stain so vile
Only so unhappy be	Blemish this, our Poet's Isle.

this period who have no special prosodic individuality Sylvester and
may be added for completeness, and put together for Basse.
convenience.   The actual verse of Sylvester [1]—perhaps the
best read (as Englisher of "Bartas") of any English poet
during the first half of the seventeenth century—is by no
means so stiff as the close and prim laurel wreath, the
palisading effrontery of the ruff, and the severely buck-
rammed doublet of his portrait might suggest.   In fact, it
is rather in diction than in versification that Sylvester is
grotesque ;   and it is noteworthy that his verse is freest
and most melodious in his rather frequent original inser-
tions.   He is, however, a strict elider and apostrophator :
and the couplet which he chiefly uses is of the indeterminate Draytonian sort, ready to take either branch
of the Y by turns, but not taking either very decidedly.
In wholly original pieces he gives himself more licence ;
and is the better for it.   In fact, Sylvester is one of those
curious persons who give one the idea that they might
have been better poets than they were : an effect at least
more gracious than that produced by the other class, of
whom Beattie is an excellent example—who would have
been better poets, if they could.   Basse, who has had late
admission [2] to the Rules of the Spenserian Sanctuary, shows
at his prosodic best in the half mock-heroic poem on the
Boarstall Walnut Tree (where his rhyme-royal rather
reminds one of Kynaston's later experiment in *Leoline and
Sydanis*).   Indeed, this mixed mode seems to have been
his forte, though he practised it little.   The two songs "The
Hunter's Song" and "Tom-a-Bedlam" are not contemptible ;
and his "Sword and Buckler"—a defence of the irregular
profession (as it has been called) of gentleman serving-man
—adopts the sixain not clumsily.   The various stanzas of
his more serious poems are respectable but undistinguished.

A subject of considerable interest and importance, The Scottish
connecting itself with something that we saw formerly, Jacobeans—
Ayton, Ker,
but capable of being sufficiently handled in short space, and Hannay.

---

[1] Ed. Grosart, "Chertsey Worthies Library," printed for private circula-
tion, two vols., 1880.

[2] Thanks to Mr. Warwick Bond, who edited him (London, 1893).

is to be found in the group of more or less strongly
Anglicised Scottish poets who represent the reign of
James VI.——Sir Robert Ayton, Drummond, Lord Ancram,
Lord Stirling, and just at the end of the Jacobean and at
the beginning of the Caroline period, Patrick Hannay.
It is well known, and, though better known than understood in detail, still comprehensible enough generally, that
poetry in Scots itself, which had been but a fading flower
for a long time, " wilted off " almost immediately after the
Union of the Crowns.   I believe that the recent studies
and discoveries of my friend Mr. George Stevenson show
that the process of Anglification is traceable even in
Montgomerie.   In the quintet above named it is simply
accomplished.   A rhyme now and then such as " allow "
to " you " in one of Ayton's poems (which same rhyme
occurs also in Hannay), an occasional appearance in the
latter of the participial *-it* mainly for rhyme's sake, and a
few Scots *oes* and *aes* may meet us, but they are quite
exceptional.   And it is worth observing that though
Ayton, Stirling, Ker of Ancram, and Hannay seem to have
chiefly lived with the Court in England, Drummond did
not.   The point, however, above glanced at, is the peculiar
accuracy of the student and practitioner in a half-strange
language.   Ayton [1] is as regular in his numbers as his

> [1] I loved thee once, I'll love no more,
>   Thine be the grief as is the blame ;
> Thou art not what thou wast before,
>   What reason I should be the same ?
> He that can love unloved again,
> Hath better store of love than brain :
> God send me love my debts to pay,
> While unthrifts fool their love away.
>
> .   .   .   .   .
>
> I do confess thou'rt sweet, but find
>   Thee such an unthrift of thy sweets—
> Thy favours are but like the wind,
>   That kisses everything it meets.
> And since thou canst with more than one,
> Thou'rt worthy to be kissed by none.
>
> .   .   .   .   .
>
> What means this strangeness now of late
>   Since time must truth approve ?
> This distance may consist with state,
>   It cannot stand with love.

friend Ben ; Ker's beautiful sonnet " Sweet solitary life "
is perfectly smooth; the long stanzas of Hannay's *Philomela*
and the sixains of his *Sheretine and Mariana* very rarely
break down or drag, while some of his couplets are as
much of the pattern that pleased the eighteenth century
as Fairfax's or even Waller's.

As for the principals, Drummond is one of the most Drummond.
accomplished verse artists of a very accomplished time.
Indeed, the skill and sweetness of his verse, with the
frequent felicity of his diction, go far, to compensate
for—if not exactly to hide—the unfortunate frigidity
of feeling which mars him, and of which one unluckily
becomes the more sensible the oftener one reads him.
Some of his sonnets are, for everything but passion, as
beautiful things as the Elizabethan period can produce,
and remind one curiously of those of Joséphin Soulary and
José Maria de Heredia in our days.   His madrigals are
better still : they are the very daintiest of sweetmeats,
only waiting for a little spirit to be infused into them,
after the fashion suspected of the Excise, and hateful to
teetotallers.   Indeed, they are sometimes (as in the cases
of " Phœbus, arise !" and the still more charming celebration
of eyes like aquamarines) so sweet to eye and taste, that
one can dispense with intoxication.   He is always best
in these short irregular pieces, where the power of prosody
is almost supreme ; while he has some very fine combinations, occasionally Platonic in tone.

Alexander Lord Stirling, with less lightness, deftness, Stirling.
and grace, had more fire in his interior.   The octaves of
his alarmingly titled *Doomsday* are resonantly moulded,
and, more than any other tailed octaves, give something
of the sound of a tail-docked Spenserian.   The *Aurora*
sonnets, with rather less finish than Drummond's, have
more " cry," nor are the varied metres of the songs contemptible.   It is noteworthy and characteristic that Stirling
is one of the last poets to use the " poulter's measure."
Here, it must be confessed, he does not get out of the
" butterwoman's rank " ; but then, as we said before, very
few do.

A moment's attention, too, should be given to the curious choruses of Stirling's most untheatrical plays. These meditative descants constituted, beyond all doubt, one of the appeals of the Senecan tragedy to an age which was nothing if not thoughtful, and so, opposed as that tragedy was to the whole drift of English dramatic taste, induced the cultivation of the form now and then. I certainly do not wish that this cultivation had been more extensive, yet I should be sorry if we had not (an absurd phrase, but with a meaning) *Monarchic Tragedies*, and especially their choruses. Whenever a man finds a form which exactly suits his meaning, or a meaning which exactly suits the form that he chooses, then the prosodic spheres sing loud or low as the case may be. I do not mean to say that they sang very loud at this achievement, but I think they sang.

At any rate, he, like the others, is certainly a careful versifier, and helps to establish the general proposition referred to above.

NOTE ON THE SATIRISTS

A NOTE will perhaps suffice on one point connected with the
serious and non-lyrical poetry of the Elizabethan time proper—
the roughness, that is to say, of the couplet used by the satirists,
Marston, Hall, and others. It is very striking. But for that
same reason it has been almost more noticed than any other
prosodic fact of the period; and if not a universal, a pretty
general agreement has been arrived at on it. This is to the
effect that the apparently deliberate licence and roughness of the
Roman satirical writers—Horace to a great extent, but Persius
even more,—in respect of rhythm and diction, was either deliberately copied by their English imitators (who certainly to a great
extent followed the Roman tone), or was accepted by them as a
sort of cloak for greater prosodic carelessness than they showed
in other respects. The most interesting and important case of
all—that of Donne—can indeed hardly be regarded as covered
by these suppositions; but Donne's prosody will be treated as a
whole at the close of the next chapter. In regard to Hall and
Marston and Lodge and Guilpin the hypothesis will serve,
though it is fair to observe that in Lodge's case—the only one
which is completely parallel to Donne's as being that of a satirist
who was also an admirable lyric poet—the discrepancy of the
two styles is not nearly so great as in Donne's.

CHAPTER IV

ELIZABETHAN LYRIC AND SONNET—DONNE

Contents of chapter.

IT was pointed out in the last volume that, at a time contemporary with Spenser, if not necessarily in all cases through his direct influence, a great change comes over the miscellaneous verse that we find, whether in so-called "Miscellany," or in any special poet. According to the mixed mode, which has been sketched in the Preface of this present volume, we have already seen something of this; but we must now fill in and complete the outline. This will best be done by taking up first the actual Miscellanies at the point at which we left them—that is to say, with *The Phœnix Nest*; then by noticing the prosodically most interesting of the scattered lyrics of the time in Romance and Drama and Song-book; then by dwelling a little on the great sonnet-outburst of the decade mainly succeeding the Armada; and lastly, by considering in particular the lyrical work of the two greatest of the younger Elizabethans, Jonson and Donne, whose influence, and in part their production, reaches forward to the "time of lilies," the late summer of the whole Elizabethan period in the wide sense, the extraordinary outburst of Jacobean and Caroline song which, in its perfect blossoming, will not come under our notice till the next Book. In Donne's case one of those licences of exception in method of which readers have been forewarned will be taken ; and his whole prosody will be considered together, for reasons which the treatment must, if it can, make clear and justify.

The identification of " R. S.," the editor of *The Phœnix Nest*, and of the further initials which indicate or conceal the authors of the fourteen most specially "woorthie wurkes" that compose this remarkable collection, is fortunately not in the least necessary to the present inquiry. Whether " R. S. " was the ghost of Shakespeare's grandfather, and " W. S. " Shakespeare himself, are questions which we may leave to those who like them. The prosodic and poetic facts fortunately remain.

The opening pieces [1] on Sidney's death are not of the most immortal garlands devoted to the *tombeau* of Astrophel ; [2] and some not immediately following verses of " N. B. " (whether Nicholas Breton or No Body) retain the blunted music of the Turbervillian period. But with the " Excellent Ditties of Divers Kinds and Rare Inventions written by Sundry Gentlemen " we come to metal more attractive. The opening sixains remind us of the overture of the *Shepherd's Kalendar* thirteen years earlier, and are not equal to it. But, with the next piece in quatrains of trochaic dimeter, they are worth sampling. [3]

[1] I follow the *Heliconia* reprint, vol. ii., London, 1815.
[2] The second, however, has the quatrain with inclosed rhyme *abba*, which, though decasyllabic, is always to be noticed when it comes early, for the sake of its *In Memoriam* derivative.
[3] Weep you, my lines, for sorrow while I write ;
  For you alone may manifest my grief ;
  Your numbers must my endless woes recite,
    Such woes as wound my soul without relief,
  Such bitter woes, as whoso would disclose them
  Must cease to talk, for heart can scarce suppose them.

There is some " fingering " here. But there is more in this—

This and still more the next (whether Lodge's or not) show us that their author had the secret—that the ball is opened, that the dancing has begun, and that the days of stumbling and hirpling are over.   And there is no relapse as long as " T. L. gent " is with us.   The beautiful short line, like the Adonic of a Sapphic, added to " All day I weep my weary woes " ;[1] the graceful wasp-waisted sixains of " Oh woods ! unto your walks my body hies " ;[2] the actual Sapphics,[3] at least in intention (which escape the jauntiness or the awkwardness of the usual English travesty of that metre almost as well as Greville's) ; and the delightful *carillon* of " My bonny lass," [4]—all show that we are really in the rose-garden, that the carols in the old sense are begun.   Things less good—things positively bad—follow.   But store of good

> Muses ! help me : sorrow swarmeth,
>   Eyes are fraught with seas of languish,
> Hapless hope my solace harmeth,
>   Mind's repast is bitter anguish.

Let it be remembered that " languish " and " anguish " were not such old partners then.

> [1] All day I weep my weary woes,
>   Then when that night approacheth near,
> And every one his eyes doth close,
>   And passèd pains no more appear—
>   I change my cheer.

> [2] Oh woods ! unto your walks my body hies,
>   To loose the traitorous bands of 'ticing Love,
>   Where hills, where herbs, where flowers
>   Their native moisture pours
> From forth their tender stalks, to help mine eyes ;
>   Yet their united tears may nothing move—

where it is again just as well to remember that " flowers—pours " was not recognised as a false concord by the grammar of the time, nor as a false rhyme by its prosody.

> [3] The fatal star, that at my birthday shined,
>   Were it of Jove, or Venus in her brightness,
> All sad effects, sour fruits of Love, divined
>   In *my* love's lightness.

> [4] My bonny lass, thine eye,
>   So sly
>   Hath made me sorrow so—
> Thy crimson cheeks, my dear,
>   So clear,
>   Have so much wrought my woe, etc.

sonnets come to comfort us, and some common measure,
" The time when first I fell in love," which, in tone as well
as in tune, is a far-off forecast of Suckling.   Nor will the
fact that the book closes with some Sapphics, quite as
bad as Southey's, remove the comfortable impression.
Qui a bu, boira ; and others will follow him in drinking
now that the fountain is once unsealed.

   Of the three collections published in the last years of *England's*
the Queen, *England's Parnassus*, being merely an anthology, _{Davison's} *Helicon* and
or rather a commonplace book from published authors, *Poetical*
need not delay us long.   But it is a prosodic document *Rhapsody.*
of the highest importance when we remember how
absolutely impossible it would have been to get together
anything like such a record of prosodic accomplishment
only twenty years earlier ;   and what an astounding
contrast would be presented by a parallel book dating
not twenty but a hundred years sooner, and representing
the entire English prosody of 1400-1500.   *England's
Helicon*, on the other hand, and the *Poetical Rhapsody*,[1]
but especially the latter, contain actual new stuff.   As
before, the authorship matters little, but the contrast of
The Phœnix Nest with the earlier miscellanies is here
repeated on a larger scale, and in more striking and
intenser fashion.   The waters of this Helicon rise from
many springs, some of which we have traced to their
actual founts already ; but almost everywhere they run
softly and smoothly, with no chafing against obnoxious
pebbles or sand-banks.   Even poor abused " Bar. Young "
writes, so far as numbers go, as much better poets could
hardly have written a generation earlier.   His notion of
expanding common measure, or rather sandwiching a decasyllabic quatrain between two " C.M.'s " in " Melisea her
Song," is no bad one.[2]   Whosoever " Shepherd Tony " was,

---

   [1] For easy access to both of which, as to much else in the contents of this
chapter, we have to thank Mr. A. H. Bullen, whose edition of the *Helicon*
originally appeared in 1887, and that of the *Rhapsody* in 1891.
   [2] Like the rest of Young's verse it comes from his translation—a most
influential one—of Montemayor's *Diana*.   Poetically, of course, it is no
great thing—hardly anything at all.   But the " twist " of the metre has, to
my ear, a rather remarkable effect, as imaging the change from mocking to
seriousness and back again :—

he had not much to learn prosodically ; and most of the others had shown, or were to show, this fact elsewhere. And it is still more the case in Davison's inestimable *Rhapsody*, with its mysterious " A. W." and its many known masters ; so much so, indeed, that we may do better to generalise only on these, and on the songs from other sources which have been mentioned.

Music and prosody.

One point of extreme importance may be dealt with first. We have seen that, in the period of the novitiate before Spenser, music undoubtedly did good by suggesting fairly complicated but harmoniously concerted measures ; yet that in some cases, in consequence of their prosodic nonage, the poets confused musical and poetical music, failing to achieve the latter in their anxiety to suit the former. In the time to which we have now come there can, of course, be no doubt that the popular fancy for music was at least equally powerful as a provoker. The cittern in the barber's shop was no bad sign for prosody ;

> Young shepherd, turn aside and move
>   Me not to follow thee ;
> For I will neither kill with love,
>   Nor love shall not kill me.
>
> Since I will live and never favour show,
>   Then die not, for my love I will not give—
> For I will never have thee love me so
>   As I do mean to hate thee while I live.
>
> That [then ?] since the lover so doth prove
>   His death, as thou dost see,
> Be bold, I will not kill with love,
>   Nor love shall not kill me !

For a still more skilful and much more elaborate composition, with poetry added, take this of A. W. the Unknown, from the *Rhapsody*, ii. 79 :—

> When Venus saw Desire must die,
>   Whom high Disdain
>   Had justly slain,
> For killing Truth with scornful eye :
> The earth she leaves and gets her to the sky ;
>   Her golden hair she tears ;
>   Black weeds of woe she wears ;
> For help unto her father doth she cry :
>   Who bids her stay a space
>   And hope for better grace.

These will illustrate the remarks which follow in the text with at least a bare sufficiency.

and we have the plain fact that, of the immense and
marvellously good lyrical production here surveyed, a
large part actually appeared as with, or for, musical
setting ; that the songs in the plays and romances
(another large part) were deliberately intended to be sung;
and that probably a very large proportion of what were
published as " poems " had the same destination, and
reached it.   Yet we find almost universally that, whether
in the songs certainly written for music or in those not so
written, Prosody has learnt how to reduce the inferior [1]
art to its proper functions—those of an accidental and
unnecessary companion.   From the " T. L." of *The
Phœnix Nest* onwards we see that she has taught these
writers to dispense with viol or flute, though they may be
willing enough to join with these—to carry their own
music in the words, not to beg it from inarticulate charity.

 The best (because the longest) known of the classes The Songs
into which this wonderful concert is divided is composed from the
of the Songs from the Plays.   These could at no time Plays.
escape notice, because, even before Shakespeare had come
fully into his kingdom, Beaumont and Fletcher were
popular, and their work happens to contain many of the
best songs of all next to his.   Jonson, perhaps from a
scruple ever so little pedantic, did not use the lyric power
which he possessed very much in his regular dramas,
though there are, of course, exceptions, headed by the
famous—

   Queen and Huntress, chaste and fair,

which has, in its prosodic movement, the stately splendour
of the goddess herself at her fullest and most undisturbed.
His masques are naturally full of lyrics, from the comic
motion (very early in this kind) of " Buzz, quoth the blue
fly " onwards.   These pieces in the masques, and some
elsewhere, are valuable for the history, not of trisyllabic
feet, but of actual trisyllabic measures, which we shall

---

[1] Inferior : being not necessarily human as poetry is, and even inferior in
humanity.   For birds beat man in all but volume of sound ; unless, as Sir
Thomas Browne might have put it, " he stayeth himself with metallic and
intestinal contrivances."

have to attack in the Interchapter ; and there is perhaps none more so than the very subtle and beautiful—

See the chariot at hand here of Love,

which was only partly and grudgingly imparted to *The Devil is an Ass*.[1]   But as the Elizabethan dramatists were one by one reinstated in the eighteenth century, and still more fully in the nineteenth, the extraordinary riches and beauty of their work in this department came more and more fully into view.   Daniel's rather prim solemnity in his regular poems becomes graceful and almost arch in—

Love is a sickness full of woes ;

and the less polished but rarer note of Dekker comes out incomparably in—

Cold's the wind and wet's the rain

(one of the very finest of all), with " Sweet Content " and " Golden Numbers " and other things, for the mere possibility and " false dawn " of which we have to look back to *Alisoun* and her company at the beginning of the fourteenth century.   And so it goes on till the very last, till Shirley's again famous and strangely adequate swansong of—

The glories of our blood and state.

Nowhere would it more be pleasing to delay and dally

---

[1] Compare the play, II. ii., and *Charis*, No. iv.   The stanza, which does *not* appear in the former place, may be given here :—

> See the cha|riot at hand | here of Love !
> Wherein | my La|dy ri|deth.
> Each that draws | is a swan | or a dove,
> And well | the car | Love gui|deth.
> As she goes, | all hearts | do du|ty
> Unto | her beau|ty ;
> And enam|oured do wish, | so they might
> But enjoy | such a sight
> That they still | were to run | by her side
> Th[o]rough ponds, | th[o]rough seas, | whither she | would ride.

(" Through," as often, is probably to be valued " thorough," and " chariot " was generally " chawyot " or " charret.")

with these delightful things,[1] and to show the cunning as well as the charm of each of them. But that way lies no end ; and, besides, they are now fortunately well or fairly well known. Only, perhaps, one may point out that nothing illustrates more remarkably the contrast of the crumbling away of dramatic blank verse, and the holding on of lyric, than these songs in the later plays, as, for instance, the faultless " Why so pale ? " and " No ! no ! fair heretic " of Suckling in the midst of the audacious doggerel of the dialogue of *Aglaura*.

The next division—the Songs and inset Poems from the Romances—was long quite unknown, or known only by a very few students ; but the late Mr. Bell made a good deal of it accessible fifty or sixty years ago, and Mr. Bullen carried on the good work more recently. This division has the special interest that it is practically all early—the work of men like Breton, Lodge, and Greene, who are in the strict and not in the large sense Elizabethans, and who even represent to some extent the præ-Spenserian time and circumstances ; not to mention Sidney, who has been dealt with. These are literally the first sprightly runnings of the new-broached cask—the first and far from discordant tunings-up of the new-strung lyre. They thus coincide (and are in some cases identical) with the constituents of the later *Miscellanies*, and exhibit the same prosodic stage. Greene and Lodge were evidently such born singers that a ruthlessly experimental mind might almost long to transfer their birth to a different period, and see what would happen. But in this, as in other cases, it can but be profane to think them anything but what they are.

Those from the Romances.

Last known, but certainly not least worth knowing, are the contributions of the actual Song-books of the period, which, until Mr. Arber and Mr. Bullen began to exhume them early in the last quarter of the nineteenth century, were literally *aurum irrepertum*. I suppose

And from the Song-books.

[1] A good number of them, after the very earliest, and down to Dryden, will be found in the present writer's collection of *Seventeenth Century Lyrics* (London, 1892), and, of course, also in most English anthologies, whether they deal exclusively or inclusively with the period.

musicians knew them ; but musicians have seldom known anything about poetry ; and I suppose lovers of poetry, seeing that they were "for music," and remembering the modern "song to be sung," shuddered and passed them by.   Yet it is strange that they should have been so long overlooked ; more particularly since they furnish one poet who is certainly no ordinary one, and who must be dealt with separately in a moment.   But they have by no means merely to speak by "their prior," though that prior be Campion.

It has, since their disinterment, struck everybody as the most remarkable proof existing of the irresistible *poeticalness* of the time, not merely that there should be so much that is exquisite here, but that so much of that exquisite stuff should be all but anonymous, or even wholly so.   It seems impossible that mere music-masters or editors like Weekes and Wilbye, Byrd and Dowland, Rossiter and Jones, should be authors of the ravishing things they published ; but if they were not, who were? When Captain Tobias Hume wanted words for an air, did he, at a spare moment, sit down and write, or open the window and invite the first-comer to compose, such a thing as that incomparable "Fain would I change that note," to the second stanza of which Mr. Bullen has done justice by inscribing it on the portal of his anthology? But we do not know ; and I suppose we never shall.

Our business, however—as I have to remind the reader, tediously to myself, and no doubt more tediously to him,—is not so much with the poetry itself as with the form of it.   And once more also we see in these song-books how "vulgate" that form was—how easily all and sundry, or at least a good many, could throw thought, original or borrowed, rare or commonplace, into shapes and garbs which poets infinitely superior to them had not dreamt of, or at any rate had not attempted earlier.   For instance, that stanza just referred to.[1]   Take away any

[1] O Love, they wrong thee much
   That say thy sweet is bitter,
When thy rich fruit is such
   As nothing can be sweeter.

of its prosodic distinctions—the masculine rhyme alternating with feminine in the opening quatrain, the restriction of the sixain that follows to sixes and fours, with feminine rhyme again in the third and sixth—and all the sweetness will be gone. Reverse or alter (I have tried the experiment) with the least possible alterations, and with sounder rhymes than " bitter " and " sweeter." *Actum est!* A few other examples might be indicated of other pieces where the prosodic character is clearly responsible for much, if not most, of the charm ; but it will be better to make a somewhat closer examination of Campion himself and of his verses in both kinds, than to select examples from the herd, however fair. As a prosodic theorist, his place will be in the next chapter ; but here he shall be saved by his works.

The " monstrous beauties," as La Harpe might have called them, may be considered first.[1] Constructed (*v. inf.*) on a system which, though mistaken, does not, like that of most " versers," from Watson downwards, fly deliberately in the face of the harmony of the English language, there is nothing to say against them except that, in the first place, they are positively things *à la chinoise*, unnaturally warped and cramped ; while, in the second, they deprive themselves, with an equally unnatural asceticism, of the congenial grace of rhyme. The five-foot " licentiate " iambics [2] of the overture " To his Book," and the longer and later inset " So numbers," etc., whether the reasoning that precedes them be good or bad, are fine blank verse of a type between the stiffer one of the

Campion.

His " versings.

Fair house of joy and bliss,
Where truest pleasure is,
  I do adore thee ;
I know thee what thou art,
I serve thee from my heart,
  And fall before thee.

[1] I use, of course, Mr. Bullen's *Works of Thomas Campion* (London, privately printed, 1889). The classical experiments are scattered as examples through the *Observations* (see next chapter).

[2] Whither thus hastes my little book so fast ?
  To Paul's Churchyard. What ? in those cells to stand,
  With one leaf like a rider's cloak put up
  To catch a termer ? etc.

University Wits and the full licence of Shakespeare—the inscrutable smile on whose face, by the way, must have been more inscrutable still when he read Dr. Campion, and found that he had been doing everything he ought to do on principles very different from the doctor's. Nearly all Campion's licences are, in his own words, " good and answerable," as they are applied.   His iambic dimeters[1] want only rhyme to be very charming, and his trochaics[2] have the right dropping cadence ; but all these are merely from his own point of view "filthy rags "— they might have been written by his adversary, Daniel, or by anybody else who could write them.   It is when he comes to his English Elegiacs[3] that he breaks down. It is impossible to imagine a more *arrhythmic* rhythm than this—the reader's voice trips and stumbles, and wallows almost as much as in fifteenth-century poetry, except that the *individual* feet are smooth enough.   Probably (though it is rather a habit of " new " prosodists) nobody ever "damned himself in confidence " more completely than Campion does here.   We really want nothing more. The system must be wrong when such a workman produces such work on it.

[1] These are catalectic, and really trochaic, for, in the apparently irresistible spirit of perversity which besets him, he gives no examples *here* of the pure iambic dimeter.   Sometimes he gives the others by themselves, as in—

> Raving war, begot
> In the thirsty sands, etc. ;

sometimes bouqueted in stanzas, as in '' Rose-cheeked Laura.''

[2] With him the trochaic must be acatalectic, whether shorter, as the curiously charming—

> Follow, follow,
> Though with mischief
> Armed like whirlwind
> How she flies still,

which he calls an Anacreontic ; or longer, as in—

> Cease, fond wretch, to love, so oft deluded.

[3] Constant to none, but ever false to me,
> Traitor still to love through thy false desires,
> Not hope of pity now, nor vain redress,
> Turns my grief to tears and renewed laments.

I only know one effect similar to this—when the tension of a type-writer goes wrong, and the carriage drags against the teeth of the rack.

His strictly lyrical measures, his ditties and odes, include " Rose-cheeked Laura "[1] herself, who would be charming with any dress in any company, but how much more with her natural graces of rhyme restored ; while as for other things quoted above, they are quite usual English verse, and require no new principles to justify them. They are passing graceful ; would they were rhymed !

"Oh how | comely it | is and | how re|viving " (is ^{His rhymed} not the appropriateness of this rather agreeable ?) to turn ^{poems.} from these poor girls with their backboards on, and their castanets taken from them, to the free, the most beautified bevy of the Airs ! When we read " My sweetest Lesbia "[2] (which is even sweeter than the original), we have not got to refer to the book, like knitting persons, to see if we have knitted this and dropped that as per rule. The verses flow as though they could and would flow for ever —reducible indeed to the broad and simple laws of now thoroughly established English prosody, but needing and brooking nothing else. And when at the other end we come to " Your fair looks urge my desire "[3] (such a different measure and such a cunning one, yet, once more, so purely and genuinely English, with such unimaginable

---

[1] Rose-cheeked Laura, come ;
   Sing thou smoothly with thy beauty's
   Silent music, either other
      Sweetly gracing.

[2] My sweetest Lesbia, let us live and love,
   And though the sager sort our deeds reprove,
   Let us not weigh them : Heaven's great lamps do dive
   Into their west, and straight again revive ;
   But soon as once set is our little light,
   Then must we sleep one everduring night.

[3] Your fair looks urge my desire ;
    Calm it, sweet, with love !
   Stay ; oh why will you retire ?
    Can you churlish prove ?
    If love may persuade,
   Love's pleasures, dear, deny not.
   Here is a grove secured with shade,
    O then be wise and fly not !

(I do not mark this for scansion, because there are *two* good and interesting ways possible.)

charms of rhyme), it is a question whether the end of this thing is better than the beginning or not, and there is really nothing to do but to turn to that beginning and go through the whole again.   Perhaps, indeed, we shall meet nothing more subtly sweet and sweetly subtle than the combination of monosyllabic feet with longer, of double rhymes with single, in the piece just mentioned.   But we shall find many to match it.

Contrast it, for instance, with a very early one, " I care not for these ladies." [1]   The general prosodic instruments of the effect are just the same—variation of iamb and trochee, of double and single rhyme, and no rhyme at all ; but they are differently disposed and applied, and the effect is proportionately varied.   Taking him altogether, it is perhaps in his use of the trochee that Campion is most distinguished and most happy.   He hardly ever overdoses us with it as Milton (I fear it must be admitted) sometimes seems to do.   Yet he does not in the least depend on it, or on the double rhyme, which is so closely connected therewith.   Such a piece, for instance, as " When to her lute Corinna sings," is rigidly iambic, decasyllabic, and non-redundant ; yet Ben himself has left us nothing more beautiful.   And the very next,[2] as it happens, is more complicated even than it looks—full of reverses, extensions, and contractions of rhythm, yet all most artfully managed.   Perhaps, indeed, some may object that it is a little *too* artful—too much of a " lesson," a diploma-piece to show cleverness, and not quite enough

[1] I care not for these ladies
   That must be wooed and prayed :
   Give me kind Amaryllis,
   The wanton country-maid.
   Nature art disdaineth,
   Her beauty is her own.
   Her when we court and kiss
   She cries " Forsooth let go ! "
   But when we come where comfort is,
   She never will say " No ! "

[2] Follow thy fair sun, unhappy shadow !
      Though thou be black as night,
      And she made all of light,
   Yet follow thy fair sun, unhappy shadow !

of a finally fused, smooth and round, accomplishment. It is, however, too beautiful to be praised merely by allowance, though it perhaps explains in a way why Campion fell in love with those "strange women" the versing creatures. But who that feels the charm of English prosody at all shall speak with measure of "Follow your saint"?[1] Here we have practically everything—audacious and unfailing conjunction of trochee and iamb, bold trisyllabic substitution with incomparable effect, extraordinary variation of pause, and telescoping of lines, all quite miraculous in effect. What such a thing as this can want with an "air" it is difficult to say; it is very easy to see that the air, whatever it is, would have no little difficulty in matching the ineffable beauty of the prosodic accompaniment.

The inchoate and extremely inferior version of "Your fair looks," in the First Book, is of the first interest as showing how Campion worked up his verse-melodies. But do we want to know what he can do with that famous prosodic weapon the refrain, and in an unusual place too? "Hark all you ladies that do sleep,"[2] with its repeated *second* line—

> The fairy queen Proserpina,

will show it. The rhythm-scheme on the whole is of the quaintest; one almost thinks that Campion must have

[1] Follow your saint, follow with accents sweet!
Haste you, sad notes, fall at her flying feet!
There, wrapped in cloud of sorrow, pity move,
And tell the ravisher of my soul, I perish for her love.
But if she scorns my never-ceasing pain,
Then burst with sighing in her sight, and ne'er return again!

[2] Hark all you ladies that do sleep!
The fairy queen Proserpina
Bids you awake and pity them that weep.
You may do in the dark
What the day doth forbid;
Fear not the dogs that bark,
Night will have all hid.

But if you let your lovers moan,
The fairy queen Proserpina

(and so throughout).

meant to combine his loves and make the last line an Adonic. But it can be scanned in a decent Anglican fashion, though he certainly meant mischief in " Come let us sound," [1] which has a strange Caedmonian suggestion.

The Divine and Moral Songs of the Second Book naturally have grave metres—some, such as that in the opening "Author of light, revive my dying sprite," approaching the majesty of the greater ode. There are some very beautiful trochaic triplets of trimeters; and some interesting quatrains with included rhyme, but not of *In Memoriam* length. Among "The Light Conceits" there is some very pretty common measure, though Campion does not seem to have cared much for this daisy of metres, and is indeed, for such a master, not extraordinarily happy in it. He is more at home in such a thing as "There is none, oh, none but you," with its three trochaics and one iambic. Campion seems always to have wanted *twists* of this kind to spur him up to his best efforts.[2]

I must regretfully omit many schemes I had noted for comment. But in "Break now, my heart"[3] we come, I think, to one of those suggestions of pure music which are not happy—a quintet composed of three lines in pure

---

[1] Come let us sound in melody the praises
    Of the King's King, th' omnipotent Creator,
    Author of numbers that hath all the loveliest Harmony framed.

[2] There is | none, oh, | none but | you,
    That from | me es|trange your | sight,
    Whom mine | eyes af|fect to | view
    Or chain|ed ears | hear with | delight.

This is not an accident; every stanza is the same.

[3] Break now, | my heart, | and die ! | O no, | she may | relent—
    Let my despair prevail ! O stay, hope is not spent.
    Should she now fix one smile on thee, where were despair ?
    The loss | is but ea|sy which smiles | can repair ;
    A stranger would please thee, if she were as fair.

It is an interesting instance of the difference between musical and prosodic scansion, that persons who go by the former would probably make these last two *amphibrachic* instead of anapæstic—

    The loss is | but easy | which smiles can | repair.

This, of course, is possible prosodically also, but less natural and elegant, as it seems to me, and certainly less naturally *paused*.

iambics and a couplet in pure anapæsts. This violent " trans-*basing* " is seldom good : nor is it here.

It is, however, about the only attempt which seems to me a failure, and we shall trace something like it down to Dryden. It would be easy to produce dozens of things which are not failures, but exquisite successes, from the Third and Fourth Books, adding yet others from the *Songs of Morning, The Masque,* etc. ; but enough must have been given to show in what a masterly fashion Campion plays over the whole gamut of sounds, the whole palette of verse-colours—every collocation and variation of the cube-integers that make up the mosaic of prosody. And what may be said of him eminently may be said of the rest of the song-writers more or less. Their results are wonderful in themselves. They are more wonderful still when we compare them with the results, not more than twenty or thirty years earlier, of men like Turberville and Gascoigne.

As in other cases, some notice has been taken of Sonnets earlier than Elizabeth's time and of some that belong to it ; but this is the place in which we are to consider the great sonnet-outburst of the ninth and still more the tenth decade of the sixteenth century—its intrinsic prosodic features, and the relation of those features to the history and development of English prosody generally. In doing this I do not think it necessary to say very much more than was said in the last volume on the general question of the Petrarchian and the English forms, or to pay as much attention as some have paid to the varying constructions of the English form itself. Whether this latter is arranged by three independent quatrains and a couplet, or by a greater or smaller interlacement of rhymes between the quatrains themselves, appears to me a very minor matter. Even Spenser's approximation of the form to his stanza does not seem to me of the first importance. The great distinctions, the real *differences*, of the two forms are, in the first place, the composition of the whole by octave

The Sonnet-outburst.

and sestet or by douzain and couplet; in the second,
and still more, the termination by tercet or by couplet.
And I have no doubt, that exquisite as have been some
—nay, many—compositions in English on the octave-
sestet-tercet plan, *the* model for our language is the
douzain-couplet. The national thirst for what Drayton
so quaintly calls "the Gemell" comes in here rightly and
legitimately; and the swift counter-twist in form of the
couplet-close suits our headlong and masterful tongue
better than the drawn-out dying of the sestet, and the
end that is no end of the tercet itself.[1]

Community of
its pheno-
mena—

It seems to me unnecessary to endeavour, thesis-writer
fashion, to discover particular characteristics in Sidney
and Watson and Barnes and Greville, in Spenser and
Drayton and Daniel, in Lodge and Fletcher and Constable
and Percy, in the *Zepheria* man and Griffin and Lynch
and Smith and Tofte. They batten their flocks upon the
self-same hill to too great an extent—whether they take
the grazing in French or Italian pastures really does not
much matter; and though, no doubt, individual poetic
capacity and quality will show here as elsewhere, the
sonnet is so tyrannous a thing in itself, and the Petrarch-
ising influence, which everywhere accompanies it, is so
concentrated and inevitable, that the general characteristics
far outrange the particular. It is chiefly where, as in
some cases, the songs and sonnets are inextricably mixed,
or mixed in such a fashion that extrication would do
more harm than good, that we need "condescend upon
particulars."

[1] The study of this subject has, for the general reader, been enormously
facilitated recently by Mr. Sidney Lee's collection, and re-issue with additions,
of the sonnet-series scattered through Mr. Arber's *Garner* (London, two vols.,
1904). As to the two main contentions of his Introduction on the originality
and the value of the poems themselves, there might be, as Captain Jamy says,
"some question between us tway," though I hope we should conduct it more
amiably than Fluellen and Macmorris. But the value of his materials
cannot be exaggerated. For myself, my being a subscriber—one of thirty,
most of whom, I fear, have joined the majority—to Dr. Grosart's exhumation
of Barnes in 1875 founded my study of the minor Elizabethans; and there
are few of the sonnet-writers who have not long been denizens of my shelves.
I only wish Mr Lee had been able to add the wretched Soothern to his flock.
"An imperfect copy in the B. M." is not the state in which I wish my
subjects to be.

In all the first group we see that strange faculty of prosodic girding and arming that had shown itself already in Wyatt and Surrey. Just as the armour which Una brought transformed the "tall clownish young man" into a very St. George, so do the sonnet-form, the sonnet-thought, the sonnet-phrase transform the rusticity which appears not merely in the Turberville group, but, as has been pointed out, in some work of Sidney's very own, into more or less thorough accomplishment. People hurl or pour contempt on the poor *Zepheria* man, who certainly did Pleiadise rather excessively, and even in some respects went back to Chastellain and Robertet rather than to Ronsard and Du Bellay for his "aureations." But I am not going to give up such things as—

> O then, Desire! father of Jouissance!
> The life of love, the death of dastard fear!
> The kindest nurse to true persèverance
> Mine heart inhearted with thy love's revere;

instance from *Zepheria*;

or

> How have l forfeited thy kind regard
> That thy disdain should thus engage thy brow?
> Which whilome was the scripture and the card
> Whereon thou madest thy game and sealed thy vow;

which last is not "aureate" at all, by the way.

No: this mobled queen is good enough though she be and of its goodness. one of the least fair of the bevy. Do not let anybody talk about imitation or translation; you cannot imitate or translate form and phrase from one language into another, or if you can "you *are* the magician." Do not let anybody say that the subject and the thought are hackneyed. I have nothing now to do with the subject and the thought. I say that the man who wrote in English such a line as—

> That thy disdain should thus engage thy brow,

even if he was translating verbally from French or Italian, was, *in his degree*, what I call a poet, and had at any rate in no small measure what prosody in the large sense can supply to poetry.

And so it is with almost all of them almost everywhere ; though, of course, in differing measure and degree.
Sidney and Spenser are the greatest ; and the Sonnet
enables them to write " With how sad steps, O Moon "
and " Like as the Culver."   Drayton is the next greatest ;
and one day it would seem that the Sonnet chose
to take him up from the second or third even to the
seventh heaven of poetry, and let him see and say
such things as no one else but Shakespeare ever saw
or said, in " Since there's no help."   The Sonnet spied
Daniel's one great gift of meditative melody and said,
" By the grace of *me* you shall write, ' Care-charmer
Sleep.' "

But these are not the most wonderful things that it
and its little (or not so little) sisters, canzon and madrigal
and the rest, effect by their combination of regulative outline with rich atmosphere of phrase and plethora of
passionate thought.   They take a man like Barnabe
Barnes, whom some people have called a fool.   They
catch him in his singing season, and carry him off with
them in their company.   He plays many fantastic tricks,
shocks the grave and precise generally, occasionally
behaves himself so as to deserve his enemy's nickname
of " Barnzy."   But all the same, he gives us things for
which, from other men of perhaps greater arts, under other
influences, we look in vain.   Or take the still smaller fry,
whom my friend Mr. Lee calls " Poetae Minimi " (if it
be so there must be an appalling range of *minus* quantities
in poetry below the minims themselves), the Percies and
Lynches, and Toftes and Smiths.   I wish I had had no
worse fortune in poetry during my critical life than to
read them.

Method of operation.   The fact seems to be that the comparatively strict and
regularly described outline of the sonnet-forms and other
similar things exactly suited the exuberant thought and
feeling and phrase and music of the Elizabethans.   It
was their Bottle of Salvation : it kept all these luxuriances
and ebulliences from merely running over and being spilt
upon the ground.   There was little danger — for there

is nothing in which bad rhythm shows so clearly and shockingly as in a sonnet—of relapse into doggerel ; there was none of the singsong of the poulter's measure and the continued fourteener ; none of the monotony of the couplet ; hardly any (even the smallest space—that of the quatorzain itself—being easy though not loose) of the cramp of the stanza.   The poet was continually "held up," but not too officiously or intrusively ; and he had or took a good deal of liberty with his go-cart.

The first of these liberties that is worth mentioning is perhaps the use of the Alexandrine, which Sidney[1] indulged in, and after him others.   Their reason is clear ; for though it is a mistake to say (as Dryden, and others who might have been better informed than Dryden, have said) that the Alexandrine was "the commonest form up to Shakespeare's time,"[2] it undoubtedly, as we have seen in many cases, and have still to see in more, imposed itself to some extent, and from curiously different sides.   It was at once one of the compromises with the longer doggerel, a part of the popular "poulter's measure," and an apparent though not real representative of the Greek and Latin trimeter.   But while it is never a success in English unless very sparingly used, and as an exception and contrast, not as a rule and staple, it is seldom less of a success than in the sonnet.   Although this form does not call for, or indeed tolerate, much positive enjambment, it demands that the individual line shall not absorb too

---

[1] In the very first of *Astrophel and Stella*—

Loving in truth, and fain in verse my love to show,

where it is most noteworthy that the famous final line—

"Fool !" said my Muse, " look in thy heart and write,"

discards the lumbering top-hamper of the other thirteen, as if the Muse had applied the uncomplimentary epithet to them also.   But, as has been hinted before, some good judges make a fight for Sidney's Alexandrine as possessing a quality of his own, nearer to the French than Drayton's.   I do not quite see this, and do not know that I should admire it if I did.

[2] It is fair to suppose that this mistake was, in not a few cases, merely the result of another—the inclusion of the fourteener under the term "Alexandrine."

much attention, and shall be intimately connected in thought-run with the rest. Now the Alexandrine in English distinctly refuses *liaison*, and, with its all but imperative middle break, excludes that variety of pause which is nowhere more necessary than in the sonnet.

in line-length: Nowhere, in fact, is that *stapleness* of the decasyllable —which is as certain in English as Dante found that of the corresponding hendecasyllable in Italian, and as is that of the Alexandrine in French—more noticeable than here. And as for excess, so for defect. As the Alexandrine is too heavy, so the octosyllable is too light for the sonnet.

in line-number. In departing, on the other hand, from the strict quatorzain, while the experimenters had, of course, plentiful Italian precedent, they cannot be said to have gone wrong in the same way as in varying the line-length. Watson, in the *Hecatompathia* (though not in the *Tears of Fancy*), took an eighteen-line form which is, in fact, merely a leash of sixains, just as the earliest English form of all had tended towards a pair of rhymes-royal. There is no objection to this form in itself, any more than to the quartets of quatrains and other things which are tried by others. Only, they are not sonnets. That there is a certain magic in numbers, all but the fools of freethought admit or rather know ; and this is part of the magic of Fourteen. Yet the douzains and dizains of *Laura* (mostly, it would seem, written in Italy, and dated from various Italian towns) are pretty forms enough : and *sua divina Bellezza* Mistress E. Caryl probably did not think so badly of them as some have done.

Other freaks. Echo sonnets, dialogue sonnets, sonnets like those of *Fidessa*, written on a continuous epanaphora (here " Most true that " ; but Spenser himself goes far in this direction, and Shakespeare some way), are, of course, of the nature of freaks. But the prosodic beauty of it is, that all these freaks obey more or less strict laws of modulation and correspondence, which oblige to the maintenance of rhythmical and metrical harmony. And the same is the case with the miscellaneous forms, not seldom intermixed, which do not even attempt to usurp the name of Sonnet, but frankly call themselves Madrigals, Canzons, or simply Songs.

The chief example of this, after Sidney himself (or even, though with much less mastery and still lesser critical power, in advance of him), is the already-mentioned Barnabe Barnes. His *Madrigals* (which, be it remembered, cannot be later than 1593, and may be some years earlier) actually anticipate Spenser, though, of course, they are practically far below him, in the use of carefully strophic compositions of varied line-length. Barnes's great prosodic fault here—a fault into which, no doubt, he was allured by the false analogy of his Italian models—is his prodigality of double rhymes, which, in such measures, and with no trisyllabic feet preceding them in the body of the line, always have an awkward effect in English. But when he gets free of this, as in 10 and 11, he sometimes achieves quite charming things prosodically, and he deserves the high praise of having quite evidently *sought* words that will suit or give his prosodic effect. He has an echo-sonnet of course, which is made additionally freakish by his deficient sense of essentially ludicrous rhyme ; but his Madrigals (16 and 17 are almost Odes) and Sestines represent his chief contribution to prosodic experiment, and, what is more, progress. His Elegies are chiefly different from the Madrigals in equality of line-length, and so less interesting to us ; but his Canzons and Odes are again very inspiriting things. The first Canzon, which is a very elaborate attempt in six sixteens and a twenty-line *coda*, despite all Barnes's usual faults of " wrenched accent," false rhyme, ill-succeeded rhythm, and fantastic or awkward phrase, is a failure of something worth attempting—and some of the Odes, even the Echo ones, are very pretty. As Dr. Johnson remarked of his cat Hodge, we have had better poets than Barnes, but Barnes shall not be abandoned to the tormentors—any more than Hodge was. For he saw, whether consciously or not does not matter, what these artificial forms could do for English poetry ; and he tried to do it with them.

Canzons, madrigals, etc. —Barnes.

And it was a thing right proper to be done ; and he did not wholly fail to do it.[1]

Let me be understood : I am not saying that Barnes and the author of *Zepheria* were great poets ; nor am I allowing—

　　　　When to the sessions of sweet silent thought,

or

　　　　Since there's no help, come, let us kiss and part,

The moral of sonnet and song. to throw their broad and star-embroidered mantles over the poetastry and the common form of many things similar in kind.　What I am endeavouring to show is the enormous assistance which these artificial measures, from the sonnet itself downwards and onwards, gave to the practice and establishment of sound and unerring, but varied and harmonious, English metre.　In this respect even the less good results were almost as beneficial as the

---

[1] His faults (which, however, are in general as easily corrigible as they are obvious), his prolixity, and his variety of forms all make Barnes difficult to illustrate ; but perhaps the following may not so ill bear out the remarks in the text :—

MADRIGAL 11

Thine eyes—mine heaven !—which harbour lovely rest,
　　And with their beams all creatures cheer,
　　　　Stole from *mine* eyes their clear ;
And made mine eyes dim mirrors of unrest.
And from her lily Forehead, smooth and plain,
　　My front his withered furrows took ;
　　And through her grace, his grace forsook.
　　　　From soft cheeks, rosy red,
My cheeks their leanness and this pallid stain.
　　The golden pen of Nature's book
　　(For her tongue that task undertook—
Which to the Graces' secretary led,
And sweetest Muses with sweet music fed)
　　Enforced *my* Muse with tragic tones to sing.
　　But from her heart's hard frozen spring
Mine heart his tenderness and heat possessed.

ODE 13

　　On the plains
　　Fairy trains
Were a-treading measure ;
　　Satyrs played,
　　Fairies stayed,
At the stop's set leisure, etc. etc.

better, not so very much less beneficial than the best.
The best, exercised *and* accomplished ; the worst, so long
as they were not prosodically bad, exercised, if they did
not accomplish. And this enormous variety of song and
sonnet—more perhaps than anything else, because in
nothing else was a certain *discipline* so constantly and
necessarily present—brought about something like a
habit of ear, which was the one thing lacking to English
prosody hitherto.

But this habit is no doubt pleasantest to study in poets
of major gift ; and we shall, according to promise, finish
the chapter with two such—Jonson and Donne—the two
great teachers of the seventeenth century with Spenser,
and in the ways in which Spenser had least to teach.
One of them, though his lyric work offers a distinct
contrast to his other, is yet very much of a piece throughout ; the other, at least at first, presents a hopeless
discrepancy. But Jonson, who thought, with all his
admiration for Donne, that Donne deserved hanging
prosodically, is not less worth our study than the object
of his admiring severity.

Except that it would have been fatal not merely to Jonson's
scheme and method, but to chronological exactitude, I lyrics.
could have wished to be able to deal with Jonson's Lyrics
before touching either his couplets or his blank verse. For
the account, in both these cases, had to be made with the
modern as well as with something of the older sense of
" censorship." Here there is nothing that calls for any
comment save that of intelligent admiration, delight, and
praise. Whether it was that Ben's classically steeped mind
found more help in ancient lyric (which is certainly not
so far removed from modern measures as couplet and
blank verse are from anything ancient) one cannot say.
The fact remains that some of the daintiest and most
delightful of English lyrics stand to his credit, and that
in lyric he hardly ever gives us anything harsh or crude.
The most famous piece of all is quite a little demonstration of the magical powers of poetic and especially prosodic
art. It is well known that the substance of this piece is

taken almost literally from Philostratus.   In the Greek,
or rather translated from it as closely as possible, it reads

thus : " Drink to me with thine eyes only.   And if thou
wilt bring it to thy lips, fill the cup with kisses ; and so
give it . . . I, when I see thee thirst and holding down the
cup, bring it not to my lips, but think that I am drinking
thee . . . I sent thee late a wreath of roses, not honouring
thee (yet I do this too), but bestowing a favour on the roses,
that they might not fade . . . If thou wilt do a favour to
thy friend, send back the remains of them, no longer merely
smelling of rose, but of thee."   What this becomes, though
everybody ought to know it, nobody shall be deprived of
the delight of reading again.[1]

Now it is to be observed, in the first place, that the four
passages which Ben has fused into this jewel of verse are
not consecutive. No two of them are even in the same letter;
and the third and fourth are separated pretty widely from
the first and second.   Philostratus never thought of
putting them together ; they were with him, though very
pretty, quite isolated conceits.   If the perfect whole which
they now present is the result of plagiarism, let us heartily
pray for the multiplication of plagiarists and out-Vida

[1] Drink to me only with thine eyes
    And I will pledge with mine ;
Or leave a kiss but in the cup
    And I'll not look for wine.
The thirst that from the soul doth rise '
    Doth ask a drink divine ;
But might I of Jove's nectar sup,
    I would not change for thine.
I sent thee late a rosy wreath,
    Not so much honouring thee,
As giving it a hope that there
    It would not withered be.
But thou thereon did'st only breathe,
    And sent'st it back to me—
Since when it grows and smells, I swear,
    Not of itself, but thee.

If it were not for " I swear " (the objection to which is not that of the other
Johnson in another case) the thing would be absolutely perfect.   Gifford (see
his notes *in loc.*) is justly severe on Cumberland for remarks on the song.
These, he thinks (and very likely they do), represent the ideas of Sir Fretful's
grandfather Bentley, whose taste was as bad as his scholarship was good.
But he is rather too severe on Cumberland's translation, which only goes a
little wrong.

Vida in the great commandment "Steal!" But there is, of course, very much more in the piece than an ingenious and lucky putting together ; there is much more even than the additions, which I have sometimes thought it might not be impertinent to italicise. The triumph, the charm, is in the way in which bits of mere prose are turned into a magical unity of living verse. The single trochee at the beginning, never repeated *as a foot*, but thrown back to by the trochaic words "only," "nectar," "rosy," etc. ; the subtle beauty of the four-times-repeated rhymes, each of resonant and suggestive quality, in the even places, and the longer-distanced ones in the odd ; above all, the ineffable and almost intolerable cadence and soar of the whole, are things that cannot be admired, studied, rejoiced in, too much. Here perhaps for the first time —for though the piece appeared in 1616, it may, as some others were certainly, have been written many years earlier—we have that marvellous seventeenth-century touch of the common measure which never appears before, which was utterly lost in the eighteenth century, and has not been very often recovered, save by accident or by very slavish imitation, even in the greatest poetry of the nineteenth. We shall fortunately come across it often, and may discuss it generally later.

The same astonishing felicity in diction and metre is observable in a large number of Ben's other lyrics ; and considering the range and power of his influence—personal and of reputation—on the younger men of letters of his time, it is only fair to give him some credit for the extraordinary accomplishment, in this respect, of English poetry between 1600 and 1650. To follow this out through the lyrical scraps in the Masques would be a pleasure in writing, as it has already been in reading ; but in that case three times three volumes would hardly suffice to carry out this undertaking equitably in regard to all our poets. But room must be made at least for some of the most beautiful of the separate poems. The The epitaphs. "honey-drop" of the trochee in his epitaphs is well known ;

and it is to me the chief reason for assigning to him rather than to Browne [1]—

Underneath this marble hearse.

This is hardly more beautiful than the undoubted " Margaret Ratcliffe " piece,[2] and not at all more so than

Underneath this stone doth lie,

which prevailed even upon Addison to shut his eyes to the " false " or at least " mixed " wit which pervades it, and to which some of us think it owes as much of its beauty as it does not owe to the form.   But the most exquisite specimen of all, that on Salathiel Pavy,[3] is structurally iambic, and only borrows the trochaic effect in the hypercatalectic endings of the alternate monometers. Here, as elsewhere, the extreme simplicity both of diction and measure, in combination with the most accomplished art, best explains the inexplicable.   It may be pointed out, too, that in every instance but two, " This little story " and " The stage's jewel," a rigid cæsura is kept up in the even lines, short as they are, and that the exceptions are more apparent than real.   This brings out the dying fall of the ending.   It cannot be accidental ; and I do not think that the effect here assigned to it is merely fanciful.

Others.   But Ben's was no single-string lyre.   There are the wonderful octosyllables of " Why I write not of Love,"

---

[1] Browne can be honeyed enough, but he cannot give his drops the *outline* that Ben can.

[2] Marble, weep, for thou dost cover
A dead beauty underneath thee,
Rich as nature could bequeath thee :
Grant then no rude hand remove her.

The *In Memoriam* inclusion, with trochaic form, may be noted.

[3] Weep with me, all you who read
This little story ;
And know for whom a tear you shed,
Death's self is sorry.

The fact that several of the odd lines have only seven syllables should not mislead.   It will be found in every case, I think, that the missing syllable rhythmically belongs to the first foot, not the last.

from which Landor, consciously or not, drew some of his best, and what is sometimes thought his most characteristic music ; the tens and eights of the Epistle to Sir Robert Wroth,[1] and the still finer tens and sixes [2] of the Epode ; dozens more instances of trochaic - iambic sevens ; the more elaborate stanza (reminding one of some of the measures popular in the last days of the Middle Ages) of the Ode to Sir William Sidney ; [3] " Her Triumph " (noted above) in the *Charis* pieces, and most of the opening *Underwoods.* In all these *the* prosodic note is the unerring fashion in which Ben adjusts his diction and cadence to the selected lengths of the lines. Many uneven metres, both old and new, are mere *faggots*—not even possessing the rough general symmetry which a well made and tied faggot has ; and this is peculiarly noticeable in the Pindarics, of which Cowley was to set the disastrous fashion. But Ben never treats his reader thus. The very excellent, doubtless, but either very hasty, or very shallow, or very ignorant people who talk with scorn about " questions of metre and quantity " would say, probably, that the only difference between a poem in tens and eights and a poem in tens and sixes must depend on the meaning. Let them, if they have eyes to see or ears to hear, look at the pair above cited together. The fact is that all natural conjunctions of metre (and the poet can only find out what are natural and what are not, by trying) have a special character, which, by the same process, he has to bring out. Some are complex and

---

[1] How blest art thou canst love the country, Wroth,
    Either by choice or fate, or both.

[2] Not to know vice at all, and keep true state,
    Is Virtue and not Fate.

[3] Now that the hearth is crowned with smiling fire,
    And some do drink, and some do dance,
        Some ring,
        Some sing,
    And all do strive to advance
        The gladness higher ;
        Wherefore should I
        Stand silent by,
        Who not the least
    Doth love the cause and authors of the feast ?

expansive, some simple and intense ; and it will be his
own fault if he does not suit them to their subjects—or
their subjects to them, as the case may be.

The *In
Memoriam*
metre.
Exactly what made Ben hit on one of the simpler and
intenser kind, which, after being tried once or twice in his
own time, was disused till, in ours, the whole sum of its
virtue was extracted, caught up, and uttered by Tennyson,
it would be difficult to say.   Inclusive instead of alternate
rhyme might seem to present itself obviously enough ; and
we have been able to indicate it—as arising probably by
accident in some stanza arrangements—much earlier.   But
the actual and continuous octosyllabic quatrain rhymed
abba has not, so far as I know, been traced earlier than
Ben Jonson's elegy " Though beauty be the mark of praise,"
which probably suggested Lord Herbert's later practice.
The piece as a whole is not one of Jonson's happiest ; and
in particular he has not wrought the diction up to the
perfection of his best lyrics.   There are obscurities of
meaning ; slight (and not quite so slight) harshnesses of
sound ; inversions which do not improve the flow, and
syllables not placed in their right situation, after the
fashion which makes " Drink to me only " and the
Salathiel Pavy piece so delectable.   But that habit by
which the prosodic virtue lies, like a Platonic statue, ready
concealed in the marble, and only wants the proper hand
to bring it out, is revealed clearly enough.   Might not the
last two lines at least of the following, if not the whole
stanza, be Tennyson's own ?—

> Who, as an offering at your shrine,
> Have sung this hymn and here entreat
> *One spark of your diviner heat*
> *To light upon a love of mine.*

There is something feminine, though nothing
effeminate, about the stanza which perhaps did not appeal
to Ben.   But his discovery of it, and his practice of
others in the two examples just noted, would have proved
him a great master of metre if he had left no other claims.
And, as we have shown, he has left many.

In the greatest of all the great Deans of St Paul's—an office which has had perhaps, on the whole, during the last three centuries, a more distinguished series of incumbents than any in Christendom—we approach one of the few well-known prosodic problems. Ben Jonson, as he had a knack of doing, proposed that problem in the Drummond conversation by the two exceedingly Jonsonian statements, that "Donne was the first poet of the world for some things," and that "Donne, *for not keeping of accent*, deserved hanging." The first, with due emphasis on its proviso, is pretty near the truth ; as for the second, it makes a very interesting pendant to that other, that Spenser "in affecting the ancients writ no language." The drawback of both these, as contrasted with the first, is that in them, as not in it, a very large proviso is *not* expressed—a proviso so large that to put it accurately and adequately in words would take several sentences. As for Spenser, we have dealt with him. As for Donne, we must deal with him now.

He has left us, speaking roughly, three classes of poetry—satires ; miscellaneous poems chiefly in couplet ; and lyrics. Now the puzzle of his prosody consists, not merely in the fact that the satires do not, as Ben calls it, and as some would still call it, "keep accent," though that is a most inadequate description of their eccentricities. It lies in the fact that his peculiarity is very much less noticeable in the miscellaneous poems, and hardly noticeable at all in the lyrics.

That Donne takes the benefit of the general law, elsewhere often stated, in regard to satire hardly needs emphasising. But that general law, while it may cover the eccentricities of Lodge or Marston, Hall or Guilpin, will hardly find a lappet of its amplest gown that can protect such a passage as this (Sat. VII.)—

> Sleep, next society and true friendship
> Man's best contentment, doth securely slip,
> His passions, and the world's troubles ; rock me,
> O Sleep ! wearied from my dear friend's company,
> In a cradle free from dreams or thoughts, those

Where poor men lie, for Kings asleep do fear.
Here Sleep's house by famous Ariosto,
By silver-tongued Ovid, and many more—
Perhaps by golden-mouthed Spenser, too, pardie, etc.[1]

The anarchy of the *Satires.*

Now it will be observed by any one who has been good enough to fall in line with the present writer, and to " read scanningly," that " not keeping of accent " is a very poor and partial key or clue to this labyrinth of cacophonies. It will, though *very* poorly, do something for " friendship " ; but it will do hardly anything for " troubles," which a man can scarcely pronounce " trŭbūlls " if he would. It is still more ridiculous to think that Donne intended any one to accent " cradle " " crădūll " and " Ariosto " " ă-wrȳ-ŏ-stōw." There is something much more than keeping, or not keeping, of accent here. Note, too, that line five begins as if " in a cra-" were to be scanned together trisyllabically, and makes a perfectly harmonious run, till you find that if you do so you have a syllable short. And note further that 3, 7, 9, not to say the same of others, are absolutely *unrhythmical,* not merely unmetrical. You cannot, except by the most enormous make-believe, get any prosodic music out of them. And yet the man who wrote them certainly wrote such a line as—

A brácelet of bright hair about the bone,

such a couplet as—

I must confess it could not choose but be
Profáne to think thee anything but thee,

with hundreds of other lines and couplets equally harmonious.

The mere Persian licence of satiric roughness will not, I say, cover this enormous difference. Sometimes I have been tempted to think that Donne and others thought themselves entitled to *scazontics*—that is to say, iambic lines with spondaic or trochaic endings, such as the ancient satirists who used the metre often preferred. But I am

[1] *Works of Donne,* ed. Chambers, 22 vols., London, 1896, ii. 205.

by no means sure that a bolder explanation, and one
thoroughly in harmony with the general results of the
inquiry on which this book is based, may not be
applicable—to wit, that Donne, recognising the classic
practice of equivalence and substitution, used it in experiment more freely than wisely, as upon the *corpus*,
admittedly *vile*, of satire.[1]

The poems which come between satire and lyric in
him, whether in couplet or stanza, are still rough ; though
less so.   The *Elegies*, which are nearest both in matter
and time to the *Satires*, and the *Verse Letters*, some of
which are in the same neighbourhood, are the roughest ;
the *Divine Poems*, which are the latest, are the smoothest.
The wonderful *Anatomy of the World*, which appears
to represent the turning-point, though it has a certain
ruggedness, resembling that of Chapman somewhat, is
not exactly rough.   If, however, we need any single thing
to show that Donne was a great experimenter in prosody,
and that he never took the trouble to criticise, polish, or
cancel his experiment,[2] we have it in that rather unlovely
though not unpowerful poem the *Progress of the Soul*.
The immense success of Spenser's stanza had naturally
set his contemporaries and successors on seeing what they
could do.   The result, as in the Fletchers' case, was
generally a conjugation of the untranslatable French verb
estropier—untranslatable unless we use a hybrid paraphrase and say "apply the strappado."   But I do not
know that an uglier deformation was ever reached than in
this ten-line stanza[3] of Donne's, which ruins itself from

The "middle" poems.

---

[1] After the first draft of the text was written I received from America an
original and very careful monograph on *The Rhetoric of John Donne's
Verse* by W. F. Melton (Baltimore, J. H. Furst, 1906).   It should be
studied by all interested in the matter ; though I am not sure that Mr.
Melton's indication of "arsis-thesis variation"—*i.e.* alternate length and
shortness of the same syllable—is quite such a *passe-partout* as he thinks.

[2] This fact, I think, is fatal to the theory that he was deliberately
engineering a "new prosody."

[3] The beauty of the actual opening couplet in the following example will
only emphasise its misplacement :—

> Prince of the orchard, fair as dawning morn,
> Fenced with the law and ripe as soon as born,
> That apple grew, which this soul did enlive,

the outset by starting with a couplet, the very worst
preparation of the ear for the distinctive rhyming which
is to follow. As no one who glances at the edition I
have used here for citation will doubt my enthusiasm for
Donne as a poet, I do not fear to speak plainly on this
part of his prosody. Indeed, it is well that he did not
lick his early poems into prosodic shape ; for then we
should have lacked the most instructive prosodic figure
between Spenser and Milton——a " first poet of the world
in some things," both poetically and otherwise, who,
exploring further in a half-explored country, stumbled in
many waste places. There is, however, no doubt that
Donne's eccentricities had not a little to do with the
severe syllabic and accentual reaction, which Milton
fortunately did not share, and against which he remained
a standing and impregnable protest. No one will suspect
me of prosodic " Popery " ; but even the wooden shoes of
the strict couplet were as seven-leagued boots to get us
away from the possibility of such a line as——

> His passions and the world's troubles rock me ;

or, if anybody takes refuge there in " woruld," from——

> Here Sleep's house by famoùs Ariòs-tòw.

" What ? what ? *Barclay* come again ? "

The utter and antinomian transformation of the
prosody between Donne's other poems (specially his
satires) and his lyrics can hardly be exaggerated. One
experiences the shock of it afresh every time one reads
this, more than Browning of the seventeenth century ;
and I confess that if I were to edit Donne, I should,
without much fear of the charge of topsyturviness, put
The lyrics. his lyrics last of the poems that are in any way certain,

---

Till the then-climbing serpent, that now creeps
For that offence, for which all mankind weeps,
Took it, and to her whom the first man did wive——
Whom and her race only forbiddings drive——
He gave it, she to her husband ; both did eat ;
So perishèd the eaters and the meat,
And we——for treason taints the blood——thence die and sweat.

in order that this transformation might work the right way. Even here there are, of course, a few lapses. In the absence of the slightest revision on the author's part —in the absence even of any evidence that he so much as saw the copy from which our prints and MSS. were taken—it was impossible that this should not happen. But these lapses are very slight, and in hardly a single case are they of the essence of the versification, as those in the *Satires* and elsewhere are. Here also, Donne is an experimenter ; and there may not be universal agreement about the felicity of his experiments. For instance, beautiful as is the song—

Sweetest love, I do not go,[1]

even among its author's, I am not sure that some may not think the bold reversal of the usual order—giving trochaic cadence first, and iambic second—a thing more bold than wise. I do not think so myself; but I should not hold any one reasonless who did. Perhaps the most inexhaustible delight is to be found in those pieces which are actually decasyllabic, such as " The Good-morrow." [2] The " nubbly " ruggedness of the satire-lines here melts honey-like into even sweetness. Nowhere shall we find a happier combination than that in " Go and catch a falling star,[3] from the rocking trochees of the sestet to

[1] Sweetest love, I do not go
    For weariness of thee,
Nor in hope the world can show
    A fitter love for me ;
    But since that I
At the last must part, 'tis best
Thus to use myself in jest
    By feigned deaths to die.

[2] I wonder, by my troth, what thou and I
Did, till we loved ? were we not weaned till then ?
But suck'd on country pleasures, childishly ?
Or snor[t]ed we in the Seven Sleepers' den ?
'Twas so ; but this all pleasure's fancies be :
If ever any beauty I did see
Which I deserved, and got, 'twas but a dream of thee !

[3] Go and catch a falling star,
    Get with child a mandrake root ;
Tell me where all past years are,
    Or who cleft the devil's foot.

the sudden spondees of the " bob " and the iambic close. It is with the trochee that Donne does most of his feats here, and unless he wrote—-

> Thou sent'st me late a heart was crowned,[1]

(of which I think far higher than some seem to do) I do not know that he has any of the greatest triumph of iambic " C.M."   But his eights, as in " O ! do not die, for I shall hate," [2] are wonderful past all whooping.   He has a marvellously sustained six-line stanza (6, 10, 8, 8, 10, 6 *ababcc*), where, though the rhyme order is the same as in the most usual sixain, the difference of line-lengths creates an entirely new music ; lighter things like " The Message," much twisted and " bobbed," and that astounding " Ecstasy," also in eights or long measure, where, perhaps, the boldest line with which poet ever dared fools—-

> And we said nothing all the day,

occurs, and justifies itself.

But one returns, somehow, to the pieces where most of the lines are decasyllabic, such as " The Dream " and

---

> Teach me to hear mermaids singing,
> Or to keep off envy's stinging,
>   And find
>   What wind
> Serves to advance an honest mind.

[1] There are many MS. versions of this, which is sometimes ascribed to Sir Robert Ayton :—

> Thou sent'st me late a heart was crowned.
>   I took it to be thine ;
> But when I saw it had a wound,
>   I knew that heart was mine.
>
> A bounty of a strange conceit !
>   To send mine own to me,
> And send it in a worse estate
>   Than when it came to thee.

Ben or Donne for many ducats !

[2] O ! do not die, for I shall hate
       All women so, when thou art gone,
   That thee I shall not celebrate
       When I remember thou wast one.

" Love's Deity," so odd is the effect of contrast with the others, as if the poet were doing it on purpose, and saying to Ben, "Oh! you think I deserve hanging, do you? Keep accent in this way, if even *you* can!" As for the famous " Funeral," it even ventures the fourteener, and vindicates its audacity in a wreath of verse as " subtle " as that which it celebrates. While if he wrote " Absence," as I feel pretty certain that he did, he has made an almost unique special mould for his thought.[1] We often say to ourselves how admirably the sense and sound suit each other in this or that poem. But here I could almost say that no other sound could possibly suit *this* sense —that we should not " enjoy but miss " it, if a foot were changed.

But I must recall the reader and myself from enjoyment—it was very hard to leave off tapping this nectar— to the sober prosodic fact that the author of most of these things certainly, of all possibly, was also the author of the jolting monstrosities above cited. Many theories— my own of a rather irresponsible experiment, Mr. Melton's of " arsis - thesis variations," a dozen others—may be brought in to account for the contrast. One thing, however, is not theory but fact, that the contrast is *there*. In other words, it was possible for the same man to produce perfect harmony in one set of· metres, almost perfect cacophony in others. In yet other words, Spenser's work was not quite done. And before Donne died, the

---

[1] By Absence this good means I gain
That I can catch her,
Where none can watch her,
In some close corner of my brain.
There I embrace and kiss her,
And so I both enjoy and miss her.

The reading of this last line is that of the *Poetical Rhapsody*, and I think the most Donnish.

And so enjoy her and none miss her,

or " while none miss her," as some MSS. have it, is possible.

And so enjoy her and so miss her,

another MS. form, is feebler.

fact that it was not quite done was shown, not merely in the older form of the couplet, but in the newer of blank verse.   So somebody had to do something more ; and at the beginning of the next Book we shall see how Milton came and did it.

CHAPTER V

PROSODISTS

A new subject of study—The attraction of classical metres—Note on Hawes's *Example of Virtue*—The "craze" for them in English—Ascham—The contempt of rhyme—Freaks of the craze—Drant—Harvey and Spenser—Stanyhurst—"Quantity" —Sidney's silence — Webbe — Nash — Puttenham — Campion's *Observations*—Daniel's *Defence*—*The Mirror for Magistrates* once more—Lesson of its prosodic freaks—Of the prose discussions—Of its later editions—Gascoigne's *Notes of Instruction* —Note on King James's *Rewlis and Cautelis*—Chapman, Jonson, Drayton.

WE have now for the first time, according to the scheme A new subject
of this Book as originally laid down, to turn, at least of study.
partially, from prosody as a matter of practice to prosody
as a matter of theory.[1]   A certain amount of the contents
of this chapter belongs, as was freely confessed, to the last
period of the last volume, and was slightly handled there
by anticipation ; but had it been dealt with then in detail
it must have been severed from its natural complement,
and left in a very unsatisfactory condition.   Moreover, it
would not have been possible to mark, as it was desired
to mark, the division between the unconscious and the
conscious dispensations of English prosody.   Henceforward, though everything that every poet does (*vide*
Preface) will still not be consciously done in obedience to

---

[1] I may as well at once refer, though I shall have to do so again and again, more specially than in this chapter, to the excellent contributions of Mr. T. S. Omond to the history, bibliography, and discussion of this part of the subject. The chief places of his work are *A Study of Metre* (London, 1903), and *English Metrists*, two parts supplementary to each other (Tunbridge Wells, 1903, and London, 1907).

rule, or in carrying out of principle, prosodic inquiry will always, as a matter of fact and time, if not always in the same persons, accompany prosodic accomplishment; and the last chapters of each of our Books will, it is hoped, represent this concomitance not inappropriately. But the first of them must begin with a fuller account (it was glanced at before[1]) of the curious measles or distemper which, dangerously but not by any means without beneficial results, affected English poetry to some extent, and English prosodic study to a much greater, for more than half a century.

The attraction of classical metres.

That the phenomenon itself[2] was a natural and necessary consequence of the general drift of the Renaissance, needs no setting forth here; that the disease (if we may so call it) attacked all Europe, is a simple historic fact. But the morbid and dangerous aspect of it was particularly threatening in England; and the fact connects itself directly with the general history which we have been telling. In no literary country of Europe (for in Germany it was a case of arrested development, not of sudden disorganisation and apparent decay) had the machinery of poetry gone so wrong as in England. The Italians were still in their greatest poetical age, and the Spaniards were approaching it. In France there had been something of a falling off in poetic spirit, though poets like Charles d'Orléans and Villon had still borne the torch high; and formal perfection had been rather over-elaborated and mis-elaborated than lost. But in England, as we have seen, practical prosody had to a great extent "gone paralytic"; and though it was recovering, the fruits of recovery were still not very great, and were not to be so for another generation.

The persons to whom the new critical nisus, so long dormant in Europe, was now extending from Italy, the

---

[1] Book iv. chapter ii. "The Turn of the Tide: Classical Influence."

[2] It should not be necessary to point out at any great length that we are dealing here only with the strictly *prosodic* influence of the classics. Their influence in other ways was, of course, enormous; though it may have been exaggerated or mistaken in some details, it cannot be denied or belittled as a whole. But it is not for us.

place of its resurrection, had before them not merely this paralysis of the prosodic vernacular in all its deformity, but also the salvage of ancient literature in all its beauty. They found Greek and Latin poetry pervaded with an ordered vigour of prosodic arrangement, such as has never been surpassed. In these new-old poets they found nothing (practically nothing) of that rhyme which was omnipresent in mediæval poetry; and they found a mathematical system of quantitative arrangement which apparently left nothing to desire, either in system beforehand or in result afterwards.

Small blame to them, then, if, especially at a time when, as we have seen, the very pronunciation and accentuation of English were unsettled and uncertain, they fell into the usual fallacy of confounding coexistence with causation, and deciding that the orderly harmony of writers like Virgil was *due to* the presence of certain metres and the absence of rhyme, that the discord of writers like Hawes [1]

[1] I am ashamed to say that I was not aware, when I wrote the note on p. Note on 235 of vol. i., that Mr. Arber had at last actually printed his transcript of Hawes's *The Example of Virtue* at the end of his *Dunbar Anthology* (Oxford, 1901), *Example of* a place where one may be excused for not looking for it, though it actually *Virtue.* includes one-third of the volume. Gratitude to him for making accessible what had been so long hidden in the Pepysian and Britwell libraries, and for filling in a gap of our knowledge, need not be in the least affected by the fact that the poem is one of the very dullest of fifteenth-century allegories, presenting nothing but a series of commonplaces, arranged with extraordinary clumsiness, and inferior to the *Pastime of Pleasure* in every conceivable respect —except that it is much shorter. This inferiority is nowhere more conspicuous than in our special province. The *Pastime* often plays havoc with prosody; the *Example* shows scarcely anything but an utter inability to manage metre at all. A very large proportion of its more than three hundred rhyme-royal stanzas conclude with frankly octosyllabic couplets.

> And tarry I did there by long space,
> Till that I saw before my face,

in stanza 4 of the body of the text, is followed by

> All wildness, I will be your guide
> That ye to frailty shall not slide,

in the next, and by

> For in what place I am exiled
> They be with sin full oft defiled,

in the seventh. And so constantly. Occasionally the poet seems to be in a state of complete uncertainty which of his master Lydgate's two favourite measures, rhyme-royal and octosyllabic couplet, he is writing, as here (stanza 81)—

and Skelton was *due to* the absence of metrical quantity and the presence of rhyme. Others before them, and abroad, had done or were doing the same thing with less excuse ; and in so doing were providing more excuse still for the English innovators. That there was no intentional treason to their native tongue is, in the case of men like Ascham, certain and demonstrable ; in the case of almost all, probable if not proved. There seems to have been in England little or nothing of the strange delusion which in Italy made even men so learned and sensible as Lilius Giraldus despise the vulgar tongue ; and though there *was* something of that distrust of it which survived as late as Bacon—though there were Little-faiths who, as he did, thought that these weak and infantine dialects had no chance with the secular strength of Latin—this very distrust took for the most part the generous form of wishing to strengthen the weakling by as much borrowing from antiquity as might be possible. The immediate and direct results of the movement were, in all but infinitesimal proportion, almost unconscionably absurd, and it might have done ruinous harm. But, as a matter of fact, it did next to none ; and in certain ways it did some good.

The "craze" for them in English—Ascham. The history of the craze has received a good deal of attention in recent times and is fairly well known,[1] though

And if a man be never so wise,
   Withouten me he getteth none utterance.
Wherefore his wisdom may not suffice
All only, without mine allegiance ;
For I by right must needs enhance
   A low-born man to a high degree,
   If that he will be ruled by me.

Speaking generally, the stanzas are merely bundles of seven-rhymed verses, the lengths of which are not so much varied as taken at random, without the slightest consideration what they are. In fact, this long-expected poem, the latest that has come under my notice, is the extreme example of the Period of Staggers. It is childish to put the blame on Wynkyn de Worde and his compositors. They may have shared the sin ; they may very probably have been unconscious of it ; they cannot have committed it wholly.

[1] A complete bibliography of the history and criticism of Elizabethan literature would be needed to do justice to the subject. Mr. Gregory Smith's *Elizabethan Critical Essays* (Oxford, 2 vols., 1904) is the best single source for texts. For a study of the special matter (including some writers and passages whom and which I have not thought it necessary to notice) see the first part of Mr. Omond's *English Metrists*, as above.

not in its earliest documents.   Curiously enough it seems
to have arisen at Cambridge, and to have chiefly prevailed among Cambridge men ; while Daniel, who finally
smashed it in one of the most admirable small critical
tractates in all literature, was an Oxonian.   But that
justification which we have already allowed to it extends
to its nurses and fosterers, after a sort at least.   It
appears to have been an offshoot of the literary and
linguistic activity, especially in relation to Greek, which
Erasmus, learning it from Oxford, taught at Cambridge
and developed there.   It has even been thought by sober
and sensible judges, that Ascham, from whom we have
the earliest accounts and advocacies of it, may have had
rather more to do with its actual inception and codifica-
tion than either the earlier Bishop Thomas Watson, to
whom he attributes the original production of an appal-
lingly bad specimen in the kind,[1] or the later Archdeacon
Drant, whom Spenser has established for us as the lawgiver of this very scrubby Parnassus.   But Watson's
verse is interesting, and I do not myself quite sympathise
with the desire which some have shown to dethrone or
disbench or gibbet (for all these images present themselves in quite orderly turn) Drant.

It is curious, if not unusual, that the earliest manifesto *The contempt*
on the subject shows at once the weak sides of the new *of rhyme.*
proposal.   Ascham in *The Schoolmaster* is very positive
about the matter, and abuses rhyme[2] with all the rather
hollow swagger of Renaissance scholarship, which sits
clumsily enough on a good-natured Englishman.   But
" rude beggarly rhyming," " barbarous and rude rhyming,"

---

[1] It may be repeated, though given in vol. i.—

All travellers do gladly report great praise of Ulysses,
For that he knew many men's manners and saw many cities.

And truly these first English hexameters were justified of most of their
children—the exceptions, as we shall see when we come to them, being no
exceptions at all.   Indeed, even Ascham, though in the place where he
quotes them he celebrates their "right quantity of syllables and true order
of versifying " (*Schoolmaster*, ed. Arber, p. 73), elsewhere (pp. 145, 146) lets
slip the words "hobble" and "stumble" on the subject.   *V. inf.*

[2] *Ed. et loc. cit.*

"foul wrong way," etc., prove just nothing at all ; and his positive arguments (not to mention certain damaging admissions) themselves prove the "wrong way." He slips on his own ground by stigmatising the metre of Terence and Plautus as "very mean and not to be followed." He asserts that rhyming was first brought into Italy by Goths and Huns—of which, as to the Goths there is evidence the other way, and as to the Huns no evidence at all. His appeal to Quintilian is so absolutely absurd that we almost suspect Queen Elizabeth's good tutor of having a simpleton side to him. What good rhyming poetry—what rhyme at all except awkward jingles like Cicero's—had Quintilian before him ?

But the admissions are, after all, the main thing. " Indeed, our English tongue, having in use chiefly words of one syllable which are commonly long, doth not well receive the nature of *Carmen Heroicum*, because *dactylus*, the aptest foot for that verse, containing one long and two short, is seldom therefore found in English, and doth rather stumble than stand *in monosyllabis*." Again, "*Carmen Exametrum* doth rather trot and hobble than run smoothly in our English tongue." After which he finds fault, not merely with Surrey's blank verse in English, but with that of Gonsalvo Perez in Spanish, and with the Italians generally for not versifying "true." This, of course, simply means, for versifying without quantity—a charge met and utterly refuted by the simple observation that the quantity of one language is not necessarily—is not even probably —the quantity of another.

Freaks of the craze.   This atmosphere of confusion and muddlement en- wraps almost all those who commit whoredom with this enchantress, except Stanyhurst partially, and Campion in a certain sense wholly. The present day has nothing to reproach them with in respect of confusing accent and quantity, and mistaking the relation between the two even when they are not confused : but they do both with a singular obtuseness. Almost from the first, as we see from the correspondence of Spenser and Harvey on the subject, there were two schools of "new versifiers"—

the less thorough-going, and the more.　The former, who have always supplied the majority of English hexametrists, and who have written the only tolerable English hexameters, accepted the ordinary pronunciation of English as far as it was settled in their day, and attempted to get hexametrical or elegiac rhythm out of this.　The others threw the whole vocalisation of the English tongue overboard, and endeavoured to introduce classical (or rather Latin) rules of quantification for individual syllables, so that, for instance, the second syllable of "carpenter" was made "long by position."　Nearly all again broke down over the great crux of the "common" syllable, which, rare in Latin, more common in Greek, is the rule rather than the exception in English.　And few had the method of the half-madman Stanyhurst, who methodically, however madly, writes "thee" for the article when he wants to make it long, and keeps the ordinary spelling when he wants it short.

The results of all this meddling and muddling in verse—to give it that title by the courtesy of Irony—are admitted by almost everybody to be among the most absurd things in literature.　The admission of Ascham, a Balaam reversed, still stands against them—they "hobble and stumble" generally ; at the best they "trot" and bump.　The great original of Watson, which we have quoted from Ascham, is a miserable thing enough ; but it is tolerable beside the grotesque (and perhaps in part intentionally burlesque) doggerel of Harvey, and the frantic gibberish of Stanyhurst.[1]　Even in iambics—as nearly indigenous as any English foot—and even in the hands of such a poet as Spenser, the ungainly shamble of this truly "unhappy verse" curiously "witnesses" its writer's "unhappy state."　And the proceeding never got out of its suggestion of marrow-bones and cleavers and salt-box as accompanying instruments, till Campion practically gave the whole case away by abandoning classical *metres* altogether, and advocating unrhymed lyric of a more or less pure English pattern.　We must, however, as in

---

[1] See the examples quoted in vol. i. p. 319.

duty bound, go through the follies of its advocates and practitioners a little more definitely.

Ascham's own remarks on what we shall not imitate him by calling his "foul wrong way" were, as we have seen, confined to generalities, and the examples which he gives, probably or certainly of his own making, in *Toxophilus*[1] are of no special interest, though they illustrate his own frank admission of the hobbling of the spavined jade, with which he wished to corrupt our English stud. But the idea was eagerly caught up from him and from Watson in their own University and **Drant.** College; and a member of the latter, Thomas Drant, appears to have drafted a complete set of Rules on the subject. I cannot quite agree with my friend Professor Gregory Smith in doubting whether these were ever committed to writing—that construction not seeming to me compatible with the remarks of Spenser and Harvey, to which we shall come next. But it is certain that, as yet, no trace of them in formal state has been discovered. Drant died in 1578, a year or two before this correspondence, and as there is no allusion to him in *The Schoolmaster*, which was published after Ascham's death in 1568, we have a clear decade in which Drant may have devoted himself to the subject. But we learn from Spenser that, before the winter of 1579-1580, Sidney and Dyer, and the coterie they called their Areopagus, had taken up the matter solemnly, proclaimed (happily without anybody obeying them) the surceasing of rhyme, prescribed laws and rules of quantities and the like. *Propter*, or at least *post quod*, it appears that Spenser himself "is more in love with versifying" (which word these sectaries always use in their shibboleth sense) than with "rhyming."

Harvey and Spenser. So also, it seems, was Harvey; but not according to the Drantian or Areopagite way. Spenser complains gently that his friend and Mentor once or twice "makes breach"

---

[1] Such as

Eight good shafts have I shot sith I came, each one with a fork-head.

Tox., ed. Arber, p. 135.

in Master Drant's rules, sending him that " unhappy verse "
of his own. Harvey, of course, was not going to stand
this ; and though very complimentary in general to
Spenser, hits some blots in the trimeters, and then proceeds
to scold at the Drantian code, which he himself " neither
saw nor heard before," and therefore " will neither praise
nor dispraise." Still he speaks handsomely of Drant.
All this is vague enough : though that " the rules " actually
existed is surely clear from a passage in Spenser's rejoinder,
where he asks for Harvey's own rules. Everybody,
however, appears (not without some reason) to have been
shy of *litera scripta* in the matter ; for Harvey in reply
thinks he had better " consult with his pillow " before he
gives them. But he then says some sensible things—as
that before you can get artificial prosody into good order,
you must agree upon one and the same orthography,
which must itself be conformable to " natural " prosody,
that is, of course, pronunciation. " *Interim* " he " dare give
no precepts." But he would gladly learn why in one
of Spenser's examples, " the," " ye," " he " being short,
" me " should be long, etc. And he declines the authority
of "five hundred Master Drants " to make *carpenter* " longer
than God and his English people have made him," whence
it would appear that one of the rules was strict " quantity
by position." On which, and on things connected with it,
he speaks very good sense indeed.

The most curious of all utterances on this matter is Stanyhurst.
Stanyhurst's.[1] The modern reader who knows anything
about him is apt, not quite justifiably, to regard this
respectable Irish gentleman and scholar as merely a
lunatic. And however thoroughly one may have acquainted
oneself with the circumstances of the case, it is still very
difficult to realise how any one, *not* a lunatic, can have
ever put to paper first, and then committed to print, stuff
which looks like the utterances of a schoolboy, to whom
some benevolent but injudicious uncle had given too

[1] In the Dedications to Lord Dunsany (and the Learned Reader) of his
translation of the *Æneid* (1582), reprinted by Mr. Arber in No. 10 of the
English Scholar's Library (London, 1880). To be found, like other things
here quoted, in Mr. Gregory Smith's book.

much champagne, and who should have been simultaneously furnished with a glossary of the most out-of-the-way words in the English language, and permission to spell them as he (and the champagne) pleased.[1]   But as regards his prosody Stanyhurst was perfectly sober. He knew that he would be accused by "the meaner clerks"[2] of "making what word he chose short or long." He insists that every foot, every word, every syllable, yea, every letter is to be observed.   And then he comes to details.   He objects to the "curious Priscianists" who are stiffly tied to ordinances of the Latins, remarking, justly enough, that the Latins had tied their own hands quite sufficiently with Greek chains, so that we need not bind double fetters still more tightly on ourselves. *Breviter* in Latin is short ; *briefly* in English is long.   It is *orātor* in Latin, *orător* in English ; and so forth.   So far so good ; but from this point he seems to deviate into one of the usual muddles between accent and quantity as if they were identical, instead of standing to each other some-times in the relation of cause and effect, sometimes not, but never actually losing their individuality.

He seems to have understood—though he rather refers to it as granted than definitely states it—the rule that in English the accent constantly tends backwards, and (as far as possible) to the first syllable of the word. But he applies this much too rigidly ; and makes his mistake worse by his confusion of accent and quantity as aforesaid.   "Honour," he says, "in English is short as with the Latins, yet ' dishonour' must be long by the former maxim ; [What former maxim?   We find none except an implication in the passage about " Orator," etc.] which is contrary to another ground of the Latins whereby they prescribe that the primitive and derivative, the simple and compound, be of one quantity. . . ." " Mother " may be long (he spells it " moother "), yet " grandmother " must be short ; " buckler " long, yet " swashbuckler " is

---

[1] If this seem extravagant, the person to whom it so seems is requested to open any page of the actual translation ; or even to refer to the specimen in the last volume.

[2] I beg his pardon, " thee meaner clarcks."

short. "And albeit that word be long by position, yet doubtless the natural dialect of English will not allow of that rule in middle syllables." He would, however, very shrewdly and correctly, have the word "and" made common. He goes so far as to charge those with ignorance who say "impérative" and "orthógraphy," denying this to be the true "English" pronunciation.

To pick up the several arbitrarinesses and contradictions of this would be superfluous. They are all too usual in English prosodic writings; and I daresay the present book is not free from them. But we may single out the remark upon "honour." It is very difficult even to be certain what he means by "dishonour" being long, if "honour" is short. It is almost stranger that his very sensible observation on "skyward"[1] did not suggest itself to him on "swashbuckler." But on the whole, what has been said already covers the situation. He cannot rise to the conception of English as of a language in which pure vowel sound has nothing *exclusively* to do with the "quantity"—the metrical capacity—of syllables;[2] in "Quantity. which "position" has nothing *necessarily* to do with this quantity, though there are cases in which it cannot be neglected; in which accent can *determine* or *entail*, though it may not *originate* or *constitute*, quantity; and in which a very large proportion of syllables are naturally indifferent or common, so that they can receive the quantifying stamp from accent itself in the general sense, from particular stress or emphasis, from position *in the verse*, and from not a few other things. His practice is of little use to us, because his apparently insane lingo—the result partly, as he himself tells us, of a desire to be different from his predecessor Phaer—can seldom be discarded sufficiently to enable us to judge his versification fairly. His theory is, perhaps, the least irrational of all its class; and the exposition of it is particularly valuable, because it preserves and emphasises for us that excessive *un-*

---

[1] "They are but compound words, that may be with good sense sundered."
[2] In other words, in which not all long syllables are made so by "long" vowel-sound.

certainty[1] of English pronunciation which lies at the root as well of these crazy experiments, as of the acquiescent dotage of the fifteenth century.

Sidney's silence.   Considering the part assigned to Sidney by Spenser in banning rhyme and blessing verse by edict of his Areopagus ; considering the numerous experiments in the new kinds which the *Arcadia*[2] contains,—it may well seem, and has seemed, odd that there should be so little reference to the matter in the *Defence* or *Apology*. Perhaps we may hope that a slight practical taste of the thing was as sufficient for the author of *Astrophel and Stella* as it was for his friend the author of *The Faerie Queene*—that " having been there " he knew better than to " go " again, finding it quite other than a little prosodic heaven.   At the same time it is necessary to point out that the controversy raised by Gosson practically had nothing to do with mere prosody.   At any rate the chief document of the earlier Elizabethan criticism for authorship, genius, and interest of almost all kinds, yields us practically nothing.   Neither does Lodge touch the point, nor Fraunce, another member of the Sidneian circle and practitioner of " versing," who brought himself a specially hard rap from the impatient ferule of Ben Jonson.[3]   It is, however, otherwise with Mr. William Webbe, whose pretty well-known little *Discourse* leaves one doubtful whether to admire him for his amiable and not ill-guided enthusiasm, or to contemn him for his extraordinary lack of scholarship and knowledge generally, his hasty adoption of ill-considered opinions, and his ridiculous attempts in the new versification itself.

Webbe.   Webbe always reminds me of the man whom Thackeray imagined as thanking his host for that host's very best Lafite, and expressing approval of it, but going on to say,

---

[1] Let me protest, in passing, against the headlong credulity with which some good folk accept the supposition that Professor This or Dr. That has " proved " how, let us say, Shakespeare pronounced. *It is impossible, unless one rose from the dead,* to " prove " this ; and though on detached points some *probability* can be reached, it must always be doubtful.

[2] On these *v. sup.* p. 94.

[3] " Abram Francis in his English Hexameters was a fool " (*Conv. with Drummond*).

"And now will you give me some of that capital
ordinaire we had?" He *has* enthusiasm for "the New
poet" (Spenser), but he does not hesitate to extol the
bastard and heteroclite doggerel which that new poet had
the sense to drop; and he produces some most egregious
travesties of his own, in which the pure, if not perfect,
music of the *Shepherd's Kalendar* is jangled and jarred
from rhyme into "verse." He is also—Cambridge man
and private tutor though he was—grossly ignorant of the
simplest and best-known facts of ancient literature.
With all this he means so well, and loves so much, that
one cannot be very angry with him.

His *Preface* contains the now obligatory fling at "the
rude multitude of rustical rhymers," etc., the necessity of
driving "enormities" out of English poetry, and the attainment of perfect versifying by judiciously conditioned
imitation of Greek and Latin. The actual "Discourse"
begins with one of the also usual Renaissance celebrations
of the venerable and divine origin of poetry, with plentiful
citations from the ancients. Hence he passes to his first
laudation of "our late famous English poet who wrote the
Shepherd's Calendar," desiderating much and not unwisely,
that vanished *English Poet*[1] of which "E. K." had spoken.
More generalities follow, and a very rickety historical
sketch of ancient poetry, supplemented by one—still more
staggering—of English, which contains, among the matters
most nearly touching us, a commendation of the *verse* of
Lydgate, and the statement that "Piers Plowman" "was
the first that observed the quantity of our verse without the
curiosity of rhyme." As to this, the least that can be
said is that it shows that Webbe used the word "quantity"
without any precise idea whatsoever.

These citations and (generally) laudations in the other
sense of poets and poetasters lead him up to fresh praise
of the *Kalendar* and its author, as well as of Harvey,
contrasted once more with the "rabble of rhyming," to
which rabble, as it happens, Spenser, so far as he is a poet,

---

[1] Yet it is probable that this was merely a treatise of "versing," and that
Spenser wisely destroyed it when he found out his mistake.

belongs, and belongs wholly in the *Kalendar* itself.   After
this he casts back once more——for short as the treatise is,
it is mostly commonplace and verbiage——to the Renaissance
common - form about delighting and profiting, " sage
advice," etc., with the old quotations from Terence and Ovid
and Martial; cites very largely from Phaer's *Virgil* ; turns
to Eclogue and the *Kalendar* yet again ; and only when
he has spent more than half his space devotes himself to
a methodical discussion of rhyme and verse.   ˙

It has by this time struck him that it is rather inconsistent to praise Spenser and other " rhymers " to the
skies, and to trample their prosody under his feet ; and he
speaks a little less disrespectfully of it.   " I may not
utterly disallow it," he says, " lest I should seem to call
in question," etc.   He is " content " (he had not been
" content " at all) to esteem it as a thing " the perfection
of which is very commendable," only he would like it
" bettered and made more artificial."   And then he
proceeds to show how this may be done, borrowing a
little dubious history from Ascham.   He analyses the
kinds of verse common at the time, truly enough pronouncing the fourteener the most esteemed of all other,
but recognising its resolution into common measure,
and then more particularly dealing with the metres of
the *Kalendar*.

Next, generalising and perhaps copying Gascoigne
(*v. inf.*) he decides that " the natural course of most
English verses seemeth to run on the old Iambic stroke,"
and shows by example how, if you change the order, the
verse will not do.   This he turns into an argument (as it
is, of course, *such* as it is) against rhyme, as occasionally
inducing awkward metrical and other inversions.   He
does not, however, disdain to suggest a rhyming dictionary,
and once more goes to his *Kalendar* for " words prettily
turned " and wound up mutually together.   But he at last
proceeds to " the reformed kind of English verse," gives
a list of feet by their classical names, admits the
difficulty of adjusting them to English, and then, after a
very few more directions, ends with abundant (and very

bad) examples of his own, and general cautions on Poetry from Horace and others.

Not much criticism of this need be given, and we need Nash. say less of Nash's well-known and as well-deserved satire on Stanyhurst, because it does not turn on any question of principle, but merely on that eccentric Irishman's application of principles.   Indeed, Nash speaks rather kindly of those similar but less harsh experiments of Fraunce, to which Jonson was to be decidedly, though more briefly hostile.

George Puttenham (*si* George and *si* Puttenham *y a*)[1] Puttenham. gave a whole third of the not inconsiderable treatise attributed to him to the subject of " Proportion in Poetry," by which he means Prosody : and no small proportion of this proportion is allotted to the new " versifying." Indeed, he starts with " feet," but for some time deals with ordinary metres, not fearing to include among them those things which excited the ever-increasing ire of neo-classic critics—" mathematical " forms in verse.   But he allows four chapters (xiii. to xvi.) to " versing."   Yet, when we come to the details, we find that odd shrinking away from the *propositum* which begins, as we pointed out, even in Ascham, and which is observable in all except methodic maniacs like Stanyhurst—to whom, by the way, Puttenham refers.   The upshot of his chapters, when we come to examine them, is, after all, notwithstanding the other contradiction to be noticed, a matter of feet, not of metres.   Now, it will certainly not be in this book that any one will come across a denial of classical *feet* in English.   The question is, how far it is possible to combine these integers into representative classical *metres*. There's the rub ; and this rub Puttenham (who frankly tells us at the very beginning that he has small love for " versifying ") persistently shirks.

Still, he has a great deal of strictly prosodic matter,

---

[1] I merely insert this because of a certain kind of critic. It does not matter here one straw whether it is Puttenham, and if so whether it is George or Richard.   But I have never thought Mr. Croft's arguments for the latter satisfactory.   For these see his ed. of Eliot's *Governor* (London, 1883) ; for Puttenham's treatise, Professor Gregory Smith's collection, or Mr. Arber's separate issue (Birmingham, 1869).

despite the enormous space given to Figures of Speech
and to the "rag-bag" of the subject. His Second Book,
"Of Proportion Poetical," is, in fact, wholly devoted to
prosody. "Poesy," he says, very properly, "is a skill
to speak and write harmonically," and he deals with
all the conditions indicated by the adverb—"Staff,"
"Measure," "Situation," etc. Staff and Measure require
no long comment, though he is very copious on them ; but
it is curious that he prefers the sixain—perhaps the least
effective of all—to stanzas both longer and shorter. He
is also very minute on "measures," and insists on the
importance of cæsura. He thinks (his argument on the
subject being to me, at least, quite unintelligible) that we
can have *no* "feet," and counts his lines merely by
syllables ; and he would, like many others to the
present day, arrange these merely by cadences, themselves
determined by accent. He is very particular about exact
rhyme ; and avails himself of elaborate diagrams to show
its arrangement, and that of line-length. Also he lays
himself open to the rather cheap ridicule of many generations since, by admitting and approving "proportion in
figure"—the eggs, lozenges, etc., which so did shock Mr.
Addison. For myself, I never could see that for the
lighter kind of poetry—such things as have since been
called *vers de société*—there was any greater harm in
butterflies and bellows than in the artificial French forms ;
though no doubt—unlike these latter—they have a certain
impertinence in wholly serious verse. On the whole,
Puttenham is extremely interesting as showing that, at
last, definite, even severe, attention was being given to
form. If he seems sometimes to pay too much attention
to the caddis and too little to the dragon-fly, why, these
things will happen.

Puttenham's book appeared, though written earlier, in
1589. In the last decade of the sixteenth century the
interest in "versing," as far as may be judged from extant
writing about it, slackened—a few sputters of the wearisome
and ill-mannered Harvey-and-Nash controversy being
the chief exceptions. In this, Harvey characteristically

took to himself the title of "inventor of the English
hexameter," a title which long stuck to him, though he
certainly merited

Ni cet excès d'honneur ni cette indignité,

whichever way we may take it.   But in almost the earliest
years of the seventeenth it came to a head again, and
was, in fact, finished, for the time, if not for all times, in
the remarkable duel between Campion and Daniel.

The peculiarity—we cannot exactly say the singularity, Campion's
for there is something of a match to it in Milton—of *Observatio.*
Campion's position as a decrier of rhyme in theory, and
a most exquisite master of it in practice, was not thoroughly
obvious during the long eclipse of his orthodox lyrical
work ; but it was all along known to any one who read
his generous and courteous antagonist's reply.   And it
cannot be too distinctly explained that his position, from
the very first, is an almost entirely different one from that
of all the previous " versers " and approvers of " versing "
—Watson, Ascham, Drant, Spenser, Harvey, Webbe,
Stanyhurst, and the rest.   The warning which Ascham
himself had uttered had been more than justified by the
ludicrous failure of nearly two generations of hexametrists ;
and there is hardly anything left of the old attitude in
Campion, except his railing at the " vulgar and unartificial
custom " of rhyming—a little awkwardly addressed to
Sackville, the author of some of the finest rhyme-royal in
the language.   He labours this point further in his first
and second chapters, with the usual hopelessly illogical
arguments from the non-practice of Greeks and Romans.
But when he leaves off flourishes and comes to business,
describing the six main feet, and (for what reason is not
obvious) ranking spondee, tribrach, and anapæst, even in
Greek and Latin, as " but servants to dactyl, trochee,
and iamb," he says, " Only the heroical verse that is
distinguished by the dactyl hath been oftentimes attempted
in our English tongue, but with passing pitiful success ;
and no wonder, seeing it is an attempt altogether against
the nature of our language."   The English dactyl is

"ridiculous"; it is "unfit for use"—confessions which, of course, sweep the English hexameter away altogether. And he would have all English prosody based on iamb and trochee, though he admits, in a rather gingerly and reluctant fashion, trisyllabic substitution in certain places —tribrachs or dactyls, rarely anapæsts.

He next deals successively with "pure" and "licentiate" iambics—the latter allowing even tribrachs—with dimeter or "English march," of course unrhymed; then he proceeds to the "English trochaic" proper; the English elegiac, the English Sapphic, and Anacreontic.[1]   He has thus described, with others which he adds, eight several kinds of English numbers, simple and compound, which he commends with an explosion at the "*fatness* of rhyme," and then concludes with a chapter on the quantity of English syllables.   Here he sets forth, with the curious mixture of acuteness and prejudice which characterises the whole tractate, the increasing abundance of common syllables in Latin, Greek, and English respectively.   He thinks that the true value is to be "measured chiefly by the accent"; but strangely pronounces the second syllable of "Trumpington" *naturally* long.   And his special rules are as arbitrary, or nearly so, as Stanyhurst's.   Perhaps it would be impossible to construct *a posteriori*, with all our advantages, a document more illustrative of the prosodic condition of the time than this.   There is the surviving prejudice against rhyme—purely irrational, but explicable because of the association of *bad* verse with it, and because of the general and generous Renaissance admiration of the ancients.   There is, further, the strongest revulsion from that badness of verse itself, and the desire to guard against its recurrence by a thorough examination of principles and a rather rigid formulation of practice. Perhaps there is something of that affectation of singularity and originality which is very human and not always—if it is sometimes—disgusting.   There was no need—Campion had himself shown it, and was to show it amply—of limiting English verse to eight or eighty or eight hundred

---

[1] For more on all these, and examples of them, see last chapter.

kinds; and even one or two of his are very good, while all without exception would be improved by rhyme. But, on the other hand, and to set against all exaggeration, misdirected ingenuity, and positive mistake, there is the renunciation, once for all, of the preposterous new doggerel —more preposterous, if possible, and certainly more perverse, than the worst of the old, if not quite so paralytic—which men of learning, and to some extent of genius, had been trying to foist into English for the best part of half a century.

There was, however, mischief enough in the piece— especially in its irrational, unhistorical, and, in the best sense, unscientific contempt and refusal of rhyme—to require serious answer; and it could not have found a better answerer than Samuel Daniel. A great poet Daniel was not, but he was a good poet in his day and at his hour; he understood the sweetness and the gravity of English poetry; and, what was of special importance for the special purpose, he was almost an impeccable metrist and rhythmist, though he had not such a command of lyrical music as Campion himself. Moreover, he was really "a scholar and a gentleman"—one who knew, and who at the same time disdained to use his knowledge with the warty incivility or the extravagant gesticulation which were too common, and unfortunately have never been too uncommon. He had a famous case as well; and the result is one of the most agreeable things of its kind, and one of the most convincing.

There may seem to be a certain oddity[1] in the opening of his piece, wherein addressing Lord Pembroke, the nephew of one of the most formidable practitioners of "versing," and in face of the chain of abuse of rhyme which we have sketched, he speaks of the use of it "having been held unquestionable." Perhaps, as was suggested above, the craze had really "gone under" for some years, or the assumption of novelty may be rhetorical. At any rate, after a proper compliment to his opponent, which

Daniel's Defence.

[1] This oddity is even double; for Campion had, as noted, chosen for *his* dedicatee a great practitioner of rhyme itself.

would have annoyed Porthos and pleased Aramis, he
takes up the most victorious and impregnable position of
all by saying, "we could well have allowed of his numbers
had he not disgraced our rhyme." Indeed, of the
"numbers" themselves he says very little. But he
founds his case at once upon the rock by saying, "Rhyme
which both Custom and Nature do the most powerfully
defend—Custom that is before all Law, Nature that is
above all Art. Every language," this golden sentence
proceeds, "hath her proper number or measure fitted to
use and delight." And to this line he keeps throughout,
never allowing himself to be tempted out of it. His
history and derivations may be vulnerable : his argument
is not. He dwells on the "added excellency" of rhyme ;
on the delight to the ear and the aid to the memory given
by its echo of delightful report ; on its actual universality.
"If the Barbarian use it, then it shows that it sways the
affection of the Barbarian ; if civil nations practise it, it
proves that it works upon the hearts of civil nations ; if
all, then that it hath a power in nature on all." There is
not such an irresistible instance of common sense logically
equipped as this in all the anti-rhymers from Ascham to
Milton. "Ill customs," it is said, "ought to be left."
"Prove the illness," he retorts. Why should we imitate
the Greeks and Latins? As for rhyme being an im-
pediment, it gives wings. And then he turns eloquently
to the general "Ancient and Modern" question, not
condemning the ancients, but once more asking *why* we
should "yield our conquests captive to the authority of
antiquity," alleging "the wonderful architecture of the
state of England" as a parallel — and urging that we
shall "best tend to perfection by going on in the course
we are in."

But Daniel is far from laying himself open to the
reproach of confining himself to safe generalities. He
points out—and it is again crushing to the whole system
of the versers—that "we must here imitate the Greeks
and Latins, and yet we are here showed to disobey them,"
taught "to produce what they make short, and make short

what they produce." "Were it not better to hold to old custom than to be distracted with uncertain new Laws?" Is not the "iambic verse" that ancient one of five feet which hath ever been used? the "dimeter" half of this verse? And so with the rest. Therefore in these eight several kinds of numbers "we have only what was our own before, apparelled in foreign titles," so that had they come in their natural attire of rhyme we should never have suspected them as other. Then he exposes some of those crotchety inharmonies which we noted above. And thus, with some remarks on his own practice and a free allowance of blank verse in itself, he closes a tractate equally admirable for matter, arrangement, and (in every sense) " manner."

So far as we know, Campion never attempted to " duply "; and he was very well advised not to do so ; while he went on with rhymed numbers, in which he was even better advised. And so the whole thing vanished away like Spenser's Orgoglio, or better still perhaps his false Florimel, when the true beauty was set beside her. Even in that curious splurt of Milton's, to which we shall come in its proper place, there is no hint of " versing " in the Ascham-Harvey or even the Campion sense, though there is an echo of the baseless abuse of rhyme. A few remarks may be made in the Interchapter on the whole thing in this phase of it, though a complete discussion of the English hexameter must still be postponed. Meanwhile we have to return. Most of the Elizabethan prosodists have been mentioned, for most concerned themselves with the craze. But some did not ; and some points in those already mentioned, not affecting this craze, may be handled.

And here we may, in the first place, recur with advantage to a book which was noticed to some extent in the last volume, but which the relegation of the prosodic studies of the period to this necessarily reintroduces. I have long been acquainted with *The Mirror for* The Mirror *Magistrates* "after a sort," by incursions and prospecting *for Magistrates* once expeditions in public libraries. But I knew very well more.

that it would be part of such an inquiry as the present to possess myself of it, and read it line by line. For the length and the breadth of that grisly plain are strewn with prosodic instances; and contain at least one remarkable, but not much noticed, prosodic discussion. It is over now. Phaer and Ferrers and Baldwin, Higgins and Niccols and the singular Blennerhassett (what relation to Skelton's girl friend, Mistress Jane?), who executed in Castle Cornet at Guernsey[1] a large loop or extension of the piece, apparently at his own instigation, are all familiar to me. The further points in this curious example of collaboration or continuation which now require notice are, first, some of its actual prosodic characteristics considered from a fresh point of view; secondly, the prosodic discussion above referred to; thirdly, the evidence of prosodic progress, which its numerous editions, extending over more than half a century of time, furnish to us by comparison. Let these be taken in order.

Lesson of its prosodic freaks.

The first is here of least importance; but it *is* important, and it leads up directly to the second. As was previously noted, the general metre is rhyme-royal, varied occasionally with others and varied in itself by certain freaks—not merely such as Ferrers' already-mentioned extension of it to regular Alexandrines, but of a more irresponsible character. Most even of the earlier writers have escaped the utter chaos of Hawes; but they allow themselves occasional Alexandrines. Once[2] the septets give place to what looks like a stanza, but is really six lines of fourteener couplet. Final stanzas are often prolonged to octaves, and in one instance[3] there is a remarkable anticipation (perhaps a suggestion?) of Giles Fletcher's cut-down Spenserian with the Alexandrine ending—a thing overlooked, I suppose, by those who will not let Spenser be of his own creation. In another case,

---

[1] I wonder if he did it in a very pleasant upper chamber of one of the towers which has a glorious view, and, when I knew it, was used sometimes as a prison and sometimes as a card-room? (It was in the latter capacity that I became acquainted with it.)

[2] i. 29, ed. Haslewood (London, 1815), "King Albanact," St. 27.

[3] i. 151, last stanza of "King Iago."

but for one decasyllabic slip, an Envoy of three stanzas is *all* Alexandrine in the Ferrers fashion. In a few cases Alexandrines and decasyllables seem to be " castered " out as carelessly as by Hawes himself. Even doggerel of an anapæstic type does make its appearance—of which more presently. Once at least [1] there is a *six*teener ; and more than once quatrains, decasyllabic or other. One Envoy provides a sort of choice of octaves or septets ; while the option is extended to nine in another (though with no Alexandrine conclusion), and in a single final stanza of yet another to eleven. The " Complaint of Cadwallader " is in continuous Alexandrine " blanks," with a few probably accidental rhymes. A curious quatrain of three Alexandrines and a fourteener appears ; and it may come almost as a shock on the unwary reader to find Skelton's *Quia ecce nunc in pulvere dormio*, with its older-world tone and air, in this newer company, and to discover that the Princes are murdered in the Tower to the broken rhyme-royal almost contemporary with the event. But this last, it is soon seen, was intentional.

These earlier and more interesting parts of the *Mirror* Of the prose have a framework of prose discussion in which the authors discussions. and their company make remarks on the pieces. Here " the matter was well enough liked by some, but the metre was misliked almost of all. Divers " even " would not allow it." [2] However, one argued that as King Richard " never kept measure in any of his doings," measure ought not to be expected in accounts of them. Nor does this seem to be merely a joke ; for the speaker goes on to say that the writer " both could and would amend in many places, save for keeping the decorum which he purposely hath observed herein." And so on another piece of the kind, supposed to be the work of a blacksmith. An odd argument : but the important point is that, in 1563 certainly, and perhaps even earlier still metre was " mis-

---

[1] The captains Euridane and Thessalone companions in the prey (i. 203).

[2] ii. 394. The two pieces will be found on each side of this prose. So also the Cadwallader blanks above referred to have a prose comment noticing their agreement " with the Roman verse called iambus " and condemning the " *gotish* kind of rhyming." But this was later—*c.* 1578.

liked," seen to be " rude," and so forth, which would have
been the regular thing not so very many years earlier.

These remarks are, in fact, of extreme value, and they
take rank before Gascoigne's *Notes*, and therefore before
everything else in the chain of evidence, showing how the
sense of rhythm *consciously* impressed itself upon Englishmen.   There are, indeed, no details ; we could hardly
expect them.   But we have evidently got out of the time
when the Lydgatian licences seemed natural ; though
Lydgate's reputation—ratified as it had been by generations—continued in a general way a little longer.   That
nearly perfect verse like Sackville's, and very imperfect
verse like that of some of the others, should find themselves side by side, is a fact of value in itself ; that, however imperfectly, a sense of the difference should exist
even in persons who had not by any means broken
themselves altogether to the more excellent way, is something very much more.   Spenser is near, though not come.
It is still something more, if not much, that Higgins, who
represents the bridge of transition between the earliest
contributors to the *Mirror* and its latest, should be aware
that people may find fault with his metre.   But the book,
as a whole, contributes a more important evidence than
this from a period later still—indeed, as late as almost
anything with which we are dealing in this particular
division of our subject.   This is to be found in the " buck-
washing," as Mr. Carlyle would have said, of Niccols.
This good gentleman is fully penetrated with the sense of
metrical regularity ; he shows the fact that he lives
not merely after Spenser and the final *rhythmicising* of
English poetry, but after Gascoigne and the fortunately
not final attempt to tie down this rhythmicising to the
narrowest limits.   Among the hundreds of new variants
initialled " N " in Haslewood, by far the larger number will
be found to be Procrustean, shortenings of Alexandrines [1]

[1] When Niccols is confronted with the " sixteener " above cited, he takes
his courage in both hands, and does not merely cut out a word or two.   It
appears in his version as
      Stout Euridane and Thessalone I did assay,
an Alexandrine being admissible in the place.

to decasyllables, and other trimmings of the same kind. A sort of White Terror has begun : you are to be nothing if not syllabically precise.

The remarkable position and the not less remarkable contents of *Notes of Instruction* have been, and will be, frequently referred to. Indeed, the little book, curiously unpretentious, is the very spring and well-head of the stream of English prosody on the preceptist side. It has been thought to be, and perhaps is, to some extent indebted—for suggestion rather than anything else—to Ronsard's somewhat earlier tract ; but there is no resemblance of principle. It is so short and so much to the point, that an abstract of it is hardly necessary. Its doctrines can be put as succinctly as could well be desired. They are, first, that accent must be attended to ; secondly, that metre must be kept—you must not wander from one measure to another ; thirdly, that there is, at the time, hardly any foot in English save a dissyllabic one—a position of the highest importance, which Gascoigne states unwillingly, saying that we " have had " others, and that they exist even in Chaucer ; fourthly, that the pause or cæsura ought to be in certain places, except in rhyme-royal, where " it skills not where it be." He mentions, besides this rhyme-royal, " riding rhyme " and " poulter's measure " (the decasyllabic couplet, and the alternate Alexandrine and fourteener), as well as octosyllabics, but makes no reference, or only an oblique one, to the new " versifying," which, indeed, at his date was little more than an academic amusement.[1] There is a most remarkable omission, in connection with that fateful limitation to the dissyllabic foot, of any reference to such work as Tusser's, which was being constantly reprinted. Probably he disdained the subject too much.[2]

Gascoigne's Notes of Instruction.

[1] There are, of course, other interesting things in Gascoigne, especially his early deprecation of poetic " commonplaces "—" cherry lips," etc. ; but they are not strictly prosodic. His peremptory adoption of " Heaven " (" Heavn " as it was commonly written) as a monosyllable, not to be lengthened except by " licence," is a precious prosodic *point de repère*.

[2] Very great indebtedness to Gascoigne, and some through him or directly to Ronsard, has sometimes been ascribed to King James the First, then only James the Sixth, in his *Rewlis and Cautelis* of Scots verse, 1584. There is also a *Note on King James's Rewlis and Cautelis.*

It is an old brocard in English history that the Wars of the Roses made English statesmen, and Englishmen generally, fear nothing so much as a conflict for succession. One might almost say that the prosodic anarchy which was contemporary with the " differing of the red and white " exercised a similar influence upon English prosodists. From this came Gascoigne's notion, and the notions which, as we have just seen, preceded Gascoigne in practice, if not in theory. From this came Spenser's shyness of trisyllabic feet, and the rarity with which the almost infinite variety of Elizabethan and Caroline lyric permits itself the galloping metres. From this came the abominable " apostrophation " of the seventeenth century, and its regularised but not much improved form in the

theory that it may represent exercises done by James for Buchanan. In itself it is rather a disappointing little book ; very clear and precise, but jejune, and giving little more than an analysis of the actual practice in recent Scots, which, as we have several times observed, was itself much more precise and regular than that of English. It has some oddities of phrase—the chief of which is the usual, though not invariable, misuse of "foot" for "syllable"—an ordinary heroic being a "verse of ten *feet*," etc. "Colours" too is used, not in the ordinary sense, nor in the technical one of rhetoric, but as equivalent to "metres." James, as we might expect, lays down his laws in a very Mede-and-Persian fashion ; and scarcely ever attempts a reason. He agrees with his English and French predecessors—perhaps authorities—in representing the iamb as practically the only foot : but allows an easement in the shape of what he calls the "Tumbling" verse, which is not so much doggerel as the alliterative line of the middle period. Within the example he gives "bob-and-wheel" trimmings. He also calls these "rouncevals" a word of many meanings and disputed origin. "Tumbling" itself has been thought to be a translation of "cadence" (*cf.* his word "flowing" for "rhythm"; but see my note, vol. i. p. 160, to which, though exception has been taken to it, I adhere). He calls pause or cæsura "section," again translating literally. He will not allow identical syllables to rhyme. He specifies couplets—oddly described as "rhyme that is not verse"; a nine-line stanza decasyllabic *aabaabbab*; a bastard octave which he calls "Ballad royal"; rhyme-royal proper, which he calls "Troilus verse"; sonnets; the tumbling variety; "common verse"; an octosyllabic sixain *ababcc*, and "cuttit and broken verse," of which his example is Montgomerie's *Cherry and Slae* stanza, but which he justly says may be and is "daily invented according to the poet's pleasure." The little tractate is by far the most exact and precise prosodic handbook that exists in any form of English before Bysshe ; and although it is not, like Bysshe's, a sort of Arian *Quicumque vult*, prescribing all the wrong things and proscribing most of the right, it is rather sapless and scholastic. The citation of the *Cherry and Slae* stanza years before the first known edition of that work may be noteworthy, especially in connection with Howell's use of it three years earlier still. See Professor Raleigh's ed. of Howell's *Devises* (Oxford, 1906).

eighteenth. From this came the grave disapproval with which Milton's *Samson*, dealing as it did with the green withes of syllabic confinement, was received by some, and I suppose also the more singular and surprising series of fictions by which others have more lately thought to show that the withes were not broken after all.

Altogether, this, or rather the nervous shrinking from the other extreme which caused it, constituted the Second Peril of English prosody. It had escaped the first, as we saw, partly by the uprising of alliteration from its hundred years' trance, and much more by the agency of the ballad. But both these had shown themselves untrustworthy agencies. It escaped the second by the aid of Shakespeare and Milton.

Some other strictly Elizabethan critics say little on prosody proper ; even Chapman, whose combined learning and pugnacity might lead us to expect aggressive rather than defensive explanation of his choice of metre, says little about it.[1] And there is a curious absence of prosodic remark in Jonson's *Discoveries*, which those who lay the utmost stress on his borrowing from the ancients might interpret in their own way. We know (*v. sup.*) from the less authentic but (with the due grains of salt) acceptable *Conversations*, that he thought Fraunce "a fool" for writing hexameters ; that he thought Donne deserved hanging for not keeping accent ; that he did not like Spenser's metre ; and that he thought the couplet, though under an ambiguous description, best of all.[2] But this knowledge comes to us only through the not exactly untrustworthy but extremely incomplete channel of Drummond's notes ; and the full deliverances, or others not reported, might very much affect his actual serious

Chapman, Jonson, Drayton.

---

[1] His curious remark as to the division of some fourteeners has been quoted above, p. 111.

[2] "He had an intention to perfect an Epic Poem . . . it is all in couplets, for he detesteth all other rhymes. He had written a Discourse of Poesy both against Campion and Daniel, especially this last, where he proves couplets to be the bravest sort of verses, *especially when they are broken like hexameters*, and that cross-rhymes and stanzas . . . were all forced." Now, whether "broken like hexameters" means a strong cæsura, or enjambment, positive people may positively decide.

opinion and doctrine. The last utterance of importance on the subject that seems fit to be handled in this chapter is the remarkable note of Drayton to the *Barons' Wars*, on his refashioning them from *Mortimeriados*, and on his altering the stanza from rhyme-royal to octave. He says (illustrating the change with interlaced diagrams like Puttenham's) that he thought the double couplet at the end " softened the verse more than the majesty of the subject would permit, unless they had been all couplets or geminels." The " couplet in base " of the octave seemed to him better ; while, thereby showing almost certainly that he had Puttenham before him, " the quatrain doth never bring forth gemells," " the quinzain too soon," while the " sestin," which Puttenham had preferred, " detains not the music long enough." To which he adds the highly characteristic conceit that the octave, like the Tuscan pillar, has a shaft of six diameters and a base of two. But (surprising and ominous conclusion !) " all stanzas are tyrants and torturers." The " geminel " or " gemell " seems to be his real love, after all.[1]

In this deliverance, brief as it is, in the asserted preference of Jonson for the couplet and dislike of the stanza, and in other things, we can see the " Prophecy of Famine " in regard to metre, which is to be gradually fulfilled, until the couplet itself is left the only authorised prosodic food. The thing would be curious, if it were not so common. " Man never is but always to be blest," and, in the very days when he has got the greatest of all prosodic triumphs in the Spenserian, there comes from the mouths of men like Drayton, who can manage stanza only less well than Spenser himself, the grumbling at it, and the cry for something different.

---

[1] My friend, Professor Elton, than whom certainly no one knows more about Drayton, rather demurs to this, and insists on the qualification as to stanzas (which I accordingly quote), "when they make invention obey their number," and on Drayton's *practice*. But this is, to me, a precious illustration of that singular *historical* character of prosody on which I myself lay so much stress. Drayton was a born (and a pretty early born) Elizabethan, and his practice followed his birth-date—thank the Muses ! But his theory looks onward, and shows the influence of the later times into which he for some space lived. And much the same is the case with Jonson.

Let Gascoigne, however, and Drayton have the credit which they deserve. Gascoigne, though he seems to acquiesce—not quite happily, but rather supinely—in a disastrous prosodic disinheritance ; Drayton, though he seems to repine, not so much after as in the midst of " the cucumbers and the melons and the garlic " of prosodic abundance,—do actually and in reality found as poets, the one the entire conscious prosodic study of English, the other the attempt to discover the poetic values and qualities of metre. For which let there be to them all due honour.

INTERCHAPTER V

IT would be difficult to find an instance where the system of halting to collect results up to the moment justifies, and in fact imposes itself, more clearly than in the present. The remark which has been made above as to Allot's *England's Parnassus* is worth recalling ; for that collection appeared at about the middle, roughly speaking, of the period covered by the foregoing Book—the period from 1580 to 1620, in round numbers—though our actual terminations are of course jagged and tallied, not squarely cut off. When we closed the last Book and volume everything, with almost the single exception of the work of Spenser, in which we deliberately anticipated, was inchoate. As we halt now, everything in the stage, or almost everything except the aftergrowth of Caroline lyric and the narrative blank verse of Milton, has reached perfection. That there is no sign of over-ripeness cannot be said ; but no reasonable person would expect, or even wish, to be able to say it.

The general characteristic of the forty years' work is that of the most daring and multiform experiment, conducted, however, for the most part, with the sureness and almost scientific certainty of success, of which Spenser set the first example, and was in a way the accepted master. It is no contradiction to the words just used that this experiment works in directions which Spenser himself never tried. The discipline and the guidance that succeed in an Arctic expedition are not very likely to be useless in an Antarctic.

That there is something a little uncanny in the run of good luck which attends these experiments may be admitted readily enough ; there is always something uncanny in great and beautiful matters. But, for a time, it seems as if things cannot go wrong. The dangerous and pernicious heresy of classical "versing" is supported for years by the greatest wits of the day, and never quite loses its hold on some of them ; but it does no harm. The mistake as to the single foot to which Gascoigne testifies, and which will do some harm later, for a time does little or none ; and its action is even beneficial as stopping the return to doggerel. And meanwhile, whatever they think and theorise about, they all "go and do " ; and some mysterious power wills it, and brings it about, that they nearly all go and do well. Each of the divisions of prosodic accomplishment in the time has a double blessing : it gives good individual results, and it helps to fortify and establish some general principle of English prosody. Even the lolloping fourteener of Surrey and Wyatt becomes the fiery one of Southwell and Chapman before it recognises its still higher possibilities in broken form, and gives us the miraculous beauty of the Caroline "common measure." The couplet gradually separates itself into its two kinds, and for a time manages to combine a good deal of the merits of both. The various stanzas, in hierarchy ascending to, and descending again from, the supreme Spenserian, recover all the beauty and more than the variety and flexibility of Chaucer. And in all, and still more in two other forms or groups of form to be specially noticed in a moment, there is, for the first time since Chaucer himself, and with this exception for the first time at all, a pervading adequacy and mastery of prosodic principle and practice.

No more do the fingers fumble with the fiddle-strings ; no more is there not merely a chance, but something like a certainty, of Pegasus going lame or snapping a sinew before he has walked or flown for a few lines. The harmony produced may be more or less beautiful ; more or less accomplished ; more or less rare ; but it is a regular and settled accomplishment—the absence of it, not the presence, is the exception and the surprise. But

what is still the surprise, and must always continue to be
so, as long as prosody and poetry last, is the endless
variety of the effects to which this new acquisition of the
general system of English verse, and this incomparable
spirit of experiment, in combination lead.   And it is in
the two kinds just glanced at that this surprise is most
constantly ready for us—that is to say, in blank verse
and in lyric ; while in both there are points, other but
certainly not minor, to consider.

That blank verse should become a school of freedom
is not astonishing, more particularly as we saw that, in
the beginning, it was a school of something quite opposite.
For as soon as the blank verser began to be familiar
enough with his instrument to recognise that it was quite
independent of rhyme—that he need not even supply the
place of that mentor by a rigid regularity of syllabic
composition—enfranchisement in other directions was
sure to follow.   Had it been much used for "papers of
verses"[1] (Gascoigne, and one or two others, be it remembered, did so use it) the punctilio might have held.   But
practically restricted to the stage as it was for so long,
the mere scuffling and heat of word-and-wit-combat were
sure to encourage—nay, to force—the discarding of unnecessary and troublesome uniformity.   Once more, the
Fortune of England thought of what was necessary, and
supplied Shakespeare to carry out the liberation in this
direction, just as she had supplied Spenser to carry out
the regimenting and drilling in the other.

But even Fortune cannot conquer Nature ; and there
was a peril in this path from which the other was comparatively free.   Everybody is the better for discipline:
everybody is not competent to manage liberty.   In fact,
if (which is luckily not yet the case) every man wrote
poetry, I am not sure that the strict preceptists would
not have a great deal to say for themselves.   This, however, is speculation.   It is mere history to say that, even

---

[1]   "These numbers [blanks] therefore are fittest for a play; the others
for a *paper of verses* or a poem : blank verse being as much below them, etc."
Crites in Dryden's *Essay of Dramatic Poesy*, ed. Ker, i. 91.

before our present period closed, the dangers of a go-as-you-please blank verse began to be apparent. But it had not, by this time, so much incurred them as shown the possibility of them. And, on the other hand, it had, in the legitimate carrying out of the great base-principles of English prosody—foot-division with substitution, pause-arrangement with licence to shift, and permission of extrametrical syllable at the end only—enriched English with such a measure as no other language then possessed, and as, in perfection, no other language has ever possessed. This measure is absolutely rhythmical and metrical — absolutely distinguished from prose, and yet uniting the virtues of verse and the shiftfulness of prose as nothing else ever has done, as it is difficult to believe that anything else ever will do. For, though there is no limit to the powers of Nature in one sense, there appears to be in her a certain generosity which prevents her depriving a perfect creation of its *differentia*, when this is once displayed. We have seen as great metres, for instance, as the Homeric or the Lucretian hexameter, but nothing has ever had the *same* merit ; and so on.

The desire for variety found almost equal—some would say greater—satisfaction in the innumerable lyrical forms of the time, but the fortunate necessity of *correspondence*[1] precluded, in the case of writers with any ear at all (and ear at this time was almost satyrically acute and universal), any lapse into disorder. It is probably a sense —and certainly a result—of this safeguard, combined with the unconquerable experimentality of the time, that accounts for the innumerable and almost unclassifiable multitude of lyric forms that meet us. We saw in the last volume that Hawes, who cannot keep himself straight even in a single rhyme-royal stanza because of his neglect

---

[1] A note on this word may not be superfluous. Correspondence, in the line or between the lines, is the note of all metre ; but in variety, and in call upon the attention, it is especially the note of lyric. And while, when you have written an undoubtedly musical line, you have *got* to make the other or the others musical to suit it, even a dubiously musical one will acquire a certain harmony from the fact of there being a pair to it. But this is *metaprosodic.*

of line composition, is regular enough in the not particularly beautiful but definitely lyrical forms of the *Conversion of Swearers*. And we saw that the " intermediates " Googe, Gascoigne, Turberville, etc., though uninspiring, were safe enough here. By our present time we have the safety *with* inspiration ; and the result is not merely the actual beauty of the songs in drama, romance, or mere music-book, but the promise and certainty of more to come, not shadowed by any of the dubieties of blank verse. The inspiration may fail—*will* fail, though not entirely for another couple of generations. But the forms are secure, and will wait for it to return.

One special point, of the first importance in prosodic history, must have its paragraph : and this concerns the fortune of trisyllabic feet and triple-time measures during this period. The central *preceptist* fact is, of course, Gascoigne's constantly to be quoted dictum : and it can summon round, and in support of it, numerous or innumerable instances of elision or apostrophation in accordance with the idea. On the other hand, we have—earlier than Gascoigne, and, if not recognised as poetry, constantly printed as verse throughout the half century —Tusser's frank, abundant, and perfectly regular practice in anapæstic metre ; a persistent if not very copious dropping into triple time on the part of the song-writers with Campion at their head ; the more and more constant *trisyllabising* of blank verse ; and the occurrence in other forms of collocations which, though they *may* be susceptible of crushing or cramming into sham dissyllables to suit theory, are more naturally and very much more harmoniously trisyllables. Here the aid of music may be cordially recognised ; for something of the kind was of the greatest importance to serve as a rallying-point against the dogmatic delusion chronicled in the *Notes and Instructions*. But on the whole, though there has now and then been a tendency to banish triple time too absolutely from this period, we must admit that it was something of an interloper—looked on askance in the more regular and full-dress forms of poetry, and taught mainly in the hedge schools thereof. But, as we have seen before, the hedge school is sometimes the depository of the truest doctrine.

Nor should there be the slightest reluctance in admitting this, or the slightest sorrow or surprise at it, even among those who believe that trisyllabic intermixture, and trisyllabic domination at times, are essential to the perfect development of English prosody. To everything there is a season ; and to every season there are certain things to which it should chiefly devote itself. The special things to which this great period had to devote itself were the enfranchising and varying of blank verse, and the thorough establishment of rhymed verse on a basis of regularity, that should escape sing-song and observe variety—regard being in all cases had to the warding off of any return to doggerel.

And so far as it is concerned—so far as the flourishing time of the authors chiefly dealt with extends—we may almost say that it did its work as impeccably as is consistent with human experiment and tentative. In the more dangerous and problematical task of delimiting the province of blank verse, it perhaps went near to overstepping, if it did not actually overstep, the bounds ; and it was left to Milton, after those bounds had been not merely overstepped but overrun in the most disorderly fashion, and indeed nearly overthrown, to take order further with the matter. But in regard to the thorough reformation, advancement, and perfecting of rhymed verse, especially in stanza form, there is no such exception to take to it. It left, no doubt, something to be done in respect of both forms of couplet, and still more of trisyllabic verse, but it cannot be justly charged with having even initiated—even given far-off symptoms of—degradation in either.

In particular, the regeneration of the stanza in almost every form, from the Spenserian, the sonnet, and the great ode-strophes, down to the smallest combinations of lyric, and its information with poetical spirit by the way of rhythm, are marvellous things to contemplate. As we have shown fully in the first volume, English, as soon as it had received its true prosody, had early shown itself prolific in elaborate stanza-forms, and before the dark quarter of the Early English moon, Chaucer had, in rhyme-royal, shown this capacity of our language for stanza in all but the highest degree. But, except Chaucer and a few anonyms, there had not been very many poets who had been able to infuse "cry" and varied music into stanza-forms, and after him everything went to pieces except in the simplest shapes of ballad and carol. The intermediate Elizabethans, except Sackville, had to some extent restored regularity, but without acquiring charm, and with a rather limited amount of variety. Now all this was changed. From the great strophes or pseudo-strophes of Spenser's odes through the sonnet, the regular long-poem stanzas from the Spenserian to the quatrain, and the zigzag designs of lyric, complexity and variety of form and out-line were combined with adequacy of music. The octo-syllable, complete or catalectic, was restored and perfected ; the fourteener spirited up ; the Alexandrine attempted ; the great staple line, the decasyllable, fingered with a conjurer's prestidigitation into almost every conceivable contour and resonance. The possibilities were, of course, not nearly exhausted, for they are inexhaustible ; even the actual development of them was to be busily continued for another technical "generation." But the extent to which they were drawn upon, and the success of the drawings, are enormous and wonderful.

Only as to the couplet have some reservations, already hinted at, to be formulated a little more distinctly. It is largely and well practised ; as we have seen, one great authority is at least asserted to have declared for it in preference to all others ; and another seems to be in two minds about it—not quite to know what to think on that point. But, beyond all doubt, a certain difficulty has been created by the fact that its great exemplar, Chaucer, is an exemplar impossible to follow exactly. Although I do not agree (while mentioning them for all

honour) with those who hold that even Spenser confused
Chaucer's decasyllables with a kind of doggerel—although
I think that *Mother Hubberd's Tale* absolutely negatives
this,—yet I feel that in the uncertainty of the Elizabethan
grasp of the couplet—in the veering and yawing between
the stopped and enjambed forms which is the evident
result, not of a designed combination of the two, but of
an irresolute and unclear grasp of either—there is evidence
that the prosodic mind was not made up about it.   That
making up of the mind is exactly what we shall have to
survey in the next two Books.   But even here admirable
work was turned out, in the enjambed form especially ;
and not a little of the same combination of method and
music which we have been noticing in other measures
displays itself here also.

Lastly—for this chapter is in a sense more of an
instalment than most of our Interchapters, and it will
have to be supplemented in the next in regard to the
whole or major Elizabethan period—this special time
deserves the high credit of having been the first definitely
to enter upon the study as well as the practice, the apper-
ception as well as the perception, of prosody.   That any
great progress was made in this direction cannot indeed
be said.   It was practically impossible that there should
be any such as yet.   The famous bull about " these
roads before they were made " applies pretty exactly.
If the Elizabethan critics had seen the Elizabethan
poems before they were made, they might have had
a better chance of understanding and blessing the
makers.   They *did* see them to a certain extent in the
making, and did not wholly fail to bless.   But the
disadvantage of their position as compared, let us say,
with that of Aristotle, is obvious and undeniable.   Further,
they devoted themselves for the most part to other things
than pure prosodic study ; they committed themselves
to some heresies when they did attempt it ; and by far
the greater part of their labours in its province was
bestowed on the worst heresy of all.   Nor did any of
them, till Daniel, take the orthodox side in a distinct

and satisfactory fashion. But we have done our best to account for this, and the aberration has at worst the praise—not such a faint praise as may be thought—of having " got itself done."

For the rest, it was too early ; and the business of the time was not really criticism of any kind. The garden had to be cultivated ; and it was.

BOOK VI

LATER JACOBEAN AND CAROLINE POETRY

CHAPTER I

MILTON

THERE is no English writer on whose prosody so much in proportion has been written as on Milton's; and the reasons for this are sufficiently evident, though perhaps the strongest of all in reality is not so apparent as some others, and the most apparent of all is not the strongest. This last is the towering reputation of Milton as a poet; yet Shakespeare is in that respect even greater, and *in proportion* Shakespeare's prosody has received far less attention. But then it is a vast, and on some not uncommonly accepted theories of the subject, a rather hopeless example; while Milton's *looks* comparatively plain sailing. Further, there is an obvious and piquant contrast - progress of the sort which attracts study, in the poet's successive devotion to rhyme and solemnly proclaimed apostasy from it, and in the hardening and ossifying of the form of blank verse that he preferred.

Studies of Milton's prosody frequent.

Reasons for this.

207

Thirdly, there is the point—obvious again to everybody likely to take the slightest interest in the matter—that Milton is a " master of harmonies " such as we have had few.   But more really, though perhaps more secretly, potent than all these is the fact that he provides a great, and perhaps the last great, turning or settling point of English versification.   Chaucer brings to perfection, as far as his time allows, all or most of the scattered tentatives and experiments of the nonage.   Spenser, after Chaucer's garnerings have been mostly wasted, and when the conditions have been changed, repeats the process in a certain sense finally, but only to a limited extent, and with respect especially to the stricter stanza - forms. Shakespeare opens up the whole possibilities of blank verse in the direction of the utmost freedom, and illustrates the freer lyric to almost an equal extent.   But the freedom of blank verse turns to licence and slipshodness, and that of lyric to a certain taste for meticulous and petty prettiness.   Then comes Milton, and leaving in his earlier work a perpetual monument and model of verse that shall have all reasonable freedom but no mere looseness—of rhymed verse that shall employ rhyme with some of its cunningest and most perfect embellishments —takes non-dramatic blank verse in hand once for all, and introduces into it the order, proportion, and finish which dramatic blank verse had then lost, and which it has hardly since recovered.   The history is indeed not over : we shall have abundance of error and right-doing, of experiment bad and good, of new perfections and new shortcomings, to record.   But we shall come to no one— not Dryden nor Pope, not Coleridge nor Keats, not Tennyson nor Browning—who occupies, in regard to general prosody, the same position as these four poets, of whom we are now to deal with the last.   For the very reason, indicated above, of the pains that have been spent by others on the matter, the treatment will have to be rather more controversial than it has usually been ; but, for that very reason it is all the more desirable to stick to our method, and to begin with a rigidly historical account of the facts.

In the poet's earliest work — postponing the early The early sonnets for notice with their fellows—it is only by the minor pieces. operation of a common and not unamiable but very uncritical fallacy that specially "vital signs" can be detected. Any fairly clever boy of fifteen with a taste for poetry, and with the English poetry up to the date of the first - folio Shakespeare before him, might have written the two Psalm Paraphrases. The more ambitious "Death of a Fair Infant" two years later, does its Alexandrine-tipped rhyme-royal deftly enough, and has a forecast of the future in the use of the compound epithet, which, however, was common enough in Elizabethan poetry. The "Trivial Masque"—as one might call the "Vacation Exercise," if more people were likely to know what *trivium* means—shows a great advance in couplet verse on the Paraphrases and, just towards the close, holds out another promise — that of the faculty of dealing with proper names. Of the Hobson pieces we need say little : Milton's mirth was always rather dismal, prosodically and otherwise. There is greater merit in the "May Morning," but it is too short to found much on ; and though the "Shakespeare" lines have been rather unfairly accused of rhetoric, conceit, and even bombast—though one or two of them are really fine and have true prosodic throb in them [1]—they call for no stay.

It is far otherwise with "On the Morning of Christ's The *Nativity* Nativity"; and whatever may be the futility of the Hymn. unfavourable criticisms of this, they are at any rate not futile as showing that the critics have no ear for verse. It was written in 1629, when all the great Elizabethans proper were dead or soon to die, and before the wonderful parade and concert of Caroline bird-song and bird-feather had well begun. The opening stanzas of rhyme-royal, if not entirely consummate, have some-

---

[1] Especially
> Under a star-ypointing pyramid,

and
> Dear son of memory, great heir of fame,

where the position of the only polysyllable among the monosyllables is no novice's work.

thing individual in them, and at any rate show much
more prosodic accomplishment than their predecessors on
the " Fair Infant " four years earlier.   But when the
" Hymn " proper begins, where are the ears—or being
there, of what length can they be ?—that miss a wonderful
nativity—speaking with reverence—in the world of
prosody itself ?   The form [1] is 6, 6, 10, 6, 6, 10, 8, 12,
rhymed *aabccbdd.*   We have seen that constructions of
this kind had been common in the fourteenth-century
lyrics, and the fourteenth-fifteenth-century miracle-plays,
and that the Elizabethan poets, even before Spenser, but
much more after his example, had also been prone to
them.   It would merely take a certain amount of time
and trouble to determine whether the particular combination schematically exists before.   What I will undertake
to say, on my faith and function as a historian of prosody,
is that the prosodic turn given to the scheme does not.
The artist is young, and he makes a few slips.   His
occasional double rhymes—there are very few of them—
were better away, save perhaps in the last stanza ; but
this does no serious harm.   The atmosphere of almost
unearthly solemnity which, very mainly by pure prosodic
means, he has thrown over the whole is miraculous.
It cannot be an accident that almost without exception
(there are, in fact, only two, and these, " around " and
" amaze," are more apparent than real) the two opening
lines in each stanza end with a monosyllable, and the
proportion of the rise in line-length from 6, 10 to 8, 12,
which gives the main distinction from Drummond, is not
likely to be accidental either.   Trisyllabic feet are very

---

[1] There is something partly like it in Drummond's *Divine Poems*, but the
splendid *coda* of 8, 12, so cunningly appended, is wanting, and the rhyme-
order is very inferior.

> Amidst the azure clear
> Of Jordan's sacred streams,
> Jordan of Lebanon the offspring dear,
> Where Zephyrs flow'rs unclose
> And sun shines with new beams,
> With grave and stately grace a nymph arose.

Compare also Sir John Beaumont's *Ode of the Blessed Trinity.*

rare; the stately, almost awestruck, tone of the verse rejects them. The great Miltonic phrase, " that twice-battered God of Palestine," is with us already; but this is not strictly prosodic, though it is always a means in prosody's hand. The double epithet, which always neces-sarily affects the run of the line (from the fact that its syllables are closer knit than those of two words), and that " science of names " in which Milton has had no rival but Victor Hugo, and which is prosodic or nothing—these are with us too. And " everything goes in "—everything works together for a steady rise in each stanza, and from stanza to stanza through the whole poem—like volumes of incense rolling higher and higher.[1] It used to be a joke to compose fancy reviews, pooh-poohing great works in literature at their appearance. I am not in the least afraid of what I should have said of " On the Morning of Christ's Nativity " if, *per impossibile* in many ways, it had been sent me in a parcel at the beginning of 1630 for criticism.

Much less need be said of the other strictly minor poems. The " Marchioness of Winchester " epitaph goes with *L'Allegro* and *Il Penseroso*, for the metre of which it is a less perfect study. The very beautiful *Arcades* stands

The *Arcades*, etc.

---

[1] Well known as it all ought to be, one must beautify and sanctify the page with a couple of stanzas—

> The lonely mountains o'er,
> And the resounding shore.
> A voice of weeping heard and loud lament :
> From haunted spring and dale
> Edgèd with poplar pale,
> The parting Genius is with sighing sent.
> With flower-inwoven tresses torn,
> The Nymphs in twilight shade of tangled thickets mourn.
>
> In consecrated earth,
> And on the holy hearth,
> The Lars and Lemures moan with midnight plaint.
> In urns and altars round,
> A drear and dying sound
> Affrights the Flamens at their service quaint ;
> And the still marble seems to sweat,
> While each peculiar power forsakes his wonted seat.

§§ xx. and xxi., Globe ed. pp. 490, 491.

in something of the same relation to *Comus*, and shows, in more ways than one, Milton's study of Lyly and Peele. The solid part, as we may say, is decasyllabic couplet instead of blank verse, and makes one sorry that we have not more couplet from him ; and the two exquisite songs are quite Peelian-Shakespearian.   So, too, the prosodic forms of " At a Solemn Music," " Time," and " The Circumcision " are chiefly interesting to compare with the choruses of *Samson* long afterwards.   But none of these requires the individual attention which must be given to the octosyllables of *L'Allegro, Il Penseroso*, and *Comus* ; to the Sonnets ; to the unique form of *Lycidas* ; to the successive blank verse of *Comus, Paradise Lost, Paradise Regained*, and *Samson*, and to the already-mentioned choruses of this latter.[1]

The octo-syllabic group.   " Where on earth did you get that style ? " said the astonished Jeffrey to Macaulay in reference to his Essay

Note on   [1] There are some metrical experiments not elsewhere tried, and therefore
Translations.   of interest, in the Translations of the Psalms, which are a good deal later than the body of the minor poems, but earlier than the blank verse.   They do not, however, require any special notice.   It is otherwise with the famous version of the Pyrrha ode of Horace.   Milton himself tells us that this is rendered " almost word for word without rhyme, according to the Latin measure, as near as the language will permit."   Now this " Latin measure " is (and it must be remembered that Milton carefully subjoins the Latin text)—

> Quis multa gracilis te puer in rosa
> Perfusus liquidis urget odoribus
>   Grato, Pyrrha, sub antro ?
>   Cui flavam religas comam ?

And Milton Englishes—

> What slender youth, bedewed with liquid odours,
> Courts thee on roses in some pleasant cave,
>   Pyrrha ? For whom bindst thou
>   In wreaths thy golden hair ?

Now it would be quite a fair question, "If you think that Milton elsewhere used trisyllabic feet, how do you account for his *not* using them here, where they exist in the original to which he says he has kept "in measure as near as the language will permit"?   It is, I say, quite a fair question, but I am not careful to answer it.   Milton sees that the trisyllabic feet of the third and fourth line are only apparent and that the measure is throughout choriambic.   What *is* rather surprising is that he did not try whether his favourite combination of trochee and iambs could not be extended to suit it.   I think Milton's ear would always have protected him against the attempt to combine dactyls with iambs or spondees in English.   With trochees they go well enough.   (See below, note, p. 255.)

on Milton. Nobody need have asked the same question of Milton himself as to the prosodic style of *L'Allegro, Il Penseroso,* and the lyrical parts of *Comus,* with its essay-pieces in the " Marchioness of Winchester " epitaph, and the *Arcades.* It is probable that Milton had no small knowledge of the octosyllable-heptasyllable, which had been almost the earliest and quite the most constant form of English metre. We know that he knew Chaucer ; there can be no reasonable doubt that he knew Gower and Lydgate ; and it would be odd if, when his " younger feet wandered " in that maze of romance [1] of which they never wholly forgot the blessed secrets, he had not even further extended his knowledge of this, *the* metre (with the romance-six) of the English versions. But his immediate creditor, though more modern, was far more illustrious, for it was nobody less than Shakespeare himself. It might not be fair—though I have no doubt about the matter myself—to allege the " cat with eyes of coal " passage in *Pericles,* which is prosodically indistinguishable from some of the best of the twin character-poems ; but it is also not in the least needful. As early as *A Midsummer Night's Dream* (if not earlier), in the opening fairy verses of the Second Act, this tripping measure—which pirouettes on either foot, iamb or trochee, with equal ease, and " twinkles interchange " of the two with almost bewildering but never-failing accuracy and intricacy combined—is one of Shakespeare's favourite woodnotes ; it recurs through this play, and in many others. Here Milton had nothing to reinforce, to reform, or to improve. He had merely to catch the key-note [2] and carry it out with such variation of his own as he might, with such perfection as he could.

Of the perfection there has rarely been any doubt.

---

[1] It may be just worth while to remind the reader that a long rhyme-royal poem on Guy of Warwick by John Lane, a friend of Milton's father, actually exists in MS. with a commendatory sonnet by the elder Milton himself. See Mr. Ward's *Catalogue of Romances in the MS. Department of the British Museum,* i. 497 (London, 1883).

[2] Some will have it that he caught it from or through Fletcher. But this is not a study of all Milton's possible sources or teachers. Shakespeare was quite enough for him, as for Fletcher himself.

Even Johnson could find no fault with the two main instances, though he probably did not like the admixture of the mode in *Comus* ; and it was reserved for the duller pedantry of John Scott of Amwell, and Vicesimus Knox, in the darkest dark of neo-classic night before the dawn Romantic, to fall foul of it.   But *they* are hardly important enough to give any valid answer to a *Quis vituperavit ?* The ear which cannot hear the music of *L'Allegro* and *Il Penseroso*, or of the even greater and certainly not less sweet close of *Comus*, must be deaf alike to the harp of Ariel and the lute of Apollo.

For variation or idiosyncrasy there was rather less room.   Shakespeare had only used the form incidentally, but he had used it not infrequently ; it is not a form of the widest range in itself, and Shakespeare (as has been remarked more than once already) had a knack of leaving very few " numbers to fulfil " for those who came after him.   Yet Milton has done a good deal, not merely by his subtle power of fingering, so as to vary scheme with theme, but also by bringing to the service of the verse those two great instruments of his own unique phrase and of the proper name.   The latter, though used with some freedom, achieves less astounding effects than in *Lycidas* and in the *Paradises*, simply because the shorter and lighter lines do not require, or indeed admit of it ; but the former is pushed to almost its possible furthest. The famous " light fantastic toe " (the metre itself) is an instance, and an obvious one : but I do not know that it is so wonderful as the selection, for its particular place and service, of such a word as " dappled," where the darker and lighter spots or streaks of the dawn are actually represented ʼby the trochaic rhythm.   Very noticeable, too, is the fashion in which the graver effect in *Il Penseroso* is attained by the use of feet which are practically spondees.   Milton, it was observed at the beginning, is perhaps the first English non-dramatic poet who uses the spondee much, and he certainly makes the most of it in such instances as the magnificent

Or that *starr'd E*thiop Queen that strove ;

while it is particularly noticeable that he scarcely ever—
I think never—clogs the trochaically cadenced lines with
these feet, but keeps them for double-shotting the pure
iambics. Not very much can be done with pause in this
short line ; but what can be, Milton does. And just in
passing, he writes that famous verse—one of his own
finest and one of the finest in English poetry, though
later ears have come to dislike the valued "ĭ-ōn "—

The Chérub Cóntempláti̇ón,

to be in future days at once a choke-pear and a stumbling-
block to Dr. Guest, and to show how absolutely wrong
that excellent scholar's general theories are.[1]

The sonnet is a very much more artificial-looking The Sonnets.
form than the octosyllable ; and Milton, since we have
abandoned Johnson's point of view, has been generally
held to be one of our most "artific*ious*" practitioners of
it. I am myself sorry that he reverted to the Petrarchian
scheme ; but it is not surprising, from his fondness for
Italian, and it may perhaps be admitted that the subjects
of nearly all his pieces invite if they do not exclusively
demand it. For the sonnet passionate or the sonnet
meditative the English form is at least the equal of the
Italian ; but for sonnets descriptive, sonnets of address
to persons, and the like, it is perhaps less good. In the
former cases the final couplet clenches ; in the latter the
final tercet softens the close—flourishes it off, as it were.
The fanatics of division and of rule generally, may be
shocked at the " Nightingale " for splitting itself absolutely
in sense and sound at the middle of the seventh line.[2]
Our side will simply say, "Why not ? " But nobody, I
suppose, putting some ugly rhyme aside, will question
the majesty of the " Three-and-Twentieth Year," though
that majesty may seem already to carry with it a certain
stiffness—a *castiliano* which is too likely to become *vulgo*.
" Captain or Colonel " is prosodically noteworthy, not

[1] Ed. Skeat, p. 184. It will be better discussed when we come to Guest
himself.
[2] Compare the "double rhyme-royal " noticed at vol. i. p. 308.

only for the extreme beauty of its close and (less favourably) for the dysphony of line six—

> That *call fame* on such gentle acts as these,

where the spondaic effect could be dispensed with, as it could not in

> Whatever clime the *sun's bright* circle warms—

but for the fact that the beauty of the sixain is largely due to three or even four trisyllabic feet—" Ema|thian con|queror "; " tem|ple and tower "; and " the Athen|ian walls." Of course, the people who believe in elision, and especially in Miltonic elision, will cry " I object ! " here. But they cannot steal the syllables from me, if they can from themselves. *Securus scando.*

So is it with " Pi|ty and ruth " and " thy o|dorous lamp " in the " Virtuous Young Lady," which is also noticeable (though scarcely more so than all these sonnets) for the very great part which the pause plays in it. Hardly in *Paradise Lost* itself does Milton use this pedal action more powerfully. In the " Lady Margaret " I believe the persons just referred to scan " fa|tal to lib|erty " " fat'l to "; but as this is a collocation of sounds which my tongue cannot express, and my ear rejects with horror, I prefer the fact to the non-fact. One need say nothing on the first " Tetrachordon " piece, except that the people who seriously rebuke Milton for splitting Mile-End between two lines seem to show that there is an absence of humour more absolute even than his own. The second must always live, in minds that care for verse, by the gorgeous line—

> Which after held the Sun and Moon in fee.

But the " New Forcers " might pair off with " Tetrachordon I." if it were not for the interesting prosodic experiment of the " tailed " sonnet. I wish I knew whether Milton did this, as he did the rhyme-split in the other, with burlesque intent ;[1] or whether it was, if

---

[1] The Italians undoubtedly did, and do, this ; see, for instance, Carducci's delightful " Pietro Fanfani e le postille," which the soul of Catullus must have chuckled at and applauded. And some precisions of "kind" would associate it especially with offensive or satiric, not merely burlesque, purpose.

perhaps only in part, a genuine experiment in a form more spacious than the quatorzain. At any rate, I rather wonder why more poets have not followed it from this latter point of view. The thing is obviously close to the old long stanzas with " bob and wheel "—things so thoroughly English that they deserved resuscitation.

The beautiful " Lawes " sonnet is doubly and trebly ours. For it shows us that Milton did not confuse musical and poetical music as so many have done and do ; that he recognised " short and long " as the capital prosodic terms, and that he objected, as all good poets have objected, to the neglect of these by composers. As for " committing," it has, I believe, been differently interpreted, but the sense seems to me not in the least ambiguous. There is, however, a prosodic side to the device adopted (of course from the Italians) by Milton, and copied almost *ad nauseam* by his followers, of beginning the sonnet with an appellative, " Harry," " Cromwell," " Fairfax," " Vane,"etc. It has, of course, a certain *arresting* effect ; and as you are not supposed to read more than one of the sonnets at once, the objection that it gets monotonous and tricky is not wholly valid. But, to my taste at least, it gives the sonnet rather too much of declamatory tone, and interrupts the steady rise which the trisyllabic metrical clause of Shakespeare (*v. sup*. p. 60) so admirably achieves. In all of these, however, those prosodic " rosin-secrets " of Milton's which have been already referred to appear, and especially his hardly excelled power of knitting the whole of a verse-paragraph into one by variation of pause and weight. To Milton, indeed, the sonnet is not much more than a form of verse-paragraph ; and (*valeat quantum*) this peculiarity, in which he is followed by Wordsworth, seems to me to put him, as a sonnetteer, not merely below Shakespeare but below Keats and Rossetti. The magnificence, however, prosodic as other, of the " Piedmont " piece is undeniable ; and though its end is weak poetically and logically, " Babylonian " saves it from the point of view of prosody, while it damns it from others. As for " On his Blindness," not only sorrows but admirations are silent when they reach a certain magnitude. It could not be better ; and it is really curious that, different as are the schemes, it is the most Shakespearian of all. Nor are the succeeding four much inferior. But the quality of the prosody in all may (without offence meant) be characterised as tending towards the rhetorical. *Here* one understands, even when one does not share, Johnson's suspicion, in another division, of the " periods of the de-claimer " as intruders into verse.[1]

Lycidas.   The opinion of the same great but strongly " condi-tioned " critic on *Lycidas* is one of the best-known things relating to prosody.[2] It is as certain as anything involving a point of taste can be, that that opinion was wrong ; it is equally certain that the fault lay in the critic's premises, not in his reasoning. If extremely regular verse, with rhymes even more regular still, is the best kind of verse— a kind from which everything else is a falling short ; much more, if this is the *only* kind of verse that is much worth aiming at,—then Johnson's unfavourable judgment on the versification of *Lycidas* is justified in every detail. If, however, any such standard as this is a fond thing vainly invented ; if regular verse and regular rhyme are good things in their way, but " irregular " verse and " irregular " rhymes good things in another, and sometimes an even better way,—then the judgment may be " antiquated." And, not in the least by childish exaggeration and con-tradiction, but in strict accordance with the principles and the observed results of this whole inquiry, we may be able to find cause for pronouncing *Lycidas* prosodically one of the very masterpieces of English poetry, displaying

[1] May I make a little excursion-protest against the interpretation of " spare to interpose " in the Lawes sonnet as equivalent to "refrain from interposing"? It is against the tenor not merely of the sonnet itself, but of the Cyriac one. Moreover, Milton knew his Shakespeare too well not to remember—

> If Clifford cannot *spare* his friends a curse,

and meant, I feel sure, " Spare *time* to interpose them oft." Why not let him be a good fellow, on the not too frequent possibilities ?

[2] It is not, however, one always exactly quoted. The actual words in the *Life* are : " *Lycidas* : of which the diction is harsh, the rhymes uncertain, and the numbers unpleasing." Perhaps I should add that I take *Lycidas* before *Comus*, partly because of its brevity, and partly to get the blank verse together.

a virtuosity at once in diction, numbers, and rhyme hardly paralleled elsewhere, and yet converting this from *mere* virtuosity — from pretentious and elaborate art — into something more like actual nature, in its unforced and ripened mellowness.

The term Monody, which Milton himself applies to this poem, has two senses in Greek; and it is probable that the poet intended to adopt both. One concerns form, and denotes a solo-piece as opposed to the combined choric ode ; the other concerns matter, and is equivalent by customary restriction to "lament" or "dirge." That Milton had the actual choruses of Greek tragedy in his mind there can be no doubt ; but he is certain also to have had before him the less rigidly concerted odes of various English predecessors, specially those two great ones of his master Spenser, to which we have tried to do justice in their place.[1] From these two modes, however, though passages of the three poems possess a not dissimilar rhythmical arrangement, he parted in the first instance by making his stanzas much less uniform. Spenser had adopted stanza-forms so long that they would hardly strike the ear as stanzas had it not been for the refrains which tip and outline them, but of pretty uniform length— eighteen lines throughout the *Prothalamion* and at the beginning and end of the *Epithalamion*, nineteen in the body of the latter. Milton discards the refrain altogether ; and attempting no uniform stanza-length at all,[2] converts the stanzas (for stanzas they still are after a fashion) into something once more like his beloved verse-paragraph— definitely finished, and corresponding to others like a paragraph of prose, but, like prose paragraphs themselves, acknowledging no obligation of corresponding length. Again, he uses that not infrequent *shortening* of the line which is indispensable to verse that is to have the choric

Originality of
its form.

---

[1] The *Prothalamion* and *Epithalamion* ; *v. sup.* i. 362.

[2] Thereby, no doubt, aggravating his "uncertainty" and "unpleasingness" in Johnson's eyes ; though the Doctor and his sect did not love even regular stanzas. Of course, Milton had the *canzone* in mind more or less directly. I need hardly keep the warning bell of "Italian" constantly ringing in regard to him. But the *canzone* is regular.

or odic effect ; but he uses it less frequently than Spenser and with very much less regularity. (Still, his most audacious and most successful innovation is in regard to the rhyme ; and there can be no doubt that it was this which most annoyed Johnson's ear, accustomed and enslaved as it was to the clock-tick of the couplet. Spenser intertwines his rhymes, of course, but he does it with considerable, if not with absolute regularity, on the ordinary stanza-plan ; though the great range of his model to some extent disguises this regularity. But Milton does not merely not attempt — it is quite clear that he deliberately eschews—a regular rhyme-scheme of any kind. He will suit his rhyme to the exigences of his individual paragraph, and to nothing else.

Thus we have a first paragraph of fourteen lines, all of five feet, except line 4, which is of three only, but rhymed *oabbaacdacdaoa*,[1] where two of the lines are blanks ; and there are only five rhymes altogether, but one of these occurs no less than six times. Now, Spenser, in his eighteen- or nineteen-line stanzas, had usually had at least eight rhymes, and had never repeated any more than four times.

Milton's second paragraph-stanza is much shorter, but more varied in line-length, consisting of eight lines, 10, 10, 10, 10, 6, 10, 6, 10, rhymed *oaabbcco*, or of two blank-verse lines enclosing (as it were) three couplets. The third discards the blank first line altogether ; and of its lines—fourteen once more—only one is not five-foot, and that is one of Milton's favourite catalectic octosyllables of optionally trochaic rhythm, though it *may* be taken as three feet only, and iambic. The rhymes are *aabcbcddeffegg*, a concerted effect approaching nearer to Spenser than the two others. The mere skeleton analysis of the rest, though of considerable importance except to "ignorant impatience," may be relegated to a note.[2] The poem

---

[1] I may remind the reader that I use *o* for a non-corresponding end-syllable. Two or more *o*'s do not rhyme to each other or to anything else.

[2] Fourth, thirteen lines—10, 10, 10, 10, 6, 10, 6, 10, 10, 10, 10, 6, 10 ; rhymed *abcabddefegfg*.

Fifth, fourteen lines—all tens but l. 7, which is a six ; *aoabbccdedfefe*.

ends with its first regular "stanza"—an octave of even decasyllables rhymed *abababcc*. But no two others are alike in length, line-composition, or rhyme-arrangement.

Thus the first, and perhaps the last, impression pro- Rationale of duced by the poem is that of the extremest prosodic the system. variety; and it may very well be that Johnson failed entirely to catch the *symphonic* effect which this variety admits and, in fact, produces.) It is not quite certain that everybody sees it now; but there is no doubt about it; and this symphonic effect is very mainly produced by the uncertainty of the rhymes themselves. With stanzas of regular length, and regularly rhymed, the individual stanza is what chiefly takes the attention; and when it is mastered, there is mere repetition. Here the attention, aroused at first by the failure of the rhyme—it was probably for this reason that Milton left *both* the opening lines of the first two stanzas blank—is reassured by the prompt appearance of it, and yet warned by the irregularity of that appearance that it must not go to sleep. The frequent but spasmodic occurrence of the *a* rhyme in Stanza One clenches this appeal, this satisfaction, and this warning at once. Never till the end—when the regular octave is probably intended to have something like the effect of the Shakespearian end-couplet to a blank-verse *tirade*—is the interest of uncertainty and chance allowed to drop; seldom is expectation defrauded by blank lines; and yet the evident possibility of these heightens the pleasure of the ear when the rhyme comes. Besides this, the recurrence has a *knitting* effect within the paragraph, while its disappearance marks the paragraph close. That this would be a very dangerous—indeed, an almost hopeless—game for any one but an exceptional master of

Sixth, twenty-one lines—all tens but the six at l. 16 ; *abccbadededfdfgghhoii*.

Seventh, eighteen lines—10, 10, 10, 6, 10, 6, 10, 10, 10, 10, 7, 10, 10, 10, 10, 10, 10, 10 ; *ababccoodeedfgfhhg*.

Eighth, twenty-nine lines—all tens except the sixth, which is six ; rhymed *abbabacddcdcecffefgh₆ihihihjj*.

Ninth, thirty-three lines—all tens except six at l. 14 ; rhymed *ababbccdeedf-ggfijijklklmlnmnpopgg*.

Tenth, twenty-one lines—all tens ; *ababbaccdedeffgfghhii*.

Eleventh, or *coda*, described in text.

harmonies to play, hardly needs insisting on.   It is a sort of game of Japanese butterflies—things which the conjurer casts into the air to flit and flutter among themselves, till it is time for them to float down and settle.   And to effect it, he has to resort to every minor device of pause and line-weighting and lightening, quickening or slacking off, with all the science of names and words that he can muster.   " Everything [once more] goes in " ; his beloved Chaucerian trick of putting one epithet before and one after the noun, which inevitably " holds up " the phrase ; the more curious but certain arrangement of a pair of epithetted nouns, where in one case the noun is mono-syllabic and the epithet dissyllabic, and in the other the values change over.   Of the names themselves, probably the greatest instance, even in Milton, occurs, as does the device just mentioned, in the famous lines—

> Sleep'st by the fable of *Bellerus* old,
> Where the *great vision* of the *guarded Mount*
> Looks towards *Namancos* and *Bayona's* hold.

I always wish Dionysius and Longinus could have known —as indeed they may know—this incomparable illustration of their joint doctrine of the " beautiful word." [1]

It must be evident to any one who reads *Lycidas* carefully, that it is in effect a piece of blank verse carefully equipped with rhyme, for the purpose, technically speaking, of providing it with a lyric vehicle.   The pause-arrangement is quite that of blank verse, modified a little by the fact of the rhyme, which relieves pause of some of the duties that fall upon it in pure blanks.   His system, moreover, has freed the poet, almost automatically, from the tendency to adopt the stopped Marlowesque line-form which, as we shall see, is so frequent in *Comus*, and he stops or enjambs as he pleases ; in fact, there are things in *Lycidas* not unsuggestive of the enjambed couplet which the author's contemporaries were abusing and to abuse. Spondees are not infrequent and very effective, as in

---

[1] It is all the more interesting that, as we know from the Cambridge MS., Milton first used " Corineus," and then substituted the far more obscure, but in the place far more euphonious, " Bellerus."

> Together both ere the *high lawns* appeared,

and the perhaps more doubtful one in

> Battening our flocks with the *fresh dews* of night,

and the certain one, again, of

> Set off to the world, nor in *broad ru*mour lies.

This last might introduce us to a still thornier point—of which I shall not attempt to grapple with all the thorns till presently—the trisyllabic feet of the piece. Once more, I have not been furnished by nature with the organs of speech needful for the pronunciation "thwrld" in any fashion that is not extremely ugly to the other organs of hearing with which nature *has* provided me ; while the natural "to the world" appears to me to add a singular charm to the line, and to contrast, in specially appropriate fashion, with the subsequent spondee itself. So, too, I have no doubt about

> Shatter your leaves before the mel|lowing year,

or "melodious tear," or "battening" in the line quoted above, or about "watery bier" and "westering wheel," or "the hideous roar."

But there is in *Lycidas* one trisyllabic foot which one might have thought indisputable by any one, and that is to be found in

> O foun*tain Are*thuse, and thou honoured flood ;

for Milton was about the last person to take liberties with a word sacred alike in classic legend and prosody. Nor do I think him likely to have called Virgil's Mincius "Minshus".; the loss of "reckoning" in St. Peter's speech would be grievous ; and it is strange that there should be, as no doubt there are, people who prefer

> And ev'ry flow'r that sad embroid'ry wears,

with its eighteenth-century snipsnap, to the winding sweetness of

> And every flower that sad embroidery wears,

or would rather force " loryate " in the place of " laureate " three lines lower, or would throw away the beauty of "perilous" before " flood " in the last line before the *coda*. So, too, those who like "thuncouth " or " thoaks " must, I suppose, have one or the other. As for me and my house, we will neither of them.[1]

The blank verse.   It is, however, beyond all question, on Milton's blank verse itself that the main attention of any student of his period must be concentrated. Indeed, that prosody, in this particular respect, is, as was remarked above, almost the only instance in which the versification of any English author has been seriously subjected to serious examination, for a long space of time, and from very different points of systematic view. This is natural enough when we remember the almost instantaneous position which Milton attained, the way in which dictators of literature like Addison and Johnson devoted themselves to him, and, above all, the fact that he was the first to establish this peculiarly English form of metre in non-dramatic poetry. Some readers would perhaps wish to have a sketch of the views which have thus come into being as an opening of the inquiry ; but I prefer, as usual, to let Milton himself speak before seeing what other people have said about him. And in most cases even this must wait till we come to themselves, lest we disturb what is almost as important to us as the history of prosody itself, the history of prosodic opinion.

The documents of the inquiry are, as everybody knows, four, but may perhaps be taken as presenting three rather than four stages of development and attitude. *Comus* unquestionably represents the poet's youth and

---

[1] I must take leave to postpone the consideration of the demur—" But it is *not* proposed to drop the *pronunciation* of elided syllables." It may perhaps be asked, " Does not the Cambridge autograph settle this matter?" No, it does not. " Imbroidrie " is indeed written there ; but " livery " appears in the alternative line for exactly the same prosodic value. So earlier, l. 12, " watrie," but l. 29, "glistering." In all these four cases the presence or absence of the *e* makes a trisyllabic or a dissyllabic foot as the case may be ; and the MS. is as obstinately yea-nay as if it were a counsellor of Panurge.

early manhood in life and literature at once ; *Paradise Regained* and *Samson Agonistes*, his age. The verse of *Paradise Lost*, published not long before the latest two, represents either successive stages, or the result of successive stages, extending over some twenty years at least. Further (to get all the facts into order and position, however well they be known), the first and the last of these documents, *Comus* and *Samson*, are in dramatic form, the *Paradises* in narrative.

The kinds of drama to which the two plays belong are not quite irrelevant to the inquiry ; but they may be considered too curiously. *Comus* gives itself out as a *Comus.* "Masque," and though specialists have, in their usual way, quarrelled about its title to the title, the plain man will not imitate them. *Comus* is a masque, because its author called (or let call) it so ;[1] because it was written to be acted by amateurs ; because it has more of the supernatural in it than ordinary plays even at that time admitted ; because it is evidently intended for music ; and because there is large spectacle and decoration in it. But it admits also much more regular dialogue, and rather more coherent plot, than the usual masque does ; and if things had so been that it had been written now, its author would probably have called it " a Lyrical Drama." Further yet, it is clear that the writer has immediately before him such things of Shakespeare's as *A Midsummer Night's Dream* and *The Tempest*, but that he is also paying special attention to the University Wits, and has not exactly cleared his prosodic mind of the mixed impressions derived from these studies. Lastly, he is full of the Greek drama, as well as of the English. Peele and Shakespeare, Marlowe and Euripides, however " confusedly " (to adopt the Shakespearian word), are before his eyes as the inspirers of his *mimesis*. The *Old Wives' Tale* is actually in some sort, though not to any great extent, his canvas. The Attendant Spirit is a

---

[1] In fact, as ought to be well known, he never, so far as we know, himself called it anything else, *Comus* itself being a later label for distinction's sake.

middle-aged and sedater Ariel, a Puck turned serious.
" Divine philosophy " gives us a sort of assonanced echo
of Tamburlaine's "divine Zenocrate" in one line, and
" musical as is Apollo's lute " walks, dropping the adjective
" bright," straight out of *Love's Labour's Lost* in the next
but one ; while Comus and the Lady "knap verses"
with each other in the truest style of Greek *stichomythia.*
The poet has in one place not shaken off "Ens and the
Predicaments," and is didactic in a way which would
have made Aristotle class him with Empedocles as
doubtfully a poet, and Quintilian put him in the "middle"
division.   Elsewhere he is altogether run off with by his
own descriptive exuberance, and may well release his
captor from all damages *de raptu suo.*   It is no wonder
that pedants of the parallel-passage, pedants of kind,
pedants of all sorts, have more or less shaken their
heads over *Comus* : while those who care for poetry,
and for poetry only, have sometimes been profane
enough to think that he never did anything much more
poetical.

The "confusedness," however, and the multiplicity of
aim and pattern certainly reflect themselves in the blank
verse.   The lyrics show nothing similar : there he had
already mastered his instrument ; it had, in fact, been
mastered for him and before him.   Here he had not
mastered it, and, except Shakespeare in rather different
conditions, nobody had.   The consequence is that the
✓ blank verse of *Comus* is obviously and multifariously
experimental.   The opening block of seventeen lines [1] is

---

[1] Before the starry threshold of Jove's court
  My mansion is, where those immortal shapes
  Of bright aerial spirits live insphered
  In regions mild of calm and serene air,
  Above the smoke and stir of this dim spot
  Which men call Earth, and, with low-thoughted care,
  Confined and pestered in this pinfold here,
  Strive to keep up a frail and feverish being,
  Unmindful of the crown that Virtue gives,
  After this mortal change, to her true servants
  Amongst the enthroned gods on sainted seats.
  Yet some there be that by due steps aspire
  To lay their just hands on that golden key

very carefully and regularly written ; but it is noteworthy
that it has not the paragraph effect at all—that the
lines, though not exactly stopped, have something of the
old bullet-mould model, and that twice the poet runs
perilously close to rhyme—"care " and " here," still more
" key " and " Eternity." [1]   In the second he warms to his
work : the pauses are more varied and the lines more broken
and vari-cadenced, while the paragraph effect, if not fully,
is nearly achieved.   In both these he allows himself the
redundant syllable ; though those who think he called
peril " per'r'r'l " may deny this.   The third and longest
still more acquires *vires eundo* ; and here there are two
striking licences clearly intended to subserve variety and
symphonic effect.   The first of these is the famous line—

> To quench the drouth of Phœbus, which as they taste,

where I should unhesitatingly make the last foot an
anapæst, where those who believe in the amphibrach
would of course bring the longest foot into the fourth
place, and where others would resort to one of their acts
of prosodic *escamotage* with an extrametrical syllable at a
cæsura.   The second is—

> Soon as the potion works, their human count'nance,

where I should (having been taught to distrust " apostrophation " by much study of seventeenth-century
originals) as unhesitatingly restore the *e* and make a very
effective Alexandrine (*v. inf.*).
      The lyrical entry of Comus himself indulges in a
little decasyllabic couplet ; and at the half-tempting,

> That opes the palace of eternity.
> To such my errand is ; and, but for such,
> I would not soil these pure ambrosial weeds
> With the rank vapours of this sin-worn mould.

It may be worth observing that in the Cambridge MS. there is a long
insertion (14 lines after l. 4), beautiful in itself, but even less paragraphic
in effect. I daresay some readers would like more reference to these
variants, but I must once more plead that I am writing three volumes, not
thirty.

[1] The blank-verse Italians have often done this ; in fact, it is excessively
difficult to prevent in Italian. In English non-dramatic blank verse it is
nearly fatal ; but that would only be found out in practice.

half-inconvenient approach of the Lady he breaks off into blanks again. They have more of the *spoken* character—that is to say, more of the strictly conversational—than the overture of the Spirit, which, naturally enough, is somewhat Senecan and declamatory. And this reappears, for all its beauty, in the long soliloquy of the Lady herself. But that soliloquy shows increasing signs of the period- and paragraph-" fingering," which is to be ubiquitous in *Paradise Lost.* Indeed, Milton has seldom given us a more accomplished verse-period than that (171–177) from

Methought it was the sound

to

And thank the gods amiss.[1]

At line 192 we have what is to me once more a pretty certain Alexandrine, such as Milton could find dozens and scores of in Shakespeare—

Is not the labour of my thoughts.   'Tis likeliest,

though no doubt some people may crumple and gobble up the end into a mere redundancy, just as in 217 they may spoil a striking phrase of the Lady—

That He, the Supreme Good, *to whom* all things ill,

by slurring it into " twom." It is to be observed that the redundant syllable is here, and continues to be, very prevalent, Milton taking his latest Shakespearian model —that of *The Tempest.*

In the speech of Comus which follows the exquisite song " Sweet Echo," the last half-dozen lines addressed to the Lady[2] are probably intended (she seems to imply

---

[1]   Methought it was the sound
Of riot and ill-managed merriment,
Such as the jocund flute or gamesome pipe
Stirs up among the loose unlettered hinds,
When, for their teeming flocks and granges full,
In wanton dance they praise the bounteous Pan,
And thank the gods amiss.

[2] But such a sacred and home-felt delight,
Such sober certainty of waking bliss,
I never heard till now.   I'll speak to her,

her sense of it in her answer) to bear a rhetorical cast of
verse, and the final spondees, "Blest song" and "Tall
wood," especially the latter, must have been designed to
impart what the Greeks called ὄγκος—stateliness and
pomp,—while the *stichomythia* that follows cannot escape
—it never does escape in Greek or English where the
lines are not enjambed—a rather ludicrous single-stick
effect.[1]   In fact, Milton has, probably of purpose, made
the enchanter's versification rather ostentatiously artificial.
But still it is of a fairly accomplished and late character,
suggesting (what is perhaps an exact enough description
of it) an attempt to write *Tempest* verse by a person who
has almost all the gifts, but not quite all the graces,
required.

It is all the more interesting to find the next scene
relapsing into a kind of verse twenty or thirty years older.
Lines 331-7 [2] are quite early Shakespeare, if not even
Marlowe — *Titus Andronicus*, if not *Tamburlaine*,—and

And she shall be my queen.—Hail, foreign wonder!
Whom certain these rough shades did never breed,
Unless the goddess that in rural shrine
Dwell'st here with Pan or Sylvan, by blest song
Forbidding every bleak unkindly fog
To touch the prosperous growth of this tall wood.

[1] *Comus.*   What chance, good Lady, hath bereft you thus?
Lady.   Dim darkness and this leavy labyrinth.
Comus.   Could that divide you from near-ushering guides?
Lady.   They left me weary on a grassy turf.
Comus.   By falsehood, or discourtesy, or why?
Lady.   To seek i' the valley some cool friendly spring.
Comus.   And left your fair side all unguarded, Lady?
Lady.   They were but twain, and purposed quick return.
Comus.   Perhaps forestalling night prevented them.
Lady.   How easy my misfortune is to hit!
Comus.   Imports their loss, beside the present need?
Lady.   No less than if I should my brothers lose.
Comus.   Were they of manly prime, or youthful bloom?
Lady.   As smooth as Hebe's their unrazored lips.

[2] *Eld. Bro.*   Unmuffle, ye faint stars; and thou, fair moon,
That wont'st to love the traveller's benison,
Stoop thy pale visage through an amber cloud,
And disinherit Chaos, that reigns here
In double night of darkness and of shades;
Or, if your influence be quite dammed up
With black usurping mists . . .

though there is plenty of overrunning in sense, the two Brothers throughout indulge in little but the cumulative fashion of verse in sound. Sometimes blocks of the different kinds come together most curiously, as, for instance, 428-440 contrasted with 441-446, and this latter again with 456-463.[1]

For the drop into couplets of 495-512 I do not think it necessary to seek any further explanation than that Milton found plenty of such drops in Shakespeare, and followed the example. They could not be bad, being his ; but, like all his few other examples, they show clearly why he never much affected the form. This, I think, we may explain by the observation that the couplet did not give him that variety of sound which he managed so exquisitely in irregularly rhymed lyric of various line-lengths, and that his mind was too orderly and logical to use rhyme, as his contemporary, Chamberlayne, did, for a mere running accompaniment to para-

---

[1] Yea, there where very desolation dwells,
By grots and caverns shagged with horrid shades,
She may pass on with unblenched majesty,
Be it not done in pride, or in presumption.
Some say no evil thing that walks by night,
In fog or fire, by lake or moorish fen,
Blue meagre hag, or stubborn unlaid ghost,
That breaks his magic chains at curfew time,
No goblin or swart faery of the mine,
Hath hurtful power o'er true virginity.
Do ye believe me yet, or shall I call
Antiquity from the old schools of Greece
To testify the arms of chastity?

Hence had the huntress Dian her dread bow,
Fair silver-shafted queen for ever chaste,
Wherewith she tamed the brinded lioness
And spotted mountain-pard, but set at nought
The frivolous bolt of Cupid ; gods and men
Feared her stern frown, and she was queen o' the woods.

. . . .

Driving far off each thing of sin and guilt,
And in clear dream and solemn vision
Tell her of things that no gross ear can hear :
Till oft converse with heavenly habitants
Begin to cast a beam on the outward shape,
The unpolluted temple of the mind,
And turns it by degrees to the soul's essence,
Till all be made immortal. But, when lust . . .

graphs constructed on the blank-verse model. At any rate, he returns at once to "blanks" when the Spirit begins a serious tirade in description of Comus and his rout, and gives one of the longest and finest stretches of it that we have yet had. The type is here not cumulative merely, but thoroughly interwoven, with plentiful diversities of redundance, trisyllables, and the like. The last-named lubricant, too, appears in the otherwise rather stiffened verse of the Elder Brother's speech, inspirited as usual by touches of passion, as in—

> And earth's base built on stub|ble.   But come, | let's on
>
> But for that damned Magi|cian, let him | be girt
>
> Harpies and Hydras, or all the monstrous forms,

in each of which I do not blink, but invite attention to the presence of the trisyllable at a cæsura.[1] Note too the broken Alexandrine—

> As to make this relation ?
>   Care and utmost shifts,

which, *as an Alexandrine,* I defy any one who goes about to break.

In line 633 we have one of those experiments—almost inevitable when experiment is once tried—which are not so successful as others—

> Bore a bright golden flower, but not | in this soil.

As in other instances, some people, I believe, manage to persuade themselves that this is harmony.[2] I cannot be quite so complaisant. You cannot get "flower, but" into one foot of any kind without extreme jumbling and cacophony ; and if you make the fifth foot "in this soil," you are burdened with a redundant syllable of much too

---

[1] *V. sup.* p. 53.

[2] It is also commonly set down as a "Fletcherism." Milton was undoubtedly much influenced by more than one of the Fletcher family, but I cannot think this awkward end-stumble one of the happiest instances. *V. inf.* on B. and F. themselves.

great weight and bulk, making a sort of spondaic ending,[1] which contrasts most unfortunately with the really and accurately spondaic ending of the very next line—

> Unknown and like esteemed ; and the dull swain.

But though I am sure that there is something wrong in a prosodic system which fails to justify, much more in one which condemns, a beautiful line, I think it absurd that any system should be called upon to beautify an ugly one ; and, further, I should regard it as strange if Milton, at the early period of his career especially, made no ugly ones. I think he has made one here.

The anapæstic last foot of 662, on the other hand—

> Root-bound, that fled Apollo.
> *Lady.*   Fool, | do not boast,

is thoroughly well in place ; and 723 offers a pretty puzzle for prudish prosodists—

> The All-giver would be unthanked, would be unpraised.

We scan it, of course, as it is printed, and make a beautiful line of it, as suitable to Comus' rapid and fantastic sophistry as anything could be. *They*, I suppose, make it—

> Th' All-giver 'd be unthanked, would be unpraised,

or

> Th' All-giver would b' unthanked, would be unpraised—

where either alternative, it may be observed, is forced in one case to break the rule which it enforces in the other, and " b' unpraised " has still to be provided for.

So also the splendid Alexandrine—

> The sea unfraught would swell, and the unsought diamonds,

must become a mere jumble of words, utterly unworthy of one of the finest concerted pieces in the medium that had yet been written. The more sober structure of the Lady's stately answer contrasts well with this " gay

---

[1] See the *actual* ending, that is to say. The last foot is, of course, if anything, an antibacchic or a very clumsy amphibrach. I do not want either.

rhetoric," as she calls it ; yet there is, after the famous
" Crams, and blasphemes his Feeder," another ebullition
of contemptuous indignation, like the

> Fool ! do not boast,

above, in

> Shall | I go on ?

And then before the long lyric Act (as we may
almost call it) which closes the Masque, and is its most
Masquish part, the blank verse appropriately ceases
with the admirable description of Sabrina's history,
haunts, and habits, which is almost more epic than
dramatic.

In a general estimate of the blank verse of *Comus* we
must, of course, take the dramatic form into consideration ;
but we need not allow too much for it.   In the first place,
Milton had practically (for Surrey, Gascoigne, etc., may
be left out of the question) none but dramatic models
before him, even if he had been minded to write plain
narrative.   In the second, he has in the piece itself little
occasion (and when he has it he does not avail himself
of it) for the jointed fabric of blank-verse conversation,
which, as we have seen, was to Shakespeare so great a
school for ease and variety of verse-making, without
really deserting the five-foot norm.   Milton evidently
affects and prefers *tirades*.[1]   Of the six or seven hundred
lines of blank verse in the piece, single speeches occupy
92, 25, 60, 27, 26, 22, 57, 67, 24, 41, 24, 46, 44, and
48.   The shorter speeches do not amount to a hundred
lines together, and, putting the exercises in stichomythia
aside, not to a score.   Moreover, though Milton avails
himself of the Alexandrine once or twice certainly, and I
think oftener, he scarcely ever tries the imperfect verse—
the verse-fragment—which dramatic " blanks " invite,
which Shakespeare managed so admirably, and which his
successors mismanaged so abominably.   His classical

---

[1] It may be just as well to say that throughout I use this word, not in
its late and limited sense, but in the origin alone of a *long* batch of uninterrupted verse, whether epic or dramatic.

models no doubt influenced him here, just as in *Paradise Lost* itself Virgil made him less precise.

On the whole, therefore, there is not much in *Comus*, outside the lyrics, which calls for a stamp of verse not equally available for pure narrative, and for the actual speeches with which narrative is usually diversified; and it could directly serve as a school and exercising ground for narrative blank verse itself.

The scholar certainly shows himself no dunce, and the recruit has left the awkward squad a very long way behind. Complete *ease* of versification he has indeed not quite attained; it is doubtful whether he ever attained this, or whether he wished to attain it. That marvellous, billowy flow of verse on which Shakespeare floats us, with an occasional break or ripple, but mostly "too full for noise or foam," is not what Milton aims at. His verses do not float : they march, and march magnificently, quickening and slackening, altering formation slightly, but always with more touch of *mechanism* in them than we find in Shakespeare, with more of the earth, and less of the wind and the water, if with hardly less of the fire, in their composition.

He has found many, if not most, of the tricks and easements of the process—the redundant syllable, the trisyllabic foot, the Alexandrine; and he makes great use of the full stop in middle line. But his use of the pause has not yet thoroughly perfected itself; and what is more remarkable, he has not yet made any fast grip of the instrument which afterwards he was to employ with such astonishing effect—the development of the verse-paragraph. He has fine periods, but his working up of them into paragraphs is very uncertain : it might almost seem as if he did not attempt it much. Even the opening passage has not the unmistakable paragraph form which one would expect; and elsewhere the nearest approach is Comus's aside before addressing the Lady. But he *has* the period—a possession on which that of the paragraph must certainly follow—in twenty fine passages, some of which have been indicated above. And he has an individual line which is already fit for almost anything, whether it tries unusual cadences, or contents itself with varying the usual from

> In regions mild of calm and serene air

to

> Commended her fair innocence to the flood,

and a hundred magnificent prosodic phrases or clauses within the lines. But when we compare the blank verse with the lyrics we see at once that absolute mastery has not been reached in the one as in the other. The *ipsa mollities* of Sir Henry Wotton's letter was surely never so justified in any of the commendatory epistles, then too frequent, as here, from

> The star that bids the shepherd fold

to the incomparable close, right on from " Sabrina Fair " to the Spirit's self - dismissal. Nobody could improve these. We feel that the blank verse, admirable as it is, and at times consummate, *is* susceptible of improvement, here and there, and as a whole.

It would be of the first interest if we had any record *Paradise Lost.* of the reflections of persons who, familiar with the volumes of 1637 and 1645, found, in one of the earliest issues of *Paradise Lost* twenty years and more after the latter of these volumes, the following pronouncement which, well known as it ought to be, must find a place here because of its importance, and of the fact that it does not invariably appear in modern editions.

THE VERSE

The measure is English heroic verse without rime, as that of Homer in Greek, and of Virgil in Latin—rime being no necessary adjunct or true ornament of poem or good verse, in longer works especially, but the invention of a barbarous age, to set off wretched matter and lame metre ; graced indeed since by the use of some famous modern poets, carried away by custom, but much to their own vexation, hindrance, and constraint to express many things otherwise, and for the most part worse, than else they would have expressed them. Not without cause therefore some both Italian and Spanish poets of prime note have rejected rime both in longer and shorter works, as have also long since our best English tragedies, as a thing of itself, to all judicious ears, trivial and of no true musical delight; which consists only in apt numbers, fit quantity of syllables, and the sense variously drawn out from one verse into another, not in the jingling sound of like endings—a fault avoided by the learned ancients both in poetry and all good oratory. This neglect then of rime so little is to be taken for a defect, though it may seem so perhaps to vulgar readers, that it rather is to be esteemed an example set, the first in English, of ancient liberty recovered to heroic poem from the troublesome and modern bondage of riming.

The abjura-
tion of rhyme.

That is to say, the man who thirty years earlier had issued, and who eight years later than that had reissued, work by far the larger part of which had been in rhyme, and who—for the moment let us put it in no stronger fashion—had certainly shown himself not unapt therein, now affected contempt and disgust at the very idea of rhyming. Nobody, so far as we know, made any observations on this anomaly ;[1] the age was, in fact, very little interested in prosodic questions as such ; and it is noteworthy that Dryden, its literary embodiment, a great practical prosodist himself and a fertile critic, hardly deals with them at all, though he tells us that he thought of doing so. And the thing still remains odd ; though we can find quite as much explanation of it as may reasonably be demanded, especially when we remember the partial relapse into the flouted form which *Samson* shows. It is known that the insertion of the paragraph was an after-thought ; and that Milton was not in the best of tempers at having to write it, is pretty evident. He was very often not in the best of tempers : but his crabbedness was probably, in this instance, not due merely to impatience of a kind of apologia.

He had much earlier, in certain famous expressions of his prose work, manifested a violent antipathy to the

---

[1] Marvell's well-known jibe at "the pack-horse and his bells" does not constitute such an observation.

" vulgar amorists," the " vain and amatorious " poets, of his
own and the preceding generation. Now to these poets and
in these poems, especially to and in those of his own generation, rhyme had been the most favourite weapon, and the
instrument not merely of the most exquisite successes,
but of some exploits which were not quite exquisite
and not at all successful. Since I have made a rather
close study of these contemporaries — more especially
from the prosodic point of view — it has been very
strongly borne in upon me that Milton must have particularly disliked the enjambed and deliquescent couplet, of
which Chamberlayne's *Pharonnida* is the longest and best
example, but which had been becoming more and more
frequent since the days of Browne. The very instinct
which had made him attempt and achieve a triumph of
irregular rhyme, fully valued and allowed for, in *Lycidas*,
would have made him shrink from this apparently slovenly
flux of rhyming lines, in a large number of which the
rhyme seems to be totally superfluous except to mark
line-ends which are no ends at all, and to provide what
his severe musical taste would probably have thought a
mere strumming accompaniment. The *Lycidas*-form
itself would have been clearly out of place in a long
narrative ; and the stopped couplet which was just coming
in was a little later than Milton, to speak from a true
historical inwardness.[1] Nor would it have allowed—
what we see from his very words, and could have seen
without them from his earlier practice, he was fondest of
—his own mastery of the " sense variously drawn out
from one line to another." Blank verse would do this ;
and he must by this time have been far too conscious of
his skill (even if it had been the Miltonic way ever to
have any doubts on this head) to fear that he could not
give harmony enough by rhythm without rhyme. Lastly,
there was the charm for such a nature—and for all
natures that have any tincture of nobleness in them—
of " things unadventured yet." And so he launches the
ship of blank verse into the sea, as yet, in fact, unsailed

---

[1] See the chapters on the couplet.

by it, with no guide but his own soul, and no chart but Shakespeare's practice.

To go through the ten thousand lines of *Paradise Lost* exactly as we went through the six or seven hundred of *Comus* would be very tedious, and it would answer no good purpose for the reader, though the writer was bound to do and has done it. There, the prosodist was slightly uncertain of his instrument ; here, he is fingering it on definite principles from first to last. There is, of course, considerable difference of opinion as to what those principles are ; and before long we may have to put the gloves on, and even to be prepared for other people Examination taking them off. But for the present we may pursue of the verse. our usual method of dispassionate examination of the phenomena, usual and exceptional, before endeavouring to draw inferences from them. As very great importance has been assigned to the actual printed text, I have thought it well to read it throughout for this purpose in Professor Masson's certified facsimile of the first edition ;[1] and where anything turns upon it I shall quote this *literatim*.

Apostropha-   The first thing of a prosodic kind which is likely to
tion.   strike the intelligent novice is the constant printed elision of the definite article, and the substitution of an apostrophe for the final *e* wherever the syllable is not absolutely required to make up a dissyllabic foot, thus—

> Fast by the oracle of God ;

but in other places "th' upright," "th' infernal," "th' Eternal," "th' Aonian." He will further observe that apostrophation is not confined to this—that "Heav'nly" and "Heav'n" occur regularly, and that some words are syncopated, without even an apostrophe, from the forms he knows best ("adventrous"). At the same time, he will, or should, remark that not merely are two syllables in words like "disobedience," "Aonian," allowed to count as one often, but that in others where there is not the

---

[1] London, 1877.

same *liaison*—" Siloa's brook," " Tempestuous fire "—no syncopation is typographically indicated.[1]

Passing from these details, if he reads the first paragraph he will find—

(1) That the lines are very regularly decasyllabic, exhibiting no redundant syllable at the end, and nothing that requires the supposition of such an one at the cæsura.

(2) That in consequence of the above-mentioned fashions of spelling, there are no even apparently tri-syllabic feet except those due to the juxtaposition of vowels as above indicated, and one where the word " Spirit " occurs.

(3) That the sense is " variously drawn out from one verse to another " after the most artful fashion, and that thus, by " verse periods," there is fashioned a " verse paragraph," which, according to choice, may be extended to the whole forty-six lines as printed in the original, or broken at pleasure into a minor paragraph and a kind of *coda*.

[1] It may be well to give the first paragraph in Professor Masson's own text, for comparison :—

> Of Man's first disobedience, and the fruit
> Of that forbidden tree whose mortal taste
> Brought death into the World, and all our woe,
> With loss of Eden, till one greater Man
> Restore us, and regain the blissful seat,
> Sing, Heavenly Muse, that, on the secret top
> Of Oreb, or of Sinai, didst inspire
> That shepherd who first taught the chosen seed
> In the beginning how the heavens and earth
> Rose out of Chaos : or, if Sion hill
> Delight thee more, and Siloa's brook that flowed
> Fast by the oracle of God, I thence
> Invoke thy aid to my adventrous song,
> That with no middle flight intends to soar
> Above the Aonian mount, while it pursues
> Things unattempted yet in prose or rhyme.
> And chiefly Thou, O Spirit, that dost prefer
> Before all temples the upright heart and pure,
> Instruct me, for Thou know'st ; Thou from the first
> Wast present, and, with mighty wings outspread,
> Dove-like sat'st brooding on the vast Abyss,
> And mad'st it pregnant : what in me is dark
> Illumine, what is low raise and support ;
> That, to the highth of this great argument,
> I may assert Eternal Providence,
> And justify the ways of God to men.

(4) That the main instrument of this arrangement is the manipulation of the pause, which in the first six lines is respectively in the middle of the fourth foot, at the end of the third (twice), in the middle of the third, in the middle of the second, and at the end of it ; while in the seventh there are *two* pauses, of equal value, at the middle of the second and of the fourth. In not a few subsequent lines he will fail to discover any pause at all ; and my ear would not quarrel with his if he found practically none in the last three lines running except at their ends. Yet, for all this variety, he will find that, various as is the cadence, it has not the range or the flexibility of Shakespeare's greatest blank-verse passages, chiefly owing to the closer normality of the lines, and to an apparent shyness of trisyllabic feet. That this shyness is always more apparent than real he may or may not be in doubt.

The continued and careful examination of the First Book will make considerable additions to this stock of observations, and will perhaps introduce some important modifications in it. Two hasty generalisations—that Milton *always* inclines to the pronunciation of " Spirit " as " Spir't " or " Sprite," and that he invariably makes " Heav'n " a monosyllable[1]—will be corrected by line 101—

> Innumerable force of Spi|rits armed

(unless anybody be bold enough, and too bold, so as to scan " Sprites armèd "), and line 297—

> On Hea|ven's a|zure ; and the torrid clime

(unless, again, the same person proposes " Heav'n's | azur|è and | "—they do things nearly as surprising).

He will further observe certain matters which interfere with similar generalisations of another kind. From the frequent crasis—on the strict decasyllabic system—of adjacent vowels, he may have thought " Siloa's brook " in line 11 meant to be scanned " Sylwa's brook." But he will find that in " th' Aonian mount " he will have to

---

[1] Cf. *sup.* on Gascoigne, and *inf.* on Mitford.

give up his theory, or else value "the" fully; and that
many other juxtaposed vowels are fully valued in similar
names, "Peor," "Baalim," etc.   It is at least possible
that his ear will revolt at the spoiling of such a line as

Of glo|ry obscured ; | as when the Sun new ris'n

by the ugliness of "Glor | yobscured," and at "glory
extinct" as "glor | yextinct."   He may kick, too, at
being told to suppress not merely the weak *e*, but a
strong vowel like *o* in

Whom reason hath equalled,

and even doubt whether Milton regarded the *e* itself
before an *r* as negligible when he reads—

Whom thunder hath made greater,

as well as whether he really meant to call "Emperor"
"Emp'ror," on the modern principle of "guv'nor" for
"governor."

Should he indeed *not* be a novice, and have some
acquaintance with the printed books of the period, he
will, or may, from the first doubt whether *any* particular
importance is to be attached to the typographical elision
of "th'"; but here he may, if not so acquainted, be left
to his mistake for a time.   Let him, suspending this, go
on to Book II.   Here he will find some really remarkable lines, such as 123—

Ominous | conjecture on the whole success,

and he will say rashly,. "Well! this settles the question
as to trisyllabic feet!   They certainly will not tell me
that Milton—a gentleman, a scholar, and a master of
harmonies, pronounced this word 'om'nous' when it is
not even spelt so."   Let him wait.   He may note the
curious slipped rhyme of "light" and "flight" at 220-
221, and certainly should note the undoubted full value
of "Michael" in 294.   But he will probably think 123
absolutely settled by 302—

A pillar of state ; deep on his front engraven,

and 313—

> Princes of Hell? for so the popular vote.

Let him wait again. Line 412—

> Through the strict sent*e*ries and stations thick,

should have some interest for him, and if he is disposed to attach real importance to printing ll. 421-422—

> Pondering the danger with deep thoughts, and each
> In other's count'nance read his own dismay,

will have more; for if " count'nance " is so of prosodic malice prepense, why not " pond'ring " ? But perhaps l. 450 will give him most to think over. This runs—

> Me from attempting. Wherefore do 1 assume ;

and to it we may return. He will admire Milton's sleight (or rather weight) of prosodic manipulation in

> Rocks, caves, lakes, fens, bogs, dens, and shades of death,

though he may think the internal rhyme of " dens " and " fens " an unlucky accident. He should observe 665—

> With Lapland witches, while the labouring moon

(not " lab'ring "), and 681—

> Whence and what art thou, execrable shape?

for the full value of " execrable." Moreover, he will find " Spi|rit " once more in 956—

> Or Spi|rit of the nethermost Abyss.

The places of Book III. shall be indicated with less comment; indeed, I am giving but a few of the hundreds that I have noted and ready for use. But I will specify line 3—

> May 1 express | thee unblamed? | since God is light

(cf. Chaucer's " in thalight," and vol. i. p. 173) ; line 5—

> Bright ef|fluence of | bright essence increate ;

line 36—

> And Ti|resias | and Phineus, prophets old ;

line 108—

> When Will and Reason (Reason also is Choice),

where *one* " Reason " *must* be dissyllabic, and both may be, with an anapæstic ending, though there also is choice of jamming these very words into " also's." And let there be added 110, " just|ly accuse | " ; 120, " sha|dow of fate " ; 131-132, " the other," printed in full twice, in the one case trisyllabic or slurred, in the other full-valued ; 195, " Conscience " (in *Comus* " Con-sci-ence ") ; 198, " sufferance," not " suff'rance " ; 461, " Spirits," dissyllabic ; 503, " Heaven " printed with the *e*, though the syllable is not wanted. In 586 a really questionable line appears—

> Shoots invisible virtue even to the deep,

which had better be reserved ; " Uriel," a trisyllable in 648, and a trisyllabic foot, or else a dissyllable, in 664 ; with two *reservanda* [1] in 728—

> Timely in|terposes, and, her monthly round,

and 731—

> Hence fills and empties, to enlighten the Earth.

In the Fourth Book, noticing the fact that in l. 5—

> *Woe to the inhabitants on earth;* that now,

the article is not apostrophated, and allowing in utmost fairness that this may have something to do with the italic type, one observes that for a long time the metre is unusually " regular." But in l. 371 there occurs what some would take as an elision of such an exceptional kind that we must return to it—

> Long to conti|nue, and this | high seat, your Heaven ;

while in 594 a quantification, happily indisputable, appears which throws light on other disputed ones—

> Diurnal, or this less volūbil earth.

---

[1] When I speak of such "reservation" and "return" I do not necessarily mean that the quotations will be separately discussed, but that they will form the basis of the general remarks to be made later.

In 720-721 occurs that collision of final and initial spondees—

> Thus at their shady lodge arrived *both stood*,
> *Both turned*, and under open sky adored,

which so did disturb the greatest of all accentualists, Dr. Johnson and Dr. Guest, and which so rejoices all foot-men, from the admirable selection of the foot for the sense.

806 is a difficult line on both schemes, but much more difficult on one than on another—

> Th' animal spirits that from pure blood arise,

where, it may be observed, apostrophation, if metrically valid, involves an excessively ugly (if even possible) sound of "thănĭmāl | spĭrīts,|" while "Thĕ ănĭ|măl spĭrĭts|" is perfectly harmonious.

There is hardly anything else in the Book that needs notice except 884—

> Employed, it seems, to violate sleep, and those,

where choice is free between the scornful appropriateness of the trisyllabic "vĭŏlăte" and the jejune vulgarity of "vi'late."

L. 141 of the Fifth is noteworthy—

> Shot para*l*el to the earth his dewy ray,

where, no doubt, the devotees of "elision before pure *l*" would say that the second was omitted to procure it. I very much doubt Milton's thus taking liberties with a Greek word, while I know seventeenth-century printers far too well to doubt *their* doing so ; but even if this liberty be conceded there remains the awkward fact that the omission makes the word better for the trisyllabic "Shot pa|ra|lel to" ; while as for the dissyllabic "par'lel," it is an ugliness to which I can allow no redemption, except that it provides a rhyme—otherwise not easy—for Lodovick Carlell.

342, I think, shows how treacherous a thing the apostrophe is—

> Rough or smooth rin'd, or bearded husk, or shell ;

for though there *is* a dialectic form "rine," it is to the

last degree improbable that Milton used it, while "husk" and "shell" point imperatively to the noun "rind."

413 is very interesting—

> And corporeal to incorporeal turn.

It must be rather a choke-pear for the "drumming decasyllabists," inasmuch as one of the "-reals" *must* be syncopated and the other not. For my own part I have no doubt that "corporeal" is simply misprinted for "corporal," which in the parallel passage at 496 of this very Book is so printed, and again at 573. This is a very common confusion, and occurs in *Hamlet*. "Incorporal" is less likely, though it occurs in Raleigh.

There should also be noted 563—

> High matter thou enjoinst me, O prime of men,

with the practical disappearance of "me," which decasyllabic scansion requires; and perhaps also 585—

> Innumerable before th' Almighty's throne,

"for a purpose to be hereafter disclosed," as the projector said in the Bubble time, and indeed sometimes says, not quite *totidem verbis*, in his prospectuses to-day.

Book Six—the famous one of the celestial battles, and, however often one has read it, a marvel alike for the magnificence of its serious substance and the utter wretchedness of the comic inset—has, to be noted prosodically, few things in number, but some of almost unsurpassed importance. The differing values of the -iel and -ael terminations in archangelic and angelic names are really of great moment—"Michael," for instance, having actually *three* values, Mī|chă'|ēl, Mi|chăĕl, and Mi|ch|āel. But the great places of the Book in prosodic discussion have usually been l. 34—

> Universal reproach far worse to bear,

and still more 866—

> Burnt after them to the bottomless pit.

These also must be reserved for the present.

In the original edition, as Milton-students know, there are only ten Books—Seven and Eight and Eleven and Twelve in the later being respectively united in the earlier as Seven and Ten. To suit this difference double references will be given where necessary. Of minor matters attention may be drawn to—VII. 15, "tempring" without apostrophe ; 73, "the Empyrean" with valued "the" ; 103, a similarly valued "the" with "unapparent" ; 127, "temperance" with the *e* neither elided nor valued except as part of a trisyllabic foot—

> Her temperance over appetite, to know ;

and the characteristic but very differently interpretable 130—

> Wisdom to folly as nourishment to wind.

More vital in itself is 236—

> And vital virtue infused and vital warmth,

of which more anon ; and still more 390—

> Display'd *the op'n* firmament of Heaven,

and 398—

> And let the fowl be *multiply'd on* the Earth.

A curious double omission of apostrophation is in 418—

> Their brood as num*e*rous hatch from th*e* egg, that soon,

and either a complete mistake of the printer or a death-blow to "pop'lar" in 488—

> Hereafter joined in her popular tribes.

On some at least the double value of the same word in the following distich will not be lost (526, 527)—

> The breath of life ; in his own Ìmage he
> Created thee, in the Imàge of God,

where "Ìmage" and "Imàge" are hardly more note-worthy than the other double testimony simultaneously given, that Milton did not in the least think "elision" necessary ; while yet another double in 533 and 534 must be noted—

> Over Fish of the sea and Fowl of the air
> And every living thing that moves on the Earth.

The remainder of the Book in the first version—the Eighth in the second—is less fertile ; but it has in 936 (VII. 299, 2nd ed.) one of Milton's curious ditrochaic (or pæonic) openings—

> To the Garden of Bliss thy seat prepared,

and a crux, the "extrametrical" syllable in 1286 (649, 2nd ed.)—

> Thy condescen*sion*, and shall be honoured ever,

which also must stand by.

VIII. (*vulgo* IX.) gives another example of "virtue" in 110—

> Not in themselves all their known virtue appears ;

and further noteworthy lines in 296—

> For he who tempts, *though in vain*, at least asperses,

and 508—

> Ammonian Jove, or *Capitoline*, was seen,

and 570—

> What thou command'st, and right thou shouldst be obeyed.

These, and especially 904—

> The sacred fruit forbidd'n ?   Some cursed fraud,

may be consulted by the curious ; but, above all, 1082—

> And rapture so oft beheld ?   Those heavenly shapes.

Does anybody really believe that Milton would have run the risk of the substitution of

> And rapture *soft* beheld ?

The Tenth Book of the ordinary arrangement—the Ninth of the original—is very rich in prosodic notanda. There is perhaps more than a fanciful inference to be drawn from the fact that while l. 12 gives us one of the supposed syncopations—

> For still they knew, and ought to have still remembered,

l. 22 gives us a full-valued Heaven in a rather remarkable place—

> From Earth arriv'd at Heaven Gate, displeased.

There are various retentions of the Latin accent—45, "impùlse"; 59, "colleàgue"; as well as one of the instances of "whether," monosyllabised according to the common theory, which also requires unusual astringents in 86—

> Of high collateral glory; him Thrones and Powers;

as again in 106—

> Where obvious duty erewhile appeared unsought.

Note also (and especially) 121—

> So dreadful to thee? That thou art naked who;

and almost more especially 178—

> And dust shalt eat all *the* days of thy life,

where it is pretty certain that Milton meant to extend the monosyllabic emphasis of the whole line to "the."

A very noteworthy line is 198—

> Because thou hast hearkened to the voice of thy wife,

where the dignity of the first phrase of judgment will be hopelessly lost if we read—

> Because | thou'st hear|ken'd to | th' voice of | thy wife,

instead of

> Because | thou hast hear| { kened to the | voice of | thy wife,
> { kened to | the voice | of thy wife,

which latter has the special argument in its favour that Milton finishes scores of lines by parallel trisyllables. And if anybody says that apostrophation could not be expected before "voice," let him look at 204—

> Unbid, and thou shalt eat th' Herb of th' Field.

The spelling of "idl*e*ly" in 236 is here mentioned
out of fairness, though or because it cuts both ways,
as perhaps does another "virtue" in 372. But passing
over some minor points (to be looked up by whoso
chooses) in 467, 468 especially, and 562, we come to a
famous Guest-choker in 581—

> Ophion, with Eurynome, the wide-
> Encroaching Eve perhaps,

where the inextinguishable wrath of the excellent Master
of Sidney shows to what extent theory will blind a
learned and acute intelligence, at once to beauty and the
reason of beauty. For the line *is* beautiful ; and the
partition of the translation of " Eurynome," besides linking it with the next, excites curiosity to know how the
second member will be translated. But to divide a word
—even a hyphen-made word—was shocking; and it
shocked.

To some ears, at least, great loss of beauty would be
caused by the omission to give full value to the italicised
syllables in 720—

> O mis*e*rable of hap*py* ! Is this the end ;

not "th' end," observe. Observe, too, the cadence in 936—

> Me, me only, just object of his ire ;

and 1092—

> Of sorrow unfeigned and humiliation meek.

There is less later ; but in XI. 34 note in connection with
the last line quoted—

> And propitiation ; all his works on me ;

while in 559—

> Fled and pursued transverse the resonant fugue,

observe what an infinite loss in "suiting the sound to
the sense " will come from substituting " res'nant " for
" resonant"; and note in 768 and 770 the curious
coincidence—more than curious when we consider what

an ear lay hard by the tongue that dictated it, not wrote it—of

> Him or his children, e|vil, he may | be sure,

and

> And he the future e|vil shall | no less.

As for the later part of the Book (which became XII.), less still need, for our purpose, be noted.   Those who are pursuing the inquiry seriously will find, among others, ll. 932 (41), "bitu|minous gurge"; 935 (44), "A ci|ty and town | whose top"; 953 (62) "Ridic|ulous and"; instances of "glory," "pillar," and the "able" and "ably" words; and so on.   More important are 1131 (240)—

> Without | Media|tor, whose high office now,

and 1419 (518)—

> By spiritual ; to themselves appropriating.

Paradise Regained.   *Paradise Regained* does not contribute quite in proportion, but it has some noteworthy lines.   Milton's not very frequent, but almost always specially felicitous use of alliteration, appears in I. 93—

> The *gl*impses of his Father's *gl*ory shine ;

and there is a bold pause, the conditions of which may be disputed, in 140—

> O'ershadow her.   This Man born and now grown up ;

while the famous crux of "bottomless" reappears in 361—

> With them from bliss to the bottomless Deep.

Here, even more than in the other, though I do not think that Milton would have hesitated to scan "bottomless" as an amphibrach, I am inclined to prefer one of his beloved, if not quite wisely beloved, choriambic syzygies (– ᴗ ᴗ –).   But both the First and the Second Book chiefly give us things noted before, excepting a complementary example (II. 154) of choriamb or antispast "as you like it"—

> Among daughters of men the fairest found ;

and II. 267-269—

> And saw the ravens, with their horny beaks,
> Food to Elijah bringing even and morn—
> Though ravenous, taught to abstain from what they brought,

where it is most important to observe that if you do not give " ra-ven-ous " the full syllabic value, which is necessary in " ravens," you spoil that play of words which Milton undoubtedly, however oddly, liked as much as he pretended to dislike rhyme. 289 gives us " bottom " with its usual accent ; and 445—

> Worthy of memorial) canst thou not remember,

prompts one to ask whether, if Milton preferred the " pure " line, he would not have written " worthy memorial," as he might have done, to get rid of at least one superfluity.

In Book III. the curious different valuations of " glory " in the different places within four lines, 117-120, first invite notice. " Ignominy " in 136—

> But condemnation, ignominy and shame,

may suggest different constructions, when taken with the existence of " ignomy." In 392 the final " battles and leagues " is corroboratory of " bottomless deep," as is "idols with God " (432) ; and 400—

> Thy *politic* maxims or that cumbersome,

may seem to some to justify Count Smorltork.

Book IV. gives at 173—

> The abominable terms, impious condition,

one of the most difficult of Miltonic lines to scan musically on *any* system. It seems to me best as an Alexandrine, the slow weight and length of which would fall in with Our Lord's distinctly mentioned " disdain," and the purport of the words themselves. " Fountain of Light," at the end of 289, is another argument for | bottomless pit | . It may be noted that Milton accumulates redundant endings here, as he hardly does earlier ; it is curious how this licence seems to be a Eurynome, or " wide - encroaching " temptation ; and the very last words, " private returned," clench the argument for " bottomless " with *un*wrenched accent.

Samson Agonistes. The prosodic interest of *Samson Agonistes* is known to be great. It consists partly in the character of the diction, which is the stiffest in Milton, and the most classicised ; partly in the blank verse ; but most in the elaborately modulated measures of the choruses, and in the fact that here the Dalila of Rhyme does actually triumph over *her* Samson, and establishes herself in his house once more after years of separation and obloquy. These choruses are rather grand than beautiful, but they all lend themselves to the strictest foot-scansion.[1]

In the blanks the chief things noteworthy are yet further experiments of the same character as the choriambic ending which we have seen so frequently attempted

[1] *Oct.,   Iamb.,* { This, this | is he | ; softly | awhile ;
   and Troch. { Let us | not break | in up|on him.
   Dec. O change | beyond | report, | thought, or | belief !
   Alex. See how | he lies | at ran|dom, care|lessly diffused,
   Hexasyl. With lan|guished head | unpropt,
   Hexasyl. hyperc. As one | with hope | aban|doned,
   Hexasyl. hyperc. And by | himself | given o|ver.
   Oct. In sla|vish hab|it, ill-fit|ted weeds |
   Tetrasyl. O'er-worn | and soiled.
   Alex. Or do | my eyes | misre|present ? | Can this | be he ?
   Oct. cat. That he|roic, | that re|nowned,
   Dec. Irre|sisti|ble Sam|son whom, | unarmed,
   Alex. No strength | of man | or fier|cest wild | beast could |
      withstand ;
   Alex. Who tore | the li|on as | the li|on tears | the kid ;
   Dec. Ran on | embat|tled ar|mies clad | in iron,
   Hexasyl. And, wea|ponless | himself, |
   Alex. Made arms | ridi|culous, | useless | the for|gery
   Dec. Of bra|zen shield | and spear, | the ham|mered cuirass,
   Dec. Chalyb|ean-tem|pered steel | and frock | of mail
   Hexasyl. Ada|mante|an proof:

Hardly anything here needs remark, except the use made of the old catalectic octosyllable beloved from *Comus* days, with its trochaic cadence, and that of half-Alexandrines or hexasyllables. There is only one monometer, towards the centre or *waist* of the scheme.

in *Paradise Regained,* and which some people call " reversal of stress." [1]

Instances may be found in 579—

> Better at home lie bed-rid, not only idle,

which no system makes really harmonious ; line 748—

> Out ! out ! hyæna : these are thy wonted arts,

which hardly any system but ours can explain satisfactorily ; line 797—

> No better way I saw than by importuning,

which is almost certainly an Alexandrine ; line 842—

> Or by evasions thy crime uncover'st more,

where the strict decasyllable needs the impossible " evăsns̄ " ; line 868—

> Private respects must yield with grave authority,

an Alexandrine more certain than ever ; and the very curious triplet of redundance in 938-940—

> If in my flower of youth and strength, when all men
> Loved, honoured, feared me ; thou alone could hate me,
> Thy husband, slight me, sell me, and forego me.

If these are not experiments, and experiments in strict foot-system with equivalence and substitution, I do not know what they are, unless you class them with all the other things reserved and most of those noted as " anomalies," which is simply confession and avoidance.

Let us call a halt now. It is not surprising that certain of the lines quoted from *Paradise Regained,* supplemented as they are by many others also cited in

---

[1] I have ventured below to image forth the effect produced on my ear and mind by accentual scansion with the aid of the shunting-yard. For a pendant as to this (to me rather absurd) phrase I must recur to the tin soldiers beloved of all properly constituted children. Can any one fail to remember how, when one had carefully arranged them in a row, they would, at a touch of a hasty sleeve or something similar, tumble against each other in different directions, and refuse to "dress"? This is just what the "reversed stresses" do.

Samson Agonistes, have somewhat disturbed the believers in a systematic and rigidly observed " elision " in Milton. Such lines in *Paradise Regained* as

> And all the flourishing works of peace destroy (iii. 80),

> Whose offspring in his posterity yet serve (iii. 375),

and

> Thy politic maxims or that cumbersome (iii. 400),

with the *Samson* example just given, are clearly not reconcilable with the limitations sometimes tabulated. No wonder that a candid believer should admit that they look as if this theory had been quite discarded. But would it not be more reasonable and equally fair to say that they look as if such a theory had never been held, or had been held merely as a stage to a wider one? Remember that the simple theory of trisyllabic feet is equally applicable to *both*—that it makes no more difficulty with the one than with the other, and sets both in harmony. Remember too that there need not be the slightest difficulty in admitting development in Milton's use of trisyllabic foot-emancipation, to some progressive extent, from the gyves of apostrophation and the strict iambic heresy. Remember, further, that even in *Paradise Lost* the precisians of elision have had to admit exceptions which were sure to pullulate. Remember, finally, how they advance the exceedingly double-edged argument that in *Paradise Lost* the exceptions are most common in those syllables which experience shows to be oftenest and best used for trisyllabic places. And join to the remembrance that what *must* have been before him—the trisyllabic practice of Shakespeare—is absolutely unlimited. To the person who will keep these things in mind it should be superfluous to dwell on them.

But let us return for a moment to the actual examination of *Samson*. The central passage, the *clou* for the whole study of the play as far as its apparent anomalies go, is the great and famous one at the opening of the Chorus after Harapha's departure—

> Oh, how comely it is, and how reviving,
> To the spirits of just men long oppressed,
> When God into the hands of their oppressor
> Puts invincible might.

It might have been thought that this passage would speak trumpet-tongued—that anybody possessed of any knowledge of Latin would see that Milton was imitating the "fantastical dainty metre" of the Catullian hendecasyllabic. But no! Inversions of stress, exchanges of accustomed rhythm for unaccustomed—all sorts of tricks, as fantastical, but not as dainty—seem to suggest themselves to those who will not accept the plain doctrine— the same yesterday, to-day, and for ever—of English prosody, since English was English. It is perfectly certain that Milton is playing his part as the Abdiel of the classical-metre craze. I would give something, little as I care for biographical details, to know whether he had read Campion—but it does not much matter. The note on the verse in *Paradise Lost*, and the observation on the *Pyrrha*, give one quite sufficient information. In these choruses he is evidently making his last and boldest experiment, to see if he cannot merely enlarge but change the bounds of English metre. It is the way of the reformer. He fails magnificently ; but he fails. He produces some exquisite curiosities, but he establishes no precedent. For once the comic verdict has no absurdity in it : " Not guilty ; but don't do it again ! " [1]

The other most remarkable passage, equally famous and equally striking, is much less homogeneous and more questionable. It consists of the opening lines of the Semi-chorus triumph over the destruction of the Philistines—

---

[1] I have sometimes thought that a stanza of this kind may have struck him as worth trying, in order to get still nearer to Latin kinds than he had done in *Pyrrha*. I do not know whether any one has noticed that it is easy enough to English *Pyrrha* exactly—

> What boy elegant with many a rose now thee
> Courts, while perfumes around everywhere drop from him ?
> For whom bind'st thou thy golden locks,
> Pyrrha, cool in a grotto ?

But it is very ugly, like all its kind.

> While their hearts were jocund and sublime,
> Drunk with idolatry, drunk with wine,
> And fat regorged of bulls and goats.

Now, here there is nothing like the almost indisputable and self-imposing metrical character of the first piece. Are we to take it trochaically, with the second line a sort of cabriole or somersault of that dactyl which is the natural expansion of the trochee as the anapæst is of the iamb, but subsiding into iambics in the third line? After this the lines continue as thus—

> Chaunting their idol, and preferring
> Before our living Dread, who dwells
> In Silo, his bright sanctuary,

and so forth, soberly enough.

Or, remembering that there is elsewhere a parallel to the first line in l. 606—

> O that torment should not be confined,

are we to take

> While their hearts were jocund and sublime

as an imitation on Milton's part of the Chaucerian "acephalous" niner, and remembering that Milton often plays tricks with "idolatry" and its congeners, scan the next—

> Drunk | with i|dola|try, drunk | with wine,

so that there will be no real or important divergence from the iambic basis throughout? Either way is possible.

There can be no doubt that if we take the second, the appearance of the two acephalous lines (knowing, as we do, that Milton knew his Chaucer well, and knowing further, as we do, what admirable use he had made of the acephalous octosyllable) is very interesting. But whichever we take, and whatever other of the *Samson* oddments we add to these, we still have, in both and in all, a further document of Milton's unconquerable tendency to experimentalise. He had begun with the anapæstic

ending in *Comus*; he continued with all the lines which
have been made subjects of question in *Paradise Lost.*
He widened his range a little—though not, I think, on
any new principle—in *Paradise Regained*; and in *Samson
Agonistes* he "makes the jump," as the French say, into
entirely new combinations.   But let it be observed that
here also he keeps his singular method.   The earlier
choruses, and parts of Samson's own speeches, are strictly
iambic in basis, though irregular in length.   The cases
where it is difficult to maintain that basis are very few.
The cases where it is simply out of the question are
almost limited to a single one.   Of this one it may
perhaps be permissible to use the old theological caution
(quite in Milton's way) as to the death-repentance of the
penitent thief.   Milton gives it that none may despair of
new possibilities in English metre.   He gives no more,
that none may presume on reckless and hazardous
experiment.

But we must return again.   The anomalies which we
have been surveying, or some of them, have struck
students of various degrees of competence and intelligence
from very early times ; and constant efforts have been
made to explain, or at any rate to "regiment" them.
Most of these efforts, and their authors, will find sufficient
place in the "Prosodist" chapters as those authors occur.
But there is one late and great exception which must be
dealt with here.   By far the most important and the
most thorough-going, as well as one of the latest of those
which I cannot accept, is that of Mr. Robert Bridges.
It would seem to appear to some people (who, I suppose,
translate their own practice into a rule for others) that to
preface a criticism with a salute is a sort of tongue-in-
cheek ceremony, if not even a Judas-like trick.   That has
not been the idea entertained by gentlemen in England
at any time of our history ; and it is not mine.   When I
say that I have had the pleasure of knowing Mr. Bridges
for some forty years ; that I have held him for
the last dozen of them as our "next poet" in English,
and for thirty at least as one of our best ; that I recognise

*Attempts to
systematise
apparent
anomaly.*

to the full the scholarship and the taste which accompany his great poetical gifts ; that I know no one who has more " fulfilled all numbers " in literature,—I speak not more " magnificently " than sincerely.   But the complement of *Amicus Plato* still abides as the rule for all servants of the Muses of whatever degree ; and that the highest poetical faculty, backed by scholarship, will not necessarily make a poet infallible when he proceeds from practice to theory is sufficiently proved by no less final instances than that of Milton himself in the matter of rhyme, and that of Wordsworth in the case of Poetic Diction.   The following is, I believe, a true abstract of Mr. Bridges' views on the prosody of *Paradise Lost*, as given in the last edition of his work on the subject.[1]

Mr. Bridges' view.

A typical blank-verse line has ten syllables, five stresses, and a rising rhythm.

There may be an extra syllable, and even two, at the end of the line ; but Milton in *Paradise Lost*, though not in *Comus*, does not allow it elsewhere, eliding it where it seems to occur.

Elision extends to words in *-ion*, *-ience*, etc. ; " open " vowels, *i.e.* vowels coming before another or an *h*, either in the same word or in the next, while *w* and *wh* for *h* may be disregarded ; " unstressed " vowels before *r* ; " spirit " sometimes but not always, and " misery," with adjectives in *-able* are made the subject of special exceptions ; unstressed vowels before pure *l* (" evil " an exception) ; vowels before pure *n* when final (not necessarily when not final) ; and some others.

Some lines have only *four*, and some probably only *three* stresses.

There is in Milton much " inverted rhythm," which may occur in every foot or stress-division, and in more than one.

Discussion of it.

I have purposely made this summary as simple as possible to avoid ostentation of complexity.   But it will hardly be denied that it *is* rather complex ; and it cannot

[1] Oxford, 1901.   The important dealing in this book with the English hexameter will not here concern us.

be denied at all that it proceeds on the general theory that Milton first adopted a strict system and then gave himself easements from it in divers directions. Wherever an apparent breach of the " ten syllable, five stress, rising rhythm " norm occurs, you have got to devise an explanation, or at least a classification, of the licence ; and sometimes even your explanations and classifications will not hold good, and you must have an " exception." Now I venture to think it unnecessary to urge at any great length, that *prima facie* the simpler explanation is always to be preferred to the more complex ; that the more numerous the epicycles and *privilegia* required for special cases, the less probable is the theory which requires them ; that, in short, one master-key is a great deal better than a whole bunch of jingling picklocks. And I believe that master-key to be provided by the system of foot-scansion, with equivalence and substitution, which has been championed throughout this book. I have allowed that trisyllabic feet had been and were still discouraged in theory, for a generation or two before and during Milton's time ; and, what is more, I have shown the cause of this discouragement. But I have shown also that they had existed ever since English poetry became English, and were only " driven in " by the mistaken theory itself.

On our system, instead of a tangle of rule and exception, everything becomes perfectly simple. Milton is writing on a norm of five-foot lines, which admits the various forms, long-short, short-long, long-long, short-short-long, and possibly here and there long-short-short and short-short-short (this rather doubtfully), just as does the Greek trimeter with which he was so well acquainted, but on a freer system of equivalence, and with the final redundant syllable allowed at pleasure. Very occasionally he allows himself, as Virgil had done in his hexameters, a fragment of a line, very occasionally what may be an Alexandrine. But generally he confines himself to the so-called decasyllable—really to the five-foot line. His business is with this, with the equivalence of feet, with the shifting of pause, and with the superior

Contrast of it with our system.

concerting effect which we have called the verse paragraph—to make as harmonious lines as he can. He
makes them ; the few exceptions dealt with or to be
dealt with presently requiring no *privilegium*, no extension of, or exception to, system, but being simply
experiments, more or less successful, under that system,
and in the carrying out of it. I think a few of them—
very few—are *not* quite successful ; and I should be very
much surprised if the case were otherwise. But I think
that the enormous majority, " not five in five score, but " at
least ninety-four and nineteen-twentieths " more," are [1]
successful, and that they form the great justification and
exemplification of our theory. Only by feet, equivalence,
and substitution can you explain Milton's prosody in a
manner worthy of Milton, as a natural, harmonious,
consistent process, and not as a tissue of provisos
and saving clauses—of Admiralty orders overruling the
Articles of War, after the fashion ignored by innocent Mr.
Midshipman Easy, and of subordinate officers producing
sealed commissions from their pockets, after the fashion
in reference to which D'Artagnan brought a blush to the
cheek of Louis the Magnificent.

The printing
argument.

For the peculiarities of printing I have, I must confess,
very little respect, though, as I have shown and shall
hope to show, they are by no means fatal to my theory
in themselves. To begin with, Milton was blind when
he wrote (or at least printed) the *Paradises* and *Samson.*
It is hard enough to get an elaborate and rather arbitrary system of will-printing carried out when you can see.
In the second place, I have myself, as the phrase goes,
"seen too many others." During the last few years
especially I have been reading—reading narrowly, and in
a literal sense literally—dozens of books, scores of
thousands of lines, written by Milton's contemporaries,
and printed in his very times. The result has informed
me, once for all, that "apostrophation" was a trick, and
almost a fetich, of the day ; it has informed me likewise

---

[1] Perhaps I ought (though it is sad to think it necessary) to remind the
reader of Porson and "The Germans in Greek."

that it was a fetich most capriciously, as well as most extravagantly, worshipped. I could give many examples;[1] but the reader, unless he likes to go through what I have gone through, will hardly appreciate the certainty of the conclusion. Yet this certainty is clenched, endorsed, made absolute by the fact that the very printing of *Paradise Lost* does *not* bear out what it is supposed to bear out—that it actually contradicts itself again and again, and that it omits almost more strikingly than it contradicts.

When the two systems come to be applied, the difference of their results must no doubt be subject to the grand caution—*De gustibus*———. There may be people whose ears are not offended by " om'nous " and " pop'lar," by " thupright," and by

Abominablunutterabl and worse,

instead of the smoothly flowing, musically rippling measure and murmur of the trisyllabically admixed cadence. But the doctrines of stress-omission and inversion seem to lead to even stranger results. I cannot understand how any one can not merely propose to scan with trochaic endings

Beyond all past example and futùre

(where *futūrus* was evidently sitting at Milton's ear rather Satanically), and

Which of us who beholds the bright surfàce

(where, as evidently, he was mentally *separating* the syllables and giving " face " its usual value), but can actually see beauty in the latter.[2] But the *omission* of stresses gives the strangest results of all. To make

As in luxurious cities, where the noise

a line of four stresses only ; much more

His ministers of vengeance and pursuit

Cacophonies.

---

[1] See *Minor Caroline Poets*, vols. i. and ii. Oxford, 1905-6.

[2] It is perhaps worth observing that "surmise," "surprise," and other dissyllabic noun-compounds with "sur-" keep the ultimate long.

a line of *three*, seems to me not only quite unnecessary—
my five "feet" being perfectly perceptible in both—but
unthinkable.   I simply cannot read, hear, or see the one
with four stresses and the other with three ; the attempt
to do so results, for me, in a mere welter of gabbled sound.

The "scanned
not pro-
nounced"
argument.

It may, however, be said, "You are kicking (and that
rather rudely) at an open door.   Have you not Mr.
Bridges' explicit declaration that he does *not* think that
there can be any doubt whether elided syllables should
be pronounced ?   Does he not go so far as to say,
'Though Milton printed "Th' Almighty," it cannot be
supposed that he wished it to be so pronounced'?   and
yet more, 'In English the open vowel is always pronounced'?   Does he not yet further admit that Milton's
own practice 'is somewhat inconsistent and arbitrary'?"
Most certainly : these citations are true citations.   I have
been acquainted with the statements ever since they were
made, and have always determined that, should I ever
have occasion to handle the matter, they should be
prominently acknowledged.   But I must observe, in the
first place, that whatever Mr. Bridges may admit, his
predecessors in the same theory of scansion did *not* admit
this.   Dryden, who was contemporary with Milton for
two-thirds of his own life, who had projected a treatise on
Prosody, and who had not improbably talked with Milton
on the subject, lays down, *totidem verbis*, that "no vowel
can be cut off when we cannot sink the pronunciation
of it."   The great Bysshe, whom it is the fashion to pooh-
pooh and keep in the background (as is the case also
with Guest, because both had the complete but maladroit
courage of their opinions), is entirely explicit on the
subject ; and he did no more than boldly formulate what
generations believed.   "Beauteous," he says, "is two
syllables, 'victorious' is three"; and he (from his own
point of view, justly) scolds Milton for making "riot" one
syllable, which it certainly cannot be unless you pronounce it "rot" or "rite."   Bysshe I understand.   I
think him wrong to a ghastly extent—hideously and
hatefully wrong.   But I comprehend his theory ; I know

whence it arose and what it meant ; I think that if you take his premisses—which I am so far from taking—it is a logical and a necessary conclusion. Moreover, his predecessors, his contemporaries and students, and the majority of the next three generations so understood him, though they agreed with him ; others, like Shenstone, so understood him, though they had the sense to disagree with him.   The printers who printed " watry " and " tendring," whether with or without the apostrophe, held the same theory and meant to express it.   To them these contractions were either not ugly, or, ugly or not, were a deliberate sacrifice to a theory of metre.   I repeat that I understand them thoroughly, and confess them to be consistent.   I should like to say, "Off with their heads ! " but that is different.

Heaven forbid that I should say, "Off with Mr. Bridges' head ! " but I must admit that his position is to me quite incomprehensible.   Pronounce these syllables and you have trisyllabic feet at once—all the trisyllabic feet that I want, and all that I contend for.   But, it seems, you must, under some strange theory of divorce of scansion and pronunciation, say that they are not trisyllabic feet.   Why ?   The ecclesiastic, in the *fabliau* so often related and utilised, who thanked Heaven "for this good carp " when he was eating his Friday capon, had a very obvious, and from his point of view sufficient, reason for his direct freedom with zoology, and his in- direct one with syllables.   But what is *prosodically* gained by calling "capon" "carp " or "caviare" "capon "? by pronouncing "riot" as "riot" and scanning it as "rot"? I cannot for the very life of me see what is the object or the purpose of these prosodic fictions.[1]   Sometimes I have thought that the influence of music (which, as I have more than once hinted, seems to me generally detrimental to sound prosodic views) may have had something to do with

[1] Of course it may be said that the whole thing is merely a logomachy— that Mr. Bridges' system of elision is after all only one of *classifying* the occurrences of "trisyllabic feet," etc.   But I must repeat my appeal to Bysshism. The system (or something very like it) " has deceived *our* fathers and may *us*."

the matter.   When a man is accustomed to the trans-
mogrification of

> When the bloom is on the rye

into

> When the bloo-hoo-hoom is o-ho-hon the rye,

it may seem to him immaterial whether you pronounce
" ominous " and scan " om'nous," whether, in your desire
to find only " three stresses " in

> His min|isters | of ven|geance and | pursuit,

you stagger wildly from " His min | " to " isters of ven | "
and thence to " -geance and pursuit."

For my part, as I have said again and again, prosodic
arrangements are to me merely the systematisation of the
way in which a man, familiar with the language and of
trained ear, reads good poetry to himself or others.   I
have no need of the rack or of the knife of Procrustes,
of the orb or of the epicycle of Ptolemy ; just as, on the
other hand, I have no organs which will enable me to
patter or skate over three short syllables in

> And in luxu|rious cities where the noise,

till I clutch, panting, the blessed *u* of " -urious."

I have compared scansion of this kind before to a
drunkard staggering from post to post ; and it also much
resembles an unskilful hurdle-racer taking his jumps now
too short and now too long.   But the most perfect simile
to my fancy is one the material of which most people
know who have been unlucky enough to be quartered in a
railway hotel on the side overlooking a shunting yard.
They will remember how, in the dead waist and middle
of the night, they were aroused, and kept awake till it was
time to get up, by something like this—

RAM ! - - - - - ra-RAM ! - - - ra-ra-ra-RAM ! - - - RAM-ra-RAM ! - - ra-
RAM-ra ! - - - RAM !

That is the tune of accentual scansion in its altitudes.

But it has also and further occurred to me, as of

course it must have occurred to others, that this prefer- Classical
ence of fiction over fact may be due to some confusion parallels and comparisons.
with classical practice, though, as a rule, the very people
who most object to trisyllabic feet, to foot - scansion
generally, are also those who object to the use, in English,
of the terms of classical prosody itself.   Now, putting
this aside, and putting aside also the minor difficulties of
that practice itself, such as the indication of elision in
Greek and its partial non-indication in Latin,[1] there is in
this connection a much greater puzzle.   Suppose that
Milton did wish to imitate at once the Greek practice of
scrupulously indicating elision, and the Latin practice of
at least sometimes not indicating it but arranging the
metrical scheme as if it were indicated.   Suppose, further,
to stretch concession as far as possible, that he believed
the Romans, if not the Greeks also, to have pronounced
what they did not scan.   After all this a huger difficulty
occurs.   Elision, both in Greek and in Latin, is fairly
universal under its own rules.   There are, of course, a few
instances of permitted hiatus, but they are very few in
proportion and are generally in somewhat exceptional
circumstances.   But Milton observes no such uniformity.
He may " elide " the *e* of " the " rather oftener than he
leaves it unquestionably hiant ; but that, on my theory,
needs no explanation, because he thereby gets the trisyllabic foot he wants.   At any rate, he never hesitates
not to " elide " it.   He may make " Spirit," dissyllabic as I
take it, a pyrrhic[2] rather oftener than he makes it an
iambus, but he never hesitates to do the latter ; the same
with " Heaven " ; the same *mutatis mutandis* with " evil."
On the trisyllabic system, once more, there is no reason
why he should not do so ; on the strict dissyllabic there
is much.   So with " -able " ; so with the liquid-followed

---

[1] I suspect, however, and may possibly again touch on the suspicion, that
this *has* a good deal to do with the matter : and I design to deal also with
the Italian practice of elision.   But sometimes, when I hear people dwelling
on Milton's " Italianation," I cannot held thinking of those brave and beautiful verses of Peacock's about " oak and beech."   You never can teach John
Milton—he never could teach himself, though he may have tried—to be
aught but an English poet.

[2] *I.e.* in *itself*, not a pyrrhic *foot*.

vowels, for which some of our flamens devise such "service quaint"; so with *io* and *oa* and *ae*.   On the one theory it is all right : they are always two, and he adds a third or not as the rhythm leads him.   On the other they are sometimes two gentlemen in one and sometimes two gentlemen in two, at a purely arbitrary choice.   Which is the more reasonable ?

The true prosodic position of Milton.

When, in short, we discard, on the one hand, non-natural imaginings, and, on the other, the earless or eyeless cavil, idol-begot, of the Bysshes and even the Johnsons ; when we subject Milton's prosody to the plain and simple system which we have seen establishing itself from the very first, and shall see confirmed to the latest syllable of recorded English verse,—all difficulties vanish, all cumbrous etiquettes and ceremonies disappear, and we are face to face not only with one of the most perfect developments of English prosody itself, but in a certain sense—and only a certain sense—with its final development.   It took, as it were, a lease of three lives, and a sequence of three works, to effect this final estatement ; leaving, of course, the development of the estate itself open to endless possibilities.   Spenser, completing the task of his humbler predecessors, restored and reconstituted English poetry once for all from the chaos of doggerel, but in so doing deprived it of a certain amount of freedom, "kept it up" very tight, and hardly, after the *Kalendar*, essayed the looser measures.   Shakespeare, availing himself of the almost infinite possibilities of blank verse on the one hand, and not neglecting those of other metres, restored and vastly enlarged freedom itself.   But his successors[1] loosened and liquefied blank verse yet further into sloppy doggerel, almost as bad as, if not worse than, the worst fifteenth-sixteenth-century mixture ; and although they wrote exquisite lyric, "turned it to prettiness" too often. Then Milton, applying the astringent of his austerely beautiful style, and the widely conditioned but never slipshod order of his measures, tightened things up again, yet with all adequate possibilities of easement.

[1] Those to whom we are coming, not those with whom we have dealt.

There is, of course, much difference in his verse, as in
his style ; and one might have thought that this difference
would act as a warning to those who, as in Chaucer's case,
insist on a cast-iron uniformity in this respect, a uniformity
ungracious in itself, and not reasonably exigible from, or
imponible on, a poet's work.   From the liquid lapses of
L'Allegro, *Il Penseroso*, and *Comus* ; from the absolutely
golden mean, between ease and stateliness, of *Lycidas*, to the
almost harsh and certainly austere modulation of parts of
Samson, is a far cry indeed.   But we have dealt with the
stages already.   Here it is only necessary to dwell, and
that briefly, on the varied perfection of the result, and on
the immense importance of it as a sealed pattern and
standing example to all future writers.   Throughout the
days of ignorance and apostrophation, in this respect as in
others, Shakespeare and Milton remained the Jachin and
the Boaz of the temple of true English prosody, between
whom any who chose could enter.   The very people who
reproved them admitted their greatness ; the very reproofs
could not but suggest to an ingenuous Shenstone or a
forerunning Cowper that it was the reprovers, not the
reproved, who were wrong.   Did anybody make a fetich
of exactly corresponding metre ?   The trochaic lines of the
smaller poems showed his folly as soon " as judging by
the result " was attempted.   Did any one lay it down that
ten syllables, and no more, are to go to an English heroic
line ?   Hundreds of lines in *Paradise Lost* were there to
sound cacophonously if you cut them down, musically if
you left them alone.   Did his own petulant malediction of
rhyme cause Israel to sin ?   All the early pieces and not
a little in *Samson* said, " Never mind what he *says* when
he is a pedant in a pet ; look what he *does* when he is a
singer in his singing robes."   And the whole work, from
the *Nativity Ode* to *Samson* itself, from the *Arcades*
choruses to the stately tirades of *Paradise Regained*,
proclaims——one cannot say unmistakably, but in such a
fashion that one can only marvel at any mistake——the
three great laws of English prosody : Foot-arrangement,
Substitution, and Equivalence.

I shall indeed be so very bold as to claim Milton, not merely—as I claim every one from Godric to Tennyson—as evidence of the truth of the system here championed, but as an open-eyed and intentional practitioner of it. Such a practitioner hardly exists[1] before Spenser ; and Spenser, though I believe he always scanned by feet, was evidently, after his earlier experiments in the *Kalendar*, somewhat shy of equivalence and substitution, which indeed were not much wanted, and might have been dangerous if too freely used, in his great stanza. That Shakespeare thought of his scansion, except in a general way as more and more expressing and satisfying the demands of an impeccable ear, I do not affirm or deny, because I believe it to be absolutely unsafe to affirm or deny anything about what Shakespeare consciously did. But from the passages in the Sonnets and in the very defiance gloved up on the front of *Paradise Lost*, from the general character of the scansion (especially the blank-verse scansion) of the successive poems, and still more from a feature to be noticed presently, I do believe that Milton *deliberately* scanned his verse as I scan it—if not to the minutest detail, yet in all general points of foot-division, equivalence, and substitution. I am not only sure that no other so well accounts for the actual result : I do not believe that any other will account at all for the production of that result, and especially for the production of some of the least, as of the most, absolutely delectable points in it. For I am by no means prepared to go to the length of some Miltonolaters, and to regard his metrical experiments as impeccably harmonious. Far be it from me to fall into the gainsaying of Guest, and quarrel with his most beautiful lines because they are "against every principle" of this or that theory of scansion. On the contrary, I have said generally that if a theory of scansion and the judgment of a good ear conflict, the theory must give way. The things that I less love in Milton do not conflict with my theory, but

---

[1] I may perhaps refer to the Preface for some remarks on the singular ideas apparently entertained by some persons on this subject.

the contrary ; and seeing that I can quite comprehend, I can almost pardon though I do not like them. A great many things hideous to me on the other system become quite agreeable, and sometimes exquisitely beautiful, on mine ; but it leaves some disagreeable. It has to account for this, and I think it does.

It is, at any rate, perfectly ready to do so. Wherever there occurs in Milton a line that the allowance of trisyllabic feet will not make harmonious, the result will, I believe, be found to be due to some use of substitution theoretically correct, but in result and the particular case unsuccessful. Now I have kept throughout the proviso, extended and suspended, that each language has its own mysterious metrical decencies and indecencies, and that these are, to my theories of versification and to all others, what the Fates were to Zeus. Milton, always impatient of control, tried, I think, to defy the Fates (like Burgoyne at Saratoga), and sometimes with a similar result. His defiances appear to me sometimes simple experiments —the strange hit-or-miss fugues and toccatas of the *Samson* choruses pretty certainly were so,—and if he had lived they would almost certainly have been turned into the things of beauty that some of them are nearly or already, as it is. In one particular, too, he was always under an influence which was dangerous, and that was his affection for Italian, and the ruling Italian foot, the trochee. He had got beautiful effects out of mixed iambic and trochaic scansions in separate lines and in the octosyllabic [1] as early almost as he got out of his poetic nonage, and he seems always to have been hankering after something of the same sort in the longer line. To this are due his choriambic endings, his ditrochaic and antispastic beginnings. There are not a few who say they like these, and perhaps some who really do. I cannot say that I do,[2] though, as I have said, they are

---

[1] Compare again Chaucer and the "acephalous" line.

[2] Thus I have no affection for his "bottomless pit" whether it be

"bottŏmless" or "bottōmless" ; and I think "universal reproach," whether

it be "univĕrsal" or "univērsal," "far worse to hear" in another sense than

perfectly justifiable as experiments on my theory, which
passes them over, duly *visés*, to the higher tribunal of the
ear.   The same is the case with an occasional accumulation of trisyllabic feet, sometimes running close to the
tribrach, and with the other accumulation, close together,
of redundantly ended lines.   I dare say I may be wrong
in disliking these, but at any rate I am not "doing in-
justice by a law."   My law licenses them all.

Conclusion on uncontentious points.

There are, fortunately, points of Milton's prosody
which lie apart from this peculiar and probably irrecon-
cilable debate.   His use of pause is unique.   Like
Shakespeare, he will put it anywhere or nowhere, so as
to achieve those "periods of a declaimer" which disturbed
Dr. Johnson, bereft of his accustomed warning-bell of
rhyme to tell him he was reading poetry.   But (and I
do not think that this has been quite so much noticed
as it should have been) Milton does not, like Shakespeare,
make the lines embrace and intertwine in the marvellous
manner which constitutes the final secret of blank verse
of the particular kind, and which, as a matter of fact, has
never been quite recovered.   His old fancy for the self-
enclosed line of the Marlowe group seems in a manner
to have persisted, though he subdues it wonderfully to
the purposes of the verse paragraph.   His use of that
paragraph was no doubt suggested (though, it may be,
quite unconsciously) by Shakespeare ; but the contrast
of dramatic and narrative requirements, as well as something in the two men, differentiates it.   It is not Milton's
way to wind up a paragraph to the highest soar of
possibility and then let it "stoop" suddenly as in those
ineffable triumphs of versification which close *Othello*.
The verse paragraphs of Milton are more like the prose
paragraphs of Hooker, which rise, keep level perhaps for
a time, and then gently slope to their conclusion.   Sometimes he arrests the slope a little before the actual lower
limit ; but he seldom finishes off with an artificial flourish,

the original.   Others are open to no sound objection, and some are beautiful
exceedingly.   But they are beauties, not indeed in the least "monstrous"
in kind, but somewhat hazardous in the individual instance.

as Thomson, in imitating him, too often did. We shall
have to wait for Tennyson before we can find any thirdsman for Shakespeare and Milton in the use of this device ;
but it was Milton who distinctly indicated it as a special
resource to English poets.

In another he has no rival in English ; while Hugo,
the only possible one elsewhere, is much more uncertain
in his use of it, and sometimes grotesque. This, it need
hardly be added, is the use of the proper name. If we
combine the tenets of the austerer sects or wings of
Christianity on both sides, the doctrine that intense enjoyment of carnal things is sin with that of Purgatory,
it is to be feared that Milton must have found the
" milder shades" not so mild in respect of his indulgence
in this pleasure. He simply intoxicates himself, and all
his readers who have the luck to be susceptible of the
intoxication, with the honey, or rather the " Athole brose,"
of this marvellous name-accompaniment. To the comparatively simple instances of it in *Comus* and *Lycidas*
may be added :—the Hebraic titles of the demon-gods
and their shrines almost at the opening of *Paradise Lost* ;
the Fable- or Romance-names later ; the shorter passage
in Satan's voyage, and that couplet almost equalling the
earlier in *Lycidas*—

> Blind Thamyris and blind Maeonides
> And Tiresias and Phineus—prophets of old ;

the inhabitants of Limbo ; the earthly Paradises in Book
IV. ; others, though perhaps less conspicuous, in the
central Books, down to the geographical illustrations of
the bridge-building of Sin and Death, and those others
of the change of nature after the Fall, and the gorgeous
catalogue of what was *not* seen from the Mount of
Speculation to which the archangel took Adam. The
taste, too, seems to have grown upon him, for short as
is *Paradise Regained* it contains—in the passage of the
tempter's feast, in the panoramas of Parthia, with the
final reference to the *Orlando*, and the parallel ones of
Rome and Athens—masterpieces of the kind, sometimes

extra-illustrated with alliteration as in the famous and delightful

> Knights of Logres and of Lyonesse,
> Lancelot and Pelleas and Pellenore,

which Tennyson imitated less wisely than well.

And so let us leave, with words in which all may agree, the last of the Four Masters of English Prosody.

CHAPTER II

THE BATTLE OF THE COUPLETS

The main currents of mid-seventeenth-century prosody—The use of
the couplet—The pioneers—Fairfax—Sir John Beaumont—
Sandys—The first main practitioners—Waller—Characteristics
of his smoothness—His other metres—Their moral as to the
couplet—Cowley—His curious position—His couplet generally
—The *Davideis*—His own principles—His lyrics—Denham
—The opposite or enjambed form—Chalkhill, Marmion, and
Chamberlayne—The constitutive difference of the two styles—
Dangers of enjambment—Note on the two couplets.

THAT Milton is the greatest single figure prosodically, as he is poetically, in the mid-seventeenth century, is undeniable. But his prosodic *influence* was not actually exerted till long after this time, and he does not represent any of the actual prosodic movements or phenomena which were most characteristic of the day. These movements or phenomena were, in the main, three—all of great importance—the Battle of the Couplets, the break-up of Blank Verse, and the culmination of Lyric. To them we must now turn.

The present chapter will be arranged in accordance with the general method of presenting, as far as possible, a chronologically continuous account of the prosodic performance of individuals, but of grouping, with a certain " before-and-after " licence, exemplars of specially remarkable prosodic developments. That is to say, it will refer to some things which saw the light during the period of the last Book, and, it may be, to some that have been already mentioned there, in order to survey intelligibly what is perhaps the main prosodic phenomenon of the first two-thirds of the seventeenth century—the emergence of the decasyllabic couplet as the staple metre of English poetry ; the flourishing side by side for a while of its two forms, the overlapped and the self-contained ; and the final triumph of the latter. This last stage we shall not here reach ; the other two will be our immediate province.

The use of the couplet. We have seen in the first volume that the couplet, if not of the very beginnings—the earth-born originals—of strictly English prosody, makes attempts to be born as early as the *Orison of Our Lady*, figures in the " heap " of twelfth- and thirteenth-century measures, and shows itself pretty frequently, if accidentally, in Hampole and in the anonymous poems of the Vernon and other MSS. during the fourteenth. It is finally established by Chaucer in something like both its forms, or rather in a form which very readily becomes either, though the temporary prevalence of the redundant syllable is against the sharpest-cut outline of ridge-backed stop.

We saw, further, that this latest and in a sense greatest triumph of Chaucer's art was comparatively little followed by his actual followers, and that those who did attempt it were almost more unlucky than with rhyme-royal. In fact, nothing shows the " staggers " of this period quite so well (and therefore so ill) as the couplet, and nothing could, unless it were blank verse, which was not then written. The octosyllable is so short, has so many licences, and can be so easily botched off after a fashion, with *cliché* rhymes and expletives, that it offers little difficulty to the *mediocris poeta* ; and rhyme-royal itself is long enough to give that poet a sort of chance (in the old provincial phrase) of " odding it till it comes even." But the couplet is at once long enough to admit, and too short to hide, the most gruesome deformities and anomalies. The early practice of it in the next century on the stage probably did not a little good, for nobody could *speak* couplets like some of Lydgate's without being sensible of their ugliness. And as soon as the strict belief in iambic feet, "keeping of accent" and the like, came in, the couplet began to be possible, and was sure to be practised. This same belief made directly, and at last successfully, for the stopped form; but it could not be admitted at once. The stanza, with its comparatively ample space, had got too much into the poetic blood of Englishmen, and they could not at once give up elbow-room. Accordingly in Spenser, Drayton, Daniel, and others, as we have seen, the character is still somewhat undetermined; it is only after the beginning of the seventeenth century that it begins to differentiate itself in an unmistakable way. Of the special stopped form, not of course the actual genesis but the intermediate origin may still be assigned, with fair if not absolute exactness, to a name already consecrated by tradition.

Whether the reader, who comes to the perusal of Fairfax's *Tasso* with a remembrance of the praises which have been bestowed upon it by poets and critics of various times and tastes, will or will not experience something of disappointment in regard to actual poetic pleasure, is a question which may be posed, but need not be discussed. The prosodic importance of this painful translator and father of witch-beset virgins[1] is quite undeniable. It is, in fact, constituted irrefragably by the fact of Dryden's well-known assertion that Waller told him that he had been influenced by Fairfax. If, therefore, he was no poet's poet he was a reformer's reformer. And let nobody interject any doubt about Waller's actual part in a certain rather questionable "reform of our numbers." The people who followed that reform believed[2] in his part in it for a century and a half, and that is the point of importance. We may make a new translation-application of *possunt quia posse videntur*, and say that the

The pioneers —Fairfax.

---

[1] See the curious story in Scott's *Demonology* or in Fairfax's own *Daemonologia* (ed. Laing, Harrogate, 1882).

[2] There is a very curious instance of Waller-idolatry in the verse prefixed by Robert Gould to the 1682 edition of Fairfax himself—

> Let Waller be our standard, all beyond,
> Though spoke at court, is foppery and fond.

influence which is acknowledged is evidently an influence which exists.   It is not necessary to waste words on the illusory objection that Fairfax, writing in stanza, could hardly have much to do with the introduction of the couplet.   He *did* write in stanza ; but his stanza was the octave with couplet close, and it is evident from the very first that he was inclined—and did not resist his inclination—to isolate this.[1]   Tasso himself had not commonly run his stanzas into one another, even to the extent of allowing less than a full stop at the end ; and his sixth lines, though they admit a little more licence, are generally full-stopped also.   Fairfax enjambs the sixth a little more, but is punctilious about the eighth.   Now we saw that Chaucer's practice, in stanza which also has a couplet ending, probably had much to do with, and was certainly followed by, his adoption of the couplet alone.   In Fairfax's case the follower (save in the small degree noted) was not himself ; but the process was the same.

Moreover, it so happened that Fairfax, by choice or insensibly, fell into a mould of line and couplet which was much closer to the stopped antithetic ridge-backed variety of this latter than anything in Chaucer.   A selection below,[2] beginning with the very second stanza of the poem, will show this ; but there has been no need to select the specimens with any care, for they are not the exception, but the rule.   There can be little doubt of the

---

[1] The edition just cited of *Daemonologia*, includes some eclogues of his own in sixain with final couplet ; the others are in continuous couplet, though partly batched in fours.

[2] If fictions light I mix with Truth Divine
And fill these lines with other praise than Thine.
                                                    i. 2.

We further seek what their offences be :
Guiltless I quit ; guilty I set them free.
                                                    ii. 52.

Thro' love the hazard of fierce war to prove,
Famous for arms, but famous more for love.
                                                    iii. 40.

In fashions wayward, and in love unkind,
For Cupid deigns not wound a currish mind.
                                                    iv. 46.

effect which they—so early, let it be remembered, as
1600—must have produced on ears which, as we see
from the result, were ready to hear.   There can be less
of that which this couplet, combined with a diction more
modern than Spenser's, not by ten years but by nearly
a hundred, must have had on later generations who
did not mind modernised romance, or rather preferred
it.   For this very reason Fairfax may not be very
refreshing now to some palates, which have no objection to Dryden or Pope, and which never weary of
Spenser, but which do not care greatly for a watery
compromise.

It is specially desirable to dwell a little on his diction
as well as on his line, because we shall see that this is
a very important element in the birth and progress of the
stopped couplet itself.   It cannot away with the slow,
gorgeous, heavily vowelled tone and rhythm of the older
vocabulary ; it wants neat, curt, sharp locutions—colours
which may be bright, but which must be decided and
definitely contrasted, not iridescent or vaguely nuanced.
Now Fairfax gives it what it wants.   Poor Collins's
malady was indeed an *amabilis insania* when it persuaded
him that Fairfax and his " magic wonders " were in
perfect harmony.   There is a great deal more of prose
and sense in Fairfax's numbers, and likewise in his phrase,
than of " magic."

The demand to which this answered was put remark- Sir John
ably by another Jacobean poet, Sir John Beaumont, in a Beaumont.
poem to the King " Concerning the True Form of English
Poetry."   This is, in fact, Sir John's principal title to an
appearance here, though it is not always mentioned in
accounts of him.   It is unlucky that we do not know the
exact date of the piece ; but as it was addressed " to his
late Majesty James I." it can hardly be later, and may
be much earlier, than the earliest date that can possibly
be claimed for the writing of Waller's " Santander " lines
(*v. inf.*), while it must be years earlier than the appearance
of those lines.   The actual form of its couplets is noteworthy, but the sense conveyed in it is much more so.

Sir John, speaking as to an expert in prosodic precept,[1] does not indeed say in so many words that the stopped couplet is the master metre, but this is evidently the sum and substance of what he means ; and if Pope had known the lines at the time when he wrote the *Essay on Criticism* he would probably have stolen them, or some of them. First, the author of *Bosworth Field* stigmatises "the *other* fellows "—

> On halting feet the ragged poem goes
> With accents neither fitting verse nor prose—

a couplet for which his contemporary and "father" Ben would have hugged him, as the later Johnson felt inclined to do, even to his enemy Adam Smith, when he heard of his love for "rhyme." Indeed, after glancing disdainfully at

> Holes where men may thrust their hands between,

Sir John goes on—

> The relish of the Muse consists in rhyme :
> One verse must meet another like a chime.
> Our Saxon shortness hath peculiar grace
> In choice of words fit for the ending-place,
> Which leave impression in the mind as well
> As closing sounds of some delightful bell.

Not merely Johnson but the austere Bysshe himself would have applauded the sentiment—

> In many changes these may be expressed :
> But those that join most simply run the best ;
> Their form, surpassing far the fettered staves,
> Vain care and needless repetition saves.

And Mr. Addison and Mr. Pope, nay their leader the great M. Boileau-Despréaux, contemptuous as he was of all things English, would have acclaimed and laurelled the man who in the depths of "the last age" dared to write in praise of

> Pure phrase, fit epithets, a sober care
> Of metaphors, descriptions clear yet rare.

---

[1] See the "Prosodists" chapter of the last Book.

It is not surprising that Mr. Courthope [1] should describe this " as an exact and critical conception of the nature of the poetic art," and should say that " a more admirable illustration of the classical spirit naturalised in English verse is not to be found in the range of English poetry." Substitute " neo-classic " for " classical " and I should say ditto to my friend very cheerfully.

Beaumont practised what he preached very fairly, but, unlike Waller (who, indeed, was considerably his junior), he could manage the " stave " without " fettering " it, and could show something of the powers which it has, beyond those of what might be more truly called the " fettered " couplet.   But he hardly deserved addition to the list of poets in the third chapter of the last Book.   Here his place is undeniable. [2]

If Beaumont has often been defrauded of his due Sandys. place among the vaunt-couriers of the stopped couplet, and if Drummond has been promoted a little hastily, another traditional pioneer, George Sandys, is perhaps again questionable, not so much in point of quality as of date.   With the odd fatality which seems to hang about the chronology of this couplet, the exact appearance of his translation of Ovid's *Metamorphoses* is uncertain.   It seems to have been published in 1621, within the reign of James, and the usually accurate and trustworthy Haslewood describes a copy.   But there is nothing in the British Museum earlier than the next edition of 1626 — Caroline, not Jacobean ;   and Sandys's other couplet work—*Paraphrases* of Job, of Jeremiah, etc.—is distinctly later, while he certainly revised the *Ovid* very carefully in 1632.   But these are not matters of much importance ;   and, once more, the position which Dryden assigns to Sandys is of itself important enough.   Any-

---

[1] *History of English Poetry*, iii. 197 *sqq.*   The poem itself may be found in Chalmers, vi. 30, 31.   Of Beaumont's other pieces, *Bosworth Field* is couplet ; but he has some good stanzas in an *Ode of the Blessed Trinity*, which perhaps had some influence on Milton's "Nativity," in 6, 6, 6, 6, 10, 12, *abbaba*, and in an *Epithalamium*, 10, 6, 12, 10, 8, 14, *abbaab*.

[2] Mr. Courthope would bracket Drummond with him : but I scarcely think Drummond so far advanced.

body, however, who turns to Sandys's actual work (it should be said that the *Ovid* is not included in the standard modern edition, that of the Rev. R. Hooper in the *Library of Old Authors*) will see at once that, though he may have a strong *nisus* towards the stopped form— a *nisus* perhaps originally determined by his anxiety to represent Ovid as much line for line as possible,—he is under no preceptist scruples in his methods, and does not always attain any very great smoothness in his results, though he sometimes does. Enjambment is quite frequent, and the pause is varied almost as freely as in blank verse. But there is certainly a hammer-stroke of emphasis in him which does foretell Dryden.[1]

The first main practitioners— Waller.

Waller occupies—or has by turns occupied and been served with notice to quit—a place of such importance in prosodic history that, especially as his volume is not great, we may consider all his verse here under the head of the metre which gained him his distinction. I do not propose to take up much space with " verifying his powers " or discussing his title. There is, in fact, too much of the gold-and-silver shield business about the discussion to make it a profitable one. More than half the modern readers who are indignant with " Waller was smooth " are so because their ideal of smoothness and Pope's or Johnson's are two quite different things. And as there seems to be no means of ascertaining exactly when such pieces as the " Santander " poem were written, it skills very little to produce such and such a verse, or

[1] Compare the openings of Job I. and II.—

> In Hus, a land which near the sun's uprise
> And northern confines of Sabæa lies,
> A great example of perfection reigned,
> His name was Job, his soul with guilt unstained.

> .   .   .   .   .   .

> Again when all the radiant sons of light
> Before His throne appeared, Whose only sight
> Beatitude infused ; the Inveterate Foe,
> In fogs ascending from the depth below,
> Profaned their blest assembly.

Sandys's prosodic interest is not limited to the couplet. The metres of his Psalm Paraphrases are varied, and include several examples of the *In Memoriam* quatrain.

such and such verses, of Beaumont, Drummond, Fairfax, and others back to Drayton, or (as can be done) Spenser himself, which have the Wallerian quality. It can be done ; it has been done here ; and there's an end of it.

What is really important is that Waller *may* certainly have written such verses as these[1] as early as 1623-24 ; that these verses have a certain quality, and that this quality was what succeeding generations admired in him, thought that he had mainly discovered, and regarded as the standard of good verse—as what all verse had better be. Let us see what this model actually is.

The standard of "smoothness," it will be seen, is pretty exactly that which, by a strange enough instance of the force of a once thoroughly inculcated convention, persons who honestly think the poets from Coleridge to Tennyson much greater poets than those from Waller to Crabbe, still put in school-books as the standard of the "regular" heroic couplet. That is to say, two lines of ten syllables each, with "accents on the even places," a division in sound if not in sense somewhere about the middle, and an exact but not identical rhyme at the end, are kept as far as possible complete in themselves, without necessarily borrowing from or intruding into those which precede or those which follow. This severance of the couplets Waller does not yet *thoroughly* observe ; but he observes all the other rules. He has no trisyllabic feet ; he has no "wrenched accents," as they call it. The motion of his mètre is as regular as that of a rocking-horse in good order and on a good floor. He allows himself expletives—especially the conjugations of " do "— in a way which will soon be tabooed ; but this is done to attain "smoothness." Further, he has, by congeniality of nature, already attained certain characteristics which, though not "in the bond," as a matter of fact always

Characteristics of his "smoothness."

---

[1] With the sweet sound of this harmonious lay
About the keel delighted dolphins play ;
Too sure a sign of sea's ensuing rage
Which must anon this royal troop engage :
To whom soft sleep seems more secure and sweet
Within the town commanded by our fleet.

develop themselves in this sort of couplet, and are recognised as a sort of *patina* or added grace in it.   Keeping
the pause as close to the middle as possible naturally
causes a slight opposition, or antithesis, of motion in the
two halves, and this as naturally invites a slight antithesis
of sense.   Corresponding epithets in the two halves help
this antithesis very much, and they duly make their
appearance ; while the same want which suggests the
expletive verb also suggests the expletive epithet.   Lastly,
not to make too great a breach, too great a rupture of
smoothness, between the lines, the rhymes are chosen with
as little echo and depth in them as possible : and even
the words within the lines themselves avoid thunderous
and long-drawn sound.

But whatever be this form's merit or its shortcomings,
there is practically no question but that Waller had a
great and a curiously *prospective* command of it.   That
the command was great, the example already quoted, and
almost any other in his work, should sufficiently show.
That it was mainly a matter of instinct rather than of
trained obedience to rule, a perusal of his whole work
will show quite as decidedly.   For instance, in one of his
very latest poems, the Epitaph on Henry Dunch, written
when Waller was eighty years old and about to follow his
friend next year, he not merely writes—

> Which, well observing, he returned with more
> Value for England than he had before—

an overrunning of the line which is quite Chamberlaynian
—but overruns the couplet itself in

> A pious son, a husband, and a friend.
> To neighbours too his bounty did extend
> So far, etc.

On the whole, however, it is evident that his genius
prompted him continually in the direction of the smooth,
stopped, antithetic couplet.   He was, of course, not its
Columbus ; nobody was.   It was only an island lying
off the inhabited continent, which had been visited
now and then, but never regularly colonised till, about

his time, the chief seat of prosodic civilisation and government was transferred to it.   But that Waller had as much to do as anybody with the transference nobody had, or is ever likely to have, better opportunities for knowing, or better brains for judging, than Dryden ; and what Dryden's opinion was we know.[1]

His prosodic interest, however, is very far from being confined to the couplet, though, curiously enough, the remainder of it has a bearing also on this.   It may be at first sight surprising, but only to those who have not considered the matter, to find that, out of this peculiar couplet, Waller is by no means infallibly or continuously " smooth."   The one thing of his that everybody knows, or used to know, " Go, lovely rose," has, of course, nothing that can be called harshness about it.   But it is not particularly mellifluous ; and among the abundant honey-pots of Caroline lyric it is perhaps rather dry than sweet.   The alternate eights of " Chloe, yourself you so excel " are better, but not extraordinary ; and I turn his lyrics over backwards and forwards, without being able to find anything that has the intense, the almost overpowering exquisiteness of music which belongs, not merely to Herrick and Carew and Crashaw and Marvell, but to Kynaston and Stanley, and even John Hall.   The best things are the catalectic trochaic dimeters of the Amoret poem, with the contrasted quatrains [2] on Amoret herself and her rival—in fact, these last eight lines are the best things that Waller ever did.   But the curious thing is that he

His other metres.

[1] The finest couplet that Waller wrote, and his most poetical passage, composed, as it happened, just before his own death—

> The soul's dark cottage, battered and decayed,
> Lets in new light through chinks which Time hath made,

is a good example of the yeoman's service that prosody can do to poetry. As a *couplet* it is not out of the way, though the variation of cæsura and the monosyllabic constitution of the last line are noteworthy ; but the effect of the thought, which *here* is the chief beauty, is much enhanced by the curiously varied values of *a* in the first line and *i* in the second.

[2] Amoret ! as sweet and good
> As the most delicious food,
> Which, but tasted, does impart
> Life and gladness to the heart.

not only never reaches the most poignant harmony, but is sometimes capable of singular discord. Even Johnson perceived the strange cacophony of the *Puerperium*,[1] which prompts a charitable reader to ask whether there is not some mistake, whether he has not got hold of a foul copy. I suppose it was written to music—that fertile source of prosodic imperfection. But then a poet with a good ear would have refused to write to this music—would have said, " You must please make your music musical *for verse.*"

There is yet another place where this excuse, though bad, will have to be replaced by a worse, and that is the piece cited below.[2] It may be observed that it is called a " Song," so, once more, the reason of the cacophony may be musical ; but it is, at least, prosodically explicable (which the other is not) on the ground of a prosodic mistake. We know—and Waller doubtless knew—how charmingly the heptasyllable, not merely of preserved iambic cadence, but of cadence definitely shifted to trochaic, adapts itself to the regular iambic octosyllable. It is very improbable that he did not know *Comus* and Milton's other minor poems, which appeared in print before his own. He certainly knew Shakespeare's triumphs in the measure, and he could not be ignorant of the more than successful attempts of Jonson, Browne, Wither, and others. But he seems not to have noticed— or noticing, to have neglected—the remarkable fact that in all these cases the rhyme is continuous and coupleted.

---

[1] *E.g.—*

> Saccharissa's beauty's wine
> Which to madness doth incline :
> Such a liquor as no brain
> That is mortal can sustain.

> Fair Venus in thy soft arms
> The god of Rage confine ;
> For thy whispers are the charms
> Which only can divert his fierce design.

[2] Say, lovely dream ! where could'st thou find
> Shades to counterfeit that face ;
> Colours of this glorious kind
> Come not from any mortal place.

He endeavoured—and the endeavour was quite justified
as an experiment—to twist the arrangement and make the
rhymes alternate. But his very first stanza ought to have
shown him that this was, in the excellent Biblical word
we have used before, " confusion." Exactly why the ear
revolts at this combination of shifted metre without
apparent rhyme it might be difficult to say ; though on
some of the symbolist systems I daresay it could be
accounted for in the manner which does not account.
But the fact can be illustrated by another little experiment, curious but conclusive. Shift the rhyme-words to
make couplet arrangement, and, though the sense will be
damaged, you will find that the rhythm is, as if by miracle,
restored—

> Say, lovely dream ! where could'st thou find
> Shades to counterfeit that kind ;
> Colours of this glorious face
> Come not from any mortal place.

I have made many curious observations in the course of
this work, but I do not know one which pleases me more
than this.

The fact is (and it may be set as people please on
either side of the account) that special aptitude and predilection for the stopped couplet seems, save perhaps in
the solitary case of Dryden, to preclude aptitude for any
other measure. It may be that this couplet is Aphrodite
Urania, and that he who loves her can tolerate no meaner
love. It may go more nearly to be thought by some that
an opposite explanation is correct. Or, without being
thus personal, it may be said, and perhaps most philo-
sophically as well as most politely, that the measure is so
extremely specialised that tongue and ear and finger,
once thoroughly subdued to it, can adapt themselves to no
other. But the fact, with the rule-proving exception of
the gigantic if not god-like craftsmanship of Dryden, is
the fact. In Waller's case I think his prosodic shortcomings account, at least as much as any quality of his
thought, for the unsatisfactory character of his lyric.

*Their moral as
to the couplet.*

Compare " Chloris ! farewell " with Marvell's masterpiece [1]
in the same stanza. The thought of the latter is better,
no doubt ; but its betterment is for less in the matter than
the limpness of Waller's measure contrasted with the
undeniable spring and soar of Marvell's,[2] or than the
tameness of Waller's diction contrasted with the rocket-
scattering quality of " rare " in the place where it occurs
and the magnificent bulk and run of the single word
" impossibility." The couplets on Myra, " The Night
Piece," [3] are very pretty and graceful, and not much less
" metaphysical " than the wildest excesses of Benlowes or
Crashaw. But, once more, both measure and diction are
flaccid ; there is no throb, no quiver, no explosive and
jaculative quality about them. In fact, one feels inclined
to play on them the reverse trick to that which we are
going to play on Garth and Pope and expand them in
decasyllables—

> [Fell] darkness which [the] fairest nymphs disarms
> Defends us ill from [radiant] Myra's charms,

etc. But this is too wicked.

Cowley—his curious position.

Cowley is a far more of a prosodic puzzle than his
fellows, Waller and Denham, and the much greater bulk
of his work might seem to challenge more elaborate
treatment than was demanded even by Waller. The
puzzle indeed is, as is *not* the case with them, one in
which the general poetical question is rather inextricably
mixed up with the special or prosodic. Waller had little,
and Denham had less, of the pure poet about him ; but
Cowley had a great deal. Even Johnson admitted that ;
and yet Johnson might have been supposed to be pre-
judiced against Cowley three or four times over, not
merely by his metaphysicality, but by the further facts
that large parts of his works are regularly lyrical in form,

---

[1] *V. inf.*, p. 334.

[2] Observe that Marvell himself is *not* an exception to the rule above. His lyrics are splendid, but his couplets, though vigorous, are not accomplished.

[3] The poem is late, but still too early for Granville's " Myra," Lady New-burgh, the object of so much admiration in her youth and of Dr. King's Yahoo-like satire in her age.

a form for which Johnson cared little ; that he was the inventor and most considerable practitioner of Pindarics, the irregularity of which the great lexicographer hated more than anything else ; and that his principal couplet-poem, the *Davideis*, is sacred in subject and not invariably or excessively smooth in form. The fact is that it is very difficult for anybody who really likes poetry in *any* form not to like something in Cowley ; but for this very reason (or the counterpart and complement of it) it is still more difficult for any one who has decided tastes in poetry to like Cowley everywhere or very much. It may be even not mere paradox to suggest that in this peculiarity lies the secret, at once of his astonishing popularity for a time and of his rapid and complete loss of that popularity. He represented all the tastes of a time of transition and overlapping ; and he could please all while none was particularly dominant. He wrote couplets better than any " metaphysical " and lyrics much better than any of the new couplet poets ; while he provided in his Pindarics an escape for those who found the couplet too monotonous and the lyrics too fantastic. He did serve many masters—with success as long as one master had not definitely got the mastery. But when this happened he went down ; and when, long afterwards, the strong man had to give way to a stronger, he did not come up again.

This not exactly Laodicean but in some respects " trimming " temperament is as noticeable in him—has indeed, by allusion and glance, been already shown to be as noticeable—in true prosodic respects as in regard of subject and of other matters. Cowley's couplet, which, let it be remembered, is not, like some others, open to any chronological scepticism, is an interesting study. In his *Juvenile Poems*, published when he was fifteen, in 1633, the year before *Comus*, they only appear in the closing distichs of the sixains of *Constantia and Philetus*, etc. But *Sylva* (three years later, and a year before *Lycidas*) is full of them. They exhibit a much less definitely stopped form than those of Waller's probably, and Beaumont's certainly, ten years' older attempts ; and are some-

His couplet generally.

times frankly enjambed.   In them sometimes, and in other pieces often, the boy-poet (he was still only eighteen) succumbs to the worst fault of the time—a fault which the pure stopped couplet (to do it justice) *did* discourage— the fault of apostrophation without the possibility of elision or of a harmonious trisyllabic foot, as thus—

> By calling th' Pope the Whore of Babylon,

where you certainly can apply a remedy worse than the disease by reading "the Pope" and "th'ore."   But this is not in a couplet.

Nor can it be said that Cowley ever gave himself up entirely, or mainly, to Wallerian "smoothness."   He could and did attain it towards the end of his life : but it is evident that he never fell into the groove in which it is practically impossible for a man *not* to give it.   And the verse of his *Davideis* deserves a brief study.

The *Davideis*.   The *Davideis* is one of those poems in dealing with which it is rather common for critics to lament the rarity with which it is read, and then to insinuate reasons why people should think twice or thrice before reading it. I have read it myself more than once, and I can see no reason why anybody, who does not read "for the subject" only, should not follow my example.   From that point of view it has the inevitable drawback of sacred narrative verse, that the main story is known, and that the teller's ekings of it can hardly interest, and may possibly displease. But this does not concern us.   What does concern us is to determine whether Cowley was justified in the rather rash and not very modest boast, made in good lines towards the beginning—

> Lo ! this great work, a temple to thy praise,
> On polished pillars of strong verse I raise.

Certainly not over-modest, and as certainly rather rash. But, as it happens, the couplet which comes immediately before this—

> From earth's vain joys, and Love's soft witchcraft free,
> I consecrate my Magdalene to thee,

is something of a justification. Indeed, there is a note
in it far above the mere tick-tick of Waller, and anticipating to no small extent the resounding line of Dryden
himself, who, beyond all doubt, paid in his youth much
attention to Cowley. Nor is the whole paragraph which
introduces these lines much less worthy of study.

And the qualities here found are frequent throughout
the poem. "Strong lines" (to use his own words, both
in and out of connection with Walton's well-known observation) abound ; strong couplets hardly less ; strong
passages of no inconsiderable bulk could be produced in
plenty to match or excel that given just now. But it is
clear that Cowley, like Dryden again, wanted, to show his
prosodic powers, more room than the narrow lists of the
Fairfaxian-Wallerian couplets could give him. He soon
expatiates into the Alexandrine. An early instance is—

> And o'erruns the neighbouring fields with violent course.

There is no doubt that, whatever the tyranny of regularity
may order, this expatiation does give to the couplet a
liberty, and at the same time a majesty, which are
unobtainable without it. And Johnson, had another man
said it, would have been the first to find this demurrer to
his own argument, "I cannot discover why the pine [1] is
taller in an Alexandrine than in ten syllables." Indeed,
he hastens to supply the demurrer himself by saying of
the other line—

> Which runs, and, as it seems, for ever shall run on,

that it is "an example of representative versification which
perhaps no other English line can equal." If you may
do "representative versification" in water, why may you
not do it in wood ?

On the other hand, Johnson is certainly right in part,
and no small part, when he says that Cowley's versifica-

---

[1] In this very line—

> Like some fair pine o'erlooking all the ignoble wood—

it is astonishing that Johnson should have overlooked the overlooking of ten
syllables by twelve.

tion is sometimes harsh to modern ears.   The line which Cowley himself thought might require justification to the most part of readers [1]—

> Nor can the glory contain itself in th' endless space,

requires it still, and will find it very difficult to get. That there was something wrong with his own ears, or his own principles, is evident from the fact that he thinks this plea of "representative versification" will cover it, and alleges among his parallels the very line we gave above, "And overruns," etc., which is perfectly unobjectionable, and another—

> Down a precipice, deep down, he casts them all,

which is, if anything, rather worse than "Nor can the glory."

His own principles.   This doctrine of sound to suit sense never lost its hold, even when Cowley himself was slighted, and it will meet us often.   It is obviously of very limited validity— at best a beggarly element of the great doctrine of verbal and specially vowel music ; while, applied as Cowley applies it, it ignores a far higher law, the necessity under which metre lies of conforming to its own nature.

In fact, no theory of foot or accent will save the bad lines quoted.   In particular, on our principles at least—

> Down a precipice, deep down, he casts them all,

commits the very worst fault that verse can commit, that of suggesting a different rhythm and line-base from that which was intended.   Had I seen this verse without its context, I should have supposed it to be one of the rough but fairly marked anapæstic lines which were then just coming in—

> Down a pre|cipice, deep | down, he casts | them all.

---

[1] His words are : "I am sorry that it is necessary to admonish the most part of readers, that it is not by negligence that this verse is so loose, long, and, as it were, vast : it is to paint in the number, the nature of the thing which it describes . . . The thing is that the disposition of words and numbers should be such as that, out of the order and sound of them, the things themselves may be represented.

These things occur far too often in the *Davideis*; but they occur side by side with others, which, in a sort of incult luxuriance, have very considerable beauty.   Nor is it quite obvious why Johnson so greatly preferred the lines on Crashaw's death, which, fine as they are,[1] are not finer than many of the *Davideis* passages, and exhibit very much the same liberties from the Johnsonian point of view of versification.   The Alexandrine, at any rate, is in constant evidence here.

It is characteristic of that contradictory quality which His lyrics. we have noted in Cowley that he is not merely inclined to eccentricity in the couplet and to regularity in lyric— we noticed this, too, in his far greater master, Donne— but that he is on the whole more timid in his diction exactly when he has the instrument that generally tempts to audacity.   He is certainly very much more of a singer than Waller; but he is seldom " nobly wild."   His most popular and perhaps his best thing—the well-known " Chronicle " of what we do not need biographers to tell us were almost to a certainty imaginary loves—is of absolute prosodic adequacy : it runs with a light, bright, regular insincerity which leaves nothing to desire in its own particular fashion.   Nor does he ever, as we have shown that Waller does, choose positively unsuccessful—perhaps positively illegitimate—measures.   But some of his also are not very happy.   Here is one which he uses more than once—

> Why, O, doth sandy Tagus ravish thee,
> Though Neptune's treasure house it be ?
> Why doth Pactolus thee bewitch,
> Infected yet with Midas' glorious itch ?
> > Ode II.

where the two shorter and central lines should certainly rhyme, or else the line-lengths should be differently adjusted.   Two other forms (*v. inf.* Odes IV. and V.) are

---

[1] The whole piece, being short, *is* perhaps the best place to study the Cowleian couplet for those who blench from the *Davideis*, and it starts with—

> Poet and saint ! to thee alone are given
> The two most sacred names of Earth and Heaven.

much better; but they are still rather, to use the old fable, clay birds prettily moulded than the same made alive.   His very favourite octave of couplets in varying line-length is sometimes better.   But both in these and in others he too often reminds us of that frightful vision of Guest's (more terrible far than the much-talked-of Lucretian nightmare of the homeless atoms sleeting in the void) of a poet sitting down to try all possible " sections "—and *not* rejecting those which are unsuccessful.   Another curious pair of metres illustrating the way in which he will keep both a bad creation and a good one will be found below.[1]

Perhaps as successful as any are his schemes for the elegy on William Hervey, and the version of Horace's *Pyrrha*, which contains some very pleasant things—not so plain in their neatness as Milton's, but daintily decked enough.   He has not lost the gift of the earlier century in trochaics; his Anacreontics include many well-known, and deservedly well-known, pieces; and the infinite variety of metre in the *Mistress* cannot, in such hands, fail sometimes to be charming.   Perhaps the finest measure of all, the opening of " The Change," [2] is merely a modification, in the last line, of the old sixain.   But

---

[1] Here's to thee, Dick; this whining love despise.
Pledge me, my friend; and drink till thou be'st wise.
    It sparkles brighter far than she,
    'Tis pure and bright without deceit;
    And such no woman e'er will be.
    No: they are all sophisticate.

.   .   .   .   .   .

When chance or cruel business parts us two,
    What do our souls, I wonder, do?
    Whilst sleep does our dull bodies tie,
    Methinks at home they should not stay,
    Content with dreams, but boldly fly
Abroad and meet each other half the way.

[2] Love in her sunny eyes does basking play;
Love walks the pleasant mazes of her hair;
Love does on both her lips for ever stray,
And sows and reaps a thousand kisses there:
In all her outward parts Love's always seen;
But oh! he never went within.

The second and fourth stanzas contract lines 2 and 4, and expand 6.

that of "Platonic Love" is very effective,[1] and the
irregularly observed form of "Called Inconstant" might
be still more so, if Cowley's phrasing, never a thing
much to be depended on, had not failed him.   He returns
here frequently to his beloved ugliness of enclosed short
lines that do not rhyme together.   On the whole, he is
rather unsuccessful in making his new schemes "run";
and it is no small relief to come—as in the famous piece
which yields the hackneyed but still admirable

> The adorning thee with so much art—

upon old ones.

But one must not be too hard on a courageous
experimenter; and the greatest of Cowley's experiments,
his "Pindaric," has yet to be noticed elsewhere.   Still,
on the whole, one should, prosodically as otherwise,
correct a little that sentence of Rochester's which so
shocked Dryden's propriety.   It is not true that Cowley
was "not of God"; but he was not quite sufficiently of
God.   There was too much wood, hay, and stubble
mixed with his nobler materials; and in some cases even
the fire of time will not burn these out and let the nobler
things remain in literature.

Sir John Denham does not require much notice. Denham.
There is no need to quarrel with the praise which Dryden
bestowed upon the famous passage [2] known to everybody,
and about the only thing that anybody, except a very
few persons, does know of its author's.   Nor is it really
of much moment that this passage was not in the original
edition of *Cooper's Hill*.   The maxim of "Saint Archi-
triclin" (as the early mediævals beatified "the ruler of

---

[1] Indeed I must confess,
When souls mix, 'tis an happiness;
But not complete till bodies too combine,
And closely as our minds together join:
But half of Heaven the souls in glory taste
Till by love, in Heaven at last,
Their bodies too are placed.

The last three lines rhyme in seventeenth-century English, and the triplet
is essential.

[2] O could I flow, etc.

the feast ") is not binding upon the poet. He may produce his wine in what order of merit pleases him ; though if it pleases him not to produce " that which *is* worse " at all, so much the better. But what is worth our notice is, that, prosodically, this passage matches rather ill with the context in which it was set. Still, the whole is of very fair couplet standard, as are Denham's poems generally. He is a little happier than Waller in his lyric metres, chiefly for the reason that he seldom or never attempts impassioned verse, and that the step from the more or less flippant couplet to the wholly flippant " verse of society " is no wide one. Very good in its way is the last stanza of " Mr. Killigrew's Return "[1] and the first of the version of Martial's most graceless epigram.[2] The octosyllabic triplets of " Friendship " and " Single Life," and the couplets of the Cowley epitaph, are also very good ; especially the latter, which are very sound criticism in excellent verse.[3] But they are nothing out of the way prosodically ; nor is anything else of Denham's. He can make a good "copy of verses "——a much better copy of verses than most can make : but that is about all. He has as much of Dryden on one side, and of Prior on the other, as consists with being in a very different class of poetry and prosody from that which Dryden and Prior illustrate.

Thus, considering their prosodies not merely as regards the couplet, but generally, we see that neither Denham nor Cowley (he, indeed, least of all), nor even Waller, was

---

[1] Mirth makes them not mad
    Nor sobriety sad.
But of that they are seldom in danger :
    At Paris, at Rome,
    At the Hague, they're at home—
The good fellow is nowhere a stranger.

[2] Prythee die and set me free,
    Or else be
Kind and brisk, and gay like me :
I pretend not to the wise ones,
    To the grave (*bis*)
    Or the precise ones.

[3] Our Chaucer, like the morning star,
To us discovers day from far, etc.

whole-hearted in practising and championing the form, and that peculiarities discoverable in their other verse affected, to some extent, their practice here.

Such, however, are the general prosodic aspects of the three chief introducers of the new form of verse in the mid-seventeenth century. But, meanwhile, the precise form and order of the stopped couplet itself were being determined, as such things often are, at least as much by Eris as by Philia—by the competition and contrast of a form and order entirely different. We have seen, repeatedly, that the couplet itself, in its earlier history, never can make up its mind which fork of the Y to take, and is nearly as often enjambed as self-enclosed. Yet the recoil from fifteenth and early sixteenth century disorder was itself in favour of the enclosed variety; and on the whole the tendency of it during the last quarter of the sixteenth was in this direction—the direction which was to be finally adopted. But as soon as the memory of that disorder became a little dimmed, and as soon as English poets generally began to be more sure of themselves, and not to require such obvious assistance as that of the line-stop, the other kind also began to be largely affected. We have seen it in reviewing prosodically the works of poets who did not wholly give themselves up to it, like Drayton and Daniel; we have seen it in poets who, like Browne and his set, positively preferred it in narrative and purely poetical poetry; while we have also seen it used, with pretty definite purpose, in satire. But as the century advanced, it acquired almost complete ascendency in some cases; and though in some, again, of these its peculiar charm was conveyed, the *toxic* quality which that charm almost implied showed itself also, and beyond all doubt caused the double reaction—to blank verse in Milton's case, to the stopped couplet in others. To some of these instances we may now pay attention. The chief of them are, beyond all doubt, John Chalkhill or whosoever was the author of *Thealma and Clearchus*, Shakerley Marmion in *Cupid and Psyche*, and William Chamberlayne in *Pharonnida*.

The opposite or enjambed form.

If we accept the only evidence [1] which gives *Thealma* to Chalkhill, his precedence follows almost as a matter of course, for the same testimony implicitly asserts it. A person who was a "friend and acquaintant of Edmund Spenser" (*ob.* 1599), and who was probably coroner for Middlesex before 1603, could not well have written this much later than 1610 at the farthest, and ought to have written it much earlier, for it is evidently the work of a young man, saturated with the *Arcadia*. Its versification, however, is quite different from anything that we have so early; it is a much greater step in the direction of enjambment than anything in Browne or in Wither. Chalkhill's verse sentences are very nearly as stopless as Clarendon's prose ones, and very much less capable of being stopped by a little charitable and judicious assistance. At my first dip I light upon a passage of eighteen lines (*ed. cit.* p. 417) without a full stop either at line-end or in line-middle. But this prolixity is of much less importance to the point than the way in which Chalkhill treats the actual *ending of the line*. It is in this that the real difference of the two systems lies. It is possible to run the two lines of the couplet pretty frequently into each other, and even not to refrain scrupulously from overrunning the second, without seriously infringing the principle of "stop." This principle is that, unless there is something special to be gained prosodically, grammatically, or elsewise, there shall be a pretty well-marked pause at the line-end, and a very well-marked pause indeed at the couplet-end. This may be said to have been observed by everybody who used "riding rhyme" from Chaucer to Drayton; and, though Browne and others violate it without scruple and without attending to the proviso, they do not seem utterly reckless of it. Chalkhill constantly, Marmion rather less often, and Chamberlayne as a rule, pay absolutely *no* attention to it—do not even seem to know that it exists.

---

[1] Izaak Walton's in the original edition. See the reprint of Singer, or that of the present writer in the second volume of *Minor Caroline Poets* (Oxford, 1906). *Cupid and Psyche* will be found in the same volume; *Pharonnida* in the first.

Very often they seem to think no more of " the end of The constitu-
the line " than if they were writing prose, except that it tive difference
is the place where you have to provide a rhyme.   If they of the two
styles.
do not make a point of overrunning it, it is simply
because they do not apparently think about it at all.
Nothing stops them ; nominative can be separated from
verb, adjective from substantive, preposition even from
case, without compunction, and, in fact, without so much
as attention or object.   The result of this is that rhyme
assumes quite a new character.   It is no longer a " time-
beater " or " flapper " except in a quite *minim* degree : it
does not tell you (at least in any definite way) that you
have come to the end of the line at all.

This may seem likely to be, and indeed sometimes is,
a source of rhythmical danger ; but these poets, to do
them justice, generally have the sense of rhythm pretty
well implanted in them, and can manage without the
staff which they so ostentatiously refuse to employ for
its staff-purpose.   When this sense fails them, the effect
is certainly not over-charming.   On the other hand,
rhyme, which is not of its nature a retiring or bashful
thing, forges for itself a quite new office.   It supplies a
sort of *obbligato* accompaniment to the rhythm.   In fact,
this couplet at its best is rhymed blank verse, possessing
the freedom, the variety, the absence of tick and click
which distinguishes " blanks," and yet adding a sort of
low guitarish accompaniment of rhyme-music.   The poet
gains immensely in range and room and verge ; he need
lose nothing in euphony.   But it would be exceedingly
uncandid to conceal, and indeed quite hopeless to attempt
to conceal, that he often does lose a good deal.

The directions of his loss are various, and, though Dangers of
some of them lead out of strict prosody, they all concern enjambment.
us, because the general case is nothing if not prosodic.
To begin with results concerning us technically least but
most important from some points of view, the looseness
of versification seems to pass, by some really metaphysical
fate, into looseness of grammatical structure first, and
then into looseness of story.   This is least noticeable in

Marmion, who has a classical pattern to keep him straight, and who also is by no means exclusively given to enjambment ; it is much more noticeable in Chalkhill, who is very rarely stopped ; and it reaches its extreme in Chamberlayne, who, though he can manage the stopped couplet well enough, and actually uses it when he thinks proper, evidently rejoices and almost wallows in the other.   A collection of instances to be given at the end of the chapter may illustrate this, and the subject generally, much better than mere talking about it can do.

There is, however, another danger, of a somewhat different character, which touches us more nearly in its direct and downright consequence as well as in its process. Composition and versification of this kind tend to destroy or impair the very thing which should be the chief justification of such poetry—the separate line and phrase, the " jewel five words long," which to some folk is the rose of poetry itself.   There is this danger even in regard to the phrase, though Chamberlayne, at least, constantly manages to save that, and is prodigal of it beyond almost all but the greatest poets.   But even he is careless of giving it to us in the line, or in definite multiples or fractions of the line.   He slops it, and spills it about, so that, were it not for the more definite rhythm, it might be a clause of the ornater prose.   Now, this cannot be right.   " *Maxima debetur* lineae *reverentia.*" [1]   It is the integer of poetry, the mistress of the poetic household, obliging indeed, and serviceable, ready to lend itself to any honest compliances, but not to be sunk and confounded in a mere mob of syllables.

In these two trios—Waller, Cowley, Denham ; Chalkhill, Marmion, Chamberlayne—the Battle of the Couplets can be seen in the most instructive and illustrative manner possible.   You may take them as group against group, as individual against individual, and not seldom as the individual divided against himself.   For this latter purpose nothing is more luminous than the contrast of Chamber-

---

[1] It may be well to observe that I do *not* think the first syllable of *linea* short, and do *not* warrant its use for this sense in classical Latin.

layne's *Pharonnida* with his verses to Charles the Second
—a contrast which, until recently, it was not easy to make,
for Singer's reprint of *Pharonnida* did not include the
lesser poem.   That the couplet, no matter in what form,
had by this time pretty well established itself as the
vehicle of such addresses, is undoubted ; but the way in
which the very captain of one side is apparently com-
pelled to desert to the other in his management of it for
this purpose, is a palmary instance, if ever there was one.
A definite subject, limited space, the necessity (or at least
the obvious desirableness) of making your appeal as
pointed and your points as clear as possible, obviously
get the better of all personal and poetical inclination.
When you say " And now to business," you take up the
stopped form as you put on a business coat, without
skirts and trimmings and furbelows.   The age at this
moment was saying " Now to business," and it took up
its office jacket almost as a matter of course.   It would
be extremely easy for the present writer to extra-illustrate
this chapter from all sorts of sources, well and little
known ; but for the general purposes of this history
almost enough should have been said.[1]

[1] I have not given many examples of the stopped couplet, because it is
well known and has undergone very little change from Fairfax's *Tasso* to
Thackeray's *Timbuctoo*.

> In Africa, a quarter of the world,
> Men's skins are black, their locks are crisp and curled,

sums it all up.   The enjambed variety is much less uniform and much less
known, and some specimens of its seventeenth-century form may be useful :—

> The rebels, as you heard, being driven hence,
> Despairing e'er to expiate their offence
> By a too late submission, fled to sea
> In such poor barks as they could get, where they
> Roamed up and down, which way the winds did please,
> Without a chart or compass : the rough seas
> Enraged with such a load of wickedness,
> Grew big with billows, great was their distress ;
> Yet was their courage greater ; desperate men
> Grow valianter with suffering : in their ken
> Was a small island, thitherward they steer
> Their weather-beaten barks, each plies his gear ;
> Some row, some pump, some trim the ragged sails,
> All were employed and industry prevails.
>
> *Thealma and Clearchus*, 2203-2216.

(Note the final stopped form.)

> When you are landed, and a little past
> The Stygian ferry, you your eyes shall cast
> And spy some busy at their wheel, and these
> Are three old women, called the Destinies.
>
> *Cupid and Psyche*, iii. 259-262.

> But ere the weak Euriolus (for he
> This hapless stranger was) again could be
> By strength supported, base Amarus, who
> Could think no more than priceless thanks was due
> For all his dangerous pains, more beastly rude
> Than untamed Indians, basely did exclude
> That noble guest : which being with sorrow seen
> By Ammida, whose prayers and tears had been
> His helpless advocates, she gives in charge
> To her Ismander—till that time enlarge
> Her than restrained desires, he entertain
> Her desolate and wandering friend.   Nor vain
> Were these commands, his entertainment being
> Such as observant love thought best agreeing
> To her desires.
>
> *Pharonnida*, IV. iii. 243-256.

Here are fourteen lines—seven couplets—without so much as a comma at the end of any one of them.   On the double-page opening from which they are taken at hazard, *eighteen* lines only out of *ninety-eight* are ended with a stop of any kind.   On the other hand, the Restoration poem (*England's Jubilee*) runs, though it is still enjambed in a way, like this :—

> Pardon, great Prince, for all our offering here,
> But weak discoveries of our wants appear ;

and

> The giddy rout who in their first address
> Cried " Liberty ! " but meant licentiousness.

NOTE ON THE TWO COUPLETS

I BELIEVE it may be not quite superfluous to draw the special attention of the reader to the fact (which I have not neglected in the text of either volume, but which cannot be too clearly understood) that neither form of the couplet is absolutely the elder. In the pre-Chaucerian examples the tendency is, if anything, to a kind of stop; and though Chaucer's own bias is rather towards enjambment, it is not enjambment of the Chamberlaynian type. Moreover, stopped couplets of almost the stock eighteenth-century kind may be found in Spenser and in Shakespeare. The form is always pulling both ways from the first: and there is no distinct tug over the line till the Restoration.

CHAPTER III

THE DECAY OF DRAMATIC BLANK VERSE

Beaumont and Fletcher—Their taste for redundance—Their attitude to their licences — Massinger — Ford — Shirley — Randolph — Brome—Davenport—Nabbes—Glapthorne—The actual *débâcle* —Suckling—Davenant—The problem—And its answer— Further instances—Goff and Cokain—*Nero* and *The Martyred Soldier—Rebellion—Andromana*—Divers Caroline plays compared with *Lust's Dominion.*

Beaumont and Fletcher. To begin a chapter with the above heading by dealing with Beaumont and Fletcher may seem a critical eccentricity, if not a critical outrage. And to begin the third chapter of our Sixth Book with two writers who were dead years before Chapman and Jonson, themselves treated in the second chapter of the Fifth, may seem chronologically unpardonable. But I do not think that very much argument is necessary to rebut any of these charges. The constant caution given here as to overlapping should dispose of the second ; and as far as the first is concerned, " I am," as Mr. Titmarsh would say, prepared "to construe anybody any day" in Beaumont and Fletcher, or in admiration of them.

There is, in fact, no doubt that in any well-arranged bird's-eye view of literary history, with a special prosodic outlook, they must appear as the first noteworthy examples of that " unscrewing " of dramatic blank verse which led, before long, to the break-up of its whole structure as a dramatic medium, and from which it required no less force than Milton's to rescue it as a vehicle of narrative. We have seen that Shakespeare himself, whose death almost exactly coincided with Beaumont's, and who *may* have worked with the pair at *The Two Noble Kinsmen*, had in his own later plays eased the screws very freely, and rather hazardously in appearance. But, then, Shakespeare was such an absolute *tregetour* with blank verse, that he could make the rocks of its Brittany vanish as easily as he could bestow a sea-coast on its Bohemia. And if we could be quite sure, as we nearly may be, that *The Tempest* is his absolutely last play, and so later than *Cymbeline* and *The Winter's Tale*, there would be good reasons for thinking that he had seen some danger in his penultimate practice, and, while not in the least giving up the advantages of redundance, had determined to guard against its disadvantages.

For the " twins," on the other hand, it is clear either that the practice had no terrors, or that they determined to brave them. The prominence of redundance, whether in the plays ascribed to Fletcher alone, to those ascribed to the pair, or in those ascribed to Fletcher and some collaborator other than Beaumont,[1] is so much of an accepted fact, that it is unnecessary to waste upon proving it space which we here want for things not generally accepted.[2] *Their taste for redundance.*

Enough, perhaps, has been said in the chapter on Shakespeare on the almost inevitable danger of this practice. But what is extremely noticeable is that Beaumont and Fletcher, luxuriating thus in one of the great blank-verse licences, appear either not to feel the *Their attitude to their licences.*

---

[1] I was rebuked twenty years ago for declining to enter into this question of distribution in my *History of Elizabethan Literature*. I am afraid that frequent reading and study, including the task of editing the text of one play, *Rule a Wife and Have a Wife*, in the most minute and careful fashion possible, has left me impenitent and of the same opinion still—that distribution is impossible.

[2] Here are a few arithmetical facts. In Philaster's last speech before the revolution at the end of the play named after him, there are twelve redundances in twenty-eight lines ; in Cæsar's magnificent lament for *The False One* (perhaps the greatest thing in the whole vast work), striking out the two awkward interruptions of Antony and Dolabella, there are twenty-nine lines, of which all but ten are redundant ; in Aspasia's picture-piece at the end of the Second Act of *The Maid's Tragedy* there are eighteen lines and eight redundances. But one need not take sledge-hammers to doors that are open.

need of the other, or purposely to abstain from it. They
have trisyllabic feet, of course, but in comparison with
Shakespeare's these are few. Nor are they very fond of
Alexandrines, though these also do occur. On the other
hand—and it is the great merit of their verse—they
have learnt from Shakespeare, or found out for themselves, almost the full virtue of the varied pause and run-
on sense, though they are less careful than he is to vary
the variation. This varied pause and run-on sense, in
fact, is almost necessary in order to carry off frequent
redundance : for a succession of single-moulded lines with
redundant endings is one of the most monotonous and
one of the ugliest things possible in blank-verse making.[1]
In fact, the exquisiteness of their lyrics shows the very
high prosodic degree which they, or one of them, probably
Fletcher, had attained. In hands less drilled to harmony,
the redundance could not but have been offensive ; and
in such hands it was bound to become so. But this
sleight of ear, and wise abstinence from "licence on
licence," kept them, if not scatheless, yet comparatively
unscathed. It made them, however, none the better
models, for the old *vitiis imitabile* is nowhere a truer
maxim than in prosody.

Massinger. The blank verse of Massinger, inferior as he is in
poetry to the twins, has in a certain sense more interest
than theirs, because it exhibits conflicting tendencies.

---

[1] Take an instance even from their own work in the speech of Archas
(*The Loyal Subject*, IV. v.). Here are very numerous redundances (only four
or five lines out of twenty-nine being without them), few or no important
internal pauses, and a general single-moulded line—

> If I had swelled the soldier, or intended
> An act in person leaning to dishonour,
> As you would fain have forced me, witness Heaven,
> Where clearest understanding of all truth is
> (For men are spiteful men, and know no pi[e]ty).
> When Olin came, grim Olin, when his marches, etc., etc., etc.

It is not easy to imagine a worse effect, and I am bound to say that the
peculiar "Fletcherian" amphibrach or antibacchic conclusion (of which
Milton's "in this soil," and similar things (*v. sup.*), are supposed to be
followings), does not arride me much, especially when preceded, as it is
often or very closely, by a pause. It has, as I said above, a "stumbling"
—as I might almost say a hiccupping—effect, which I cannot think agreeable
or artistic.

We know that he worked with Fletcher ; and if we did not know it, the approximation of some of his verse to that of the more usual pair would be obvious to any careful reader.   Indeed, I believe the " enumerators " rank him next to Fletcher, though a good deal below him, in point of " weak endings," which are evident enough in most of his best and worst passages.   Nay more, he sometimes experiences the drawbacks of the practice more than Beaumont and Fletcher do ; for he is less careful to vary and lengthen the internal pauses, and not unfrequently has a full stop at the redundant syllable, a thing only tolerable in very special cases.   On the other hand, his proportion of redundant lines is certainly smaller ; and he seems to have realised the truth that they are seasonings, or at most side-dishes, not *pièces de résistance*.   The consequence is that two closely connected but not quite indistinguishable types of blank verse emerge in him— the one nearer to Fletcher and " dissolution," the other to Shakespeare and the perfect middle way.   Indeed, here for the first time we can speak of resemblance to the greater and earlier writers with some special propriety. More than one student of the Elizabethan drama, since it was possible to study it as a whole or nearly so, has noticed in Massinger, and in him first, distinct " literary " quality—the evidence of writing in a school.[1]   And this is, I think, as clear in the passages where he tempers redundance with arrest, and thus is at his highest, as in those where he lets the Fletcherian volubility carry him away.

Ford is so much less inclined to redundance that, Ford. reading him independently and in no conscious relation to others, it might seem, in him, no more than the exception which occurs, as we have seen, almost from the first. Indeed, his blank verse generally is of a much older type than that of any one mentioned in this chapter ; and it sometimes, as in the remarkable piece of lurid bombast

---

[1] I do not refer to mere citations and references, such as those dealt with in Dr. E. Koeppel's interesting essays on *Ben Jonsons Wirkung*, etc. (Heidelberg, 1906).

(and yet not quite bombast neither) which may be cited below from *Love's Sacrifice*,[1] carries one right back to the University Wits. Nor in his greater plays does the staple of verse ever approach the dressing-gown-and-slippers form. It is impossible, in our very limited knowledge of Ford's history, to decide whether this is a case of a man writing late in life (as he seems pretty certainly to have done) and deliberately or unconsciously observing the fashions of his youth, or of one making (in this case deliberately beyond all doubt) a literary study of his forerunners and adopting a standard according to the older of them. Probably there is something of both ; there is almost certainly something, whether much or little, of the second. For Ford, though very far indeed from being the least, is certainly the most artificial of all the giant race before the flood ; he smells most of the lamp ; he betrays most clearly that *renchérissement* which we can only express in English by the doubly disreputable aid of paraphrase and slang. It is almost if not quite a necessary consequence of this, that his blank verse is the least flowing and varied of any. But it ought to be set to his credit that it is an almost perfect instrument for the class of subjects which he proposes to treat. The consummate and universal Shakespearian form would expose the " extra-naturality " of the *Broken Heart* and *'Tis pity she's a Whore* too much ; the loose Fletcherian would make their excesses disgusting.

In neither Massinger nor Ford, however, can there be said to be much abuse of the trisyllabic foot ; while the very peculiarities which have been mentioned save Ford, and to a rather less degree Massinger, from the great danger of all, slipshod and clumsy enjambment. This cannot be said of the last scene or " Shakescene " of the Shirley. company, James Shirley. The literary tendency which

---

[1] iv. 1.   *Duke.* Forbear ; the ashy paleness of my cheek
         Is scarleted in ruddy flakes of wrath ;
         And, like some bearded meteor, shall suck up
         With swiftest terror all those dusky mists
         That overcloud compassion in our breast.

Here, as of old, it does not matter in the very least that there is no stop either at " cheek " or " mists." The line *as such* is bullet-moulded.

has just been noticed is more noticeable in Shirley than ever : he not only collaborates with other men—that had always been done—but he finishes their work, writes new plays which are obvious refashionings of old, follows parts of old plays freely. He is, moreover, of his own time as well as of theirs, and though not by any means so great a sinner in the special sins of that time as some, he is not free from them, as the speech of Fernando in Act II. Sc. i. of *The Brothers*, one of his best and most serious attempts, will show.[1] Nobody, I suppose, will charge the present writer with looking too much awry on prosodic licences. But I do not see how it is possible to regard such things as the line-breaks at " what," and still more the thrice-continued one at " to," " thou," and " shall," as other than extremely ugly blemishes. It is true that Shirley rarely—as we shall see in a moment many of his fellows do—complicates this licence with others—redundance, trisyllabic feet of the clumsiest kind, and ill-rhythmed lines or lines of quite haphazard length, till verse disappears altogether in a slough of the most awkward prose. But in this overrunning of the line which must be taken in conjunction with the tendency to overrun the couplet (see last chapter), he is a most offending soul. One turns a leaf and finds—

> He had better cool his hot blood in the frozen
> Sea, and rise hence a rock of adamant
> To draw more wonder to the north, than but
> Attempt to wrong her chastity.

---

[1] I dare,
With conscience of my pure intent, try what
Rudeness you find upon my lip, 'tis chaste
As the desires that breathe upon my language.
I began, Felisarda, to affect thee
By seeing thee at prayers ; thy virtue winged
Love's arrows first, and 'twere a sacrilege
To choose thee now for sin, that hast a power
To make this place a temple by thy innocence.
I know thy poverty, and came not to
Bribe it against thy chastity ; if thou
Vouchsafe thy fair and honest love, it shall
Adorn my fortunes which shall stoop to serve it
In spite of friends or destiny.
(Ed. Dyce, i. 212.)

Here a fight might be made for "but" if it stood by itself; but the neighbourhood of "frozen" with its totally unjustifiable divorce from "sea" is not likely to dispose any one with an ear to mercy. And what on earth was there to prevent his writing—

> He had better cool his hot blood in the sea
> Of ice, and rise a rock of adamant?

That is, in fact, the question; and it is a question which can only be answered, "The spirit of the age was there to prevent him, and he was not strong enough to withstand it." Not that Shirley is a bad blank-verse writer by any means; these very passages, which were chosen at the purest hazard to show his vices, show his virtues as well.[1] He really has at times, and not so seldom, form, fire, *timbre*. I am not certain that he has not sometimes more of these than either Ford or Massinger, though he has nothing like their dramatic power. But the epidemic of looseness is on him, though not in its worst form. With Minerva willing he can write the beautiful last lines of Amidea, which are so interesting to contrast with Otway's similar exaggerations of Fletcherian sentiment, and the still more beautiful lament of Florio over her, where, be it observed, redundance appears strongly to express passion in the old way. Nor does he require strong situations; although facile in these he can furnish ordinary blank verse as well as Middleton or Heywood (as per dip in *The Young Admiral*, p. 123), and sometimes extraordinary blank verse (as in *The Cardinal*, p. 343). His prowess in lyric is well known; and that he should sometimes slip in the manner above indicated is a great sign of the times.

To find, however, this sign in complete ascendant, we

[1] The very beautiful one (noticed long ago by Farmer, and in a note to Dyce's ed.), ending—

> And with it many beams twisted themselves
> Upon whose golden threads the angels walk
> To and again from Heaven,

is not far from the others.

must pursue the line of evidence (as it was not necessary to do in the last chapter on the subject) through some of the minorities.   Not all are guilty, yet even in the innocent we may observe that they are, as a rule, the older.   Thomas Randolph,[1] as became a son of Ben and a scholar, is quite free from the roughest impeachment. Randolph's verse may not be of the first quality as poetry ; his subjects do not give it much opportunity of being so. But it is strong, free, well-ordered, and able to avail itself of all lawful things without being brought into bondage to any.   The speech of Mediocrity at the close of *The Muses' Looking-Glass* is an excellent piece of blank verse of a good pattern ; and neither here nor in the other plays shall we find anything that can truly be called bad.   The frequentation of Ben indeed appears to have been to some extent sovereign against verse-paralysis.   " Dick " Brome, whom he " had for a servant once " and whose promotion to the status of playwright he welcomed in nearly his best manner, was a person whose own manner obviously " better suited prose."   The character of his happiest plays—and they are very far from unhappy—invites it, and he does well in it.   But when he has occasion to give verse, which he does not infrequently, it is quite competent and in fact rather interesting, because it takes all the liberties—redundance, trisyllabic feet, etc.   It is never, perhaps, very poetical, but also it never falls into mere chaos.   The general blank-verse scheme is perfectly well maintained.

Another minor of the third decade of the century, Robert Davenport, is also, at his best, fairly " tight and shipshape and Bristol fashion."   Now this is the more remarkable because his plays are not well printed ; and Mr. Bullen in his reprint of them has taken no liberties, though he makes a few suggestions.   There is plenty of very rough verse in him.   I do not know that it can

Randolph.

Brome.

Davenport.

---

[1] Of course his claims are not limited to blanks.   He has good couplets ; capital ''broken and cuttit verse '' in the '' Anthony Stafford '' Ode and other pieces ; excellent octosyllabic triplets in his '' Epithalamium.''   But it is all rather forged than fused.

be acquitted entirely of symptoms of a break-up. The trisyllabic feet are often mere slurs, mere patter; and there are numerous passages where one would very greatly prefer mere prose, and may indeed suspect that mere prose was meant. But these very shortcomings imply that he has over all an impression and atmosphere of the true blank verse—which impression and atmosphere are the very things that are wanting in some writers to whom we are coming.

Nabbes.   The same is very much the case with the still later, looser, and more pedestrian Nabbes. There is really not much more need for him to "drop into verse" than there is for Brome, but he does it, and does it by no means badly. He even sometimes, as in *The Unfortunate Mother*, resolves to be nothing if not poetical, and carries out his resolve without too much failure from the merely formal point of view. Only, once more, when he employs the two, one can often hardly help saying, "Why not write prose entirely?" and when he sticks to verse, "Was it necessary to take so much trouble?" For, once more, blank verse is, in the double sense, nearest prose; and it has to be in many ways careful lest it knock down the partition between the two houses.

Glapthorne.   That much-abused, and it may be admitted not very much-deserving, playwright Glapthorne occupies perhaps a somewhat middle position. As there is no reason why some of his plays should have been more carefully printed than others, one can only suppose that he himself was more careless in some of them. Take Sir Martin's speech in the first Scene of the fourth Act of *The Hollander*, and you will have to rewrite it in its earlier or latter parts to get any kind of pure blank-verse rhythm into them; yet the middle is of very fair quality. Contrast Wallenstein's speech and that of his son on opposite pages of the Pearson reprint (48, 49); take numerous speeches of Doria in *The Lady's Privilege*. They might seem to have been written by different persons: it is difficult to imagine that any one who had been sufficiently broken to the writing of blank verse to produce some of them, or parts of some, could possibly be guilty of others or parts of others.   Yet an example of this kind is a convenient and valuable bridge between those which we have just been examining and those which we are now to examine.   That the school of Fletcher generally tended to laxity, and the school of Jonson to correctness, may be true enough.   But there must have been something in the air which affected the former to produce something more than laxity.   For Fletcher is seldom or never unrhythmical : men like Glapthorne, and, still more, men like the remarkable pair to which we are coming, with even Shirley to keep them company, are.

Of Suckling we may certainly say, as we said of Shirley, that his metrical prowess in lyric is well known ; indeed, it is much better known.   Some half-a-dozen pieces of Suckling's are familiar, to the fairly well-read general reader, for one of Shirley's.   It is true there is the doggerel *Session* ; but putting what is said elsewhere aside, the most accurate and punctilious metrist in the world may write doggerel deliberately.   Take up Suckling's plays and you will meet on every page doggerel that is *not* meant—that has no conceivable reason for being meant—as doggerel. There is a specimen on the third page of *Aglaura*—not an extreme one by any means, but a fair average.

The actual *débâcle.* Suckling.

This opens, not with a casual Alexandrine which Shakespeare might very well do, but with rhymed Alexandrines—things uncommonly difficult to smuggle in, even with a special purpose, in blank verse.   Then it at once settles down to rather shambling decasyllables of the ordinary kind.   All of a sudden occurs a clumsy octo-syllable—

> Would come should make me master of,

paralleled lower down by another and clumsier—

> It cannot be long, for sure fate must.

The example, it has been said, is not an extreme one, but it already makes one think of the Lydgatian chaos which we struggled through of old.   Here is a worse—

Thor. Softly, as death itself comes on
        When it doth steal away the sick man's breath,
        And standers-by perceive it not,
        Have I trod the way unto their lodgings.
        How wisely do those powers
        That give us happiness order it ! etc. etc.

Now I do not say that by "arranging" you may not pull a verse here and a verse there straight after a fashion, but I do say that the whole is hopeless.   And one could parallel it and outdo it, a hundred times over, from Suckling.

Davenant.   But there is another case which is almost as strange as Suckling's.   Davenant, if not one of the greatest, was one of the most thorough men of letters of his time.   He belonged to the older race, not merely by his perhaps mythical relation to Shakespeare, but by his certain association with Fulke Greville and others; to the middle by his friendship with Hobbes and all the wits of the First Caroline period and the interregnum, as well as by nearly forty years' practice in letters and the theatre; to the newer age by his friendship and partnership with Dryden, and the powerful assistance which he gave to the return to rhyme on the stage.   He was not only more of a poet than is sometimes thought, but a good deal of a critic; he could write correct and stately verse enough in *Gondibert* ; and one or two of his lyrics—the early lines on Shakespeare, the famous "Lark" song, and others—could no more have been written by a man without an ear than Suckling's could, though they may not have quite the same airy grace.   Yet Sir John himself is not a greater sinner than Sir William in respect of chaotic and barbarous blank verse.   The third line of his first play, *Albovine*, which dates as early as 1629, runs—

        Verona which, with the morning's dim eye—

an almost Occlevian abomination in its shapeless decasyllabicity, without corresponding rhythm.   Suppose, charitably, that there is something wrong here—there certainly is, but not in this sense—and turn the page to

get a whole speech of some length in verse, that of
Hermenegild to Paradine——

> Rhodolinda doth become her title
> And her birth.   Since deprived of popular
> Homage, she hath been queen over her great self.
> In this captivity ne'er passionate
> But when she hears me name the king, and then
> Her passions not of anger taste but love :
> Love of her conqueror ; he that in fierce
> Battle (when the cannon's sulphurous breath
> Clouded the day) her noble father slew.

Now I venture to say that this is immedicable.   To
the sanguine and complaisant ear some scraps of
rhythmical promise, " Her title and her birth," " She hath
been queen," and similar rearrangements, may suggest
themselves.   But it will be found that nothing of the
kind " will *do* " : it only leaves nubbles of shapeless and
concordless phrase wedged between the experiments.
Of course, if you slash with a Bentleian hook, and simply
throw the slashings away, you can do something with it ;
but that is not the way *we* behave round this mulberry
bush.   Even the last resource of throwing the whole into
prose——a thing which doubtless at this time may be done
in some cases with advantage and perhaps justice——will
leave it in no better condition.   For then it will be the
scraps of rhythm that intrude themselves awkwardly ;
and moreover, the order of the words is not prose order.
It simply has to be taken for what it is——blank verse,
but hopelessly bad blank verse——knock-kneed, mutilated,
awkwardly sliced at line-ends, with no pause-composition ;
as inartistic as anything can possibly be.

> Battle (when the cannon's sulphurous breath

is about as vile a thing metrically as I remember ; and
if anybody says that you can put it all right by reading
" battalia " or some similar form, I can only once more
reply that, no doubt, if things were different they would
not be the same, and that if Venus Anadyomene is
allowed to be substituted for Venus Hottentotiana there
will doubtless be an improvement in colour, outline, and

the rest.   Moreover, it *is* the same everywhere, both in
this play and in others.   You may think, now and then,
that you have got out of the stones of stumbling and on
to fairly level ground ; but you will assuredly find yourself
sprawling headlong, before a score or so of lines have
been read.   Even when some sort of rhythm is kept it
is only by aid of reckless splitting of adjective from
subjective, preposition from case, noun from verb, without
the faintest excuse or atonement of special poetic or
rhetorical effect.   It is bad blank verse—and there's an
end of it.

The problem.   Now what does this mean ?   How could a man who
could write the "Ballad on a Wedding," or "'Tis now
since I sat down before," sit down, either before or after,
to write such stuff as this, believing it to be any kind of
tolerable verse whatever ?   How could an equally or more
hopeless thing be done by one who could accomplish the
workmanlike, if not wonderful, quatrains of *Gondibert*,
the decent couplets of the *Siege of Rhodes*, and divers
lyric measures, without tripping ?   How, much more, could
a man like Shirley, who was neither a mere dilettante
like Suckling, nor of a generation that was actually and
already breaking away from blank verse like Davenant,
occasionally condescend to it ?   Why did Glapthorne,
small as may be his actual inspiration, fail to produce at
least as respectable verse as men a little earlier, with no
greater gifts than his, could turn out ?   And why in other
writers do we see the same sort of "rot" spreading ?   The
answer is, I think, twofold.

And its
answer.   In the first place, the degradation, strange as it may
seem, can be set down in part to that very imitation, that
very "literary spirit," which has been noticed.   It must
be remembered that the growth and the failing of blank
verse were not separated from each other by any considerable stationary period of orthodox and settled
practice.   They overlapped each other with a copious
and complicated overlapping, and the pupils could, with
the greatest ease, take the irregularities which their
masters had permitted themselves on the way to per-

fection as steps on the way to perdition. Further, though I believe too much rather than too little stress has been laid on the long-suffering shoulders of the printer, it must be remembered that the printed editions of Shakespeare and the rest are not exactly things "to *lippen* to," to place implicit and unquestioning faith in. But, most of all, it must be remembered that the most perfect blank verse is (from certain points of view) a tissue of exceptions and irregularities, and that it requires but a very little blundering in the use of these to make it a complete failure.

And this brings us to the other fold of the answer— that there *was* a spirit of such blundering abroad, and that by its works we know it.

The overlapping mentioned above confuses the vision ; while perhaps if we endeavour to get the two sets of phenomena separately envisaged, there is a danger of regarding them *too* separately. But, on the whole, when we consider the total effect of the work reviewed in the last chapter on this special subject, and the total effect of that reviewed in this, two different spectacles do seem to outline themselves to the mind's eye. The one is of a house, or houses, in process of building—in various stages of the process, in fact. Here the walls are half-reared ; there the complete "carcass" is finished, and even perhaps roofed in, but the interior is in various stages of imperfection. Here you have only the joists of a floor ; there the frame of a staircase clinging to the walls ; or all this done, but no decoration, no paper or painting. On the other side we have a house or houses in the process of pulling down, and at some stages of that process not very distantly resembling stages in the other process of building up. But to the fairly acute and careful observer the two things are very different. The "fervency of the work" is constructive in the one case, destructive in the other. In the one the workman is making himself a *pou sto* for further advance ; in the other he is hacking away the brick-work under him, making the plaster fly, tumbling down the beams and planking.   There is not much doubt as to what the result will be in the respective conditions.

As a contrast of the two styles I do not think it too freakish to take two writers, each of whom has been rather a by-word with literary historians than a familiar study with readers—one of whom, indeed, is still not easy to study.   I refer to Thomas Goff, of *The Raging Turk*, and Sir Aston Cokain, of *The Obstinate Lady*.   Goff was indeed an older man than Cokain by some sixteen or seventeen years ; but the former's plays were being acted at Oxford (*c.* 1630) just at the time when the latter was at Cambridge ; and we know from Cokain's too chary revelations about the older playwrights that he must have been theatre-bitten pretty early.   Moreover, the date of the second (collected) edition of Goff[1] coincides very nearly with the appearance[2] of Cokain's work—the date of composition of which we do not know at all.   There is very good ground for thinking that it preceded the shutting of the theatres.   Anyhow, and giving full value to their difference of birth-date, they represent, all the more completely for that, the older and the younger generation of First Caroline playwrights. Now Goff, whose work is even in other respects rather better than it has sometimes been represented as being, is a most respectable if by no means a heaven-born blank-verse writer.   He drops into couplet sometimes—one would expect him to do so—at the end of scenes and speeches, and sometimes elsewhere.   Yet his blank verse, as blank verse, is orderly enough ; you will not find a real "hobbler," certainly not due to the printer, at all frequently.

But with Sir Aston it is quite different.   His plays vary a little in this respect.   I think *Ovid* is rather more regular than *The Obstinate Lady* and *Trappolin*.   But even in it, and much more in the others, the "rot"[3] appears.   Most people know that uncomfortable affection

---

[1] 1656. This, of which is my copy, is not a common book, and the earlier separate editions (1631-33) of Goff are very rare indeed.

[2] 1658.

[3] This, let it be remembered, was a contemporary word applied almost exactly in the modern cricket sense.

of the muscles or sinews, or whatever it is, which makes
a man Mr. Ready-to-Halt without notice, and without his
in the least expecting it.   This happens to Cokain
constantly; he is never safe from it; and not seldom
he simply "hirples."

Another comparison is fortuitously suggested by the
presence of the plays in the same volume of Mr. Bullen's
invaluable collection, but is in itself much more than
fortuitous.   The fine anonymous play of *Nero*[1] was *Nero* and
published in 1624, or just at about the turning-point *The Martyred*
of blank verse.   Henry Shirley's *Martyred Soldier* dates *Soldier.*
fourteen years later, in 1638, when blank verse was far
down the hill.   That the first piece was evidently by
some one of greater talent than Shirley the lesser—
perhaps even than Shirley the greater—does not affect
the question.   For certainly Suckling, for instance, had
talent enough for a dozen Chettles or Haughtons; and
yet Chettle and Haughton write very decent "blanks."
But the *Nero* man, whoever he was, and whether he writes
just at the time when his play appeared or earlier, writes
with his verse-team perfectly in hand.   Some of them
may trot and some may canter—he evidently wrote late
enough to allow himself a good deal of redundance,
though not of the Fletcherian kind,—but the whole sweep
well together in almost every instance—a few misprints
and the like excepted.   The example to be given below
is a fair average one.[2]   Just compare it with Belisarius'

[1] This play was made accessible to a larger public than Mr. Bullen's
subscribers in an omnibus volume of the useful " Mermaid " Series
(London, 1888).
[2] To make it "average" I avoid the specially fine speech of Petronius
known from Lamb.

  Nero. Aye, now my Troy looks beauteous in her flames;
      The Tyrrhene seas are bright with Roman fires,
      Whilst the amazèd mariner afar,
      Gazing on the unknown light, wonders what star
      Heaven hath begot to ease the aged moon.
  (The rhyme is quite characteristic and possibly intentional.)

  Belis. Methought one evening, sitting on a fragrant verge,
      Closely there ran a silver gliding stream:
      I passed the rivulet and came to a garden—
      A paradise, I should say, for less it could not be,
      Such sweetness the world contained not as I saw.

speech from the *Martyred Soldier* which has been put
side by side.   It is not the contrast of bad verse with
good merely, or of a moderate verser with a better.   We
are in a different country——or, to go to the former
metaphor, the horses break step, pull different ways,
stumble, start back, do everything that they should not
do.   You cannot "touch up" such verse ; it must be
wholly taken to pieces and re-made.

A few examples from separate plays in Hazlitt's
"Dodsley" may also be given——it would be easy to multiply
them by the hundred.   Listen to the excellent Thomas
Rebellion. Rawlins in his *Rebellion*, two years later than *The
Martyred Soldier*, and two years before the closing of
the theatres.[1]   One thinks curiously of that fine speech
of Greene's heroine fifty years before——

> Why thinks King Henry's son that Margaret's love
> Hangs in the uncertain balance of proud Time ?

and then perhaps, one may think likewise of Baudelaire's
sonnets on *Le Lever* and *Le Coucher du Soleil Romantique*
and transfer them to the sunrise and sunset of blank
verse.   If poor Philippa's poet——she is, as one of the
characters says, "a fiery girl," and her speech is noways
wholly contemptible——had just avoided those two hideous
break-downs——

> Bring all the rough tortures

and

> Practised Sicilian tyranny, my giant thoughts,

the "uncertain balance of proud Time" would not have
put her so far below Margaret.   But his ears were
stopped and his hand was careless.

---

[1] Canst thou, proud man, think that Philippa's heart
Is humbled with her fortunes?   No, didst thou
Bring all the rough tortures
From the world's childhood to this hour invented,
And on my resolute body, proof against pain,
Practised Sicilian tyranny, my giant thoughts
Should like a cloud of wind-containing smoke
Mingle with heaven ;
And not a look so base as to be pitied
Shall give you cause of triumph.

Take yet another [1] from that curious play *Andromana*, *Andromana.*
which, though not printed till 1660, is probably " before
the flood "—if not much before.   The speech of Plangus
is a very " moral " of the hopeless stuff of which we are
now speaking—of verse run prose, and prose run mad,
or rather of something that is neither pedestrian verse
nor bombasted prose, but a sort of gallimaufry of both,
corresponding with an almost alarming exactitude to the
rhyme-royal of two hundred years earlier, and making
one inquire in an uneasy fashion whether similar things
may not happen x hundred years later.

Readers who really take an interest in the subject Divers Caroline
might indeed do worse than take up, say, the twelfth, plays com-
pared with
thirteenth, and fourteenth volumes of Hazlitt's " Dodsley " *Lust's*
and run over the pages, stopping whenever they see *Dominion.*
blank-verse passages in plays of the First Caroline time—
Habington's *Queen of Arragon*, Mayne's *City Match*, May's
Old Couple, Cartwright's *Ordinary*, Rutter's *Shepherd's
Holiday*, Fisher's quaint *True Trojans*, Berkeley's *Lost
Lady*.   Almost without exception they will discover for
themselves, as it would take pages on pages of citation
here to discover to them, the unscrewing of blank verse
in all its stages, and the fact that even men who can be
perfectly well trusted with verse of other kinds, such as
Habington and Cartwright, appear to have lost all real
grip of *this* kind—though they may not be quite so
extravagantly chaotic as some others.   The degeneration
takes various forms, and exhibits, as we have said, various
stages.   Now it is not much more than a slight exaggeration of Fletcherian redundance ; now this is extended to
the ugly splittings of connected words so often noticed ;
now it passes into chaos proper—the medley of nondescript inharmonies.   And then between *The Rebellion*

---

[1] 'Tis more impossible for me to leave thee
Than for this carcass to quoit away its gravestone
When it lies destitute of a soul to inform it.
Mariners might with far greater ease
Hear whole shoals of Sirens singing
And not leap out to their destruction
Than I forsake so dangerous a sweetness.

and *Andromana* themselves let such a reader find *Lust's Dominion*, printed at about the same time as the latter and twenty years after the former.   The prosodic effect is like nothing on earth but the bucket of cold water that used to be employed in early and Spartan Turkish baths, destitute of modern frippery and luxury of equipment, at the University of Oxford æons ago.   No matter whether this " Lascivious Queen " is Marlowe's or not— he has had worse things ascribed to him as his creatures, and she could hardly have a better creator.   The point is the absolutely different structure of the verse—its vigour, majesty, "brace"—as against the slipshod, "slamacking," dissolute facility of the others.

CHAPTER IV

CAROLINE LYRIC, PINDARIC, AND STANZA

Special character of this lyric—And special influence of Jonson and
Donne—Some general characteristics—Special metres—The
Caroline C.M.—L.M. and *In Memoriam* quatrains—The pure
or mixed trochaic measures—Herrick—Carew—Crashaw—
George Herbert—Vaughan—Lord Herbert of Cherbury—
Marvell—The general—Digression on " Phillida flouts me "
and foot-division—" Pindaric "—Its rise in Cowley and its
nature—The inducements to it—*Furor poeticus*, etc.—Its
intrinsic attractions—Its history—Cowley's own practice—
The decay of stanza—The quatrain.

THE first subject of the present chapter forms one of the
most delightful bodies of matter to be met with in the
course of our whole inquiry ; and it appertains to that
inquiry in a peculiarly important fashion.   Yet it will not
perhaps be necessary to treat it at a length greater than,
if so great as, that which we have given to periods and
products very much less interesting and less obviously
capital.   The reason of this is that its contents are, in a
way, results, " finals," " last fruits of much endeavour," in
their particular sphere, rather than examples of that
process of exploration and experiment which takes fore-
most place in a genuine history.   And it may be further
remarked, in the manner of general preliminary, that, on
the whole, varied as are the forms of this lyric, *mere*
variety is not its chief feature, and that its greatest results
are attained in one or two well-known and long-established
arrangements.   For mere variety, the earlier Elizabethan
and the First Jacobean periods probably beat our present.

And special
influence of
Jonson and
Donne.

Here, more than anywhere else, the triple influence which has for so long been a settled fact to all fairly intelligent and well-read students, but which is constantly being advertised as a new discovery—the influence of Spenser, Jonson, and Donne—is exerted. Here, indeed, it culminates. But here, as the peculiarities of the subject made necessary, the two younger poets worked more strongly than the eldest. We have, indeed, in our dealings above with Jonson and Donne themselves, outlined a good deal that might have been said here.

Some general
characteristics.

Attention has been already directed to the very startling difference in Donne, and to the less startling but still existing difference in Jonson, between the almost invariable smoothness of their lyric and the not infrequent roughness of their other measures. A similar distinction will be found, varying not seldom in individuals, but constant on . the whole, in the very large group which we have now to survey by representatives so far as its purely lyric constituents go. Whether music is here in any large part the beneficent agent or not does not matter ; the fact of prosodic accomplishment remains. And the fact also remains that this prosodic accomplishment, remarkable as it is everywhere, tends, as has been said, to concentrate itself specially upon one or two forms —the common measure, the octosyllabic quatrain, and the catalectic iambic-trochaic dimeter, either in couplet form or in arrangements. The effects produced by these are positively miraculous during a space of fifty years at the outside—at the inside probably not much more than five-and-twenty. But in variety and curiosity of lyrical experiment, though certainly this is not wanting in the time of Herrick and his mates, the period yields to its predecessor, and still more to the great lyrical revival of the nineteenth century. And in one very remarkable respect it still hangs back. It has been too positively said that for real triple time—for measures not merely admitting the trisyllabic foot, but based on it—we may seek in vain or with little result here ; and it has been too positively replied, on the other side, that this is a mistake. But if the literal truth is rather with the last-named disputants, the real is rather with the first. There *is* a certain amount of anapæstic verse, especially in the ballad or popular division. But it is seldom resorted to by the best poets ; and when they do use it they seem to think it unnecessary to be careful, or necessary to be careless. It does not reach even the point of excellence which we shall find in the later or Second Caroline division, to be treated in the next Book ; and it never, or only in the rarest flashes, comes anywhere near the splendid bravura of " Young Lochinvar " or the ineffable poetic witchery of the great Chorus of *Atalanta in Calydon.*

The subject will still be best dealt with, for the most part, in our usual way by surveying the work of different poets in order, partly chronological, partly of importance. But there are some of the special developments of metre just noticed which must be specially handled ; and first of the first—that marvellous spiritualising of the " common measure "—the eight and six or broken fourteener.

We have seen it arising in Ben and in Donne. Never, perhaps, was there a case more illustrative of the maxim *reculer pour mieux sauter* ; for the common measure, and its matrix the fourteener, had been, as a rule, the dullest and woodenest of First Elizabethan forms. Nor had the pioneers of the great stage done much for it. But now the new wine fills the old bottle, not to bursting, but to a marvellous transformation of its limp and flaccid outline. Of the poets under the combined influence of Spenser (who himself never tried it except in the *Kalendar,* and the doggerel headings of the *Faerie Queene*), Jonson, and Donne, hardly one fails with it. There is scarcely an adventurer from Herrick to Sedley who is not at his best when he touches it. The exact mechanical devices of this sudden attainment of the sublime cannot, of course—they never can—be given with actual certainty. They appear to me, however, after long analysis of the best examples in all the Caroline poets, to be at any rate connected with a rather strict *separation* of rhythm, if not of sense, at the line-ends ; a very careful selection of

Special metres. The Caroline C.M.

strong and sonorous syllables for the "long" places ; and a rather unusual proportion of foot-ending coincident with word-ending, so that the beats of the wing which is achieving the "tower" are distinctly felt. But the examinations of Mercury will never fully reveal the secrets of Apollo.

L.M. and *In Memoriam* quatrains.

No very different processes seem to effect the parallel exaltation of the "long measure" or octosyllabic quatrain, which, in the one glorious example of Marvell, attains the very highest place and in many others a place not far below. It must, however, always seem strange that the *In Memoriam* variation, once reached by Jonson and copied by Herbert and Sandys, should not have been more widely cultivated. We have seen that Ben himself did not fail to strike, though not constantly or certainly, the true tone of it ; nor, as examples later will show, did his chief follower. But it was seldom tried by any one else. And yet its special quality—of meditative melancholy music—is easily adjustable to "metaphysical" thought. It should have allured poets, from Crashaw and Vaughan to Kynaston and Hall, as, according to Izaak Walton, the juice of yew-berries attracts fish. The way, in particular, in which the second line of the included couplet positively invites epexegesis—added comment or imagery on what has gone before—should have been a perfect godsend to them. But the time was not yet.

The pure or mixed trochaic measures.

The special gift of the iamb, in spring and soar, though not absolutely limited to these metres, is more particularly shown in them. But the raising of the trochee to a higher power, which also characterises the period, is very much more diffused. In one case it is the line or stave which has special virtue, in the other the foot itself. The English trochee is, in fact, rather an uncanny foot—in which saying I am not merely alluding to its latent tendency to play Jacob to the iamb's Esau. It is (let us remember our Anglo-Saxon) Lilith—older than Eve, in a manner— dethroned by her, but never quite forsaken ; "kittle" to deal with, but of magical and witching attractions when taken in a kind and coming mood. There had been a good deal of practice with it in the strict Elizabethan times, mainly in the form of the catalectic octosyllable : we have pointed out the effectiveness of it in Shakespeare's lyric passages. It had, as has been also pointed out, been in the same way very largely practised in Jacobean time by Browne, Wither, and those about them, as well as by Fletcher, while Ben himself has done beautiful work with it. But it was reserved for the group of his "sons" and their schoolfellows to bring it to the highest perfection ; and in particular it forms one of the favourite instruments of Herrick—so much so that at this point we may pass into our more usual method of handling, and take poet by poet, illustrating metres and forms more generally as the opportunity presents itself.

With Herrick, indeed, there is a particular and interesting difficulty which is not found quite to the same extent in any other poet. The relation between style and metre, or between prosody and phrase, is, of course, always intimate and almost inextricable. It is especially so at this particular time. But not even in Milton is it so difficult to adjust the nice calculation of less or more in these two respects as in this elder in birth, companion almost exactly in death, of whom we may be half-glad and half-sorry that we have not Milton's expressed opinion. We must try, however, to make the sifting.

In Herrick's very first lines,[1] as they meet us—the Herrick. Dedication to Prince Charles—we find something notably metrical—that he has hit on the device of the specially emphasised "you" to vary and "pedal" the line—a device which Dryden, not so many years afterwards, was to adopt. The fifth line of the second Hesperid—

> The *poor and private* cottages,

is perhaps an example rather of phrase than of " numbers "

---

[1] If I venture to refer to my own edition in the *Aldine Poets* (2 vols., London, 1893) it is only because I there carried out what I have always desiderated in others—the numbering of the poems right through. Herrick's mote-like cloud of poemlets urgently demands this, though I daresay I made slips in it.

in its felicity ; but not so the second of the eighth, a famous thing—

> In sober mornings do not thou rehearse
> The holy incantations of a verse,

where the lengthening out of the words " the " " holy " and " incantations " shows the master of harmony at once. When a man is avized of a trick like this, he will go far ; and before long he *has* gone far in the marvellous couplets to Perilla, which end—

> Then shall my ghost not walk about, but keep
> Still in the cool and silent shades of sleep.

But one might fill a chapter—nay, a Book—with examples of Herrick's metrical legerdemain on this system. We must, alas ! confine ourselves to specimens of it in different arrangements.

His Jonson combinations, such as No. 106, in couplets, decasyllable, and octosyllable, deserve no special notice. He is better in stanzas like that of the Southwell " Epithalamie," and still more the justly famous " Corinna Maying." And the more he shortens his individual line, the better, as a rule, he is ; for that unerring phrase of his saves him from the difficulty which most poets find in avoiding awkward inversions or compressions of diction in such circumstances. The wonderful " To Violets " (No. 205) is perhaps greatest in this, but there are many nearly as great. And in most varieties, as in the most famous of all, " Gather ye rosebuds," we shall find that the trochee, either as principal or as substitute, plays a great, perhaps the greatest part, of the music. Nowhere, perhaps, does his fancy for it appear more strikingly than in the beautiful

> Charm me to sleep ; and melt me so
> With thy delicious numbers—

the said numbers dwindling down to what some would call amphibrachs (" My fever," " 'Mongst roses," " For Heaven "), but what I should call monosyllabic feet and trochees, or catalectic iambic monometers, which are the same thing. You clearly want the double foot. "To Meadows," another of the famous things, is probably the greatest piece in pure sixes that we have. I do not think that Herrick meant "flowers" and "hours" in the first verse (the only "doubtfuls") to be dissyllables. More elaborate, but perhaps not greater prosodic art, is shown by two of its companions in the general knowledge, "Fair Daffodils" and the "Night-piece to Julia"; and it is interesting to see how, in both, the iambic and trochaic bases are "legerdemained" the one into the other. The equally masterly "Mad Maid's Song" has a sort of sub-species of general Caroline common measure to itself: the verses sob more; they float "on a broken wing," to quote a great parallel in matter. No. 535, "To Electra," is undoubtedly in triple time; but it is not one of the best, and it is very important to notice that even in this the trisyllabic feet are rather substituted than staple.

He does not require extremely elaborate measures. I think it may even be said that he does not specially shine in them. "The Wounded Heart" (No. 20) is quite sufficiently done, but would hardly be selected by any one as a diploma-piece; nor "His Answer to a Question" (No. 26). But turn to the continuous hepta-syllables of "The Loss of his Mistresses" (No. 39) and note the difference. If ever there was an "O of Giotto" in the lighter prosody, it is

> ·   Only Herrick's left alone.

And he seldom tries this metre without succeeding in it perfectly. In the full iambic octosyllable (happy as he is) he is never quite so happy; but his serious decasyllabic couplets are quintessential. Anthea (see the one quoted above, and 55 and 74) seems to have had the best of them,[1] but they are all choicely good.

On the other hand, in that common measure which, as has been said, is the masterpiece and cynosure of the

---

[1] As she did in the common measure "Bid me to live," and other forms. I should like to have known Anthea.

time, he is less certainly happy, though at times " past all whooping." " The Rock of Rubies," which offended Hazlitt (and made him offend), has something too much of the hardness of its subject ; and he can elsewhere be mechanical and even singsong in the measure. Yet " Bid me to live " itself is one of the unapproachable things——pure effluence of pure essence of prosody.

In " To his Valentine " (No. 94) we have another example of the " Phillida flouts me " problem (*v. inf.*). It may be——

> Choose me | your Va|lentine,
> Next, let | us mar|ry.

It may be——

> Choose me your | Valentine,
> Next let us | marry.

Both are beautiful. I am not going to dictate, but it is fair to say that undoubted trisyllabic feet are rare in Herrick, though they exist.

The two greatest things in *Noble Numbers*, " The White Island " and " The Litany," are also its two most remarkable prosodic experiments, though there are others. On the whole, what has been said of Herrick above remains true.

Carew.   In the work of his chief brother in " the Tribe," Carew, while there is a good deal of similarity in prosodic atmosphere, and especially in the way in which diction and versification almost refuse to be distinguished, and quite refuse to be divorced from one another, there is one great prosodic difference. Carew avoids almost entirely the more eccentric and variegated metrical experiments. The prosodic contours of his pages are mostly level enough : there is hardly any zigzagging and vandyking. Simple couplets or quatrains, triplets, quintets, sixains, serve him ; and if he takes up the fretwork saw in the song " A Beautiful Mistress," he tires of it soon, and relapses into regularity. But out of this regularity he gets the most marvellous effects. He has been accused of artifice, labour, sterility, monotony ; one can only borrow the famous and almost contemporary wish, and sigh for more people to be monotonous, artificial, laboured, and sterile in this fashion. The heroics of the opening piece are beautiful, but not exceedingly ; the octosyllabics of the next, "To A. L.," are among those things of prosody before which it were almost best to be silent— so impossible is it to analyse the secret of their charm, and yet so intense is the feeling of it. Only, one can discern part of the mystery in that sudden " tower " which the poets of this period have mastered, and which appears in all their greatest things. Here Carew proceeds for some fifty verses or so, not by any means in a maundering or wool-gathering, but in a pleasantly wandering, strolling, flower-picking fashion. And then there is the sudden explosion of passion—

> O ! love me then, and *now* begin it !
> Let us not lose this present minute,

where at the end every vein of the verse swells, every nerve quivers.

I have had frequent occasions of noting the singular success of quintets when they *are* successful. I wish I had been at Norwich in time to give Sir Thomas Browne a hint to extend the *Garden of Cyrus* in this direction. And in Carew's

> When thou, poor excommunicate,[1]

I could have pointed him to certainly not the least of those which follow *The Cuckoo and the Nightingale* in various applications of this number.

He has his own variety of the common - measure triumph of the time in

> I was foretold, your rebel sex,

where the *r* and the *s* will demonstrate what two bare letters can do in a line, and where the final couplet

---

[1] When thou, poor excommunicate
　　From all the joys of love, shalt see
　　The full reward, and glorious fate,
　　　Which my strong faith shall purchase me—
　　Then curse thine own inconstancy.

caps the double quatrain mirifically.[1]   I am not sure
that the trochaic sextets of "Disdain Returned" are a
great success; though the virtue of its sentiments has
conciliated some admiration.   But it is not the fault of
the foot or of Carew's use of it; nothing anywhere in
English can match the trochees of

> Read in these roses the sad story,

at least in the mixed mode; for the iamb plays a pleasant
chassé-croisé all through.   The splendour of the enjambed
decasyllables of "The Rapture" is well known; and
though the poem may be shocking from some points of
view, nothing shocks prosody but false quantities or
halting rhythm.   Fortunately there is the "Elegy on
Donne" to show the same mastery of the same metre in
a fashion harmless to the youngest and most inflammable
of young persons, or nearly so.   For I am not sure that
there is not a *tarte à la crème* everywhere for those who
hanker after such things.

And lastly (for we must not dwell too long on a single
songster in even this chorus of singing birds), Carew's
best known and most universally admired piece, "Ask
me no more," though I cannot say that it appeals to me
as strongly as do a dozen others, shows his prosodic
power admirably in the rise and fall of each stanza.   I
think it is a little artificial, this regular *forte* of the question couplet in each stanza, and *piano* of the answer, but
there is no doubt that the artifice is faultless of its kind.

Crashaw.   The use of the word "tower" a little above will, it
may be hoped, have suggested the name of Crashaw to
more than one reader; and certainly there is no greater

---

[1] I was foretold, your rebel sex
    Nor love nor pity knew,
And with what scorn you use to vex
    Poor hearts that humbly sue;
Yet I believed to crown our pain,
    Could we the fortress win,
The happy lover sure would gain
    A paradise within.
I thought Love's plagues like dragons sate,
    Only to fright us at the gate.

example of that phenomenon in English prosody—I doubt whether there is so great a one in any other—than the famous invocation of St. Theresa, the "rocket"-like quality of which has long ago been recognised. But this remarkable poet has another prosodic "record," in quite the opposite way, for his equally famous "Wishes." Carew is never really playful; and though Herrick often appears to be so, it is very serious playfulness. Great as both are in their and our way, it is an artful, if not an actually artificial greatness. Crashaw appears to have been a thoroughly natural person; he could not, with his wits, have been guilty of the extravagances of "The Weeper" if he had not been. Compare him with Cowley, and you will feel the difference at once; while I am not sure that he has not in this respect the actual advantage over Suckling. His constant and very felicitous practice, sometimes in Latin and sometimes even in Greek verse, no doubt helped his English prosody.[1] But he has little prosodic mannerism, or rather he has it in so many kinds that it is difficult to isolate. "The Tear" is like Herrick. Sometimes he has those prosodic ambiguities or amphibia which have been noticed as specially interesting at this time. For instance, the beautiful fragment on the marks of Christ's wounds[2] is no doubt in intention iambic. But a nineteenth-century Crashaw could hardly have prevented himself from moulding the lines—

> Are in another sense,

and so on, as they are arranged in the note, though of

---

[1] And his octaves, from the Italian of Marino, are noteworthy.

[2] What|ever sto|ry of their | cruelty, |
   Or | nail, or thorn, | or spear have | writ in thee, |
   Are | in ano|ther sense
      Still | legible.
   Sweet | is the dif|ference :
   Once | I did spell |
   Ev|ery red let|ter
    A | wound of thine|—
   Now | (what is bet|ter)
   Bals|am for mine. |
            (*Poems*, ed. Waller ; Cambridge, 1904.)

As usual, dactylic or amphibrachic arrangement is also possible.

course with some alterations. Every line, it will be observed, but

> A wound of thine

goes well so, and even that is not hopelessly refractory on principles of substitution.

George
Herbert.
In prosody, as in other things, Crashaw's special master, George Herbert, is difficult to write of critically, without giving the perhaps uncritical reader a wrong impression. Here, as elsewhere, he is rather good than delicious. I do not, as I have said or hinted before, think any the worse of him for arranging Altars and Easter Wings of verse. I am not with Mr. Addison on this point, and a poet is quite welcome, for me, to write Easter eggs of verse as well as wings—if he likes, and will make the shell and white and yolk poetical. But there is more of the mechanical in Herbert's prosody than is shown merely by the adoption of these mechanical forms ; and it is only when the fire of his poetry burns hottest that inspiration takes the place of mechanism. Plain eights, or "long measure," suit him as well as anything—

> I got me flowers to straw Thy way,
> I got me boughs off many a tree,
> But Thou wast up by break of day
> And brought'st Thy sweets along with thee—

which (it may strike the reader) would be better still if, like his brother, he had adopted the *In Memoriam* form, and put line 2 first.

His sonnets are sometimes very good, and so are many of his mixed modes, especially a quatrain of 8, 10, 10, 8. In fact, he is scarcely ever bad prosodically, any more than in other ways ; but he has not the rarest touch of Vaughan. his fellow-disciples, Crashaw and Vaughan. While of Vaughan himself it may perhaps be said with some truth that the thought usually has the upper hand of the form with him—the malt is above the meal. If he wrote that wonderful anonymous piece that Mr. Bullen discovered in the Christ Church library, he showed more prosodic fingering there than anywhere else. Usually in his finest and best known things, " The Retreat," " The Watch," etc., the prosody is fully *adequate*, which is saying a very great deal, but it does not attract attention to itself. Some people, of course, would say it should not ; on which point I give no opinion.

Herbert's elder brother, though a very much worse poet than the author of the *Temple*, is more interesting prosodically, because of his adoption, from Jonson probably but not certainly, of the *In Memoriam* metre, and of his making rather more progress with it than Jonson had made or than Sandys did make. The explanation of his advance is simple—that he gave himself more practice in it, and that such practice, except in the hands of an almost impossible dullard, must necessarily bring out the peculiar qualities which are inherent in the measure. It is curious that his first example, " The Ditty," is not wholly of this metre, but, as it were, settles down to it after a first stanza where the last line is a fourteener, and a second which strikes out of the form altogether into one totally different. But from the third to the end the model is kept, and the fourth, despite a certain awkwardness of phrase, develops the peculiar bird-sweep, the circular rise and fall, very fairly— Lord Herbert of Cherbury.

> For whose affection once is shown,
>   No longer can the world beguile ;
>   Who sees his penance all the while
> He holds a torch to make her known.

But the much longer " Ode " is uniform from the first, and contains some still better examples, with one Helot, a stanza with double rhyme in the first and fourth, which is instantly fatal.[1] Herbert also tries what we may call the lengthened *In Memoriam* (though in all probability

[1] While doubling joy unto each *other*
   All in so rare consent was shewn,
   No happiness that came alone
   Nor pleasure that was not *another*.

This, which will be found at p. 94 of Professor Churton Collins's edition (London, 1881), is a curious and excellent example, showing how *touchy* the ark of prosody is.

the true form was actually shortened from it) in decasyllables; but the subtle charm of the thing is hidden
here.   That he brought it out at all is the thing, and for
so doing one may pardon him a good deal—sophist and
coxcomb, Bobadil and something like traitor, as he was.

Still one cannot help wishing that it had been somebody else who had hit on the measure.   For instance,
who could have brought out its capabilities much better
Marvell. than Andrew Marvell?   Marvell is a sort of *bridge* in
prosody: we shall have to deal with his couplets in
the next Book; but the lyrics belong wholly to this.
For the (widely) Elizabethan power of " fingering "—of
getting the utmost possible out of metres borrowed or
invented—not the greatest poet in English or in literature
is Marvell's superior.   In that favourite and, as we have
seen, constantly-practised measure of the earlier time, the
catalectic octosyllable, he does not much practise; but
the full form is his, almost in perfection, in the " Bilbrough "
and " Nun Appleton " poems of places, the incomparable
" Bermudas," the " Fawn " poem, the " Coy Mistress " with
its well-known couplet [1]—one of those which strike a
certain terror, so " passionately and irretrievably " does
the sound meet the sense—and others.   In the transcendent common measure of the period he has not given
the most transcendent example; but in " long measure "
he has given the best of all—a thing often referred to,
to be given here, but above comment.[2]   The " Horatian
Ode " is a sort of compromise prosodically between
English and classical metre, a kind of transnotation, a
little artificial, perhaps, and non-natural, but how exquisite![3]   " The Coronet " is one of the finest symphonic

[1] And tear our pleasures with rough strife
Thorough the iron gates of life.

[2] My love is of a birth as rare,
As 'tis for object, strange and high—
It was begotten of Despair
Upon Impossibility.

Where observe that part of the secret is exactly the opposite to that of the
common measure—the *overrunning* of the foot by the word-ending.

[3] I do not say much about this remarkable piece, triumph as it is prosodi-

things of the whole period since Spenser, in very long stanzas, almost of the Pindaric kind. If, once more, we find a Donne-like contrast in the perfect artistry of these and the roughness of his couplets, we shall not be very much surprised.

But warning has been given more than once that we The general. must not linger too long in this island of a harmless Alcina—the Caroline lyric. In the " cuttit and broken " verse which King James, in one of his Solomon-moments, had characterised as depending on the invention of the poet—though if he had been quite Solomonic he would have added, " when once the rhythm is implanted in the general ear "—these men can do almost anything. From the best known to the least, from Suckling and Lovelace to Kynaston and John Hall, they get prosodic effects which at other times far greater poets cannot get at all— do not even attempt to get, or, attempting, fail miserably. They may be mere reeds by the river; yet the great god Pan has touched them and shaped them, and the ineffable music follows. Only it is important for us to put in the reminder that it could not have followed but for the patient experiment of generations from Spenser, nay from Watt and Surrey onward—that Pan is doing no sudden miracle : that the reeds have been planted, and watered, and trained, and are no mere wildings.

So also it is impossible to go through the later song-books and the miscellanies of the time and point out beauties. But even in these there is one famous piece on which we may pause a little, as on an example.

" Phillida flouts me," [1] indeed, is one of the most Digression important texts in the whole range of our scriptures for on " Phillida
flouts me " and showing, first, how differently it is possible to scan the foot-division. same collocations, and, secondly and much more also,

---

cally, because of its slight artificiality. It requires some assistance with the voice. You *can* make it a little singsong, if you are profane enough. Very slow time is required to bring out its beauty. In fact, it is a chief instance of the " fingering " above mentioned.

[1] The date of this charming thing is very uncertain. It appeared in *Wit Restored* (1657), but it is probably much earlier, though whether earlier than other examples of the metre or not is a question probably unanswerable.

how great is the excellence of foot-division against a mere counting of syllables on the one hand, and of "stresses" on the other. It may possibly not have occurred to everybody—it was certainly many years after he was thoroughly acquainted with both poems that it occurred to one person—that the metre of "Phillida flouts me" is essentially the same on syllabic, and quite potentially the same on accentual principles, with that of Longfellow's "Skeleton in Armour." The disposition of the lines is indeed slightly different; but the lines themselves are the same—one of six syllables and one of five; and for half of each stanza the actual disposition is identical. Yet, putting the *tune* of "Phillida" out of the question, the prosodic movement is entirely different, and nothing but foot-division will exhibit the reason or system of that difference. Syllabically, there is no difference at all; accentually, both may be scanned almost at pleasure as "two-stress" or "three-stress" lines. Justifications of all these statements will be found below;[1] but one of the arrangements will utterly destroy the plaintive dropping "innocence" (in both senses) of "Phillida," and both will rob the "Skeleton" of its martial and stormy sweep. To get the former you must scan "Phillida" in the longer lines as a dactylic or a

---

[1] Oh! | what a | pain is | love,
    How | shall I | bear it?
  She | will in|constant | prove,
    I | greatly | fear it.
    .   .   .

Please | her the | best I | may,
She | looks a|nother | way,
A|lack and | well-a-|day,
    Phil|lida | flouts me.
Or
  Oh! what a | pain is | love, etc.

The second syllable being common—or rather depending much on the time given to the first—and so yielding a dactylic start throughout. I need hardly ask the reader to remember Drayton and Agincourt in this connection.

And | as to catch | the gale,
Round | veered the flap|ping sail;
Death | was the helms|man's hail,
  Death | without quar|ter!
Mid|ships with i|ron keel
Struck | we her ribs | of steel,
Down | her black hulk | did reel
  Through | the black wa|ter!

On the other hand, pure iambic scansion, which the stress system invites (and which would make of the opening of Phillida a kind of decasyllable broken, with redundance, into 6 and 5), utterly destroys both—

Oh whāt | a pāin | is lŏve,

And ăs | tŏ cātch | thĕ gāle.

trochaic with short monosyllabic foot appended ; and you must take as the shorter lines dactyl *plus* trochee, or two trochees separated by a short monosyllabic foot. To get the latter you must rely on the central anapæst, with an anacrusis of one strong monosyllable, and an iamb, or monosyllabic foot alternately on the other side. If Longfellow had carried out this principle in his hexameters, and let them fall into the same movement with four anapæsts in the middle instead of one, the namby-pambiness of *Evangeline* would not exist.

I think it may be not impertinent to lay a little further stress on the importance of this instance in the argument for foot-division. On the strict syllabic calculus there is, as has been shown, no difference in the metre of the two poems ; on the strict accent, stress, or beat system there need be none ; and there is none on a very sufficient construction of both. But when the requirement of *feet*—of the attachment of unstressed, unaccented, unbeaten " short " syllables to the stresses, accents, beats, or " long " syllables in certain schemes—is met, then the difference—the true difference, the difference corresponding to nature and effect—emerges. It is the same, but in much more striking measure or degree, as the difference between the two scansions of Coleridge's pattern hexameter-elegiac and of *Boadicea*, referred to at vol. i. p. 8. And I must again urge that the syllabic system and the stress system have no means of terminology, no device of any other kind, for indicating the nature of this attachment. The evasive phrase of " rising " and " falling " is utterly inadequate. Our system and our terminology can do it without effort—and will do it as a matter of course. It is no doubt possible that there are some ears so constituted that they do not hear the feet in their actual composition ; but they must be passed by.[1]

It is possible that some readers may be surprised at not finding " Pindaric " verse estated in a chapter to itself ; ' Pindaric.'

---

[1] In connection with " Phyllida," I should like to refer students to Mr. Ker's paper on the *Arte Mayor* (*v. sup.* i. p. 408 *note*), though I must postpone the application.

but such a chapter would suit awkwardly with strictly historical method, and would be more appropriate to that of kinds, which others use.   So envisaged, it would have to begin with Spenser and end with Mr. Swinburne, which would not suit us.   It is, however, at our present point and in our present chapter, of sufficient importance to demand a section of rather more than ordinary " self-containedness," though we shall not find it necessary here to deal with, or to illustrate from, any poet except Cowley. The degradations of the style in the later part of the seventeenth century belong to the next Book, together with its partial rescue at the hands of Dryden ; the eighteenth-century exercises in it, and the attempts of Gray to raise them, to the last of this volume.

Its use in Cowley, and its nature. Although the Pindaric movement is rightly and indissolubly associated with the name of Cowley, it would be a great mistake—an even greater one than is common in such cases—to regard him as its only begetter.   That it should have specially commended itself to him is, indeed, no wonder.   It suited that restless and enterprising, but rather facile, eclecticism which was partly displayed in the last chapter ; and he probably thought that he might find in it something of a refuge from the see-saw between " metaphysicalism " and " prose and sense " which we notice in him so often.   But he would not have drawn after him anything like the portion of the poetic (or at least versifying) host that he did draw, if it had appealed merely to his private idiosyncrasies.   There were other and important inducements to it, which were public and general.

The inducements to it. *Furor poeticus,* etc. In the first place, and affecting not merely England, but all Europe, there was that odd devotion to, or at least belief in, *furor poeticus,*[1] which was accepted by the latest sixteenth and all the seventeenth century as safety-valve or sauce for the equally accepted doctrines of poetic rule and reason.   You were allowed to be mad ; it was creditable for you to be mad ; and under whose auspices could you be mad so respectably as under those of the

---

[1] I must refer to the numerous passages on this subject in my *History of Criticism*, vol. ii. (Edinburgh and London, 1902).

" Theban eagle "? But this consideration was not specially prosodic or specially English ; there were others that were both. In the first place, we can trace all along the century, from Drayton to Bysshe, a certain growing weariness of the stanza, or at least of the chief recognised stanzas. Rhyme-royal was almost sure to die down for a time after its long and partly glorious history of nearly three hundred years. Its nearest rival, the octave, has always been something of an alien—a visitor welcome, but not exactly naturalised—in English. The very splendour and completeness of the success of the Spenserian seem to have daunted imitators : as we have seen, they took everything from Spenser except his stanza, and made clumsy alterations of that. The quatrain was to be tried almost simultaneously with the Pindaric—and to fail. In fact, it is quite clear that the age was losing its taste for stanzas of all kinds except in lyric of moderate size. On the other hand, fast as it was settling towards the couplet, it had not yet definitely made up its mind which of the two forms of this it would prefer : and Cowley at least was a man of prosodic brains and prosodic practice, both more than sufficient to tell him that the couplet's danger was monotony for the reader and cramp for the writer.

Now the irregular Pindaric stanzas and lines, lengthened *Its intrinsic* or shortened at the pleasure and judgment of the poet, *attractions.* and both adjustable to a poem of almost any moderate length—that is to say, to any of the " occasional " subjects which were more and more appealing—might seem to be free from all objections, and to promise all sorts of com- modities. No form of cramp, whether of those incidental to the couplet or of those incidental to the shorter but regular and identical stanza, seemed to threaten them. They invited, without exactly imposing, the favourite and fashionable metaphysical exaltation, digression, par- enthesis. They suggested the variety and the sweetness of rhyme without tying the poet down to the necessity of giving it at absolutely regular intervals. Their harmony fell in with the musical tastes of the time ; in fact, they

were in manner larger lyrics—lyrical "magnums." As
for patterns, not merely Pindar himself and the Greek
choruses(troublesome strophic arrangement being prudently
dropped), but the Italian canzone, Spenser's own two
great odes, and other things presented themselves. Nor,
in fact, to any one of very moderate versifying faculty
were special patterns in the least necessary. The general
rhythm of English prosody having been by this time
sufficiently established, only individual incapacity could
go far wrong. A fifteenth-century Pindaric is a thing
too awful to think of ; though, in fact, not a few fifteenth-
century rhyme-royal stanzas are like small Pindaric strophes
written by a bad poet and stupid man. But there was
no such danger in the seventeenth, except that the
individual stupidity would, of course, have its way in this
form or that.

Its history.   That Cowley says nothing of all this (or practically
nothing) in his actual Preface to his Pindaric Odes will
surprise no sensible reader. From his words you might
think that he began by translating two actual Odes of
Pindar into something more or less resembling their
original form in English, and then was tempted to extend
the practice to original composition. Very likely this
was the actual conscious historical genesis of the matter
in his case. But the order of conscious thought and the
order of actual evolution are pretty notoriously not
identical ; and, as I must again and again remind readers,
there is perhaps no case in which they need have coincided
less than in prosody. It is sufficient that Cowley *did*
adopt these irregular semi-lyrical stanzas or paragraphs ;
that they almost immediately "made a school" ; that
they produced, during the last half of the seventeenth
century and much of the eighteenth, some of the very
worst verse (poetically, not always prosodically) to be
found in the English language ; but that, though again
and again corrected into Greek form by poets who were
also scholars, they have practically maintained themselves
to the present day, and have shown themselves quite as
able to provide a poet with wings to soar as they are to

provide a poetaster with weights to sink. In fact, interesting as some of the regularly strophic arrangements[1] are, it may be doubted whether English is not of the "rebel sex" in poetry, and does not take such things rather impatiently. At any rate, it is a very significant fact that Milton, a scholar if ever there was one, the possessor of an ear the infallibility of which was only limited by his nonconformist temper and his unconquerable tendency to experiment, a craftsman able to do almost anything he liked with "numbers," did not adopt strict correspondence of form in *Lycidas*, or even in *Samson Agonistes*.

As for Cowley himself, it is of course very easy to show that his Odes are "not" several things; and most particularly that they are not Pindaric or choric, being usually an uncertain number of irregular stanzas, corresponding to one another neither in number nor in position of line, and arranged on no system of rhyme-tally. But this, apart from the question of mere nomenclature (and even perhaps, to some extent, in respect of that), is a merely technical, not to say a merely pedantic, objection. Take them for what they are, not for what they are not, and it is impossible to deny them great capabilities, which, in their very form, Dryden was to develop admirably in the "Mrs. Anne Killigrew" especially, and which, whether as regulated by Gray and Collins or remodelled afresh by the poets of the nineteenth century, were to add vastly to the stores of English poetry. Here, as elsewhere, Cowley wants the anecdotic "that—!" As in the *Davideis*, he accumulates and agglomerates fine things, and things not fine at all—harmonies and cacophonies, curiosities and mere oddities, in the most pell-mell fashion. As in the Lyrics—and this is specially important and unfortunate—his irregular schematisation is merely hit or miss, it may "come off" or not come off, almost at the hazard of the dice. Yet it makes one think of some of its author's own words. It is a "large garden" to the

Cowley's own practice.

----

[1] They date, the reader may be reminded, back to Ben Jonson at least, and were attempted by Cowley. Congreve's essays in them are in front of us.

"small house" of the couplet, and it afforded an invaluable place of escape, and exercise, and contemplation of nature to those whom the couplet cramped and confined.

The decay of stanza.
The quatrain.
We may conclude the chapter with a few further words on the curious phenomenon which was noticed above, which will be found glanced at in the only prosodic document of the period, and which is one of its most important historically—the growth of discontent with stanza. Of course, there are plenty of long poems of the time which use this—Kynaston's *Leoline and Sydanis*, More's and Joseph Beaumont's great philosophical treatises, numerous others. Nor is there much return, if any, to the disorder of the fifteenth-century rhyme-royal—a disorder which is practically reproducing itself in blank verse. The mere stanza forms, now that some general sense of rhythm was diffused, were sufficient to prevent that. But the longing for the "geminell," which discloses itself in those curious observations of Drayton's long before, almost inevitably brings distaste of the symphonic forms with it. If they end in a couplet, why not have the couplet alone? If they do not, why don't they? That seems to have been the unspoken drift of the thought of the time, indicating itself even in such an apparently contradictory symptom as the Pindaric : indicating itself directly in the contraction of the stave to a mere quatrain in the first place, as a preliminary to reduction to the lowest term short of blank verse. The principal example of this, Davenant's *Gondibert*, belongs in time to the present Book and chapter, but the discussion of the measure had best take place when we come to its greatest practitioner, Dryden. Davenant, whose curious reasons for choosing it are noted elsewhere, manages it with fair skill, but certainly does not evade or conquer its defects.

The chief of these is the peculiarly soporific effect—an effect, as we shall see, not fully evaded or conquered by Dryden himself—of the form when repeated uniformly or at great length. *Gondibert* might have been a prose heroic romance of some interest ; as a verse one

(putting poetry out of the question) it is almost more difficult to *read* than its contemporary and rival *Pharonnida*,
though Davenant tells his story clearly enough, and
Chamberlayne with an almost total absence of clarity.[1]

[1] The experiments in new *short* stanzas, such as the excessively awkward
10, 8, 12 of Benlowes' *Theophila*, point the moral.

CHAPTER V

PROSODISTS

Barrenness of the compartment—Jonson a defaulter—Joshua Poole
or "J. D."

Barrenness of the compartment. THIS chapter will probably be the shortest of the volume, except the corresponding one in the next Book, yet it is not, nor is that, introduced merely for the sake of symmetry. That after the very considerable interest taken in many if not all questions relating to poetry during the Elizabethan period proper, there should be, during a period so closely united with it in poetical practice, an almost total disuse of poetic theorising, may seem odd. But there is no doubt that, as a matter of fact, the first half of the seventeenth century with us is exceptionally barren in all kinds of critical exercise, and most barren in prosody.

Jonson a defaulter. Jonson, the principal exception in criticism generally, had intended to be an exception here also. At the beginning of his unfinished *English Grammar* he not only, as he was by tradition almost bound to do, glances at prosody, and makes a distinction between English and the classical languages in point of quantity, but promises something of a discussion "in the heel of the book." That heel, however, played him or us a worse trick than did the heel of Achilles; for it never, so far as we know, came into being at all. One naturally regrets this; for a prosodic treatise from the man who not merely was a great master of the practice, but who thought Fraunce a fool for writing in quantity, and Donne worthy of hanging for not keeping accent, ought to have

344

had something worth reading in it. Yet, after all, it might have been disappointing.

There is, however, one exception[1] late in the period and itself rather enigmatic, but curiously " up to date " and therefore important. In the first half of the century there lived a certain Joshua Poole whose birth-date is unknown, but who was entered at Clare Hall, Cambridge, in 1632, and appears to have passed the final years of his life up to 1646, when he died, as master of a private school at Hadley near Barnet, which had been set up by, and in the house of, a certain Francis Atkinson. To this Francis Atkinson he dedicated a book called *The English Parnassus*, which, however, did not appear for ten years after his death.[2]

Ungracious as it may seem, it has to be said that this Joshua so far as he himself is concerned, leaves us completely in the wilderness. His book (evidently suggested by those of Fabricius, Mazzone da Miglionico, and others on the Continent) is an English *gradus*, giving a dictionary of rhymes, another of epithets for leading words, and a third part containing no uninteresting, but to us no important, anthology of illustrative passages. It is, in fact, one of the (except indirectly) mischievous " Poetry-made-easies " with which we have nothing to do. But when it appeared, it appeared with a second Preface " being a Short Illustration of English Poesy," with which we have a great deal to do, and which has been rather strangely neglected. This Preface is signed " J. D.," and it will naturally be asked who this J. D. was. There is unfortunately not the faintest scrap of evidence on the subject. It is, of course, impossible

Joshua Poole or "J. D."

[1] We need hardly make one for Davenant, though he has one paragraph in his long Preface touching on his stanza—the decasyllabic quatrain. He thought it would be less tiresome to the reader than the couplet, and less to the singer or composer than the stanza. For he seems actually to have hoped that this long poem would be sung, as Hannay seems also to have done with his not quite so long and more lyrical but still exorbitant *Philomela*. The fact is curious. Nor need more than mention be given to the slight references of Wallis to the classical metre craze in his *Grammatica Linguæ Anglicanæ* (1653).

[2] The first edition (London, 1656, or 1657 ?) appears to be extremely rare. Of the second (1677) I have a copy.

not to think of John Dryden, who, like Poole, was a
Cambridge man ; who was five or six and twenty at
the time ; who had long before written the " Hastings "
lines ; who had just taken up, or was just going to take
up, his residence in London ; who was about to write
his first characteristic poem on Oliver Cromwell ; and
who is traditionally, though not very trustworthily,
asserted to have done more or less hack-work for the
booksellers about this time. But, except the chronological and circumstantial one, there is no link between
Dryden and J. D. whatsoever. The style is not in the
least like his, and there is (with one very trifling exception to be noted presently) no connection, that I at least
can discover, of reading, allusion, or opinion.

Still, J. D. is not to be neglected ; he gives us, in fact,
our only important and detailed document between
Daniel and Bysshe. He flourishes a little to begin with,
but at least endeavours to come to close quarters by
adding to his statement that " harmony in prose [a
faint remembrance of Dryden's " other harmony of prose "
arises] consists in exact placing of the accent, and an
accurate disposition of the words " ; that " poesy consists,
besides, in measure, proportion, and rhythm." He knows
Sidney, Daniel, and Puttenham's book (though not as
Puttenham's) ; and he even knows the examples of
fifteenth-century poetry which Ashmole had just published
in the *Theatrum Chemicum.* He has no delusions about
" Spondey [*sic*] and dactyl," and quotes the person who
sent Ben Jonson a copy of verses beginning thus—

Benjamin immortal, Johnson most highly renownèd—

which, by the way, is quite as good as most of its kind.
And he notes (which is quite noteworthy) that " all kind
of historical poesy was performed by most of the
European languages in stanzas *till of late.''* He describes
other kinds from lyric to didactic, and then turns
to symphony and cadence. He objects to rhymes
of different accent (" náture " and " endùre ") ; to long
parentheses ; to the contemporary enjambment (for which

he has no word, but which he illustrates), and, very strongly, to apostrophes and words "apostrophated"— an objection priceless to us ; also to double rhymes, which he thinks "speak a certain flatness derogatory to the dignity of the Heroic" ; to polysyllables ; to rough rhythm (he quotes Sir Thomas Urquhart) ; to identical rhyme ; to assonance and to gradus-epithets, wherein it may be thought that he galled the kibe of the defunct Joshua's heel somewhat. But here he stops, or merely goes on to give some details about Joshua himself.

I think a good deal more nobly of this than some have done—in fact, than anybody has done, so far as I am aware. It is not, of course, very *durchgehend* : it is (and I confess this is part of its interest to me) rather like an intelligent article on the book and subject, by somebody who was turned on for the purpose ; and I daresay it was this. But it at least shows that the writer knew something, had thought something, and had observed something in regard to that subject ; and of such things in these early days we have astonishingly little. He fixes on the great and crying evil of "apostro-phation," which was to become all the more mischievous because it was to drop some of its warning deformities. He is aware of the other evil of excessive and slovenly enjambment. It is perhaps necessary to have read more verse of the time than most people have read to know that the danger of allowing mere assonance was much greater than is commonly thought,[1] and he protests against this. He was right about the danger of numerous double rhymes ; and, again, it was a pressing danger of his time. He presents, in all these respects, a curious contrast by anticipation to the *a priori* prosodists of the eighteenth century with whom we shall have to deal towards the close of this volume, and who, when they take account of English poetry at all, too often seem to think that nothing but the existing practice of

---

[1] To take a single writer, and not a bad one, Shakerley Marmion in *Cupid and Psyche* rhymes "bor*n*" and "for*m*," "ocea*n*" and "swa*m*," even "asc*ribed*" and "den*ied*."

it is to be taken into account, and give no intelligent consideration even to that. In short, while they were blind, he was at least one-eyed and saw with his one eye. Now we know in what kingdom the one-eyed man is king ; and, once more, for prosodic discussion, if not prosodic practice, this seventeenth century is a most remarkable *Royaume des aveugles*.

INTERCHAPTER VI

IT is of the first importance that we should look round and " collect," at the point which we have now reached. The *annus magnus*, the larger period of Elizabethan poetry, has ended, or is ending, and an entirely new dispensation, prosodically as well as otherwise, is beginning or has begun. Prosodically, as poetically, the Pisgah - sight backwards about 1660 — even without Milton's latest work—is of quite astoundingly developed range, variety, and beauty, as compared with any such survey possible about 1580. In fact, Pisgah has changed its place, and is not on the threshold of the Promised Land, but on its farther limit. But for us the goodly heritage is less an object of contemplation than the way in which it has been occupied.

The points, to speak without any metaphor, to which attention has to be directed in the period of the last Book are : the position of lyric ; the decadence of blank verse and of the stanza ; the advance, in a certain direction, of the couplet ; and (changing the principle of arrangement) the work of Milton. Something has been said, even of the general kind, on each of these points already ; but we must now bring the generalities together.

The condition of lyric brings out for us a most important era or epoch in prosodic history. We here reach a point where the prosodic possibilities of a given time are fully developed—where you can " get no more of them." The poet has his instrument in absolute perfection, ready to his hand ; and, so long as he has the power to use it, his performance is absolutely perfect also.

Instead of having—as Wyatt, for instance, had had—
plenty of power to play, but an instrument breaking
down under his hand at every moment, he has one which
is mechanically perfect, which leaves nothing to desire in
the doing of its part, and which merely leaves him to do
his.   It is, in fact, so perfect as an instrument that comparatively little power is necessary to bring out its effects
up to a certain point—though the greater the power, of
course, the better.

There are sufficient reasons, besides the rather Molièr-
esque, and more than rather unphilosophical (yet not
perhaps quite irrational) reason, that the virtue of the
time was lyrical, why this perfection should be specially
shown in lyric.   One perhaps is that lyric is, after all, the
central, the highest, the most natural and essential form
of poetry ; so that the more poetical a time is the better
will it show in lyric, and the more favourable the
mechanical aids and circumstances, the better will lyric
show in them.   But it is possible to be more precise, and
also more "in our own division," than thus.   In the first
place, there had been from Wyatt to Shirley more than a
century and a quarter, from Spenser to Shirley more
than three - quarters of a century, of constant and
voluminous practice in lyric, with the modern English
pronunciation and quantity-valuation more or less settled.[1]
The greatest triumph of the time, and one of the greatest
triumphs of English or any prosody — the ineffably
beautiful "common measure" of this time—was actually
the last ἐπιγέννημα, the final growth and flower of nearly
four hundred years' practice of the fourteener, continuous
and broken, from Robert of Gloucester and the Judas
poem onwards.   The octosyllabic couplets, either full or
catalectic, were older still, and trace themselves directly
to the "heap" of Layamon ; while the "long measure"
is a variation of them which must have been hit, deliberately or by accident, soon after they themselves emerged.

---

[1] I am aware that some high authorities think that pronunciation in
Shakespeare's time differed greatly from ours.   Save in a few well-known
cases, not themselves of much importance, I cannot agree with them.

As for the more variegated forms, the "broken and cuttit" measures, they had been practised during the whole major Elizabethan time, till it would have been strange indeed if such perfection as practice can give had not been reached.   But there is something more than this.   There is in lyric at once a constraint and an easement, neither of which exists, to the same extent, in continuous verse, though there is more of it in stanza narrative than in couplet or "blanks."   You *must* pay some attention to your form ; if you do not it will give you constant jogs and nips of reminder which only the dullest and most callous can neglect.   And, for the most part, the shortness of the lines, the frequent recurrence of the rhymes, and other things of the same kind, while they require a certain effort, confine that effort within moderate limits, and do not offer the tempting but dangerous expatiation of the continuous verse.   But the instrument, like all good instruments, can be ruined by bad playing, and nearly as much so by simply not being played upon ; and we shall see in future Books how this actually came about.

With the stanza-forms of narrative which come nearest to lyric, the case was the same with a difference.   They had actually reached perfection (in the rhyme-royal of Chaucer and of Sackville first, in the Spenserian *novena* afterwards) much earlier than lyric, and it was the way of the world that they should die off first—that they should take their turn of the application of the law that nothing endures—that the one fair, good, wise thing shall not stay in the hand that grasps it—nay, that the hands shall slacken their grasp of the thing.

Besides, your epic or your romance is, after all, another guess matter from your copy of verses ; and it is one thing, as Sir Francis Kynaston shows us with his lyric and his romance, to turn out a perfect song of three stanzas and another to produce an even tolerably perfect poem of five or six hundred.   And for a third cause of decay we must remember the concomitant growth, in the period, of blank verse and of the couplet.   The rose will always wither ; but the withering of *hesterna rosa* is made more conspicuous, and at least seems to be actually hurried, by the blooming of *rosa hodierna*. Once more, it may be rather unphilosophical, rather question-begging, to say that the stanza is more poetical than the couplet or the blank, and that therefore, as generations get more prosaic, they will like the stanza less, and the couplet or the blank more. But if philosophy is divine, *un*-philosophy is exceedingly human.

Undoubtedly the chief and central prosodic fact of this period is the rise, if not yet the thorough establishment, of the couplet itself. We have traced this rise with, it is to be hoped, sufficient care, and with it the struggle of competing forms which accompanies and in a way constitutes it.[1] And we have not attempted to conceal the fact that though the enjambed couplet may be much the more beautiful at its best, it is very much the uglier at its worst, and is specially likely to be bad. In fact, it may be said without exaggeration, that it is, if not exactly a spurious form, something of a hybrid—that its graces are the graces, not so much of the couplet itself, as of the stanza, or of blanks with rhyme added. There is something Bohemian, something even contraband, about its charm ; and it is scarcely necessary to add that it is not the only thing contraband or Bohemian that is charming. On the other hand, the graces of the stopped couplet are from the first, and tend to be, more and more, graces of order and rule. It is not necessarily staid or stiff : it can be lively enough. Nor is it by any means necessarily flat or dull : it can assume majesty and display vigour with any form of verse you like. But it lacks—especially as it breeds itself more " in-and-in "—atmosphere, suggestion, *aura*. It is, though very far from the most elaborate, the most mechanical and metallic form that prosody has ever known. Now, metal has plenty of resonance. You can make large brass instruments with it, and frame pianos

---

[1] I think it impossible to lay too much stress on the way in which the excesses of the enjambed couplet and the broken-down blank verse *drove* men to the stopped form.

with it, and construct all sorts of musical things, down to
Jews' harps, with it. But you cannot, they say, make a
fiddle of it that shall be good for anything, though you
can of almost all the trees of the forest, and even (so
says legend) of a dead woman's bones.

It was this severer and more prosaic but more
genuine form to which the taste of the time was really
directed, though for a season the actual quantity of
couplet production tended the other way. This last fact
was probably due, first, to the survival of a taste for stanza
forms; secondly, to something less creditable—to the other
fact that the enjambed couplet *looks* the easier of the two.
As a matter of fact, and as further practice showed, it is
just the other way—at least if you try not merely to do,
but to do well. It is excessively difficult to keep the
enjambed couplet at a high level of excellence : only
master the few and easy tricks of its rival, and, as the
satirist says—

> You or any man
> Can reel it off for miles together.

They did not know that yet ; and they were half
enraptured by the Wallerian smoothness, half afraid of it
as of something new and uncanny. But the stopped couplet
had not yet had its enormous luck of falling into the
hands of a craftsman who, while he developed almost all
its own proper qualities, enriched it with others, not
perhaps more of its essence than those of its enjambed
rival, but much more consonant to the prevalent tastes, and
much less liable to abuse. And so in this Book we leave
it half way : entering, but not entered upon, its kingdom.

In this last point the fortunes of blank verse, as we see
them from the advantage-ground of 1660, or thereabouts,
are curiously similar ; for Milton had to some extent
" come," and was coming to a much greater. But in all
others they are as curiously different. Blank verse is, unlike
the stanza (lyrical or narrative) and the couplet, a new-
comer. It has even " come in ten thousand strong "
and carried everything before it, for a time at least, on the
stage, displaying, in the hands of Shakespeare, powers

which no metre has ever excelled, and in those of not a few others, powers which few metres have ever equalled. But it has gone almost as rapidly as it came, in one if not in all senses of going. The relaxation—the actual bone-dissolution—which came upon one form only of the couplet has come upon it universally, and in a far more malignant form. It will be said of it in a year or two, and said with a certain colour of truth, that it is "too mean for a copy of verses"; both against it and in its favour, that it is so like prose as to be unobjectionable as a medium of conversation on the stage. And this is scarcely forty years after

> We are such stuff
> As dreams are made of, and our little life
> Is rounded with a sleep,

had been first printed, perhaps scarcely fifty after it had been first written. What is still more singular, the dramatic perfection, thus lost, has never been exactly recovered since. But—though the loss is not quite yet, *Comus* being at any rate dramatic in form—it is about to be freshly started as a non-dramatic medium in a form almost as glorious as Shakespeare's own, and destined to constant revival, if not positive progress, to the present day.

It cannot be too often repeated that, in prosody as in poetry generally, Milton, though he is in his time, is not of it. But the statement may be taken too absolutely; and perhaps it is sometimes made under something of the same misapprehension. In his early work he *was* of his time in his lyrical sweetness and perfection, as well as in his special fondness for, and proficiency in, the mixed iambic-trochaic octosyllable-heptasyllable. He was of it in his refusal of stanza for his great later poems. But he was conspicuously *not* of it—not merely in his rejection of the couplet, not merely in his complete freedom from its tendency to degrade and maltreat blank verse, but in his exaltation of that medium to the place and function described at the end of the last paragraph.

The natural consequence was that his influence, though immense, was not immediate. There are stealers from

Milton—that odd person Baron, for instance—quite early, but there are no real imitators of him, early or late, in his own life.   Dryden's admiration, great and genuine as it certainly was, did not lie in the least in the direction of form.   He "tags" Milton's blanks while he is in love with rhyme for stage purposes ; and when he has taken a new mistress, his own kind of blank verse, fine as it is in *All for Love* and the rest, is not Miltonic at all.   Nowhere does Milton, for his own lifetime, and for long afterwards, dwell so much apart as in the sphere of prosody : it is only by a sort of cosmic alteration that the star of his soul begins to shed its influence here.

On the other hand, looked at from a greater altitude and with wider range, he is one of the very greatest facts of English prosodic history ; and as such we have given him room accorded to hardly any one else.   Separated as he was from all the immediate or nearly immediate prosodic interests and symptoms of his own time, he supplies infallibly, though no doubt undesignedly, all or almost all that is necessary to correct the faults of that time, to confirm, while extending and vitalising, its merits. Moreover, he does something for English prosody at large which had to be done at some time, though not perhaps necessarily in this.   His *parergon* in the sonnet, interesting and important as it is, still is a parergon.   His blank-verse paragraph, and his audacious and victorious attempt to combine blanks and rhymed verse with paragraphic effect in *Lycidas*, lay down indestructible models and patterns of English verse-*rhythm*, as distinguished from the narrower and more strait-laced forms of English *metre* which lyric and stanza had already made safe, and as against the ungirt and unstayed lubricity of the unstopped couplet, the brisk insufficiency and commonness of the stopped.   That by Pause, Equivalence, and Substitution— these three—you can secure perfect English poetic form ; that, to secure it in perfection, whether you add rhyme or not, you must attend to these,—that is the doctrine and the secret of Milton.   It was long before it was understood —it is not universally understood or recognised even now.

But it was always *there* ; and as enjoyment and admiration of the results spread and abode, there was ever the greater chance of the principle being discovered, the greater certainty of its being put into perhaps unconscious operation by imitation.

And so Milton in a sense completed, though of course he did not in the least arrest, the work which had been begun by Chaucer long before, which had been resumed by Spenser and carried on by Shakespeare, and which had fallen into his hands almost directly from Shakespeare's own. In this lease of the three lives English poetry and English prosody had been developed in a fashion still wonderful in our eyes, but certain, and fully evidenced by the results which we have been analysing from our own point of view. They were now to contract operations and reverse principle in the odd way in which, throughout literary as throughout political history, people (and the English people very particularly) have chosen to relinquish the fruits of victory, and run counter to their own previous practice and theories. But there was something to be attempted and done still, though on a smaller and less striking scale ; and with this we shall be concerned in the rest of the volume.

BOOK VII

THE AGE OF DRYDEN

CHAPTER I

DRYDEN

Variety of Dryden's metres—His general prosodic standpoint—His
    practice — The Hastings elegy — The *Heroic Stanzas*—
    Astræa Redux and its group—*Annus Mirabilis*—The couplet
    in the Heroic plays—Its changes—And conversion to blank—
    Dryden's blank verse—His lyrics—Other songs—The Odes—
    The Hymns, etc. — The couplet in the Translations — In the
    later poems generally—The *Prologues*, etc.—The Satires—The
    didactic and narrative pieces — Triplets and Alexandrines —
    Note on Alexandrines in continuous verse.

AMONG the numerous, and nearly always significant,
differences between Dryden and the poet who continued
(and in one sense finished) his work, there is hardly any
more striking, though there are several which have struck
more, than the fact that while Pope is practically *homo
unius metri*, Dryden is remarkably *polymetric*. To some
slight extent, indeed, the fact that there is hardly anything
of his more widely known than the *Ode on St. Cecilia's
Day* has kept in mind the other fact, that he was not a
mere couplet-monger. But the singular fancy which has
made some editors of the *Poems*, even while admitting
Prologues and Epilogues which are almost purely dramatic,
keep out the Songs in the very same plays which are
not dramatic at all,[1] has obscured the full truth from
the general reader. That full truth is that, here as elsewhere, Dryden was far more above, and less of, his age
than Pope. In the first place (and here Pope is not to
blame for not sharing his advantage), he was nearly as

---

[1] They are in the "Aldine" edition, but not in the "Globe."

much of the past age as of that succeeding the Restoration, having spent almost half his life in the former. But, in the second, he had what was all his own, a restless and catholic spirit of exploration and appreciation which made it impossible for him to stay in one groove. The inconsistency with which he has been reproached by short-sighted persons in his criticism is really, and in its results invaluably, one side of this Ulyssean restlessness; his metrical proceedings are another, and for us here a most interesting one.

His general prosodic standpoint.

According to a remarkable passage [1] of the Dedication of the *Æneid*, it is only the envy of Fate which has prevented us from having Dryden's theory as well as his practice to deal with. But from the remarks which precede it, and which deal with what he strangely calls " cæsura " (*i.e.* "elision "),[2] there is some chance that Fate here, as so often, has been cruel only to be kind. There is, indeed, some matter in his remarkable statement that the French and Italians know nothing of feet, of which a less transparent and Golden-Age-like equity than that which rules in this book might lay hold, and claim Dryden for a convert. I shall not do this; though I shall be able to show that he was with us in spirit. Nor shall I deny that his *Prosodia* might, as do so many of his criticisms, show an odd mingling of preceptive inadequacy and impressionist correctness. But I fancy that he had the " sweetness-of-Mr.-Waller " delusion too strong upon him to have done more than expound, magisterially, the narrower system. Yet I may invite special attention to the words " no vowel can be cut off before another when we cannot sink the pronunciation of it," because this clearly bars that singular system of " elision and no elision " —of a metrical scansion which is independent of and

---

[1] This should be returned to in the " Prosodists " chapter of this Book, but had better be given here as well :—" I have long had by me the materials of an English Prosodia, containing all the mechanical rules of versification, wherein I have treated, with some exactness, of the feet, the quantities, and the pauses."

[2] " There is not, to the best of my remembrance, one vowel gaping on another for want of a *cæsura*, in this whole poem."

contrary to rhythmical pronunciation—with which we have had to deal in Milton's case. Dryden could never have reached the wooden precision of Bysshe. But I should imagine that Bysshe does not do much more than *lignify* the system which in Dryden's hands would have had flesh and life, though not all the life and the flesh that it might have had. But, for the present, to his practice.

His Juvenilia are well-known to be few in number and not very remarkable in quality. The extravagant meta-physicalities of the Hastings elegy (1649) were not inconsistent with future development; indeed, and from our special point of view, they hardly present anything that is noteworthy to any one who has read much of the poetry of the immediate period. It is, however, noticeable that though this was the very flourishing time of the enjambed couplet of *Pharonnida*,[1] this boy of seventeen prefers the closed form, and achieves something distantly like the clench and stroke of his own future in such single lines as

His practice.
The Hastings elegy.

> To bring a winding for a wedding sheet,

and even in distichs like

> Graces and virtues, languages and arts,
> Beauty and learning, filled up all the parts.

He was no doubt not superior to the apostrophation of his time; and would, for instance, have scanned, if he did not actually write, l. 35—

> Were fixed and conglobate in his soul and then,

"in 's soul," unconscious or afraid of the far superior rhythm of " con|globate in|." Nor should I lay much stress on " filth(i)ness " in l. 54 and " cab(i)net " in l. 64; while " to hang " in l. 84 was probably " t' hang." [2] The

---

[1] Part of which was written six or seven years *before*, while the whole of it was published ten years *after* Dryden wrote.

[2] Perhaps these three lines should be given if only to show how fine the second is (*properly* scanned)—

> The very fil|thiness of | Pandora's box,
>
> The cabi|net of a richer soul within
>
> Or to hang | an antiquary's room withal.

apostrophation mania stuck at no cacophony in these days. But, in fact, both this piece and the Hoddesdon lines next year, where, in the last places of the 16th line—

And look the Sun of Righteousness in the face,

we must take it as "i' th' face," are things rather not to be missed than to be dwelt upon—they tell us nothing *real.* It is with the *Heroic Stanzas* of 1658-59 on Cromwell's death, written when Dryden was in his twenty-eighth year, that his poetic career begins.

The *Heroic Stanzas.*   In these stanzas there is still something of what hasty judges call that "unoriginal" character which is so noticeable in Dryden—as it is also in Chaucer, Shakespeare, and other persons of that class. He accepts a fashionable form of the moment—the decasyllabic quatrain—which, in the decadence and deliquescence of the enjambed couplet, the immaturity of the stopped one, and the popular weariness of the more elaborate stanzas, Davenant had tried in *Gondibert,* that heroic poem which, according to the principles of its Preface and the opinion of Mr. Hobbes, was going to revolutionise English poetry. The supposed advantages of this quatrain are theoretically evident. It gives more room than the couplet; it does not invite to prolixity, or break up the narrative, to the same extent as the longer stanzas may seem likely to do ; and at the same time its form tightens up, and applies a styptic to, the flowing looseness which at this time was a special danger. Practically, these advantages are over-balanced, as even *Annus Mirabilis* was to show finally, and as *Gondibert* had already shown, by a coincident combination of the *dis*advantages both of couplet and stanza, and an almost unavoidable stiffness. You cannot vary your stops as in blank verse or the Spenserian, there is not room enough : and the recurrent divisions necessitated by the stanza lack at once the conciseness and continuity of the couplet, the variety and amplitude of the rhyme-royal, octave, or Spenserian itself. The *Heroic Stanzas* naturally show their disadvantages more than the *Annus*, though not more than their original in

Davenant. But there is already a new " mighty line," less magnificent than Marlowe's, but hardly less vigorous, and much more manageable. This appears in the very opening, but it is specially noticeable in stanzas 13-16 [1] and elsewhere. Only, it may be observed that pauses of importance literally occur *nowhere* except in the 1st and the 58th line, with a result in stately monotony, which is more interesting than felicitous.

Considering the return to the quatrain in the *Annus*, *Astræa Redux* it is probable that it was mainly a feeling that Usurper *and its group.* and King should not be celebrated on the same instrument which made Dryden, only a year or two later than the Cromwell period, revert to the couplet as the vehicle of his three poems on the Restoration, *Astræa Redux*, the *Coronation* poem, and the lines to Clarendon. The difference is extraordinary. That the metre of these things should excel the mere Juvenilia is nothing ; the point is that they far excel all couplet verse of their kind by Mr. Waller or by anybody else, in force, and strength, and *timbre*, if not yet in deftness and agility. There is a sledge-hammer stroke about the verse of

XIII

[1] Swift and resistless through the land he past,
　　Like that bold Greek, who did the East subdue ;
　And made to battles such heroic haste,
　　As if on wings of victory he flew.

XIV

He fought, secure of fortune as of fame,
　Till by new maps the island might be shown,
Of conquests, which he strewed where'er he came,
　Thick as the galaxy with stars is sown.

XV

His palms, though under weights they did not stand,
　Still thrived ; no winter could his laurels fade :
Heaven, in his portrait, shewed a workman's hand,
　And drew it perfect, yet without a shade.

XVI

Peace was the prize of all his toil and care,
　Which war had banished, and did now restore :
Bolognia's walls thus mounted in the air,
　To seat themselves more surely than before.

Astræa Redux,[1] for which, save in casual lines, I do not
know where to look before it : and this giant's pulse is
kept throughout. There is interest in the pause (or its
absence), and interest in the rhyme ; but the greatest
prosodic interest of all is in this redoubtable march of
metre, which suggests, not so much Gray's (borrowed) car
and two horses as the image of a warrior in complete
steel, riding slowly through the press and dealing mace—
rather than sword—strokes as he goes. There is also one
very curious and interesting device [2] which is employed
throughout, and which consists of " powdering " (as we
may call it) the verse with repetitions of a particular

[1] Now with a general peace the world was blest,
While ours, a world divided from the rest,
A dreadful quiet felt, and worser far
Than arms, a sullen interval of war.
Thus when black clouds draw down the lab'ring skies,
Ere yet abroad the winged thunder flies,
An horrid stillness first invades the ear,
And in that silence we the tempest fear.
The ambitious Swede, like restless billows tost,
On this hand gaining what on that he lost,
Though in his life he blood and ruin breathed,
To his now guideless kingdom peace bequeathed ;
And heaven that seemed regardless of our fate,
For France and Spain did miracles create ;
Such mortal quarrels to compose in peace,
As nature bred, and interest did increase.

[2] Our setting sun, from his declining seat,
Shot beams of kindness on *you*, not of heat ;
And, when his love was bounded in a few
That were unhappy, that they might be true,
Made *you* the favourite of his last sad times,
That is, a sufferer in his subjects' crimes.
Thus, those first favours *you* received, were sent,
Like heaven's rewards, in earthly punishment :
Yet fortune, conscious of *your* destiny,
E'en then took care to lay *you* softly by,
And wrapped *your* fate among her precious things,
Kept fresh to be unfolded with *your* king's.
Shown all at once, *you* dazzled so our eyes,
As new-born Pallas did the gods surprise,
When, springing forth from Jove's new-closing wound,
She struck the warlike spear into the ground ;
Which sprouting leaves did suddenly inclose,
And peaceful olives shaded as they rose.

Compare with this the opening of *Verses to the Duchess*, where the " you "
stop is even more skilfully played on.

word, sure to be pronounced with more or less emphasis, and so providing, as well as the regular setting of the rhyme,[1] a peculiar accompaniment of sound that almost produces the stanza effect, and in a manner makes up for the absence of pause-variety.

It would be easy, but probably idle, and certainly in- *Annus* conclusive, to guess *why* he reverted to the quatrain in *Mirabilis.* *Annus Mirabilis.* Probably, being as yet inexperienced in the varied powers of the couplet, and particularly struck at the moment (as we know from the *Essay of Dramatic Poesy*) with its dramatic capabilities, he thought that, in a narrative of stirring but individual scenes and accidents, the stanza would be better ; while he was still not a little under the influence of Davenant. At any rate, he did use it, and showed (as he probably convinced himself) both its full capabilities and its almost inevitable limitations. It has gained, in his hands, a great deal of vigour, variety, and flexibility ; while it has certainly lost no weight since he used it seven or eight years earlier. And his practice in couplet has clenched his epigrammatic power in single lines. The way in which he vignettes most of his numerous descriptions always makes me think of an old chart of the History of England which used to exist in my childhood, with framed cuts, like book-plates, of battles, and beheadings of kings and kesars, arranged round its margin. The Bergen blunder, the great three-days battle, the dock-yard scenes themselves, the second battle, the burning of " the Fly " (as Ulie used to be called), and above all the fire, are admirably done in a sort of convention of their own ; and the argumentative and other connecting passages already confess Dryden's almost unequalled skill in that semi-poetic kind of verse. The diction is

---

[1] Dryden's rhymes almost deserve a special appendix or note. Here, for instance, *A. R.* 106, 147, we have "chronicles" rhymed (as is not uncommon with him later) "chronic*lees*," and " hour " to " travellour," which latter word elsewhere takes " stars " and " wars " for companions. I believe that we may generalise these latter rhymes thus : "Any combination of letters may, in rhyme, take any sound which it sometimes has, though in another word."

often extremely felicitous, and in some parts, especially the famous " stanza of the heads,"[1] the stanza itself accompanies the meaning with a wonderfully suitable and original music. But, on the whole, the effect is still stiff and monotonous. The " rocking-horse " undulation of the quatrain—with its equal lines, very seldom strongly stopped internally, most frequently end-stopped in themselves, and in almost every case with full stop at the end of each stanza—would send one to sleep if it were anybody but Dryden who is writing ; and comes more nearly than it should to doing this, as it is.

For some dozen years after the appearance of the *Annus*, Dryden put forth nothing of importance, in poetry strictly so called. But his poetical, and especially his prosodic practice was continued and immensely extended during the whole of this long time. Indeed, it may be justly taken as his final stage of exercise. When we leave him with the *Annus*, his verse, though of the most eminent promise and even accomplishment, has not shaken itself quite free : it is good but laboured, effective

---

[1] The last of four which will give a good specimen passage :—

CCXX

So scapes the insulting Fire his narrow jail,
   And makes small outlets into open air ;
There the fierce winds his tender force assail,
   And beat him downward to his first repair.

CCXXI

The winds, like crafty courtesans, withheld
   His flames from burning, but to blow them more ;
And, every fresh attempt, he is repelled
   With faint denials, weaker than before.

CCXXII

And now, no longer letted of his prey,
   He leaps up at it with enraged desire ;
O'erlooks the neighbours with a wide survey,
   And nods at every house his threat'ning fire.

CCXXIII

The ghosts of traitors from the bridge descend,
   With bold fanatic spectres to rejoice ;
About the fire into a dance they bend,
   And sing their Sabbath notes with feeble voice.

Scott calls the last "this most beautiful stanza."

but unfinished. When we meet it again in *Absalom and Achitophel*, the freedom has been finally obtained, the finish definitely put on.

As far as the decasyllable, his great staple, was concerned, this mastery had been brought about in a double line of practice. At the very moment when he was writing the narrative *Annus* in quatrains, he was, as has been pointed out, championing the couplet for dramatic purposes in the *Essay*. As before, what notice we must give to his arguments, good or bad, will come best elsewhere ; it is his practice with which we are here concerned.

This practice was copious enough in the "Heroic" plays ; and it soon conferred upon him complete facility of a certain kind. It could not take a Dryden long to learn the "rhyming and rattling" which he labelled contemptuously later. And a Dryden could not learn this without learning a great deal else with it, and unlearning some things. The Heroic play had a convention of style and sentiment, as well as a convention of metre. The two had no necessary connection, but they were, in the usual course of human things, certain to react on each other. The extravagant sentiment and passion, the trick of sword-and-buckler interchange of short speeches, and the declamatory bombast which was fashionable, found in the couplet a very ready instrument. The worst of it was that this instrument was *too* ready, and carried the effects required of it over the line into burlesque. This defect—naturally enough caught up and reflected by the parodists of the *Rehearsal*, etc.—is patent and flagrant in the earlier plays up to the partly beautiful and partly absurd *Tyrannic Love* : and Dryden has not entirely cured it in the triumph of the style, that unique *tour de force* the *Conquest of Granada*. But by this time, and in many instances earlier, he has contrived to get out of it, or into it, an effective rhetorical form constantly, and occasionally a really great poetic vehicle. In particular, he has discovered and applied, as nobody had applied before, the "driving" power of the couplet —that faculty of, as it were, ramming things home,

The couplet in the Heroic plays.

Its changes.

which is as much its special virtue as the plangency of rhyme-royal, the descriptive and pictorial capacity of the Spenserian, the universal adaptableness of blank verse, or the half melancholy meditation of the enclosed *In Memoriam* quatrain. This driving power is, of course, sovereign for the *pointes*, the *sententiae*, the γνῶμαι, which are at once the solace and the sin of the " heroic " style ; and it is scarcely less useful in the passages of sentiment or of rodomontade, while it makes the wit and gallantry combats, if more dangerously near to the comic, more comfortably free from the wearisome, than blank-verse *stichomythia*.

In the very process of growing weary of his long-loved mistress, " rhyme," Dryden experimented in *Aureng-zebe* with a slightly different form of couplet itself—a form more enjambed, less wedded to the sharp hammer-stroke at the end of each distich, approaching nearer to the blank-verse period or paragraph, and so inevitably tending towards the adoption of that period or paragraph itself. This produced among other things the famous " criticism of life," which has ranked as the most purple passage of his plays, and which any poet might be proud to have written. But the form of this, finer at the best, is flatter when not at its best, and more insidiously invokes the question, " Why rhyme *at all* ? " [1]

---

[1] It, with an earlier sample of the other style, will probably suffice for specimens. We need no "awful" (or rather ludicrous) "examples" ; for though the metre usually emphasises the absurdity it does not create it.

> Fair though you are
> As summer mornings, and your eyes more bright
> Than stars that twinkle in a winter's night ;
> Though you have eloquence to warm and move
> Cold age and praying hermits into love ;
> Though Almahide with scorn rewards my care,—
> Yet, than to change, 'tis nobler to despair.
> My love's my soul ; and that from fate is free ;
> 'Tis that unchanged and deathless part of me.
>   *C. of G.* II., III. iii.
>
> When I consider life, 'tis all a cheat.
> Yet, fooled with hope, men favour the deceit ;
> Trust on, and think to-morrow will repay :
> To-morrow's falser than the former day,

He heard that question, and answered it by taking to
blank verse itself; and a very interesting study his blank
verse is, both intrinsically as a contrast to the dramatic
blank verse of "the last age," and in connection with the
extremely difficult problem to determine why, when we have
produced in the last two centuries narrative blank verse
not unworthy of its ancestor Milton, we have never
produced dramatic blank verse in the very least degree
worthy of its ancestor Shakespeare. For a hundred years
after Dryden there is no dramatic blank verse that can
touch Dryden's from any point of view, whether we look
at it as verse to be spoken or as verse to be read. For
a hundred years more till the present day we have not
unfrequently had dramatic blank verse which has been
perhaps what we are pleased to call more "poetic" than
his; but then, at least in the humble judgment of the
present writer, it has never been anything like so
dramatic.

The stock test passage is, of course, the description of
Cleopatra on the Cydnus, and though I hope that I have
shown myself not obliged to stick to stock passages, it
appears to me puerile to go out of the way to neglect
them. Few nowadays will take the view once entertained
by great admirers of both poets, that Dryden is here
Shakespeare's equal; none, perhaps, that which was
certainly once entertained by people not small, that he
is Shakespeare's superior. We are not quite over the
border between poetry and rhetoric, but we are approaching it, if not actually in the debatable land between them.
The march is more perceptible than the flight, the toga
more in evidence than the singing robe; and yet the
piece is poetry, and, what is more, good poetry, and, what

Lies worse, and while it says we *shall be* blest
With some new joys, cuts off what we possessed.
Strange cozenage! none would live past years again,
Yet all hope pleasure in what yet remain;
And, from the dregs of life, think to receive
What the first sprightly running could not give.
I'm tired with waiting for this chemic gold,
Which fools us young and beggars us when old.
                                        Aurengzebe, IV. i.

is still more, good dramatic poetry.[1]   Dryden's blank
verse is, indeed, a construction of quite peculiar quality,
and it serves as a fair test in the few "doubtful" plays
which have been attributed to him, as well as sometimes
in those where he collaborated with others.   In its most
perfect example, *All for Love*, which has just been sampled,
the poet has made great efforts to attain the Shakespearian
fluidity.   He has come nearest to it in the passage cited,
in the interview with Cleopatra on the return from Parthia,
and the last scene before Antony's death.   He has
achieved much by the ordinary means—by the variation
of the pause, and the provision of full stops in the interior
of the line ; and he has even sometimes come near to
that effect which we compared formerly to the running of
quicksilver through a tube to alter its balance.   But
Dryden's fluid is denser and less "quick" than Shakespeare's ; or (to vary the metaphor) he takes breath more
perceptibly, and at more frequent intervals.   Lee has the
advantage of him in this respect, though Otway has not.
The truth evidently is that the tendency of the couplet to
emphasis was too thoroughly congenial to Dryden, and
had been developed by him too frequently and familiarly,
not to impress itself likewise upon his blanks.   Yet they
are, after his very first beginnings, seldom or never
wooden, and not often merely rhetorical. In still later plays,
such as *Don Sebastian* and *Cleomenes*, they provide a very
stately and by no means stiff medium of dramatic speech.

It must not, however, be supposed that Dryden had
never tried blank verse till he became disgusted with the
couplet.   On the contrary, his early plays—some of them

---

[1] She lay, and leant her cheek upon her hand,
And cast a look so languishingly sweet
As if, secure of all beholders' hearts,
Neglecting, she could take them : boys like Cupids
Stood fanning, with their painted wings, the winds
That played about her face.   But if she smiled,
A darting glory seemed to blaze abroad,
That men's desiring eyes were never wearied,
But hung upon the object :   To soft lutes
The silver oars kept time ; and while they played,
The hearing gave new pleasure to the sight,
And both to thought.   *All for Love*, III. i.

written before the fancy or fashion for rhyme had come in—contain plenty of it, and in some it disputed the place with the couplet itself. *The Wild Gallant* is in prose ; but *The Rival Ladies* exhibits the competition of the two verse-vehicles.[1]   Dryden was too much of a craftsman, and had too regular an ear, ever to permit himself the worst excesses of blank verse that is blank of every verse-characteristic except the division of the lines —of the hideous mingle-mangle of which we should have seen enough.   His model is evidently that of Beaumont and Fletcher in their less inspired passages—a good many redundant endings, a free use of fragmentary lines, and so forth.   But it is noticeable that he has not risen to the secret of the verse-paragraph ; and that his lines, whether they have an actual stop at the end or not, are mainly of that " self-contained " kind of which we have said so much. To this last characteristic, indeed, he always more or less adhered—in fact, it was closely connected with his mastery of the closed couplet.   But, in spite of it, he managed later to achieve a very fair paragraph.   We have seen that Milton, whose paragraphs are hardly sur-passable in their way, and who certainly had no small influence over his junior and admirer, was in no such very dissimilar case.

But besides this immense and double exercise in the His lyrics. great dramatic and epic line, Dryden gave himself, in the plays, another, of which we have no examples from him before them and only a few outside of them, while the whole division is perhaps the least known of his work. These songs are invaluable to compare, not merely with that Second Caroline lyric contemporary with them which (at least in the masterpieces of Dorset, Sedley, and Rochester) has preserved a certain vogue, but with the *First* Caroline

---

[1] The uncertainty which exists as to his part in *The Indian Queen* makes it difficult to draw any conclusions from that play except as to the lyrics, which Sir Robert Howard, *alias* " Crites," *alias* " Sir Positive At-all," simply could not have written.   But there can be little doubt that he " buckwashed " the body of the play a good deal ; and it is at least noteworthy that there are alternate rhymes in it (*e.g.* the speech of Acacis in II. i.).   Generally in this, and in the later plays for some years, the couplet ousts blank verse altogether.

variety, and the songs in the Elizabethan drama generally. They are of much greater poetical merit than is usually allowed ; but on that we must not directly dwell. Our main point must be their prosodic character ; and to bring this out we may best take the whole together, including those written in plays subsequent to the resumption of non-dramatic verse in the Satires, and the few that exist unconnected with plays at all. The two great points to be brought out by the examination will be found to be : first, the power shown by the poet in manipulating measures far removed from the regular decasyllable ; and, secondly, the appearance and power of the *anapæst*—a foot which, as we shall see, was to provide part of the Asturias in which the faithful of true English prosody were to take refuge, during the triumph of the couplet and of syllabic uniformity, in the eighteenth century.

However much or however little of *The Indian Queen* may be Sir Robert Howard's, there can, let it be repeated, be very little doubt that the lyrics are Dryden's. They include the octosyllabic incantation (Dryden was fond of incantations)—

> You twice ten hundred deities,

largely changed to trochaics in its Second Part ; and a more varied "Song of Aerial Spirits." But it is noticeable that in neither of these is the dissyllabic foot exceeded. Nor is it in the songs of *The Indian Emperor*, one of which is very beautiful.[1] One might have feared from these that, as far as Dryden was concerned, English lyric was to suffer the fate which French had already undergone, and was to become merely iambic staple lines cut into varying lengths. But in *The Maiden Queen* we come across a measure which Dryden was to practise several times, and which is curiously susceptible of two very

---

[1] Ah, fading joy ! how quickly thou art past,
Yet we thy ruin haste.
As if the cares of human life were few,
We seek out new,
And follow fate, which would too fast pursue.

different scansions. It may have been suggested to him by music ; but, as has been pointed out more than once, even if we were quite sure that it was, and that the music which suggested it was definitely in double or definitely in triple time, that would not settle the question.

Now this measure, which is also that of

> From the low palace of old Father Ocean

in *Albion and Albanius,* and of the extremely beautiful song in *Cleomenes,*

> No! no! poor suffering heart, no change endeavour!

may obviously be taken as

> I feed | a flame | within, | which so | torments me—

iambic hendecasyllables—or as

> I feed a | flame within, | which so tor|ments me—

dactylic tetrameter or anapæstic trimeter with anacrusis and redundance, as may be preferred. We may return to this ; meanwhile a stanza of each shall be given below.[1]

The pure anapæst appears first in *Sir Martin Mar-all,*

[1] I feed a flame within, which so torments me,
That it both pains my heart, and yet contents me ;
'Tis such a pleasing smart, and I so love it,
That I had rather die than once remove it.

From the low palace of old Father Ocean,
Come we in pity your cares to deplore ;
Sea-racing dolphins are trained for our motion,
Moony tides swelling to roll us ashore.

No! no! poor suffering heart, no change endeavour!
Choose to sustain the smart, rather than leave her.
My ravished eyes behold such charms about her,
I can die with her, but not live without her.

In this last, which is the finest, there is least temptation to "trisyllabise," and most in the second. As for the first, it has been objected that you cannot "stress" *that, which, and,* etc. I demur. "And" I hold to be, at pleasure, one of the longest and one of the shortest syllables in English. As for the others, compare Spenser's tricks in his elegiacs ; and remember that these trisyllabic measures were only in the go-cart. But I admit a choice.

which has two examples,[1] neither of the specially poetical
kind, but both good light tripping examples of the mere
metre, as are some [2] of the lyrical additions to the travesty
of *The Tempest.* Dryden's exact share in both these
plays is unknown ; and there are reasons for thinking it
mainly " buck-washing." But if anybody claims the first
set of songs for Newcastle, and the last for Davenant,
he will meet with no protest from me. There are no
competing claims in *An Evening's Love*, and here
Dryden shows what a master of lyric he was. The
cadence of

> You charmed me not with that fair face,

though purely iambic, has not a little in it of the
ineffable throb and soar of the First Caroline wing ;
while

> After the pangs of a desperate lover

(which seems to have become deservedly popular) has
a delightful anapæstic lilt, and is very interesting to
compare with the hybrid pieces mentioned just now.
Here there is hardly any possibility of the iambic base
having been meant—the dropping of the redundant
syllable in the even lines being fatal ; while in yet a
third example—

> Calm was the even and clear was the sky,

the odd lines themselves merely complete the just
anapæst. The gradation is of the first prosodic interest,
and the execution of three such songs by a master of the
heroic couplet must have been invaluable for the retention
of the liberty of English prosody. Nor was Dryden
satisfied even with this good measure, for he added a
fourth song, the pretty

[1] " Make rea|dy fair la|dy to-night " and " Blind love | to this hour Had
ne|ver like me | a slave un|der his power."
[2] For instance—

> Where | does the black | fiend Ambit|ion reside
> With the mis|chievous de|vil of Pride.

> Celimena ! of my heart,

before the play ended.[1]

The gorgeous fustian of the couplets of *Tyrannic Love*
is diversified by three lyrics of good quality, though not so
good as the set just quoted,—an anapæstic duet of " Astral
Spirits," and two solos—one in Pindaric form, and one of
very soft and flowing trochees.

That palmary example of the heroic play, the double
Conquest of Granada, does not contain much lyric, but what
it does is very noteworthy. The " Zambra Song,"
" Beneath a myrtle shade," is the very triumph of its own
peculiar style, with the sleepy voluptuous grace of a portrait by Lely transposed into metrical expression, and only
falling short, by the traditional yet all-important " that—! "
of the highest lyrical rapture. It has no rapid movement,
and requires none.[2] On the other hand, the later—

[1] Part of all four must be given :—

> You charmed me not with that fair face,
>   Though that was half divine ;
> To be another's is the grace
>   That makes me wish you mine.
>
> After the pangs of a desperate lover,
>   When day and night I have sighed all in vain,
> Ah ! what a pleasure it is to discover
>   In her eyes pity who causes my pain !
>
> Calm was the even, and clear was the sky,
>   And the new budding flowers did spring,
> When all alone went Amyntas and I
>   To hear the sweet nightingale sing.
>
> Celimena ! of my heart
>   Nothing shall bereave you.
> If with your good leave I may
> Quarrel with you once a day,
>   I will never leave you.

The two last lines of this last have a delightful explosion—

> It will | be the | *devil and* | all
>   When we come together !

[2] Perhaps the second stanza is the most beautiful—

> From the bright vision's head
> A careless veil of lawn was loosely spread ;
> *From her white temples fell her shaded hair*
> *Like cloudy sunshine, not too brown nor fair ;*
> Her hands, her lips, did love inspire ;
> Her every grace my heart did fire,
> But most her eyes, which languished with desire.

> Whatever I am and whatever I do,
> My Phyllis is still on my mind,

consists entirely of the freest-flowing anapæsts—a little shallow and "jingly," but perfect in mere motion ; and the same may be said of that in the Second Part—

> How unhappy a lover am I.

Poetically, neither of these two is the equal of "Beneath a myrtle shade" ; but the trio shows, as well as possible, from the prosodic side, how this poet was master of the double mode, now languorous, now nimble.

Marriage à la Mode, the next play, practically opens with a most interesting combination of these modes, such as Dryden had not yet tried. This combination—an iambic common measure quatrain followed by an anapæstic one with an internal rhyme in the third line—has been widely imitated since, and has an excellent bravura effect.[1] It is followed by a still livelier composition entirely in anapæsts,[2] the freshness of which—as I remember after some thirty years—made a highly

---

[1] Why should a foolish marriage vow,
    Which long ago was made,
  Oblige us to each other now
    When passion is decayed ?
We loved and we loved, as long as we could,
  Till our love was loved out in us both ;
But our marriage is dead when the pleasure is fled—
  'Twas pleasure first made it an oath.

[2] While Alexis lay pressed
    In her arms he loved best,
  With his hands round her neck,
    And his head on her breast,
He found the fierce pleasure too hasty to stay
And his soul in the tempest just flying away.

Modern readers, accustomed to these easy measures, may forget that they were *not* easy two centuries and more ago. Such things, for instance, as the varied refrains, with internal rhyme, of "Calm was the even"—

  For when, with a fear, he began to draw near
  He was dashed with a Ha ! ha ! ha ! ha !

or

  And just as our bliss we began with a kiss,
  He laughed out with Aha ! ha ! ha ! ha !

anybody can write *now* ; but this is because Dryden and others wrote them for the first time *then.*

respectable editor who declined, as likely to shock the public, an essay of mine on Dryden, inquire innocently " why I had not put this in ? "   There is certainly nothing like it that I know of in English before, for rattling and galloping melody, except " Calm was the even," cited before.

That rather dull play *The Assignation* relieves itself with another symphony,[1] that of the hybrid hendeca-syllables mentioned above with a shorter *coda*, which at once links this scheme (and possibly the others) to " Phillida flouts me."   But it was not likely that Dryden would waste good lyrics on a piece of occasional rubbish like *Amboyna*.   The blank verse (such as there is of it) is so bad for the most part that one cannot help suspecting that the public of that day *liked* bad blank verse—perhaps for the same reason for which Mr. Fitz-Boodle's beloved liked bad oysters—because they were accustomed to it. For the same reason also—the whole purpose of the thing being popularity—he gave then, in the " Sea-fight " song, one of the half-doggerel Pindarics of which we find so many examples in the song-books of the period.   But the octosyllabic couplets of the " Epithalamium " are smooth enough.

It may seem extraordinary that the " opera " of *The State of Innocence* (which, by the way, is a much better thing than those who have not read it, but who very properly hold that Milton was a greater poet than Dryden, may think) should contain no lyrics.   It may be that the author of *Paradise Lost*, in giving his famous and characteristically gracious permission to " tag," may have

[1] Long between love and fear Phyllis, tormented,
Shunned her own wish, yet at last she consented.
But loth that day should her blushes discover,
" Come, gentle night," she said,
" Come quickly to my aid,
And a poor shame-faced maid
Hide from her lover ! "

Earlier there are some lively *three*-anapæst lines—

For 'tis of a nature so subtle
That if it's not luted with care, etc.

barred lyric patching. But I think there is a simpler
explanation. The piece was never acted ; if it had been,
Dryden would probably have inserted songs. Still, it is
certainly not a negligible thing that none occur in the two
next plays, *Aurengzebe*, that fine curtain to the " Heroic "
series, and *All for Love*, that still finer overture to the
blank - verse succession. Dryden, however, as careful
students of him know, though not a man of mere whim, was
subject to curious ebbs and flows of special interest. This
tidal state of his mind has brought upon him the reproach
of inconsistency in criticism—it is a much better explanation
of such apparent irregularities in practice as those which
we are now noticing.

It was not merely his return to comedy in *Limberham*
which induced him to revert to lyric, though that ill-famed
production contains two pieces, " 'Gainst keepers we
petition " (fair rollicking ribaldry), and a sentimental song
from the Italian. There can be no doubt that the lyrical
part of *Œdipus* is among his contributions, and not among
those of Lee. It has been observed that he liked
incantations ; and it may be added that while he has left,
proportionately, but few catalectic octosyllables, those
which he has left are rather varied in style, and always
good. The scene in question is almost (not quite wholly)
in the trochaic heptasyllable, and while obviously inspired
by *Macbeth*, is not unworthy of the inspiration. The
earlier song to Apollo, less successful, is equally interesting, because of its combination—without blending—of the
strict and the equivalenced octosyllable. Do this in odd
lines, and not in regular batches, and you have *Christabel.*
There was no room here for the hand-gallop which the
light cavalry of Dryden's poetical army had mastered as
thoroughly as his infantry had mastered the march of
the couplet and the blank line. But he found a place for
it in *Troilus and Cressida.* Let it be observed in connection with the question of " Music *v.* Prosody," that the
prosodic and poetic quality of this piece is immensely
improved by the *omission* of the " vain repetition " required
by the setting. A short piece of *In Memoriam* metre in

The Spanish Friar is also spoilt by this damnable iteration
—one of the worst injuries which music does to poetry ;
but Dryden more than recovers himself in the other lyric
of that play, " Farewell, ungrateful traitor," which joins
the music of the seventeenth century to that of the nineteenth, and Dryden to Mr. Swinburne.[1] The single song
in the *Duke of Guise*—the second play in which Dryden
collaborated with Lee—has less poetical merit, but is a
pleasant in-and-out measure. On the other hand, practically
the whole of *Albion and Albanius* is lyrical, though of
the libretto kind. Hardly more than the two songs,
" Come away," and that formerly noted—

> From the low palace of old Father Ocean,

need notice. In the great play of *Don Sebastian* he put no
lyrics ; but *Amphitryon* has several, and good ones, though
rather too musical. The second " opera," *King Arthur*,
has over the first the advantage that its bulk is blank verse,
not libretto mishmash and recitative—perhaps also that
its setter, Purcell, was a very different person from
" Monsieur Grabu," who performed the office earlier. It
is not, however, only thanks to him that " Come if you
dare " is the best known of Dryden's songs ; and many of
the rather numerous others are pretty, though one would
be much improved by a slight alteration of the measures
which would anticipate some well-known later movements.
It must, however, be confessed that

> Fairest isle, all isles excelling,

though pretty in itself, has a certain fore-echo of eighteenth-

---

[1] Farewell, ungrateful traitor !
  Farewell, my perjured swain !
Let never injured creature
  Believe a man again.
The pleasure of possessing
Surpasses all expressing,
But 'tis too short a blessing,
  And love too long a pain.

May the reader be respectfully reminded that " swain " was not hackneyed,
and " craytur " not a vulgarism, then ? (Cf. as to the metre Drayton, as
quoted above, p. 102 *sq.*)

century namby-pambiness.   It is a comfort to be back
in *Cleomenes* with that last and best of the hybrids so
often noticed, which is one of Dryden's greatest lyric
triumphs.   It is impossible to understand how any one
reading it can deny him lyric poignancy and "cry." This
is the only lyric in the play ; and though his last piece,
Love Triumphant, contains three, one of them is by
Congreve, and another, on jealousy, is not of much account ;
the third—

> Young I am and yet untried,

is the best here, but not of its author's best.

Other songs.   To these songs in the plays have to be added certain
detached examples, printed in the *Miscellany* or otherwise
attributed, which may or must be Dryden's—the smoothly
flowing "Farewell, fair Armida," and its answer in anapæsts ; " The Tears of Amynta for the Death of Damon,"
a trochaic *placebo* and *dirige,* where sentiment does not
exclude pathos ; the galloping *gaillardise* of " Sylvia the
fair in the bloom of fifteen," and the less questionable
in subject, but equally pretty, " Lady of the May " ; the
older-fashioned and really charming " Ask not the cause,"
and its companion, " Go tell Amynta, gentle swain " ;
" Chloe found Amyntas lying " ; " Happy and free, securely
blest " ; " Fair, sweet, and young, receive a prize " ; and
" High state and honours to others impart " ; the Secular
Masque ; the songs for *The Pilgrim* ; and yet others.
These, with the two Cecilia Songs, reserved for treatment
with Dryden's other odes, make a very considerable total
of lyric : and I have often wished that, in these days of
innumerable reprints, some one would make a book of
them together.

Such a book would not only do, to perhaps our greatest
poet of the second order, a justice to which he has long
been a stranger; but it would help to bring out a point
of literary and prosodic history which has almost entirely
escaped attention, for the reason that when the facts were
known nobody was likely to draw the inference, and that
since people have been likely to be interested in drawing

the inference they have generally been ignorant of the facts. This point is the immense importance of the coincidence and persistence of Dryden's practice in lyric, and especially in the lighter triple measures thereof. He was establishing the supremacy of the couplet, and bringing it about that people were to think—not merely (as even Ben had been inclined to think) that it was the best of all measures, but that it was practically *the* measure, which every other measure would be if it could—that real poetic virtue and orthodoxy were hardly to be found elsewhere. Yet at the same time he was providing, in these lyrics, a perpetual door of escape from the prison, a perpetual warning and protest against the over-generalisation.

The Odes—with which, if we call *Alexander's Feast* The Odes. " Cecilia Major," we may join the ten-years earlier " Song " for the Saint's Day, as " Cecilia Minor "—constitute a sort of bridge between the quatrains, couplets, and blank verse on the one side, and the pure lyrics on the other. The "Anne Killigrew" ode or epicede is the severest of all, confining itself to iambics strophically treated : and its famous opening stanza has always, and deservedly, been reckoned as one of the finest examples of its kind. The longer *Threnodia Augustalis* on the death of Charles I. is on the same model, but for obvious reasons not quite such a success, though it contains fine passages. Although Horace and English Pindaric are as opposite as possible, the famous verses in the translation of Od. i. 29, " Fortune, that, with malicious joy," are neither more nor less than magnificent.[1] The two Cecilias, being definitely intended

---

[1] This, which, with its sequel, was a special favourite of Thackeray's, must be given once more. I do not know whether it or the better known (Anne Killigrew) stanza is the finest example of English Pindaric.

> Happy the man, and happy he alone,
> He, who can call to-day his own :
> He who, secure within, can say,
> To-morrow do thy worst, for I have lived to-day.
> Be fair, or foul, or rain, or shine,
> The joys I have possessed, in spite of Fate, are mine.
> Not Heaven itself upon the past has power ;
> But what has been has been, and I have had my hour.

The rest, with " Fortune, that, with malicious joy," and " I puff the

for musical setting, and not hampered by the epicedial gravity, combine the Pindaric and the strictly lyrical appeal ; and are thus very interesting. The opening stanza of the older and shorter piece is a fine example of Pindaric ; and the short stanzas attempting to express the characters of the different instruments, though perhaps *tours-de-force*, still exhibit the " force " of Dryden. He put it to even greater trial, and with more success, in *Alexander's Feast*—" Cecilia Major "—where he intermixes the dissyllabic and trisyllabic measures. The effect is undoubtedly artificial ; but it is artful as well, and must have exercised, owing to its unbroken popularity, an influence enforcing—silently and unmarked it may be, but not without result—the same lesson to which attention has been drawn above. If the great Mr. Dryden condescended to these " irregular " numbers, could they be utterly childish and inartistic?

The Hymns, etc.

One other division of Dryden's work outside the couplet calls for notice, though, like some other work not brought together for convenience, it may be later than the resumption of couplet itself in the Satires. As certainly known, the body of his hymn-writing is a very small one, but there are at least strong reasons for thinking that it ought to be very largely supplemented.[1] And as it happens, the prosodic characteristics are noted as strongly as possible in the certainly genuine cases. Indeed, they supply the main argument for the addition of the " doubtfuls." These certain pieces are the paraphrase of

---

prostitute away," is a little less sustained, good as these things are. But the examples referred to, and many others, including not a few from *Threnodia Augustalis* itself, contrast most strikingly, not merely with such stuff as Swift's and other Pindarics, which we shall notice, but with not a little of Cowley. Dryden hardly ever fails in real symphonic effect ; the others too often simply empty sackfuls of wooden bricks of different sizes.

[1] See the present writer's revision of Scott's *Dryden* (Edinburgh, 1893) xviii. 269-281, for some account of the Hymns in the Roman Catholic Primer of 1706 and their attribution to Dryden, with some carefully selected specimens, and for reference to Mr. Orby Shipley's and other fuller treatments of the subject. I was prevented, as there explained, from discussing the matter fully, and this would not be the proper place for doing so ; but I have seen no reason to alter my opinion that the probability of their being Dryden's work is very great indeed.

Veni Creator (which has been glanced at already in connection with the fourteenth-century version[1]), the *Te Deum*, and the *Hymn for St. John's Eve.* In these and in many of the new claimants for his authorship there appears that peculiar massive strength, thoroughly under command and not in the least clumsy, which is Dryden's great prosodic note. The *Veni Creator* is in octosyllables,[2] the *Te Deum* in heroics, and the *St. John's Eve* in a combination of the two ; but all are alike in the massive resonance of the single line.

And so we may return to his couplet work itself, still postponing, however, the central display of it in the Satires.

The couplet in the Translations

In so vast a quantity of verse of this kind as that contained in the Miscellanies, the *Juvenal*, the *Virgil*, and the *Fables*, it is, of course, inevitable that there should be some passages where the poet settles into common form. But there is an astonishing number of passages and lines, colouring and characterising the whole, in which he does not do this. He avails himself, of course, of his various licences (*v. infra*), including what I was, I confess, surprised to find when I went through the *Virgil* some years ago—numerous examples of the fourteener. But he does not really need these for prosodic effect, though they are convenient to him, as even Pope found the Alexandrine convenient later, in rendering lines and phrases which demanded additional room in English. His variety is really the result of the variety of his individual line and couplet. In the speeches something of the old " heroic " emphasis returns : you could not expect the author of *Tyrannic Love* and the *Conquest of Granada* not to remember his swashing blow when he came to such convenient matter as the Fourth Book of the *Æneid* or the later negotiations. But it in no respect prevails through-out. Further, the *Juvenal* differs from the *Virgil*, the *Lucretius* from the *Juvenal*, and all from the more modern " translations " in the *Fables*. *The Flower and the Leaf* is

---

[1] Vol. i. pp. 131, 132.

[2] See above, p. 378, for remark on his too seldom shown command of this metre. Of the lighter or Hudibrastic form of it we have from him only the *Epistle to Sir George Etherege*, which, if not consummate, is good.

perhaps the most remarkable example of the singular
adaptableness of this apparently massive instrument to the
fantastic graces of the delightful original. *Theodore and
Honoria*, equally good in itself, is less surprising; because
Dryden's majesty is conceded, and his lightness is not.
In fact, when the varied craftsmanship of these pieces
is considered, and when the certainly erroneous "major"
of the eighteenth century—that all metres would be
couplet if they could—is granted, we need feel no
prosodic wonder when we find even such a man as Ellis,
who knew nearly the whole range of English poetry up
to his own time, and could appreciate it, estating some of
these examples as "topmost."

This translation-couplet is (of course, in the *Virgil*
most of all) specially valuable for the important
comparison with Pope. Dryden's theory of the process
itself is well known—that you should rather strive to
bring home a parallel or analogous effect in the language
of translation, than endeavour to render exactly and
literally the language translated.[1] It naturally follows
from this, that though he used a uniform vehicle in almost
every case his management of it varied—a variation
rendered easy to him by the elastic character of his model
of couplet generally. That he often uses his own
favourite weighty current—which runs to the end of the
second line and resounds there with the slap of a wave on
the shore—is natural enough; natural also that he should
often develop that antithetic arrangement both of rhythm
and epithet which the form almost inevitably invites, and
which was rather to tyrannise over it later. But he
himself allows no predominance to either of these. The
fine description of the stallion in the Third Georgic[2] is

---

[1] Its merits could not be better vindicated, nor could its faults be better
brought out, than in the passage from Horace above given. This is magnificent, but it is not Horatian.

[2] I. ii. 120.   Here at least one line—

Sharp-headed, barrel-bellied, broadly-backed,

is quite Shakespearian or Miltonic in its bold independence of the mere
mechanical mould of line which was going to be made a fetish, and in its vivid
profile of the object.

one of the many which refute Wordsworth's most
unjust remark, that "when Virgil has his eye on the
object Dryden always spoils the passage." The fact
is that the Lake School, including even Coleridge
himself, are never to be trusted on the Augustans—
thereby supplying yet another instance of the almost
universal truth about a period and its immediate predecessor.

But it is time to say something of the general result of *In the later*
these various practisings : in the tap and rally of the sharply *poems generally.*
stopped couplet, in the more "linked" quality of the enjambed,
in the partly individual, partly associated blank verse, and in
the lightness and variety of lyric. When Dryden returned
to the couplet itself in non-dramatic verse after his dozen
years of interval, he showed a really astonishing command
of the form which he had by this time elaborated, and
which he afterwards preferred. It has been observed in
all countries—from Greece to France—which have been
addicted to the rather ignoble practice of first submitting
to tyrants and then taking vengeance on the tyrants'
families, that this vengeance has always been peculiarly
savage and lasting. And it has been so seen, outside
politics, with regard to the stopped couplet, which
domineered over England prosodically for nearly a century
and a half. Full justice has rarely been done to it,
though the enjambed variety, which the stopped one had
itself ousted, has, as in other cases, been allowed to escape
the penalties. Yet no one with a catholic ear and a taste
for the subject can well help admitting Dryden's form of
it (as he was to practise it for the last twenty years of his
life, from *Absalom* to the *Fables*) as one of the noblest
vehicles of verse ever put together. Neither he nor
any one else during its flourishing time explored quite all
its capabilities. It is, indeed, false to say of Dryden, as
Landor said in a phrase the other part of which is just
enough, that he is "*never* tender or sublime." Tenderness
and (in one sense at least) sublimity are not the regions
that he haunts most gladly, though the famous and
beautiful *confiteor* in the *Hind and the Panther*, and the

charming if slightly metaphysical [1] "daughter of the rose" addressed to Mary Somerset, do not require much development in their respective ways to reach these regions. But the things that the verse does are so many, and are done so admirably, that one hesitates to say what it might have done or might not. To begin with, it has entirely lost the touch of stiffness, not to say clumsiness, which characterised it in the group of poems on the Restoration. It is no longer a giant's club or mace or *morgenstern*, not even an irresistible but somewhat unmanageable axe. It is a sword, with the power of the two-handed kind and the alertness of the rapier miraculously adjusted to each other, so that neither interferes, and both contribute. In satire it stings and swings with a lightness of motion as great as the depth and sureness of its blow ; in argument it has the clearness as well as the weight of prose, with an added cogency of rhythmical phrase. Metaphors have been and still may be lavished on the consummateness and the variety of its achievement of its own ends—above all, on the extraordinary ease and temper of the prosodic as well as the intellectual composition. Dryden never overbalances either line or rhyme ; he has recovered almost before his lunge is finished, yet it *is* finished ; and at the same time he never approaches the monotony which is Pope's great fault, and from which Akenside and Churchill could only escape by having recourse to Dryden himself.

The *Prologues,* etc.   To appreciate the full range and power of this extraordinary form, it is necessary to take in the *Prologues* and *Epilogues*, which, from their great variety of subject, reinforce the examples of its capacities in the most desirable manner. With them, with the great satires and didactic pieces, and with the more original part of the *Fables*, we have such a body of exemplification of the possibilities of a particular form as exists nowhere else in our subject save in the dramatic blank verse of Shakespeare, the epic blank verse of Milton, the stanzas of Spenser, and perhaps the octosyllables of William Morris. The "stal-

---

[1] I suspect he owed a little royalty on this to the much-abused Cleveland.

warts " of Pope would, of course, challenge this ; but I am
not afraid of them. Pope's couplet may have higher if
narrower perfection, but it is a peak, not a range : and if,
in its mathematical and mechanical regularity, it escapes
some flecks and flaws which Dryden's carelessly exhibits,
it has corresponding disadvantages. Dryden's antithesis
is scarcely ever merely verbal and expletive as Pope's is
often, and Pope's seldom attains the absolutely final
touch of Dryden's in such lines as—

> They got a villain, and we lost a fool,

where you will find that, turn and re-turn the thing as
you like, it only becomes more crushing, for the *retention*
of a villain is surely as unsatisfactory as the getting of a
fool. There is also a sort of buoyancy in Dryden's
couplets which no one else, except some clever pupils of his
own like Churchill and Canning, has succeeded in attaining. Here is a chance-medley from the Epilogue to
Albion and Albanius—not of the best nor of the worst—
which will illustrate what I mean—

> The saint who walked on waves securely trod
> While he believed the beckoning of his God ;
> But, when his faith no longer bore him out,
> Began to sink as he began to doubt.

In this buoyancy he has at once merged the necessity of
pause and the danger of the self-moulded line ; the point,
whatever it is, is taken as Condé took (or did not take)
Lerida—" at a hand-gallop."

The adaptation of a medium of this kind alike to The Satires.
satire, to didactic, and to narrative could only be effected
by extraordinary craftsmanship ; but it is done. The great
satiric triumphs in the series from *Absalom and Achitophel*
to *The Hind and the Panther* are still comparatively
well known, but probably few people have given themselves
the trouble to realise how much the mere prosody contributes to them. Such satiric " whole-lengths " as those of
Shaftesbury, Buckingham, Oates, Bethel, Shadwell, Settle,
require no ordinary combination of qualities in the verse
that is to carry them out. It must be swift, but not

desultory or wanting in weight ; solidly moulded, but not
monotonous.   It must build up the satiric structure as
Burke later prided himself on building his prose, with
equal and accumulative attention to the idea and to the
imagery.   It must be always well in hand, serious without
passion, and disdainful without loss of temper.   Everywhere in the measure, as well as in the sense, perfect
command has to be manifested : the poet cannot afford to
miss a hit, to fire in the air, to boggle anything ; and he
does not.   It is almost enough to say that the passage of
Pope's satire which most reminds one of Dryden is the
character of Atticus, and that the principal thing which
reminds us again that it is *not* Dryden's is the deadly
earnest of it—the absence of the Olympian quality.   Pope
attacks on the level, or from below, and sometimes from
behind ; Dryden always from above.   And if it be said,
" Oh ! but all this is characteristic of the meaning, not the
form," one can only say, " Pardon ! "   To the present
writer at any rate, all the characteristics just mentioned are
as noteworthy in the form as in the sense, or more so.   We
have once more " riding rhyme "—verse moving easily,
fluently, for all its formidable punctuation.   Only the
chevauchée is no longer Chaucer's graceful " taking the
air " on horseback.   It is little more disturbing to the
rider : he takes his exercise almost as nonchalantly as
Chaucer himself.   But it is an exercise of sword-hand as
well as bridle-hand.   He does not " accompany each blow
With a Ha ! or with a Ho ! " like The Bogle ; he is less
gesticulatory.   But he is like that redoubtable champion
in another respect—

> [For] he *always* cleaves his foe
> To the waist !

The didactic and narrative pieces.   But the argumentative use of this couplet is almost
more remarkable than the satiric, and much more unique.
Here Pope is altogether inferior ; the didactic and argumentative parts of the *Essay on Criticism*, the *Essay on
Man*, and the rest are amateurish, desultory, feeble, when
compared with the serried reasoning of *Religio Laici*, and

the great church-battle of the *Hind and the Panther*. Whether such things should be couched in verse at all is another question ; but one may certainly alter the old hyperbole, and say that if the Gods argued cases in verse, they would use the verse of Dryden. Its curious freedom from the obvious and salient *trick* which damages Pope's, its strange faculty of combining without running on, and even what some call its "prosaic" quality, assist it mightily in this respect : as does a certain other faculty, instanced in the great satiric pictures above noticed, of attaining the verse-paragraph in couplet itself.

Nor is it much inferior in description and narration of a kind ; though how far it would have proved suitable for long, varied, much incidented narrative, one can hardly say. I never can feel quite so certain as Scott did that

> Dryden, in immortal strain,
> Had raised the Table Round again

but for the misconduct of King and Court in making him toil on to give them sport. The couplet, unless enjambed, is not a very good medium for long narrative ; but in its shorter examples in and out of the *Fables* it proves a very fair vehicle—in *Theodore and Honoria* more especially. Yet undoubtedly it is greatest in satire ; and it is there so great that when we think of the Second Part of *Absalom* or of *Mac-Flecknoe* there is no room for anything but laughter *and* applause. The thing is the very triumph of the particular branch of poetic and especially of prosodic art.

Two of Dryden's means for keeping off monotony Pope deliberately discarded under the idea of "correctness"— bane of all prosodic thought ;[1] and each of these, the triplet and the Alexandrine, deserves mention.

The original persuasive to both is, of course, clear enough—it is simply a sense of too narrow room in the Triplets and Alexandrines

[1] There is no point on which I feel more strongly than on this *pseudo-*correctness. Its whole mother-idea is wrong. Varieties of verse are not aberrations from a norm : they are on equal terms with it, children of the same parents. It is not even the eldest son : it has no rights that they have not. You might as well expect a clock to go with the pendulum always perpendicular as verse to go rightly with an unvaried line.

ten or twenty syllables. But it is improbable that any one could practise either without feeling their use as a corrective of monotony as well as a promoter of ease. I have never been able to persuade myself that the giving up of them was not one of those rather unreasonable, though it would seem quite inevitable, "tightenings up" of rule which have spoilt almost all games at one time or another. The triplet has no doubt a slight tendency to burlesque, and, if used often, throws the general effect out of character; but then it is the poet's business to guard against these results. Both in descriptive and argumentative verse it is of great importance, and has something of the effect of a parenthesis—that figure hated of the vulgar, and beloved by the elect. As for the Alexandrine, we have made the antiquity of that licence at least probable; and it is one which should never be given up either in blank verse or couplet; for while eminently useful in point of sense, it is invaluable for varying, without too much irregularity, the cadence and composition of the measure. To expand it still further to a fourteener, as Dryden has (*v. supra*) sometimes done, is indeed, perhaps, going too far; but in about the only instance of this which occurs in original and important work[1] it seems likely that the common idea of "suiting the verse to the sense" had a good deal to do with the extravagance. The Alexandrine proper has no burlesque effect unless very clumsily handled. As for Pope's well-known "wounded snake" gibe, it is enough to reply that the poet has no business to let his snakes be wounded, and that nothing glides much more smoothly or briskly than an *un*wounded snake.

It is indeed, perhaps, true that the peculiar weight and massiveness of Dryden's actual decasyllable enables it to stand the "thrust" of these additions better than a lighter and slighter staple may do. And yet it seems rather absurd to deny it the epithet "light." There is

---

[1] Thou leapst o'er all eternal truths in thy Pindaric way.
The Medal, 294.
Dryden was pretty certainly thinking of Cowley's note quoted above.

already nothing " heavy " about the passages which scorch and scathe for ever in the two *Achitophels*, and the *Medal*, and *Mac-Flecknoe*, or about the peculiarly graceful description of *The Flower and the Leaf*, which here owes nothing prosodically to the rhyme-royal of the original. The truth is that, barring the absence of that diviner æther which had left English poetry, and was scarcely to return till Blake conjured it back from some of the cloudy regions of his Forbidden Countries of prophecy, there is hardly anything wanting to Dryden's prosody. It not only did one thing supremely, even though that may not have been an absolutely supreme thing ; but it did an astonishing number of things well, and more than well. One feels, however much one may worship the earlier Caroline fancy and the later Romantic imagination—however conscious one may be that Dryden is not Blake or Coleridge, Shelley or Keats, Tennyson or even Browning — a sort of indignation at having to apologise in any way for him. We may with him, pro-sodically as well as poetically, as a whole be on Earth and not in Heaven. But (as Browning has been mentioned) his Earth is so good that it seems a little impertinent, and more than a little ungracious, to inquire, while we are on it, whether Heaven is not best.

NOTE ON ALEXANDRINES IN CONTINUOUS VERSE

IT may be objected to the remark on Pope (*sup.* p. 390) that he made ample amends to Dryden's Alexandrines elsewhere, in the equally well-known compliment to their "long resounding march and energy divine "—not to mention that his objection is specifically limited to *end*-lines. But it is clear from his *Letter to Henry Cromwell*, which is in part a sort of prose redaction of the passages in the *Essay on Criticism*, that this objection was wider. For he there condemns " the too frequent use of Alexandrines, which are never graceful but when there is some majesty added to the verse by them, or where there cannot be found a word in them but what is absolutely needful." One may indeed *literally* accept this statement ; but if it is examined it will be found to amount to nothing more than that " Alexandrines are never good, but when they are good "—and so to intimate an evident prejudice against the use. It is somewhat curious that neither the partial return to Dryden after Pope's death, nor the completer reaction against Pope at the Romantic revival, dispelled this prejudice. I have endeavoured to show that in Chaucer, in Shakespeare, and even in Milton, Alexandrines may be admitted with no loss and great advantage. Yet, except Keats, most nineteenth-century poets have been shy of them : although Keats's own use in *Lamia* shows how excellent they may be. The fact probably is that, as has been hinted above, not all poetical building is strong enough to stand their thrust.

CHAPTER II

CONTEMPORARIES OF DRYDEN IN LYRIC, PINDARIC, AND COUPLET

Arrangement—Relation in form to predecessors—" Orinda "—
Aphra Behn—Sedley—Rochester—Dorset—Others—Otway—
Halifax—Mulgrave—Congreve—Walsh—The later Pindarics
—Sprat, Watts, etc.—Otway again—Swift—Yalden—Con-
greve again—Couplet verse—The minor heroic dramatists and
the satirists—Roscommon—Mulgrave again—Others—Pomfret.

THE poets to be mentioned in this chapter have not Arrangement.
usually held a great place in histories of English literature,
nor perhaps have they deserved such a place. But some
of them have been ranked rather too low even as poets,
while as prosodists they (or at least the lyrists among
them) are worthy of distinct if not very prolonged attention. The chapter would have gained not a little if we
had separated the lyrical part of Dryden for its purposes ;
but that great poet has lost so much by the neglect to
consider his lyrical work, not merely in addition to, but
in connection with his other, that the scheme actually
adopted seems preferable. Here we shall handle those
contemporaries of his who dealt with his staple metres
and styles—reserving Prior among the younger, and
Butler among the elder, as captains of yet other hosts in
the next. The first, or lyrical group, is a large one, and
fringes out into minor poets and contributors to *Drolleries*
and *Miscellanies*, and the famous *Pills to Purge Melancholy*
(later in date, but mainly contemporaneous in stuff), after
a very copious and floating manner. Its work, however,
can be studied not only sufficiently, but perhaps best, in

that of a few persons—the famous quartette of Restoration song-writers, Dorset, Rochester, Sedley, and Aphra Behn, heading others, from Mulgrave to Congreve, with a few isolated persons like Katherine Philips for the earliest period, Philip Ayres for the middle, and William Walsh for the last.

Relation in
form to pre-
decessors. Perhaps the prosodic note in regard to the persons to be discussed in this chapter, lyric or not lyric, is that hardly one is of sufficient individuality to require much separate study. The interest which they possess is interest in relation to the great prosodic forms already developed, or in process of development, accordingly as they may show decadence or new beginning ; and the new beginnings will be shown rather in the next chapter than in this. The very first question which should put itself to the student of prosody, who has set himself at the right point of view, is, " What is their attitude towards the two greatest forms of earlier Caroline lyric, the common measure and the octosyllabic quatrain ? " And it so happens that these, with the enlarged forms of both which come from the addition of a couplet, or two interspaced lines, changing the quatrain into a sixain, are the chief, though not the only, forms that they use.

The answer can be sufficiently general, though it will require a certain amount of proviso and qualification for individual instances. The peculiar grip of the measure which we have noted in the First Carolines has not gone ; but it is going. For the observation of this, Katherine "Orinda." Philips is a peculiarly useful subject. " The matchless Orinda " lived but a very few years after the Restoration itself, but she died young ; she was born in the very same year with Dryden, and she was not much the elder of Sedley and Dorset, both of whom survived into the eighteenth century. She is also, in temper, rather older than her date : serious, metaphysical, and if prosaic at all, prosaic because she cannot help it rather than otherwise. Yet the prose encroaches on her, will she nill she, in this metre of soar and throb. Her admirers put down her submission to the encroachments as a result of " artistic restraint "—a very convenient thing, but perhaps just a little too convenient for the *mediocris poeta.* Sometimes (examples may be given below)[1] she can soar ; but she cannot always.

For some years past, her graceless junior poetess, Aphra Behn. Aphra Behn, has had her proofs restored to her in this matter. Critics and anthologists have reminded the forgetful general reader of that marvellous

Love in fantastic triumph sat,

which, as a last triumph of Caroline mastery in these measures, exceeds the best things of Sedley and Rochester, because it can not only tower, but maintain itself as the summit of the soar, and stoop to the finish of its flight as masterfully as it rose. There is not a weak point in this strange achievement; even the "did" of the third line is not a mere expletive.[2] If this was the poetry by which Rochester, in a partly unquotable piece of doggerel, makes her swear that the bays were her own, Apollo might well say that it was hard to deny her. But though there are good things, prosodically and otherwise, in the rest of her verse, she never reached such a height as this elsewhere, at least in that poetic music which prosody creates.

The tones of this music are still in the two much more graceless poets of the other sex (for they were both ill-

---

[1] *Caroline Poets* (Oxford, 1905), i. pp. 485, 612 :—

> I did not love until this time
> Crowned my felicity,
> When I could say without a crime
> I am not thine—but Thee !
>
> .   .   .   .   .
>
> As men that are with visions graced
> Must have all other thoughts displaced,
> And buy those short descents of light
> With loss of sense, or spirit's flight, etc.

[2] Love in fantastic triumph sat
> Whilst bleeding hearts around him flowed,
> For whom fresh pains he did create,
> And strange tyrannic power he showed.
> From thy bright eyes he took his fires,
> Which round about in sport he hurled ;
> But 'twas from mine he took desires
> Enough to undo the amorous world.

natured, which poor Aphra is nowhere charged with being)
who have just been mentioned. They attained it, but with
much less sureness of touch. One knows that Sedley has
got it, and one hopes that he is going to keep it, in the
famous piece beginning—

> Love still has something of the sea,
> From whence his mother rose.

Sedley. But he does not keep it ; and though the rest of the
poem is not bad, it is not better than hundreds of others
written during his life-time. In " Phillis is my only joy "
he has sought a lighter and more varied form, derived
rather from Suckling than from the great joint tradition
of Ben and Donne. It is prosodically notable, in particular,
for the skill with which the iambic and trochaic cadences
are combined and contrasted. And this contrast-combine
—a purely prosodic device—is noticeable again in the
" Knotting " song, where it curiously enhances and is
enhanced by the use of the refrain. Read by themselves
these three poems create a very high idea of Sedley's lyrical
powers, though no one is so entire and perfect as the
Aphra piece. Read among the rest of his verse (which need
not be ill-spoken of), they seem rather chance-medleys.

Rochester. Rochester, on the other hand, had a much more constant
command of the lyrical secret than either the knight or
the lady. But the evil angel who made him from a brave
man into a coward, and who seems to have been able
also to turn him from a scholar and a good fellow into a
spiteful fribble, appears to have been further able to
prevent him from ever keeping a poem up to its best
level. The first distich of

> An age in her embraces past
> Would seem a winter's day,

runs Sedley's opening close, in the exquisiteness of the
harmony got out of quite simple words ; and the conclusion of the stanza—

> Where life and light with envious haste
> Are torn and snatched away,

is not unworthy of it. But the rest is unequal, and

sometimes purely flat. Much the same is the case with
the long-measure—

> Absent from thee I languish still,

and with others, though it may almost be said that none
is without prosodic melody. The most sustained is the
completely trochaic

> My dear mistress has a heart—

very charming, and perhaps worthy of being ranked next
to Aphra's in thoroughness of success in verse in its own
kind. Even here the demon has made him careless of
rhyme.[1] But in it, and in one or two others, there is no
failure of rhythmical command : while in some—" 'Tis
not that I am weary grown," and " All my past life is
mine no more," are examples in different keys—this
command is consummate.

Charles Sackville had poetry " by kind " ; but it did Dorset.
not take in him these rarer and more haunting forms,
though they might have been thought exactly corre-
spondent to the clangour and witchery of his great
ancestor's[2] rhyme-royal. He is rather a middle term
between Suckling and Prior in light verse of society than
a music-maker in words ; and skilful as is the run of the
famous

> To all you ladies now at land,

happily as the ballad touch is caught and half burlesqued
in it, its fluency and ease are more remarkable. than
its range or variety of tone and harmony. In fact,
Dorset always turns to the caricature. The brilliant lines
on " Dorinda "[3] (Catherine Sedley, who proved her

---

[1] Not " weak " and " break," which was then quite justifiable, but the
rhyming in one short poem of " wander " *and* " wonder " to " asunder."

[2] By a curious set of chances, though Thomas Sackville was the *first* and
Charles the *sixth* Earl of Dorset, and though no less than 170 years inter-
vened between the birth of Thomas and the death of Charles, there were a
bare thirty between their lives.

[3] Dorinda's sparkling wit and eyes,
    United, cast too fierce a light,
  Which blazes high, but quickly dies,
    Pains not the heart, but hurts the sight.

" sparkling wit," among many other things, by the best
epigram ever attributed to a king's mistress) are
thoroughly characteristic. The first stanza reads like a
beginning in the old metaphysical style with the old
metaphysical soar a little but not so very much vulgarised;
the first distich of the second keeps the tone ; and then
the last does what itself describes, turns sharply round
and " thrusts its brightness in your face," with complete
travesty and denial of all passion. A *tour de force* of
this kind could only be achieved when prosody has gone
very far, for it needs absolute sureness of touch; but the
touch has to be imitative rather than original, rhetorical
rather than poetical. Even in his best though not his
most popular thing—

> Phyllis, for shame let us improve,

though he is almost serious, there is something like the
same ἀγχίστροφον, the same quick twist and shift in the
close. But it must be admitted that

> Most *miserably* wise,

admirable as it is, deserves the admiration for a pure
prosodic merit, the position of the tetrasyllable " miserably "
(with strong stress on one of its four naturally short
syllables, and the others hurried over), between the two
naturally strong monosyllables " most " and " wise."

Others.   The character which appears so eminently in the best
things of Aphra, of Sedley, and of Rochester ; less
eminently but more evenly in " Orinda," and to no small
extent, proportionally speaking, in Dorset's handful of
verse, is widely scattered, though seldom in large volume,
throughout a great host of forgotten or but name-remem-
bered minorities. One might compare it to the light of the
Queensland opal, which, instead of being concentrated on
one pervading glow of colour and fire, as in the Oriental

> Love is a calmer, gentler joy,
>   Smooth are his looks and soft his pace—
> *Her* Cupid is a blackguard boy
>   That runs his link full in your face.

and Hungarian varieties, is peppered over the substance of the stone in small sparks and flakes. Not to do injustice to the Colonies, it must be granted that Queensland peppers her opals more generously than the minor Second Carolines cared, or could afford, to do with theirs. Still it is *there*, as, practically speaking, it never is in the eighteenth century till we come to Blake, or at least Chatterton. Otway, a powerful dramatist, was a very Otway. weak poet. But the little piece " The Enchantment " is a curious poetic-prosodic study——its music floats so oddly between the Æolian harp of the seventeenth century and the harmonicon or hurdy-gurdy of the eighteenth. The first stanza, though it is no wonder, actually invites the hand to keep time, with the sleepy magic of the earlier measure ; the second is colder, and the third colder still, but not quite " Edwin and Angelina " yet. Halifax Halifax. (Montagu) may have been something of a statesman, but was even less of a poet than Otway.

But in no one of these, perhaps hardly even in any of Mulgrave. the preferred list before except in Rochester, is the old touch to be found so frequently, yet so flawed, as in Rochester's chief enemy, himself another type of Restoration character, the valiant, brutal, honourable, covetous, long-lived, many-titled John Sheffield, Earl of Mulgrave, Marquis of Normanby, and Duke of Buckingham[shire]. He has got the touch, a little worn but unmistakable, in

> I must confess I am untrue
> To Gloriana's eyes,

for the common measure ; he has got it for the long in " The Dream "—which, by the way, is obviously misprinted in Chalmers. In fact, though never quite in quintessence (which puts him below Rochester), he has a full dozen of right pieces——" The Warning," " To Amoretta," " The Venture," " Despair " (which is in the " short " measure, the split " poulter's," less used than the others since Elizabeth's days), " Reconcilement," and others. Nay, though it is perhaps unfair, one can hardly read Sheffield's lyrics without remembering the persistent association of Dryden's

name with his in regard to couplet verse. One lyric of
the Earl's (he was only Duke quite late, but inherited the
Earldom as a child), the dialogue "Between an Elderly
Shepherd and a very Young Nymph," is Dryden *aut
diabolus* ; unless his lordship was a most successful ape of
the poet whom he got into scrapes, patronised in bad as
well as good senses of the word, did *not* help to starve,
but did help to bury, or at least to entomb.

The touch is almost gone in Philip Ayres, pleasant
as are some of his verses ;[1] but it exists in Flatman and
Bancks, and others yet lower. And it is—let it be
repeated, as we are leaving and losing it—in the main,
though not wholly, a *prosodic* touch, provided by skilful
or lucky fingering of the stops and vents, the light and
heavy places, of the line, which gives value and *nuance*
to the result. Already in Congreve, and even in Prior
(who for that reason among others is reserved for the
next chapter), it is being exchanged for a merely even
beat—for rhythm with some resonance and swell, but
without soar and stoop.

Congreve.   Yet Congreve has some of it, and so, though much
younger than most of them, he may be made the last
of this batch. He is as exceptional in it as elsewhere,
in drama and in prose. We shall deal presently with
his Pindarics. Some of the smaller pieces have the
felicity of Prior with a certain *air de grand seigneur*, the
solace of Congreve's sin, which Prior could never reach.
Thackeray set the seal long ago upon "Pious Selinda" ;
the song—

> False though she be to me and love,

if it be but Bristol diamond, is Bristol diamond of the
best kind. Amoret, Sabina, Aminta, Cloe, though it may
be feared that they might have something to complain
of Mr. Congreve, must have been difficult to please
indeed if they were not satisfied with Mr. Congreve's
verses. They are not exactly prosodic magic, but they
are astonishing prosodic conjuring, and about the last
of their kind.

[1] See *Minor Caroline Poets*, vol. ii. pp. 261-365.

Between the lyrists proper and the Pindarisers who consciously or unconsciously sought to make up for this loss by mechanical irregularity, one small poet, but remarkable prosodist, may be picked in the person of "knowing Walsh." There was reason for the respect with which both Dryden and Pope regarded him—the one from the position of established monarchy, the other from that of eager aspiration. Small as is Walsh's poetic baggage, it is, from the prosodic point of view singularly varied and not ill-composed. He has the common measure, not quite untongued of its magic ; he has actually a sonnet, and not such a very bad one ; he has stanzas of various kinds, once popular, but ten years before his own death to be banished by Bysshe from the English Parnassus ; he has anapæsts which are not worse than some of Prior and much of Moore ; long measure ; at least one couplet of rhymed fourteeners curiously unlike in rhythm to anything that had been written for nearly a hundred years, or was to be written for another hundred ;[1] and one piece in anapæstic mono-meters which is equally quaint and effective in prosody and in point.[2] Whether he was, as Dryden says, "the

[1] I see her smile, I see her kiss, and oh ! methinks I see
    Her give up all those joys to *him* she should reserve for *me*.
These couplets come at the end of the eight-lined stanzas of "Jealousy," arranged 10, 10, 10, 10, 8, 8, 14, 14, *ababccdd*. Most have prosodic blood in them ; indeed, some readers may prefer this—
    Nay, in the fury, in the height, of that abhorred embrace
    Believe you thought, believe, at least,you *wished* me in the place.

[2] A despairing lover goes to a precipice to commit suicide.
    When in rage he came there,
    Beholding how steep
    The sides did appear,
    And the bottom how deep ;
    His torments projecting,
    And sadly reflecting
    That a lover forsaken
    A new love may get,
    But a neck when once broken
    Can never be set ;
    And that he could die
    Whenever he would,
    But that he could live
    But as long as he would,
           etc. etc.

best critic in the nation "—it is well known that with
contemporaries who were his friends, and sometimes
without that limitation, Dryden's praises require a little
discounting—or was not, he must have possessed a very
remarkable ear, open to the notes of various quills as
no other then was except Dryden's own. He need not
be taken very seriously as a poet ; but as a versifier he
must always hold a remarkable position.

The later
Pindarics.

Sprat,
Watts, etc.

In pity for the reader I shall not say very much about
the later Pindarics, although I have had no pity upon
myself in reading them. The chief result of being
married to their muse, however, is a not unpleasant
amazement. From Sprat, Cowley's immediate pupil and
biographer, with his description of angels embodying
themselves—

> For which they fetched stuff from the neighbouring air

(I have always wished to read " fair "), to good Dr. Watts
with his not wholly dissimilar description of humanity
itself as

> Arrayed in rosy skin and decked with eyes and ears,

they are truly marvellous. Even from Johnson's Essay
on Cowley a shrewd person might perceive that the
" metaphysical " reproach is chiefly levelled against, or at
least largely evidenced from, Pindaric ; it is certain that
fancies and conceits which are charming in the lighter
lyric seem most barbarically bedizened in this form. Its
attractions, however, are likewise very easily perceivable,
putting aside mere fashion, which had a good deal to do
with it. It gave the reader the variety which, no doubt,
he really missed, though he did not think so, in the
couplet. It had the more subtle charm of giving the
writer, if not exactly *carte blanche*, at any rate almost as
much freedom from galling and cramping punctilio as
might consist with anything but the absence of rhythm
and rhyme altogether. Very frequently, too, he did not
trouble himself much even about these. Sprat certainly

did not.　He has, in the ode above quoted (the glorification of Cowley himself), such lines as—

And in natural embraces lay,

or, again—

And their light some human shapes do dress,

which, if they are anything, are Chaucerian *acephala*.

In this undress—freed alike of the restraints of stanza and couplet, and by prescription entitled to pay not much attention to sense—the poet could ramble on as long as he chose, and come to an end of his ramble when he chose likewise.　Sometimes he achieved quite a respectable piece of rhymed and rhythmed prose of a rhetorical kind : as in one out of a hundred possible examples, Halifax's Ode on the Marriage of the Princess Anne to " Est-il-possible ? "　Sometimes he produced *Otway again.* something like the following sprout of the brain of the author of *Venice Preserved*—

Never would he learn as taught,
But still new ways affected, and new methods sought.
Not that he wanted parts
To improve in letters and proceed in arts ;
But as negligent as sly,
Of all perverseness brutishly was full,
By nature idle, loved to steal and lie,
And was obstinately dull.

It may be feared that most people who read the average Pindaric of the late seventeenth and early eighteenth centuries will find it obstinately dull.　That it need not be so is certain ; the famous stanza referred to a few pages back from Dryden's " Anne Killigrew " ode is enough by itself to prove that, and can be backed by others.　But the Pindaric—like blank verse and like all verse that is apparently loose—is far more difficult than things that look easier.　It *is* easy to write it badly : in fact, bad Pindarics and bad blank verse merely require a very little practice to be as easy to write as bad prose.　A statute enjoining either use in Parliament, or platform, or pulpit would be no hardship on any but the merest *crétin*.

But to write *good* Pindaric simply means the ability to produce a good word-and-line symphony ; and the man who can do this can do anything.

Swift.   Dryden, himself hardly greater as poet than as critic, of course knew this perfectly well both in theory and by practice.   And, though he was as good-natured in the one capacity as he was unassuming in the other, he could hardly have passed any other than the judgment which earned the undying enmity of " Cousin Swift " on the Pindarics of the latter.   Swift's other verse, with which we shall deal in the next chapter, is far from deserving or justifying the doom ; and if the words were ever pronounced at all, it is nearly certain that the form in which they are usually *not* quoted, " You will never be a *Pindaric* poet," is the true one.   The odes to Temple and to the Athenian Society (that to King William is in quatrains and of a different stamp) are not precisely absurd.   It is difficult to imagine Swift being that.   Nor do they hobble like some of the examples just quoted.   They are rather like the contemporary and subsequent French verse of the same kind from Boileau to Escouchard Lebrun—prose of a rhetorical kind, carefully cut into patterns and tipped at the edges with rhymes.   They are, in fact, what, to unintelligent or excessive criticism, Dryden's own verse has sometimes seemed to be.   One of the best stanzas, or rather part of one (for Swift allows himself even more expatiation than most of his fellows), may be given below.[1] It will be seen that, putting aside the ideas, which do not specially concern us, the prosody is sufficiently correct, according to mere specification, and the diction, of its own

---

[1] The eager Muse took wing upon the wave's incline,
    When War her cloudy aspect just withdrew,
    When the bright sun of Peace began to shine,
And for a while in heavenly contemplation sat
    On the high top of peaceful Ararat ;
And plucked a laurel branch, for laurel was the first that grew,
    The first of plants after the thunder, storm, and rain ;
        And thence, with joyful nimble wing,
        Flew dutifully back again,
    And made a humble chaplet for the King.

The whole stanza has twenty-six lines.

inflated kind, not specially frigid or inappropriate. But
the varying lengths of line are ill-assorted, the rhymes ill-
distributed, the words scarcely ever placed—perhaps the
chief exception is

On the *high* top of *peaceful* Ararat—

so as to give colour and light and ordonnance to the parts
of the composition. And this is the general fault of what
may be called the middle Pindaric—that which steers
fairly clear of extravagance or bathos, but merely steers
clear of them, and does not attain sublimity or splendour.

One point just mentioned—the juxtaposition of line-
lengths—is of the highest importance in the prosodic
criticism of the irregular Pindaric. Swift does not begin
badly in the stanza just quoted ; his first quintet of
Alexandrine, two heroics, Alexandrine, and single heroic,
" squads " well enough together, and the as yet uncoupled
" drew " gives the hearer a rhyme to expect on old *Lycidas*
principles. But the fourteener and Alexandrine that
follow are out of keeping, and the subsequent octosyllabic
couplet and single heroic more out still. The hungry ear
pricks up and is *not* fed.

And so constantly. Harshness or insignificance—these Yalden.
are the two curses of the minor Pindarics. The eminent
Yalden, in whom Johnson discovered " one stanza of
exquisite beauty," wrote the " Hymn to Darkness " (in
which this occurs) in a regular quatrain of a heroic, two
octosyllables, and an Alexandrine ; but he " Pindarised "
freely, and it is quite clear that he used Dryden to correct
and corroborate Cowley. His proportions are better than
Swift's ; but that is about all that can be said for him, except
that he has a noticeable tendency to reduce the range of
his lines, and use a very large share of decasyllables. In
other words, he is something of a deserter from the
Pindaric proper—the very essence of which is length-
variety.

It is not necessary to multiply examples of it ; and I Congreve
should hardly be thanked for doing so even if it were. again.
But Congreve once more calls for notice in connection

with it, both for his irregular and his regular odes.
Johnson, who was disproportionately kind to the famous
passage in *The Mourning Bride*, has made up for it by
rather sharp strictures on the frigidities of Congreve's
Elegies ; but these were usually in couplet. "On Mrs.
Arabella Hunt Singing " is a very pretty Pindaric, with an
unusual harking back to the metaphysical diction which
after all suits it best, but which doubtless made Johnson
hate it. The translations from Horace, though Dryden
had set the example, could hardly be good. But the
regular Odes, with their critical Preface, have the greatest
interest for us in the example which they set to Gray,
and some in themselves. It is to be feared that very few
of the compositions of which we have been speaking,
including his own, escape the sweeping description : " A
bundle of rambling incoherent thoughts, expressed in a
like parcel of irregular stanzas, which also consist of such
another complication of disproportioned, uncertain, and
perplexed verses and rhymes." He excepts Cowley—that
he did not except Dryden, to whom he was always faithful,
and who had deserved his fidelity, is probably due to the
fact that Dryden did not *call* his Odes Pindaric. As for
Congreve's own "regular" attempts, they deserve fair
commendation ; but with the remark (which may shock
some readers) that it is doubtful whether regularity by
itself is here, any more than elsewhere, a gain in English.
The mere correspondence of strophe, antistrophe, and
epode derives its attraction for the ear mainly from the
musical accompaniment which all English poetry is better
without ; and if irregular stanzas are as good as the best
of Cowley and Dryden, they will gain nothing from the
fact of there being another like them elsewhere. If they
are bad, the absence of something like them may be a
possible good. The advantage of the regular Ode is
chiefly that it is more troublesome, and so less likely to
be written by those who had better not write at all.

Couplet verse.   The Pindaric, however, was, as we have endeavoured
to show, commonly a false escapement from the couplet ;

the truer ones will be considered in the next chapter. In this we may content ourselves with considering the minor couplet - work itself—sometimes of poets already mentioned, sometimes of yet others—which fills the forty years of Dryden's supremacy in it, and the ten more or thereabouts before the advent of Pope. Butler's and Prior's heroics, according to the scheme adopted here for all the more remarkable prosodists, will go with their productions in the forms more specially their own.

The principle of primogeniture, by which the whole or nearly the whole of the property of a possessor passes to a single representative, has been regarded as an unjust arbitrement of law, or a lazy expedient to save trouble. Yet it is sometimes the principle of Nature herself, in cases where neither of these reproaches applies. There was no reason why the lessons of sixty years, from Fairfax onwards, should profit hardly any one but Dryden, or should profit others only after they had passed through his hands. Yet, as a matter of fact, it practically was so. The minor heroic dramatists have no doubt been too little studied ; but a familiarity of a good many years with them enables me to say confidently that nobody need trouble himself much about the management of the couplet in any one of them from Crowne to Lee.[1] So, again, stress has sometimes been laid, if not exactly on Dryden's obligations to Marvell and Oldham in satire, at any rate on their priority to him in this kind. As to the aspect of this which concerns manner of handling, it is not ours to speak. Prosodically, it is safe to say that he learnt nothing, and could learn nothing, from them. According to the old satiric tradition, they roughen the Wallerian couplet a little ; but that is all.

These are not, however, the couplet-poets to whom memory generally recurs as to those of " Charles's days."

The minor heroic dramatists and the satirists.

---

[1] Crowne's curious *Destruction of Jerusalem* is the best place to look in for this purpose. Lee is far better in blank verse ; in fact, in his best single lines, or very short batches, he beats Dryden himself, leaves Otway miles behind, and is on the whole nearer to Shakespeare than any other " post-diluvian." The couplet brings out his tendency to rant.

Marvell was a survival, and Oldham a quickly-nipped precocity. The "mob of gentlemen," and (shall we say?) the herd of their led-poets, must be expected and need not be refused.

Roscommon.   The respectable Roscommon deserves priority, not so much on account of his unspotted bays (which, unless the spotlessness be also prosodic, would not concern us) as because he was one of the oldest of the group—very nearly as old as Dryden himself—and because, as a matter of fact, his bays *are* unspotted in this respect likewise, though Longinus would have been glad of him as an instance of the small satisfaction that faultlessness can give. If you take "smoothness" as the be-all and end-all of the couplet, and the couplet as the finest form of verse, one really does not see who is to be put above Roscommon. Pope himself can scarcely give him points (or rather can give him nothing but *point*), and is much more careless and licentious in rhymes, though Roscommon doubted rhyme, admired Milton, and experimented in blanks. In pause he is equally impeccable; he isolates the couplet carefully (Dryden himself is here quite chaotic and anarchic beside his lordship). Nor is he exactly flat: the famous couplet about immodest words is worthy either of Dryden or of Pope. Clear as he is, you cannot call him shallow; and though Johnson himself denied him vigour he is not anywhere really feeble. What he lacks is almost everything, not mechanical, that makes poetry. He is totally *uninteresting*. And I cannot help thinking that Johnson's own very lukewarm approval of him is due partly to a secret sense that Roscommon is rather an awful example of what a poet according to couplet orthodoxy would generally be.[1]

Mulgrave again.   Roscommon himself speaks with respect of Mulgrave, to whom indeed the *Essay on Translated Verse* is addressed; and "sharp-judging Adriel" has some decent

---

[1] It is curious that Roscommon's only recorded vice was gambling. From his verse one would imagine that nothing with more chance in it than chess could have attracted him. It must have been the need of relief from the couplet that drove him to the cards.

couplet to add to his already-mentioned lyrics. If he wrote that in the *Essay on Satire* which has variously been assigned to him alone, to him and Dryden, and to Dryden alone—

> Was ever prince by two at once misled—
> False, foolish, old, ill-natured, and ill-bred ?

he touched, at least this once, one of the apices of the style. Dryden has no better example of the slap-in-the face distich, or of the gesture and motion of verse which it requires. But it is fair to say that in his undoubted work—the imitation of Habert's *Temple de la Mort*, the *Essay on Poetry*, the curious " Vision while on his Tangier Voyage " (a piece not unprophetic of Pope's " Unfortunate Lady " in style and cadence), and the semi-Pindaric Ode on Love (it tries to be Pindaric, but is always settling down towards mere heroics)—things not much less good can be found. His ear for rhyme, though not technically incorrect, must have been blunt ; for he has the same *a* sound in eight successive lines of the *Temple of Death*, making in effect a miniature assonanced *tirade*. But as far as the mere " scantling " of the stopped couplet goes he has very little to learn. He will not, or he cannot— at any rate he does not—attain that " fingering " of it which allows Dryden to introduce many of the advantages of blank verse. But in this way again he is an ancestor of Pope's, who (perhaps for that very reason) alternately adulated and lampooned him. On the whole, " Adriel " is one of the poets whom an historical study of prosody distinctly exalts, though it may not finally put him very high. To have almost a strong reminiscence of the seventeenth-century common measure, and quite a strong anticipation of the Popian decasyllable, is something.

Dorset's couplets are few and unimportant—rather Others. rough too, though, as might be expected, witty ; and Stepney, who " made grey authors blush," need only have made them reflect how very easy it was to get this tune by heart. But John Pomfret (I once called him Thomas, Pomfret. and, to expiate that inexpiable, have bound myself never hereafter to mention him without his right Christian name) deserves a little more notice here, partly because of Johnson's famous assertion about "The Choice," and still more because he is perhaps the capital example among minor poets of the time of the oscillation—whether in doubt or for relief it is impossible to say—between Pindaric and couplet.

The piece of which it was thought, a century and a quarter ago, by the person who had the best right to speak of any man living, that "perhaps no composition in English had been oftener perused," is itself couplet—indeed, one may almost say that it could have been in nothing else—at any rate, that the harmony between matter and metre was evidently pre-established. All but the best and all the worst characteristics of life and literature in the eighteenth century are there, just on the eve of the century itself : good sense and good nature ; rather easy morals ; a moderate and conventional intellectuality, and a sensuality neither coarse nor *raffiné* ; a certain selfishness, but not of a shocking kind ; a not too ardent patriotism, and even a queer kind of piety, which allows itself considerable easements and licences. And all this is just reflected in the verse. It does not flow like Denham's great example, but it is not a mere stagnant ditch. It is like a "canal" of the period—stimulated to mild wavelets by gentle breezes, the paddling of water-fowl, the dip of an oar here and there, and the prospect of a slight cascade at the end. As an adjustment of prosodic means to (by courtesy) poetic ends, one must feel a certain admiration for it. But one does not want it again.

There is, however, nothing else to be found in Pomfret's couplet verse ("Love Triumphant over Reason," etc.), and when he tries sterner themes, as in "Cruelty and Lust" (a versification of the atrocity attributed to Kirke and to others before him), his verse is quite unequal to them. In fact, he can fall pretty low. The distich—

> Oxford submitted in one year to Fate,
> For whom her passion was exceeding great,

deserves a place among the choicest examples of the bathos, and plumbs the prosodic depth as successfully as others. The Pindarics of such a writer must have interest, and they have accordingly been kept for this place. A mere glance at their titles—"The Divine Attributes," "Eleazar's Lamentation over Jerusalem," "A Prospect of Death," "The General Conflagration," "*Dies Novissima*"—does a tale unfold.

> The lightning with its livid *tail*
> A train of glittering terrors draws behind,

is one of their own graces. The man wants to be sublime, and is so far critically gifted that he sees no chance of sublimity with his own form of couplet. But what is the Sublime if it is not the Pindaric? Let us be Pindaric and we shall be sublime. He *is* Pindaric in the sense which Congreve stigmatises Pindaric, as thus—

> Matter produced, had still a chaos been :
> For jarring elements engaged,
> Eternal battles would have waged,
> And filled with endless horror the tumultuous scene ;
> If Wisdom infinite (for less
> Could not the vast prodigious embryo wield,
> Or strength complete to labouring Nature yield)
> Had not, with actual address,
> Composed the bellowing hurry and established peace.

The "Prospect of Death" is rather better than this: something of that strange "calmed and calming" effect which seems to be often produced, when men really bring themselves to contemplate the enemy, is on it and in it. But the double lesson of the Pindaric and the couplet of this time has been almost sufficiently enforced.

That lesson is : first, that the Pindaric, at least as we find it from 1650 to 1750, is essentially an *escapement* from the couplet ; and, secondly, that it is, for any automatic or mechanical effect that it may have, an extremely inefficient escapement. Irregularity is a capital thing in its way ; but mere irregularity for irregularity's sake is, if not quite so monotonous as mere regularity, rather more tiresome

and considerably more irritating.   The mediocre couplet
sinks gently from the hands, which fold themselves, it may
be, to a blessed sleep ; the mediocre Pindaric provokes them
to cast it away, and induces a wish that one could cast
it at the author.   Between them, when they are both bad
enough to be amusing, there is, perhaps, not much choice; but
of this amusement a little goes a long way.   The important
thing for us to notice is, that the very indefiniteness of
outline in the Pindaric deprives it of such almost automatic
virtue as belongs to the sonnet, to the greater stanzas, to
the couplet itself, and to some extent, as we shall see
shortly, to continuous measures like the octosyllable and
the anapæst.   It is a shape that shape has none, except
that which the writer has taste and power to give it.   If
he has the taste and the power, well and good ; but in
that case he will probably write well in any metre.   If he
has not, he will probably write rather worse in it than
in any other.

CHAPTER III

THE OCTOSYLLABLE AND THE ANAPÆST—BUTLER, SWIFT, AND PRIOR

"Hudibrastics" and *Hudibras*—Their congeniality—The rhymes—
Improper use of the name—Practice of the metre before and
after 1700—Swift: his octosyllables—The anapæst—Retrospect
of it—Examples up to "Mary Ambree"—And "A Hundred
Years Hence"—Remarks on this—Prior—His relation to the
couplet—His prosodic remarks—His Pindaric—His "improved"
Spenserian—His octosyllables—His anapæsts—The charm of
the metre—Other points in him—His double rhymes.

WE have seen, in the last two chapters, how the couplet
flourished, greener with Dryden's bays, during the forty
last years of the seventeenth century; how the more
delicate and exquisite lyric dwindled under its shade;
and how the apparently robuster Pindaric was but a—
let us say a cabbage-stalk-staff, against its tyrannous
domination. But the domination was not quite universal.
Prosody still had its Asturias or its Horeb in the provinces
of two other metres: one the oldest of all in English
properly so called, the other an early derivative of forms
still older. These are the iambic octosyllabic couplet,
and the various combinations of the anapæst.

By one of those coincidences which it is not unreasonable to regard as something more, the five-hundred-years-
old metre of Layamon and the *Paternoster* received a
most important reinforcement and redevelopment at the
very moment when its rival, the heroic monarchy, was
finding its Richelieu in Dryden. It had, we have said,
never been abandoned; and it had, in the preceding three-

quarters of a century, received exquisite illustration from Shakespeare and Milton themselves, as well as from many lesser men.   But its employments had been occasional and minor ; and its most consummate practice had been in the mixed form with catalexis, which gives a trochaic alternation.

"Hudi-
brastics" and
Hudibras.
It was now to be made the vehicle or medium of a much more daring enterprise—to serve as the metre of a poem of length and importance such as it had not known since the days of the romances, and of a style which recalled nothing in English except the extravagances of Skelton, and a few burlesques of romance itself.[1]   And it was to be used for this purpose in a fashion, and on a subject, which made it the most popular poetical reading in English for years, and by a man who was Dryden's own equal (though only on one of the many sides of Dryden's genius) in satiric power, his superior in learning, and the equal, if not the superior, of almost any poet in a certain narrow and eccentric but most vigorous idiosyncrasy.   Dryden (*il était orfèvre*) wished that Butler had written *Hudibras* in heroics.   It is improbable that he could know the fact that Butler had, most characteristic-ally, written the quite homogeneous *Elephant in the Moon* (a satire on the Royal Society, to which Dryden himself belonged) both in "short" and "long" verse, as he himself calls the latter.   I say characteristically, because the proceeding shows at once the shrewd, practical, almost scientific temper of the man, and his curious sardonic attitude.   For the very process is a kind of "covered way," as we shall show later, to attack the weaknesses of the heroic, and its liability to *cliché* and stuffing.   But this comparison is decisive as to the poet's wisdom in selecting the shorter form for his longer poem.   If he had wished to attack the earlier Roundheads as Dryden

---

[1] The question of the exact relation of the "Hudibrastics before *Hudi-bras*" of Sir John Mennis and Dr. Smith in *Musarum Deliciæ* (1656) and *Wit Restored* (1658) to *Hudibras* itself is, in the old sense, a "nice" one. But it is hardly one on which we can enter here.   There are worse subjects, among those waiting for separate treatment, than the progress of burlesque verse from Skelton to Butler.

himself attacked the later Whigs—satirically indeed, but with satire of an argumentative turn : to convince as well as to persuade, to overthrow as well as to ridicule—the heroic would have been his weapon.[1]   But in his case the conviction and the overthrow were accomplished : he simply had to keep the vanquished enemy "on the run" with an avenging swarm of light troops, to sprinkle them, after their reprobation, with a fiery rain of endless sarcasm. For this the nimbleness of the octosyllable, its natural skip and flutter as compared with the stride and sweep of the couplet, were essentially suited.   And Butler knew exactly how to manage this skip and flutter : how to let it drop now and then into a sly gentle run, and how to wake it up with a perfect pirouette of some astounding rhyme, which enables him to plunge upon the foe and stick poisoned banderillas in his hide.

People complain that *Hudibras* is difficult to read now ; and perhaps it is, for in order to appreciate it *Their congeniality.* thoroughly a great deal of literary and historical knowledge is wanted.   Men have forgotten what the petty and irresistible tyranny and spite of a gang of triumphant Nonconformists—without letters, the sworn foes of art, hypocritical, morose, pedantic in spite of their illiteracy—must have been, and was.   But anybody who can take the prosodic point of view, and who will give himself the very slight trouble required to understand Butler's object and plan of attack, will be rather sorry than glad when he comes to the end of " The Lady's Answer." He will most assuredly mix no sorrow with the gladness of his appreciation of the thing as a work of art, and feel no grudge at the time spent upon it.   In fact, the only fault to be found with the poem, from our point of view, is the difficulty—in fact, the impossibility—of properly illustrating its prosodic character.   In one sense, no doubt, almost any passage is a fair sample ; but in another no single passage is a fair sample at all.   Nothing but the whole, or an extract altogether beyond our means, can

---

[1] Nor must I be understood for a moment as meaning that he was not master enough of it.   He has left examples that are quite competent.

shew its variety in monotony, its endless fertility in metrical as in other resource, the way in which the conjurer's "bag of tricks" is absolutely inexhaustible in playing with this little handful of sixteen syllables normal.

The rhymes.   So also, though not quite to the same extent, the famous eccentricity of the rhymes is very difficult to illustrate, and impossible to generalise.   Such well-known things as "philosopher" and "Alexander Ross over," such less-known and more audacious ones as "benignly" and "pigsney," in hypercatalectic lines—the latter looking like a survival or revival of the old Wyatt licence of rhyming on the redundant syllable—throw light only on themselves, and the actual places where they occur; not on each other, or on the general system.   In fact, that system may be said to be one of perpetual "surprise rhymes"—of making the terminal curvet contrast with the steady roll of the line itself.   For this purpose, evidently, a bad rhyme is as useful as a good, and rather more so, provided only that the author be not suspected of making it by mistake—a suspicion which will rarely attach to Butler. Indeed, it is one of his not very recondite but admirably managed devices to amble along peacefully for quite a period of couplets, regularly flowing and nicely "poppling" with decently resonant jingle and nothing more, before and after he plunges down one of his cascades, or spouts up one of his geysers of extravagant rhyme.

Improper use   It is scarcely to be wondered at that the extraordinary of the name. cleverness of *Hudibras*, its wide popularity, and the way in which, when that popularity ceased as regards actual reading, it took its place as an acknowledged classic, should have caused even an illegitimate association between it and the metre of which, after all, it made something like a catachresis.   "Hudibrastics" became, however improperly, almost as recognised a title for the octosyllable as "Skeltonics" had properly become for the short doggerel; and even so late as the beginning of the nineteenth century we find demurs to the use of them in serious poetry, when they were taken up by Scott.

But this was not of the slightest importance.   What

was of much, was that by this popularity, this merit, this established classical position of *Hudibras*, the octosyllable was at once appanaged, and entrenched in its appanage, against the tyranny of the heroic. It became, as it were, a Rochelle or a Sedan for prosodic independence, and one out of which the independents never allowed themselves to be either cajoled or coerced. For some time, indeed, it was not much practised : its rival was the newer mistress. Dryden, as we have said, has it once or twice in different forms, and showed his usual mastery in it ; but it was not his doxy. Rochester and his fellows tried it a little, and when they did, chiefly in the older half-trochaic form of Wither. Aphra uses it in *The Lady's Watch*,[1] but merely as an alternative—in fact, as one among dozens of other measures ; and the eclectic Walsh turns out a copy of verses in it with his usual skill. That curious poetaster King (not to be confounded with his cleverer but more ill-conditioned namesake in the next generation, the Jacobite and renegade Principal of St. Mary Hall) used it for his *Art of Cookery* not at all ; but alternated it with heroics for his *Art of Love*, trying it also in several other poems, one of which, " Orpheus and Eurydice," furnishes a passage which used to be familiar in the older *Speakers* and extract-books.[2] One might bring in Congreve and even Parnell here ; but both probably owed additional stimulus, besides that received from Butler, to two great writers—who are thought of commonly as eighteenth-century, but who belonged for nearly half the life of one and for two-thirds of that of the other to the seventeenth—Swift and Prior. Availing ourselves of the usual licence, we may take Swift first with such of his versification as has not yet been noticed. Prior is of such importance in this History that we may take, not only his octosyllables and his pre-eminent contribution to the other "escapement,"

---

[1] In this metre' is the agreeable passage which Mrs. Blake pitched upon, "told by a spirit," in Bysshe (*v. inf.*, and Mr. Swinburne's *Blake*, p. 130—a passage by which, forty years ago, Mr. Swinburne was my introducer both to Aphra's work and to Bysshe's name).

[2]   A roasted ant that's nicely done
        By one small atom of the sun, etc.

the anapæst, but all his rhyme together at the end of the chapter, with some account of the previous history of this anapæst between.

Swift : his octosyllables. The importance of Swift himself is indeed very great from the point of view which we are chiefly taking in this chapter. His Pindarics are almost negligible, except by the historian (by whom they have not been neglected), and they are merely glances of the backward face. But his octosyllables are very noteworthy. With less grotesque and more polish than Butler's, they have at least equal *diable au corps*, and they actually presented themselves as examples of light but not burlesque versification to " Spleen " Green and many others. For pure narrative, neither directly comic nor directly romantic, he made them, as in *Cadenus and Vanessa*, an admirable vehicle ; and if (of which I myself have never had the least doubt) he really wrote the lines about the

Offending race of human kind,

the preservation of which we owe to Chesterfield, he made this Tartar bow of a weapon into a catapult of the most appalling force and range. Just as the Caroline common measure shows to the utmost how deft manipulation of word-sound can give charm and witchery, so do these octosyllables show how the same manipulation can express contempt—annihilating, or too contemptuous even to care to annihilate.

He could, however, write Butler a little modernised when he chose, as, for instance, when he horrified Dr. Guest with " Aristophanes " and " profane is," or Hibernically dared " Ganymede " and " any maid." And his pure doggerel, as in the immortal " Mrs. Harris's Petition," shows a quite admirable ear, as in fact do all his odds and ends of verse with their wild rhymes and fantastic breakdowns of cadence.[1] It may be that he never was exactly a poet, Pindaric or other. But he was no mean versifier,

---

[1] " O'Rourke's noble fare," is but one instance among many that could be given.

and it is curious that nearly all his verse ranges itself among the escapes from the heroic couplet.

Swift tried the pure, non-doggerellised anapæst not very infrequently ; but it was not a measure likely to be at its most perfect with him either in its playful or its passionate modulation.   It was, however, at this time that it came forward as an "above-stairs" metre, and, as fashioned by Prior chiefly, took, with the octosyllable as fashioned after Butler by Prior and Swift himself, a definite position, if not exactly *against* the couplet—for the metaphors of hostility are merely metaphors—at any rate as an ally and exponent of moods different from those which find their sufficient expression in the couplet itself. *The anapæst.*

It was, of course, no new thing, though its continuity from very early times has perhaps never yet been vindicated till now, and though some critics and historians have laid rather undue stress on its non-appearance in "literate" poetry during the Elizabethan period.   The anapæstic foot, or, if not definitely that, a sporadic suggestion of anapæstic rhythm, may appear in Anglo-Saxon—though to my ear it is almost always merged in the trochee.   But, as we have shown in the preceding volume, it appears as a substitute and equivalent from the very dawn of Middle English poetry ; while as a dominant it is more or less distinct in the Lewes poem, in the rhythms of *Retrospect of it.*

My tru|est trea|sure so trai|torly ta|ken

and

Alas | that e|ver the speech | was spo|ken,

with others.   It replaces the trochee as the "ground swell," the underlying rhythmic character, of the revived alliterative verse: and in the doggerel that comes from the clash of this and the broken-down decasyllable of the fifteenth century it is one of the most prominent features, and even forms.   Nor at last in Tusser is there any more doubt about it : it has as much method, if as little music, as any metre that ever was metred.

Despite, however, this long sap and definite lodgment at last ; despite the attraction of the rhythm for the natural man ; despite the help given by triple-time accompaniments in the music which was so universally cultivated,—it is undeniable that *pure* anapæstic measures —nay, pure or basic trisyllabic measures of any kind—are not prominent, and are even strangely latent, in Elizabethan literature.[1] My own explanation of the fact is, in the main—though it may seem too "metaphysical" to some, —that unconscious horror of a relapse into doggerel which I have urged before.   But I should lay much stress, as a secondary cause, on the working of this horror in the great pastors and masters of the poetry of 1580-1650. Although Spenser did nothing more epoch-making than his trial of the anapæstic admixture in *The Shepherd's Kalendar*, nothing is clearer—indeed, his very abandonment of the path he had opened proves it—than that he did not care for quick, dancing, galloping rhythm.   We know that Jonson thought the heroic the crown of prosody. As for Donne, if he had thought about the matter at all, it is probable that he would have thought both the regularity and the celerity of the anæpaest canter rather common and popular.   At any rate, this class of measure is mostly wanting except in pure songs, and present rather seldom in proportion even there.

But two words which have just been used give the key of the fact, that if it was seldom admitted above stairs it was constantly in evidence below.   It *was* "common and popular," and the commons and the populace took good care that it should not die.   Most people know that despite all the pains that have been spent upon the ballad-poetry of the sixteenth and seventeenth centuries, there is, in

---

[1] Humphrey Gifford has had for a century and more, and certainly shall not lose through any tactics of mine, an honourable position for his "Something made of Nothing at a Gentlewoman's request" (*Posie of Gilloflowers*, ed. Grosart, 1875), published as early as 1580—

> Ye gladly would have me to make you some toy,
> And yet will not tell me whereof I should write, etc.

And I have given examples from the song-books.   But the text is true *on the whole.*

nearly all cases, insurmountable difficulty in settling its exact dates.   The obvious impossibility of deciding how long a ballad was composed before it appeared in print at all ; the perishableness and the undatedness of broadsides ; the bewildering promiscuity and cross-inclusions of collections, Garlands, Drolleries, and the like,—make dogmatism, except of the rashest and most worthless kind, impossible save in a very few cases.   Moreover, there is the extremely interesting and important fact that, in many early examples, owing to the presence of that equivalence which has been so fully exhibited and discussed in the preceding volume, it is difficult to say off-hand whether the *basis* is really iambic or anapæstic.   *The Nut-Browne Mayde* herself, though the enormous majority of the actual feet are iambs, has a distinct tendency towards anapæstic rhythm : I have even known people who were under the impression that both it and *Chevy Chase* belong to the anapæstic brigade.   But when we get into the region of known tunes, " Derry Down," " Packington's Pound," etc., there is no further doubt of the anapæstic basis, though the prosodic construction on it is often very ramshackle. If " Tie the Mare, Tom boy " is really of Henry the Eighth's time or even of Mary's, there is no doubt of the measure being securely established by then, which, be it remembered, was little, if at all, before Tusser.   If we could be certain of the date of " The King and the Miller of Mansfield " we should know when the anapæstic suggestion and substitution which is observable in the earlier versions of the story, as far back as " John the Reeve," settled into a definite anapæstic measure.   But it would be altogether unreasonable scepticism to doubt that " Mary Ambree " was composed immediately or very shortly after the date of the events it mentions—that is to say, 1584.   And allowing for the roughness of the printing, " Mary Ambree," if not excessively poetical, is as good cantering rhythm as a body can want for working days.[1]

Examples up to " Mary Ambree."

[1] In Scotland, Montgomerie's " Hay ! now the day dawis " (*v. sup.* vol. i. p. 285), gives contemporary evidence of well-settled anapæstics, themselves, no doubt, not new things.

At any rate, from that time, or about that time, onward, there is no doubt that these measures have taken the popular ear ; and we find them, not indeed to any great extent in the choicer and more aristocratic song-books (which we have examined already) of the earliest years of the seventeenth century, but in all their more miscellaneous successors of the miscellany kind up to D'Urfey's famous *Pills to Purge Melancholy.* Very many of the contents of this book, though they did not appear till 1719, date much earlier. How many readers, half amused with the gaiety and variety of D'Urfey's collections, half disgusted with their roughness and ribaldry, have stumbled with delight, as I remember doing long ago, on the charming, if not uniformly charming verses to which Mr. Swinburne, I think, with his unfailing instinct, has been the chief critic to do express justice?[1] They begin well enough—

> Let us drink and be merry, sing, dance, and rejoice,
> With claret and sherry, theorbo and voice.
> The changeable world to our joys is unjust,
> All treasure's uncertain, then down with your dust !
> On frolics dispose your pounds, shillings, and pence,
> For we shall be nothing a hundred years hence.

There is no grating on the axle-tree of dry wheels, still less any dropping off of the wheel itself and dragging of the whole chariot, as we so often find earlier. But the third stanza is the triumph—

> The most beautiful bit, that hath all eyes upon her,
> That her honesty sells for a hogo of honour—
> *Whose lightness and brightness doth shine with such splendour*
> *That none but the stars are thought fit to attend her—*
> Though now she be pleasant and sweet to the sense,
> Will be damnable mouldy a hundred years hence !

---

[1] But let poor " Captain Shandon " have his due. Maginn had written a glorious Tory ballad on the theme long before, starting with the actual first lines and going on—

> So sings the old song, and a good one it is ;
> Few better were written from that day to this.

(Mr. Montagu's *Miscellanies of Maginn,* 2 vols., London, 1885, vol. i. pp. 34 *et seq.*)

Of course, the middle couplet here is sheer poetry—Remarks on this. something transcending mere prosody. But what you transcend, once more, you must use as a means and stage in the transcension or trans-scansion ; and the prosody helps the poetry mightily here, as everywhere. Observe how even in the first stanza, but still more in the second and noted, the progress is like the easiest and most graceful hand-over-hand swimming : the singer pulls him-self up the ladder of song with the confident, effortless quiver of each successive foot-beat. Observe the immense advantage obtained from the redundant endings and the double rhymes ; not universally used, but occasionally, as a sort of launch-out in the progress with an echoing extension to the sound. It is impossible to conceive anything better suited as rest, as refreshment, as alterative, after the vigorous insucculence of the couplet even at its best, than this abounding torrent of various melody.

Dryden, as we have seen, had perfectly well known where to find the springs of it ; but, once more, it was not these springs of which he was the high priest or head dispenser. Nearly twenty years before D'Urfey published his *Pills*, though perhaps as much after these verses were written, Bysshe had, as we shall see in the next Book, made a kind of prosodic rogue and vagabond of the anapæst, which he would not name or admit to be an anapæst at all. But perhaps after they were written, perhaps not, the measure had been taken up by a poet who died a year or two after the *Pills* appeared, and who had made himself one of the most popular of his time, while he also possessed scholarship and social and political position. Almost the founder, according to current literary tradition, of the department of "verse of society" in English poetry as to tone and matter, he was in many ways remarkable as a mere prosodist, though perhaps few under this description would recognise, as all would under the former, the person of Matthew Prior.

Prior[1] is a remarkable illustration of a subject on Prior.

[1] The new edition of his poems by Mr. Waller (2 vols., Cambridge, 1905-7)

which, from certain indications, he would have written very well, the ingratitude of mankind. Because he was a diplomatist (and apparently no bad one) they have decided that he was not a poet, or at any rate not a great poet. Because he amused them, they have, sometimes at any rate, decided that he could not do anything else. But this is to a great extent *non nostrum*, as still more are his unfortunate deficiency in personal and political heroism, his alleged proneness to low company and the worship of Venus Pandemos, and other things. Not so his prosodic position, which is, if the present writer has not deceived himself for a good many years, that of a definite though no doubt half-unconscious rebel against the heroic couplet. In fact, it was—again if I do not mistake—this taint of sedition in him which was at the root of Johnson's very damaging but very unfair criticism. For a universally known saying of the Doctor's about *Paulo Purganti* shows that his objection was not moral.

His relations to the couplet.

But, it will be said, he *wrote* heroics. He did ; and it would be very odd if he had not written them. *Solomon*, which he thought his masterpiece, and the world (according to the world's unkind habit) did not, is in couplets. It is ; and there are some fine ones in it. But, again, he could hardly have done otherwise, hoping, as he did, to make the public take it for a masterpiece. Moreover, the Preface of this very poem contains a distinct expression of discontent with the form. He wrote others. Again he did. But his ordinary couplets are, as heroic couplets, very ordinary ; nor can much more be said of any of his pieces in the metre. It is when he is free from it that he curvets, that he expatiates, that he displays the "careful and perspicuous art" which Mr. Dobson so justly ascribes to him, the "charming humour of lyric" that had been earlier awarded him by Thackeray ; above all, that power

has added much to our knowledge of him. Prosodically, however, we need only draw attention, among the new matter, to the charming anapæstic triplets of "Jinny the Just" and to certain very terrible "blanks" which he never published, and which shall therefore be reserved to the next Book, with their more carefully finished kin, his translations of Callimachus.

"of making verse speak the language of prose without being prosaic, of marshalling words without seeming to displace a syllable for the sake of rhyme or rhythm," the ascription of which is one of the highest proofs of Cowper's gifts as a critic.

It may perhaps be permitted to insist a little on the remarkable evidence of conscious interest in different prosodic forms displayed by Prior. It is well known that this is by no means the rule with poets—some of whom seem even a little to resent the idea that they do not sing otherwise than as they must. And those who have read this book with any attention will know that it has (except in the earliest time) seldom been less the rule than at the time with which we are dealing. Milton has left no theory but the outburst at the beginning of *Paradise Lost*, and the enigmatic allusions in the sonnets. Dryden tells us that he was going to write about prosody ; but never seems to have done it. Hardly anything, indeed for a century before Prior, since Drayton's remarks on the various epic stanzas, corresponds to Prior's own observations in the Preface to *Solomon*, and those in that to the *Ode to the Queen*. That the experiment announced in the latter, and carried out in the Ode itself (*v. inf.*), is disastrous, is of much less importance than that it is an experiment. The *Solomon* passage, which, I feel sure, excited Johnson's hostility, is of too great moment not to be given, as far as its more important utterances go.[1]

His prosodic remarks.

The validity and general drift of Prior's censure will be illustrated later : the point for us here is that it shows in its author a very considerable sense of the importance of prosody, and especially a sense of discontent and a desire to explore. Remembering this, let us examine his

His Pindaric.

[1] "Heroic with continued rhyme, as Donne and his contemporaries used it, carrying the sense of one verse most commonly into another, was found too dissolute and wild, and came very often too near prose. As Davenant and Waller directed and Dryden perfected it, it is too confined. It cuts off the sense . . . produces too frequent severity in the sound. . . . It is too broken and weak. . . . It loses the writer when he composes, [and] must do the same to the reader." He "dare not determine," but is "only inquiring," whether blank verse and stanza be "a proper remedy for [his] poetical complaint."

practice. The exact order of his work is not always easy to determine, for, busy as he was in another service from that of the Muse, he published no collection of his work for some twenty years after he began to write. But this matters little. He seems to have begun, as it was almost certain that a man of his date would begin, with couplets and Pindaric. It is to the latter that Mr. Dobson has laid the just and great compliment above quoted. But, as that admirable metrist himself would be the first to admit in cross-examination, you want, in poetic art, something more than carefulness and perspicuity, though these qualities will give you all but the very best prose. And it is one of the dangers of the Pindaric that when it escapes bombast or unkemptness, and does not attain sublimity, its resemblance to fine prose is apt to appear in a damaging fashion. That Prior fully saw this may or may not be the case; that he felt it, his subsequent history shows. He did not abandon Pindaric entirely: in that age he could hardly do so; it was then, if not your only wear, your wear occasionally by obligation, like *canons*, or a silk hat, in other ages. But it was evidently not his choice, and on perhaps the most distinguished occasion on which he might have used it he actually substituted his unlucky but not uninteresting experiment with the Spenserian.

His "improved" Spenserian.

Whether he knew the alterations which Giles and Phineas Fletcher had already made in this stanza cannot, of course, be positively stated. It is not impossible; for *The Purple Island* appeared only some thirty years before his own birth, and the work of Cambridge poets has always been rather carefully cherished by tradition in their University. If he did, he should have taken warning by them "not to move Camarina." As a matter of fact he is less successful than either. His proceeding is to add a line, making the stanza a dixain, to remove the picking up of the *b* rhyme at the fifth, and, retaining the final Alexandrine, to make the rhyme-scheme *ababcdcdee*. By this egregious device he gets indeed that "regularity" to which his age sacrificed everything; for instead of the in-and-out structure of the original you have simply two quatrains and a couplet, the extra length of the tenth line being the only instance in which everything is not exactly matched and batched.   But, *ipso facto* and inevitably, he loses the unique and miraculous *cohesion* of the stanza, and the charm of linked sweetness by which that cohesion is at once accompanied and accomplished.   In fact, the attentive and fairly accustomed ear is cheated into the expectation of a sequence of *Gondibert* or *Annus Mirabilis* quatrains, and then shocked by the intrusion of a bandy-legged couplet in the procession.   However, as has been said, there is large licence and plentiful pardon for experiment. Prior made no other false step in this direction : in fact, to use his own words elsewhere and on another subject—

Matthew thought better, for Matthew thought right

to take up, instead, the octosyllable (which had been brought into fashion again by Butler), the anapæst (which, as we have just shown, had been working its way up in the social-prosodic scale), with common and other lyrical measures, and to treat them in his own way as escapements and expatiations from the couplet.   This he still practised in translations, in satiric styles, in the usual "balaam" of epilogues, etc., and (oddity number two !) in the rehandling (which reads to us most like designed burlesque) of the *Nut-Brown Maid.*

To attempt to distinguish exactly between Swift's handling of the octosyllable and Prior's would partake of the nature of hair-splitting.   Both start directly from Butler.   But between them and their original there is, in the first place, that remarkable though indefinable change of modern for not modern English to which attention must be often drawn ; for though *Hudibras* was published after the Restoration it is wholly retrospective in tone. In the second, there is a corresponding alteration of manners ; and in Prior's case, if not in Swift's, a consider-able softening of temper.   Where Butler makes us think —to take the companion literature—of the *Satire Ménippée* and even of Rabelais, they make us think of Molière and

La Bruyère.   And, to frame and adjust the proper
prosodic equivalent of this, they, and especially Prior,
banish or reduce the roughness, the curvets, the extravagances, of the Hudibrastic.   They leave it, or make it,
much more than what Cowper in his earlier verse, less
happily than in his later prose, described as

> Dear Mat Prior's easy jingle.

For "jingle" is derogatory, and in fact incorrect ; while it
at least suggests a quite wrong sense for "easy."   They
revive that old quality of the metre which has been
spoken of as a danger in the mediæval epoch and in
Gower—its extraordinary *fluidity*.   Butler had purposely
broken its amble into flings and plunges ; they restore the
ambling movement, but they take care that its monotony
shall be relieved, partly by felicity of phrase, partly by
slight but sufficient starts and quivers.   In the three great
modern *fabliaux*, in the superlative "English Padlock,"
the equally great "Epitaph," the "Conversation," and all
the rest, including even the very early lines to Fleetwood
Shepherd, this process appears.   *Alma*, like to Butler in
subject, is also rather liker to him in versification : at least
in parts.   But in all, whatever the date and whatever the
subject, there is to be traced the desire of substituting,
for Butler's idiosyncrasy, an easy descant with charm of
rhythm and rhyme superinduced or transfused through
the clearness and workmanlike efficiency of prose.

It seems as if he meant, if he could, to do something
of the same sort with the other couplet in *Solomon*, but
did not dare for fear of falling into the "dissoluteness and
wildness of heroic with continued rhyme."   It is not
surprising that, with such sentiments, he kept the triplet,
the Alexandrine, and the occasional incomplete verse of
Dryden.   And indeed, in one or two places, he did
venture positive enjambment, as, for instance, close to
the beginning—

> Happiness, object of that waking dream
> Which we call life, mistaking ; fugitive theme
> Of my surprising verse, etc. ;

where it is noteworthy enough that he actually dares a tri-syllabic foot, or at least one that can only be dissyllabised by the appalling pronunciation "*fewdgtive.*" He also makes no indistinct attempts at a much more varied pause than couplet orthodoxy allows—making strong stops at the second syllable frequently, and once or twice at the first. But he never gets out of it, and he could not get the combination of ease, variety, and fluency for which his soul longed.

It was, as we saw, very different with the octosyllable, His anapæsts. and it was almost more different still with the combined measures and with the anapæst. This last, indeed, Prior was the first literary poet to instal in regular literary use. Dryden, as we have seen, had done it, and done it admirably ; but in definite " songs "—generally so-called, sometimes marked out as such by refrains in the old " derry-down " manner, and always of the song type. Prior extended the employment—widened, as it were, the admission from that of a mere performer in the music-gallery to that of an actual *débutante* on the floor of the ballroom. I cannot remember anything earlier like the famous " Secretary," which was written as early as 1696. It matters nothing that there is French accentuation—there are a good many instances of it in Prior, as was natural in a man constantly speaking and writing French. There is no fault to find with such a couplet as

> This night and the next shall be hers, shall be mine :
> To good or ill fortune the third we resign.

And with it the lighter English poetry entered, for all purposes, and not merely for theatrical or musical ones, into the possession of a new medium. How charmingly " der Herr Secretaris " employed and exemplified it, everybody at least ought to know. Somehow one cannot imagine

> As Cloe came into the room t' other day

in any other measure—the misdeeds and ingratitude of the " ugly hard rosebud " must have remained untold or

ill-told, even by Herrick, otherwise. And it is the
same with

> Dear Cloe, how blubbered is that pretty face—

quatrain this time and alternately rhymed, with its glorious
challenge at the end to grammaticasters. While as for
" Down Hall," the versatile foot there provided the lighter
narrative poem with a vehicle as incomparable for its own
purposes : and was as ready to accommodate the epigram
when " Bibo " and others required it.

The general advantages of the regular installation,
among the methods of recognised poetry, of a measure so
inspiriting, so various, can escape no one ; but some
niceties of its prosodic property may escape notice, and
deserve indication. For instance, it opens the way to a
whole class of word-values which the iambic excludes, or
only admits when mixed with the anapæst itself. Take,
for instance, such a word as " laudable." In strict iambic
you must give that word a secondary accent, as some
would say ; must provisionally lengthen its last syllable, as
I should. There is ample justification for this ; it would
have been actually spelt, in the rougher MSS. of Middle
English, " lauda*bull*." But doing this weakens the length
and strength of the legitimate " laūd- " and slightly alters
the balance of the whole word. Now in that unkind
account of the different fashion in which, on different
occasions, poor Florimel bore her pleasing punishment—

> Ten months after Florimel happened to wed
> And was brought in a *laudable* manner to bed,

the strict and proper value of the word reappears with
delightful effect, and enables the full stress to be laid on
the right syllable. So, again, in the incomparable " Cloe
Jealous " itself, and in one of Prior's most ravishing lines—

> The God of us versemen, *you know, child*, the Sun.

If " child " occurred in an iambic line, though it would be
quite possible to put it in the place of a short syllable, the
admissibility of spondees in that measure, and the natural

tendency of the word to length, would give a temptation towards the lengthening of it.   Whereas, used as it is like " dear," " friend," etc., as a mere appellative, with no weight laid on it, it ought not to be so lengthened.   Here the metre itself forces the shortening, and you get the careless, coaxing negligence which is wanted.[1]

It is, in fact, hard to be equal to this occasion, which is one of the most memorable in the history of English prosody.   From the " ugly hard rosebud " that fell into Cloe's neck has come a progeny of roses among the most exquisite that the garden of English poetry holds : that " little Dutch chaise on the Saturday night " carried with it volumes of unwritten verse of the most adorable quality, besides the visible and printed Horace between which and the nymph the spare form of Prior sat bodkin. For a time, indeed, only its lighter capacities were noticed ; though Byrom, and Shenstone, and Anstey developed these well.   But when the greater Muses awoke once more, then it was seen, and it has been seen ever since, what the anapæst could do : then, like its own Jinny, " it answered the end of its being created."   " The Grave of Sir Arthur O'Kellyn," and " Lochinvar," and " Bonnie Dundee," and that less popular but wholly delectable " When the dawn on the mountain was misty and grey " ; " I come to thy garden of roses," and (to suit all tastes), " The Assyrian came down " ; " I saw from the beach," and " The Battle of the Baltic " ; " The Revenge," and the " Voyage of Maeldune " ; all the great things in it from " The Lost Leader " to " Prospice " ; the master-chorus in

The charm of the metre.

---

[1] The newly revealed and most amiable as well as "just" "Jinny" (was she the same as " *Coy* Jenny " who protests and vows elsewhere ?) adds some pleasing instances of the metre's virtues, which may be sampled :—

> Thus still whilst her morning unseen fled away,
> In adorning the house, and in making the tea,
> That she scarce could have time for the psalms of the day—
>
> And while after dinner the night came so soon,
> That half she proposed very seldom was done,
> With twenty " God bless me's, how this day has gone ! "
>
> While she read and accounted, and paid, and abated,
> Eat and drank, played and worked, laughed and cried, loved and hated—
> As answered the end of her being created.

Atalanta and " Dolores,"—one could fill pages with the mere
titles of only the best serious things that this bountiful
and abounding measure has given us—things which could
not have been given without it.   The trisyllabic measures
are the cavalry of versification ; and for English at least
the anapæst is

The clipper that stands in the stall at the top.

Other points
in him.
His double
rhymes.   Although, however, Prior's accomplishment, and still
more his example, in the domiciling of the anapæst and
the octosyllable are his greatest achievements, they are
not his only ones, and there are some minor points in
them and in others which deserve mention.   He was
particularly happy in the smaller quatrains—" common "
and " long."   Not, indeed, that he had much (if he had
anything) of the soar and reach which we have noticed in
the last chapter and which died out in his own earlier
time.   But he could substitute for it a quaint neatness which
was reinforced and exchanged with a curious melancholy
sentiment, noticed by all the best judges, but not forming
part, perhaps, of the popular conception of him.   One of
his main secrets in this respect seems to me to have
consisted in a singular and almost magical sense of the
power of double rhymes, by themselves or intermixed.
If the immortal " Child of Quality " had been in masculine
rhymes throughout, it would not only have been a false
concord with the subject, but ruinous to the concordat of
subject and metre.   The extraordinarily fine lines " written
in Mézeray " may seem to be rhymed double or single
quite at haphazard, but they are not ; and, in particular, if
any one will care to substitute a monosyllable for the last
word instead of " weary," which Prior has bought at the
not inconsiderable expense of making it rhyme with
" tarry," he will see " how vast the stroke is and how wide
the wound " (as Dr. Watts pindarically observes of the
death of the Reverend Mr. Gouge).   His anapæsts, and
especially his alternately rhymed ones, gain almost as
much from this variation of play ; but it is perhaps most

noticeable in the shorter and mainly iambic measures. For instance, in the very wicked jests on Helen and her eyebrows and the kitten, half the sting of the last would be lost but for the echo in the double rhyme of " sorrow " and " morrow." Substitute once more, and see.

So, yet again, in the mocking English ballad on Namur, the double rhymes, which are here not very numerous (Prior was in his apprenticeship), have the effect of increasing the mock, just as they have in the Mézeray piece of emphasising the moral ; their function, in fact, being in both cases that of emphasis—of drawing attention to whatever is the point.

But perhaps nothing distinguishes him more from most of his predecessors in the use of the anapæst, and indeed from not a few practitioners in other metres, than that naturalness—that " never seeming to force a syllable " which Cowper so justly commends. The older anapæstic writers hobble and drag terribly. Any three syllables are good enough for them. Whereas with Prior a bad foot is an exception. It does occur, for instance, in the " Cloe Jealous " piece, where the admirable Shakespearian borrowing—

> Let us e'en talk a little like folks of this world,

itself a capital example of his style, is ushered at the end of the verse before by the clogged stumbling discord of

> and as old | Falstaff says.

You can do a great deal with English prosody, she is the most obliging of damsels ; but you can't make " Falstaff " a pyrrhic without her protesting, or at least making a wry face. Very seldom, however, does he do anything of this kind. And it is only fair to add that if he never quite reaches the soar and throb so often spoken of, he never sinks into the pit of bathetic singsong which was yawning for the ballad-measures, and into which they usually fell even before his death. The well-known *Garland*[1] presents a battered and hackneyed appearance, rather because of

[1] The pride of every grove I chose.

its diction than of its versification, which is far from unhappy. And the " worse answer " (which, accordingly, only not one person knows for twenty that know the better) to " Cloe Jealous," [1] is also quite above the ordinary. To recur to the Mézeray lines from a point of view not yet noted, the idiosyncrasy of Prior's handling of the romance-six is particularly observable. This was to be, for what sins of its own it is hard to say—possibly for those old ones not quite expiated by *Sir Thopas*—a great favourite, and a terrible victim, with the eighteenth century. Especially after Gray, but even before him to no small extent, it suffered from attention on the part of those appalling Odes—Odes to Peace, and War, and Poverty, and Riches ; Odes to Miss B., and to " A Gentleman Recovering from the Measles " ; Odes on the Qualities of a Good Washerwoman, and on the Sensations of being Transferred from the Blue Bed to the Brown—which were the darlings of the eighteenth century, and are the stupefaction of its successors. So Prior uses it, in its simple form, little or hardly at all. But he lifts and chequers it, lengthens it with thought and adorns it with phrase, drops lines and adds syllables, till, in these altered but related versions, it proves itself one of the best vehicles for serious-humorous verse ever devised.

It is possible that this estimate of Prior's importance may seem extravagant to those who are content to take traditional opinion. But I think that even here I have been able to present some evidence to support it ; and I have not much fear that any student who has followed this book without finding himself shocked by its general principles, and who takes the trouble to study Prior directly, will think me very wrong. Some of the minor points which I have indicated may seem doubtful to such a student ; but doubt about them will not shipwreck belief in the main contention advanced, that the secure establishment, in an honoured station, of two such metres as the octosyllabic couplet and the anapæst in its various combinations, was a matter of immense moment in face of the

---

[1] Yes, fairest proof of Beauty's power.

domination and reputation of the heroic. I formed my opinion of Prior in these respects a very long time ago : before I had any definite intention of treating this subject systematically, and indeed before I had much noticed the prose documents which show that he paid conscious and theoretical, as well as empirical, attention to prosody. And the more I have studied both the subject and the poet since, the more convinced I have been on the matter. He does not, of course, rank as a prosodic influence with Chaucer, or Spenser, or Milton, even with Dryden and Pope. But he occupies a position different from others and only possible at a peculiar stage of prosodic history—that of a man who, as prosodic civilisation advances, takes care that one good custom shall not corrupt it, that room shall be found for different sorts and aspects, different spirits and administrations.

CHAPTER IV

PROSODISTS

Continued poverty of the subject—Dryden—Mulgrave, Roscommon, etc.

THE remarks which were made in the corresponding chapter of the last Book apply to the present almost equally. Although it will not exactly be, as that was, a *capitulum unius hominis,* there will hardly be as much to say of any one person as there was there of Joshua Poole—or rather of " J. D." This must be, of course, all the more surprising in that the other J. D., John Dryden, is of this time, and that in him we have an example of the poet-critic hardly exceeded by any in history : a consummate practitioner in certain kinds of prosody, and a man quite obviously interested in the particular subject, who is constantly approaching it, who expressly laments the lack of " an English *Prosodia,*" and who had thought of supplying it. But something sealed his lips ; and even when he talks about " numbers," compliments Mr. Waller on his achievements, and so on, he never tells us *exactly* wherein " the sweetness of numbers " consists. We know " in a sort of way " ; but it is only in a sort of way. He thinks [1] Chapman's *Homer* characterised by " harsh numbers, improper English, and a monstrous length of verse," [2] and supposes that when Mulgrave and Waller read it " with incredible pleasure and extreme transport " (as

---

[1] Dedication of *Examen Poeticum* (Ker's *Essays of Dryden,* ii. 14).
[2] Observe that, as noticed above, he himself by no means eschewed the " monstrous " fourteener, though, of course, he did not use it continuously.

some of us also do), it must have been the Homer that
delighted them, and not the Chapman.   But decasyllables
alone will not satisfy him, even when they are fairly
stopped ; for he thinks[1] Sandys' *Ovid* "prose."   He
says[2] "that he might descend to the mechanic beauties
of heroic verse," and tells us[3] elsewhere that he "has long
had by him the materials" (which, unluckily, he never
worked up) "of an English *Prosodia* containing all the
mechanical rules of versification."   So that as Jonson
disappointed us in the first half of the century, so does
he in the second.   Yet we get some hints from him.
He objects, in the passage last quoted, to elision, which
he calls cæsura, and hints (saying he had "given them
to his friends") at the reason of the sweetness of
Denham's famous lines, which one may guess to have
been the strong cæsura in the proper sense, and the
antithesis.   He frankly thinks that we are "ignorant
what feet ought to be used in Heroic Poetry"; says he
borrowed the idea of using the Alexandrine from Spenser ;
and has other tantalising glimmers which never come to
a light.   That he thought "thousands" of Chaucer's
verses such that "no pronunciation could make them other
than short of half a foot or even a whole one," is a well-
known example of practically blameless ignorance.

If such a man as Dryden, with his practice in poetry
and his interest in criticism, can give us nothing more
definite than this, we are not likely to get very much
from Roscommon and Mulgrave on the one hand, or from
Rymer and Dennis on the other.   Nor do we.   Mulgrave
of the many titles, in his *Essay on Poetry*, talks of
"harmonious numbers," and says that the language "must
soft and easy run," but that is about all, and it does not
do us much good.   The "unspotted" Roscommon in

Mulgrave, Roscommon, etc.

---

[1] *Ibid.* (Ker, pp. 9, 10).

[2] *Discourse of Satan* (Ker, ii. 110).

[3] *Dedication of the Æneis* (Ker, ii. 217).   This last passage is the longest
and fullest, but provokingly *general*.   Its most valuable remark of a strictly
prosodic character is that quoted above on Milton—that what you elide you
must not pronounce.   (For more on this and the whole, *v. sup.* p. 360, at
the opening of the present Book and of the chapter on Dryden.)   But the
text had perhaps better be given at the close of this chapter.

his *On Translated Poetry* is a little more precise, and talks about "accents on odd syllables," of "vowels and accents regularly placed"; but this does not take us much further. Rymer ran down Shakespeare, and Dennis held him up; but neither in any place grapples at all closely with actual questions of prosody; though we are sure that their standard of "harmony" would have been pretty much the same as that of the two noble lords.

The fact seems to be that, till the very end of this time, there were two checks operating against the production of any definitely prosodic treatise. It was practically impossible, considering these general views about "harmony," "sweetness," etc., that anybody should take a complete view of the subject, and include even Elizabethan, much more older poetry, in his survey. But, on the other hand, there was not as yet a sufficient supply of the new verse to serve as a basis of study; and that verse, as preferred and validated, was exceedingly monotonous in kind. Its producers, yet once more, were too much occupied in producing it to discuss it, and it was only after Dryden's death that Bysshe, greatly daring, took upon himself the office of *législateur du Parnasse anglais*. To tell the truth, we need not regret the absence of treatises at this time. They might have been curious; but they might also have been disgusting.[1]

[1] To Prior justice has been already done, and he is as much of the next Book as of this. The Dryden passages referred to above are as follows :—

"You may please also to observe, that there is not, to the best of my remembrance, one vowel gaping on another for want of a *cæsura*, in this whole poem : but, where a vowel ends a word, the next begins either with a consonant, or what is its equivalent; for our *W* and *H* aspirate, and our diphthongs, are plainly such. The greatest latitude I take is in the letter *Y*, when it concludes a word, and the first syllable of the next begins with a vowel. Neither need I have called this a latitude, which is only an explanation of this general rule, that no vowel can be cut off before another when we cannot sink the pronunciation of it; as *he, she, me, I*, etc. Virgil thinks it sometimes a beauty to imitate the licence of the Greeks, and leave two vowels opening on each other, as in that verse of the Third *Pastoral*,

Et succus pecori, et lac subducitur agnis.

"But *nobis non licet esse tam disertis*, at least if we study to refine our numbers. I have long had by me the materials of an English *Prosodia*, containing all the mechanical rules of versification, wherein I have treated, with some exactness, of the feet, the quantities, and the pauses. The French and

Italians know nothing of the two first ; at least their best poets have not practised them.   As for the pauses, Malherbe first brought them into France within this last century ; and we see how they adorn their Alexandrines. But, as Virgil propounds a riddle, which he leaves unsolved—

> *Dic, quibus in terris, inscripti nomina regum*
> *Nascantur flores, et Phyllida solus habeto—*

so I will give your Lordship another, and leave the exposition of it to your acute judgment.   I am sure there are few who make verses, have observed the sweetness of these two lines in *Cooper's Hill*—

> Though deep, yet clear ; though gentle, yet not dull ;
> Strong without rage ; without o'erflowing, full.

And there are yet fewer who can find the reason of that sweetness.   I have given it to some of my friends in conversation ; and they have allowed the criticism to be just.   But, since the evil of false quantities is difficult to be cured in any modern language ; since the French and the Italians, as well as we, are yet ignorant what feet are to be used in Heroic Poetry ; since I have not strictly observed those rules myself, which I can teach others ; since I pretend no dictatorship among my fellow-poets ; since, if I should instruct some of them to make well-running verses, they want genius to give them strength as well as sweetness ; and, above all, since your Lordship has advised me not to publish that little which I know, I look on your counsel as your command, which I shall observe inviolably, till you shall please to revoke it, and leave me at liberty to make my thoughts public.   In the meantime, that I may arrogate nothing to myself, I must acknowledge that Virgil in Latin, and Spenser in English, have been my masters.   Spenser has also given me the boldness to make use sometimes of his Alexandrine line, which we call, though improperly, the Pindaric, because Mr. Cowley has often employed it in his *Odes*.   It adds a certain majesty to the verse, when it is used with judgment, and stops the sense from overflowing into another line.   Formerly the French, like us, and the Italians, had but five feet, or ten syllables, in their heroic verse ; but, since Ronsard's time as I suppose, they found their tongue too weak to support their epic poetry, without the addition of another foot.   That indeed has given it somewhat of the run and measure of a trimeter ; but it runs with more activity than strength : their language is not strung with sinews, like our English ; it has the nimbleness of a greyhound, but not the bulk and body of a mastiff.   Our men and our verses overbear them by their weight ; and *Pondere, non numero*, is the British motto."

INTERCHAPTER VII

THE summing-up at this point need not be voluminous; but it is by no means a superfluity. In the forty years, more or less, which are covered, as far as their main prosodic symptoms go, by this Book, we find, for the first time, something like a "tyranny," in the strict Greek sense, established in English prosody. Partly owing to the operation of the various causes and processes which we traced in the last Interchapter; partly owing to the astonishing craftsmanship and the overpowering pre-eminence of a single poet,—the more or less decidedly stopped couplet has not merely triumphed over all its rivals as a vehicle of long narrative poems, but is bidding for something very like poetical monopoly. All the stanzas—even its own nearest relation, and, for a time, rival, the quatrain—are discountenanced and disestablished for this purpose of narration; while, on the other hand, its peculiar suitableness for argumentative purposes puts didactic poetry more on a level with narrative than it has ever been before—tends, in fact, to give the principal place in poetry to that to which Aristotle hesitated to give the name of poetry at all. Assisted by the extra-ordinary state of disarray and decadence into which dramatic blank verse—the rival which had driven it from the stage seventy or eighty years earlier—has fallen, it plays a return match with that rival, defeats it utterly, and holds the stage itself almost completely for a time, and more or less for most of the time.[1]

---

[1] Crowne's *Caligula* is generally selected as the last important heroic play. But there were certainly others; and it continued for at least a century. The curious *Battle of Aughrim*, by a certain Robert Ashton, with which Thackeray

But its successes in these, the greatest and most important divisions of the prosodic field according to general estimation, are perhaps not really so remarkable as the way in which it tends to regard itself, and to be regarded, as a sort of universal standard, a Sir-Positive At-all, who is fit for anything and an expert in everything. The beautiful lyric of the early part of the century dies slowly ; but it dies. The sonnet goes into a period of almost complete occultation. Prologues and epilogues—those gangways between poetry and drama, which, in their earliest forms, had had rather a tendency not to be even decasyllabic—adopt the couplet as their regular and almost (though not quite) their only wear. It invades the provinces of other metres in the smallest " copy of verses " ; and but for the influence of one or two persons—notably Prior and Swift—might capture them.

But what is more striking still, its reputation and acknowledged claims are even greater than its actual achievements. We have seen, in the last chapters of the last two Books, that, during its rise and growth, a curious dumbness has come on the preceptist side of prosody after the very considerable loquacity of the strictly Elizabethan period. Yet, in such utterances as we have been able to catch and interpret, there has been an obvious general idea that the regular couplet is the *ne plus ultra* of verse. This idea is on the verge of being formally stated and codified, of being accepted in practice and in theory, and of holding its position as popular orthodoxy for a full hundred years, if not longer. Nay, after another hundred has completely passed, and a third has been entered upon—during the writing of this very book, of this very part of it,—I have seen expressions in newspapers of the specially literary kind which seem to show that in some quarters it is popular orthodoxy still. There is no need of pointing out here the advantages and disadvantages of this singular promotion " *vice* everything else superseded." They have been, or will be,

deals in *The Irish Sketch Book*, is said to be as late as George the Third's reign. It is heroic *ad absurdissimum*, and yet obviously serious.

fully set forth and dealt with. It is the fact that we have here to lay down—to *constater*—as the dominant fact of the stage with which we are dealing, and that which must be constantly borne in mind in proceeding to and through the next. But it is important that the reader should not forget that the success of the couplet has been obtained under peculiar conditions. In the first place, there never was such a " one-man " period in English poetry as the last five-and-twenty years of the seventeenth century ; though there have been perhaps " no-man " periods. There was nobody who could be put anywhere near Dryden ; and it was this overpowering, this *hervorragend* eminence—to give the thing the best word for it in any European language that I know—that did so much to establish the couplet, which was Dryden's usual vehicle.

But special pains have been taken to point out that Dryden himself is by no means, as Pope was practically to be, a couplet metrist only—that he is an expert in very different metres, in fact in nearly all ; and also that his true couplet is by no means the stopped couplet pure and simple. The easements of the Alexandrine and the triplet, if they interfere with its purity, enlarge its variety and flexibility very much. They will perhaps create a longing for variety and flexibility which will not even be satisfied with them, but will be made keener when they are withdrawn.

Here also it has to be noticed, as so often, if not so invariably, that the time of the flourishing of tyranny is the time of the sowing and even the growing of the seeds of liberty. At the very moment when the heroic couplet is driving the rabble of half-disbanded blank verse from the stage, Milton is rearranging and reforming the measure in a fashion which will not perhaps serve for dramatic practice, but which for the first time will make it available for the far wider and finer uses of poetry at large. From being " too mean for a copy of verses," he is making it fit for the greatest poetry ; and in so doing is laying bare and illustrating principles which will react with tremendous effect on other measures, and will tend to make men specially discontented with the stopped couplet itself.

At the very same moment likewise (*Paradise Lost*, and *Hudibras*, and Dryden's first heroic plays, are close to-gether [1]), Butler's peculiar revision of the octosyllable, if it may seem to confine that venerable metre to but a part of the ground which it has hitherto occupied, en-trenches it in that part in the strongest possible fashion, and makes it sure of popularity because it amuses. Nay, later, with a reversal of things as humorous as its own nature, people will speak of poems like Scott's own as being written "in Hudibrastics." Always and anyhow, it will provide for the other couplet an alternative of the most opposite, at any rate of the most supplementary and complementary, character.

But a newer and hitherto less recognised force in resistance and escape is to be found in the trisyllabic —practically the anapæstic—metres, which, developed by slow progress from the débris of "the heap," and playing, like the heroes of romance, the part of scullion or lackey for a time, are taken up even by Dryden himself, and by others as media for song-writing in and out of plays ; recognised by degrees as invaluable alternatives for miscellaneous verse ; and finally established by Prior as possible vehicles for something more—capable of narra-tive, inimitable in social lyric, employable in a thousand different ways.

These are the most dangerous foes of all to the couplet, because they do more than provide alternatives, they suggest things disastrous, nay destructive, to the strict decasyllabic form of the couplet itself. When the full form of such words as "every," "violet," "dangerous," is seen to be perfectly melodious, why torture them into the ugly cripples "ev'ry," "vi'let," "dang'rous"?—which last an ordinary Englishman would feel inclined to pronounce like "dangle." When you find that you can say "the eye" and "the immense" without the least cacophony,

---

[1] *Hudibras*, 1663-8 ; *Paradise Lost*, 1667 ; *The Indian Emperor*, 1667, but acted, 1665.

why blurt out the monstrosities of "thimmense" and
"theye"? "Oh! but," say precisians, "these are different
kinds of verse." You look back on your Shakespeare,
whom you are told, though with some cautions, to admire ;
you look even on your Milton ; and you find that in the
same kind of verse there are feet which you cannot but
regard as trisyllabic. And it will go hard that you will
begin to ask, Why this Procrustean artificiality? Which
when you do, the strict decasyllable is doomed.

Its doom, however, was not to come upon it rapidly ;
it was to enjoy pride of place for some three generations
more, and it was even to be, if weakened, refined and
polished still further. No "Mene Tekel" was at all
traceable on its palace walls in 1700. And meanwhile,
under the shadow of its throne, there grew up among other
things a fresh crop of prosodic study, which, after the
almost fallow of the last chapter and its predecessor on the
subject earlier, will give us plentiful matter. But we
must first survey the final triumph of the couplet itself in
Pope ; and then its decadence (though it was not exactly
that), and the strengthening of the opposing metres.

BOOK VIII

THE EIGHTEENTH CENTURY

CHAPTER I

POPE AND THE LATER COUPLET

As was observed previously, Pope is practically *homo unius metri*. The few pieces which he composed in any other would not fill a dozen pages, and (as it has been said of the contemporary French lyric and the Alexandrine) these very pieces are seldom more than decasyllables cut into lengths. Of the faith of which Bysshe was the humble but undoubting lawgiver, Pope was the not at all humble, and, whether undoubting or not, unhesitating high priest, as well as victorious champion. The couplet, the pure couplet, and nothing but the couplet, is the prosodic heading of every page of his verse, save the few noted. "There is one metre, and Pope is its prophet," was the doctrine of the greater part of the eighteenth century. From one point of view, therefore, he may seem to demand very brief handling, and from any point he must demand less than poets of equal position who have been more polymetric. But, on the other hand, it is under him that we should deal with the couplet itself, so as to keep the connection of poets and poetry, and to

Pope's metrical unitarianism.

447

lighten what would be otherwise an unduly heavy Inter-chapter.

His couplet, and its form.

The Popian couplet is, in its own way, a Quintessence, an Entelechy ; and nothing *qui tient de la Quinte* arrives at perfection at once.   Whether he composed his works as early as he said he did, or as early as we know he did, they are still remarkably precocious, and it was not to be supposed that he would at once discard the easements and licences which Dryden had permitted and transmitted. Yet, as we see from Garth's *Dispensary*, there was already a tendency to reject both the Alexandrine and the triplet, and it was one of Pope's special characteristics to be sensitive to such perhaps not quite skiey influences, and to express them early, forcibly, and in a way finally.   He laughed at the Alexandrine before he practically abandoned it : except in very early work he never seems to have been much given to Dryden's triplet, though he never quite abandoned this either, using it occasionally with an obvious desire for special—generally for comic—effect. In the case of these two poets the style certainly was " *de l'homme même*," as the probably better reading of Buffon's maxim runs.   Not merely the range of Dryden's interests, and the weight and vigour of his understanding, but a certain *bonhomie* which distinguished him, are reflected in his metre ; Pope's narrower accomplishment, and his slightly viperish disposition, find their natural utterance in his. But accomplishment is a very delightful thing, and the viper, though a formidable, is really a beautiful beast.   It is very interesting to watch the gradual, though by no means tardy, polishing and lightening, and in the process the necessary whittling or filing away, of the measure. With the discard of the Alexandrine and the triplet, or their very unfrequent use, not only is an approach made to the imaginary " purity" of the style, but another and still closer one is also made to its uniformity, and yet another, closest of all, to its maximum swiftness.   This latter desideratum is further secured by a certain not easily describable but most perceptible lightening of the rhymes—a large proportion of Pope's final words are monosyllabic,—and an avoidance, not prudish, but evident, of long and heavy vocables in the interior of the lines themselves. The first line is allowed to run into the second in sense, though there is generally reserved a perceptible halt in sound to mark it ; but one couplet is never allowed to run into another except for some special purpose, and seldom at all. The pause is kept as nearly as possible to the three charmed centre syllables, fourth, fifth, and sixth ; and though antithesis in the halves is seldom as striking as it sometimes is in Dryden, it is perhaps more uniformly present ; while that between line and line, or between both halves of both lines, is not uncommon.

One drastic but dangerous device for securing the undulating penetration of the line had been obvious from the very first in Fairfax, and much more in Waller ; while, though avoided to a great extent by Dryden's masculine strength and his fertility of ideas, it had become very prominent in Garth and was never relinquished by Pope. In fact, it is probable that to his dealing with it is due the popularity of some of his most popular passages. This is the use, either at one place in the line or at corresponding ones towards its two ends, of the "*gradus* epithet," the filling or padding, the *cheville* as the French call it, which, when overdone, is perhaps the worst blemish of the style. There are passages—examples will be given below [1]—in

The "*gradus* epithet."

---

[1] The *Rape* passage will be found further on (p. 453), cited for an additional purpose.   Here is the Garth :—

> With ~~breathing~~ fire his pitchy nostrils blow,
> As from his sides he shakes the ~~fleecy~~ snow.
> Around this ~~hoary~~ prince from wat'ry beds
> His subject islands raise their ~~verdant~~ heads.
>
> Etérnal spring with ~~smiling~~ verdure here
> Warms the mild air and crowns the ~~youthful~~ year.
>
> The vine undressed her ~~swelling~~ clusters bears,
> The labouring hind the ~~mellow~~ olive cheers.

Read, omitting the interlined epithets, and you get perfectly fluent octosyllables. It is hardly necessary to say that no novelty is claimed for this demonstration. The *locus classicus* for it is the Introduction to *The Lay of the Last Minstrel* ; but, as Scott there observes, "it had often been remarked" before. In fact, Pope himself frankly suggests it in the *Essay on Criticism*.

The Dispensary and *The Rape of the Lock* where you can convert the decasyllable into the octosyllable for several lines together without detriment to sense or poetry, by simply taking out these specious superfluities. No doubt, in Pope himself especially, there are others where you cannot; but the temptation is a besetting one, and the second-rate poets fall into it almost to a man.

The *Pastorals.*　　With Pope, however, as with other poets *majorum gentium*, we must trace the successive shapings of this famous instrument. Let us take his word for it that the *Pastorals*, though not published till 1709, were written five years earlier, in their author's sixteenth year. The first six lines will well illustrate the process above outlined; but if space would permit, the illustration might be extended to the whole piece :—

> First in these fields I try the *sylvan* strains,
> Nor blush to sport on Windsor's *blissful* plains.
> Fair Thames, flow gently from thy *sacred* spring,
> While on thy banks *Sicilian* Muses sing ;
> Let *vernal* airs thro' *trembling* osiers play
> And Albion's cliffs resound the *rural* lay.

Now this, by the omission of some of the *gradus* epithets, becomes—

> First in these fields I try the strains,
> Nor blush to sport on Windsor's plains.
> Fair Thames, flow gently from thy spring,
> While on thy banks [the] Muses sing ;
> Let vernal airs through osiers play
> And Albion's cliffs resound the lay—

where, if anybody prefers it, the fifth line may run—

> Let airs through trembling osiers play ;

for " vernal " and " trembling " are equally good illustrations [1] of that <u>antithetic epithet with no antithesis in it,</u> which is the curse of the style, and which Pope, though he often avoided it later, did not always, even then, avoid.

---

[1] Of course, I know that he took the idea from the famous " inhorruit veris adventus " (or " vepris ad ventum " !) of Horace. But this does not affect the point. In fact, it could be made, if it were worth while, to support it.

This sample, purposely cut short in order not to take an unfair advantage, shows at once, but I think without appeal, the intensely *artificial* character of this versification, and its attendant diction. Poetry becomes an abacus, where a certain but limited number of beads can be slipped on or off, arranged in corresponding groups to suit taste and demand. Dictionaries of phrase and rhyme become, as they were in the "Maronolatrous" period of the Renaissance, allowable and almost indispensable, and the Temple of Apollo is a sort of poetic exchange or clearing-house.

Yet in these, and in their professed companions the *Messiah* and the First Part of *Windsor Forest*, it would be either idle or uncatholic to deny an extraordinary dexterity at the game, such as it is. The wonderful *nerve* of Dryden (which Pope was hardly ever to reach, except perhaps in the really magnificent close of the *Dunciad*) is not there ; and the matter is *publica materies* enough. But the "careless verses," which Langton in a tell-tale phrase complained of (as Boswell tells us) in Glorious John, are absent likewise—the whole is swept, garnished, polished (furniture-polished ?) to a miraculous degree. There are even no triplets, or scarcely any, though there is an Alexandrine now and then ; and the triumph of this kind of poetical rhetoric can hardly go further than the famous "Messiah" passage.[1] Here the beads are of the best quality, being supplied from no less a treasury than that of Isaiah ; and the hand arranges and shifts them on the wires with all the skill of an infant phenomenon. It is already *virtuoso* poetry of all but the

The Messiah and Windsor Forest.

---

[1] The swain in barren deserts with surprise
　Sees lilies spring, and sudden verdure rise ;
　And starts amidst the thirsty wilds to hear
　New falls of water murmuring in his ear.
　On rifted rock, the dragon's late abodes,
　The green reed trembles, and the bulrush nods.
　Waste sandy valleys, once perplexed with thorn,
　The spiry fir and shapely box adorn ;
　To leafless shrubs the flow'ring palms succeed
　And od'rous myrtle to the noisome weed.
　　　　etc.　　　　etc.　　　　etc.

highest kind ; and by continual practice it is going to be made higher still. The game is played with all the unnatural strictness of Bysshism. " Barb'rous," " wat'ry," even " vi'let," " th' enamel'd," " hov'ring," " O'er 'em," stud the diction with their maimed and crushed forms like " L'Homme qui Rit " or the tortured pygmies of whom Longinus speaks. One almost wonders that " Belerium " and " Verrio " escape the apostrophe or the *y*.

The *Essay on Criticism* and *The Rape of the Lock.*　　If we turn to the *Essay on Criticism,* said to have been written some four or five years later than this group, it is interesting to find something of a declension from this rigid playing of the game, not an advance in it. The Alexandrine is indeed stigmatised in the famous verse that exemplifies it ;[1] but there are numerous triplets, which is explained by the fact that the poem is argumentative, and that, in consequence, the author not merely feels the twenty-syllable cramp much more sharply than in descriptive and imitated substance, but naturally recurs to the licence allowed himself by the greatest master, except Lucretius, of argumentative poetics. The constraint and the pattern are both removed in *The Rape of the Lock* ; and the triplet accordingly disappears. But the *gradus* epithet and its antithetic distribution appear more than ever—for equally obvious reasons. Point and sparkle, which they supply at a tolerably cheap rate, are especially necessary ; and there is another subtle influence which may be seen in operation from Chaucer downwards in almost all our greater poets except Milton, Wordsworth, Shelley, and Tennyson, in whom the sense of humour was weak or intermittent, and Byron, in whom it was kept down by egotism and affectation. The poet, to what extent consciously it is difficult to say, caricatures himself and his methods as a means of adding zest to the caricature of other things and persons. This may seem to be considering too curiously as to the cause ; the effect is certain. The famous and, in its rococo way, really

---

[1] It is only fair to Pope to remind the reader, again, that he also fully admitted and illustrated its merits in the line on his and its great master—

The long majestic march, and energy divine.

beautiful opening of the second canto exhibits it in a fashion which a few italics ought to bring out sufficiently ; while the other fashion in which the verses " split " right down the paragraph—like a bit of starch when you drop water on it—and the odd ridge-backed appearance which they present, may be pardonably illustrated by a very slight violence to their typographical arrangement in a note.[1]

The diagram, I think, does not bring out unfairly the curious jointed-doll character of the metre. Hardly even Johnson's prose antitheses are more exactly proportioned than these : "ethereal," " purpled," and " silver " in different lines ; " white " and " sparkling," " Jews " and " Infidels," in the same ; while the way in which the verse runs up the hill, halts, and then runs down again, is positively acrobatic in its deftness of mechanic agility. For the subject nothing could be better : nothing, at least in a poem of any length, could well be so good : but then the subject is—the subject.

The *Elegy on an Unfortunate Lady* answers the objection started in the final words of the last paragraph, and shows once for all *qualis artifex* Pope was, and how ridiculous it is to ask the question " Whether he was a poet ? " (I do not say that it is ridiculous to ask " What

The *Elegy on an Unfortunate Lady.*

[1]
Not with more glories   in th' *ethereal* plain
  The sun first rises   o'er the *purpled* main,
   Than issuing forth   the rival of his beams
  Launch'd on the bosom of   the *silver* Thames.
Fair nymphs and well-drest youths   around her shone,
    But ev'ry eye was fix'd   on her alone.
      On her *white* breast   a *sparkling* cross she wore,
    Which *Jews* might kiss   and *Infidels* adore.
      Her *lively* looks   a *sprightly* mind disclose,
    Quick as her eyes   and as unfixed as those.
     Favours to none   to all she *smiles* extends,
      Oft she rejects   but never *once* offends.
    Bright as the sun   her eyes the gazers strike,
    And like the sun   they shine on all alike.
    Yet graceful ease   and sweetness void of pride
  Might hide her faults   if Belles had faults to hide.
    If to her share   some female errors fall,
    Look in her face   and you'll forget them all.

sort of a poet was he?"). The general scheme of verse is the same; but it is altered with marvellous ingenuity to suit the particular matter. It is an enormous confession, though one made quite safely to the immediate readers — who did not in the least apprehend it,—and perhaps even made unconsciously by the poet, that the double arrangement—the centred *crease*—of every line is largely given up. There are lines, and many of them, which have hardly more middle pause than in Shakespeare, save a fictitious one.[1] The *gradus* epithet and its antithetic use are not absent;[2] but they are rarer and subdued, as if purposely. Old rhetorical devices—epanaphora[3] especially—are brought in to heighten the style; to be "sources of the sublime," as Longinus says. The piece has always been something of a puzzle, and all the exertions of the commentator as to "Mrs. W." have not quite cleared that puzzle up. But it remains Pope's best serious thing, untinged by satire — for this last appears even in the *Dunciad* "curtain." And it would have been interesting to see whether, if he had made larger practice in the language of the heart, instead of that of the head and the spleen, he could have given yet further range and *timbre* to his poetic speech.

Eloisa to Abelard. It is only necessary to turn to the other piece which is sometimes coupled with it, *Eloisa to Abelard*, to see the return from the piano to the pianola. Here too, of course, old Mr. Pope would have been justified in saying "these are good rhymes," but perhaps nobody would be justified in saying much more. That the artificiality which is the curse of the couplet can be vanquished has just been admitted: it is proved not merely by the *Unfortunate Lady* and the *Dunciad*-close in Pope, but in

---

[1] And separate from these kindred dregs below
       .   .   .   .   .   .
    Thus, if Eternal justice rules the ball,

where there is even something like the abhorred and condemned pause at the first syllable!

[2] They are worst in the opening lines, where the poet has not warmed to his work.

[3] "By foreign hands" thrice repeated.

Johnson by the almost equally magnificent and much more certainly sincere termination of *The Vanity of Human Wishes* (where, however, there is a strong infusion of Dryden), by Tickell's splendid " Cadogan " epicede, and elsewhere. But it has always got to do everything that it knows to keep the art from being too obviously uppermost, and too suggestively exclusive. *Eloisa to Abelard*, though it is the best of its group, does not do this. Its last line—

> He best can paint 'em who can feel 'em most,

is unlucky in more than its apostrophes. The painting of the poem is admirable, but of the feeling it is impossible to say much ; and this extends to the most as well as to the least mechanical part of the execution. The undoubted truth, and still more undoubted *pointe*—

> All is not Heaven's when Abelard has part,

or

> Nor wish'd an Angel when I loved a Man—

the frequent tags from Dryden, which only bring out the difference of method, the " roseate bowers " and " trances ecstatic " and the rest—leave us sadly cold. It is very neat—very neat indeed ; but neatness is not exactly poetry.

The group, however—the *Eloisa* itself, *Sappho and Phaon*, and the Chaucerian attempts,—supplies a very interesting opportunity of comparison with Dryden's similar pieces, as illustrating the capacities of the two couplets for this kind of work. Many different judgments may, of course, result from such a comparison ; but there is one on which there should not be much controversy. Both forms admit the variety of subject in a remarkable manner ; but Dryden's does this by accommodating itself to them, Pope's by bringing them all under its own species. One can fully understand, though one may not share, the satisfaction which this latter process gives to those who think the particular couplet the highest of created things poetic ; but, without that premiss of

Interim comparison with Dryden.

feeling, one may prefer the way in which such exceedingly different things as *The Flower and the Leaf* and *Theodore and Honoria*, for instance, are rendered with almost a full representation of their difference, as compared with the rather too uniform interpretation of *Sappho and Phaon* on the one hand and *The House of Fame* on the other. Certainly the hall-mark is there ; but a hall-mark is required to certify something of which we cannot judge without it ; we had rather be left to our own hall-marking in matter of which we can judge.

Although it would be rather absurd to speak of the verse which has been surveyed as *juvenilia* — for Pope was never exactly juvenile, just as he was never at all senile—it may in a sense be all classed together, inasmuch as it is divided from the great achievement of the Moral Essays and Satires by the famous interval which the poet described (in his wontedly amiable manner both as to inclusion and omission of coadjutors) as

Pope translating ten long years with Broome

The *Homer.* (" Fenton with them," as it might be put legally). This interval is curiously parallel to that which Dryden experienced in no very different length of years, as a result of his dramatic avocation from poetry proper, between *Annus Mirabilis* and *Absalom and Achitophel.* The results corresponded to the character of the poets. Dryden, who had begun with infinite " body " and a quite new grip of verse, emerged from his *corvée* with roughnesses smoothed, but with the secret of variety unimpaired. Pope, who had begun by an imitative correctness, came out with increased and concentrated deftness of practice, but with something like a definite committal to one form of verse.[1]

It is, however, most interesting, and should supply a fresh evidence of Pope's craftsmanship, to find that though his thirteen years' practice in translation is in a sense a

---

[1] " Definite "—but, of course, not *absolute*. Enough of the old satiric freedom remains to enable him now and then to roughen his lines effectively. (For his own views on the couplet see note at end of chapter.)

"loop"—that though he comes back at the end of it to his old style like a giant refreshed, he has not been pursuing that style with slavish exactness or constancy inviolable meanwhile.   The fact is that, like a wise man, he evidently had consulted Dryden's translations afresh before he attempted his own, and that he to some extent recurs to the Drydenian model rather than to his own. He is, perhaps, rather more faithful; and this fidelity itself keeps out the antithetic *gradus* epithet—to some extent only.   In the same way, Homer does not so very frequently admit, and certainly never invites, the antithetic or "ridge-backed" division of the line itself.   On the other hand, he does invite the Alexandrine; and Pope finds this by no means "needless," and manages to make it by no means "slow."

Still, the whole medium, deft as it is, has much more monotony than Dryden's, and its peculiar character is almost sufficiently indicated by the well-known fact that there is really very little difference between the work of Pope's coadjutors and his own—a fact which ought to be taken in conjunction with the anticipations of Garth and Young, and the "tune by heart" of all the couplet-warblers of the rest of the century.   The Popian line is indeed so thoroughly "standardised"—its parts are, like those of a cheap watch, made so perfectly interchangeable, that in its mere prosodic influence there is hardly any secret effect left possible.   Had Pope chosen to use more such feet as that of which he recognised (or perhaps only half recognised) the beauty in "The freezing Tanais," to Johnson's equally illuminating astonishment,[1] the case would have been different.   But, as it is, it is hardly even a case of the well-known fiddle-and-rosin character.   The

---

[1] "I have been told that the couplet by which he declared his own ear to be most gratified was this—

"Lo where Mæotis sleeps, and hardly flows
The free|zing Tana|is through a waste of snows.

But the reason of this preference I cannot discover."—*Life of Pope.*

We can.   The vowel music is good; but it is the tribrach that does it.   At the same time I could wish that the *-is* were not repeated so correspondingly.

rosin as well as the fiddle is within the reach of Hoole as well as of Pope.   There is, of course, a difference, and a vast one, between Pope and Hoole ; but that wants a different simile.   The glass is the same glass almost exactly ; but the wine poured in is very different.

The quality of the wine which Pope poured out for his guests in the *Essays* and *Satires* is well known. People may call it amontillado or absinthe, vermouth or vitriol, as they like ; in fact, it, at different times, deserves well enough each of the four descriptions.   But we are here concerned with this wine only in connection with its glass.   It is certain (to drop the metaphor) that no other form of verse has ever been devised which would have suited the matter so well ; while there is no other example, in all literature, of a single metre (except perhaps the Lucretian hexameter) in such absolute adaptation to the temper and mood of the poet.   Pope may have lisped in numbers : he certainly thought in couplets.   Moreover, now that he was free from translation, he went back, naturally enough, to his own more special form, and brought that form closer and closer to its highest—or lowest—terms.   Here you may turn pages and pages without finding a triplet ; while the Alexandrine is never used unless for some very special purpose.   There is hardly such a thing as a rough, a loose, or a limping line. We think most naturally of the purple patches : the " Atticus " libel, written earlier no doubt, but polished and published now ; the *Dunciad* conclusion ; the scores of passages only less famous, and the hundreds or thousands of couplets, lines, or phrases, which are (or recently were) part of the language of every educated Englishman.   But this is in a way unjust ; for the difficulty—not quite the impossibility—would be to find anything that is not perfect according to its own standard of perfection.

Nor should it be forgotten that, narrow as that standard is, its conditions, both positive and negative, include some of very great prosodic value.   After the stress already laid in these volumes on the advantages of prosodic freedom, and on the special and immemorial privilege of English prosody in that respect, no more need be said on that side. But it must be remembered that this freedom, as in all cases, was dangerously likely to pass into a tolerance of anarchy. Anglo-Saxon prosody, to say the least, had not been remarkable for definitely metrical—that is to say, measured—rhythm.[1] The struggle to attain and maintain this, in the thirteenth and fifteenth centuries respectively, had not been a light or short one ; it had been well-nigh lost in the fifteenth, and in some respects rather jeopardised in the seventeenth itself. It was therefore none the worse, in the long-run, that for a time regularity, even of an excessive and meticulous kind, should be inculcated. The danger of this " entering into the soul "—which had been very great in the thirteenth century, and not slight in the sixteenth —was now past. The accumulated patterns of English verse included by this time examples of liberty and variety too great and too numerous. For a little while it could well be tolerated, as we see when we look back on the whole life of the subject, that bandage and bearing-rein should be applied. Even for the century of exuberance which was to follow, the preparation was probably of the greatest value ; while the results of that preparation itself in the middle or applied styles of poetry were such as no literature can afford to despise.

Pope's essays in metres other than the couplet are, it has been said, few and unimportant : they are certainly *Pope in other measures.* not worth dealing with elsewhere in connection with those metres themselves, and we may therefore best interpolate a paragraph before proceeding to notice the couplet in the hands of the rest of the school. It was impossible that any one of them should be exactly bad, prosodically speaking, but they were evidently written mainly as exercises and with no zest or gust. It is

---

[1] I say this in full knowledge of the elaborate and rather pathetic systems of "stresses" and "half-stresses," $\times$ *s* and *'s* and *'s* and the like, which have been devised to supply what is invisible and inaudible without them.

perfectly clear that the "St. Cecilia's Day" Ode would not have been written if Dryden had not written on the same theme before; and few will contest the superiority of the earlier master. Warton, indeed, exhibits one of the mistakes of the century when he stigmatises the attempts at triple time as "burlesque, low, and ridiculous"; but the poet is but ill at them, and obviously uncomfortable till he comes back to his decasyllables. Instead of the verse being fused, it is built; and that is fatal in lyric. Something of the same fault recurs elsewhere. The "Ode on Solitude" is not unmelodious, but "The Dying Christian" is still only cut-up couplet, as is "The Universal Prayer." The octosyllables deserve no special characterisation. The "Verses to Lady Frances Shirley," the "Challenge," the delectable "Song by a Person of Quality," and the famous "Lines on Lady Suffolk" are all the work of a consummate man of letters, who clothes the thing he is writing in the appropriate prosodic garb. But things nearly, if not quite as good, have, by taking the proper patterns, been written by men who had no pretensions to be poets at all in the sense in which Pope certainly *was* a poet; and things infinitely better have been written by some who were hardly as great poets as he.

After Pope.   Since the very qualities of this couplet make it more uniform the more it tends to perfection, it follows that while it is in that perfection it has little history. From Pope to Crabbe in time, and from Pope to Hoole in another scale of reckoning, it has few vicissitudes, and hardly more than one sectarian difference, as we may call it. This is, indeed, somewhat important, being a reaction in the hands of Churchill (or perhaps of Savage first), and after and from him in those of Cowper, to something more like the Drydenian model. But this is not encouraged by the theory, and still less by the practice, of Johnson, the dominant literary influence of the time, and it never becomes ruling or orthodox. It has, however, not a little influence in the unsettlement of the prosodic autocracy, which is the main feature of the period.   The couplet, like other autocrats, cannot afford to transact with liberty in any way : alone it has to make the happiness of its people.   As soon as they find other charmers, or as soon as it relaxes its chains, its day is done.

We must remember, however, that Johnson's two Johnson. short but remarkable couplet pieces were published, the one when Pope was still alive, the other when he had not long been dead.   Their author had, it need hardly be said, a great and just admiration for the earlier master of the couplet ; and with that unerring sense of kind which is one of the better features of Classicism, his Prologues, though with somewhat less licence, are Drydenian in stamp.   But the other form was certainly much more to his liking.

In *London* especially, the "splittable" form—which tempts one to treat it like those rolls they call *pistolets*, and bend it backwards into halves—is very frequent. Antithesis and balance, both in prose and verse, were such delights to Johnson that he was bound to prefer the form that supplied them most freely ; and besides, his general critical tendencies would always have led him to select the variety nearest to the apparent norm as the best.   Even in *London*, however, the *gradus* epithet does not make very great conquest of him ; though it does sometimes, as with

> Some *pleasing* bank where *verdant* osiers play,

and where one does not know whether the bank or the osier ought to blush most at its companion.   Usually, however, Johnson's vigour and fecundity of thought make this unnecessary ; and in the conclusion of *The Vanity of Human Wishes* he has reached one of the oftenest-quoted triumphs of the style.   It is curious how the dangers and temptations of that style are surmounted here.   Not a word is otiose in

> Must *dull suspense corrupt* the *stagnant* mind.

The contrasted colour and value [1] of

> Roll darkling down the torrent of his fate

might be the text of no short lesson in prosodic art. The middle-creased lines are varied and intermingled with straight-running ones, till the " fold " effect is wholly obliterated, and the piece has almost the virtue of a blank-verse paragraph—praise for which Johnson would not have been grateful. The *rise* of the rhythm is extraordinary ; and it is pleasant to see how the poet has resorted to the good old device of *epanaphora*—" For love " ; " For patience " ; " For faith " ; " These goods " ; " These goods "—in order to gain the upper levels of the air. And if the halved or folded verse makes its appearance once more at the end among these, it is all in the right way of the rhythm : the wings themselves are folding as the poem sinks to the rest and resignation that itself expresses.[2]

It is well known that Johnson actually " coached "

---

[1] The picture of the line is good : its resonance almost better. Notice how the dissyllables " darkling " and " torrent " not only correspond with each other, but adopt in a cross contrast, interesting to compare with Johnson's similarly adjusted contrasts of *meaning* in prose, the sounds of the monosyllables " roll " and " fate." The *a* of " darkling " is related (we will not say " exactly," in order not to excite a *querelle d'allemand* with the phoneticians, but) *generically* to that of " fate " as the *o* of " torrent " to that of " roll."

[2] Where then shall Hope and Fear their objects find ?
Must dull suspense corrupt the stagnant mind ?
Must helpless man, in ignorance sedate,
Roll darkling down the torrent of his fate ?
Must no dislike alarm, no wishes rise,
No cries invoke the mercies of the skies ?

.   .   .   .

Yet, when the sense of sacred presence fires
And strong devotion to the skies aspires,
Pour forth thy fervours for a healthful mind,
Obedient passions, and a will resigned ;
For love which scarce collective man can fill ;
For patience, sovereign o'er transmuted ill ;
For faith that, panting for a happier seat,
Counts death kind nature's signal of retreat.
These goods for man the laws of Heaven ordain,
These goods He grants who grants the power to gain ;
With these celestial Wisdom calms the mind,
And makes the happiness she does not find.

Goldsmith and Crabbe ; it is equally well known that Churchill and Cowper were rebels to his influence.   But all these and one or two others may follow him in this notice, which, in fact, need not be long ; for, except that they are by no means always " strong," Gyas and Cloanthus[1] themselves deserved no more individual mention than the average eighteenth-century coupleteer.

The couplet work of Thomson, Tickell, and one or two others, especially that of Young and Akenside, has been, or will be, incidentally mentioned ; but here, if anywhere, is the place to mention Savage.   I have very little respect for Savage as a poet ; and when he has been praised, I think he has generally been overpraised. But it is only fair to say that in his rambling, ill-conditioned, bombastic verses there is already something of that return to Dryden which, as has been said, is the most important fact, outside the actual achievements of Pope and Johnson, to be mentioned in this chapter. As Savage, we know, was a very careful proof-corrector, it must be supposed that he had some principles of correction ; and among them a more or less definite prosodic standard may have been one.   This standard in *The Wanderer* (which is as early as 1729), in *The Gentleman*, and other pieces, is not very different from Pope's.   But it is otherwise in *The Bastard*, which is probably Savage's sincerest poem, though it is impossible to say whether he had merely persuaded himself into sincerity.   The solidity of run, the absence of hinge and fold, which distinguishes Dryden, are to be found in the famous

> No tenth transmitter of a foolish face,

in

> His body independent as his soul,

in

> Warm championess for freedom's sacred cause.

Even when he balances, the balance has Dryden's, not Pope's, mark on it—

[margin: The partial return to Dryden.]

[margin: Savage.]

---

[1] But Gyas and Cloanthus pulled a good stroke in the regatta ; and so did some of these.

> Conceived in rapture, and with fire begot,

or

> Who most shall give applause where all admire ;

while sometimes, as in

> On that kind quarter thou invad'st me not,

the whole character of the line, in composition, rhythm, and phrase alike, is of the older, not the newer type.

Churchill. But Savage was a man of the seventeenth century, though of just its close. Churchill was more than a generation younger, and had he reached the statutory days of our life, would have actually seen the nineteenth. His partial desertion of Pope for Dryden as a model is itself part of a general *literariness*, which has perhaps never been quite sufficiently realised. Everybody who has written on him has seen that he studied his heroics from Dryden and Pope, his octosyllables from Butler and Swift. But I do not know whether anybody has noticed that much of his verse is a mere cento from these authors, from Shakespeare, and from others. If you were to print Churchill with the borrowed phrases in different inks, the page would look like a harlequin's coat. This was not plagiarism—the passages were generally known as a rule, and nobody could hope to escape detection in conveying them. Nor do I think that it was either barrenness or pure laziness. It was simply that Churchill (who, let it be remembered, was a very young man at his death) wrote in great haste, was full of his books, and so, being in a hurry, sent out his thought clothed in the wardrobe of his memory. It is probably, therefore, less by distinct design than because of the mixture of influences and origins that his verse comes to wear an older appearance than that of Pope, whom sometimes he follows close enough to give the work the air of imitation and even burlesque. Still, that this work, which was undoubtedly popular (as most work which is ill-natured and deals with current events and living characters is for a time), had an anti-Popian effect is indubitable ; and it had perhaps most of this on Cowper, his school-fellow and admirer. But before coming to Cowper we may say something of the " ruck " of the Pope school itself, of Goldsmith, and of Crabbe.

Pope is to such writers as Pitt of the Vida translation, of the *Virgil* which is not Dryden's, and other things, much what the other Pitt "was to Addington,"—as a capital to its suburbs. Indeed, much more also ; for suburbs sometimes have more character than the capital, and the Popelings certainly have not more character than Pope. Indeed, most of them have no character at all ; and one turns the pages of Chalmers without being able to hit on a single patch of colour—not in the sense of anything purple or splendid, but merely in that of something distinguished. They all have the prize-poem style : they are reeled off, sometimes very decently, but that is all. " How a thousand more ? " you say to the author ; and if you are wise, stroll on without making a bid.

Of course, there are exceptions ; and Goldsmith is Goldsmith. the chief of them. But then Goldsmith was a poet in his way, and he might, like his great friend's other friend, have said that he tried to be a coupleteer, but poetry was always breaking in. Moreover, as was said, that great friend certainly coached him—in *The Traveller* more particularly. Both it and *The Deserted Village* are studies prosodically curious in a minor way. *They* are like prize poems in which a poet should have written the piece (good-naturedly or mischievously) for a school-boy and kept within the model as well as he could. Much of the charm of the *Village* is due to Goldsmith's delightful style and his charming temper, which soften and humanise the rather icy glitter and contour of the couplet. The finer pieces in *The Traveller* are distinctly Johnsonian. On the whole, the two are among the most gilt-edged assets and securities of the couplet-stock—but——— !

Although Crabbe far outlived Cowper, and is, in fact, Crabbe. our main link of connection, biographically, with the next volume, his prosody is of a much older type than Cowper's, and should be despatched first. With hardly more than one important exception (the alternately rhymed octo-

syllables disposed in batches of four, or six, or eight, in
Sir Eustace Grey, The Hall of Justice, Woman, etc.), his
work, as known ever since his death, is in the heroic
couplet. These octosyllables resemble the work of
Mickle and one or two other late eighteenth-century
writers who were acquainted with Percy, and to some
extent (as Crabbe was certainly) with the Elizabethans ;
and who get out of the form a narrative medium, rather
jingly and cheap, but swift enough and by no means
ineffective. In particular, the octaves of *Sir Eustace
Grey,*[1] which are rhymed *ababbcbc* (the individual quatrains
reminding one strikingly of Mickle's *Cumnor Hall*), contain Crabbe's most imaginative work ; but this piece
was written well within the nineteenth century. It is
particularly noticeable for the boldness of enjambment,
not merely between line and line, but between the halves
of the stanza ; while a further licence, which would have
shocked Crabbe's earlier contemporaries, is taken in
extending the two first stanzas, to a dixain and a nine-
lined stave, by extra lines differently rhymed in the two
examples. Probably, as the subject of the piece is a
madman, Crabbe either permitted himself˙ or infinitely
aimed at a corresponding irregularity.

The heroics. There is nothing of the kind in his voluminous heroics,
where the prosody, perhaps as much as anything else,
procured him the famous, if rather unjust, label of " Pope
in worsted stockings." Johnson, as it happens, was
fond, we know, of these latter garments in the non-

*Sir Eustace
Grey,* etc.

[1] He used this form also in *The World of Dreams,* which is not very
dissimilar in subject. Of course, in noticing this form and the couplet I do
not mean to imply that Crabbe used no others. On the contrary, both in
his previously known *Juvenilia* and other miscellanies, and in the new work
which has been made accessible by the Master of Peterhouse's valuable edition
(3 vols., Cambridge, 1905-7), there is a fairly large variety ; but nothing
requires special *prosodic* notice, except, perhaps, the curious combination of
metres in the unfinished " Tracy," which starts with rather un-Spenserian
Spenserians, has a couplet body, and a rhyme-royal tail. Bysshe and
Johnson would have shaken their heads at this unequal yoking of the elect
couplet and the uncircumcised stanzas. Some would assign to Dryden a
larger influence, in respect of couplet, over Crabbe than may seem to be
admitted here. It undoubtedly exists, especially in his better passages, but
not, I think, to the same extent as Pope's generally. He does, however,
use the Alexandrine with some freedom.

metaphorical sense ; and Crabbe took his Pope to some extent prosodically through Johnson. The actual revising of *The Village* could hardly fail to leave its mark, as in the case of Goldsmith ; but the influence and principles of Johnson impressed themselves so widely, in the impalpable fashion to which we have often drawn attention, that the mere drilling, in the case of one poem, was not probably the whole source of resemblance. When Crabbe is in his trivial moods, so happily and hardly to excess parodied in *Rejected Addresses*, the Popian and Johnsonian antithesis brings out the triviality. When he is more weighty the Johnsonian emphasis helps to communicate the weight. In his few finest passages—that splendid autumn picture in "Delay has Danger," which has united the mightiest suffrages, and others—he does not alter the form of the couplet much. But the crease-arrangement which has just achieved the unpardonable distich—

> We saw my Lord, and Lady Jane was there,
> And said to Johnson : "Johnson, take a chair,"

positively lends itself to the added strokes of gloom and failure. Not merely the lines, but the half-lines, cumulate and amplify the effect like fresh weights piled on a sufferer under the *peine forte et dure*.[1] But, except at such

---

[1] Early he rose, and looked with many a sigh
On the red light that filled the eastern sky ;
Oft had he stood before, alert and gay,
To hail the glories of the new-born day :
But now dejected, languid, listless, low,
He saw the wind upon the water blow,
And the cold stream curled onward as the gale
From the pine hill blew harshly down the dale ;
On the right side the youth a wood surveyed,
With all its dark intensity of shade ;
Where the rough wind alone was heard to move,
In this, the pause of nature and of love,
When now the young are reared, and when the old,
Lost to the tie grow negligent and cold—
Far to the left he saw the huts of men,
Half hid in mist, that hung upon the fen ;
Before him swallows gathering for the sea,
Took their shotr flights and twittered on the lea ;

major moments, it must be owned that the correspondence
of the ribs of the worsted stockings is rather irritating
and painfully suggestive of machine-weaving.[1]

Cowper. His early poems. With Cowper it is different, and the difference is
highly interesting, though his couplet work contains
nothing so good as his best things in other metres, and
indeed nothing that can vie with the astonishing description just quoted from Crabbe.   The few examples in the
early poems—which, it has specially to be remembered,
were all composed before, and some much before, 1763—
the " Lines written in a fit of Illness," and those on the
" Death of Sir William Russell," give us absolutely
nothing distinctive : they are fairly smooth and even
fairly. vigorous examples of the common type, and that
is all.   But when, nearly twenty years later, he issued
the volume of 1782, the major part of which consists
of couplet poems, a considerable difference is apparent.
It is quite plain that he has studied Churchill, who was
his school-fellow, whose short career had come to an end
during Cowper's own period of eclipse, and whom he
praises elaborately, but not uncritically, in one of these
very poems.   His own ear, however, was far too fine,
and his scholarship too considerable, to imitate or not
to deplore Churchill's " careless mood " in " striking the
lyre."   But he, like Churchill, shows many traces of
recurrence to Dryden ; he is rebel to the Johnsonian
influence which steered back to Pope.   Nor is it improbable that two other causes worked powerfully—his
intense interest in his subjects, which made it impossible

And near the bean-sheaf stood, the harvest done,
And slowly blackened in the sickly sun ;
All these were sad in nature, or they took
Sadness from him, the likeness of his look,
And of his mind—he pondered for a while,
Then met his Fanny with a borrowed smile.

[1] It is curious that the very early *Inebriety*, though, naturally enough, a
pastiche to some extent, has rather more spring and vigour than the later
work.   And even in that later work Crabbe, who had an odd kind of
humour, may be allowed the benefit of intentional mock-heroic sometimes ;
as perhaps in the " Lady Jane " distich itself.   For the blank verse of *Midnight* see next chapter.

for him to write a mere " copy of verses," and that secret *nisus* towards blank verse which was fortunately to display itself later.

At any rate, these couplet-poems, though the very subjects that interested him have come to tell against them now, and though his unpractical and worse than academic treatment of them has helped to make the division the least readable part of his work, have interest for us. *Table Talk* would seem to have meant to keep *Table Talk,* fairly close to Pope : it has the dialogue form that he etc. affects ; and there are other Popian vestiges. But strange new cadences—

> In honour's field advancing *his firm foot*—

meet us almost at once. The couplet seems to be straining at enjambment ; and the line, as in

> The fleeting forms of majesty engage
> Respect,

does not hesitate to break the restraint. Independently of the division necessitated by the interlocution, the whole structure tends to the paragraphic ; and the conversational form itself forces the pause into very exceptional places. It is even in one instance [1] (followed, as it happens, by an Alexandrine) (l. 308) at the first syllable, though there is a secondary pause at the fifth, as if by way of apology. And just before [2] there has been one at the second, without anything after it to break the current of the line. There is an actual " prosodist " passage in this *Table Talk* where for some forty or fifty lines (500-550) the writer sneers at " creamy smoothness," at

> The clockwork tintinnabulum of rhyme ;

while a little later comes the universally known sentence on Pope—

---

[1] No.   His high mettle, under good control,
  Gives him Olympic speed and shoots him to the goal.
(Note the Alexandrine.)

[2] Agreed.   But would you sell or slay your horse?

> But he (his musical finesse was such,
> So nice his ear, so delicate his touch)
> Made poetry a mere mechanic art,
> And every warbler has his tune by heart ;

which may be almost called the " notice to quit " of the couplet in this form.

But he who lodged it did not at once observe it for himself, and *The Progress of Error, Truth,* and the rest all employ the same medium—a couplet which in the main follows, but frets at and occasionally half kicks over, the rules of " smoothness," at which it has been mocking. Sometimes he comes closer to Pope, or at least to Young, who has a certain premonition of Cowper in many ways. Sometimes he goes back to the Alexandrine, as just now noticed, or at *Expostulation,* l. 499—

> And while the victim slowly bled to death,
> Upon the tolling chords rung out his dying breath,

where the principle which Johnson criticised as laid down and put in practice by Cowley, is evidently followed once more.

Tirocinium. Of his later returns to the style, which he so fortunately deserted in *The Task,* the most important is, of course, *Tirocinium,* where it was well in place. There is absolutely no such vehicle for regular satire—satire which is not merely playful but which means business, which intends to " burn, sink, and destroy," if it can —as the couplet. Both—all four, if we join Young and Churchill to Dryden and Pope—of Cowper's masters had shown that to demonstration ; and he proved himself one of the aptest of their pupils. One-sided and excessive as the piece may be in thought and purpose, it is, as satire, not much the worse for that ; and in form it is quite excellent. In fact, it is by far Cowper's best piece in the couplet for craftsmanship and adaptation of means to ends.

Yet we must not forget " My Mother's Picture," where, with true poetic power, he manages to make this vehicle, if not exactly a " bauble coach," a carriage for something

very different from satire ; or " The Needless Alarm,"
and others in which he brings out its capacities for
playfulness. " Anti-Thelypthora," though it has pained
some good people, is unexceptionable as heroi-comic verse
—in fact, it is in parts not inferior to Canning's " New
Morality" from this point of view. " The Colubriad "
is pure burlesque, and very excellent burlesque ; but
though burlesque certainly is sometimes a form of dis-
sembling love, it was by no means the form that the
couplet wanted at this particular time. There was no
danger to blank verse in the " Lines to the Immortal
Memory of the Halibut," for blank verse was young and
strong. There was a good deal in " The Colubriad," for the
couplet was old and could not stand being unceremoniously
handled—all the more so that it had been handled with
rather too much ceremony. Once more, all Cowper's
dealings in different ways with couplet are " notices to
quit "—except in its satiric divisions, and in some even
of these. Even in " My Mother's Picture " one cannot
help feeling how much better blank verse, or stanza,
would have suited the occasion.[1]

---

[1] This chapter is so dominated by Pope that it may be better to give
here, rather than with the " Prosodists," his views of couplet scansion as
contained in the " letter to Cromwell " (1710), already cited *sup.* (p.
392) :—
    " 1. As to the hiatus, it is certainly to be avoided as often as possible ;
but on the other hand, since the reason of it is only for the sake of the
numbers, so if, to avoid it, we incur another fault against their smoothness,
methinks the very end of that nicety is destroyed : as when we say for
instance,
            But th' old have int'rest ever in their view,
to avoid the hiatus in
            The old have int'rest.

Does not the ear in this place tell us, that the hiatus is smoother, less con-
strained, and so preferable to the cæsura ?
    " 2. I would except against all expletives in verse, as *do* before verbs
plural, or even too frequent use of *did* or *does*, to change the termination of
the rhyme ; all these being against the usual manner of speech, and mere
fillers-up of unnecessary syllables.
    " 3. Monosyllabic lines, unless very artfully managed, are stiff, languish-
ing, and hard.
    " 4. The repeating of the same rhymes within four or six lines of each
other, which tire the ear with too much of the like sound.
    " 5. The too frequent use of Alexandrines, which are never graceful but

when there is some majesty added to the verse by them, or where there cannot be found a word in them but what is absolutely needful.

"6. Every nice ear must, I believe, have observed that in any smooth English verse of ten syllables, there is naturally a pause either at the fourth, fifth, or sixth syllables ; as for example, Waller :—

> At the fifth :   Where-e'er thy navy | spreads her canvas wings.
> At the fourth : Homage to thee | and peace to all she brings.
> At the sixth :   Like tracks of leverets | in morning snow.

Now I fancy, that to preserve an exact harmony and variety, none of these pauses should be continued above three lines together, without the interposition of another ; else it will be apt to weary the ear with one continued tone—at least it does mine.

"7. It is not enough that nothing offends the ear, that the verse be, as the French call it, *coulant* ; but a good poet will adapt the very sounds, as well as words, to the things he treats of. So that there is, if one may express it so, a style of sound ; as in describing a gliding stream, the numbers should run easy and flowing ; in describing a rough torrent or deluge, sonorous and swelling ; and so of the rest."

CHAPTER II

BLANK VERSE AFTER MILTON

The meaning of "after"—Roscommon—John Philips—Broome and Fenton—Addison, Watts, and others—Gay and Prior—Thomson—Somerville—Armstrong—Young—Digression on dramatic blanks—Southerne—Congreve, Rowe, and Addison—Exaltation of the soliloquy—Return to *Night Thoughts*—Akenside—Blair—Glover—Cowper—Early blank verse—*The Task*—*Yardley Oak.*

The meaning of "after."

THE present chapter is one of those where convenience requires, and real symmetry does not forbid, that we should double back a little from the main stage of our Book. But its title contains, in a double sense, the justification of this proceeding. All non-dramatic blank verse that follows the death of the author of *Paradise Lost* is "after him" in the two senses—posterior to him, and imitated, as best the imitator might, from him. The remarkable effort of Thomson himself does not escape this description, though it furnished, not an independent, but an additional and slightly altered model. From these two, and thus from the one, descends all blank non-dramatic verse—of dramatic blanks we may speak later—till quite the close of the eighteenth century. It is a sign of the comparative paralysis of poetry during this century that no one seems to have thought—Young is the only possible exception, and we shall deal with him presently—of adapting afresh from Shakespeare and others, and moulding a non-dramatic form different from Milton's.[1]

[1] In fact, most of the early eighteenth-century pieces in the metre are

The idea that Addison's criticism was necessary before Milton could be "got read," as Mr. Carlyle used to say, has been, or ought to have been, long ago dispelled ; but it is certain that people were not in a hurry to imitate him.   The exception which in the fullest sense proves the Roscommon. rule here is that of Roscommon.   Not only did that ingenious earl translate the *Ars Poetica* into blank verse ; but he shocked precisians by inserting, at the end of his much more famous *Essay on Translated Verse*, a solid block of blanks, very oddly paraphrased or abstracted from the Sixth Book of *Paradise Lost* itself.   This is a sort of Miltonic cento.   The Horatian piece very properly avoids all imitations of the Miltonic style, which could not but have had the effect of sheer burlesque.   But as blank verse it betrays no grasp, on its author's part, of Milton's real secrets—pause-variation, line-composition, and architectonic of the lines when composed.   It is, indeed, a strong justification of the use of that couplet which its writer had employed, but discountenanced, for didactic purposes.   Roscommon, in fact, falls back on the old " single-mould " line before Shakespeare,[1] and as he has not, and could not with propriety have had, the magnificence of diction which lightens that mould in the University Wits, the effect is not exhilarating.   This kind of thing, for instance, will give the enemy of blanks plentiful opportunity to blaspheme—

> Quintilius, if his advice were asked,
> Would freely tell you what you should correct,
> Or if you could not, bid you blot it out,
> And with more care supply the vacancy.

What is the advantage (except perhaps that it is rather easier learnt by heart) of this over, " If Quintilius were asked his advice he would freely tell you what you should

---

formally described not as " in blank verse," but " in the manner of Milton." The chief exercise of the other kind, apart from actual drama, that I remember is Dr. Ibbot's *Fit of the Spleen* in the fifth volume of Dodsley.   If this was the Ibbot who died in 1725, it is interesting as being early, and has the additional interest of being wonderfully bad ; but it has no other.

[1] The presence of this mould may be traced further in the blank-verses of the eighteenth century right onward to Cowper, and sometimes in him.

correct ; or if you could not, would bid you blot it out,
and supply the vacancy with more care " ?   The heroic
has nothing to fear from a competitor like this, and one
ceases to wonder at the frequent assertion or insinuation
throughout the succeeding century, that there is little
difference between blank verse and prose.   In the actual
extract, as will be seen, there is *none*, except slight
inversions of order, and an ellipsis or two.

In fact, there was some excuse for the idea which John Philips.
evidently prevailed, that, except for dramatic purposes,
the fortunes of blank verse were practically bound up
with Milton's gorgeous diction, his peculiar syntax, and
his various mannerisms.   The next attempt to practise in
it was—perhaps less oddly than it may seem at first sight
—made by way *both* of parody and of serious following.
Less than twenty years after Roscommon's, and thirty
after Milton's death—a year or two only after Dryden's—
John Philips, a young Christ Church man, delighted first
Oxford and then London with *The Splendid Shilling.*
The piece is certainly good, and, like all good parodies of
good things, rather recommends than discredits the form
that it burlesques ; but it is puzzling to observe the
particular direction of the applause towards its novelty in
kind.   Even Johnson accords it " the uncommon merit of
an original design."   But this is not our business.   It is
certain that Philips was one of the numerous and not
ungenerous tribe who never make fun of anything with so
much zest as of the things they love ; for he stuck to
blank verse in both his serious poems—*Blenheim* and
Cider.   For the bombast and the absurd pseudo-classical
machinery and mannerism of the first, he has been
severely and in part deservedly, but perhaps excessively,
blamed by Macaulay and others.   *Cider* is far better.   If
such things as Georgics are to be done in verse at all, it
establishes blanks as an excellent vehicle for them ; and
as for form, there is no doubt that it is right to regard
Philips as a predecessor, and probably a preceptor, of
Thomson.

In the parody, however, inevitably and to some extent

legitimately—in the serious poems less legitimately, but more damagingly,—the defects of mere imitation, and of going to Milton instead of to Shakespeare for pattern, are apparent.   The omission of articles and possessive pronouns ; inversion, apposition, the arrangement of two parallel phrases in the same line with epithet preceding in the first and following in the second, or *vice versa,*— these things and others are naturally exaggerated.   Yet the very exaggeration must have drawn attention to the style, and to the medium generally.   And it is extremely well worth noting that in the encomiastic fragment printed by Johnson, from the pen of Edmund ["Rag"] Smith, that eccentric and rather ne'er-do-well, but very clever and scholarly friend of Addison and Philips himself, describes this style as "very particular, because he writes in blank verse and lays aside rhyme."   So that, at the beginning of the reign of Anne, to lay aside rhyme and write blank verse was still "very particular."

Broome and   There is no reason to doubt that Philips's own work,
Fenton.   both comic and serious, did something to diminish that "particularity" ; but there can be no doubt likewise that Addison's criticism of Milton, when it came, did even more to dispel the notion that blank verse was "too low for a poem, nay for a paper of verses," and that its sole justification, even for drama, was its similarity to prose. Further, it seems, to me at least, that the sense, unconscious it may be, of the oppression and obsession of the couplet, which was forcing some to the octosyllable and the anapæst, would necessarily force others to blank verse. Before the century saw the end of its third decade— indeed, when it had scarcely completed its first quarter— the measure was further relieved of the sense of not being "proved" which still rested on it.   By an odd, but quite comprehensible and much more than coincident coincidence, both Pope's coadjutors in the great couplet venture of that first quarter—the translation of Homer— relieved or consoled themselves with blanks.   Broome, at a time which I have not identified, did part of the Tenth Book of the *Iliad* "in the style of Milton."   Fenton,

probably much earlier, paraphrased the 14th chapter
of Isaiah in the metre, and did " in Milton's style " the
Eleventh Book of the *Odyssey*.   In none of these attempts
is there much merit ; but they are attempts.

But besides, and between, these larger ventures there are
small ones of which notice should be taken.   The exact
date of Addison's translation of part of the Third *Æneid*
in imitation of Milton is not, I think, known.   But from
its order in his poems, it should come somewhere between
1701 and 1705, which would be a probable enough date ;
for though it might be earlier it could hardly be later.
It is not good.   Not only has he not succeeded in
catching, or even it would seem in comprehending,
Milton's texture of verse, but even single lines are rarely
Miltonic, and the imitation is chiefly confined to borrow-
ings, or not very clever imitations, of phrase.   The piece
could hardly have encouraged others to follow it.   In
Watts's remarkable *Horæ Lyricæ* (see next chapter) there
are several blank-verse pieces, one of them dated 1701.
Some may be even earlier ; while the whole collection
was published in 1706, when one of its complimentary
introducers, Mr. Joseph Standen, had the audacity to
make the same experiment.   Watts is happier with the
measure than Addison ; and Standen has caught something (whether from Milton direct or from Watts, it is
difficult to say) which we do not meet commonly elsewhere.   In fact, I am not sure that the passage of Standen
given below[1] is not better than anything else in the
measure before Thomson, though Watts's " To Sarissa " is
a little more artful and various.   That he had not reached
the root of the matter, however, is shown by his finishing
one of his verse paragraphs with a redundant syllable.

Addison, Watts, and others.

[1] Amazed, we view
The towering height stupendous, while thou soar'st
Above the reach of vulgar eyes or thought,
Hymning the Eternal Father : as of old,
When first the Almighty from the dark abyss
Of everlasting night and silence called
The shining worlds with one creating word,
And raised from nothing all the heavenly hosts,
And with external glories filled the void.

In any case, these various attempts, though serious and not unimportant as symptoms, are mere " copies of verses," obviously tentative. And Gay's *Wine*, 1708, though a substantive poem, is not of great substance. As Mr. Austin Dobson (I think quite correctly) says, it suggests Philips rather than Milton as its direct inspirer in more than the title. But perhaps the most curious of all are the blank-verse experiments of Prior in the recently printed [1] Longleat Poems. To speak frankly, they are curiously *bad*—full of redundancy, although narrative ; full of gasping and unrhythmical movement. But he never published them, and we do not know their date. If, as the company in which they are found suggests, they are late, he was evidently trying on dramatic models (and not good ones) rather than on narrative. But it is scarcely fair to comment unfavourably on mere *brouillons*. He had, however, finished and published, in not dissimilar but less chaotic blanks, two translations of Callimachus which have, I believe, found favour with some good wits. I cannot like them ; the very first line—

> When we to Jove select the holy vic*tim*

has an awkward stumbling effect which is constantly repeated ; and Prior commits the fault (largely followed, as we shall see) of converting his Miltonic *pauses* into abrupt *stops*, which break down the line instead of merely keeping it in measure variously weighted. I sometimes think he meant, but did not dare, hendecasyllables throughout —and that he had better have dared them.

It was very different with the poem which James Thomson, after difficulties, got published in 1726, and which was completed in the course of the next few years. *Winter* and its sister *Seasons* not merely established blank verse, as Prior and Swift had established the octosyllable, and as the first of these had at least established the anapæst, but did more. They practically introduced a new form of the metre that they established. Thomson's is not, as all previous blank verse since Milton had been,

(marginal note: Gay and Prior.)

(marginal note: Thomson.)

---

[1] Ed. Waller, Cambridge, 1907.

more or less direct *imitation* of Milton : new elements and features, some good, some not so good, make their appearance. In fact, Thomson deserves to rank in the genealogy of non-dramatic blank verse between Milton and Tennyson. Of course, he does not achieve, or attempt, any absolute independence of his great exemplar. He could not have achieved, and he was too wise to attempt. A little even remains of the " corrupt " following of Milton which Philips and the others display.   Thomson's finer sense avoided, for the most part, excessive discarding of articles and particles, prodigal apposition, and even to some extent, though to a less, persistent inversion and " geometrical " disposition of phrase. But he kept, and even (though in a new fashion) exaggerated, the Miltonic buckram and affectation; while he had not the Miltonic fire to warm and lighten these things. But Thomson was really a person of prosodic genius——his double record with blank verse and the Spenserian proves this,——and he succeeded in new-moulding the measure in a way which Smith might have again called " very particular," and which nearly all eighteenth-century writers of it followed. In one very important respect he, indeed, comes short ; and that is the management of the verse-paragraph. It is not that he wishes to neglect it : quite the contrary. Typographically, he is very careful of his paragraph ; and, what is more, he has invented a peculiar mannerism of his own to distinguish and mark it off otherwise than typographically, in the shape of the curious end catch-lines more or less identical in form, which every tolerably careful reader of the *Seasons* must have noticed.[1]   But he is not able, as Milton had been and as Tennyson was to be, to modulate the whole music of a paragraph into a perfect symphony, and to make the reader feel that its prosodic career ends exactly with the career of the thought.

---

[1] And Egypt joys beneath the spreading wave.

And Mecca saddens at the long delay.
    etc.   etc.   etc.

Nor could he arrange these symphonies with the same gorgeous accompaniment of proper-name sound.   But, on the other hand, he is a much more definitely pictorial poet than Milton ; and he makes the structure of his paragraphs prosodically subservient to his pictures with no little skill.   The lines are touches ; they build up the subject to eye, if not to ear, and in order to do this, something more than the mere " brick-upon-brick " of the common blank verse was wanted.   Thomson is particularly fond of that kind of enjambment which consists in multiplying full stops and colons in the middle of lines ; [1] and he has borrowed, from Spenser rather than from Milton, the device of linking one paragraph to another with a " turn of words."   He likes to throw up his verse with a monosyllable of some weight and strength at the end ; and he utilises prosodically the exacter nature-painting which in general poetic history is his glory, by putting the distinctive words for colour and shape in notable places of the verse, so as to give it character and quality.   Even his rather too distinct " poetic diction," his fondness for the forms in y, for heavy Latinisms and the like, are definitely defensible as expedients to get blank verse out of the old reproach of being measured prose.

(Johnson, therefore, was at least sufficiently justified—he usually was, save when some special disqualification was present—when he said, " His numbers, his pauses, his diction, are of his own growth " ; and the reference to pauses shows, among a thousand other things, what a critic Johnson was when he would let himself be.   There is nothing more characteristic of Thomson's blank verse than its peculiarly broken character.[2]   The breakages are not such as cause roughness, but such as hinder continuity. All good verse is serpentine ; but Thomson's serpents are rather like those very excellent ones which are compounded

---

[1] Nor does he *break* the verse quite so much by these as Prior had done before, and as Glover was to do after him.

[2] In the well-known picture of the Advent of the Rain in *Spring*, there are *four* full stops in mid-line out of *six* lines ; in the Harvest Storm (*Autumn*), *six* semicolons, heavily paused, towards the middle of *ten* consecutive lines.

(for the use of childhood) of a large number of sections artfully strung together. His lines and sections of lines are not interfluent, but conjoined : the resulting structure is a sort of mosaic. This, with his peculiar diction, is the source of the artificiality which for the last century or so has been charged against him ; and there is a modicum of truth in the charge. But it is extremely probable that these brilliant bits of verse—these tesselations of marble of divers colours, if not of positive gem-substance—did a great deal to reconcile his readers to the absence of the rhyme-stroke and flash ; while there is no doubt either, that the style also suited what his frank but friendly critic (who tried to read *Liberty* when it appeared, and never tried again) characteristically calls his "enumeration of circumstantial varieties." Yet even in *Liberty*—false, frigid, hollow, pedantic, sciolist as it is—such passages as the well-known one on the Retreat of the Ten Thousand justify the unusual mercy which Johnson shows to this blank verse.

But, though undoubtedly Thomson's horsemanship, to vary the metaphor, savours for our modern taste rather too much of the *manège*—though he owes the bit more than is perhaps consistent with absolutely perfect riding, —this is not quite invariable with him. There are passages, and a good number of them, where, if he does not exactly throw rein on neck, he never makes the curb ostentatiously felt ; and these constitute a very agreeable set-off to, and relaxation from, his more artificial style. Nay, more—and it is in this that his merit very largely consists,—he knows how to interpose fluent and unchecked lines in the very passages where break and check are generally prominent.

If it be said that even these reliefs from artificiality are not quite artless enough, the objection, though a little ungracious, cannot be met with a blank denial. It may, however, be demurred to as excessive, and it may be met, most successfully of all, by a consideration of the reasons and the circumstances. It must be remembered that it was Thomson's mission—a mission which, let it be also remembered, he achieved, though perhaps, as so often, unconsciously enough—to refashion blank verse so that it might assist, in the graver and severer regions of poetry, the efforts which the octosyllable and the anapæst were making against the inordinate and exclusive domination of the heroic couplet. For this purpose the pure Miltonic model, which had hitherto been followed, was clearly insufficient. To begin with, it required a Milton to manage it ; and anybody who endeavoured to do so was but too likely, whether he meant it or not, to slip into a caricature of a Milton. Again, it was almost necessarily bound up with the Miltonic diction, which was by this time in parts obsolete. And for a third remark, it might not unjustly be pronounced, like the first project of Tennyson's *Princess*, too "grand, epic, homicidal" for the semi-pedestrian didactics and descriptions which the time wanted.

On the other hand, there was the danger, not only of the meanness and lowness which had long attached itself to the very idea of blank verse, but (not to adopt quite such derogatory language) of the flatness and prosaic quality which Roscommon, its first post-Miltonic practitioner, had actually displayed. On this side it was as much in need of raising, varying, decorating, as on the Miltonic side it was of humanising and adapting to miscellaneous needs. And all this had to be done with due regard to eighteenth-century notions about poetic diction, dignity, decency, and the rest of it.

That Thomson was immensely assisted by his nature-studies, by the interest which his landscape-painting enabled him to offer to his readers so as to make them forget the absence of their usual douceur or bonus, rhyme, is undeniable. But this should not make us disregard the technical skill which he showed in beating out, and throwing into system, the peculiar music of his verse. His natural gift for this—a gift which in other times might have made him one of the greatest of verse-smiths —is, as has been said, shown in his Spenserians, which, of all the numerous imitations of Spenser which amused their writers and annoyed Johnson at this time, are simply the only ones that come near the motion and the music of that Pactolus-Mæander, the Spenserian river of song.   The fingering of the stanza, in the First Part of the *Castle of Indolence* especially, is nearly faultless : it is the inferiority of the lexicon that, whenever the subject admits of it, prevents Thomson from coming quite close to his master.   Nay, there are a few places where he is actually not far off.[1]   Other measures he hardly tried ; and in his few lyrics the curse of the century, which we shall notice more particularly in the next chapter, was much on him, especially in that matter of diction.   Yet the opening verse of " Tell me, thou soul of her I love " could not easily be better in its own way, and approaches a way better than its own.   His heroics are undistinguished ; but a man can hardly be expected to distinguish himself in a style which he deliberately declines.   And, in fact, he needs no ekings from these minor performances. The Spenserian imitation of the *Castle of Indolence* would have been a very great prosodic achievement had it stood alone, and it is still greater as showing up, and contrasting with, the more independent variation on Milton in the blank verse.   But that blank verse itself, if it has not given us his very best poetry, is certainly his main prosodic title-deed.   It is great in performance, and greater still in example.   The colour-passage[2] in the Newton poem in particular must have been, to every poet of that time and immediately afterwards, who read

---

[1] Especially, of course, the great " Shepherd of the Hebrid Isles," but also others.

[2] First the flaming red
Sprung vivid forth ; the tawny orange next ;
And next delicious yellow ; by whose side
Fell the kind beams of all-refreshing green.
Then the pure blue that swells autumnal skies,
Etherial played, and then of sadder hue
Emerged the deepened indigo (as when
The heavy-skirted evening droops with frost),
While the last gleamings of refracted light
Died in the fainting violet away.

No bad paint-pot to " chuck in the face of the public " when that public is besotted with *drab* !

it with eyes to see, a casket of jewels much richer than itself, with the key in the lock. The somewhat too high stepping pace could easily be modulated ; the somewhat formal and even rigid diction could in due time be suppled and simplified. But here once more was an important metre got ready for various poetic uses ; and for this we say " O " to Jemmy Thomson, not in the manner of the scoffer at *Sophonisba*, but in that of Man Friday—who came into the world just seven years before *Winter* made its appearance.

Thomson, when the subject of cider came up in *Autumn*, made a not unnatural reference to Philips as the second

> Who nobly durst, in rhyme-unfettered verse,
> With British freedom sing the British song,

thereby ignoring Roscommon, but suggesting, not too officiously, himself as the third. But his own example soon made the keeping of numbered order impossible and superfluous. In little more than a decade from the completion of the *Seasons*, three verse-writers obtained, by dint of blank verse, a permanent place in the history of English poetry, and a fairly prolonged hold on the attention of English readers. These were Somerville, Armstrong, and Young.[1] Those who look only at the dates of *The Chase, The Art of Preserving Health*, and the *Night Thoughts*, may think my order incorrect. But Armstrong had adopted the measure in that early and eccentric effort of his which, as Chalmers observes with exquisite decency, has " very properly been excluded from every collection of poetry," and which remains as an example, not, it would seem, of Rabelaisian naughtiness, not of catchpenny rascality, but of that strange

---

[1] Mallet was, of course, earlier still, with his *Excursion* (1728) and his *Amyntor and Theodora*. But the association of this much-abused person with Thomson was so intimate, and his blank verse is so clearly *calqué* on his friend's, that it does not require much notice. The interest of the problem whether he or Thomson wrote *Rule Britannia* is hardly prosodic. The body of that famous piece has no great prosodic distinction, and the effective contrast of its chorus is due to the music.

mixture of solid perverseness and partial want of humour which marked and marred the career of a man who was Thomson's cherished friend in his youth, and whom the Burney girls liked in his age.

Somerville has left a great deal of work in other Somerville. metres besides blank verse ; but little of it is of any value, save in so far as it displays a certain knack of adaptation to *any* metre—heroic or Pindaric, Hudibrastic as improved by Swift and Prior (in this last he is very copious), or some of the easier lyric measures.   His comparative earliness in the blank-verse field gives him more interest here ; though Johnson would not, as in Thomson's case, suspend his implacable enmity to the form, and lays down the law that " if blank verse be not tumid and gorgeous it is crippled prose."

His blank-verse poems are three—*The Chase* itself ; the short supplement of *Field Sports*, which deals with falconry mainly ; and the burlesque *Hobbinol*, which particularly displeased the great lexicographer.   The latter, indeed, shows his usual judgment in putting his finger on the excellence of shortness in the *Splendid Shilling*.   Perhaps he did not see, or, seeing, resented the fact, that his own " tumid and gorgeous " prescription constantly lends itself to burlesque.   In fact, in this transition stage of blank verse one is never absolutely certain whether the writers are writing seriously or not.   As was observed above, there are passages of *Blenheim* and others of *Cider* which read to us nearly as much like burlesque as the *Shilling* itself.   Thomson, with all his art, is constantly coasting the danger : of Armstrong and others we may speak shortly.   *The Chase*, however, escapes this danger fairly. The subject is as well suited to the treatment as a great part of Thomson's is, and the writer, who duly acknowledges Thomson's precedence, has very fairly assimilated his method.   Indeed, in his opening he has followed Thomson's " broken style," to Johnson's displeasure—

> The Chase I sing ; Hounds and the various breed,
> And no less various use.   O thou great Prince, etc.

Johnson thought these "bad," being no doubt disgusted at the trochee after the first pause.[1]

Armstrong.

But Somerville, at least, never actually caricatured this style except when he meant to do so. Whether as much can be said of Armstrong is not certain.[2] The subject of his tabooed poem is so essentially heroi-comic that the amount of intentional burlesque in it is quite impossible to decide. But there is at least no probability that he meant any in *The Art of Preserving Health*, though he certainly seems to us to have achieved it. In diction, at any rate, the famous "gelid cistern," and other things, are at once the evidence and the obloquy of the "tumid and gorgeous" conception of blank-verse style, while in construction the "broken" system of Thomson is pursued throughout.

Young.

With Young the case is altered. Young was a very odd person in many ways, and he still awaits thorough critical examination. When, at the age of at least sixty, he began to compose the *Night Thoughts* in blank verse, he had almost run the gamut of the poetic forms of his day. He had written full-dress heroics in *The Last Day*, and had written them not ill; he had written satiric heroics in *The Universal Passion*, practically before Pope, and had done things in them that Pope was scarcely to excel. He laid himself out to write various kinds of lyric —trying dangerous short measures in *The Ocean*, not much-improved long ones in *Imperium Pelagi*. And what is more important to our present purpose, he had been a not unsuccessful tragic dramatist.

It is this last exercise which reflects itself in the blank verse of the *Night Thoughts*, as everybody calls it, though its head-title is really *The Complaint*.

Digression on dramatic blanks.

It may therefore be proper here, and indeed almost necessary, to interpose a slight account of dramatic blank

---

[1] The blank verse of Dyer, whose very different *Grongar Hill* is noticed below (p. 532), is almost wholly Thomsonian, and needs no special notice.

[2] He seems—but rather late, and as afterthought when he saw his mistake —to have claimed burlesque intention for his *péché de jeunesse*. But any one who can see much difference between it and the *Art* in this respect must have an even finer eye for distinctions than Scythrop had for consequences.

verse between Dryden's return to it and Young's famous
"lugubrations," as somebody once called them.   We saw
how Dryden himself, supporting his usual craftsmanship
with a study not merely of the older dramatists but of
Milton (whose verse, independently of his known admiration for it, he must have come to know pretty closely in
"tagging" *The State of Innocence*), elaborated a form,
inferior indeed to that of the giant race, but at its best
very good.   It is probable that his contemporaries owed
as much to him in this respect as in most others.   Crowne
is best at the heroic, but he can write blank verse of
this second-growth kind fairly.   Lee is sometimes almost
magnificent, but inclined to the bombastic ; and Otway is
by turns bombastic and mean—indeed, the weakness of its
blank verse is one of the main faults of *Venice Preserved*.
Southerne, who was actually alive when the *Night* Southerne.
Thoughts appeared, may perhaps be recommended, as
well as any one, for a study of the late seventeenth-
century dramatic kind outside of Dryden.   It is rather an
interesting study, but only the result of it must be given
here.   Southerne's verse is rarely contemptible either from
frigidity or bathos.   *Isabella*, and *Oroonoko*, and *The Fate
of Capua*, and *The Spartan Dame*, and the rest, employ a
very respectable kind of versification, but one which
neither exhilarates nor saddens, nor indeed affects in any
particular way.   You feel that the writer is using verse
instead of prose, just as he might at the present day wear
a frock-coat instead of a jacket on occasions of ceremony.
It is not a badly cut frock-coat : it is of tolerable broad-
cloth and decently brushed.   But as for "sceptred palls,"
and that sort of thing, you may look elsewhere.

The famous passage which Johnson so overpraised, Congreve,
though he did not mispraise it quite to the same extent Rowe, and
as is generally believed, will suffice for Congreve : it is, Addison.
indeed, a fair "copy of verses" in the dramatic descriptive
style, but not much more.   And Rowe, despite his pretty
minute study of Shakespeare and his peculiar "intro-
mittings" with Massinger, is rather behind Southerne as a
blank-verse smith.   In particular, he falls constantly into

that clumsy use of the redundant syllable to which all periods of bad blank verse are prone when they do not reject it altogether.   And then there is the great Mr. Addison's *Cato*, which was in Young's and everybody's hands, and to which the author of *The Revenge* and *Night Thoughts* had contributed complimentary verses.

It is to be feared that it is not in everybody's hands now ; but portions and parcels of it still must or should be known.   Even an age which is rapidly forgetting all letters probably has a dim inkling of

> big with the fate
> Of Cato and of Rome,

and of

> 'Tis not in mortals to command success ;
> But we'll do more, Sempronius, we'll deserve it—

(of which it has been justly said that the position of the verbs would have been more really modest and not much less true if reversed) ; and above all, how Plato, if not Cato, " reasoned well."   Indeed, this last passage, of some substance, may call for a few comments.   It is, no doubt, a fine piece of work ; but independently of general artificiality there is a curious prosodic note of unreality about it.   In the first part the redundant syllables are accumulated as if to disguise the " *Drang nach* couplet " ; in the second, where the lines are strict, they seem to cry for rhyme.   The *sense* is in distichs, with a triplet at the end ; the pauses are mostly central ; the verses quiver for their absent tips.

Exaltation of the soliloquy.

Return to *Night Thoughts*.

There is a point in connection with this famous *Cato* speech which is of great importance, not only as regards Young's plays, but as regards the *Night Thoughts* themselves.   If any one will think of the matter, it will probably strike him as odd that not merely the most famous passage, from a literary point of view, in *Cato*, but the acme of the fable itself, is couched in the form of a soliloquy.   Shakespeare's soliloquies may contain some of the greatest poetry in his plays, and they are all-important in the task of drawing character ; but, generally at least, they take the place of choruses, explaining, completing, commenting on the action, but not constituting it.   Here, it is evident, the case is altered.   And as a result of the alteration, the soliloquy comes to occupy, with blank-verse writers—dramatic first, then non-dramatic—an altogether disproportionate place ; and its style, as they understand it, becomes the general style of blank verse itself.   Certainly the *Night Thoughts* consist of one enormous chain of such soliloquies—of travestied and prosaised series of " To be or not to be " and " If 'twere done when 'tis done." This gives us, as is well known, fine passages now and then ; but it is far less favourable than the Thomsonian description and cataloguing to the development of the full powers of the metre ; and it gives to the whole an unreality which is fatal to any such development.   In fact, not a night-thought but a nightmare suggests itself of a play even more enormous still,—a play dwarfing mediæval and Chinese entertainments—from which all this should have been cut out and the parts which justified its existence thrown away.[1]

A little more analysis, however, may be given to this remarkable variety of the great English measure, not only because its very great popularity (now, I suppose, absolutely decayed) had much to do with popularising the measure itself, but because it is really curious.   One thing noticeable at once is that Young, however strong the dramatic influence may be on him, avoids the redundant syllable, the unskilful use of which was once more ruining blank verse with dramatists.[2]   Another is that he exhibits a kind of return to the single-moulded form, though he by no means refuses enjambment as far as sense goes.   And

---

[1] Although sad experience, dearly bought if not dear, would enable me to write a good deal on eighteenth-century tragedy, I cannot think it necessary.   Johnson's *Irene* is the only other piece that may insist on notice.   Its versification is exactly what might be expected from its author's expressed opinions on verse in general, and blank verse in particular.   It is ornate in diction, careful and even deliberately varied in form ; but really monotonous and fatiguing to the reader from the very fact that it has obviously been a piece of fatigue-duty to the writer.

[2] The amazing Lillo when he tries it (*George Barnwell* is in prose, with only a drop or two into verse) cannot get on without redundancy.

though he no doubt intended no trisyllabic feet, he is rather fond of those words which give the real trisyllabic, or, as Shenstone (perhaps about the same time) called it, "dactylic" effect, while saving the countenance of eighteenth-century prudery by an appearance of elision. His pauses are fairly frequent, but, like Thomson's, they are rather more rhetorical than poetical — induced by the simple close of a sentence or a clause, or by a special stress of argument or illustration, rather than by rhythmical necessity or beauty. In fact, sometimes, and indeed rather frequently, he has a succession of these rhetorical pauses, in or near the middle of the line, which has a very teasing and disturbing effect. He is rather fond of alliteration, of "turns of words," and other mechanical or semi-mechanical devices of the kind. As a matter of course, the rhetorical interrogation and interjection are among his most constant aids. If it were not for the perpetual false emphasis (the older editions are half italics, and in a way these are in place), for the (to us) glaring artificiality, and for the incessant monotony of tone, there would be a good deal to admire in the *Night Thoughts* prosodically as otherwise. As it is, admiration of a kind is due ; but "admiration of a kind" which is felt to be "due" is a very long way from love.

Akenside.   Something of the same curious mixture of feelings is excited by another poet of this time—it is unnecessary any longer to observe strict chronological order, though it must not be wholly neglected—whose most famous poem is in blank verse. I mean Akenside. I do not know whether the curious and characteristic praise which Johnson gives to him of having "fewer artifices of disgust than his brethren of the blank song" was intended to apply to the first or to the last version of the *Pleasures of Imagination.* Akenside was one of those poets who have a habit of pulling their work about. Having written one of the finest pieces of orthodox couplet verse to be found in the mid-eighteenth century—the *Epistle to Curio*—he proceeded not exactly, as has been said, to transform it into, but to postscribe it with, a clumsy collection of awkward stanzas worthy of the worst Pindaric type, except that they are uniform.   And not content with correcting the *Pleasures* (Thomson himself corrected *The Seasons* so freely that I believe there is no complete edition [1] of the variants, though Mr. Logie Robertson has given many of them), he simply rewrote it.   Fortunately both versions are in Chalmers.   The object of the rehandling would appear to have been to make the verse less Thomsonian.   This has been, to some extent, achieved ; but, as often, and perhaps most often, happens in such cases, without the attainment of any very individual substitute.   The rhetorical turn which is so prominent in all the blank verse of this time reaches its highest point with this poet.   It is strong in Thomson, though fortunately less so in *The Seasons* than in *Liberty* ; stronger in Young ; but strongest in Akenside.

At the same time, I should be very sorry to be thought to belittle Akenside as a blank-verser.   In this respect, as in nearly all others, he is a difficult writer to deal with ; there is so much to admire in him and so little to enjoy.   His verse recalls that dreadful phrase of his own and at least two more generations, " a fine woman," more, I think, than that of any English poet. As far as blanks are concerned, however, it is very much in his favour that the second version of the *Pleasures* is far better verse—less stiff, less severely Thomsonian, than the first ; and that perhaps his very best work in the metre is to be found in the opening fragment of a Fourth Book which is dated as late as 1770.   Here we are not only almost alongside of Cowper, but very nearly in presence of Wordsworth ; and so have got hold of a rope which will pass through the hands, not indeed of Tennyson exactly, but of Shelley and Browning.   The prosodic phrase in particular is very remarkable, and strangely uneighteenth-century both in pictorial and prosodic composition.   The fine woman is, paradoxically and beatifically, shading off into a beautiful girl.   But

---

[1] One is said to have appeared recently in Germany.

Akenside has always been to me a greater puzzle than almost any other English poet.

Blair. The pulpit had its turn unmixed (for there is no pulpit in Akenside, and a good deal of platform in Young) with Blair's *Grave*, published very close to the blank-verse poems of both. The shortness of this poem ; the inevitableness, in a more than Wordsworthian sense, of its subject ; and the not inconsiderable vigour of its treatment, secured it a reputation which it can hardly lose whenever it is fairly read. For if the manner is not to us now congenial, it has a historic interest which it could not possess for contemporaries. The handling, from the prosodic side, differs curiously from Young's in the studied profusion of redundant syllables, which makes the soliloquial character even more striking.[1] In fact, *The Grave* would provide, if cut up into five-and-twenty line lengths (it has not quite 800 in all), useful soliloquies on Death to more than thirty different tragedies. Yet it is noteworthy that the fine concluding quatrain (which also purposely or not ends, stage-fashion, with a couplet) has no redundancy ; nor have most of the best lines. Had Blair given himself more practice he would probably have discovered how dangerous it is outside of dialogue. But his poem is, after all, but a highly rhetorical sermon in verse, addressed almost obviously to an audience ; and much that would be improper elsewhere is not so here.

Glover. By the middle of the century, then, and in fact before the deaths of Pope and Swift, blank verse had thoroughly established itself—not for all kinds of poetry, but for not a few of the most popular and dignified. It was thus an even more formidable rival to the heroic than the octo-syllable or the anapæst, though it was less of a relief therefrom. One example of a somewhat different kind from any yet noticed, and challenging the heroic still more directly, has been postponed, because its author long

---

[1] Blair has sometimes been thought to derive in this respect specially from Fletcher and the other Jacobean playwrights. One need not question his knowledge of them. But I think it has been insufficiently noted how strong the tendency of the soliloquy, in Shakespeare himself, is to redundance.

afterwards expanded it and continued it with another. This was Glover's *Leonidas*, the first nine books of which appeared more than a dozen years indeed after Thomson had shown the way, and seven after Somerville had stepped into it, but as much before the almost simultaneous deliverances of Young, Akenside, and Blair. It was not concluded till more than thirty years later ; and *The Athenaid* was posthumous. This latter "stupendous and terrible" poem extends to thirty books. The Spartan hero, even in his later appearance, had contented himself with twelve ; but his books are individually longer. At one time of my life I had a certain acquaintance with both ; but I have never been quite sure how much of my remembrance is nightmare, how much ghastly fact. I have, however, done my duty sufficiently, I think, on the present occasion to make the dream, if it was a dream, reality.

Glover outlived Johnson, and there is therefore no life of him in the *Lives*, while I do not remember any reference in Boswell. This is a pity, for it would have given an interesting opening for a fresh exercise of the critic's untiring, though as we have seen not undiscriminating, devil's advocacy against blank verse.

For Glover really has something of his own, though whether it is a good or a bad something is a different question. *Leonidas* is at first, and could not but be, Thomsonian in a way—the way of strongly "broken" verses, short sentences to make the breaks, and so forth. But the narrative substance of both his works (one may add *Sir Isaac Newton*, and *London, or the Progress of Commerce*, which are both of a length more suited for readers of this world, and are more like Thomson in theme, while the former actually repeats a subject of his) almost necessitated some difference. Glover sought or found the means of that difference in pushing regularity to an extreme, and out-Bysshing Bysshe.[1] He prided

---

[1] Who would no doubt have greatly approved him, as Pemberton (*v. inf.* chap. iv.) actually did. Indeed, Glover was very highly thought of in his day.

himself, we are told, on *never* admitting a trochee in place
of an iambus ; and though it would hardly be worth
while to hunt that needle through a hay-stack of more
than twenty thousand lines, it certainly does not obtrude
itself.   He is so careful to block even the possibility of
a   trisyllabic   foot,   that   he   prints   " gen'ral,"   " ev'ry,"
" delib'rate."   Warton, who rather admired him, admits
that he does not avail himself of the great privilege of
blank verse to run his verses into one another with
different pauses ; and that fault which we have noticed
in Young—strong breaks without variety—is almost im-
possibly burlesqued in such passages as this—

> Mindful of their charge,
> The chiefs depart.   Leonidas provides
> His various armour.   Agis close attends
> His best assistant.   First a breastplate arms
> The spacious chest ;

where one really begins to think that Glover (who was a
city man) imagined that there was a run on blank verse,
and tried to stop it by telling the sum out in half-guineas
slowly on the counter.

These things help to produce—though they might not
by themselves entirely suffice to produce it—a general
flatness which is dully excruciating.   Glover is seldom, if
ever, bombastic, as most of the other blank-verse writers
of this time are.   His inversions are not violent ; nor
does he often overplay the cards of Miltonic omission of
articles or of apposition.   An absolutely absurd single
verse or phrase is not very common with him.   But the
midwife (no doubt a descendant of Shadwell's, as pro-
phetic and as laconic) had laid her hand on his head at
his birth and said, " Be thou *flat* " ; and except in *Admiral
Hosier's Ghost* (under what special disenchanting influence
one does not know) he never discredited the prophecy.
His verse not only cannot soar : it can hardly flap its
wings.   It toddles regularly along after what Johnson
(in another context) calls " the manner of the heavier
domestic fowls."   When we look at its inanity ; when we
look, on the other hand, at the faults of the " tumid and

gorgeous " school,—it is not surprising that in the middle of the century the heroic for a time shook off its competitor, and blank verse hardly came into competition again till the deferred advent of Cowper.[1]

If the "Verses written at Bath on finding the Heel of a Shoe" were really Cowper's first original attempt, as they seem to be his first extant, he began—and our poetical knowledge of him begins in any case—with the form to which, after abandoning it, he was to return, and in which he was to do his best work for bulk and merit combined. And though the subject almost necessitated the imitation of Philips and the burlesque Miltonese, there are odd anticipations of his later and serious style.

> This pond'rous heel of perforated hide

is burlesque, of course, but it need not be ; and the three last lines—

> Betrayed, deserted, from his airy height
> Headlong he falls ; and thro' the rest of life
> Drags the dull load of disappointment on,

are not burlesque at all. They are good lines too ; but it is evident that the writer has not escaped the " centripetal " habit of pause induced by the couplet.

When, half a lifetime afterwards, Lady Austin's fortunate fancy for blank verse induced him to write *The Task* therein, it was almost inevitable that he should at least begin in the same falsetto. In fact, the first batch of *The Sofa*, set beside "The Heel," shows little difference in this respect. But between the school-boy— actual or just emancipated—of eighteen, and the man of fifty-three, there is, besides a sad experience of life, an experience, not so sad, of poetry, his own as well as others ; and the range of his command of the instrument

(margin: Cowper. Early blank verse.)

(margin: The Task.)

---

[1] Crabbe's but recently published *Midnight* (see the Master of Peterhouse's edition, vol. i. p. 74, Cambridge, 1905) was probably *written* earlier than the appearance of Cowper's first volume, and when Cowper had himself written nothing but burlesque "blanks." It is crude, of course, and rather too dramatic in cast, but contains some fine lines and verse-clauses. It might not have been a bad thing if he had used it as a staple. For, as has been maintained more than once, Crabbe was really rather a novelist than a poet.

is very much enlarged. Although he has not yet quite grasped the full scope and reach of the Miltonic pause, he is much less centripetal ; at any rate the pendulum allows itself a wider swing before it seeks the centre. The worst of it is that while he has certainly not attempted to shake off burlesque, it is not clear that he has attempted any more to shake off the sham gorgeous style. Cowper's humour is so gentle, and at the same time so pervading, that it is difficult to be certain on this point. But though it directly succeeds a passage of undoubted *burla*, I would not be too sure that

> Oh may I live exempted (while I live
> Guiltless of *pampered appetite obscene*)
> From *pangs arthritic* that infest the toe
> Of *libertine excess*

is in the same case. Armstrong, and even Thomson, would have written these very lines quite seriously ; and immediately afterwards there is no doubt about the matter.

> For I have loved the rural walk through lanes
> Of grassy swarth, close cropt by nibbling sheep,
> And skirted thick with intertexture firm
> Of thorny boughs ; have loved the rural walk
> O'er hills, through valleys, and by rivers' brink

escapes the falsetto altogether.

It was this nature-description that was to give Cowper, in a far greater degree than that in which it had already given Thomson, escape from the buckram prison of eighteenth-century metre and diction. The famous landscape of the plain of the Ouse which follows before long, though still strictly decasyllabic, and even apostrophating words like " fav'rite," avails itself of nearly all the licences —varied overrunning, shift of pause or absence of it altogether, and contrasted weighting of line—which the strict decasyllable admits. The passage of the trees—so interesting to contrast with Chaucer and Spenser—is not much further ; but it is hardly necessary to recapitulate the well - known " beauties of Cowper." He relapses into burlesque, and into that—we cannot call it in his case insincere, but—hollow and unreal tone of satire which mars his couplet poems. But again and again he gets free ; and then the verse gets free likewise. The famous pair of frost pictures—the frozen river and the palace of ice,—both admirable, are worth comparing minutely, in order to perceive the greater freedom and prosodic intricacy of the seen picture, the more rhetorical and artificial beauty of the read and fancied one.

But Cowper's greatest blank verse, after all, is not yet. It is to be found, as is fitting, in his greatest poem—the unfinished result of one of the last flashes of light that visited the cottage of his soul and kept it for a time from the power of Our Lady of Darkness.

Yardley Oak begins, if not ill, not particularly well, *Yardley Oak.* and before half-a-dozen lines are read we come upon one of the worst instances of the worst imitation of Milton's least good things—

> As now and with *excoriate forks deform,*

a phrase which (since at this moment it is evident that there was not a fragment of burlesque in Cowper's intention) confirms the interpretation put above on the " pangs arthritic." [1]   But the *awen,* the poetic inspiration, is too strong on him for much of this rubbish, and before the twentieth line is reached there opens a short but splendid paragraph, which takes most of the secrets, not only of Milton, but of Shakespeare—even, whether he meant it or not, the trisyllabic foot in " swallowing " and "embryo." There is a slight fall for a few lines, and then, at the fiftieth exactly [2] there begins once more a magnificent tirade, which anticipates Wordsworth not a

---

[1] Cf. below, in the finest context of all, "*prominent* wens *globose.*"

[2] Time made thee what thou wast, king of the woods,
And time hath made thee what thou art—a cave
For owls to roost in.   Once thy spreading boughs
O'erhung the champaign ; and the numerous flocks
That grazed it stood beneath that ample cope
Uncrowded, yet safe-sheltered from the storm.
No flock frequents thee now.   Thou hast outlived
Thy popularity, and art become
(Unless verse rescue thee awhile) a thing
Forgotten, as the foliage of thy youth.

little in spirit, and excels him (save in " Tintern Abbey" and one or two other places) in form. And there is hardly a descent afterwards, though if there is any it becomes ascent again in

Thine arms have left thee.   Winds have rent them off.

It is possible that if Cowper had been able to finish, to revise, and to print this great poem, he might have done harm to it, under the false impression that he was staying it with elisions and comforting it with apostrophations.   But that does not at all matter to us. What we want—what is the real substance of our history —is not what people thought they ought to do (except as a very minor matter), but what, under the joint influence of their own souls and the time-spirit, they *did*. Now what Cowper did in *Yardley Oak*, when we look at it in itself and compare it with his earlier blank-verse work, is clear, and his own prosodic state is clear from it.   He has long outgrown the notion that blank verse is, if not essentially, *preferentially*, as we may say, burlesque ; and he has nearly outgrown the notion that it must be gorgeously stiff.   He has almost entirely given himself up to the " periods of a declaimer "—to the system which, while retaining the integrity of the line to all reasonable extent, varies its internal constituents as much as possible in pause and impetus, and combines it with others, by assumption of them in whole or part into verse-clauses. Of the greatest secret of all—admixture of trisyllabic feet —he may or may not have been consciously conscious. We have already printed two of the Shenstonian dactyls, "swallowing" and "embryo." We may add "veteran" (l. 4); " Heaven," of course, in trisyllabic combination constantly ; "reverence"* (l. 8); " reasoners "* (l. 30); "fostering " (l. 39); "ambiguous " (l. 43); " recovering "* and " desperate "* (ll. 48, 49); " prominent " (l. 65); " to inflict "* (l. 67); " various " (l. 69); "tortuous " (l. 96); "rivulets" (l. 113); "millennium " (l. 136).   And he has, once at least, separated adjective and substantive at a line-end.[1]

[1] He was excused the penalties of dull
Minority.

What matter if not a few of these (those to which an asterisk is affixed) are, as they appear to be from the very carefully printed edition of Mr. Milford,[1] apostrophated in the MS.? The wonder is that they are not all so, for the habit had been ingrained in something like four or five generations. But some are not; some could hardly be, by a poet with such an ear as Cowper had. And, in any case, the acute observation of Shenstone himself[2] remains applicable. The poet has evidently sought those words which, play whatever ugly typographical tricks or fantastic fictions you like with them, have trisyllabic *value*; and it is by dint of this, in combination with the variations of pause, the over- and inter-runnings of line, and the rest, that he recovers the Miltonic effect, and in fact differentiates it with a new movement. He has turned away from the pond, and has drunk of the stream. He has not drunk much : but others will drink more.[3]

[1] Oxford, 1905.
[2] *V. inf.* chapter on " Prosodists."
[3] After the text was printed, Professor R. H. Case brought to my notice the *Fables done into Measured Prose* of Walter Pope the astronomer. The quality of its blank verse appears to be pretty accurately designated in the title. But the date (1698) is early and interesting.

CHAPTER III

EIGHTEENTH-CENTURY LYRIC, ETC.

Preliminaries—The Transition—Addison, Parnell, and Rowe—
Hughes—Gay—Granville, etc.—Watts—Byrom—Shenstone
— Spenserian imitation — Akenside — Smart—Collins—The
" Ode to Evening "—The others—Gray—The " Elegy " and the
minor Odes—The two great Odes, etc.—*Note*, Mason—Goldsmith—Cowper—Chatterton—The Ballad—The 1723 Collection—The *Reliques*—Evans—Some minor lyrics—The hymn-
writers—Charles Wesley—Toplady—Cowper again—Note on
latter eighteenth-century anapæst and octosyllable—Dyer and
Anstey.

THE above heading may alarm some readers, and prompt
others to suggest the celebrated mode of treatment which
is supposed to have originated either with regard to the
Irish snake or with regard to the Icelandic owl.[1] But
the one set should be consoled, and the other corrected,
by the remembrance of three persons at least—Collins,
Gray, and Chatterton—who will fall to be substantively
mentioned here, though Blake will be postponed.

Preliminaries.   Nor, from the point of view of prosody, is even the
remainder so dry a biscuit as it is sometimes thought to
be. The highest spirit of poetry is, no doubt, almost
uniformly lacking in it. But even so it is interesting to
trace the extraordinary intimacy of the connection of
spirit and form ; while in the history of the great prosodic

[1] It seems to be one of the great unsettled points of literary history
whether " There are no snakes in Ireland " or " There are no owls in
Iceland " is the original form of the chapter, and whether this form was due
to Horrebow or to Van Troil. Some good men, relying on Johnson, plump
for Horrebow, snakes, and Iceland.

kinds—especially the common or ballad measure—this period, though it may represent eminently the " minima " of our title-motto, is, on that very account, specially interesting. It cannot but be useful to watch, even if we can rather feel than explain, the process by which the ineffable rhythm of the seventeenth century, which at once sets the commonest thoughts commercing with the skies, changed into the jog-trot hardly caricatured in Johnson's famous parodies, and seriously exhibited in this stanza—

> Within an unfrequented grove,
>   As late 1 *laid* alone ;
> A tender maid, in deep distress,
>   At distance made her moan,

which was written sometime before 1740, by the Reverend William Thompson, Fellow of Queen's College, Oxford, imitator of Spenser, one of almost the first flight of blank-verse writers after his all but namesake, etc., etc.

We saw how Dryden, throughout his life, managed, partly by actual poetic survival of spirit, and partly by his consummate craftsmanship in varying the forms of lyric, to preserve some of its quality ; and how a few of his earlier contemporaries actually retained, though in an uncertain fashion, something of the unearthly tone of the earlier music. The degradation, though not yet quite at its uttermost, of the instrument, may be seen in a man like Duke, who has interspersed his more serious work, mainly couplet in form and translated in matter, with a few songs not quite contemptible ; and the effort to supply the place of the vanishing beauty with new charms may be traced distinctly in Prior, whose establishment of the anapæst indeed positively˙ widens the range of the lyre. On the whole, however, the lyric of the latest seventeenth and almost the whole eighteenth century steadily *flattens*. That it, too, like blank verse and like the octosyllable, is used as a variation and relief from the couplet, is true of all its forms, and not merely of the new anapæstic ; and this once more enforces the lesson which we shall gather up and codify

The Transition.

in the Interchapter.   But poetry does not change its character in proportion to the changes of its position and attitude.   As in French, so in English, the fatal image of prose cut into lengths survives.   The prevailing sing-song does not help, but rather intensifies, this effect ; and nowhere is the artificial poetic diction of the century more strongly prominent.   It is perhaps not least because the necessary biblical phrase, free from the taint, is substituted in religious poetry, that this poetry acquires such remarkable relative excellence, and, in the work of Charles Wesley, Smart, Cowper, and others, becomes more positively poetical than most of the profane.

Addison, Parnell, and Rowe.   The process, and this curious phenomenon in it, become manifest almost at once.   Addison's verse, couplet, blank, or lyric, is nowhere very stimulating ; but it nowhere possesses such spirit and body, such throb and quiver, as in the stanzaed octosyllables of

> The spacious firmament on high,

and the modest cadence, not enchanting but not merely jog-trot, of

> How are thy servants blest, O Lord !

and

> The Lord my pasture shall prepare.

Parnell is mostly Drydenian in his songs ; but he too can practise something like the Miltonic (*not* the Hudibrastic) octosyllable in the " Night Piece," and the " Hymn to Contentment," and some sacred poems.   Rowe, who has very little name for a poet with most of us, keeps perhaps more prosodic freshness in his lyrics than most of his contemporaries.

> When in fair Celia's eyes I gaze,
>   And bless their light divine ;
> I stand confounded with amaze
>   To think on what they shine,

has something of the past swell, the dying wave, of the old Jonsonian volume.   Side by side with it we find examples of the new tripod anapæst, which Byrom and

Shenstone were to popularise, which was a favourite with the eighteenth century, but which, even in Cowper's hands, was never quite satisfactory till somebody turned it, by making the odd line hypercatalectic, into the glorious measure of the addresses to Araminta and Dolores. The short-stanzaed poem to Miss Anne Devenish, whom he afterwards married, is pretty and uncommon ;[1] and the Willow song is partially caught. He may have " had no heart " for Mr. Pope ;[2] but he managed to put some into the prosody of these songs.

In another of the Addisonian set, however, the degradation of lyric is much more strongly exhibited. Although the members of the "little senate" received, like those of others, at least sufficient salaries of praise, John Hughes seems to have been a man of parts, learning, Hughes. and amiability ; and he has the credit of going outside stock subjects for that of his rather popular tragedy *The Siege of Damascus*, which takes one of the most romantic episodes of the early Caliphate. But I cannot say, as " L. Duncombe *e Coll. Mert.*," a youthful poet who died in his teens said, of Hughes—

> Aonidum decus ille dolorque sororum,

as far as English lyric was concerned, though he seems to have been very prone to the composition of it. He wrote Odes on the House of Nassau, in the half-regularised Pindaric; others with less ponderous credentials; lesser songs in common measure, long measure, heroic

---

[1] As on a summer's day
In the green wood shade I lay.
The maid that I woed,
As her fancy moved,
Came walking forth that way.

By accident or intention, he improves on this lower down by an internal rhyme—

Then the nymphs of our green,
So trim and so sheen,
Or the brightest *Queen* of May.

[2] Pope seems to have been curiously exercised about the hearts of the Rowe family. He was also much shocked at Mrs. Rowe for marrying again six years after her husband's death.

quatrains, a good many of them in various forms for
music.   He even had the modest assurance to rearrange
Dryden's " Cecilia Major," and the more lawful ambition
of writing masques.   Yet in all this variation of measure
one hardly meets one thing thoroughly " hit off" in
rhythm and cadence ; though they are all decently
measured off.   Reading him has made me think of a
passage in *The Irish Sketch Book* where " the waiter holds
up the bottle and asks me how much I'd have."   Mr.
Hughes holds up his verse, and asks us how much and
in what form we would have it, and he cuts it off or
pours it out to the bespeak.   I think he is about happiest
in a not very common adaptation of the common
measure.[1]   The thought and phrase are commonplace
enough ; but the measure is " lifted along " rather well,
and the reduplication of the seventh line sends it home
gallantly.   Yet when by the accident of Chalmers's compilation we turn a page or two and stumble on

> I must confess I am untrue
>   To Gloriana's eyes,

noticed before and written by Mulgrave, a contemporary,
though an older contemporary, of Hughes, the sense of
what has been lost is itself strangely driven home.   Even
in Congreve, actually one of the Addison set, the same
sense arises : we hear what we shall hear no more.

Gay.   To some readers this last sentence may seem hard on
Gay ; and on Gay I should be very sorry to be hard, for
I think that others have recently been too hard on him,
and he was always prosodically competent.   But those of
his continuous metres which come nearest to lyric—his
famous octosyllables——are not very lyrical ; and his almost

---

[1] The Graces and the wandering Loves
       Are fled to distant plains,
   To chase the fawns, or deep in groves
       To wound admiring swains.
   With their bright mistress there they stray.
       She turns her careless eyes
   From daily triumphs ; yet each day
   Beholds new triumphs in her way,
       And conquers while she flies.

equally famous lyrics are a little damaged prosodically by the comment which his best and most competent living critic, Mr. Austin Dobson, has made on him—that he was a musician.   The fact is—and we have had occasion, and shall have more, to apply the distinction— that there are certain poems which are musically and certain others that are prosodically melodious.   Some, no doubt, are both ; but few.   "Black-eyed Susan," " 'Twas when the seas were roaring," " Daphnis stood pensive in the shade," and others of Gay's are of the former kind. Everybody knows the tune of the first ; I, at least, do not know the tune of the two others, but I cannot imagine them without one.   I never think of a tune in connection with even Cowper's things ; and though I know the settings that have been put to " Drink to me only " and the " Night Piece to Julia," and other things of that kind, the prosodic music of their words is to me independent of them.   This may be some private sin or fault, yet I cannot help thinking that there is a real difference corresponding to the distinction ; and Gay, I have said, seems to me to be set on the further side by it.

The useful Chalmers (who should be more of a favourite with the public than he is, I fear) has again supplied an interesting contrast by beginning his next volume, after that which Gay closes, with Lansdowne, " Granville the polite."   Neither Granville's politeness nor Granville, etc. his Toryism had made Johnson kind to him as a poet ; and I suspect that the unkindness was partly due to a fact, which, besides his other graces, makes me rather partial to Lansdowne, namely, his prosodic quality.   Johnson is not very severe on songs in *The British Enchanters* which seem to me rather feeble copies of Dryden's not best manner ; but he is so on the numerous verses to Myra, afterwards Lady Newburgh, and long afterwards the victim of atrocious lampoons, written by another Tory, though rather a renegade one, Dr. King[1] of St. Mary Hall.   Whether Myra deserved her earlier or her later

---

[1] King had some skill in verse, and was ingenious in Macaronic.   But he is too dirty for anything.

vates most, I do not know ; but I do know that in
Lansdowne's celebrations of her there is a faint shadow or
flavour, a sort of distant rose-scent, of the cadence and
the melody of older days.   There is nothing of it in
Yalden, who follows; and in Tickell, who follows *him*, there
is the *minus* quantity.   Tickell was a really great hand,
as we have said, at the couplet,[1] and the famous verse
from his " Colin and Lucy "—

> I hear a voice you cannot hear,
>   Which says, I must not stay ;
> I see a hand you cannot see,
>   Which beckons me away,

may raise fair expectations of his lyric in some gentle
minds.   But mere antithesis was easy to a coupleteer ;
and the rest of the piece is in the desperate jog-trot,
which, after ruining the gutter-ballad of England earlier,
was at this very time, when the real ballads of England
and Scotland were being resuscitated, obtaining a mastery
over both countries in modern work.

But the reader need not be alarmed ; I am not going
to bestow upon him all the tediousness for which I have
ample notes from ten mighty volumes of Chalmers himself—ten more, though less mighty, of Dodsley and Pearch,
and I do not know how many of other collections,
selections, and separate issues.   It was desirable to sample
regularly at this junction (or rather separation) of the two
centuries ; but henceforward it will be better to concentrate the treatment either on persons who have a
distinct prosodic importance of the individual kind, or on
special forms illustrated from greater and smaller people
alike.   Of the former, some of the names may astonish,
but I think that I can make their claims good without
Watts much difficulty.   We have seen that Dr. Watts is one

---

[1] The splendid lines on Cadogan, which caught Thackeray's attention—

> Thou music, warbling to the deafen'd ear ;
> Thou music, wasted on the funeral bier,

are preceded by some rather literal borrowing from Dryden ; but both here,
in the Addison poem, and elsewhere, Tickell is fine.   If he had been less so,
Mr. Pope would probably have been less angry with him.

of the examples of Pindaric eccentricity ; but even in this style he is far from technically ineffective.   It is the ludicrous disproportion of making a world-cataclysm out of the death of a dissenting minister, the worse than metaphysical folly of describing the human frame as

> Arrayed in rosy skin and decked with ears and eyes

(as if it were one of the old paste-pigs, with currants for these latter organs, which used to be displayed in pastry-cooks' shops), not any defect of versification, that makes Watts's Pindarics absurd.   His also noticed blank verse shows prosodic independence at least ; and his lyrics are, when tried in the proper court, not contemptible. The *Moral Songs* (which for some reason or other people will call *Hymns*) may be goody and platitudinous, but, prosodically, they are very early and very deft examples of forms that were by no means commonplace.   ."The voice of the sluggard" would have been a most early-rising voice if it had complained in fluent anapæsts a few years before ; and the same may be said of the lambs, and the rose, and the Summer Evening.   People would certainly not laugh at the measure of "Good Resolutions"[1] if it happened to clothe naughty ones ; for the trochees are most cleverly handled, and the postponement of the full line to the second place, instead of the commoner arrangement of giving it the first, is excellent.

The *Divine Songs*, which also commonly receive, and with more reason, the name of *Hymns*, luxuriate less in the metrical way.   They are, naturally enough, in the three great recognised hymn measures which, as we have seen, result from different manipulations of the aboriginal couplet, the " Common," " Short," and " Long."   And although Watts has scarcely the touches of pure poetry which we find in Charles Wesley and in Cowper, his

---

[1]   Though I'm now in younger days,
      Nor can tell what shall befall me,
   I'll prepare for every place
      Where my growing age shall call me.

This is " very light and good," and one can easily imagine a positive *gaillardise* written to it, and actually including these first lines.

handling of the familiar descants is far from despicable.
The later poet who sang—

> The dogs, and the birds, and the little busy bee—
> O ! it's all sing-song in the Watts countree !

was not quite fair.   In the less familiar hymns, the
common measure keeps its stateliness ; the long, its grave
and rolling flow ; the short, that quaint variety which,
at its rare best, it extracted from the jog-trot of the
" poulter's."

But it is in the *Horæ Lyricæ*, Sacred and Profane, that
Watts's prosodic power and range are best seen.   His
remarks on the subject, which will be quoted in their due
place, are as sound as possible in principle, though we
may doubt some of his applications ; and his practice
shows singularly wide range of experiment.   He even
tried Sapphics,[1] failing, of course, but not uninterestingly.
Some of his ode-measures in the shorter scales are far
from contemptible ; and, naturally enough, he has here
more temptation to bring out the prosodic qualities (noted
above) of the three great sacred measures than in the
" Songs for Children."   He is rather fond of one of the
best combinations[2] of that fine unit the quintet, 10, 10,
10, 8, 12, *abaab*, where it is one of the most agreeable of
minor prosodic studies to see how the awkward and jolting
triplet of Benlowes composes itself into graceful motion
by the prefixing of the first two lines.   We have spoken

[1] When the fierce North-wind with his airy forces
Rears up the Baltic to a foaming fury ;
And the red lightning with a storm of hail comes
Rushing amain down.

These, no doubt, inspired both in form and subject (" The Day of Judgment ") Cowper's " Hatred and vengeance."

[2] Happy the feet that shining Truth has led
With her own hand to tread the path she please,
To see her native lustre round her spread
Without a veil, without a shade,
All beauty and all light, as in herself she is.

Here " please " is a subjunctive, and the rhymes are more old-fashioned
than wrong.   The fact is that Watts, who was actually born within the third
quarter of the seventeenth century, was a belated metaphysical who had
turned to dissenting pedagogics.   He is really worth reading.

of his blanks, which are here ; he can do the continuous trochaic dimeter catalectic excellently, and his romance-sixes—a measure which the century was to use freely, with some fine results, but more failures—are very fair. In short, he has variety, and he has craftsmanship.

The agreeable author of   Byrom.

> God bless the King—of Church and State defender,

was even less of a poet in the highest sense than Watts, and he was most tyrannically voluminous.   But he has importance for us in the fact that, from the first occasion on which he distinguished himself by the famous verses, printed in the *Spectator*, on " Jug " or Joanna Bentley—

> My time, O ye Muses, was happily spent,

he did all that he could to practise and popularise the anapæst.   Thereby, of course, he directly and indirectly produced a great deal of doggerel ; but thereby, also, he helped to stake out, embank, and bastion that fort of refuge which we have described above.   Even in them-selves, too, the " Phœbe " verses, the great history of the combat between Figg and Sutton, and other poems, are very welcome, and Byrom has done things of merit in other metres.   But it is as a writer of the anapæst that he concerns us.

He was wise enough to use it mainly, if not wholly, in the dimeter or four-foot sizing, which is its most natural arrangement in English.   Shenstone, who comes next on   Shenstone. our list, preferred another form, which has been noticed already, and made it extremely popular.   For my own part, I do not share Dr. Johnson's objection to the crook and the pipe and the kid *because* of their crookship or pipeship or kidship.   But I do think

> The crook and the pipe and the kid

(which does not actually occur as a line, but might) to be rather a vile metre.   In the first place, even when it is most pretty, its prettiness is of the insignificant kind, which is worse than piquant plainness ; in the second, it

is horribly monotonous ; and in the third, there is a
peculiar kind of "ramshackleness" about it, a tendency
to "come to pieces," which excites a sort of petty alarm.
I have pointed out before how close it is to, and how
happily genius can make it into, one of the most glorious
of lyrical measures in English ; and the smallness of the
alteration, with the astonishing difference of result, is one
of the choice marvels of prosody.[1]   But in itself I cannot
away with it ; not even Cowper's "Catharina" can induce
me to grant more than a reluctant exception and exemp-
tion.   The fact is that Shenstone—a real name, as we
shall see, in prosodic theory, a rediscoverer of the lost
land of promise and possession—is not a great prosodist
in practice.   His elegiac quatrains are very tame : there
are, I suppose, five hundred of them, and the whole
would not supply small change for one of Gray's worst.
Of his Odes, the best prosodically is "The Princess
Elizabeth," where the trochees are made to race with
considerable skill ; and some of his common measure has
a faint far-off echo of the old divine music.   For Shenstone was a poet, though his prose shows it even more
than his poetry.   And though the poet cannot do
without the lyre, the lyre will generally show its quality
only when the poet touches it.

Spenserian imitation.   He may serve, as well as another, as a peg whereon to
hang a very short discourse on the minor Spenserian
imitations [2] of the century, which are so curiously
abundant.   No one of them comes anywhere near the
Castle of Indolence in merit ; and though there are one or
two pretty and well-known things in Shenstone's own
Schoolmistress, he is not even the most successful of the
other imitators before Beattie.[3]   Most of them, though to

[1] It has also great serio-comic qualities, discovered and exhibited in
Thackeray's "Chronicle of the Drum."
[2] I do not apologise for inserting it here ; the Spenserian stanza is the
most lyrical of all narrative forms.
[3] Of Beattie I would rather not talk much.   I once wrote of him that
"he would have been a poet if he could," and I cannot go any further now.
But there is no doubt that he was a most successful schoolmaster to bring
folk to poetry in his own day and long afterwards ; indeed, I have been told
by quite young people that Beattie so brought them.   And I am not like

a rather less extent than those of Chaucer at this time, show very little sense of the qualities of their original. Under the singular delusion that it is only the quaintness, not the music, of the Spenserian diction that unites it so close to the verse, they pepper the words of Spenser (or travesties of them) as hard as the caster will let them. They have conceived a still more singular notion of his "simplicity" (an application of the word which "simply" deprives it of all meaning), and though they are not wrong about the tenderness in him, they seem to be quite unaware of the splendour and the stateliness, the long-drawn sweetness and elaborate art, which he displays. Nobody except Thomson ever gets anywhere near to the resonance and colour of the stanza. But the constant practice of it is still noteworthy, as a sign of the haunting desire for something different from the couplet.

The importance of Akenside in blank verse has been Akenside. dealt with ; but it recurs in connection with lyric, and it may be profitably taken, from our point of view, in connection with that of another poet, Smart, who, from being mainly a name, has of late years become much more. Both have interest in themselves prosodically ; both have more when taken in conjunction (as they have not been always taken) with Collins and with Gray.

Perhaps to no one—certainly not to Gray—was Johnson more unjust than to Akenside, and perhaps nowhere is his injustice more easily accounted for.[1] He did not dislike Akenside's principles in politics more than I do ; but he positively hated Akenside's principles in versification—for which I have much tolerance. Once more we have the complaint of "harsh" diction, of ill-constructed stanzas, of rhymes dissonant, unskilfully disposed or too far from each other, perplexing to the ear, and so on. Akenside is not Milton ; but it would

---

that severe allegorist of the forties (was it Bishop Wilberforce or Mr. Adams ?) who delivered over to the Black Cherubim a great teacher of young soldiers for not fighting the good fight himself quite consistently.

[1] It has been duly recorded above that he gave a certain faint praise to the blank verse, but it was chiefly that he might point out what a poor thing blank verse is at its best.

be quite worth while for any student who is still puzzled
by Johnson on *Lycidas* to read Akenside and Johnson on
him.   The fact, of course, is that these Odes have not
the regularity of the couplet, and, moreover, that they
are resorted to in order to get rid of the regularity of the
couplet.   It is this which gives them, like all their
fellows, interest for us ; it is even this which gives them
a certain merit for us.   But it could not be expected to
give them either merit or interest for Johnson, to whom
the couplet was actually the crown and sum of things
prosodically possible or desirable.

Yet it was impossible for Johnson to go wrong
without also going right.   He has undoubtedly "fixed"
Akenside's great defect when he says that "his thoughts
are cold " ; and it would be difficult to meet with a
simple counter-denial his denial to this poet of "the ease
and airiness of the lighter, the vehemence and elevation
of the grander ode."   In fact, if my theory is right, the
very fact that these eighteenth-century odists and lyrists
generally were seeking relief from the couplet, would
always be prejudicial, would sometimes be fatal, to their
complete success.   For the artist to try to be unlike
something or somebody else is nearly as cramping and
distorting as for him to try to be like something or
somebody else.   Your deliberate high jinks, your organ-
ised orgies, are always rather sad things ; and the
lighter and grander odes of the eighteenth century are
too often the one or the other.   There is something of the
fearful joy of a barring-out in their irregularities.   "See
how playful—see how Pindaric—I am " is a too common
suggestion.   Yet Akenside is sometimes very near
success, as far as his measures go.   He is specially given
to the romance-six in its eighteenth-century form—
which he sometimes varies by shifting the first hexa-
syllable to the second place,—and others of his forms are
further variations of the same.   It is almost a pity that
he did not " Pindarise " the stately blank verse " Hymn to
the Naiads," one of the most remarkable examples of his
icy elegance.   It could not have lost warmth as the

"Curio" Epistle did, for it has none to lose ; and a more irregular outline would have suited it well. The best icebergs and glaciers, I am told, are always irregular ; stalactites,[1] which Akenside also suggests, certainly are.

For once, if not for once only, *furor poeticus* actually Smart. developed out of *furor vulgaris* in the well-known case of Christopher Smart. The regular collection of Smart's poems (to be found in Chalmers), which is fairly voluminous, is in prosodic, as in other respects, of the most ordinary eighteenth-century kind. Some positive irregularities of metre may be accidental ; most varieties of the popular lighter measures are treated with respectable skill, and the crambo ballad, with its Hudibrastic rhymes to "Harriot," is just worth noting in a History of Prosody. But in prosodic, as in other character, the *Song to David*, which was actually excluded from the orthodox collection, and, though published, could not be found by the industrious Chalmers (who had to content himself with an extract from a review), is utterly different. This, again, is in the romance-six, which, after the dying down of Pindaric, became almost the "common measure" of Ode during the century. But it has wholly changed its character. It shakes off entirely that original sing-song which *Sir Thopas* hit so unerringly ; it shakes off equally the somewhat heavy march which at this time it commonly affects ; the subject, of course, puts the quaint grace of Gray's Cat-and-Goldfish piece out of question. But Smart——or rather some certainly not evil spirit which at the time had possession of him——has poured into it a flowing fervour of thought and expression which compulsorily transforms its motion and sound, its outline and colour. It becomes utterly alive, full of panting and glowing life, throbbing with fervour of the very kind that eighteenth-century poetry most lacks. Its movement is of the most various and minutely divided character, and yet it is perfectly symphonic and continuous as a whole. The dead twigs of ordinary eighteenth-century line and stave have become fiery flying serpents——not maleficent

[1] Cf. Théodore de Banville.

at all, but dazzling and delightful with their fire and their flight. The matter of the *Song* you will get much better, and even much better put, in Isaiah and David himself; but its manner is its own, and, for the time, unique.

It has been hinted above that it would be well to take Collins and Gray rather less as if they were earth-born prodigies than has sometimes been done, and rather more as in connection with their fellows and their time. No doubt they constitute the third, as Prior may be said, roughly, to be the first, and Thomson the second, of the warnings addressed to the couplet. But the actual form of this warning was much less novel than that of the anapæstic or of the blank - verse secession. Even the regularising of the Pindaric had been long anticipated by Congreve. In other respects there is little positively new of the prosodic kind in either poet except their patterns and the spirit of their fingering.

Collins.

Collins began with couplet, and not very good couplet ; though the refrain construction of the Second Eclogue already shows an *anima naturaliter lyrica*. How that soul showed itself in the handful of Odes and the " Fidele " Song, there is not much need of saying. But except in the unrhymed " Evening " there is nothing so very new in the actual form. In that, no doubt, there is something very new. We shall meet with this uncovenanted [1] rhymeless-

The "Ode to Evening."

ness not seldom ; and it would be premature to discuss it in its first example, which, however, it may not be premature to say, remains by far the most successful ever written. In fact, we ought to be particularly grateful for it, because it shows, with as little adventitious aid as possible, how exquisite Collins's ear was. Yet it is impossible not to think how much more beautiful it would be *with* rhyme.

The others.

But the other Odes, which do not thus break with the usage of the time, illustrate, from one side even more effectively, the difference which fresh studies and individual gift combined will produce, in this as in other matters.

---

[1] I use these words because Campion unrhymed his verse on an elaborate covenant, and sometimes at least with a definite challenge.

Most poets since Dryden had been good Latin scholars, and some had been more or less fairly acquainted with Greek. "Rag" Smith is said to have been more than fairly so; but the Greek *influence* is certainly less perceptible in any of them than the Latin. Collins is full of it; and its importance, especially in regard to metres of the choric kind, cannot be exaggerated. Moreover, there was his own influence—the indefinable—working too. But the conventionality which had been and was to be fatal to most of his brethren was also, as the *Eclogues* had shown, strong on him; and not a few even of the Odes show it. The first—that to "Pity," in the romance-six of which we have said so much—is the queerest jumble conceivable of tags of Monmouth Street expression—"scene," "turtles," "British shell" (which does not in the least mean a larger edition of what the British grenadier carried in his pouch), and so forth. But there is something in its cadences which is not as the Yaldens or even as the Akensides. "Fear," with its Epode stuck in the middle, is even a wilder jumble, with the pent-up music still struggling to get free; while "Simplicity" seems to drug itself with a quasi-Miltonic regularity. But the lyric scheme of the "Poetic Character" insists on being attended to; it is not, like the usual eighteenth-century strophe and stanza, a congeries of lines with little individual and less symphonic harmony. "Mercy" is doubtful. But who shall overpraise the opening strophe of "Liberty" as poetry or as prosody? Its substance is, if not exactly naught, naught better than Akenside. But its form abolishes the substance; for we know that only the chosen ones—the aristocracy, or for the special occasion the monarchy, of poetical man—can so write. "Liberty" to write like that, will enable no one to write like it.

Patriotism shall protect the shade of Colonel Ross from critical remarks of any kind, and the golden hair of Peace in her turn shall be borne swift from our grasp. Nor were it mannerly to say much of "The Manners." But "The Passions" and "The Death of Thomson" and the "Popular Superstitions of the Highlands" and "Fidele,"

—who that has any sense of the music of words can speak unbribed of these?   Perhaps the famous first is not improved by its having been written directly for setting ; as in all pieces of the kind, from Dryden's downwards, the transitions and variations are sometimes not strictly prosodic, but tampered with to suit the composer's convenience.   In all, the conventional diction appears, and we could no doubt do with less Personification ; though I rather doubt whether Personification is so deadly as the first Romantic school thought.   But in all the four that command over words to make them musical, that fingering, that vivifying of dead schemes into live measures which is what we are questing for through this long history, makes its appearance.   The symphonic variety of the "Passions"; the ineffable sweetness of the octo-syllabic quatrain in the "Thomson" and "Fidele"; the stately decasyllables, woven into statelier stanzas, of the "Highlands,"—we may go far indeed in the eighteenth century—we may travel indeed from its China to its Peru —without finding such prosodic delights in diction and measure together.   Add "Evening," add the incomparable "How sleep the brave"; and one may say "If Fate had not bound him ; if he had improved on these Odes as they improve on the *Eclogues* ; if he had shed the stock diction and phrase as he had tuned up the stock metre, what might not Collins have done?"

Gray. Gray has nothing like this prosodic witchery ; but he is, here as elsewhere, a very great artist.   The magnificent praise which Johnson, captious as he may have been about other things, has given to the substance of the "Elegy" might almost be repeated of its form.   The difficulty of the decasyllabic quatrain has been dwelt upon before in these pages.   Gray has not only surmounted that difficulty ; he has not only got something uniformly good out of the metre, but he has made it uniquely good.   Nothing like it had been done before (*voyez plutôt* the egregious Hammond),

The "Elegy" and the minor Odes, and everything since, approaching the kind, has been imitated from Gray.   He that reads it, to keep close to Johnson's admirable phrase, persuades himself that this must

have been what the stanza was meant for. Dryden had tried
to make it splendid, and even his magnificent craftsmanship had, on the whole, failed. He, and Davenant and
others had tried to make it subservient to narrative; and
it had refused to be so made. Hammond and the rest
had tried to make it graceful, dainty, what not; and the
lame foot of Failure had kept up with them easily enough.
Gray first caught its curious faculty for *subduedness*—for
minor keys of thought, emotion, description—and brought
this faculty out without a false note from first to last. This
sense of what measures can do, and this knack of making
them do it, distinguish him throughout. His minor Odes
do in the same measures what all the other eighteenth-
century odes come short of doing. Some people whom I
revere do not like "the pensive Selima"; from Johnson's
criticism one would conclude that he did not. It seems
to me perfect. But it is perfect as a caricature of the
eighteenth century itself; and it is quite possible that
Johnson saw, did not choose to see, and did choose to
punish, that.

As for the two great regularised Pindarics, the John- The two great
sonian criticism about the stanza being too long, and the Odes, etc.
ear being kept waiting for its pleasure, is, of course, merely
the *aeternum vulnus* of the slighted couplet. There is
nothing like leather, and this is not leather. No such
objection will be made here, and undoubtedly there are
many fine prosodic phrases in the pair. But the extreme
artificiality of the diction is far more seldom melted or
veiled by a real rush of melodiously adjusted sound;
and the adjustments themselves partake too much of
artifice. It is by no means certain that Gray's best
work, prosodically, is not the simple and beautiful
" Vicissitude." The virtue, again, of the Norse translations and imitations lies in their imagery and *dramatis
personæ* much more than in their metre; and though the
Long Story is worthy of Prior, and has touches that are
not in Prior, these touches are not metrical. Those who
cannot distinguish may be shocked at Gray not being
put higher here; his position will not, I think, be shock-

ing to those who can. He did great work ; but with the exceptions noted, and one to be added presently, it was not done in our division. Indeed, in part of our division —that which concerns Diction—his work was very dubiously good ; for in few eighteenth-century poets is this stiffer and more artificial than in Gray. But the final regularising of the irregular Ode,[1] and the marvellous modulation of the quatrain, remain to his credit ; while he is almost wholly an anti-coupleteer.[2]

Goldsmith.   We should have dealt almost sufficiently with Goldsmith as an example and pillar of the quasi-reaction towards the couplet. There is no doubt that a great support was given to this by the *Traveller* and the *Deserted Village*, reinforcing as they did, with a lighter and brighter variation, the magnificent character of the *Vanity of Human Wishes*. And both in them and in the minor poems there is noticeable a *suppleness* of prosodic gift which has often distinguished Irish poets. In the days when I used to review minor poetry by the measured cubic foot, I nearly always found that volumes by Irish writers, though they might not be in the least superior as poetry, could " rhyme and rattle " much more deftly than the others. The anapæsts of " The Haunch of Venison " and " Retaliation " are not only the best since Prior, but are perhaps more regularly good than Prior's longer copies—certainly than " Down Hall." " The Hermit " has terrors, but we shall talk of them under the head of the ballad ; and it may be observed that in the brief common measure song—

The wretch condemned from Life to part,

---

[1] And whether this is altogether "to credit" may be seriously doubted. The original Greek choric arrangement is magnificent, just as the minor Greek arrangements of Sapphic and Alcaic are exquisite ; but, for all that, neither the one nor the other need suit English.

Mason.   [2] This does not mean that he could not or did not write couplets. His " very ineligible friend," Mr. Mason, one of the paltriest and most pretentious poetasters who ever trespassed on the English Parnassus, need not delay us long. His couplets are tinsel ; his blank verse is wood ; his Hudibrastics are straw ; and his odes are plaster. Four good lines stand to Mason's name at the end of twelve bad ones in the epitaph on his wife in Bristol Cathedral, and these four lines are Gray's

these terrors are quite absent. His Hudibrastics are at least good ; and the jog-trot which he can hardly have meant in " Edwin and Angelina " comes in well in the " Mad Dog " elegy and " Madam Blaize." In fact, all the smaller pieces are prosodically adequate and more ; while the anapæsts are prosodically consummate in the lighter kind, and do not attempt any other.

Cowper, the last poet of the exclusively English Cowper. eighteenth century, and by the facts of his unhappy history representing a singular combination of different time-influences, is not less interesting prosodically than otherwise, even if we leave out of sight the blank verse formerly noticed. He is not like Chatterton (*v. inf.*) and Blake (who published, the one before, the other contemporaneously with him), a nineteenth-century poet antedated ; nor has he, like Smart, been taken up, not exactly into the seventh heaven, but well into the first, by the inspiration of insanity.[1] Insanity, alas ! was only coming in its final stage when he wrote the greatest of all his lyrics ; and it was the insanity that quenches, not that gives, poetry, and hope, and life. But he was, like Collins and like Gray, an eighteenth-century poet in whom there were germs of something not eighteenth-century ; and the half development of these germs affected his lyric not less than his blank verse, even at its latest and greatest development. Many of his best things, if not all, are in the ordinary and popular eighteenth-century metres ; but in nearly every case he manages to give them, if not an entirely new turn and life (he sometimes does this), at any rate the best life and the best turns. Scores of poets had practised the trochaic dimeter catalectic, and had fitted it for a range of epithets extending upwards from trivial to beautiful. He took it for " Boadicea," and made it magnificent. " John Gilpin," besides its more commonly recognised charms, is one of the best examples of the happy faculty which the century possessed of burlesquing itself. " The Royal George,"

---

[1] It was in the early stages of this that he wrote the Sapphics referred to under Watts.

effective as it is, is a little uncertain in its metre ; but its best stanzas are almost up to " Boadicea " in movement. Those naughty lines which mystified poor Lady Austin, and which (though certainly a man between two ladies—both widows, too !—is in a terrible quandary) seem to show that " William's " subsequent account of the transaction was one of his few derogations from an otherwise stainless gentlemanhood—

The star that beams on Anna's breast,—

recover for common measure much of its ancient soar. He nearly succeeded in raising to something better the rickety jingle of the anapæstic three-foot without redundance. The beauty of his best hymn-measures is unquestioned. And, finally, the splendid and terrible " Castaway " is one of those examples (the singling out and characterising of which is one of the pleasures of writing such a book as this) which get out of particular measures, on one particular side at least (for the facets of some measures are numerous, if not infinite), almost everything that this side can give. When one reads these steady, hopeless staves — accomplished, but not finical ; carefully subdued, but not to any extravagant point ; reminding one of the stories of men who have dressed themselves, not foppishly, but with especial neatness, before committing suicide— it seems as if superficially calm despair could take no other form—as if this measure were " quoted and signed " for the utterance of Wanhope. It is perhaps so fated. Bishop King's famous " Tell me no more," though far less gloomy, is despairing too. But in many other examples there is nothing of this ; and none but a great prosodist could have found it out and declared it, for the world to shudder at, if it be in shuddering mood—to wonder at, if it knows how to wonder.

Chatterton.   I have kept Chatterton to the last single mention for several reasons. He could not, considering that all his work was over and done thirty years before the century closed, be reserved, like Blake and Burns, for the next volume. And there is the additional argument against doing so that, in his non-Rowleian poems, he is, prosodically as in other respects, simply the most ordinary of eighteenth-century hobbledehoy poetasters. Nowhere, in the vast deserts of this verse, is a stretch so utterly bare of oasis as the " Poems in the Modern Style." Hardly anywhere is there such an interesting, though such a bewitched and bewitching oasis, as the " Rowley " poems themselves. The desert, no doubt, has made some irruption with its sands even here ; but it is astonishing how the return, however clandestine and however ill-guided,[1] to the founts of the older English has refreshed matters prosodically and otherwise.

The most interesting thing for us by far is the way in which Chatterton learnt from Spenser—it could hardly by any possibility have been from any one else—the great *Christabel* variation itself in " The Unknown Knight " or " The Tournament." It begins with pretty steady iambics, one shortened line—

> With manie a tassild spear,

giving an effect which is not Christabellian, though it does foreshadow the *Lay of the Last Minstrel,* and may have been in Scott's mind. But so far no other feet have been beyond risk of doubt or question allowed, though there have been some of Shenstone's " dactyls," " clarion," " champion," etc. After some thirty lines, Chatterton breaks into anapæsts, and before long he has felt the true intermixture.[2] He does not quite hold it, stumbling into decasyllables.[3] But it is noteworthy, and of the

---

[1] If Chatterton took liberties, liberties far more unjustifiable have been taken with him. The publishing of the Rowley poems as wholes in modern spelling, and the "improving" of them by original emendation, or even by moving gloss into text, are both things to be contemplated with amazement.

[2] But when he threwe downe his asenglave,
Next came in syr Botelier bold and brave,
The death of manie a Saraceen, etc.

[3] So great the shock their senses did depart.

This has led to a theory, as to Spenser's own practice, which will be best discussed when we come to *Christabel* itself.

noteworthiest, that Spenser had done the same: and most of the piece is very fair, if accidental, *Christabel.* Nor should notice be omitted of the strange fact that while both Coleridge and Scott could hardly have failed to know Chatterton, yet neither of them refers to him. There is no other single feature in the Rowley poems of such importance, so striking, or so strange ; but the breath of a new prosodic inspiration blows at intervals through the whole of it, and more than atones for the preposterous misspelling and the " marine store " jumble of real, mistaken, and manufactured archaisms. The intervals are sometimes trying, as where poor John Lydgate (who, as Heaven and we know, has prosodic sins enough of his own) is saddled with eighteenth-century doggerel common measure, of which, before the sixteenth, there is no trace in English. Rowleyfied Pindaric is also rather terrible ; and clumsy stanzas suggesting a sort of hotch-potch of the Spenserian, Prior's ugly variety of it, and the octave, are not much better. But some short regular lyrics are breath from Heaven.

> I kenne syr Roger from afar
> Trippynge over the lea ;
> Ich ask whie the loverds son
> Is moe than mee ?

should make any ear that deserves to hear prick itself up. And as for the great " Minstrel's Song in Ælla," this, once more, is one of the chief and principal things—one of the turning points—of our story.

The remarkable thing about this[1] is the almost un-erring skill with which the variations of the metre are adapted, and the still more wonderful judgment with which the vowel values adjust themselves. One of the improvers upon Chatterton, neglecting the latter point,

---

[1] O ! synge untoe mie roundelaie,
O ! droppe the brynie teare wythe mee,
Daunce ne moe atte hallie daie,
Lycke a reyning ryver bee ;
    Mie love ys deade,
    Gon to hys deathe-bedde
    Al under the wyllowe tree.

has actually substituted the feeble word "gird" for "dente" in one stanza, and the perfectly different "grow" and "blow" for "gre" and "bee" in another. Such experiments chiefly show the need of inculcating the true principles of prosody, and its absolute dependence on individual cadence and sound.

The stanza and the song just given are Chatterton's greatest prosodic feats, and those of which one thinks most fondly as one visits or revisits the mighty church that inspired him, on its knoll looking half down upon, half up to, Bristol city. But the prosodic afflatus is all over the Rowley poems. The "Ballad of Charity," in subject a rather common-place though beautifully varied version of the Parable of the Good Samaritan, is the first resurrection for many a day of rhyme-royal with an Alexandrine ending. It has not a few charmingly moulded lines, and there are many to be found elsewhere. At any rate, here once more is "fingering"—the touch of string and stop which turns line and stave from dead things to live ones —that makes the clay birds take wing and sweep and flutter and cry. And so "Glory! Glory!"—as Salvation Yeo (who must have seen St. Mary Redclyffe often enough, though it is to be feared not with the proper feelings) has it of the discovery of another ocean by Englishmen.

This chapter, however, would be incomplete without The ballad. a survey of the part played by the ballad during the century—a part which is of the very highest prosodic importance, though of the least intricate. It will even be better still to reserve the directer and greater part of the Scottish element to take together with Burns in the next volume, only reminding the reader in the interim, that Watson's collections when the century was quite young, and those of Allan Ramsay a little later, undoubtedly exercised great influence ; that Allan himself was in communication with Pope, Somerville, and other English poets ; and that Scotland, through Lord Hailes, had a finger even in Percy's *Reliques*. It will be sufficient here to give the history, during the century, of the English ballad as written or collected by Englishmen in the narrow sense, or men resident in the South, no matter from what part of the kingdom they drew their extraction.

At the beginning of the time this English ballad was at its absolute nadir as regards literary reputation ; and in the *Garlands* and other collections, as well as in broadsheet form, had to a large extent deserved that position. But there must have been a stirring of the waters somewhat far back in the seventeenth century ; since the inestimable Percy Folio is attributed to about its middle, and we know that not very long after that middle, Pepys began to make his collections, and others theirs. And according to the operation of that mysterious but comfortable law of which the oldest expression is found in one of our own documents—

When bale is hest, then bote is nest,

and which we have seen prosodically illustrated through-out these two last Books, the ballad began to exhibit its lifebuoy properties just when English prosody generally seemed settling towards elaborately but monotonously

The 1723 rhythmed prose. The first *Collection of Old Ballads*
Collection. *corrected from the best and most ancient Copies extant* appeared in 1723, three years before D'Urfey's *Pills to Purge Melancholy*, which in a way may be called the second, though it contains much other matter. The earlier collection is attributed to " Namby Pamby " Philips, and if it be his, is by far his greatest literary work, estating him in a position much above that of writers of better original verse. And it is not insignifi-cant that it has a motto from Rowe, defending ballad writers from the obloquy generally thrown on them. One must not, of course, expect in this collection any attempt to criticise or sort the wheat from the tares ; it was, in fact, much better that there should be none, for it would probably have proceeded on a wrong method. The historical introductions are now historical curiosities mainly ; and the illustrations much the same. As all the pieces, no doubt, were taken from printed copies,

the singsong and jog-trot which had invaded and mastered the ballad during the past two centuries are triumphantly in evidence. But this need not disturb us. In his first volume, taking it alone, Namby gave them the "King and the Miller of Mansfield," divers "Robin Hood" pieces, "Chevy Chase," "Sir Andrew Barton," "Johnny Armstrong's Goodnight," "Lord Thomas and Fair Ellinor," "Gilderoy"; he gave them such verse as—

> Queen Elenor was a sick woman
> And afraid that she should die,
> Then she sent for two Friars of France
> To speak with her stealthily,

which, for all the abominable libel of which it is going to be the vehicle, has virtue enough to take Bysshe and all Bysshism on its sinful shoulders and carry them off to their own place. And again and again in the two others you come to measures every one of which, while it knocks the fetters off the feet of English poetry, teaches those feet at the same time how to run freely. Here are the well-stamped coranto of the "Spanish Lady," the swinging anapæsts of "Pretty Bessee," the floating lilt of "The Lass with the Golden Hair." No matter about good text or bad text; no matter about incongruous admixtures and prosaic degradations. The circles which arise when you cast stones like these into the waters will widen and widen till they cover the whole pool.

It is tempting, but would be improper, to dwell further The *Reliques.* on individual instances of influence. The next important *point de repère* is Percy's book itself. Here, too, one has to keep the foot carefully, in order not to stray into general poetic influence; but it can be kept. And let us remember also, that it does not, for our purpose, matter one scrap how Percy doctored and blended his material. What he gave to his age is the point. The gift was certainly a mighty one—meddle and make as he might, he could hardly mar worse than the seventeenth-century ballad-mongers had done; and his contributions to the education of the reading were all-important. *His* "Chevy

Chase " is no longer the castrated and translated version which Namby had given, but

The Percy out of Northumberland,

with the real swing and sweep ; and the same is the case with many another, if not with all others. The exact age, the real genuineness of his pieces, have really nothing to do with the importance of the fact, for us, that they came before the generation of 1765. The numerous variations of the ballad measure itself must have been priceless as tending to disturb the deadly singsong which, as we have seen, had settled on it. No matter who wrote " Sir Patrick Spens," no matter where and when it was written : it could not but be antidote to the bane of Percy's own ballad style. The zigzag and the *discordia concors* of " Edward " must have been sovereign for eighteenth-century complaints. The Lewes Ballad itself was there—a document of which then hardly any one could be expected to understand the full significance, but which was at any rate put on record and exposed to access. " The Nut-Brown Mayd " reappeared without the obliging but ill-parted companion to which Prior had yoked her. " The Heir of Lynne," again, whatever questions may be raised about it, stirs and enlivens the dead bones of the long measure, just as other examples do those of the short. The admirable cadence of " Mary Ambree " varies " Pretty Bessee " exactly in the difference of the spirit of the two young ladies ; and " Brave Lord Willoughby " in the same way teaches that lesson which (it is to be hoped not quite *ad nauseam*) we have so often urged here, that the possible fingerings of the same measure are in many cases almost infinite. Even allitera-tive metre this admirable Doctor exhibited to his fortunate patients, though it is not probable that many of them assimilated the medicine ; and he selected some of not the least beautiful of seventeenth-century compositions to temper and complete this his exhibition of English poetry and English prosody. Many hard things have been said of Percy, sometimes by pedants, sometimes by persons for whom that word itself would be too hard, but who for the occasion were made somewhat pedantic by special interests and special studies. To any one who judges from the general point of view of literature, he must always seem one of the most profitable servants that this literature has ever had : and fortunately *our* special interest and subject only intensify appreciation of his work.

Still there is no doubt that he did not learn the lesson of his own work as fully as he might ; and that, either in consequence of this or of evil habits of older date, he set a very bad example in two ways. One was that of tampering with the actual ballads, which does not much concern us ; the other, that of imitating them with a *prava imitatio*, which concerns us very much. The results were shown throughout the rest of the century. Except Chatterton and Blake, no one before Southey and Coleridge showed any real grasp of ballad metre ; no one before Coleridge, any real grasp of ballad diction. The error is shown in Percy's own original work more than sufficiently, and in that of many others ; and it appears glaringly in the third great ballad collection of the century, that of Evans.[1] Evans.

Far be it from me to be hard on this good bookseller. Not only did he extend Percy's selection of ballads considerably, especially in the Robin Hood part, but he ransacked the 1723 collection and other sources with some care, and had at least the wits to include Chatterton among his moderns, or the fortunate folly to believe him an ancient. His book must have done good.

But it may also have done some harm, and has certainly the record of more. Mickle, who, though not a bad man, was a great fashioner of not very good modern antiques, is believed to have had much to do with the collection, and things like "The Prophecy of Queen Emma,"

---

[1] There are two issues of this. The first appeared originally in 1777, with a second edition in 1784 ; the other in 1810. This latter, much the handsomer and better book, is also immensely improved by additions, omissions, and corrections—most of the namby-pamby imitations being cast out neck and crop. But this very fact, and its date, make it of no great use to us as a document even at that date ; and quite out of place here. What follows above will therefore be restricted to the first issue.

said to be written by "Mr. Mickle the very ingenious translator of the *Lusiad*, author of *Almada Hill*, an excellent poem, etc.," abound. Now we do not want, and nobody ought ever to have wanted, such stuff as—

> O'er the hills of Teviot beaming,
>   Rode the silver dawn of May,
> Hostile spears and helmets gleaming,
>   Swelled along the mountains gray.

There is no solace in *this* sin; it is only the sin of a solace which is for the moment in abeyance. When they Chattertonise spelling they are more dreadful still.

But there is no need to dwell on this. It was inevitable: it was the scum of the fermentation which Percy had introduced. And before long the good wine was to come in *The Ancient Mariner*, who indeed was, let it be remembered, "Auncyent" and "Marinere" at first, and did otherwise bedizen and bedevil himself.

Some minor lyrics.

But it would be somewhat curmudgeonly to leave this much-abused century—which was, after all, let it be remembered, one of the wisest in history, though its wisdom was narrow—with praise merely of its fishings-up of pearls in lyric which were not its own. It *had* some of its own besides those which have been mentioned in dealing with its greater writers; and some of these, if not quite of the purest Orient, such as only a very base or a very foolish Judean would deliberately throw away. The charming toy-symphony of Pulteney's "Strawberry Hill,"[1] and the admirable anapæsts[2] which he and Chester-

---

[1] Since Denham sang of Cooper's,
      There's scarce a Hill around
    But what in song or ditty
      Is turned to fairy ground!
    Ah! peace be with their memory,
      I wish them wondrous well;
    But Strawberry Hill, but Strawberry Hill,
      Will ever bear the bell!

[2] Had I Hanover, Bremen, and Verden,
      And likewise the Duchy of Zell,
    I would part with them all for a farthing,
      To have my dear Molly Lepell!

Pronounce "Verden" with the proper English value of *er*, and give "farthing" its then correct form of "farden," and the rhyme will be spotless.

field jointly wrote for Molly Lepell, are capital prosodic examples of the wit, and the merriment, and the good temper that set off the wisdom. Scores of other well-known things, from " The Girl I left behind me " onwards, show that improved sureness of rhythmical grasp on which we have commented, and shall comment. I do not know who wrote this " Girl," but I am nearly certain that much greater poets than he would have been unable to keep the ring and swing of his measure, as he does, only a generation or so before. Nor does anybody seem to know who wrote the sweet and gracious address to " My Winifreda,"[1] which appeared in a miscellany edited by D. Lewis as early as 1726 ; but whoever it was, he had that very rare gift of making each line catch up the last, and so establishing an unbroken chain from beginning to end of the *karole.* Far later, how did Mrs. Crewe's mother secure the wonderful throb (almost early seventeenth century in its character) of certain stanzas[2] in the " Prayer to Indifference " ? That she may have at times. been sorry for having married " out of the window " that typical fine gentleman, Mr. Greville, is highly probable. The final lines—

> Half-pleased, contented I will be—
> Content but half to please,

can be interpreted better from certain passages in Fanny

---

[1] With its well-known last stanza—

> And when with envy Time, transported,
> Shall think to rob us of our joys,
> You'll in your girls again be courted,
> And I'll go wooing in my boys.

This very agreeable thing (" Away ! Let nought to Love displeasing ") has, I believe, been often reprinted. I met it last in Mr. Arber's *Pope Anthology* (Oxford, 1899), pp. 208-9.

[2] I ask no kind return in love,
> No tempting charm to please ;
> Far from the heart such gifts remove
> That sighs for peace and ease.

> Nor ease nor peace that heart can know
> That, like the needle true,
> Turns at the touch of joy or woe—
> But turning, trembles too !

Burney's *Diary* than many puzzles of the sort. But the instance of passion—of whatever kind—quickening the actual structure of the verse, is curious, and not too common in the century.

These instances have been taken from anonymous or non-professional verse writers ; but the patient explorer of the preserves mentioned above [1] will find not a few reliefs to mere prose and mere singsong in the minor poets of the time. Harry Carey may have been chiefly inspired by music when he wrote " Sally in our Alley," and (*if* he wrote it) " God save great George our King." But the lyrical motives to be found in that little read and certainly very minor poet Langhorne [2] show once more how, when prosodic form is once thoroughly accomplished, it remains, so to speak, out of commission, but ready : a hulk it may be, dismantled and moored in some out-of-the-way creek, but always capable of being fitted out, and manned, and manœuvred by the right poet.

The hymn-writers. Charles Wesley.

So, too, some further reference should perhaps be made to the hymns which constitute no small part of the lyrical achievement of the time. Here it may be thought specially rash to attempt to separate the purely prosodic character from the musical on the one hand, and the strictly religious-sentimental on the other. Yet I believe it can be done. [3] Take any of the masterpieces of Charles

---

[1] As it was once frivolously put—

> For poetical curios whoso would search,
> Let him look in the volumes of Dodsley and Pearch.
> It is wondrous how many quaint ends and queer odds lie
> Concealed in the store-house of Pearch and of Dodsley.

[2] I have dwelt elsewhere on the singular beauty of Langhorne's stanza—

> Where longs to fall that rifted spire,
>   As weary of the insulting air ;
> The poet's thought, the warrior's fire,
>   The lover's sighs are sleeping there.

(Of course, he printed it "th' insulting," but he knows better now.) The whole poem "The Wallflower" (Fable vii. of *Flora*), rococo as it may be, has a strange and delightful languor of rhythm and phrase.

[3] And it must be remembered that, as was pointed out at the very beginning of this *History*, hymns, from their constant communication *ad vulgus*, have a strange power of *disciplining* the general ear. " If only they did not do it so badly ! " says some one. Amen. But when they do it well ?

Wesley, of Toplady, of Cowper. Several of these, and several dozens, scores, hundreds, or thousands more of other hymns, were composed for the same old tunes. All of them, without exception, have the same inspiration of sentiment, and even the same mould of biblical diction. That part of the difference of the good ones from the bad ones arises from the better handling of the thought, is, of course, not to be denied. But I think it can be shown also that a good deal arises from the purely prosodic manipulation of the measure, from the ransacking of the lexicon, and the fingering of the selected vocables. They say Charles Wesley wrote between six and seven thousand hymns— a sin of excess for which he perhaps deserved a very short sojourn in the mildest shades of Purgatory, before his due translation upwards for the best of them. Of these best take even such as " Hark the herald angels sing," [1] or " Jesu, lover of my soul," which it is difficult even to read without hearing the well-known tunes. But resist that temptation, wax your ears like Ulysses, and you will find that the mere word-music is fingered throughout in the most absolutely adequate manner : while there is something more for us in his transformation of Cennick's crude and "string-halting "

> Lo, he cometh, countless trumpets
> Blow before his bloody sign,

into the gorgeous

> Lo, he comes with clouds descending ;

which the Reverend Martin Madan of *Thelyphthora* fame naturally tried to spoil.

Toplady is an even better example, for " Rock of Ages " owes much less to its tune than the others, or rather is much more easily separable from it. Almost any "crooning " kind of accompaniment, fitting the feet, would suit it ;

Toplady.

---

[1] I quote it thus because otherwise nobody would recognise it. Wesley wrote " Hark how all the welkin rings." The alteration, with some others, is apparently due to Whitefield, and is one of the few good to many bad examples of tampering with hymns. These may be traced in Mr. Julian's invaluable *Dictionary of Hymnology* (London, 1892 ; new ed. 1907).

that is to say, it is independent of any; it is like the
great Latin hymns which carry their own music with
them; and accordingly all the attempts to "Latin" it are
as bad as are the Englishings of, say, *Dies Irae.* Every
word, every syllable in this really great poem has its
place and meaning: a fact of which the respectable
persons who change "eyestrings break" into "eyelids
close" and "riven" into "wounded" are no doubt as
ignorant as those who have tampered with Chatterton.
And I fear it must be said that the hopelessness of the
late Dr. Grosart as a critic (he was invaluable in other
ways) is nowhere better shown than by his remark that
Toplady was "no poet," unless it be by the fact that he
deplores the comparative ignoring of

> Dateless principle, arise !

which is prosodically weak, verbally awkward, and chiefly
suggestive of an epitaph on the head of a nondescript
college whose birth-year was unknown.

Cowper.   But, of course, the chief interest here is in Cowper, who,
though he may never have gone quite so high in this
particular line of ascent as Wesley and Toplady, scattered
and squandered himself much less than the first; is not
nearly a "single speech," like the second; and, besides, is
a poet, apt at many if not all weapons, and not merely
a singer whose lips are specially and solely touched by
the coals from the actual altar.   It has been said above
that his variety, even in profane work, is rather remarkable; it is almost more so here, because the tendency of
hymns—with their few metres, their well-known tunes,
and their stock subjects—is towards monotony.   But
Cowper gets strikingly different and strikingly good
effects out of most of his measures and many of his
themes.

> Oh ! for a closer walk with God,

though its rhymes shock the captious modern, possesses a
curious plaintive dreaminess, contrasting with the skip and
hop of

> Ere God had built the mountains.

No finical and Philistine dislike of the phraseology ought to blind any lover of poetry to the wonderful tranced adoration of the movement of

> There is a fountain filled with blood ;

and I do verily believe that

> Hark, my soul, it is the Lord,

suggested its well-known tune imperatively, though the tune is but a feeble echo of the prosodic music.

> What various hindrances we meet

is weaker—in fact, one of the weakest ; but not so

> God moves in a mysterious way.

Indeed, one may say, without irreverence, that the way in which this prosaic century ceases to be prosaic in divine poetry *is* rather mysterious.

A paragraph or so may suffice — because there is nothing at all new or very special about the individuals— for the continuation of the work of Prior and Swift in anapæst and iambic octosyllable. But it could not be wholly omitted, because of the immense importance of these measures as strongholds of lighter and freer movement ; and it may be placed here not improperly, because both are constant vehicles of lyric. Both were utilised all through ; but the most important document of the octosyllable was lodged early in the shape of Dyer's beautiful *Grongar Hill*, which coincided in date with the earliest of Thomson's Seasons. Dyer afterwards relapsed into blank verse, on Thomson's own model, where he is of no particular importance. In *Grongar Hill* he is of much ; for he there went not to Swift or to Prior, but straight to Milton, and wrote such mixed measure as had not been seen since " Comus "—

> On the mountain's lonely van.[1]

They shook their heads for more than a couple of

Later eighteenth-century anapæst and octosyllable.

Dyer and Anstey.

---

[1] I have always wondered whether he meant " van " in the *local* sense— " Brecknockshire Van," " Carmarthenshire Van," etc.

generations over the mixture ; but it could not fail to do good.

Of the many practitioners of the lighter continuous anapæst, Byrom, who has been noticed above, and Anstey of the *New Bath Guide*, stand out perhaps most prominently. Anstey did not confine himself to the anapæst, but wrote (even in this book) in octosyllables and other forms. Yet it is for his handling of the triple measure that he is deservedly celebrated. Indeed, he stands to Prior in this class very much as Thomson stands to Milton. He had the advantage of a still further modernised language ; and I really do not know that much advance has been made upon him in the mere *handling* of this delectable instrument for light satire since. And, once more, the extreme popularity of the book helped to popularise the measure, and to fix its principles, all unconsciously, in the ears of those who read it. His other works were of little or no value ; indeed, as Horace Walpole is rather fond of repeating, the additions to the *New Bath Guide* itself are inferior ; but the first chronicle of the Blunderheads helped to fix the anapæst as the favourite measure of the later eighteenth century for easy verse. Not merely was it used for definitely satiric purposes, as in Goldsmith's *Retaliation*, and in much of the political work which was such a feature of the time ; but people of all sorts and conditions, from men of full age and sufficient position, like Dr. Burney, to school-boys or undergraduates, like Southey, wrote doggerel diaries in it—a distinct testimony, if not in very valuable material, to the general sense of its being at the opposite pole from the couplet. The octosyllable was similarly—one need not say degraded, but—hacked in *Doctor Syntax* and others of Combe's productions ; but here the example of *Hudibras* was of older standing, and showed less of any prosodic feeling peculiar to the time. In both cases, however, the metres did run a certain danger of appearing to justify the comparatively menial position which had been once assigned them ; and we get few, if any, very fine serious examples of either till the

Romantic movement has well begun. Their inherent virtue, however, was sure to be recovered in the case of the octosyllable, discovered in that of the anapæst, when great poets began to practise them ; and meanwhile they served the purpose of a foil to excellent effect. In fact, *Grongar Hill* (which always continued to be read as part of the century's own work) was a perpetual testimony to the poetic power of " Hudibrastics," and the real poetic quality of the anapæst needed nothing but trial to develop it.[1]

[1] In the above chapter it has been necessary to omit detailed comment on some interesting and accomplished prosodic forms, because they present nothing new in general principle, and nothing striking in individual treatment. For instance, Gray's stanza in the "Spring" Ode—a combination of common measure and romance-six with lengthened third and sixth lines— is very much better worked out than any stanza-form in the *York Mysteries*. But in mid-eighteenth century the perfected work is of far less importance to our history than the imperfect work was in the bridge of the fourteenth and fifteenth.

CHAPTER IV

PROSODISTS

Revival of prosodic study — Bysshe — The rigour of the syllabic game — Importance of this — Watts — Gildon — Brightland, etc. — Pemberton, Mainwaring, Harris — Say and Home — Burnet, Tucker, Herries — Sheridan — Steele — Tyrwhitt — Walter Young — Nares and Fogg — The Upper House: Shenstone — On "long" rhymes — On "dactyls" — Gray — His *Metrum* notes — Johnson — Note on Goldsmith, *note* — " Decasyllabomania " in him and others — His arguments on pause — John Mason — Mitford.

Revival of prosodic study. THE show which we were able to make under this head, in our last two chapters devoted to the subject, was exceeding poor and beggarly — so much so that even the small room accorded to them might appear to a hasty judgment to be mere waste of space and abuse of method. But no such judgment can be passed, even by the hastiest, on the present, except indeed by those who openly profess want of interest in the whole subject ; and to such one may without churlishness retort, *Quaere aliud diversorium.* The eighteenth century, from its very opening years, devoted itself to prosodic inquiries ; and though most of these inquiries were, from the point of view of the present Book, conducted under almost totally wrong principles, and by hopeless methods, they tended, like the work of all blameless heathens, to better things. Nor is it unfair to credit them, as a whole, on the one hand with a sort of healthy if unconscious reaction from the rather unsatisfactory poetic practice of the time, on the other with a direct preparation for the greater poetry that was to follow.[1]

[1] I have, in this chapter, to acknowledge, with the greatest alacrity and satisfaction, the help that I have received, in preparing it, from my friend Mr.

The present writer has been already taken to task, in Bysshe.
more than one quarter, for exaggerating, in his *History
of Criticism*, the importance of Edward Bysshe's *Art of
Poetry*, 1702. He has only to observe, as little contu-
maciously as possible, that *here* this importance cannot
be exaggerated, and that any one who takes the trouble to
learn a little about the subject is not likely to dispute it.
As a personal man of letters—indeed, as an authority
who speaks not as the scribes—Bysshe is, if anybody
likes it, immediately above or immediately below nullity.
Practically nothing seems to be known about his life ; the
Art itself,[1] with the exception of a few pages, is mere
compilation—a rhyming dictionary, and one of similes,
etc., after the fashion of Poole's ; while outside it he
appears to have merely translated and done other hack-
work. But (and a very slight study of literary history
will show that the case is not isolated) he seems, somehow
or other, to find himself expressing what everybody had
been thinking more or less confusedly for more than a
generation ; and what almost everybody was to think it
proper to think for more than one or two generations
more. Dryden had died at all but the full threescore
and ten, two years before Bysshe wrote ; and during the

Omond's work on prosody, especially his *English Metrists* (Tunbridge Wells,
1903), and its enlarged form (Oxford and London, 1907). Mr. Omond and
I approach the subject from rather different sides. As he justly says, in
some kind remarks about this book, it is planned as a history "rather of our
verse itself than of what critics have said about it." And Mr. Omond takes
great, perhaps chief, interest in the points which seem to me at best
"previous." But I do not think that there is much difference between us
on *results* ; and I have not the least hesitation or shamefacedness in referring
my readers to him on some other points which do not interest me, and are
not, I think, really relevant to my work. At the same time, I acknowledge,
as frankly, that he has put me on the track of some interesting prosodists,
and has saved me from dealing with not a few uninteresting ones. Nothing
that he writes can be safely neglected by students of the subject. In so
far as I think it necessary to deal with the questions which mainly interest
him, and which he dealt with first in his *Study of Metre* (London, 1903),
an excursus on "What is a Foot?" with which I hope to conclude this
work, will give my views. It could not really, according to those views, be
written satisfactorily save after a survey of the whole facts.
   [1] It appeared, as stated above, in 1702, and was frequently reprinted. I
use the "Third edition with large improvements," London, 1708. It
appears that Bysshe was a Sussex man, and may have been connected, in
blood as in name, with Shelley. Which would be humorous.

whole of Dryden's life—nay, before it, in the practice of Waller, and in the practice and principles of Beaumont—the stopped regular decasyllabic couplet had been more and more establishing itself as the perfect form of verse. But, as we saw in the last two chapters under this heading, people were strangely shy of entering into any detail about "numbers": it almost seemed as if it were held unlawful to utter the sacred principles.

The rigour of the syllabic game. Bysshe had no such scruples; probably he was one of the clear-headed but stupid men who have none. His Preface is mere ordinary "talkee-talkee"; but his "Rules for Making English Verse" (which, with examples of some length and frequency, fill thirty-six pages) show a perfectly clear conception, an undoubting mind, and a considerable faculty of drafting. "The structure of our verses, whether blank or in rhyme, consists in a certain number of syllables; not in feet composed of long and short syllables." He is so particular about this, which certainly is the hinge of the whole question, that he works it out with rather superfluous arithmetic—explaining that verses of double rhyme will always want one more syllable than verses of single; decasyllables becoming hendecasyllables, verses of eight syllables turning to nine, verses of seven to eight. "This must also be observed in blank verse"—an iteration which will not seem quite damnable when you perceive that the syllable is the "Faith" of Bysshe's creed—that everything depends on it, and that it must be specified in every case. Once let an uncertain number of syllables in, or permit the syllables in any way to group themselves or coalesce, and Troy falls. Then of the several sorts of verses. Our poetry, he thinks, admits, for the most part, of but three verses—those of ten, eight, or seven syllables. Those of four, six, nine, eleven, twelve, and fourteen are generally employed in masques and operas and in the stanzas of lyric and Pindaric odes. We have few entire poems composed in them; though twelve and fourteen may be inserted in other measures and even "carry a peculiar grace with them." In decasyllabic verse two things are to be considered—the seat of the accent and the pause. The pause (he works this out rather elaborately) ought to be at the fourth, fifth, or sixth syllables. The strongest accent must be on the second, fourth, and sixth. One does not quite see why he says nothing about accent in the last four places ; and indeed he is less explicit about the second half of the line throughout. Perhaps the possibility of a redundant syllable bothered him. And he says less about accent generally than about pause, though he is sure that " wrong placing " of it is as great a fault in English as a false quantity was in the classical languages. To make a good decasyllable you must be careful that the accent is neither on the third nor fifth—a curious crab-like way of approaching the subject, but bringing out in strong relief the main principle of all this legislation, " Thou shalt not." The verse of *seven* syllables, however, is most beautiful when the strongest accent *is* on the third.

More curious still is his way of approaching tri-syllabic metres. As such, he will not so much as speak of them. " Verses of nine and eleven syllables," it seems, " are of two sorts." " Those accented on the last save one " are merely the redundant eights and tens already spoken of. " The other [class] is those that are accented on the last syllable, which are employed only in compositions for music, and in the lowest sort of burlesque poetry, the disagreeableness of their measure having wholly excluded them from grave and serious subjects." The guileless reader [1] will hardly suspect that these nasty idle things are neither more nor less than anapæstic ; though for some extraordinary reason Bysshe does not even mention the full twelve-syllable form under any head whatever. [2] I suppose the "lowness and dis-

---

[1] I can honestly say that when I first read Bysshe I did not know what he was talking about till I came to his examples.

[2] *His* " verses of twelve syllables " are " truly heroic "—in fact, Alexandrines. Yet he must have been perfectly well aware of the existence, in no less a poet than Dryden, of such lines, not merely as

She had heard of a pleasure and something she guessed,

agreeableness " of the thing was too much for him, and
as he had disallowed feet he had, at any rate, some logical
excuse in making nothing of them.   He admits triplets
in heroic, and repeats his admission of Alexandrines and
fourteeners, concluding this section with a funny little
sniff.   " The verses of four or six syllables have nothing
worth observing," though he condescends to give some
from Dryden.

Under the head of " Rules conducing to the beauty
of our versification," and with the exordium, " Our
poetry being very much polished and refined since the
days of Chaucer, Spenser, and other ancient poets," we
find that you must avoid hiatus ; *always* cut off the *e* of
" the " before a vowel ; never allow even such collocations
as " th*y* *i*ambics " or "int*o a* book " ; never value such
syllables as " amaz*e*d " and " lov*e*d," but always contract
them ; avoid alliteration ; never split adjective from
substantive, or preposition from verb, at the end of a line.
" Beauteous " is but two syllables, " victorious " but three.
You must not make " riot " one syllable as Milton does.
" As Milton does *not*," one says ; though, of course, Bysshe
would have thought " -ot ascends " as a foot a thing
too horrid to contemplate.   You *may* contract " vi'let "
and " di'mond," and if you do, should write them so.
" Temp'rance," " diff'rent," etc., are all right ; and you
may use " fab'lous " and " mar'ner " (not Silas).   But
Bysshe acknowledges that " this is not so frequent."   And
he rejects or doubts some of the more violent and most
hideous apostrophations,[1] but has   no   doubt   about
" t' amaze," " I'm," " they've," and most others.   Rhyme is
not very fully dealt with, but for the most part correctly
enough—so far as Bysshe's principles go.   Stanzas of
" intermixed rhyme " (like rhyme-royal, the octave, and

---

which he would probably, on his own abominable devices, have scanned
" she'd," but as

<blockquote>What they meant by their sighing and kissing so close,</blockquote>

which is proof against " apostrophation."

[1] Such as those of " b' " for " by " and " wh' " for " who."

the Spenserian) " are now wholly laid aside," for long
poems at least ; but he gives a good many examples of
them for all uses, and seems more sorry for than angry
at Spenser's " unlucky choice."   Shakespeare, it seems,
invented blank verse to escape " the tiresome constraint
of rhyme."   Acrostics and anagrams " deserve not to be
mentioned."

Now, no doubt, there is not much originality in this ; Importance
and I need scarcely defend myself from the suspicion of of this.
agreeing with it.   But, in the first place, I shall, as a
historian of English prosody, be very much obliged to any
one who will point out to me anything at all like it earlier
as a coherent, thorough-going, practical code of rules for
the making of English verse.   Secondly, I shall be very
much obliged if any one will point out to me a flaw—
there are gaps, but a gap is not necessarily a flaw—in its
theory.   Thirdly, I shall be most of all obliged to any one
who will disprove my contention that what Bysshe here,
in his downright way, codified and mummified was the
actual creed of almost everybody from a time pretty well
before Bysshe's probable birth to a time many years
after his probable death.

It does not matter that Gildon sneers at the tractate.
It does not even very much matter, on the other side, that
it was rapidly and repeatedly reprinted, and that it remained the popular handbook of English verse during something like the whole century—Blake,[1] of all people in the
world, being apparently in the habit of consulting it long
afterwards.   The point is that, as has been said above,
Bysshe caught up and uttered, in hard and fast sym-
bolic terms, the creed of the eighteenth century itself,
of not a few years before the eighteenth century, and of
a good many after it.   Within the year 1907 I saw a
letter from a no doubt most respectable person to a
literary paper, saying that he, the person, had seen
Coleridge's verse in *Christabel* much praised, but was this

---

[1] See in Mr. Swinburne's *Blake*, pp. 130, 131, the pleasant story of Blake
and his wife (on spiritual suggestion) trying *Sortes Virgilianae* on Bysshe,
with results from Aphra Behn and Dryden's *Virgil* respectively (*v. sup.* p. 417).

verse really " regular " according to orthodox views? We
know what Bysshe would have told him ; we know what
Bysshe did tell him a hundred years before *Christabel*,
and two hundred before his own respectable letter.   I do
not think it is quite fair to Bysshe to say, as my friend
Mr. Omond does, that he "represents the traditional
view."   Where is the evidence of "the tradition"?   In
what preceptist writer before him?   In *practice* before
him it exists; but he brought this practice out, formulated
and crystallised it.   I think he was utterly wrong—wrong
most of all in discarding feet ; wrong in dwelling too
much on accent; wrong in countenancing "elision"; wrong
in his estimate of various metres ; wrong everywhere
and every way except in some points of rhyme.   But
he was wrong with a fascinating and logical sequacious-
ness ; and he was wrong, as a theorist, in the manner of
a real and eminent heresiarch.

Watts.   Seven years later than Bysshe, Watts in his Preface to
Horae Lyricae has some interesting prosodic remarks.
At this early time (the Preface is dated May 14, 1709)
he tells us that he had endeavoured to give his couplets
" the same variety of cadence, comma, and period " [*i.e.* the
lesser and the greater pause] which blank verse glories
in."   " It degrades," he continues (and remember that
Pope was only just beginning to publish) " the excellency
of the best versification when lines run on by couplets,
twenty together, just in the same pace and with the same
pauses.   It spoils the noblest pleasure of the sound ; the
reader is tired with the tedious uniformity, or charmed
to sleep with the unmanly softness of the numbers and
the perpetual chime of even cadences."   But even in his
" essays without rhyme " he has not " set up Milton for a
perfect pattern," though he " shall ever be honoured as
our deliverer from the bondage."   It seems that "the
length of his periods, and sometimes of his parentheses,
runs" the good Doctor "out of breath"—on which occasions
one might have hoped that the hospitable Lady Abney
was ready with some cordial not spoken against in the
Scriptures ; but, in fact, it was a year or two before he

became her guest. "Some of his numbers seem too harsh and uneasy." But it is evident that he is thinking even more of burlesques of Milton than of Milton himself. "In Pindarics" Watts "has avoided the excessive lengths to which some modern writers have stretched their sentence," and he lays down the golden rule, "the ear is the truest judge." These are generalities, of course ; but whether he goes right or wrong in them (and he does both) they seem to me to be at any rate in the right vein, and a good deal more important than the accent-and-quantity battle which was before long to begin.

Charles Gildon [1] seems to me, on the other hand, of Gildon. very little importance, except that he was one of the first to adopt the heresy of denoting verse by minims and crotchets, and that, in what Mr. Carlyle would have called rather a "high-sniffing" manner, he puts down Bysshe with his bare accents and syllables, and insists on real "numbers"—though it is very difficult to attach any precise meaning to this fashionable word. Gildon had some parts and some literature ; but there was a good deal of Grub Street in him, which sometimes took the special form of the pedant and sometimes that of the coxcomb. And I have never known anybody who endeavoured to express prosody in terms of music without coming to grief.

Another and rather earlier opponent of Bysshe, John Brightland, Brightland, in his *English Grammar* (1711) also condemns etc. the reliance on accent, and insists on quantity ; but has little detail. He, Gildon, and one or two others [2] may have had something to do with the raising of the "accent *v.* quantity" battle just referred to. It has been fought at intervals ever since ; it shows not the slightest signs of settlement ; and indeed it never can be settled : because

[1] Who wrote on the subject in *The Complete Art of Poetry* (1718) and *The Laws of Poetry* (1721). (Pope's remarks (*sup.* p. 471) are of 1710.)
[2] The excellent Maittaire, who had the grateful task of producing some good editions, and the ungrateful one of teaching young Stanhope (see Chesterfield's *Letters*), thought that English verses "commonly consist of five feet, governed more by accent than quantity." He also informs us that "exercises of poetry of some length are called poems : those that are shorter, copies of verses."

it is almost impossible to get a set of definitions of terms which any two combatants will accept.[1]

The fight, however, went on, in this section of it, for a considerable time, sometimes extending over the whole field of ancient and modern poetry, sometimes limiting itself to the classics, sometimes to English. I have read most, if not all, of the texts,[2] but have found very little in them which needs notice here, and a curiously general unsatisfactoriness by results. The *Observations on Poetry*, for instance, of Henry Pemberton (1738) would treat Milton *more ultra-Bentleiano*, and alter every line which contains a trochee, reading—

And *rolling towards* the gate her bestial train,

etc.; while for the same reason the whole of *L'Allegro* and *Il Penseroso*, "those otherwise excellent pieces," is black-marked. "Pause is the only available source of variety"; and Pemberton greatly admires Glover. Edward Mainwaring (1744) is again disastrously musical, as in fact most of them are. He wants "tierce minors" and "tierce majors" in poetry; and is one of the

Pemberton, Mainwaring, Harris.

---

[1] I may take for example myself and my friend Mr. Omond, who, I believe, agree pretty generally as to results, and cordially as to the necessity of "feet" or something of the kind. But Mr. Omond, while he objects as I do to making accent the basis of English prosody, thinks it impossible that accent can create quantity. I feel quite sure that it can, or rather (for "create" may cause misapprehension) can give "brevet" rank in quantity. But then that is because we do not agree in the definition of the word quantity. To me, quantity is simply that which fits a syllable for occupying a "long" place in a foot, or that which only fits it for a "short"; and I use "long" and "short" just as I might use "black" and "white," to denote the difference of the two constituents of feet, which I am quite as ready to call Greek and Trojan or anything else.

[2] I began making up my leeway (I had known not a few long before) for the *History of Criticism*, and have completed the process, or nearly so, for this book. With the exceptions which will be noted above, I have never had a more thankless task. The much-abused scholastics knew, and knew thoroughly, what they were talking about. Most of these eighteenth-century prosodists hardly knew anything of English poetry. The great Dr. John Foster, for instance, in his *Essay on Accent and Quantity*, which contains some glimmerings, bases the enormous generalisation, that "our dissyllabic nouns are for the most part trochaic and our verbs iambic," on the small class or identically spelt nouns and verbs ("cóncert" and concért, etc.), where the distinction had actually been made, for convenience' sake, not long before his own time.

first to suggest the trochaicising of standard iambic
metres—

>   And | mounts ex|ulting | on tri|umphant | wings.

He laments, memorably, that though Milton has the
numbers that he likes, "they are generally confounded
by prosaic stops." Harris of *Hermes* fame has a little
about poetry, and redeems his terrible description of
Milton's verse as consisting of "ten *semipeds*" by
admitting that each of these animalcules can "carry a
pause." Samuel Say (1744) is above all things an
elocutionist, and great on "making the sound suit the
sense." He too is musical ; and perhaps owes to this his
exaggeration (of a doctrine which up to a certain sense
is true) that "every syllable in English is common." But
when we try the result-test he shrinks up at once, as they
all do ; for he thinks Prior's *estropiement* of the Spenserian
"noble," "the noblest of the Poems." Lord Kames
(same year) in the *Elements of Criticism* takes the extreme
opposite line to that of his brother on the bench, Monboddo
(*v. inf.*). He is an apostle of correctness ; even Pope is
sometimes too lax for him.[1]

In the same year with Foster and Kames, an odd
person named Daniel Webb wrote *Remarks on the Beauties
of Poetry*, following them up seven years later with
Observations on the Correspondence of Poetry and Music.
Webb is a quaint mixture. He attacks Pope for monotony, and praises Shakespeare and Milton for variety. But
he has this very odd misunderstanding of Shenstone's
(? *v. inf.*) plea for the "dactyl" : "Some are of the opinion
that a dactyl may take place in the pentameter. This

Say and Home.

---

[1] As I rather took up the cudgels for Kames in my *History of Criticism*
on some points, I am bound to say here that his eighty pages on Versification
contain very little of value.   He thinks

>   This nymph, to the destruction of mankind

(as happy a line for its prosodic adaptation as may be) "harsh," because "the"
is lengthened ; and reduces "Scotch metaphysics" to the almost unbelievably
absurd, by alleging that there cannot be a pause *even in melody* between
adjective and substantive, because "a quality cannot exist independent of
a subject."

verse consists of five feet or ten syllables. If, therefore, we appropriate three syllables to one foot, there must be a foot of one syllable, which would be contrary to nature." One could have no better instance of the depth to which the syllabic idea had entered, and the harm it had done ; hardly any better example of the preposterous fashion in which these writers approach their subject.

Burnet, Tucker, Herries.   There was a great outburst of prosodic work in the seventies of the century.   Not only did Monboddo's work [1] then begin to appear (1773), but in the same year came a treatise [2] by " Light-of-Nature " Tucker, under his usual pseudonym " Edward Search," and another [3] by John Herries.   As everybody who is familiar with the *Light of Nature* itself would expect, Tucker's tractate is amusing ; but it is much more phonetic than prosodic.   He experiments in hexameters, but thinks the iamb *the* English foot, and in fact is, like most people in this chapter, not " at the point of view."   John Herries anticipated, though on less magnificent scale, a notion of Guest's—trying to arrange accented and unaccented syllables in all possible permutations and collocations, of which he makes 178.   Elocution is always at one ear of Herries, and Music at another ; and they distract him properly.   At one moment he thinks that an accented syllable is not always long (which is true enough when you can *escamoter* the accent) ; at another, that accent and quantity *very seldom* coincide—which is absurd from almost any point of view ; and, at a third, that the *longest* syllables are accented—which throws the whole thing into chaos again.

Sheridan.   Two years later came that victim of Johnson's in-justice, " Sherry," to demonstrate in his *Art of Reading* how unjust the Doctor could be.   Of course, being a teacher of elocution, he is M. Josse, and his profession plays him some tricks.   Of course, likewise, he might

[1] *The Origin of Language.* He deals largely with accent and quantity "in the *ab*stract " ; approves of Milton for "breaking the measure" ; actually likes the "bottomless pit " ; and has many glances in his usual way—often wrong-headed but never stupid.   Still it is all *a priori*.
[2] *Vocal Sounds.*   [3] *The Elements of Speech.*

know more than he does. But that "we *indolently* adopted French prosody" is about as true as it is false in regard to what he was thinking of. It is a great thing at this time to have a man dismissing the valuation of "echoing" as "ech'ing" with the term "absurd"; and one would much rather have a man believe, as he does, in the pyrrhic and the amphibrach than believe in nothing but the iamb. And he is so good on the pause that it may have been the reason of Johnson's objection; while if he depreciates rhyme and extols blanks—once more he *is* M. Josse. No! "Sherry" shows no dulness, either by nature or in art, here, though he is rudimentary.

As to Joshua Steele and his *Prosodia Rationalis*, I find myself, perhaps for the first time, in total disaccord with Mr. Omond, who thinks very highly of him. That, in Mr. Omond's own words, Steele "proclaims that verse is essentially matter of musical rhythm, and applies musical methods frankly and fully to the notation of metre," naturally does not prejudice me in his favour; but I hope I have shown myself fairly superior to mere prejudice already, and in this particular matter I may appeal to my treatment of Mason and Mitford below. I do not care what system a man adopts, so that his system brings out the beauty of good English verse, and the ugliness of bad. But the proof of the prosody to me is in the scansion; and even Mr. Omond himself admits that Steele's scansion is "utterly wild." I should say that it was contemptibly and impudently ridiculous. He scans [1]

O happiness! our being's end and aim,

O | happiness | our | being's | end and | aim,

and gravely adds, "whosoever would pronounce with propriety must allow at least six cadences by the aid of proper rests" in, apparently, any heroic line. Sometimes there are eight. He has "met no one to whom this was

---

[1] Let me observe that I have no objection to *anacrustic* scansion as such. It is sometimes necessary, often optional, and it forms the basis of my own theory as to English hexameters; but as applied to the heroic or to most if not all iambic schemes, it simply turns the whole measure topsy-turvy.

enunciated who was not immediately convinced of its truth and utility" (I wish *I* had met Mr. Joshua Steele). He thinks that Milton, "making use of his natural senses," arranged the first lines of *Paradise Lost* for scansion thus—

Of | man's | first diso|bedience | and the | fruit Of | that for | bidden | tree | whose | mortal | taste Brought | death | into the | world | and | all our | woe | Sing | Heavenly | Muse.

He calls, of course, the English heroic a " hexameter," and the Latin hexameter an " octometer." Now really ! I own that I cannot at all share Mr. Omond's admiration for Steele's mere theory ; and I have grave doubts about the point for which he praises him most—the inclusion of the pause, as a matter of course, in the constituency of the line. *Some* pauses should no doubt be so included. I myself believe in "the pause-foot" as a reality, and an important one. But the ordinary pause is not a foot ; and you can have the most beautiful lines, and any number of them, without a pause at all. All Steele's notation seems to me a musical-mathematical supererogation, if not a musical-mathematical hallucination. Yet I could tolerate it if it had led him to any good results.

His results are not good : they are bad, absurd, revolting. He can have had no more notion of the true prosodic music of any piece of English verse than the swine have of the pearls—not so much as the cock had of the *iaspis*. When Mr. Omond says that " real students will hail Steele as a master," I can only say that I regretfully take my name off the books. I am not a real student. I will not hail Steele as a master except of utter prosodic chaos. The only object of prosody—its only business, its only reason for existence— is to give English verse a true interpretation. His interpretation is utterly false.

Tyrwhitt.   Fortunately, the true method vindicated itself in this same year, 1775, for then appeared Tyrwhitt's *Chaucer*. Here there was no substitution of theory for study of fact. On the contrary, the actual verse which had

always been beautiful, which made its beauty felt, as in
Dryden's case, even to those who mistook the facts, was
cleared, manifested, exhibited as it was.   You cannot
have two better examples of a prosodist in his right
mind and a prosodist out of it than Tyrwhitt and Steele.
Tyrwhitt himself still did not know quite enough ; he
should not have held our verse to be *wholly* " of Norman
origin."   But he admitted the trisyllabic feet (which are
not of Norman origin), and this takes the mischief out of
his perhaps still too great belief in syllables and accents.
He had only to *learn* a little more ; he could *hear*
already.   Steele, it is obvious, was absolutely without
ear for poetry, whatever he may have had for music.[1]

With regard to the *Rythmical* [sic] *Measures* of Walter Young.
Walter Young, contributed to the Royal Society of
Edinburgh, read in 1786, but to be found at p. 550 of
Part I. of its second volume of *Transactions* (1790), I
hoped something from Mr. Omond's first note on it as
" good and original."   And I got it duly out of the library
of the University of Edinburgh, where it had possibly
reposed unread (unless Mr. Omond consulted it there)
since it was first shelved.   But his later and fuller
notice, in his complete *English Metres*, may relieve others
from following my example.   Young is again purely
musical : he begins with *a priori* musical considerations,
as far as prosody is concerned, and with very few illustrations from actual verse.   Once more we have the beginning
with an odd syllable, which seems obligatory in such cases.
Blank verse is " hardly verse at all."   It appears to require
some argument to prove that " words may be arranged in
rhythm," which, considering that poets have been doing
it for some thousands of years, is rather superfluous.
" Eight is most easily conceived as two fours [not by
me !].   Sixteen is *always* conceived as four fours "—

---

[1] It is fair to say that his work was a sort of incidental parergon, arising
out of letters to Monboddo, and that he turned from it to schemes of doing
good to his negroes in Barbadoes.   So the world had no more

Nice clever books from Josh Steele the philanthropist.

I hope the negroes were the better.   I am sure the world was not the worse.

except by the unworthy writer of this book. In reading
Milton you must " sacrifice the measure to the sense."
Again, there is nothing for it but Mr. Carlyle's immortal
sentence—" All these propositions I content myself with
modestly but peremptorily denying." But why go beyond
the Reverend Walter Young's latest and best possible—
perhaps his only—defender? " Would that there were
more such essays to cite, *and that the author of this one
had given more of his attention to our own verse.*" As to
the last half, I can say, " Thou sayest it "; but if he had,
I think he would have burnt his essay.

Nares and
Fogg.   Only two other preceptist prosodists of the eighteenth
century (postponing those, such as Sayers, who are
directly connected with the Romantic movement) seem
to me to deserve notice here. They are Robert Nares
and Peter Fogg. Nares [1] is of some interest because he
illustrates a special point of time in the story. He refers
to " the fate that has befallen Chaucer "; dwells specially
on " words that have changed accent, or are the subject
of dispute respecting it "; tries once more the hopeless
task of giving general rules for quantity—" a vowel
followed by a consonant is short " : a rule which I should
cheerfully adopt with the addition, " except when it is
long "; and winds up with the suggestion—a favourite
one at various times as a counsel of despair—that " the
elder poets meant rather to indulge themselves, and
diversify their measure by the admission of a super-
abundant syllable, than to suppress the vowel." [2]   Fogg,
who, it must be remembered, is very late,[3] is evidently well
acquainted with his predecessors, and he has glimmerings,
saying that you " extend " a syllable by " lengthening
the vowel *and* dwelling on the consonant," thus showing
that he really has a notion of the foot or " isochronous

---

[1] *Elements of Orthoepy* (1784).

[2] The mixture of truth and error here is interesting and almost pathetic.
The good man rightly revolts at the " suppression " of a vowel ; but he only
allows it to survive in a limbo of extra-metrical " superabundance." That it
is as full-franchised a denizen or citizen of the metre as any other syllable is
not to be thought of.

[3] *Dissertations* (1796).

interval." But there is not much in him ; and, in fact, his dissertations on the subject are only two out of many.[1]

I have not much fear of Mr. Omond's misunderstanding me ; but I shall be very sorry if there seems to others to be anything superficial, perfunctory, or flippant in this account, so far, of eighteenth-century prosodists. Almost all the persons yet named seem to me to exhibit the very worst fault of neo-classic criticism, the tendency to construct rules from *a priori* considerations of one kind or another, or from an absolutely insufficient portion of the facts, and then to apply them to those facts as if the facts themselves were bound to give way. The exact points from which they start, and the exact quantity and character of plant and material with which they may be furnished at this start, no doubt vary considerably. Some—most, indeed—start with music—with the occasional clothes instead of with the universal body. Some start with mathematics—with the measuring rod instead of with the substance to be measured. Some—perhaps the truest children of their century—start with considerations of human pleasure, and of the particular pleasure derived, or supposed to be derived, from orderly succession, etc. A very few, like Bysshe himself (who really does not seem to me by any means the greatest fool of the group), do start with actual poetry and poets, but either confine themselves to, or arbitrarily prefer, those who exhibit certain limited forms. Nobody, so far as we have gone, even attempts to make an examination of English poetry as a whole, or even to collect a large number of different poetical examples that give him pleasure, and to examine their characteristics. And the result is that even the good remarks that are found here and there in them are haphazard, partial, likely to be contradicted, or at least confronted with bad ones, on the

---

[1] I gather references to some other writers in this note, that those who are curious about them may look them up, either in the original or in Mr. Omond's book. For my purpose they have little or nothing. John Brown's ("Estimate" Brown's) *Dissertation on Poetry and Music* (1763) ; Hawkins's *History of Music* (1771) ; Beattie's *Essays* (1776) ; Blair's *Lectures* (1783). Some writers on English hexameters, etc., including Goldsmith, I keep for the special treatment of that subject later. (But *v. inf.* p. 561, *note.*)

next page.   While, as for general results, you get
Pemberton preferring Glover to Milton ; you get the
absolutely Bedlamite scansions of Steele ; you get Nares
suggesting that if one comes upon a superfluous syllable
in an elder poet, one had better conclude that it was the
elder poet's fun, and pass on.   Once more, by their fruits
ye shall know them ; and for the fruits of this Covent
Garden I have no use whatsoever.

The Upper   On the other hand, there are five writers of this time,
House.   Shenstone, Gray, Johnson, Mason (not the poetaster), and
Mitford, who seem to me to deserve close attention,
though their utterances differ much in bulk, and though
the reasons for dealing with them are curiously various.
Shenstone. Shenstone, for instance, has left us but a few hints on the
subject scattered about his *Essays*.[1]   Yet I know nothing
much more momentous in this history.   When we remember
that he died in 1763, and that, in the lazy leisure of The
Leasowes, these posthumously published essays were
probably, if not certainly, jotted down for twenty or thirty
years previously, the following short and casual remarks
may seem to some—they certainly do to me—more
important in the history of English prosody than scores
of volumes of wrangling about accent and quantity, or than
limbos full of impossible notations that make eight feet
out of an English heroic.   They are as follows :—

> "Rhymes in elegant poetry should consist of syllables that
> are long in pronunciation, such as 'are,' 'ear,' 'ire,' 'ore,' 'your,'
> in which a nice ear will find more agreeableness than in these—
> 'gnat,' 'net,' 'knit,' 'knot,' 'nut.'

> .   .   .   .

> "There is a vast beauty, to me, in using a word of a particular
> nature in the eighth and ninth syllables of an English verse—I
> mean what is virtually a dactyl.   For instance—

> And pikes the tyrants of the watry plains.

> Let any person of an ear substitute 'liquid' for 'watry' and he
> will find the disadvantage.

> .   .   .   .

---

[1] Especially in those on " Books and Writers " (*Works*, ii. 157-180, 228-
239, in 3rd ed., London, 1768).

" As there are evidently words in English poetry that have the force of a dactyl, and if properly inserted have no small force on that account, it seems absurd to print them otherwise than at length—

> The loose wall tottering o'er the trembling shade."

These may seem scanty texts upon which to base On "long" high distinction for a man. But let us remember when rhymes. they were written, and what they mean if you look at them in the light of history. The first indicates a perception of vowel-music—(*not* of mere " sound suiting sense "), and is moreover opposed to the whole practice of Pope and his school, the dominant school of the time, which tended towards the " short " rhyme, in order not to interfere with the swift transition from one half of the couplet to the other, and the quick resumption of the second couplet after the first. Of course, you will find plenty of " long " rhymes in Pope ; but they are obviously not intended to be dwelt on—to leave a sort of smoke and fringe of detonation and flash after them. They are whip-cracks, not powder-explosions.

The second and third, moreover, are still more important. On " dactyls," Shenstone's " dactyl " is open to misapprehension, but it etc. is quite clear (though we have seen that it, or something like it,[1] was actually misapprehended) what he meant. He meant trisyllabic feet—neither more nor less. He obscures it by printing (if he really would have printed it, for he never saw these proofs) " watry " ; but he prints " tottering," and " tottering " is enough to make the whole " apostrophating " and strict decasyllabic theory not merely totter but fall to the ground. Now this was what was wanted, and this, I maintain, was what the author of the " Pastoral Ballad " did in these few words. In three sentences he restores echo to rhyme, and he restores undulation to rhythm.

The contributions of Gray are less scanty, and therefore Gray—his *Metrum* notes.

---

[1] Shenstone's words were not published till long after Webb wrote. But Shenstone was a great letter-writer, and the literary men of the eighteenth century were a much smaller and more closely connected body than those of later times. Still there may be some earlier utterance of the kind, and if so Mr. Omond probably knows it.

at least equally important, but their importance is of a
different character. They consist of some seventy or
eighty pages [1] of fragments intended for the *History of
Poetry* which Gray began, but left to Warton to accomplish,
at least, in great part. And it so happens that they deal
almost wholly (they are grouped under the general title
Metrum) with what Warton [2] almost as wholly neglected.
They would thus, whatever their bulk and merit, have had
the immense *moment* of directing study for the first time
to historical consideration of prosody, and must so
outweigh a whole library of *a priori* theorists.

But independently of this general gist and tendency, they
show that, even as it was, Gray's prosodic acuteness was as
great as we should expect from a man who joined very high
proficiency in the practice of poetry to scholarship quite
unusual in such practitioners. That he altogether mistook
" riding rhyme," or rather frankly confessed that he did
not know what it meant, is nothing. He probably missed
the connection with the actual " ride " to Canterbury ; and
every student knows how an initial miss of this kind will
set one wholly in the wrong way, or groping in vain for
the right. But he more than made up for this mistake
about Chaucer by detecting, for the first and almost the last
time, till a comparatively recent period, the secret of
Spenser's *Oak and Breer* and *Fox and Kid* verses. Whether
Coleridge knew these notes before he published *Christabel*
(they were printed by Mathias in 1814), it is impossible
to say. But if, by any chance, he could have heard of
them while he was at Cambridge (where they were actually
lying in MS.) it would throw a great light on what went
on about the Quantocks a few years later. At any rate,
Gray hits the white. " The measure, like our usual verse
of eight syllables, is dimeter iambic, but admits of trochee,

---

[1] Gray's *Works*, ed. Gosse, i. 325 *sq.* (London, 1884).
[2] For which reason he makes no independent appearance in our text. His
neglect of prosody is all the more curious that he was a by no means unimportant practitioner in it, helping, among other things, to revive the Sonnet.
But he not only says very little about it, but is curiously careless and clumsy
in what he does say—muddling up rhyme-royal with octave, calling (like
Dryden, but with far less excuse) the fourteener an " Alexandrine," and so on.

spondee, amphibrachys, anapæst, etc., in almost every place."
I will give him the "amphibrachys" as his fee for the rest,
though the line[1] in which he introduces it (for he actually
scans half a score) I should myself take differently.   And
I do not agree with him as to the "trochaic" scansion[2]
of "August"; but there is nothing preposterous about it.

The important point, however, is that, hit or miss, Gray
takes the texts, and, instead of cramming them into iron
boxes, measures them off with a leaden rule, or takes a
cast of them in duly yielding plaster.   Even about the
final *e* he went nearly right,[3] though by conjecture only.
He saw that the Alexandrine must, as a rule, have the
middle cæsura, and that there is no "must" in regard to
others.   His list of texts shows astonishing reading for
the time, and his scheme of metres for them almost as
astonishing accuracy.   On rhyme ("pseudo-rhythmus" as
he calls it) there is the same learning.   He is acquainted
with the *Life* of St. Margaret and with the *Moral Ode*;
and (probably on hints or helps from Percy) he shows a
very fair understanding of alliterative metre.   Although
he is far too kind (almost unintelligibly so, but see vol. i.)
to Lydgate and the "smoothness" of his verse, his note
on the subject is, whether right or wrong, full of interest.
But his title to enter the Upper House of eighteenth-
century prosodists, his patent of prosodic nobility, consists
in his being the first to be directly and unflinchingly

---

[1] And in|terrupted | all his other speech

seems to me simply heroic.   Spenser often relapses into this, especially in
"May."

[2] Then lo ! Perigot, the pledge which I plight,
A maple ywrought of the maple warre.

Anapæstic rather, I think.

[3] Mr. Omond has pointed out what I had not noticed (though I was aware
of some things similar in the *Rambler*), that in the examples to Johnson's
Dictionary, twenty years before Tyrwhitt, some of the Chaucerian *e*'s are
valued.   Perhaps Gray got his idea from this, as he may have got his knowledge of the *St. Margaret*.   His prosodic studies probably suggested the
remark, in the letter which Horace Walpole wrote, but did not send to
Chatterton, about the Rowley metres having not then been invented.   This
remark is partly true and partly false ; but is made from a point of view which
not many men in England had then reached, and certainly out of the range
of Horace, who thought the poems were written "in the Saxon language."

historic.   That was the *via salutis*, and he was the first to enter on it—almost the first even to point it out.

Johnson.   The error of belittling Bysshe as a beacon is evident when we come from him, a very small man, to a very great one, no less than Samuel Johnson himself.   That Johnson learnt his views on prosody from Bysshe would, of course, be an absurd proposition, though he must have known the book, and could not well but have generally approved it.   That he judges from a bench practically planked out of its principles must be obvious to all, except the curious persons who say that the ballad writers of the fifteenth century are not witnesses for our view of prosody, because they did not at the moment think of it.   For Johnson as for Bysshe, rhyme is almost a *sine qua non*.[1]   For Johnson as for Bysshe, the counsel of perfection, the standard of excellence, in English verse, is a couplet of twenty syllables exactly arranged, with an accent at the 2nd, 4th, 6th, 8th, 10th, in each line, and a rhyme at the end of each, and a pause as near as possible to the centre of each.   All the surprising judgments, all the dubious arguments which we find in the *Rambler* and the *Lives*, come from this primary creed.   Yet, as indicated in a note above, the very examples of his own *Dictionary* provided texts for setting folk right ; and in many cases, no doubt, did so set them.

The "places" for Johnson's prosodic utterances are mainly three—the *Dictionary*, the *Rambler*, and the *Lives* (I put the *Dictionary* in front, though it did not appear before the *Rambler*).   The prosodic *doctrines* of the *Grammar* in the *Dictionary* are unflinchingly Bysshian. Everything goes to syllables ; iambs and trochees are validated almost alone, though the anapæst has a sort of

---

[1] Johnson would probably have agreed with the sentiments, though he would have doubly disliked the language, of the late Mr. T. H. Nolan of St. John's College, one of the authors of *The Oxford Spectator*, and a great loss to his University and to literature by his early death.   Nolan, who was swift of foot and swifter of wit, used to say, "Blank *werse* is usually the comparative of——bad."   "It is very well, sir, but you should not [pun or] swear," would have been the sage's remark, I suppose ; though he would doubtless not, as Nolan possibly would, have admitted that the maligned thing *might* be the superlative of very good.

recognition. The strict regularity of the accents constitutes the harmony of the lines. There are scarcely any
licences except synalœpha, synæresis, etc.—in other words,
the abominable apostrophation, which, in fact, is *not* a
licence, but a crime committed to prevent having recourse
to what is thought licence.

These briefly announced principles govern all the
prosodic remarks in the *Rambler* and most of those in
the *Lives*. It is on them that Johnson objects to the fine

> *both stood,*
> *Both turned,* and under open sky adored,

of Milton's description of Adam and Eve praying. It
is these that make him denounce as "remarkably inharmonious "—

> *where thy* abundance wants
> Partakers, and uncropped *falls to* the ground.

By applying them he condemns Cowley's really exquisite

> And the soft wings of Peace *cover* him round.

For these reasons Milton's "elisions," as he calls them—
that is to say, his trisyllabic feet—are an abomination
to him. For the sake of these or others closely connected
with them, he brands some of the best pauses of
Paradise Lost as "inharmonious," "defective," "losing the
very form of verse"; and they require few additions, or
even only a little working out, to enable us to understand
the famous condemnation of *Lycidas*, the disapproval of
the Spenserian stanza, the description of the ravishing
songs in *Comus* as "not very musical." All these things,
preposterous in themselves, lose their preposterousness if
you once remember the major premiss. *The perfect form
of English verse is a line of ten syllables with the accent
resting on every second syllable through the whole line ;* to
which one might add, *followed by another line of the same
kind which rhymes to it, after which the sense is not continued without a break.* Johnson's wide knowledge of all
the English verse which followed his rules, and of not a
little that did not; his extraordinary mental alacrity,

perspicacity, and vigilance; the clear legal fashion in which he could, whenever he chose, put his arguments and his judgments,—make him by far the greatest authority on his side, and, in fact, if the paradox may be allowed, an authority still even when he is seen to be absolutely wrong. There is no flaw in the connection of his conclusions with his premises; and these premises are never disguised, concealed, minced, or half comprehended by the person who relies on them. It is true that they are pure assumptions, and, what is more, assumptions in the teeth of evidence; but all that is previous. *If* Diana of the Ephesians is great; if the drumming decasyllabon of ten syllables only, and five immutable accents, and a very slightly mutable pause, is the God,—everything else follows.

"Decasyllabomania" in him and others.

In fact, I cannot doubt that decasyllabomania is at the root of almost all, certainly of a great many, prosodic aberrations. Originally entertained as a shelter and refuge from the jargon-and-doggerel-welter of the fifteenth and early sixteenth centuries, it establishes itself to such an extent in the English mind that the very revolt against it cannot drive it out. Like the infernal power in Mansoul, it is expelled only to maintain, or rapidly recover, lodgment in high and low places alike. We are seeing what it does with Johnson during its tyranny. We shall see it lurking in Mitford, despite his actual championship of "triple time." It is present, in the most singular fashion throughout, with Guest: the crusader of sections and accents and Anglo-Saxonries generally is evidently of opinion that when you once give up the more excellent way of accent and alliteration, there is nothing for you but pure Bysshism—though, of course, he never mentions the name of Bysshe. It drives Dr. Abbott into the most astonishing conditions of extra-metrical syllables and slurs and the like. And I am by no means certain that the puzzle, as it seems to me, of Mr. Bridges' elaborate system of metrical fictions— co-existing with the confession that all the syllables he has ruled out are pronounced—is not due to the ghostly

presence in the background of this idol with its ten
syllables, its five regularly placed stresses, and the rest
of its (I beg pardon, but the word is Miltonic and
irresistible) " trumpery."

At any rate, the constant presence of this arbitrary
standard, and the almost unconscious reference to it,
supply a much more satisfactory explanation of the
saugrenu judgments that we find in Johnson than the
mere physical fact that his hearing was dull ; just as the
other fact that his sight was bleared only supplies a very
vulgar solution of his indifference to " prospects." That
there was a connection in each case no sensible man will
deny ; that the connection was wholly, exclusively, and
sufficiently causal few sensible men will maintain.
Johnson's tendency—the tendency of many of the better
sceptics to embrace one " substance of a doubt " as
noble, and refuse to allow any dram of eale to do it to
that dram's nature—is well known. He chose here to
adopt the decasyllabic couplet of the most rigid construction as orthodox ; and all right-hand defections
and left-hand fallings off from this were bad—at best
with differing degrees of badness. Lines ought to be
regular in length, and the lines of *Lycidas* are not ; so
its numbers are harsh and unpleasing. Rhymes ought
to recur at regular intervals, and (as Bysshe had boldly
said) had better not even be alternate ; so the rhymes
of *Lycidas*, as " uncertain," are bad. You want in poetry
sharp effects and quick returns ; so the Spenserian stanza
is unpleasing again. The line should always obey the
precept *festinare ad eventum* ; so Collins's lines " clogged
with clusters of consonants" deserve reprobation.
Alternate accent is a law, transgression of which can
at best be venial ; and so spondees are questionable, and
trochees, in iambic metre, intolerable. The most instructive, and to sharp-eyed readers the most ludicrous
example of this, is the way in which Johnson, after a
fashion which he would have " downed " and shouted
over at once in another man, hints gingerly side-reasons
for edging the pause closer and closer to the middle.

" If a single syllable is cut off from the rest, it must either be united to the line with which the sense connects it, or be sounded alone. If it be united to the other line it destroys its harmony ; if disjoined it must stand alone, and with regard to music be superfluous. For there is no harmony in a single sound, because it has no relation to another." To which one has only to answer—" *Negatur !* "

His arguments on pause.

Even more paralogical and question-begging is the argument against the use of pause at the second syllable from end or beginning. " When two syllables are abscinded from the rest, they evidently want some associate sounds to render them harmonious." For myself I always suspect the word " evidently " ; and one *had* been under the impression that " two was company." But the climax, both of ingenuity and insufficiency, is reached in the argument against pauses (which he admits to be better) at the third or seventh. " As the third and seventh are weak syllables [by his own arbitrary hypothesis only, remember], the period leaves the ear unsatisfied, and in expectation of the remaining part of the verse." Now one had thought that this " expectation " was precisely what the poet should encourage. But, as will be seen, the series of arguments leaves only the consecrated fourth and sixth—for even the fifth as " weak " is inconvenient. The others are " the noblest and most majestic which our versification admits," and that on the sixth is the very best of all. Now, as a matter of fact, one does not require to go beyond his own examples of all the pauses (except that at the ninth, too terrible to think of, I suppose), to see that every one can be as " noble," as " majestic," as any other. I should have said myself that nothing could deserve these epithets better than his example [1] of the pause at the first, and, according to him, worst. But the whole thing is evidently working up to a

---

[1] Defaming as impure what God declares
    Pure ; and commands to some, leaves free to all.

It is positively amazing that any one should miss the immense advantage, poetical as well as rhetorical, of this particular pause.

foregone conclusion. The pause ought to be as near the middle as the "weakness" of the actual middle (which must be weak) will allow it ; therefore everything else is wrong—with modified degrees of wrongness perhaps, but wrong.[1]

In 1749, the year of the prospectus of the *Dictionary*, John Mason. there appeared a couple of little tractates, in sequel to each other, on *The Power of Numbers and the Principle of Harmony in Poetic Compositions* and on *The Power and Harmony of Prosaic Numbers.* Neither had any author's name on the title-page, but they are known to be by one John Mason, a dissenting minister and a teacher of elocution. The poetical tractate contains not a little which puts the axe to the insane root of the tree of decasyllabomania, as well as incidental remarks of an invaluable kind. Like so many of these prosodists, Mason invites a Biblical phrase, by the way in which he goes a-wandering after musical analogies ; but it does him little harm. He begins, if abstractedly, yet happily enough, by setting up *pleasure* as the object of verse : and the examination of the source of that pleasure as his immediate object. Then he starts with " Times," and excites qualms by laying it down that a single time makes a short syllable and a double time a long ; but he relieves us soon by saying that the single times are some longer, some shorter, "and the double times often more than double the short." So too, though he enters slightly into the accent-and-quantity logomachy, he comes out of it unscathed ; and (with the same possibly

---

[1] Perhaps Goldsmith ought to have a place in this "Upper House" for Goldsmith. his eighteenth "Essay" on "Versification," and a remark or two elsewhere, especially that in *The Bee*, viii., on "the unmusical flow of blank verse." This, which is not very happy, is probably an echo of Johnson, whom, how-ever, he certainly does not follow in his view of rhyme in his "Versification." The fact, I suspect, is that his soul "did huddled notions try" here as else-where. More has been promised on his attitude to English hexameters, etc. But he has the merit of asserting that "to assert that modern poetry has no feet is a ridiculous absurdity" ; of recognising that "Spenser, Shakespeare, Milton, Dryden, Pope, and all our poets abound with dactyls, spondees, trochees, anapæsts, etc." ; of admiring Collins's *Evening*; and of extolling varied pause. If he had "settled his love" a little more, he might have been of greater consequence.

unscientific but profoundly rational "transaction" as in the former case) decides that "that which *principally* fixes and determines English quantities is the accent and emphasis." There is much virtue in your "principally," and, as long as we see and cling to it, there is no danger of intabescence.[1]

Safely entered on this *via media,* Mason is able to throw out all sorts of precious observations which we may gather up without attending at all to his musicalities. Quoting—

And many an amorous, many a humorous lay,

Which many a bard had chanted many a day,

with the scansion reproduced, he observes on them : " This, though it increases the number of the syllables, yet it sweetens the flow of the verse, and renders the ear perfectly reconciled to the irregularity of the metre." And after pointing out that there are fourteen syllables instead of ten in the first, and twelve in the second, he adds : "The ear, which is ever the best judge in this case, finds nothing in them redundant, defective, and disagreeable, but is sensible in them of a sweetness that is not ordinarily found in the common iambic verse." It is a good many years now since, having never previously heard of Mason, I saw these tractates advertised in a catalogue and bought them ; but I remember quite well the joy with which I read this sentence, noticing its date. There are others nearly as good, especially several dwelling on the "inharmony" of anything like a regular cæsura ; and though he is excessive in some of his comments on Milton, yet he is right in the principle on which he bases them, that *too* heterogeneous "numbers" will overthrow iambic verse. Coleridge has actually done this in *Christabel* once or twice, and, as has been admitted above, Milton in his experiments sometimes went near to doing it, though I think Mason hypercritical in the

[1] Virtutem videant, intabescantque relicta.
You can " intabesce " in *both* directions here, unfortunately.

instances he selects.   Let it be added, but (in order to
send somebody if possible to him) without detail, that he
has a most interesting solution of the "problem" why
Dryden thought the Denham lines "Though deep yet
clear" so admirable.   But his sweeping away of the great
prosodic heresy of the age—his appeal to the Cæsar of
the ear about plusquam-decasyllabic lines—is his warrant
for admission here.

The last prosodist to be mentioned in this place is Mitford.
William Mitford, the historian of Greece.   Mitford's
scheme and range are distinctly ambitious; and he is not
below them in a volume [1] of four hundred pages.   He
begins with an approximation of poetry and music, spends
much time on vowel-sounds, and binds quantity strictly
to time, separating accent from it.   Then he passes to
rhythm or cadence, and admits in poetry as well as
in music both "common" and "triple" time.   The
"mechanism of verse" succeeds; and then we have a
long, and for his time most creditably well-informed
chapter, on the history of versification.   But the new
historical and comparative spirit is far too strong in him
to allow him to be content with this.   Seven chapters
and about a hundred pages are devoted to the harmony
of Greek and Latin; six chapters (or sections, as he calls
them) and about seventy pages to modern languages other
than English; while some eighty pages more contain general

[1] The *second* edition of an *Inquiry into the Principles of the Harmony of Language* (London, 1804). The first, much shorter, had appeared thirty years earlier. Mr. Omond thinks it "clearer and more pointed." Perhaps it is, but it almost necessarily lacks, except in small measure, the invaluable historical survey in which, to me, the great merit of his second consists; for in 1774 the texts were seldom available, and Mitford, then quite a young man, had hardly had time to read what were. He is theoretic mainly; indeed, the two forms differ so much that comparison of them is not easy, though I have spent a good deal of time in working with them side by side. He thought in the earlier book that "modern poetry will not allow the inter-mixture of common and triple feet"; that "we *know* that a certain number of syllables and a certain disposition of pause are necessary." He observed that "the dullest ear [mine must be very dull] will perceive the difference in length between 'banner' and 'banter.'" He admits that elision, *except* of "the," is objectionable; gives very little analysis of English verse; thinks "stărry" *short* [! ! !], and pronounces the "bottomless pit" verse "not an English heroic."

observations on euphony and cacophony, on grammar, and on divers minor points including orthography.

The book is certainly, in its enlarged form at any rate, by far the most satisfactory result of combined theoretic and historical inquiry that had yet been seen. Like Mason, and *not* like Steele, Mitford is helped to useful observation by his attention to music. But at the same time it led him into errors, as it always does ; for it is perfectly certain that poetical music and musical music, though allied, are two separate things, often found in company, but sometimes quite dissociated, subject to decidedly different laws, and though often assisting and developing each other in the most remarkable degree, yet only to be confounded with dangerous results. Still the most careless attention and the least cultivated ear could not but perceive that the accepted and fashionable prosody of the neo-classical school was miserably limited in comparison with music ; that the omnipotent couplet required all sorts of distortions and liberties to be taken with it before it would suit musical setting at all ; and that the things that went best to music were the metres which were scornfully admitted at best as playthings and pastimes. Yet everybody admitted, and talked of, " the music of verse." This was necessary, for the thoughts might and did divide themselves this way and that.

It was partly, though not wholly, from the weight attached by Mitford to musical considerations that he was led to champion the accentual theory of English prosody. He did so *totis viribus* ; and appears to have been led to do so partly also by a too absolute insistence on time as the foundation of quantity on the one hand, as well as by a remnant of the old hard and fast deca-syllabic theory on the other. Nor did his distinction of common and triple time lead him to the true theory of trisyllabic substitution, but, on the contrary, to that unnatural, unnecessary, and, if widely adopted, intolerable system of " extra-metrical " syllables which has, strangely enough, from time to time found patronage among the elect. Yet among these elect Mitford must certainly be

ranked.   Whether his main theories be right or wrong,
his system of inquiry is a most valuable one, proceeding,
as it does, first on the broad and safe ground of historical
investigation of the actual literature, and secondly by an
appeal, not to *a priori* rules, but to the effect on the ear.
And it frequently leads him to excellent results ; while,
be he right or be he wrong, his evidence for actual
pronunciation, etc., is invaluable.

Thus, for instance, we get in him a most interesting
and historically important contrast with Gascoigne.   That
early and acute critic, as we saw, regarded " heavn " as the
normal pronunciation of the word, and " heav-en " as a
licence, to be sparingly and doubtfully used.   Mitford,
among some excellent remarks on trisyllabic feet (for he
does admit them, though he sometimes prefers " elision "),
has the curious and rather hazardous *obiter dictum*,
" Thus we find ' heav'n ' and ` giv'n ' printed for ' heaven '
and ' given,' though to pronounce ' heav'n ' or ' giv'n ' as one
syllable *is impossible.*"   He objects—very arbitrarily, but
very naturally, from his accentual point of view—to the
use of the terms trochee, anapæst, etc., but he uses them
himself.   What he means by saying (p. 95) that " rhyme
is without analogy in music " can only be guessed ; and
when he pronounces it to be " wholly unrelated to
melody " one cannot even guess, unless " melody " is used
in a most improperly technical and limited sense, which
again exhibits the danger of confusion.   But his indication
of its office as a time-beater is, I think, novel, and of the
first importance.   He exhibits not merely the inadequacy
of the limitations of the central pause, but the fact that
great Pope himself had not observed them.   He admires
what he calls " aberration " of the accent (*i.e.* the substitution of trochee for iamb), with a complaisance which
is creditable to his ear, but rather fatal to his accentual
theory ; and he has the attention to observe anapæstic
rhythm, or, as he prefers to call it, triple " cadence," in the
revived alliterative verse, though he may have gone wrong
in carrying it back to the older forms.

But the most important, nay the capital thing, is that

he should have thought of going to these older forms *at all*. Beside this, his attention to, and his opinions on, such questions as whether English verse is quantitative or accentual ; whether quantity depends solely on time ; whether accent consists in " loudness " or " sharpness " of tone ; [1] whether rhyme has no analogy in music ; and the rest,—become entirely unimportant. If a man gives you bread *you* do not (except from the most delicate sentiments of humanity) care whether he gives himself stones or thistles. Now attention to the actual course— to the actual phenomena—of English prosody was the bread that was wanted ; and this Mitford gave, if not perhaps always with the right results to himself. Others who followed his example were sure to come right sooner or later.

[1] This minor battle is a good example of the way in which this kind of prosodist becomes a κυμινοπριστοκαρδαμογλύφος, not with parsimonious but with pettifogging intent.

INTERCHAPTER VIII

THE break which we have now reached is not one merely resorted to for convenience, because enough has been put into the present volume. It corresponds, not quite in the same way, but in equally important degree, to that at the end of the first. There, after four centuries of constant but for the most part quite *untheorised* practice, a little theory and a great deal more practice, culminating in the work of Spenser, had practically put English poetry into possession of its prosodic estate, though that estate was only to a very small extent even explored, and hardly in the least degree regularly surveyed and mapped. Here, two centuries more have almost completed the exploration, though certainly not the occupation. But they have, for the last two-thirds of them, witnessed a most curious withdrawal from the largest and fairest part; while, though there has been a great deal of work done in the surveying direction, little, if any of it, has been done on right principles.

In the first third of these two hundred years—the period covered by the first two Books of the present volume, and extending from the establishment of Shakespeare to the publication of *Paradise Lost*—the positive addition to the amount of prosodic exercise is almost incredibly great in value, as well as in amount. From the certain appearance of *Venus and Adonis*, coinciding very probably with that of its author's first published plays, to that of *Paradise Lost* itself, is little more than one reputed lifetime of threescore years and ten. Yet it includes, with one other of scarcely greater length, the greatest bulk of the greatest poetry that we have ever known. And this poetry (which is the chief point of interest for us) takes a quite astonishing number of forms, and practises them to quite an astonishing degree of perfection. In these seventy years blank verse rises,[1] perfects itself, declines, falls, and is (by Milton) raised again—a five-act chronicle-play in prosody absolutely without parallel elsewhere. It rises to such a height in its two zeniths that absolutely no metre, in our or any other language, can surpass it as a vehicle of poetry. It falls, at its fortunately single nadir, to such a depth that hardly the dog-rhythm of the fifteenth century outstrips it in sinking. At the opposite pole in the system of vehicles for long poems, the continuous stanza reaches, in the Spenserian, its most consummate achievement, and in other forms one not much lower ; while similar arrangements for shorter pieces—the sonnet as a single and uniform type, with the innumerable outlines of the greater lyric—match anything in other tongues and other times for perfection. This same perfection, on a smaller scale and in simpler fashion, but in almost more remarkable degree, is shown by the manipulation of quite ordinary schemes—mostly very old, and, it might have been thought, hackneyed, such as the quatrains of the common and long measure—which acquire a prosodic power that they had never known before, and which they have seldom known since. Experiments are made, not so perfectly happy, but not unhappy, with longer integers —the Alexandrine and the fourteener.

Meanwhile, between blank verse and the stanzas, an interesting change, or rather a set of interesting developments, comes upon the heroic couplet. Never practised with real success since Chaucer himself perfected it up to a certain point, and receiving, to all appearance, a severe rebuff to its prospects by the preference on the stage of blank verse, it is taken up for non-dramatic purposes slightly by Spenser, indirectly and as part of something

---

[1] If anybody objects that the actual rise was earlier, it can hardly be carried reasonably beyond the first plays of Peele and Marlowe ; and this will only extend the threescore years and ten to the fourscore.

else by Fairfax, but directly by Drayton, Daniel, and many others, even before, much more after, the beginning of the seventeenth century. By degrees there appears, in the practice of it, a separation, if not a direct opposition, between two forms, which, by Chaucer himself, and in the earlier Elizabethan practitioners, had been almost indiscriminately used — the stopped and the enjambed. For a time nobody devotes himself very extensively to the first; but the apparent advantages of the second induce plentiful use, and by degrees no small abuse, which, in its turn, encourages, by reaction, the development of the stopped form. And there is apparent, also quite early in practitioners of the latter, something which has not been visible before—a disposition not merely to prefer, but to impose.

It is, however, noticeable in this abundant time that there is a tendency, outside of blank verse, to adopt trisyllabic feet in songs for music only. The idea— which we have seen turned into something like a precept even earlier—that there are *no* trisyllabic feet gains ground; though it never establishes itself entirely or exclusively in practice, though not a few beautiful examples of "triple time" measures exist, and though the admixture (actual, if not confessed) of these is the very secret of the perfection of blank verse itself.

Then there comes the strange and heavy change, the beginning of which has been described in Book VI., and the progress of it in the following Books, the last two of this volume—a change of the most complicated and far-reaching nature as regards poetry itself, but gathered up and symbolised prosodically in a singular fashion by the exaltation and almost idolising of the stopped couplet. This exaltation, as we have taken care to point out, though it was largely due to the influence of a single poet, was not due, by any means, to an inability on his part to excel in the measures which he discountenanced. Dryden, it has been shown, could and did write excellently in a very great number of metres, and I see no reason to believe that he could not have written in others still. There

are passages in his almost unread lyrics which make it
not rash to say that he could have managed, if not in
"the best and most orgillous," at any rate in no ill fashion,
even the Spenserian *novena*, even the *In Memoriam*
quatrain.   But beyond all doubt his influence helped
immensely the set of the time towards the stopped,
antithetic, more or less rigidly decasyllabic couplet.
At any rate, it did triumph.   I do not know a more
remarkable instance of the completeness of that triumph
than a fact not yet noticed, though the passage containing it has been quoted, that Shenstone, a practitioner
of other forms, and at the moment a protester against
the rigid mode, uses the term "English verse" as
synonymous with the heroic line.   This rod had not, as a
matter of fact, quite swallowed up all the others ; but it
had actually made some progress in the swallowing ; and
it was the general theory of preceptists on the subject
that it ought to do so.

For prosodic theory seems to have adjusted itself to
prosodic practice in a manner curious and almost uncanny.   As we have seen, the last forty years of the
seventeenth century furnish practically no prosodic
treatise, and only a very few prosodic hints.   Yet the
next has not seen its second twelvemonth close when up
starts Bysshe with a precise and carefully drawn code,
every principle of which is directly adapted towards this
model ; which only admits one other as capable of being
in any way ranked with it, and which rather more than
hints that, except for subordinate and popular purposes,
no others should be used at all.   Moreover, though a few
protests are made against parts of this code, and more
against its grounding itself on "accent," it is quite clear
that the majority of the prosodists—and there are, as
we have seen, many of them—are with Bysshe in the
main.   It is the exception when they take anything but
the heroic as their subjects for illustration and demonstration ; and though a few of them—especially the
mélomanes (the solace of whose sin is that they cannot
well help admitting "triple time")—do admit trisyllabic

feet, it is scarcely ever on any extensive comparison of different ages, types, and kinds of English poetry. The couplet might long before have taken the motto of the Superintendent Fouquet—*Quo non ascendam ?*—but it was now in the position of Fouquet's master and tormentor—a sort of *Roi Soleil* of English metres.

Almost, but not quite. Even Bysshe, as we saw, had to recognise one not exactly rival but lesser potentate— the octosyllable ; and the octosyllable, strengthened, when the couplet had not yet gained its full authority, by Butler, had been further fortified by Prior and Swift, and made available for purposes peculiarly germane to the temper of the eighteenth century. Although much of the spirit of lyric had been lost for the time, the forms remained, and were sure to keep some of the spirit itself floating and lingering about them. The anapæstic metres, again mightily assisted by Prior, had established a scheme of sound, and, to some extent, diction, widely different from, and, to some extent, destructive of couplet verse-morals. Above all, the restored blank verse of Milton, though nobody imitated it for a long time, began at last to attract practitioners, and to prove itself the most formidable rival of the couplet itself. The others could be tolerated, because few of them aspired to, and none of them was very well suited for, the business of " long poems " ; but this was the main business of blank verse. Moreover, blank verse had of old lent itself, and was sure to lend itself again, to all the things which are most incompatible with the rigid couplet—which are pitch, and fat, and hair to destroy that dragon. Tri- syllabic feet, enjambment, free variation of pause,—all these things blank verse brings with it ; and all are fatal to the couplet in its triumphant form, if not in others.

Let it not, however, be for one moment supposed that I wish to represent the stopped couplet as an Ahriman of English poetry or prosody. It was very much the reverse : and if it had not been for the fact that its popularity, coinciding with, and in fact brought about by, an excessive devotion to " prose and sense," tended to tyranny, there would be little to be said against itself, and much in its favour. For one thing that it did we ought to be perpetually grateful to it. It is evident enough *a priori*, and has been sufficiently illustrated from the other side, that the innate and ingrained freedom of English verse has a dangerous *nisus* towards anarchy. Already, by 1700 (in fact, by 1650), there had been two periods in which this danger had become a reality—the chaos, chiefly in rhyme-royal, of the line in the fifteenth and earliest sixteenth centuries, and the shameless *dévergondage* of blank verse, and, to a rather less extent, of the enjambed couplet, in the mid-seventeenth. Milton, it is true, tightened up blank verse again ; but Milton, as we have shown, allowed himself so many licences, and in fact achieved his great effect by allowing himself so many, that he might have been a deceptive example if he had been much followed at once—which, as we have seen, he was not—and if people had thoroughly understood his methods. Blank verse, in fact, can never, of its nature, be a safe guide to strict order, though it is an invaluable one to the recovery of liberty ; it depends too much on the individual. And, indeed, much of the blank verse of the eighteenth century itself is evidently afraid of its own franchises, and is almost stiffer than the couplet.

For stiffness is not *necessary* to the couplet, though regularity is ; and it cannot be denied that a course of regularity was by no means unsuited to the British constitution, prosodically speaking, at this time. A great advance had been made in settlement of pronunciation, and it was desirable to bring verse into accord with this, both in respect of accent and in respect of rhyme. As a preliminary of recurrence to full equivalence and substitution of feet, it was very desirable to get into the poet's mind a strict notion of what feet were ; and this the decasyllabic couplet—even when it is chopped up by preceptists into ten syllables with no feet at all—infallibly provides. Nobody with any ear could read twenty lines of Dryden, or of Pope, or even of much worse poets, without perceiving the five feet as distinctly as he perceived his own five fingers. People like Steele might, but then they had practically stopped their ears. No doubt these feet were sometimes not beautiful on any mountain—rudimentary, monotonous, hard ; but for the purpose they were all the better, because they were quite unmistakable. Having got to conceive them as unities, human nature was sure, sooner or later, to inquire with itself whether their identity did not admit of variation of kinds ; and as soon as this was done, the tyranny was overpast. The couplet was drilling the people to rebel against itself.

But it did something else likewise—something not perhaps greater, for nothing could be greater than the opportunity at least for realisation of the foot—but something more obvious and not less important. It made people—to a limited extent once more, but once more in a manner certain to spread and germinate—perceive the necessity of attending to general rhythm. Up to the time of Dryden one is constantly met—except in Shakespeare and Milton—with extraordinary and almost unintelligible break-downs in this respect. It is not merely in extreme cases like that of Donne, which have been dealt with in their proper place, but in almost all others—except a few of the lyrists who were preserved by their form—that we meet these. The virus or bacillus of the fifteenth-century doggerel had not met its phagocyte. That phagocyte was cultivated and supplied by the couplet. Here you simply *could* not be unrhythmical, unless you were prepared to brook not merely the grave rebukes of the preceptists, but the "Away with it!" of the natural man, which met you at once. The couplet might, after a comparatively early period, be unprogressive ; it might simply " mark time" ; but it did mark it, and in an unmistakable and imposing manner. Now, marking time is not much fun ; it is monotonous ; it is tedious ; it is (to look at) rather ridiculous. But it is the foundation of all good marching and running, and of all good progression whatsoever.

The couplet marked time quite admirably, and it taught its enemies and supplanters—who need not have been enemies or supplanters at all but for human unwisdom—to go and do likewise.

Some of them were not very quick to learn, and blank verse especially stuck in the rudiments. But for blank verse it was all the better ; for the disorderliness of the broken-down model of the second quarter of the seventeenth century was a terrible danger, and the Miltonic standard was for a long time too high for the neophytes. So blank verse marked time too, and at least cured itself of the hideous shuffle of men even like Suckling and Davenant.[1] The octosyllable, which had not nearly so much to unlearn, learnt a great deal under teachers like Butler, and Prior, and Swift. The anapæstic metres, the faults of which were not so much degradations as mere acquired imperfections of youth and bad company, gradually perfected themselves, with the general fear of rhythm before their eyes. Only lyric, which had little to learn and still less to unlearn, disappoints the examiner ; and that is because lyric, the purest *form* of poetry, most requires something more than form to make it admirable.

Its actual forms, moreover, and the suggestions of more, had been so thoroughly put on record by the preceding century, that as soon as the " something more " was ready they were certain to be utilised. And lyric, though it needed the assistance less, profited also by that disciplining of rhythm which has been dwelt upon : while everything else, including the couplet itself, was being more and more prepared for the divine inspiration when that inspiration was ready.

Nor, though it is on the skirts of prosody, should we omit here to salute (what has been already saluted in the last chapter in the person of its capital and crowning example, Tyrwhitt's *Chaucer*) the immense assistance

---

[1] The awkward blank-verse attempts even of such a metrist as Prior (outside of his *Callimachus* versions, and perhaps in them) give a striking example much later.

which the eighteenth century gave, by its editions and commentaries on the great writers before the couplet accession, to that historic study of actual English prosody which is the one thing needful. It is scarcely hyperbole to say that a man who will take Chaucer and Spenser, Shakespeare and Milton, to a lodge in some vast wilderness, read them and use his wits on them without prejudice and without precedent theory, can hardly fail to hit on the truth of the whole matter—that even short of this, study of any of them may, and probably will, give him light and leading. Spenser and Milton needed no great editorial aid, for they had both (with whatever exceptions in Milton's case) seen their work in print, if they had not actually seen it through the press. But Shakespeare was not very well served by his early editors and printers, and Chaucer was very ill served by some of his. In endeavouring to set things right, the early eighteenth-century editors of Shakespeare no doubt patched and pieced too much ; but still they removed many obvious, and some not so obvious, copyists' and printers' blunders. Until Tyrwhitt it was difficult for any one, not a rather exceptional scholar, to understand Chaucer's prosody at all.

How great was the assistance to prosodic study of this editorial labour, and of the study in well or badly edited copies of the literature of the past generally, may be seen by comparing the two editions of Mitford's *Harmony*. The first may please students of the " previous question " better, with its wide-ranging theory ; the second, though cramped perhaps a little by that theory, is still the first honest attempt to take the facts of the subject from the beginning, and at least *adjust* theory to them. Previously this could not be done. Of the beneficent effects of the process—the *only* process really possible or profitable— we have seen something in Chatterton ; we are postponing two other examples—in practice, not in theory,— those of Burns and Blake. But it is necessary to remember that all the great writers of the Romantic movement were affected by this resurrection of the past.

For in these studies, as in almost all others of the human kind, the future is merely a blank, and the present is partly a puzzle. In them, more than in others, the past is a possession. We have it, and if we choose we may know and understand it. Without such knowledge we shall never decipher the puzzle of the present, or be ready to understand the writing that is to fill the blank of the future. With it we have kept our hold on the life of the subject, and are prepared for whatever that life may bring.

INDEX

INDEX

THE END

Printed by R. & R. CLARK, LIMITED, *Edinburgh.*

A HISTORY OF
ENGLISH PROSODY
FROM THE TWELFTH CENTURY
TO THE PRESENT DAY

By Professor GEORGE SAINTSBURY

Three Vols. 8vo.

Vol. I. From the Origins to Spenser. 10s. net
Vol. II. From Shakespeare to Crabbe.
Vol. III. *In preparation.*

SOME PRESS OPINIONS ON VOLUME I.

THE ATHENÆUM

" A thing complete and convincing beyond any former work from the same hand. ' Hardly any one who takes a sufficient interest in prosody to induce him to read this book ' will fail to find it absorbing, and even entertaining, as only one other book on the subject of versification is : the ' Petit Traité de Poésie Française' of Théodore de Banville. . . We await the second and third volumes of this admirable undertaking with impatience. To stop reading it at the end of the first volume leaves one in just such a state of suspense as if it had been a novel of adventure, and not the story of the adventures of prosody. ' I am myself quite sure,' says Prof. Saintsbury, ' that English prosody is, and has been, a living thing, for seven hundred years at least.' That he sees it living is his supreme praise, and such praise belongs to him only among historians of English verse."

THE TIMES

"To Professor Saintsbury English prosody is a living thing, and not an abstraction. He has read poetry for pleasure long before he began to read it with a scientific purpose, and so he has learnt what poetry is before making up his mind what it ought to be. It is a common fault of writers upon prosody that they set out to discover the laws of music without ever training their ears to apprehend music. They theorize very plausibly at large, but they betray their incapacity so soon as they proceed to scan a difficult line. Professor Saintsbury never fails in this way. He knows a good line from a bad one, and he knows how a good line ought to be read, even though he may sometimes be doubtful how it ought to be scanned. He has, therefore, the knowledge most essential to a writer upon prosody. . . . His object, as he constantly insists, is to write a history, to tell us what has happened to our prosody from the time when it began to be English and ceased to be Anglo-Saxon ; not to tell us whether it has happened rightly or wrongly, nor even to be too ready to tell us why or how it has happened."

Professor W. P. KER in the SCOTTISH HISTORICAL REVIEW

"The history of verse, as Mr. Saintsbury takes it, is one aspect of the history of poetry ; that is to say, the minute examination of structure does not leave out of account the nature of the living thing ; we are not kept all the time at the microscope. This is the great beauty of his book ; it is a history of English poetry in one particular form or mode. . . . The author perceives that the form of verse is not separable from the soul of poetry ; poetry ' has neither kernel nor husk, but is all one,' to adapt the phrase of another critic."

LONDON: MACMILLAN AND CO., LTD.

THE ACADEMY

" It is a careful attempt, based upon an exhaustive examination of the whole of the available material, to do for English Literature what has never yet been done in any systematic or co-ordinate fashion. When the three volumes of which the work is to consist are published, a blank in the history of our literature will have been filled. . . . That the work will bring peace in the ' fair field full of fighting folk ' whereon modern scholars of Prosody ' clang battleaxe and clash brand,' is not to be hoped ; rather will it bring a sword, for the central idea of the book runs counter to many widely-received and much-debated theories. We have no desire to enter upon the field, and will content ourselves with saying that after a careful study of the book, after checking it again and again in the light of opposing views, we have little hesitation in stating that Professor Saintsbury has set the history of English prosody upon a firm basis, largely because he has remembered ' that the Rule comes from the Work, not the Work from the Rule,' and because he has been wise enough to take his examples from amongst the experimenters in novelty just as readily as from the writings of the great. . . The present instalment has convinced us that the whole subject is being dealt with in masterly fashion, and we are confident that the remaining volumes will be worthy of their theme. For Professor Saintsbury has that quality which made Hazlitt one of the first of critics, he has *gusto*, he loves literature."

THE OXFORD MAGAZINE

" The first volume of Professor Saintsbury's History establishes itself at once as the standard work on the subject. . . . His treatment is thoroughly exhaustive, and is distinguished by his wide learning and his usual skill in the handling of vast masses of detail. The book is not only a history of prosody. The student might do worse than take it as quite a useful guide through the rich but confusing store of poetry of the twelfth to the fourteenth century. For the author has adopted the admirable plan of giving in his copious footnotes not only illustrations of his judgments, but also valuable information as to the best available printed form in which the work he discusses is to be found."

THE MORNING POST

" Most of the books yet written on English prosody are prosy. Professor Saintsbury's ' history ' (at any rate in this first volume) is never prosy, and is frequently even breezy. One might think it almost impossible that a competent critic, who regards his work seriously, should discuss the most difficult and controversial points of early English versification in so lively a spirit without detracting from the quality of his work. But Professor Saintsbury has attained this desirable end, and his comments on some of those ancient or modern experts with whom he happens to differ on matters of metre or rhyme are fully charged with attic salt. .   A work which, if the whole is as excellent as this first part, will be a highly valuable addition to history and criticism in a difficult and comparatively little-studied field of literary inquiry."

THE DAILY NEWS

" It is difficult to imagine anyone better qualified than Professor Saintsbury to undertake a work of such highly specialised character as a detailed historical study of English prosody. He has wide knowledge and remarkable power of research, as well as a capacity to handle thorny problems with convincing originality, and, above all, an unconquerable enthusiasm for a subject which to many, even among those who know and love English poetry, must seem dull and uninspiring. He makes the dry bones live."

LONDON : MACMILLAN AND CO., LTD.

N. 1300.7.08.

ImTheStory.com

Personalized Classic Books in many genre's

Unique gift for kids, partners, friends, colleagues

Customize:

- Character Names
- Upload your own front/back cover images (optional)
- Inscribe a personal message/dedication on the
  inside page (optional)

Customize many titles Including
- Alice in Wonderland
- Romeo and Juliet
- The Wizard of Oz
- A Christmas Carol
- Dracula
- Dr. Jekyll & Mr. Hyde
- And more...

CPSIA information can be obtained at www.ICGtesting.com
Printed in the USA
LVOW062044060613

337276LV00005B/851/P